The Ossie Clark Diaries

The Ossie Clark Diaries

Edited and Introduced by
Lady Henrietta Rous

BLOOMSBURY

First published in Great Britain 1998

Bloomsbury Publishing Plc, 38 Soho Square, London W1V 5DF

PHOTO CREDITS

Colour section
David Bailey © Condé Nast Publications Ltd: pages 2, 15, 27 *left*; Chris Barham: page 14 *top*; Albert and George Clark collection: pages 26 *top, right & bottom*, 27 *top & bottom*; Annette Green © Condé Nast Publications Ltd: pages 8, 9 *top & bottom*; Bernard Mignault © Condé Nast Publications Ltd: page 3; David Montgomery © Condé Nast Publications Ltd: pages 14 *bottom*, 21; Johnny Rozsa Photographs: page 31 *top & bottom*; Sport and General Press Agency: pages 12-13; Eric Swayne: page 19.

Text pages
Norman Bach: pages xxiv, lvii; A. Baumann/Rex Features: page 355; Shirley Beljon: page 32; Clive Boursnell: page lxii; Mauro Carraro/Rex Features: page 223; Albert and George Clark collection: pages xiii, xvi, xviii, xxiii, xxxi, lviii, lxv, lxxii, lxxv, lxxvi, lxxvii, 22, 29, 70, 74, 216; John Dewe Matthews: pages xxxvi, xlii, xlv, 13, 40, 332; Terry Disney: page xxi; David Gwinnitt: page 146; G. Hanekroot/Sunshine/Retna: page 97; C. Hopper: page xxvii; Mitch Jenkins/Retna: page 105; Maurice: page xxxv; Lorenzo Poccianti: pages 254-5, 311; Michael Putland/Retna: page 37; Rex Features: pages lxvi, lxviii-lxix, 386; Snowdon: page xxix; *Women's Wear Daily*: page xl.

Endpaper captions and credits
Left page: Model Gala Mitchell wears an Ossie Clark chiffon dress in a Celia Birtwell print (photo: Celia Birtwell). Upper inset: Another chiffon dress by Ossie Clark in a Celia Birtwell print, modelled by Patti Boyd (photo: Albert and George Clark collection). Lower insets: *left* Ossie with Albert (photo: Albert and George Clark collection); *centre* David Hockney at work on *Mr and Mrs Clark and Percy* (photo: Albert and George Clark collection); *right* Ossie on holiday (photo: Maurice).
Right page: Ossie Clark (photo: Norman Bach).

A CIP catalogue record for this book
is available from the British Library

ISBN 0 7475 3901 4

10 9 8 7 6 5 4 3 2 1

Text design by Bradbury & Williams
Printed in Great Britain by Clays Ltd, St Ives plc

Contents

Foreword

Lady Henrietta Rous

Ossie Clark and I met at a society wedding in late 1982, through his interest in the Edwardian cut of the outfit I wore. The snowy-haired R. A. Craigie Aitchison introduced us. 'He really wants to meet you; he likes the dress you're wearing,' Craigie motioned in his inimitable accent. Although Clark's name was familiar to me, I had never been party to the sixties scene of which he was the emblem. Sitting on a gold chair upstairs in the Turf Club, in an idiosyncratic tweed suit, he examined the frock with an expert eye. He was immediately intimate. Upon a simple enquiry, he told me, 'I'm so depressed, I'm going to see a psychiatrist next week. I went bankrupt last year.' His uncompromising frankness was refreshing after the social la-di-da.

I sympathised and invited him to stay at our family home in Clovelly, north Devon. He arrived at our local station with his black-and-tan Cavalier King Charles in a basket so as to avoid paying the train fare. My mother came a couple of days later, a little old-fashioned and shocked to find her house taken over; there was a clash of outlook.

'I can't stand these upper classes and their double double,' Ossie muttered; 'it's just like at Cecil Beaton's. The guests were so rude about him, then *sooo* nice to his face when they met him, and he was equally two-faced about them. Anyway, I'll cook supper,' he commandeered. 'More red pepper!'

'I wish my daughters were better career girls,' my mother sighed.

'I can see with Henri it's just "one more cigarette",' Ossie countered drily and, I fear, shrewdly.

I really fell for Ossie after that visit: I felt compassion and puzzlement for someone of that enormous and proven talent being in such a bewilderingly precarious position. (I could never understand how he was never helped more radically by his extremely famous, rich friends.) I found Ossie a basement flat in Redcliffe Road. He used to arrive – always beautifully dressed that summer – at the flat where I was living in Manchester Square touchingly early, with a single rose in his hand. He would sit for hours quietly reading and, however he felt, was always a creative and reviving presence. Little lunch parties were organised to introduce him to new clients. I approached a certain *Vogue* columnist and asked her why she did not use him more. Her reply was: 'If a horse has fallen at the fence, do you back him?'

Besotted, I devoted the whole summer to him. We went to parties together. Still the star, he had known more dazzling events, but was glamorous, stimulating and fascinating company.

He lent me a skin-tight leather outfit – wild and wonderful, studded with silver and with huge shoulder pads – and took me to Catherine Guinness's wedding to Jamie Neidpath. Ossie designed many dresses for her and knew her in New York in Warhol days. I was amazed to hear quite varied people remark years later on the stunning effect of her wedding dress. I met Lord Spencer, the late Princess of Wales's father, hiding behind a bush 'to avoid the press', while Raine danced.

Early on we had rows as well. Memorably one evening four of us went to dine at San Frediano in Fulham Road. A roughneck at an adjoining table insulted Ossie, or his dog. Ossie retaliated by throwing a glass of wine over him. We, all over the top, were thrown out and went on to a night club. Ossie French-kissed a girlfriend of mine. I slapped both their faces. Ossie whacked mine back on both sides, quite hard. It was salutary. I remember he had a short fling with the friend, which I found very upsetting. I was briefly furious with them both.

Our intensely emotional love affair lasted a matter of months. He was really still mostly involved with his boyfriend Nick, who had left him. Ossie could be cruel and he sometimes 'snipped away', as he put it, at feelings when they became intense – as many of his friends had painfully experienced. There was a period when I refused to see him for six months. After our reconciliation came a close, bonded friendship and mutual care, concern and compassion for twelve years.

I think I did understand his depression, and like him I revelled in a sense of beauty and glamour. Of course, I had not begun to see the worlds he had. Ossie considered I had led a sheltered life by comparison.

Proudly one day, he appeared in red-carpeted Manchester Square with a delicious chocolate cake for his second son George's fourteenth birthday. I felt the love and tender regard between the two and George's pride in Ossie. We went to the National Gallery together – Ossie was inspired at selecting pictures to look at: it was wonderful, educative and stimulating. His way of seeing opened new vistas.

I was so grateful to Ossie; I had been to Camberwell Art School and had got into the Courtauld to study art history, and I knew I had some decorative and aesthetic sense, but experiences such as this gave me enormous respect and admiration for those who were God-given creators. Ossie was not only a truly original cutter, dreamer and perfectionist, but also incredibly rewarding as a person. Coming from my background, I hated the often confining and obvious forms of cliquiness, snobbery and class categorisation. It was enlightening for me to know someone so interesting from such a different world. Ossie with his intellect and instinct cut straight to the heart of things. He was gallant and very, very warm.

In the years when Ossie wasn't really being very productive, he still felt inspired to design me the most exquisite clothes. I know I was the only person at certain dark moments who encouraged him. Together we chose six colours of silk from Pongees in Islington. Ossie made a skirt, knee-length, with eighty-four panels, like a wonderful balletic creation, with a purple fitted corseted top and romantic puffed sleeves. The colours were yellow, turquoise, red, green, pink and mauve. He was a stickler about tights, shoes and combinations. And honest: 'Your legs are not your greatest asset, Henri.' This dress was later photographed in Los Angeles and I wore it in Monte Carlo to Craigie Aitchison's exhibition (he was the visionary, white-haired painter who had orchestrated my first encounter with Ossie at Cosmo Fry's wedding). I immediately acquired a new admirer: Prince Rainier's chamberlain, no less. He rang the gallery and asked, '*Qui est cette fille delicieuse?*' and described the dress.

As Ossie matured in outlook through adversity, so did his education. I remember him reading Proust through and through in Redcliffe Road. Later he read social diaries and historical biographies and was mostly assiduous about returning the books he borrowed. His uncompromising personal integrity was the hallmark of his work, but did not help him in his practical or productive life. One very rich client once asked him to do another dress in blue, like the pink one he had earlier designed for her. 'It's like asking Picasso to paint another picture in a certain way,' he remarked. 'My dresses are like Bentleys; they are quality and last for ever.'

In the autumn of '94, Ossie invited me to stay at Dave Gilmour's house in Lindos on the Greek island of Rhodes with his second son, George, and a former van driver and lover, Roger Dixon, 'a horse coper with gypsy blood'. He was on terrific form, but very high and excitable. (People had recently been sniffing eagerly at his designs – romanticism was coming back. The Japanese were very keen.) Ossie organised delicious meals very bossily, and insulted my drawing and poetry-reading abilities. The first evening, I went to bed hating him, only to be woken at 7.00 a.m. to hear his metallic Buddhist chant – even worse. We made up; he encouraged my drawing and took some outrageously good photographs. I asked him if he missed a certain friend. He said, 'Well, I certainly miss his American Express card.'

He decided not to take the charter plane home, so that he could spend another night in the presence of the new moon – he had inherited a strong mysticism from his mother. Of course we couldn't get on a flight for three days and were forced to buy extra tickets.

On the final morning we left for the airport at 6.00 a.m. Ten minutes out of Lindos the car ran out of petrol. Ossie chanted, while I implored locals driving to work to assist. A dashing huntsman with two pointer dogs and a black moustache stopped. Eventually, petrol was siphoned from his Land Rover to ours. I remember Ossie spitting some out. I also remember him writing in his diary, 'Henri leapt around blaming everyone but herself. I changed and help arrived.' 'Put your foot down,' said a practical Greek who had also assisted. 'You will just make it.' And miraculously we did.

ACKNOWLEDGEMENTS

To Ossie, whose genius and captivating spirit left the world such a rich legacy – testified, I hope, in some measure here.

First of all, of course, I would like to thank Ossie's adored sons, Albert and George, for honouring me by entrusting me with this challenging and fascinating project.

I would like to thank wholeheartedly the following people for their patience and helpful advice in piecing together Ossie's life: Celia Birtwell for her love, generous humour, insight and responsiveness; and Ossie's family – his niece Margaret Clementson for her refreshing balance and endless help, his sisters Kay Clark and Gladys English, his brother John Clark, his niece Carol Hammond and his nephew Jimmy Melia. The much-slandered Chelita Secunda must be thanked enormously for her knowledge of people. For their time, knowledge and professional insight I am indebted particularly to Suzy Menkes, Vanessa Denza, Vanessa de Lisle, Percy Savage, Liz Smith, Sandy Boler, Meriel McCooey, Susannah Handley, Caroline Charles, Mary Quant, Jeff Banks, Ann Chubb, Norman Bain, a wonderful source of memory and understanding, and Georgina Howell. Those who remained loyal to Ossie and adored his clothes include Gill Goldsmith, Marianne Faithfull and Candida Betjeman. Thanks too to close and long-term friends such as Carla Ames, David Hockney, Dave Gilmour, Patti Boyd, Guy Burch, Adie Hunter, Edina Ronay, Jose Fonseca, Pam and Sid Procter, Jenny Dearden, Johnny Dewe Matthewes, Bernard Nevill, Tony Howard, Nicolette Meeres, Andy McKay, Bella Freud, Kevin Whitney, Al and Karen Radley, Duggie Fields, Molly Balaban, Stevie Buckley, Monty White, Nikky Waymouth, Martin Wilkinson and Elizabeth Wyndham.

Those who gave helpful insight include Ben Brierly, Christopher Gibbs, David Mlinaric, Marie Helvin, Jane Rainey, David Oxtoby, Leslie Poole, Jennifer Little, Chrissie Lewis, Clive Bendon, Melissa Chassai, Jenny Runacre, Brian Clark, Michael Fish, Neil Zarach, Alastair Derbyshire, John Maybury, Lynette Williams, Maureen Smith, Tony Jones, Shirley Jones, Michael Huet, Jane Normanton, Tony Tucker, Zandra Rhodes, Kari Anne Jagger, Lady Stockton, Bertie Hope-Davies, Raynes and Patrick Minns, Sheila Oldham, Tony Calder, Polly Hope, Vanessa de Lisle, Catherine Tennant, Kenny Sneddon and Darko Lugger.

I am also thankful to those who worked with Ossie, particularly Kathleen Coleman and Quidejeta, and to Ossie's close Buddhist friends Denise Golding, Bill Weston and Sarah Lamb, Rosita Yarboro and Justine Silver.

Thanks are also due to all those who diligently have empathised with the project and helped edit and work the computer: Chris Manby, for her heroic efficiency and presence, Will Anderson for unstinting devotion and sympathy, Samantha Matthews for her intelligent efficiency, Richard Smith-Bingham for his humour and academic professionalism, Suma Ghosh for her enthusiastic interest in fashion, John Massey, Ben Murphy, Emma Lucia, Alison McIntyre, Miranda Wood, Huda and Charlotte Gregor and especially Lisa Hodgkins the *Vogue* librarian.

Also: Sue of Panda typing services, Peter Hamna at Clovelly and the Estate officer for their help; Mr Ian Peel from the South Bank University, who rescued me from tears when the computer and printer played up, usually before a deadline; Ann Barr for her editorial insight so generously given; Patrick Kinmonth for his rigorous intellect and reassurance; Michael Bloch, Sandy Boler and Virginia Ironside for sympathetic and professional advice; Antony Mockler and Gwenda McEwen for their hospitality and waspish criticism.

Thanks also to Dr Cantillon who put me in the ambulance when I was in agony during, but not because of, preparing this book and to the lovely nurses at St Thomas's; to Hedley Marten for his invaluable moral support and help; to saintly Andrew Rae for sympathy and endless technical expertise. And lastly, of course, to my wonderful soothing agent, Luigi Bonomi, and his assistant, Amanda Preston, at Sheil Land; David Reynolds, who admired Ossie so much; Monica Macdonald who has worked so hard and with perception; Alexander and Graciella Grigg; my sister Caroline for endless love and sympathy and my niece Mary 'Bubsie' Gibbs; and Margaret and West de Wend Fenton. To Camel and Noah, my two cavaliers, who gave solace and diversion.

Will the reader please note: Ossie had a vivid and salty tongue; the choice of passages in the book is in no way an attempt to portray anyone unflatteringly – no harm is intended. Ossie's aim was to create with humour, feeling and insight a record of his time.

London, September 1998

Introduction

Ossie Clark was born on 9 June 1942 in Walton Hospital, Liverpool, in the middle of an air raid during which the hospital was hit. His mother, Anne Grace Clark, had been in labour for seven days – 'He didn't want to leave his mother,' joked his sister Kay later. A doctor on the delivery ward immediately noticed something remarkable: 'He's got great fists, he's going to do something with those hands.' Anne had been expecting a girl (she had even decorated Ossie's room in pink) so she asked the midwife to suggest a boy's name – she chose Raymond, and that's what he was christened. However, the family was later evacuated to Oswaldtwistle, where they lived behind a shop. It was there that Ossie spent the first seven years of his life and developed a strong local accent about which he was teased when the family later moved to Warrington: 'You're a real Ossie,' and the nickname stuck for life.

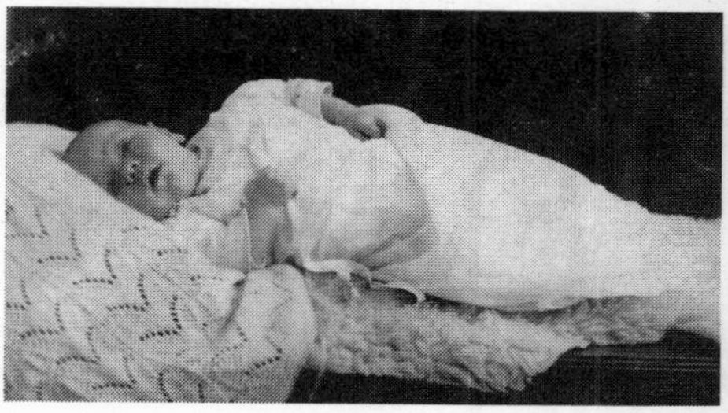
Ossie Clark, aged six weeks, 1942.

Ossie was the youngest of six children. Gladys, a tailoress, was already 18 when he was born and would wheel him around in his pram. After Gladys was Kay, then aged 16, who would later become a jazz singer. Then Beryl, 12; Sammy, 8, who would later join the army and eventually die of a heart attack in his thirties; and John, 4. Though closest in age to Ossie, John was of an entirely different temperament. He enjoyed football and other sports, while Ossie preferred to listen to the robust repartee of his older sisters. Their humour and love of a good story was certainly something he shared later on in life, though it was in fact John who went on to be professional entertainer.

At the outbreak of war in 1939, Ossie's father, Samuel Duncan Clark, had been too old to serve and was put in charge of the naval victualling at Risley. Samuel had travelled the world as chief steward on a P&O liner, and I recall Ossie once showing me his near-perfect naval records, laughing but saying proudly, 'He was chief boot-boy and always got 10 out of 10!' Samuel also had a talent for music and played in a jazz band on the Cunard ships that sailed from Liverpool to the USA. He could play guitar, mandolin – which he also taught his wife how to play – banjo, ukulele and balalaika, and this musical background led to both John and Ossie becoming choristers at the huge St Oswald's church in nearby Winwick. The boys excelled sufficiently to sing in Chester Cathedral and York Minster and, at the age of 12, Ossie won a medal for his singing at Darley Dale.

Samuel would return from each of his long journeys with great bolts of cloth and exotic presents from far-flung places for his children, who would rush down to the quay to meet the ship with their mother. Gladys recalls that however long their father was away Anne would 'never think of looking at another man and never uttered a swear word in her life'. Theirs was a household that represented old-fashioned matriarchal values – Anne was the focal point for many lives and inspired loyalty and respect in her family and friends. Ossie always said, 'It was a marriage made in heaven,' and perhaps this model of happiness later influenced his own romanticism. John thinks their mother poured so much love into Ossie that it 'turned him the way he was'. He was apparently breastfed until he was two, which may help to explain his emotional dependency. Certainly Ossie and his mother shared a lasting mutual devotion. It was also from her that he inherited his superstitious nature. Whenever there was a full moon she would tell the children to go outside, look at the moon and turn the coins in their pockets for good luck. The mystical sense of the powers of the planets and the natural world stayed with him throughout his life.

When Ossie was seven the family moved to the village of Orford near Warrington. There, the family enjoyed a lively, creative and happy rural existence. The semi-detached house had concrete floors, and a staircase and a little front garden with a lilac tree and a bicycle shed. Across the road were open fields in which they went for long walks, picnics and bike rides. By this time the three girls were married and had left home, though the boys were soon joined by Kay's two children Carol and Jimmy Melia, who became like a brother and sister to Ossie. Kay was working as a jazz singer and earning her living in London.

According to Jimmy, Ossie's father was more aloof than his mother. 'The women in the family were always friendly, it was a happy atmosphere. But his father liked to watch the football every Saturday night and everyone had to be quiet as he listened to the results as he religiously did the football pools. There was John, Carol, Ossie and myself and sometimes we would be squabbling together – his eyebrow would twitch with annoyance, he'd tell us all to shut up and then disappear behind his copy of the *Liverpool Echo*.'

Ossie was a mischievous child. A little boy living in the same street once showed him how to steal a Dinky car from Woolworth's by sliding the box up the sleeve of his jacket. When the pair arrived home they were questioned as to where the toy had come from and subsequently ticked off and barred from visiting town. Beryl's daughter Margaret remembers a visit to the house when she was about two: "Ossie was a basket. He took me in my pram to Orford Park to meet his friends and play football – he was so engrossed in the game that he returned home without me!' Shirley Conrad, a neighbour at the time, remembers Ossie as a pleasant and well-mannered boy who was always smiling. She recalls Ossie making clothes for his dolls even at the age of eight, painstakingly cutting the pieces of fabric and fitting each doll with great concentration. Carol remembers him designing her a bikini when he was not yet 10 – he had watched Gladys sewing complicated patterns and wanted to emulate her with his already skilful fingers.

Creative flair went hand in hand with human warmth in Ossie's family. His mother had learnt to knit for the First World War effort, and at the age of eight was making mufflers, jumpers, scarves and hats 'for the cannon-fodder being wiped out in Europe', as Ossie dryly informed RCA students in a lecture he gave there in 1996. 'She had terrific colour sense, and I'm sure I inherited a lot of my style from her. She put unusual colours together – some very soft and subtle and then some unusually dark. "You must", she said, "have light to appreciate the depths".'

Ossie failed his 11-plus exam. From the local school in Orford he was sent to Beaumont Secondary School where he stayed until he was 15. There he had the good fortune to have an art teacher, Roy Thomas, who was fanatical about fashion and ballet. Thomas would sometimes throw pieces of chalk – or even the blackboard eraser – at misbehaving boys, so Ossie sat at the back of the class with his friend Peter Fearon to avoid the missiles. Fearon recalls that very early on Thomas recognised Ossie's talent and would hold up his drawings to show the class.

Ossie begin to draw clothes: shirts, jackets and suits, all with unusual details. When Fearon mentioned that his mother liked to sew, Ossie asked to be introduced to her. The meeting was the first of many. Ossie would visit and talk about his designs, or sit cutting out paper patterns or sewing and altering the clothes he was working on. He took great delight in these creative sessions and his brain was always teeming with ideas. Says Fearon, 'He told me then that his dream was to become a fashion designer.' Although Ossie was teased at school about it, he never strayed from his chosen path. At home he would study Gladys working – he would borrow her fabrics, consult her on how things should be done and occasionally they would create things together. Gladys recalls making their mother's outfit for John's wedding in 1961 – Ossie made the hat. 'It was the same green as the suit, covered in silk voile roses and was very beautiful. Each rose was deepest pink in the centre and shaded out to nearly white.' Ossie designed himself a collarless suit – the first ever 'Beatles' suit.

At the age of thirteen, Ossie was offered the choice at school of training for either engineering or the building trade and chose the latter because the engineering master was a bully. He was given access to teachers who taught architecture and learnt many skills he later deemed invaluable – he once told me that the subject had taught him about proportion, height and volume. In the meantime Roy Thomas telephoned Ossie's mother and recommended that Ossie attend classes on Saturday mornings at Warrington Art School. This he did, despite contradictory advice from his headmaster, who thought the classes a waste of time and suggested Ossie keep art as a hobby and get a 'proper' job.

A teenage Ossie at home in Warrington. His precocious fashion drawings hang behind him.

Anne gave Ossie her full support and he was eventually accepted into Manchester Regional Art College in 1958 at the age of 16. He was not required to submit a portfolio and was admitted on the strength of a few outstanding drawings of ballet dancers and some fashion pictures based on American magazines. He received the princely grant of £6.6s.8d per term, which his mother augmented by giving up smoking and going out to work – for the first time in her life – as a home help.

During his first term at Manchester Ossie caught the five to nine train from Warrington Central each morning and lived on two shillings a day.

He also took pills prescribed for his mother. This was the beginning of what would become a lifetime's abuse of both prescribed and illegal drugs on which he became dependent for work and recreation.

The college was a red-brick Victorian municipal building with a huge exhibition hall and a glass domed roof over a central atrium where jazz bands would play, situated near the Northern College of Music and the BBC in Oxford Road. The post-war generation enjoyed a time of great change within many art colleges, and Manchester in particular had an interesting mixture of students from varied social backgrounds – it was fast becoming a place where the working class youth could express themselves.

Ossie was part of a very charismatic group of people convinced of their own talent, whether they were artists, actors, writers or musicians. He was extrovert and already a precocious stylist: he wore flares he'd made himself and 13-inch winklepickers, a trilby hat and a long black ex-army coat; his hair was dyed black, meticulously cut short in the fashion of the day. Jane Normanton, a fellow student at the time, recalls thinking, 'Wow, you can do that in London, but not here! He was determined to go places.' Ossie was popular and worked hard – when shows were imminent until late at night. He was a little impatient and would commandeer, saying things like, 'Don't say "frocks", say "dresses"!'

One of Ossie's most influential contemporaries was a wild, charismatic textiles student called Mo McDermott whom Ossie first met in 1959. It was Mo who introduced Ossie to Celia Birtwell, whom he would later marry. She was at that time studying textiles at Salford College. Celia remembers Mo saying to her, 'I know this extraordinary guy and he's at Manchester Art School and you've got to meet him.' She says, 'He was wearing one of those leather sleeveless pre-Beatles pullovers that he'd made himself and this round-collared shirt with a tie. He used to come to my home because my mother could sew; he'd talk to her about the problems he was having at Manchester.' Ossie nicknamed Celia 'Beakie' – a term of endearment which he was still using well after the breakdown of their marriage.

The 'in' group of the period, of which Ossie was a prominent member, met at the Cona Coffee Bar or the Twisted Wheel, and included Alan Whitehead, Krishna Banji (later known as Ben Kingsley), Mo McDermott, Celia Birtwell and Jenny Dearden. Jenny had known Ossie since the age of 14 and was one of his early girlfriends. She recalls how he used to make her little outfits and looked after her. 'He was very intelligent, kind, gentlemanly, and protective,' she says.

In his RCA lecture Ossie remembers how he wept after the first pair of trousers he tried to make twisted round his legs when he tried them on and the tutor explained how you 'close the outer seam and turn over, then you balance and mark'. This tutor was tailor Louis Huet, a Belgian expert in leatherwork who early on in his career made outfits for the Beatles from a shop called Togger in Stockport. Huet was a perfectionist and amazed at Ossie's later success, as he found him a 'distracted' student!

Ossie during his college days in Manchester.

Ossie went to Paris several times and other students would chip in to help him with the fare. Gladys remembers that he did work-experience at Christian Dior, just sweeping the floor, 'to study a large fashion house and get the atmosphere there'. In his RCA lecture Ossie recalled, 'On my first trips to Paris I saw the Dior collections which to my eyes were so exciting – being crammed into the back of this huge salon and seeing exquisite clothes being paraded in front of these wealthy women. Barbara Hutton arrived with two Pekinese dogs and sat on a blue moire couch and stopped the show now and again saying, "Divine! I'll have it in both colours," regardless of the price. I saw Coco Chanel, which was truly amazing, with Susie Parker modelling.' He added, 'I also saw Pierre Cardin, who made this collection of clothes which was mad but wonderful at the same time . . . John Tyra [one of Ossie's tutors] also bought the first pair of square-toed Roger Vivier shoes which were so elegant in comparison to the shoes in Manchester – it was the difference between an orchid and a dandelion.' Lynette Williams, who was in the year below Ossie, also went to Paris. On one trip Ossie was consigned to doing three days in a toile school – 'He was not too pleased about this,' she says, 'as he wanted to be a free agent.'

Williams remembers Ossie as quiet and dedicated, a little lost sometimes. 'He could be caustic and occasionally aggressive; there were certain people he wouldn't associate with – he knew he was going on to do better things. The other male students would laugh, as he was always with the girls but showed no sexual interest in them.' One night after a party, too late to get home, Williams and a girlfriend spent the night with Ossie – him in between them in the bed. He said, 'You've got nothing to worry about,' and they didn't. However, Ossie seemed horrified at this point by the idea of homosexuality and wasn't interested in pursuing it at all.

In a small class of fifteen students Ossie was soon on first-name terms with the staff, and they encouraged him to apply for grants and bursaries. He later acknowledged the support of two of his tutors in particular, Ms Ryder and Ms Tyra, as invaluable. It was they who encouraged him to take the entrance exam for the RCA in London – his interview was successful and he was awarded a scholarship.

Bernard Nevill and Janey Ironside had been on the interview board. Nevill remembers that Ossie and fellow student Anthony Price stood out for their chutzpah, confidence and vitality. Ossie recorded, 'I was interviewed by Janey Ironside, later to become a dear friend. She was a truly startling woman, like a magic person. I visited Ennismore Gardens when I was doing the exam and was amazed that so much love and care went into what the students were being taught. The huge windows overlooking gardens and plush furniture were just another world to a little hick boy from the north.

'When I got the Royal College after being the bees knees in Manchester, I was given two and a half metres of white poplin and a pattern and told to make this shirt. Well, I put it together okay and so did the girl who came with me, but I was amazed to see some of the students could hardly thread a needle. I thought, how on earth did *they* get here? But Janey could see – she made the final choice. She saw that each one had a talent – it could be drawing or it could be making clothes or it could be ideas or the way they were passionate about a period. In fact, there was a boy in the year before called Normain Bain, who came from Scotland and had worked as a librarian until he was 24, when he learnt about the Royal College. He brought his drawings but he couldn't sew to save his life . . . he did the most extraordinary designs. He went and looked at the Chanel Collection and when he returned he said, "If they tell me I've overdone it once more, I'll say look at Chanel – she had peacock feathers, carnations, black lace, pink ribbons . . ."'

Norman Bain testifies to the technical proficiency Ossie acquired at Manchester: 'In the north at that time the technical colleges were excellent. When Ossie arrived at the college, he was more or less perfect technically. He would finish exercises in a trice and then wish to go out and party. He could do everything without too much trouble. He had superb concentration.

Concentration and energy are the key to all major successes.'

Ossie's first digs in London in 1961 were in Elgin Avenue, Maida Vale, at his sister Kay's and cost four pounds a week. By the time Ossie arrived in London his Manchester soulmate Mo McDermott was settled there and had discovered a network of lively, smart and ambitious people with whom he associated. This set included David Hockney – then still a student at the RCA – for whom Mo was life-modelling. Celia Birtwell had followed Mo south and was working as a waitress in Hades Coffee Bar. Reunited in London, Mo, Ossie and Celia spent a lot of time together. Mo was self-educated, self-assured and openly gay, and his company seemed to give Ossie the confidence to face up to his own hitherto ambivalent sexuality. However, Ossie was drawn to Celia's romantic, Botticellian face and was stimulated by their common interests. She had a room in John Manasseh's house in Addison Road and recalls, 'Ossie used to visit me there. John wanted to refurbish the house so I went to live in this flat off Ladbroke Grove. So Ossie and I shared a bed and somehow had this little relationship.' This is an understatement, for Celia clearly adored and understood Ossie – though his sexual propensities must have been obvious to her – and he was very attracted to her physically and valued her lively, responsive spirit and intuition.

Hylan Booker, an American who was in the same class as Ossie and worked closely with him for three years, told me how he adored him. 'As a student he was always so good and pulled one's own standards up, even if his attitude did not always conform. Janey Ironside had a special relationship with her students – it was very personal, very warm, very open. We blossomed because we were so encouraged. She was quiet and authoritative. It was extremely stimulating because we had such talented students – Janice Wainwright, Zandra Rhodes, Sally Tuffin and Marion Foale; John Bates the milliner and James Wedge came in as instructors. Grace Coddington would come in as a model. They were really the good old days – the feeling was good and it lasted. Ossie was a rebel and pooh-poohed conventions. Within our year he was the most excellent pattern cutter. He was brave, fabulous, debonair and witty; he was always able to say something sardonic but he was bursting with talent. He was also incredibly competitive – he was a true designer and had great confidence.' Ossie was very inventive at discovering new sources of inspiration, combining high and low fashion. Like his contemporaries, Ossie would trawl the Portobello Road for ideas, but he also loved the Victoria and Albert Museum, where he examined exquisite clothes from the past, such as the splendid thirties silks seductively cut on the bias by

Ossie is at the centre of a posed photograph with fellow students, taken before a show at the Royal College of Art in 1965.

Madeleine Vionnet. Vionnet, Schiaparelli and Molyneux had a huge and enduring influence on Ossie's work. He had a keen sense of history, and the intricacy, romance and perfectionism of these designers inspired him. 'Ossie was hooked on glamour,' says his teacher Bernard Nevill.

The first design Ossie and Celia worked on together was a paper dress for Molly Parkin, editor of *Nova* magazine. Ahead of its time, it was an ephemeral thing, small, simply designed, slightly fitted over the ribcage, and the beauty was in the printing. They sold for 5 shillings – all the students wanted them. 'They were done on mail order in three sizes from home,' Celia recalls. 'Jane Asher modelled in one – I remember one in lime-green and orange with Poiret designs I had transcribed.'

At about this time, Ossie forged a significant friendship with David Hockney, and for a short time they became lovers. While it seems probable that Ossie and Mo went to bed together, this was Ossie's first documented homosexual experience. Hockney was seemingly innocent, but confident and already hugely accepted by the world. Ossie was longing for the confirmation of fellowship and sophistication and needed to experience new excitements and challenges. 'He introduced me to sex, drugs and rock and roll,' Hockney later said of Ossie. Set apart from conventional society by their sexuality, the two men soon had the world at their feet.

Years later, Ossie recalled the thrill of his first trip to America with David in the summer of 1964, which was to shape and tighten his fashion sense, and open up the glamorous world he wanted to inhabit. He met Bette Davis and Dennis Hopper, and was mobbed by fans at the Hollywood Bowl when mistaken for George Harrison. He returned to the Royal College with swathes of Pop art material which he used in his last student show – an event unlike anything seen before: a dress with electric lightbulbs flashing down the hem made the headlines and was televised. Ossie became a household name overnight. Janey Ironside gave him the roll of honour and he was the only one of his year to graduate with a first-class degree.

The climate of the time could not have been more conducive to Ossie's quirky, extreme nature. As the groundbreaking designer Mary Quant put it: 'After the war and its privation and fear, the older generation thought things might return to the situation before. It simply didn't. There was a negative and gloomy vacuum. It had to be filled. We cut through it and created a fresh look. Out of the vacuum came a burst of energy and optimism. We started very young and were very fortunate and very confident.'

Ossie's early financial success came through the maturity of outlook, pro-

Ossie in shades at the top of the Empire State Building with David Hockney (top left), Derek Boshier (top right), Peter Phillips (middle right) and Pauline Fordham (centre), 1966.

fessionalism and expertise of those behind a shop called 'Woollands 21', which opened in Sloane Street in 1961. Vanessa Denza, who ran the store, recalls: 'It was such a small crowd in London and Chelsea then. I knew all the press who were writing on fashion. I knew a lot of painters and the photographers. Everything was done in a very central area. There were loads of parties. Martin Moss, later Managing Director of Simpsons, was the powerhouse behind the 21 Shop. It was designed by Terence Conran with wonderful furniture by a New Zealander called David Bishop.' Moss considered Ossie 'the outstanding student – fascinating, but he was unstable in a way' – an instability noticed later by one of his clients, Stella Astor, who felt even after Ossie's huge success he was not quite at home with himself. The transition from the self-styled 'hick boy' from the north to London's most avant-garde couturier and trend-setter was phenomenally rapid and surely put great strain on his psychological resources. He was truculent to people who interviewed him and simply grunted his way through a TV interview. Ossie has admitted that he was 'too successful too young and didn't have the strength of character to cope with it then.'

HEADY DAYS – 1965-1974

Ossie's first knock-out coat, with Pop art images fused with psychedelic material given to him by the American painter Robert Indiana and Bridget Riley's op images, was recorded in a *Vogue* photograph by David Bailey in 1965. Utterly contemporary, stark and bold in its apparent simplicity, the construction of the silk satin coat is deceptively elaborate. There are broad black and white stripes travelling diagonally over the collar to meet wavy rhythms on a white background, just about the bust. Suddenly this strong swirl is intercepted by more black stripes which descend to the knee. "I want to dress frilly people in colours that confuse the eye," Ossie stated with a confidence and sophistication remarkable for his years. Despite having only just graduated, Ossie constructed his dress with professionalism; the machine work criss-crosses over and over again. In the *Vogue* photo Ossie stands alongside

Celia and Ossie and dog Beulah.

the model, pale and pencil thin in black with a modish Beatles haircut.

Before Ossie left the Royal College his talent had been spotted by Alice Pollock, who became a vital factor in his success.

Although she had had no formal training, Alice made dresses and children's clothes. She had set up a shop named Quorum in Ansdell Street in 1964. Enormously confident, practical, extravagant and trend-setting, she instinctively recognised Ossie's compatible talents.

Celia Birtwell remembers the day he first got the job. 'He said, "I have met this extraordinary girl born the same month, same day, same year as me. I think she's an amazing person and she really wants me to design." Ossie did a collection for Alice and she asked me to do one print the first evening, then three or four, and gradually I would work from home and do the designs. I'd often want to talk to him about them but you couldn't. It was just do this! or do them or do whatever you want and I'll put it on my table and I'll work with them. Bit by bit it evolved. He did the chiffons, he did the snakeskin jacket, the leather jacket, the bomber jacket, the whole thing began to take off.'

Ossie had a small but devoted team working with him at Quorum. Kathleen Coleman began work there as a sample machinist, after training at Harrods and Marshall & Snelgrove. She was technically brilliant and worked for Ossie for seventeen years. Kathleen used to work designs out with Ossie and then stay up all night to finish the elaborate pieces that were too complex for factory production. He merely had to explain something to her and she was off to whip it up. 'I worked on all the shows. He wanted to do it all himself but he wasn't always able to work things out. At first he only let me do the hard bits – if he couldn't put a sleeve in, or a zip on a collar. He christened all his dresses. One suit was called 'Blanche' after a pattern cutter, others were 'Star', 'Lapis' and 'Daisy Flower'. 'Ziggy', created in 1972, was a best seller. There was another straight dress with a spiral which only I knew how to sew. I had to teach Isobel [another machinist] how to do the designs.' Kathleen revered Alice Pollock, but criticised the fashion firm Radley who later took over Quorum. She felt they constrained Ossie's wondrous free spirit.

Just as Ossie relied on Alice Pollock's energy and business sense for the production and sale of the dresses, so he drew on Celia for emotional stability and creative stimulus. Their first years together were relatively innocent and optimistic. Ossie admired her looks but suffered terrible jealousy. He told me how people stopped in their tracks open-mouthed to stare at this 'sex kitten in sailor pants' in Galeries Lafayette in Paris. In 1964 after his success in America with Hockney, he persuaded her they should live together and they moved to 8a St. Quintin Avenue. Celia had been amazed that Ossie rang from America to say how much he missed her. 'He was very persuasive and a strong character. I relented. At first we were this funny little couple. He would go out and party and bring nice friends home. I would enjoy that. He was always very, very exciting. He'd go down the Portobello Road and bring back another vase or another this or another that. Or be saying, "Let's do this". So his contribution was marvellous. Because I'm more domestic, placid and down to earth. I let him run at his pace. I felt he had to make his own life in a way, otherwise it wouldn't have worked.'

What did work was the creative partnership between Ossie and Celia: their chiffon dresses enchanted the world, and are still invoked as design classics. 'Celia Birtwell created some of the most beautiful dress fabrics of the period, characterised by Art Deco forms and Audubon botanical sketches in offbeat colours – prune, dead rose, saffron, a myriad of blues – that decked satin moss crêpes and wispy chiffons. Her bold Egyptian prints and trellis-like patterns fused and flowed round the body,' said Sandy Boler, editor of *Brides*. 'Ossie used crepe and gauze in a way it had never been used before. His cut and Celia's prints were indivisible. They were innocent and sexy at the same time – delicate, divine and utterly desirable.'

In 1965, Ossie and Celia moved from St. Quintin Avenue to a pretty house in Blenheim Crescent, Notting Hill, owned by John Lafflin. For £10 a week, they rented one floor overlooking a Carmelite Nunnery. 'We had a view of three separate gardens and used to watch the nuns planting vegetables,' Celia recalls. 'We worked in the bedroom and had a little balcony and a black poodle called Beulah. Ossie never left for work at any set time. He would bring back six albums – Jimi Hendrix, the Beatles, whatever appealed to him. He was terrific fun to be with and I loved his zest for life and music, but he became more and more impatient. When he met Alice he had a different social set and they took drugs together. This was when his character began to change, but at the beginning he was oh so lovely.'

In the spring of 1966, Ossie had his first fashion show for buyers in a barge moored at Little Venice, impressing both Prudence Glynn, editor of *The Times* fashion pages and Molly Parkin, editor of *Nova* magazine. Later that year Quorum moved from Kensington to a prim white building at 52 Radnor Walk in Chelsea. Downstairs the walls were dark with huge mirrors and a

In the kitchen at Blenheim Crescent, 1967. Celia and Ossie found the letters that decorate the wall in a junk shop.

OSSIE

resplendent white leather sofa. Upstairs was the office and atelier. This address soon became a prominent feature on the map of swinging and aristocratic London. By August the *Daily Mail* was declaring: 'Ossie Clark and Alice Pollock are showing people what they should be wearing in 1967. Their small London boutique has boomed into a wholesale business selling as far apart as Scandinavia and the West Indies. Quorum skirts are 6 inches above the knee at the last count. The three models in the picture reveal yonks of slender leg swathed in clothes of striking class and elegance. One is a consummately cut white tunic with pink straps, the second a shirtwaister in satin with long sleeves and elegant cuffs, the third a little sleek black jacket top and a dress which seems to be a good 12 inches above the knee tapered around the top.' The dresses Ossie produced were infinitely softer and more refined than Mary Quant's mini-skirt.

Candida Betjeman (daughter of the late Poet Laureate and a long term friend of Ossie's) bought two of his dresses for her honeymoon. 'It was the closest I ever got to understanding the art of making women's clothes and the importance of the cut. I rate people who do things beautifully, because they are enrichers. All my daughters wear the balldress Ossie designed for me for the 1990 Chatsworth Ball. It is red and ballerina length with yards of silk chiffon billowing out. Even now [1998] Imo has had a great success with it at Glyndebourne.'

Ossie had broken the mould. Up till then debs had still worn twin sets and pearls. Wearing Ossie meant being part of it all. The Beatles dropped in. Twiggy would save money to buy Ossie's extravagant frilly blouses, as later would the American star Fay Dunaway; Elizabeth Taylor was famously photographed in the shortest of Ossie's mini dresses. Karen Radley, who worked at Quorum remembers that Sharon Tate (the wife of Roman Polanski who became one of Charles Manson's victims) was photographed in Ossie's full-length python coat with a mink lining not long before her murder. In the shop, Karen once almost fell over the actor Warren Beatty, brought in by Julie Christie. Brigitte Bardot spent £350 ($600) on a pair of pave velvet and crêpe pants. Liza Minnelli's costumes for the film *Cabaret* were designed by Quorum.

The Rolling Stones' Brian Jones lived over the shop when he wasn't staying at the Ritz, and ordered Ossie's floral shirts by the dozen. Ossie recorded in his diary: 'Brian Jones and Keith Richards took to wearing the satins printed by Celia and the skin-tight jewel-coloured trousers from a stash of pre-war corset satin Alice Pollock found. I made men's shirts with frills in chiffon, in crêpe with a one-sided silver collar and a leather jacket of metallic blue snake.' Quorum, a crashpad of louche grooviness, not only attracted the attentions of the police after the famous Stones drug trial, but of the rag trade spies. Whenever Ossie invented a new sleeve design they would infiltrate the shop and disappear to copy it on the High Street.

Famous for his innovations, Ossie discovered the first snakeskins in a dark cavernous leather warehouse. 'What's that?' he asked, touching the skins of twenty-six pythons which had been on a roller for twenty years. 'They sprung to life and lay opened before me.' He bought them for 'thirty bob' a foot. Suddenly snakeskin shorts and hot pants were produced and worn with Biba boots.

The first Ossie Clark collection was bought by Henri Bendel of New York – the first export of a talented British designer's work, rather than of dependable British wool and waterproofing. His inventions so impressed Manhattan that lesser talents immediately copied them for Seventh Avenue – all the devilish snakeskins, the chiffons, the midis that swept away the minis, the flared riding coats, the soberly tailored men's jackets constructed for beautiful girls.

Marit Allen, English *Vogue's* 'Young Ideas' editor, soon realised Ossie was

Entwined with his Quorum partner, Alice Pollock, in a photograph by Snowdon. Ossie's chiffon shirt and scarf are printed with Celia Birtwell designs; Alice wears one of her crêpe de chine dresses, 1969.

setting a prototype with each new collection. She set up a *Vogue* sitting for Norman Parkinson, who photographed Jean Shrimpton wearing Ossie's leather motorbike jacket, gaucho pants and fluid maxi coat. 'It let me in for a series of awful encounters with the editor [Beatrix Miller]. She felt she had to justify everything to Condé Nast in New York, and felt the clothes were outside high fashion. It would be the first time *Vogue* had put its weight behind radical subculture.' Vogue published the picture.

The stars kept coming. Marianne Faithfull, singer, girlfriend of Mick Jagger and star of *Girl on a Motorcycle* (1968), visited Quorum, loved Ossie's clothes and bought a suede suit trimmed in python with fluted peplum. The model Verushka came into the studio in Radnor Walk to be photographed for the *Telegraph* magazine. Britt Ekland bought a long beautifully fitted python skin coat for £150.

Ossie was the first designer to fuse rock music and fashion, and this wild combination seared into contemporary consciousness. Marianne Faithfull brought Mick Jagger to Quorum and Ossie instantly fell under the rock star's spell. 'My first sight of Jumping Jack Flash was his tongue, which appeared from behind the curtain of the two changing rooms, followed by his face, which broke into the grin I was destined to know so well . . . There was no conceit, he was very natural, coy, camp almost, a joker, self-confident, sensuous lips, a winning smile broke over large teeth – I noticed the expensive cosmetic dentistry, the expressive blue eyes that creased up with laughter and the fake cockney accent.' Marianne told me: 'I knew Mick and I knew Ossie. I thought they were made for each other and they were. Mick needed somebody who could express what he saw himself as being. They were kindred spirits. Mick had a vision in his head of what he wanted to be and Ossie implemented that vision.' Mick's first jump suit, which could be unzipped on stage, was designed by Ossie. And later he made the famous satanic black cape that Jagger wore at the infamous Altamont Festival in the USA.

To all those who attended Ossie's fashion shows they were unforgettable points in their lives. Patti Boyd (girlfriend of George Harrison and later wife of Eric Clapton) modelled for Ossie. She described him as wildly undisciplined, but a perfectionist in every detail, staying up the night before a show to finish his creations and select the music that would fit in with his dresses. 'The only time I walked the catwalk was for Ossie,' she said.

The most spectacular of Ossie's early shows took place at Chelsea Town Hall in 1967. It was reported on the Pathé Newsreel. Chelita Secunda recalls how the models, including Patti Boyd and Marianne Faithfull, 'danced,

Mick Jagger pictured in one of the many catsuits designed by Ossie for him to wear on stage.

sashayed and twirled up and down the catwalk. Gala Mitchell, his favourite model, almost fell off the end.' Celia felt 'shivers down my spine. It was the breaking down of those old stodgy rules.' Ossie was given thirty bouquets of flowers, and his niece Margaret Clementson remembers him driving her back to Linden Gardens in the Buick. 'I only realised how famous Uncle Ossie was when there was a vast bunch of lilies with a card from John Lennon and Yoko Ono. It said, "Sorry, good luck, I hope it goes well."' Despite this heady celebrity, Ossie never forgot his family, proudly inviting them to all the shows, to share his success. He designed dresses for Kay to sing her jazz numbers at Ronnie Scott's, and repaid kindnesses from other family members by extravagantly offering them clothes from the shop. Margaret was embarrassed at his generosity then and was happy to repay him later on when he fell on hard times.

Notes in Ossie's jottings testify to the unusual and hectic organisation behind the shows: 'If we don't go on soon the birds will get too hot.' These carnivalesques were invariably an hour or two late starting, with Ossie determined to ensure the kind of flamboyant display that became one of his contributions to the developing art of showing fashion. David Hockney recently described them as marvellous 'theatre'.

Ossie stated that he wanted 'to make a woman aware of her body', and in pursuit of this ideal he brought in a new style of model. They were no longer 'tall things that swayed at you as they walked down the cat walk', but characters in their own right. Gala Mitchell, with her sculptural bone structure, big eyes and theatrical style, looked particularly good in leather jackets. Others who modelled were KariAnne Jagger (Mick's sister-in-law, whose captivating dances on the stage inspired the Hollies' song which begins "Hey Carrie-Anne, what's your game now, can anybody play?"); Amanda Lear (Salvador Dali's muse and as good a performer as KariAnne); and Lady Carina Fitzalan-Howard, daughter of the Duke of Norfolk, whom Alice had discovered walking down the street.

Ossie always dressed Marianne in black. He thought the most beautiful part of her body was the top bits, so he would show a lot of her breasts, then arms, shoulders and neck would be bare. He would also put gloves on her. Whenever she puts gloves on she thinks of him. The dresses he made for her to model would go in at the waist and come out in stiff taffeta, a tulip shape and quite long. The fashionable audience was enthralled by the new style of expression and they begged for more. The emphasis was on hedonism and display rather than hard-headed commercialism.

After refining the mini skirt, which Mary Quant popularised, but which Ossie claimed to have foreseen (there is a picture taken in Manchester in 1959, in which Ossie's girlfriend Anne Siddell wears a mini he had designed) Ossie and Alice Pollock produced the midi skirt in April 1967. This was hailed as the 'Bonnie and Clyde look'. The fashion pages reported the same year: 'Ossie moves fashion boundaries again, when he produces the maxi skirt mark 2.' He made coats that invoked a 1940s nostalgia. In a Parkinson photo for *Vogue* the model wears huge goggles and pilot's helmet with Russell & Bromley boots. Ossie's characteristic subtle but perfect sculpturing around the bosom, midriff and legs lends the coat a timeless distinction, recalling Ossie's teenage Oxfam discoveries of the largest and longest ex-army coats. In *Vogue* a year later a David Montgomery photograph shows a model wearing a superb classic long coat by Ossie, beautifully shaped around the bust, waist and thighs, in mist pink tweed. Meriel McCooey, the former *Sunday Times* fashion correspondent says her favourite outfit of Ossie's was a ballerina-length teddy bear coat made of fake fur material. Celia Birtwell possesses another Ossie coat with intricately fluted pleats, made in black gaberdine.

Ossie's greatest triumphs were the chiffon dresses he produced with Celia Birtwell. As the fashion design Caroline Charles says, 'Ossie epitomises the quirky nostalgia of thirties clothes. His use of Celia Birtwell prints made them doubly desirable. They were the most exciting designs of the times and I remember them with a tingle of pleasure.' *Herald Tribune* correspondent Suzy Menkes extends the tribute: 'Where often British designers mask lack of technical skills with frills and furbelows, Ossie was that rare thing – a romantic designer with a classic base. It was very important in the sixties. There was that taut, tight silhouette. Women's sexual power was controlled. It followed the body. It was the beginning of androgny.'

Ossie also developed the corset. He said himself in 1984, 'It took three years to get the corset shape perfect. Now it fits everyone from Marie Helvin to Marianne Faithfull.' St Laurent had declared, 'The laced corset is the symbol of sexuality' and observers saw the truth of this in Ossie's creations: 'A woman isn't just a woman in an Ossie, she's a super female blazing away at every man in sight.' Ossie brought out the delicacy, the sensuality, and above all the sexiness in the female shape.

He could twirl strips of bias cut chiffon into a fluted asymmetric smock. He cut on the bias like nobody else, straight into the cloth. Adie Hunter, who worked as Ossie's PR for five years, reminisces: 'My most memorable moment was seeing him cut on the floor at ten o'clock one night. It was the most incredible pattern on the bias called "the Daisy Whirligig Dress". I felt privileged to be there at such a moment of genius. It was like a Picasso, like a Leonardo da Vinci. He made the dress in marrocaine, which Celia had done the prints for. Marrocaine is quite an old fabric they reintroduced. It's stronger than crêpe de chine and soft.'

It was Celia's inspiration with the romantic prints that completed Ossie's designs. They allowed his sharp cut to relax into something softer and more heart-stoppingly seductive than his erotic leather jackets and tailored coats.

By now Ossie was being hailed as the 'King of the King's Road', and photographers would head down the King's Road to Radnor Walk. But Ossie's wild liberality, 'Take another dress, darling', does not run a successful business: by October 1968 Quorum was mired in debt. This time Ossie was lucky – Al Radley was thrilled by the chance to take over the shop. Radley Fashions had gone public in August 1968 and this was one of its first acquisitions. However, all did not go smoothly. Monty White, Radley's chairman, says: 'We were meant to have a business meeting with Ossie. Alice Pollock was away. Ossie was floating. Our arrangement was to meet Ossie at midday. He whizzed in completely preoccupied. He said he had to fly to New York at 5 p.m. and had to get some new shoes from the Chelsea Cobbler. He disappeared. He never returned. When Alice turned up on Monday, she was very businesslike.' Radley Fashions bought a 65 per cent stake in the two companies which ran Quorum: Ossie Clark (London) Limited, and Alice Pollock Limited. Under the deal, Ossie was given a salary and got a royalty based on sales. Despite the rather unpropitious beginnings to Ossie's relations with Radley Fashions, the partnership lasted from 1968 to 1977, and brought Ossie's designs to people who could never otherwise have afforded them.

Al Radley's aim was to develop Quorum from being the preserve of a fashion conscious clique into a shop for people who cared for fashion at a more affordable price. The company turned round Quorum's £70,000 debt and employed Rosie Bradford, an ex Royal College designer, to adapt Ossie's dresses for a wider market.

Monty remembered that sometimes Ossie simply didn't turn up at all. 'He had tremendous chips on his shoulder. He was producing work of genius, but it was all so ephemeral. He came into the shop but if he felt the attitude was wrong he would say angrily, "My soul has gone into these garments and you are treating them like dirt."'

'Ossie was a perfectionist and wanted to be absolutely in charge of what was turned out. He didn't really like delegating to a team,' Al Radley told me. Ossie did however enjoy financial security for the first and last time in his life. He was given a percentage of the sales, and earned £23,000 in 1973. 'He was thoroughly spoilt,' Celia believes, and certainly Al pampered him in many ways. He took him to Italy, Paris and Hong Kong. In Hong Kong Ossie was newly divorced, and had confided to his diary his despair at the loss of Celia and his sons Albert and George. He was gloomy and unpredictable, which overwhelmed any remaining sense of self interest.

Radley did keep Ossie's feet on the ground, despite the designer's resistance – by nature he hated the pressure of producing regular commercial shows – and structured the business side as best he could. He moved the Quorum shop from Radnor Walk to the King's Road. 'Photographers from all over the world raced down to our shop, just like the Chelsea Football Club today.' Ossie had a large atelier in Burnsall Street, but he missed his old workroom in Radnor Walk, where people had dropped by at all times of the day and particularly at night, when he tended to work.

Patti Harrison modelled a Quorum/Radley concoction in 1969, a tunic top and pants cut to emphasise the silhouette of her slender body. In photos

Ossie is standing alongside, almost more Twiggy-like than the skinny model herself. An enthusiastic store-buyer remarked, 'He's real fashion – utterly original – a genius. His first wholesale range has sold like a bomb.' 'We now produce 3,000 of one dress instead of three,' said Ossie.

Perhaps inevitably there were fallings out: Al Radley insisted on the importance of 'working in a sequence' and producing fresh ideas all the time, and he became exasperated with Ossie. Brian Shack, the accountant, fell out with both Ossie and his PR Adie Hunter, and by 1973 even Alice Pollock had argued with Ossie. Later he recalled, 'I snipped with Alice,' but never explained how or why.

Photographed on holiday c.1970 by Maurice, a friend of Tahlita Getty.

Adie makes clear how different were Ossie's working methods from those required by Radley. 'He accelerated at the last moment. At two in the morning he'd still be making something, almost his best stuff was coming up, he touched his genius – and then he'd stop. He never had the discipline to carry on. He'd have the show and the big accolade. He'd be up there – then go off on holiday. He'd then come back depressed. You just had to accept that was how he did it. Celia didn't like it either.'

Ossie's 1970 show, appropriately called 'Revolution', was held in a mews behind Berkeley Square and became immortalised in people's memories. The rock star Jimi Hendrix was there, and Patti Boyd, with her 'ankles like glass', sailed down the catwalk in creamy chiffon and a scarf fluttering with a design of pale blue birds. As Norman Bain recalled, 'with all Ossie's shows there was a wonderful feeling which came from within'. One photograph showed the model Sue Worth with strappy white sandals in a floral dress showing a tantalising amount of cleavage.

By 1971, a chagrined Courrèges was protesting, 'French women seem so easily influenced by outside sources. Haute couture is as good as dead. The streets of Paris are beginning to look like the Portobello Road.' Ossie understood: 'Youth is spreading its own tastes over the world, and it spells the end of the French way.' Ironically, and much to Radley's annoyance, Ossie was courted by Didier Grumach for Mendes, a French manufacturer who also made off-the-peg couture for Yves Saint Laurent. Ossie was invited to give a show in Paris that April. His fragile organisational discipline is vividly described by Suzy Menkes. 'As a bourgeois journalist, I arrived an hour early at the airport for the plane to Paris. Just as the doors were shutting, a raggle taggle gaggle arrived dressed in night-for-day clothes – jackets with red and black patterns. Someone was wearing a chiffon dress with dragons down the side. Of course it was Ossie with his group, which included Vanessa de Lisle. When we arrived at Orly, people smiled and shrugged their shoulders wryly, and threw their hands up saying "Les anglais!", expressing the eccentric mad spirit of the group.

'They had a bit of paper with no address or booking or anything. Ossie had been drinking on the plane. We eventually found Grumbach in a dubious street near the Madeleine. Ossie was so prima donnaish, but on one level so wonderful. It was a magical band of creative people. Ossie was "farfelu", like a wonderful dragonfly. It's sad it ultimately didn't get anywhere.'

The French loved Ossie calling him 'divin, excentrique, erotique'. Tellingly, they reported the dresses 'ne correspondent pas a notre vie, mais

Ossie and Celia with George and Albert, Linden Gardens, 1971.

seduiront surement les hommes (don't reflect our lives but will undoubtedly seduce men)'. Ossie restored that Edwardian naughtiness to gay Paree – hips swayed, bottoms bounced, arms were encased in leg of mutton sleeves. Marit Allen raved about this show: 'Ossie Clark's collection was a fantasy of the finest silks, cut velvet and dotted chiffon cut into parachute frills and knife-edged pleats, plunging necks and clinging insets. A satin guitar set as a stomacher in plum crêpe was his favourite. There were incredibly contoured seams across the back with knife pleats springing from the jacket insets, long skirts alive with the cut, flare and frills, pleats and peplums, and his ultimate raincoat cut, which flared from the riding mac fabric – long puffed sleeves and a huge collar. Audacious and incredibly feminine.'

Life ran at a hot pace for Ossie that year – he had to race back to London to complete his Ossie Clark and Radley collections. He had been thrilled to bits by the French success, and his home collection was pronounced 'much more Londony'. However, no lasting business came from the excursion. Recently Al Radley explained why. 'After the show several appointments were made with important fabric suppliers from Lyons; Ossie just never showed up.' At other times Radley would take Ossie to Interstasse, the huge fabric emporium in Germany. 'There were warehouses upon warehouses of cloth. It was exhausting covering it all, but Ossie just didn't want to do the legwork.'

Suzy Menkes's assertion that, 'The Royal Court Show [25 May 1971] in Sloane Square was the most extraordinary moment in the history of fashion', was understandable hyperbole. After the Paris show in April, it combined technical innovations with pure glamour. David Hockney had designed the programme with a drawing of Celia. Set to begin at midnight, the show was not ready to start until 2.30 a.m. Ossie had ordered Black Magic chocolates in their distinctive thirties boxes for every seat, but because it was Eastertime, the boxes turned out to contain bunnies and chicks. 'Ossie came to me hysterical, furious and screaming,' Norman Bain said. 'Because he wanted the art deco box to complement the mood of the designs.'

Model Penelope Tree was there in a see-through blouse with David Bailey in a liquorice black suit. The restaurateur Michael Chow was in a cerise satin blazer, heading a contingent of oriental trendies. Lord Harlech, former ambassador to Washington, was there to see his daughter, Alice Ormsby-Gore, modelling. David Hockney fell asleep in the seat of honour in the front row. Norman Bain commented, 'Even the fans became restless when it was 2 a.m. and the show hadn't begun. Suddenly Linda and Paul McCartney were smuggled in next to me. She was groomed to one inch of her life and flooded with scent. Flash bulbs started popping off. I simply don't understand how they have any retinas left! One had a brief awareness of what it is like to be that famous.'

There was a screen of transparent gauze as in a pantomime, and light came out from behind the curtains; through this you could see Ossie dressing a model. Patti Boyd twirled in a cape-topped dress that showed her breasts beneath. Carina Fitzalan-Howard and Gala slid on in ruched tarts' dresses worn with heavily sequinned platform shoes. Models gyrated across the flowery set in Ossie's latest figure-hugging dresses. Shoulders, cleavage and nipples were teasingly revealed in slashed-away shapes, boldly printed in scarlet and black. Ossie got a standing ovation.

The show in London incarnated a look that said 'it's chic to be vulgar'. Ossie declared he was deliberately designing to bring out the tart in the woman: 'Right now I am in a dress mood.' Said Alison Adburgham in the *Guardian* on 13 July 1971: 'Let's hope he will disembarrass himself of the prevailing Forties influence and create a new look relevant to the Seventies.'

Ossie had another memorable show at Nikki Waymouth's house (Augustus John's former studio), 26 Mallord Street, Chelsea. Nikki Waymouth, (née Samuels) was an heiress, who later married the American fashion jeweller Ken Lane. The opulent house, provided an ideal backdrop, with the models descending its narrow spiral staircase. Patti Harrison, an Ossie fan, came out of her hermitage in Henley to model for him; Bianca Jagger flew in from Jamaica. 'The models wore fitted bellboy jackets with pointed fronts and printed reveres. Soft blouses were gathered at the waist, there were curvaceous jumpsuits and wispy chiffons. There were big tucked coats and prints on fine jersey. Everywhere there were big rounded shoulders and narrow waists. The effect was feminine, sexy and stunning,' said Suzy Menkes, who even then put in a plea, 'Wouldn't the ideal be for a benefactor to step forward, who would set up Ossie Clark in his own studio, and organise production on a streamlined basis with couture standards?'

'Bianca insisted on having her own bedroom as a dressing-room, and as the star of the moment, rolled up one and a half hours late after having her hair done by Ricci Burns, her personal hairdresser,' recalled Adie Hunter. 'Tony Howard and Jeff Dexter did some very good music. The models were not really catwalk models; Ossie liked them to dance and just move as they felt.'

Throughout this period Ossie was living at a breakneck pace. He crashed his silver Buick Riviera in 1968, three minutes after getting the insurance cover for it. That winter he stayed in New York in a borrowed apartment, with ice skaters skating below in Central Park. Jimi Hendrix and his girlfriend Sandra visited him there, and Ossie remembered, 'He whispered in my ear "I believe I am a prophet from outer space and I won't be here very long."'

Ossie's charisma and status as a boundary-breaking designer meant that he held place of honour in a wide variety of social scenes. The painter Kevin Whitney recalls, 'When I first met Ossie I felt about him as I would of a pop star. There would be a frisson at any party if Ossie Clark bothered to show up.' In London Ossie's renown was such that even the venerated society beauty Lady Diana Cooper (daughter of the Duke of Rutland and widow of diplomat Duff Cooper) demanded at June Churchill's house in Victoria, 'Where is this person everybody's talking about? I must see him. Point him out!'

Ossie's set included some of the most fascinating people of the era. Cecil Beaton entertained Ossie and Mick Jagger at his house, Broadchalk, in Wiltshire. Jagger invited Ossie to stay at Villefranche in the south of France. Ossie famously visited Tony Richardson's La Garde Fresnais, where he behaved outrageously and threw a gaggle of ducks into the heated swimming pool. In 1969 he and Celia holidayed in Marbella with John Aspinall's half-sister, Jennifer, and Tony Little. In London he spent every night in clubs like the Aretusa, the Speakeasy, Tramps, and Yours or Mine.

'I met Ossie in the Sixties when I was acting,' says Edina Ronay, actress and now fashion designer. 'We were part of a gang that included Manolo Blahnik and Patti Clapton. Ossie would always dress us up and take us out.' Tara Brown, the ill-fated Guinness heir killed in a car crash in the Fulham Road, was amongst Ossie's many glamorous intimates.

He holidayed in Marrakesh with Paul Getty's wife, Tahlita, Christopher Gibbs (close friend and mentor of Mick Jagger and the society antiquaire), Jesse Downe – the streetwise Adonis, and Oliver Musker (boyfriend of Marianne Faithfull, after the Jagger split, who later married a Lambton daughter, Rose). He zoomed over the Atlantic to his shows in New York and was famously arrested in Macys for trying to take his own clothes out of the shop in 1967. He fraternised with the Andy Warhol group and experimented with drugs, drag queens, alcohol. This and his temperament sometimes got the better of him. In New York he preferred to lie in bed in a duplex decked in Lichtensteins than see an important buyer.

By 1970 Marianne Faithfull was supplanted in Mick Jagger's life by Bianca. Ossie became her personal couturier and friend. He told me: 'Darling, we were bosom. Many's the time I've spent the night on her sofa in her room.' He designed the dress for her wedding to Mick in St Tropez in September

1971. He dined with the Rolling Stones in Monte Carlo and smoked opium with Anita Pallenberg. 'It tastes like poppies,' he noted.

A BOOK, LILIES AND A TELEPHONE

David Hockney's 'Mr and Mrs Clark and Percy' painted in 1971 is the most visited painting in the Tate Gallery. Its formality may well be attributed to Gainsborough, but the painting encapsulates a potent triangular relationship. Hockney explained, 'I took two months to complete the picture. I was always in their apartment. We were all three of us very very close. Celia was slightly pregnant at the time. Somehow Ossie is sitting and Celia standing. It's really because I thought the dress looked better that way.'

Ossie is sitting to the right of the balustraded window, his bare feet buried in a rug. Celia is upright, feminine and in control. The soft tendrils of her hair wave prettily round her head. She is dressed in a long sinuous black Ossie-designed gown which has a slightly medieval quality. Ossie, the knight in modern garb, looks passionate, introspective, Celtic. In the flat, light floods the room. The objects on display are significant: a book, lilies and a telephone. The picture shows Hockney's insight into and love for his two subjects, but Hockney is far from a dispassionate observer, he has feelings for Celia and a greater affinity for her more genteel background. 'Her father like my father was self educated. Ossie's family encouraged him, but weren't quite as aware of the value of education.'

Tahlita Getty drinks with Ossie at an after-show party, 1971. Both wear Ossie Clark velvet suits; Tahlita's has suede insets, Ossie's is brown, trimmed with silk braid.

People remain fascinated by this painting. In the decade before it was painted the three had produced works of edge and elegance. Whilst the three had had their separate impact, they were psychologically entwined. The painting hinted at the complication of three icons, but like an allegory held its silent mystery.

Early on Ossie and Celia had been passionately in love. Celia described it as a 'thing of the mind'. In their work together they had a very unselfish relationship, but with his increasing success Ossie, 'hooked on glamour', would party party party and indulge in drugs, influenced by his friends in the pop world. 'This is when he began to turn nasty,' says Celia. Ultimately Ossie became increasingly sexually unfaithful; Celia was more and more hurt: 'I would wait up till three a.m. for his little Mini to return.'

As a source of domestic and creative strength, her input to his life was fundamental. But the dragonfly Ossie, too attractive for his own good, mesmerised by speed and exotic adventure, did not want to confine himself to the mundanities of marriage. In 1969 he felt, 'I was too young to be saddled with the responsibility of a mortgage.' Celia, who had wanted a child of his, despite his proclivities, became pregnant with Albert in January of that year. Celia's father, Albert, wrote and persuaded Ossie to marry her and give the young Albert legitimacy, and so, in August, with David Hockney and Ossie's sister Kay as the only witnesses, they married in Kensington Registry Office. That evening Ossie took Celia to an elegant Indian party at artist Rory MacEwen's in Tregunter Road.

The day after, Ossie took off on honeymoon – solo – to Barbados. Chelita Secunda recalls sitting next to him on the plane looking 'glum, glum'. When she asked why, he replied, 'I got married yesterday.' Hockney recalls, 'We laughed at the time. We thought it was an odd way to start, but Ossie was an odd person.' Later in his diaries Ossie recalled: 'Women were fighting over me and I felt like a prize fighter. I was in love with someone else at the time.' Significantly, Ossie was not present at the birth of either of his two sons. But this did not preclude him from being a tender and adoring, if unreliable, father. He proudly enjoyed the boys growing up and naturally they were very fundamental to him as mainstays of love, beauty, growth and affection, but the regular work and caring was all down to Celia.

Hockney gradually realised that all was not quite right in the marriage, and the violence Ossie occasionally committed against Celia was born of 'frustration'. Devastated himself by the breakup with Peter Schlesinger, Hockney relied increasingly on Celia's soft femininity and emotional ballast. 'I couldn't have done without her. It was Celia that became the shoulder that I leant on. She was very, very funny.' Celia responded to Hockney's appreciation of her looks and varied expressions. She became his muse. His only significant pictures of a woman (aside from his mother) are of her, often dressed in the beguiling Ossie chiffons.

In 1973, according to Hockney's dealer John Kasmin, 'Celia and David were staying in Lee Marvin's house in Malibu, where he did some beautiful

David Hockney on his brown leather sofa in Powis Terrace, 1972. Mo McDermott's tree stands in the background.

watercolour paintings of her, and they were both very nervously contemplating a consummation of their emotional relationship into a physical one.' Hockney took Celia to an Elvis Presley Concert in Las Vegas, but then, according to Kasmin, 'Ossie arrived and interrupted everything, giving everyone angel dust.' Ahmet Ertegun from Atlantic Records flew Ossie and Celia to New York where Celia remembers spending a week with the two boys in a flat owned by Henry Geldzaler. 'Ossie disappeared with Mick and Bianca Jagger, and left me there. I remember the oven exploding.'

By 1974 Celia 'felt driven to the edge of the precipice,' according to Chelita. All through the period when the marriage was degenerating, Ossie had maintained a social life of astonishing intensity, and his appetite for speed, glamour and distraction was simply incompatible with a stable home-life, marriage and childrearing. Ossie's sexual attraction to young men was a key part of his fast-paced and undomestic lifestyle. As Celia recalled, at the Royal College Ossie had crushes on straight men, whilst having girlfriends such as Sandra Keenan and Stevie Buckley. Many years after the divorce, Celia reflected: 'At the time Ossie grew up in the North, homosexuality was taboo. Although he camped it up at Manchester, with his effeminacy, he probably felt very isolated. It was only when he met Mo MacDermott, who was also sexually ambiguous and a kindred spirit, that he felt he could express himself sexually. Our meeting was rather out of order. I happened by accident. It threw a spanner in the works of his life and in mine. He was homosexual and I was straight. He did have an appetite for boys, and he would show this off in front of me. I couldn't stand it. Jealousy is the most horrible emotion.'

Although Celia was still in love with Ossie, his sexual interests lay in other arenas. Finally, in need of more physical affection, she had an affair with the illustrator Adrian George. When he found out, Ossie broke her nose. Hockney, always a frequent visitor to their home, had bought her a very precious diamond ring that year. Ossie never forgave Hockney for supplanting him in her heart. He made fun of Hockney and referred to him as 'Mr McGoo'. Adrian George he nicknamed 'the rat'.

In May Ossie returned from a trip to New York resolving to start afresh with Celia and change his habits. Yet he still socialised wildly with the glamour set – the Rolling Stones' Ronnie Wood, the Lambtons, and Bianca Jagger. He completed dresses for society weddings such as Stella Astor's (granddaughter of Nancy Astor, the first female MP). He had romantic trysts with other female admirers and lurched from crisis to crisis.

Ossie's home life was pretty erratic. He divided his time between 55, Linden Gardens, Notting Hill, the flat Celia and he had rented since 1968, and David Hockney's huge apartment in Powis Terrace, where Mo lived in the basement.

Ossie had bought 56, Cambridge Gardens, a large house off Ladbroke Grove, Notting Hill with a £7,000 deposit obtained from the sale of a David Hockney painting (given as a wedding present in 1969 to him and Celia) to the Friends of the Tate Gallery. He decided that Linden Gardens was too small for the whole family and longed for Celia to come and live there with the boys. She refused, and was intent on divorce. As with all marital breakups, friends and family take sides: after he attacked Celia, she saw her "lawyer lady", and Hockney accompanied her to Al Radley's for him to witness her bruised face. In the autumn Ossie went to a Hockney vernissage in Paris, where he was driven to remorse upon seeing Hockney's beautiful portrait of Celia. 'How could I have done that to her?' he said.

BLUE

After the divorce in October 1974, Ossie went to Hong Kong with Al Radley, and was consumed with longing for his wife and children. He said at the time, 'I will do anything to save the marriage for the sake of the children,' and went so far as to threaten suicide, 'because I cannot see any point in continuing life with my financial millstones and the future not being as I planned it.' That year Ossie had a £10,000 overdraft, and in June yet another threatening letter from his bank. He often reflected in the diary of '74, 'I have no one to turn to.' Hockney remembers Ossie insisting, 'I need a Kasmin in my life,' and later concurs: 'My life was reasonably organised, I did have someone to look after the business side. Today there are more young entrepreneurs, who would have picked up someone of that talent for mutual benefit. I told him to trust Al Radley, let him handle it.' Ossie resented the commercial pressures and would reply, "I am an artist".'

In December, as Celia drove Ossie to the airport, he noticed that Celia was no longer wearing her wedding ring. He spent Christmas on his own, heartbroken. In 1975 he was manifestly bereft and lonely in Cambridge Gardens. This period is marked by him as the start of his later depressions.

Bringing up two sons Celia needed a more stable basis for her life than Ossie could afford her. Hockney felt Celia had 'a bit of a rough time. She had the harder times because she had the children to bring up.' She forsook her career to bring up the boys. 'I helped teach George to walk in 1973 in Malibu,' Hockney recalls. 'It was felt Ossie could look after himself.' The tragedy was Ossie could not. He needed Celia, her balance and anchor, and felt he had lost the most precious things to his heart.

His early success and the intensity with which he lived – with or without the help of drugs, pills and extreme emotional swings – obscured a sense of reality, that had already been fairly blurred. As Hockney observes, 'Ossie's Buick was so wide it took a long time going round that corner into Linden Gardens; he was slightly richer than I in those days and had more flash taste. His tendency was that he worked hard for a month, then he stayed in bed all day and went out every night. He seemed to know how to live; I didn't live that way, I worked.'

'Each time he had a wonderful collection,' Celia says, 'he'd say at the end of it, "I've worked out these new theories. I've worked out that and that, and this time I'm going to produce a collection and I'm going to build on it." He never did. Before each collection he'd take the black bomb, stay up all night and make twenty dresses. Usually the last dresses were the most amazing ever. Afterwards he was absolutely worn out on speed because he was burning up too much energy. So they would sit around saying, "He must have a holiday." Nobody could make him go on and do it because of his state. That's what I think it was. He couldn't plan it. He couldn't make his body obey him.'

Singer, model, friend and steadfast supporter of Ossie, Marianne Faithfull, 1973.

In the sixties Ossie had been centre-stage; in the seventies, although his life remained glamorous beyond most people's dreams, he found it increasingly hard to adapt to the changing ethos. Ossie had thrived in the optimistic, hedonistic spirit of the sixties, but felt ill at ease during the less forgiving recessionary seventies. With the fashion shift from his wizardly creations to cartoon images by Mr Freedom to punk, Ossie no longer shared the media spotlight with popstars. More than his financial and emotional difficulties, this marked the real start of his decline. He simply went out of the fashion limelight, and for a person of Ossie's emotional brittleness, that was the unendurable insult.

As Marie Helvin, who modelled for Ossie early in her career, put it, 'These days fashion is so much more serious. It's become a big business, and there's not as much room for individuals and eccentrics as there was in the sixties and seventies. Ossie was too fragile in an emotional sense.' Because his aspirations had been so high, and he wanted them to be met constantly, he retained an arrogance about some things not being good enough. As a friend from 1975 onwards, Marie Helvin was struck by a streak of negativity in Ossie's character. She found he had 'an intuition verging on the psychic,' and recommended that he talk with his shrink about his unwillingness to say 'yes yes instead of no no'. Ossie was very much into Jungian therapy, and had experimented with many different therapists.

From his student days onwards Ossie had been dependent on stimulants; he seemed to be a manic depressive – his extreme productiveness and creativity would be counterbalanced by extreme lows. As a child of the sixties he often felt drugs were both the clue and the answer. Money naturally came into it. Ossie was as glamorous as it was possible to be, but didn't have the money to sustain that glamour. His finances were a constant source of perplexity and anxiety. In the mutually massaging world of rock and fashion Ossie was on the same level as his peers and influenced by them, but was not insulated by vast wealth as they were. This made him vulnerable, as he discovered later when he was out of that orbit and had to borrow money from his wealthier friends for the exotic trips that were his life blood. With poverty came resentment, and fashion loves only success.

Ossie's Diaries begin in 1974, and from then he can tell his own story. To help the reader, I have provided a brief introduction to each year.

Henrietta Rous
London, September 1998

Ossie's Stream of Consciousness

His Life before the Diaries

In late 1988, when Ossie had reason to believe that his diaries were likely to be published, he wrote thirty pages in his 1988 diary in which he recalled his life before 1974, when the diaries begin. He had been reading James Joyce and was encouraged by his psychiatrist, Michael a'Brook, to write this in 'stream of consciousness' style. Short passages which make no sense to the reader have been removed. Otherwise, what follows is unedited. The spellings and date sequence are Ossie's.

1955

I start junior art school on Saturday morn.

9 June: My 13th birthday. I received a brand new sports bicycle – a Dawe's (or was it a Raleigh Sport's) with 4 gears, cream with a red trim.

1956

8 June: Great Ormond Street Children's Hospital, Carshalton. John Cigarini's 11th birthday, wheeled into the operating theatre miming to a cardboard guitar to have his balls dropped.

9 June: Nicholas Mustapha Theodorus Balaban, birth. St Teresa's Hospital, Wimbledon. Two months later Ankara, Turkey, where he lived till he was seven. DH's 18th birthday – National Service conscientious objector, Bradford, Yorkshire. Most menial jobs in a hospital ward. Don't forget the testicles, David, bah ah ah ah.

George Harrison; Michael Phillip Jagger; Marguerite Littman teach, Southern drawl; Elvis Presley Top 10; Collet's – gentleman's outfitters, hosiers and glovers – specialised in stiff collars.

1952

Kay came to London.

Jimmy Francis Melia visits Warrington.

Premonition in the front room – the front doorknocker, the front door locked the back door always open. 'If you 'ad mucky 'ands on my trousers I'd be right cross.'

The art of the Super Groupie.

I'll have a party and you shan't come, tea without sugar, bread without butter, yum yum, pigs bum.

Mary Anne, she locked the door and she turned the key – I believe you, thousands wouldn't. We'll have two when God comes round with the money cart.

1953

January: Beryl to Singapore. Born 31st. Port Said – Sammy a boat, *Empire Windrush*.

1954

John.

In Doze Daze.

'Ready Steady Go, Man, Go' – Little Richard on Radio Luxembourg, the great liberator.

Walt Disney – 'Mrs. . . Will you stop sitting on that baby!'; Tinker Bell; *Alice in Wonderland*.

'Well now since my baby left me, I've found a new place to dwell. . .'

1956

After Rockingham club or the Arts and Battledress, drinking in an after-hours club called Claire's Copa Club. Christopher Gibbs meets Michael Rainey.

My father – 'Sam, will you talk to your son!' No television – when did *6.5 Special* start? The Saturday afternoon ritual: the football results. Sunday lunch: family favourites, mum scraping veg, he carving the lamb. I always tried to be out before *Billy Cotton's Bandstand*. Wakey Wahhhkey. 'If I were a blackbird I'd whistle and sing.' When I told him of my first trip to the USA – 'Well, son, I must've been to America 100 times but you've seen 100 more things than I ever saw and you've only been once.'

1964

Rio de Janeiro Christ erected, Al Capone, shit street.

1957

Nijinski died, having been insane for the last 25 years.

'You're a foolish woman, Mrs Clark, let him have a proper job and have art as a hobby' – advice from the headmaster. Roy Thomas the art teacher – *Elle* magazine, *Vogue*, Diana Vreeland. Beaumont Secondary Technical School: Art, Building, Construction, and Geometry. GCE – three.

My mother went to work for the first time as a home help; she gave up smoking cigs to send me to art college. Mum's three-course breakfast: a cup of tea, an Aspro and a good cough.

Fiona Campbell; Walter; Barbara Gohlen; Jennifer Hocking; a young medical student M. a'Brook; Dicky Buckle; the Diagliev exhibition; 'Mitzukoo' by Guerlain; 'Why do fools fall in love?' – Radio Luxembourg; Sugar Pie Di Santo, soulful dress.

My dad answers a knock at the front door (unusual) early evening: 'Is your Ozzie in?' – enquires. 'Ozzie? You've got the wrong house, there's no Jews here.' Door slams. Dad's cigarette case left each night on the fire place, Woodbines, offering one on a bus going to see mum in hospital when hysterectomy.

1962

John's wedding – fab, yer hair looks fab.

1955

'Blue Suede Shoes'; 'The Ballad of Davy Crockett'; *Billboard*; E. Presley – didn't know what the E stood for.

Kay working on a US airbase in Germany – 'If he had a hard-on he didn't mind showing it.'

Singing the blues; little Guy Mitchell; Tommy Steele; Aunt Mary's jokes (when did she die?); James Dean; Marilyn Monroe; Marlon Brando; Brigitte Bardot; Jean Alcock – no balls; Beatrix and Bongo's coffee bars; Bill a'Robie's weekend – meeting Harry Webb, I think he's a queen and I always have; the greens; the cockin's; Kevin Harrison who thought he was a car, always revving up; my brother John working at the Vulcan foundry; Jody Reynolds; my brother Sammy getting Jean Bailey pregnant; Chess records; Taffy's death.

Warrington: my first job after school, scrubbing the chopping blocks with wire brushes. 'Eh, lad! Ya'nesh', said the butchers. I faked dedication to *The Archers* to escape by quarter to seven. 13 years old, Choirboy, St Oswald's. Later came the two nights and weekend petrol-pump attendant. That summer before starting RCA: £2 a day, 12 hours, catching the shit at the back end of a pea-viner.

1956

Elvis: 'Hound Dog', 'Don't be Cruel'; the Teds lounging in pink day-glow socks at the Boys Club, Mr Fairclough his pebble glasses steaming up; the jukebox at the Rendezvous coffee bar; Anthony Tucker applied to Eartha Kitt at Belle Vue Boxing Stadium, the day the circus left town; Wilf, hash; Marion Hanson wearing the first sack-dress when everybody pale-pink lips, fifties jive-skirts, nylon petticoats.

Burton Wood Air Base: American cars with fins; suicide blondes, one Yank and they're off; 'Hi! My name's Chuck'.

1958

Daphne Teague; the man with a turd caught under his braces looped a turd; the ouijie board predicting Patricia's pregnancy.

Henry Moore, Michaelangelo, the sending up of the students' sculpture, the design projects. Derek Howarth – 'Imagine you are invited to a country weekend house party, shooting, long walks, formal dinners, decide what you will require bearing in mind packing' etc. etc. Presumably I had to imagine I was aware of how the other half lived – crazy fondue party.

1958–9

Intermediate year, Manchester Regional College of Art (first term on approval). The 5 to 9 from Warrington Central, 2/- a day and a packed lunch. Other male Jeff Baker, mostly upper-class girls instead of finishing school. Jane Evans, Robinson maiden name, the latest champagne from Paris, blacked up as Nijinski the ghost on the landing of the mill house, Bury. Lindsay Altringham – the costume research in Plah fields – 'Don't use the public toilets, they are used by undesirables.' Learning how to sew, to tailor a pair of trousers, the first attempts disastrous.

Rebel-rouser Duane Eddie: 'Summertime Blues' 1958, 'C'mon Everybody' 1959. Dean Martin; Volare; Norman Bain story; Robbie had left college; first blue overlay; Bobby Rydell; Dame Vera Lynn.

'There was a boy, a very strange enchanted boy, they say he wandered very far, very far over land and sea, just to love and be loved in return.'

Lonnie Donnegan; skiffle; freight train; Nancy Whisky; Frankie Avalon; Bobby Darin, whop bop a loo bop; Don't, Hazel – first girlfriend creeping around the dancefloor of the Boys' Club; the only time I appeared in drag, wearing the first attempt at a long evening dress at the College Christmas Ball, the photo's. A weaver to weaver teddy-boy jacket, 6-19-6, no, 7 guineas. Beatle-crushers, trousers so tight with zips.

'Excuse me, dear! I buy my shoes at Derber's.' 'Where do you buy your hair?' Derber's in Oldham where we all got factory reject cheap enough, Celia and Valerie wearing white stilettos – Sophia Loren. Adam Faith who had a record player in a car; Mo pimping even then. 'What Do You Want if You Don't Want Money? Wish you wanted my love, babe.' Austin Healey? Set in the dashboard, didn't work.

1959

BH selling Herald Tribune in Paris; 'Maybe Baby' sings Buddy Holly; Didsbury textile dept – Mr McEnernie.

Met Mo McDermott, an only child, the Cona coffee bar – Russian tea.

The left-wing jazz club: Tubby Hayes, Phil Seaman with Kay later.

Fashion school. 'Off the shoulder, on the hip'; Joyce Ryder and Joan Tyrer, bell-bottomed hipster trousers; Vivienne Berg and Ester Cohen, first taste anti-Semitism; Celia's descendants Slav Viking; jiving with Celia in the Copa Cabana Club, Albert Square; Mo with Ilene Knowles; Mo chalking white under his nails; Peter Blancmang and Lawrence Harvey – Central Library and theatre – first queen, never used soap/water on his face, did bathe but it had to be loaded with potions; Alan Whithead and Mo went to St Ives in the summer; Billa Robe who met the spotty Indian looking boy Harry Webb; Brian Morris and Mo drew characatures of Celia in her latest dress, striped Swedish cotton (run up by her mother, put on three daughters). I took to calling her 'Beakie', Beakie Be-Bop-a-Lula.

1960

'Money', Barrat Strong – 'The best things in life are free, but you can give them to the birds and bees, I want some money.'

Motown; Vernoti girls; hot pants; 's'truth, overtalented and undereducated' – Georgina Howell wins *Vogue* talent contest, goes to work there.

Genet Cocteau; Bergman; Eisenstein. Hollywood: Jean Harlow; glamour; silk, satin, sex, lace, louche, lascivious, love. 'Will you still love me tomorrow' – Shirrels 1961; no dancing with Ilene Knowles – 'Catch me dear, I'm the last trolley.'

Eartha Kitt on *Sunday Night at the London Palladium*, 'Hold on, junior, this is the last public engagement.'

Pill-heads, purple hearts, blues; Miles Davis.

1959

In Worthing PP meets Bill Franklin at art school. Born 1942 in Rustington Sussex. Went to Canada a little boy, 21 came back, lived with her Granny – already experimenting heroin.

'Ee, lad, you've got crabs' – Dad told me if one person on board ship had them everyone got them.

Meeting Trevor and Glynnis.

Jack Kerouac – *On the Road*, the Beat is the word.

1962

Bobby's bar at Piccadilly: One day a Jaguar stopped about 7.30 as I was walking along Oxford Road, Manchester. I was wearing a shoulder bag and a round-necked suede jacket, with my flared jeans I'd made myself and the buckles undone on my winklepickers. I'd cut my hair very short and it was dyed black after bleaching it, which didn't suit whatever. Mo saw it, Mo went out and got it, he quite suited the blond, blue-eyed description. Edwardian striped suit, white colour Liberty print, thin silk tie, pleased with the new look I'd contrived – my hero was Tony Perkins, psycho. Dad saying, 'You might as well go the whole way and put a skirt on.' The car had slowed down and its owner cruised me as I continued walking to catch my train home to Warrington – what should I do? I knew exactly what was going on and could quite easily have changed course but I was intrigued with the blatant approach. I could've changed lane but without any hesitation (pretending I hadn't even noticed) the car door opened. Barring my way a thick cloud of cigar smoke – a middle-aged man with a friendly smile and a knowing twinkle in his eye which said, 'I know that you know that I know.' 'Am I going the right way for Piccadilly?' he asked, but I didn't know that he meant Piccadilly London, so I said yes, straight on to the Central Library. 'Where? There? Are you going that way? Do you want a lift?'

1961

Spring: 'If you shout loud enough, Raymond, and long enough, Raymond, you'll always get what you want' – Joyce Ryder. First trip abroad to see the Couturier Collection in Paris, Jane Parker's mother gave me a £1 note, 'Avez un autro chambre S.V.P.?' Chiffon southwesters at Pierre Cardin; Dykey models at Chanel; Nina Ricci; Barbara Hutton at Dior with two dogs on an empire-grey covered couch, ordering in twos.

August: John marries Christine Turnstall, embarrassing how many pictures I'm in. Was I still in the church choir?

1961

Wept when I read of Nijinski. Thesis: 'The effect of clothes on his personality' – Leon Bakst, Diagliev, Les Ballets Rousse, Le Apres Midi deb un Faune de Debussy.

I hitch-hiked to London with Maureen, eight hours in a lorry from a transport caf to visit Mo, and at the V&A meticulously copied from rare books some already apart at the binding. A Jewish hairdresser tried to rape me in Maida Vale, Celia and Mo knew him. I think we must have been staying with my sister, I was quite struck by Maureen. He's a rebel – the crystals, blues in the night.

Hitchhike baby – an aborted attempt to thumb a lift to South of France. We only got as far as Dunkirk, a flooded bathroom via Ostende and Brussels.

Celia first meeting: introduced by Mo; her parents – Albert, Edward Lear and Phyllis. We met the night of the fifteenth episode of *Coronation Street*, a very arty chemist, jars of coloured water, rose-pink and green. Ena Sharples is based on Mo's mother – 'Fancy running out of tinned salmon, she should have stocked up.' She called Annie.

My first pair of winklepickers from Stan the man, £6. Mo ordered them, came too big.

Mo's address in Salford? Hair net – 'Sit down and have your tea,' all prepared neat as a pin kitchen. His dad a sea-faring man like mine, he turned his hearing aid off when he came home. 'Will you be mother?' 'Shall I wet the tea?'

'I know what you're up to in London, selling your arse.' – Mrs McDermott. Royal Oak tube, graffiti in the ladies' toilet – 'My boyfriend shoved his dick up my fanny and I loved it'; the pompous woman at Hardy Ames, irate cross-legged showing all her drawers, so dignified. Ken Russell's TV Monitor – Celia and Mo on telly in the background and dancing, Pauline Boty in a wheelchair in the Albert Hall (Peter Blake and Derek Boshier), made me want to leave home that very night. David Hockney excluded – 'Ken, to be honest I don't know how to handle it' – 'it' being homosexuality.

Met David Geddes working on the Xmas post delivering parcels – tales of London. The angel, Leslie Poole. The Christmas party in the fashion school when DH stole the only bottle of whisky, Anne Upton's quote if anybody had first noticed Pamela Procter – a very striking blonde wearing silver jewellery she had made herself 'fardee', big smile – yes, I was disappointed she wasn't in my year.

The RCA fashion show – the beautiful girl in a temper, ripping the black seam of a long skirt, too tight. Saw Albert Finney as Billy Liar, Royal Court Theatre. Marat Sade play, Glenda Jackson RSC. Celia actually working but in the Aldwych theatre wig creations – put on your high-heel sneakers, wear your wig hat on your head. Paul Schofield's beard, Claudia Cardinali's smile. Alice Pollock working for Woodfall Films, Tony Richardson and Lenny Bruce at the establishment – *That Was The Week That Was*.

Entrance exam to the Royal College of Art. Celia working in the Hades coffee bar, 'D'ya like ma fucking frills?' Dressed like BB, blue jeans and Victorian blouse, boots with a lavatory heel. Exhibition Road, Sandra Keenan in a red leather coat on the Bakerloo line from Harrow. Kay living in Elgin Crescent Avenue with Joan Small, made her my clothes – 10 quid a dress. Shoplifting in Liberty – Mo the expert. Raven tresses – Kay Pearson, 'do you think my accent's very pronounced?'

DH drawing Spender (longing for Gervase), drawing Auden, painting Mo and me from Maybridge. His advantage his eccentric father reading Proust instead of the shopping list, National Service. 'Don't forget the testicles, David', said in a voice like a Walt Disney donkey, Hee Haw. With Kasmin in Las Vegas, drawing in a motel room to play the crap games and fruit machines. The Kasmin gallery openings in Bond St, the dinners, the opening Charlotte St; moving to Paris.

Jane – 'Basically, the reason our marriage is over was the number of hairs in the bathroom sink. He to her very cruel, she masochist. When I asked Kas – 'Actually, Ossie, I didn't want either.'

1962

Mo working for Adam Pollock, living Ladbroke Grove, already life-modelling for DH at RCA.

Spring, before RCA autumn term: David Hockney taught me how to see, he saw me first (even though he was already blond) and bought me a lunchtime drink. Norman Stevens – teaching, painting, Manchester. He, DH and David Oxtoby – Bradford RCA. Together they left 1962, the year I started. Norman Steven's buttock; my sister Kay's room while she worked in Turkey where she smoked the Cherass; Mo's flat in Ladbroke Grove, his smart London friends, neighbours – Yvonne Morrell, Nicolette Meeres. The glamour of the third-year students, Tony and Helen Messenger, Mike Upton bronzed from holidays in Greece with PP. Drinking in Hennerkes on Portobello and the bargains on the market Saturday morning, a strict ritual. Vangi Harrison, Yolanda Sonnabend – the theatre. Ralph Katcy; Brian Morris; Eddie Squires; Pauline Fordham working for Sally Tuffin and Marion Foule. Michael Wishart – 'Could you drop me at my club? The Gigolo in Kings Rd. Do you know it?'

April Ashley meets Noel Coward – very ill just before he dies, his face a mass of blotches, in a wheelchair – 'Don't get up.' 'Please, I always rise for a lady'.

AA exposed as a sex change in the *News of the World*.

1963

With Michael Caine, Edina – AA at the bar very friendly, Pickwick Club.

'Gottya, you little bleeders, now give me your autograph' – enter the Fab Four, Earlstown, Frodsham. Carol my niece had cornered them, I'd migrated south a few months before, missing their meteoric Liverpool local lift-off to megastardom. Meanwhile sore feet sighing in the RCA new building, Kensington Square. Homesick, poor, rent saved £3, 17 shillings, in the gas meter a shilling. Going to see 'Billy Budd' and bursting into tears -'It's so unfair, it's so unfair,' I wailed. 'There there,' soothed Jane Parker.

1961

Bobby Vee, 'Rubber Ball'; 'Green Onions', Booker T and the MGs; Stax Records; Bob and Earl, 'Harlem Shuffle' – shake your tail-feather baby.

Summertime blues working at Lever Bros at Crossfields past Bridgefoot, dreaming of dresses and Celia, crude men and vulgar-mouths insinuate sex hand-in-hand, complement the filthy task. Sampling raw tallow for water in great barrels stacked high, remove the huh, cap, huh, steel drum. Unscrew the cap slowly, ever so slowly to insert the dipper, gingerly in case it farts or flobs out all this evil smelling shit to cover you up.

Celia went to Greece with Mo to see the Oriole oracle – poetry in motion, 'Oh, a tree in motion.'

1963

Janey Ironside: black, always dark glasses, clutching her bag having plucked up Dutch courage with gin to stealthily teeter in. Pure Chinese red lips. She hadn't spoken to any first-year student all year. First task the noticeboard, everyone whispers silence while Mrs Herbert-Smith pins the single white sheet of foolscap through a cloud of smoke, fag dangling dangerous (half of ash), precariously near from scarlet mouth, 'Who is that boy who wiggles his bottom when he walks?' she asks.

October 2nd: The second year begins, a new pecking order – Maurice Woodruff; Lionel Bart; Peter Sellars; bar of Claridge's, let's have some fun – no grassing.

1962

Late spring: the soup kitchen, Chandos Place. Pauline Boty: the first time she noticed me, sunbathing her bikini bottom sprawled out in the garden. Phillip Saville was her current chap, beau lovers by the score. Freckles, innocent blue eyes, lips so full, a look direct eyeball to eyeball, melt away like Tom and Jerry heavy as mercury down a drain, or foolish as I did then – What subject should she paint? I'd suggested flags of the major powers, (Derek Boshier, Dick Smith, Peter Blake) China, Russia, America. 'Naa! S'bin done!' Green as the grass we lay in corn, in sunlight, as the storm clouds lift the golden rays from her smile. Those lips I was eventually to kiss, so soft like crying tears absorbed into a downe pillow, maudlin, too pretty. Always swanking.

I moved into a flat with John on Westbourne Grove, Miss Morphy treading the overlocker. John Polaris, Mr at first, Herbi chain-smoking. The Hans Yudas; Hardy Amis; The leopard lady – Julie Christie; Do Bessant.

Celia lived with Pauline Boty in Addison Rd – Robina in illustration, Ian Dury, poltergeist. Caught shoplifting with Celia, innocent and unaware in Galleries Lafayette. She wore trousers, people stopped in their tracks to stare. She caused quite a commotion, and from balconies ignorant laughter, envy in the eyes of women staring open-mouthed from French windows at this sex kitten in sailor pants.

Mo in 1962 – Ladbroke Grove, top floor redecorated weekly, oftener if possible. Stolen glass ashtrays, hessian and pink felt walls, my body lies over the ocean. First Hockney print – later the pyramid and palm. DH – Pam

Bum, the boy who painted his baseball sneakers turquoise and orange strips and white.

Alan Hughs – 'I've brought me toothbrush', from Birmingham, already enamoured of Phillip Prowse, already nicknamed Lena and Betty Borer.

Joe Pridera; Cecil Beaton's diaries, the all-night cafe on the corner.

My sister meets the Kray's, pipe-down to hear her sing.

'Everybody's Doing the Locomotion'; Amadeus; La Duce doing the Madison in the Gigolo.

1961

Otis Redding; Sam and Dave.

Tony Radenco's blow-job in Redcliffe Gardens.

DH's gift to Mo after a trip to Egypt for *Sunday Times*, stolen drawings turn up later for verification and David takes it back, in reprisal for Mo's consuming 144 bottles red wine in a matter of minutes while DH in Paris drawing Celia.

1963

Home for Christmas – cold winter.

Taken up seriously by DH.

1964

Trip to Paris with Mo (after US trip): the carousel and Madame Arthur; met Patrick Procktor, eccentric artist, become aware of a group forming – DH, PP, Kasmin and Jane, George Lawson, Wayne Sleep, Kitaj – taken to expensive dinners, introduced to wine, described as 'the campest thing on two wheels', taken to the ballet and opera.

Bernard Neville and Glebe Place – met Derek Jarman.

'Get her, she hasn't even heard of the new look'; The Gigolo; Cecil Beaton courting DH and borrowing Jeremy Fry's brown convertible roller to join DH for lunch at Broad Chalk – example of Cecil's social graces.

LATE 1971

Celia second pregnancy.

1963–64

Winter: 17 Powis Terrace, David's studio while he in California working at UCLA. A single bed in the corner, a single paraffin stove, 'Get up and work, work, work' written in red on waking. 'I'm just going to the beach', he says on the phone – walks the high wire of life and applauds the crowd for being brave.

Celia and Ossie photographed by Norman Bach at his flat in Putney.

1966

First meeting Jesse Downe. Lucien Freud next door, looked 17, glossy dressing to match his hair.

Saw Peke's whip act – Raymond Revue Bar – first underhand move.

Tara Brown and Mick Rainey, Rainey had all the style.

Selling acid when it was still legal, when was it made illegal?

1963

Greece, Mykonos. The ancient Greeks had an obsession with male genitalia. Maria Callas; Paul Babb; Brian Godbold; Hilary Dyer; Stevie Jams.

After the summer Celia came to live with me in the room above the bicycle shop I'd painted aubergine dark-red. *Rubber Soul*, her legs all golden from the sun and bitten by cat-fleas, she kept them covered up with a sheet, her knees up in bed. Yvonne's room, cat's gone, 'look' – she put one leg out to the matting on the floor, half fleas leapt straight on.

Jennifer Green: first Jewish princess, first wedding suit, first met Gala Mitchell bored in a mink coat – 'there's nothing in the Sunday newspapers for me'.

Addison Gardens. Clive Goodwin later married Pauline Boty – pregnant – dies soon after.

Tony Little; Gordon Deighton; Jenny Aspinal; Clive Arrowsmith's cowardice in 17 Powis Terrace – 'You've got evil eyes,' said the drunk who forced his way in after being beaten up by a prostitute.

Bill Gibb and Kaffe Fasset in Lansdowne Crescent.

Meeting Dickie Buckle above a bank in Covent Garden, Edwardian opulence, the Karsavia Cocteau poster. Anthony Page gives me a telephone number of Jimmy Mathis for my forthcoming NY trip.

Grace Coddrington – college shows.

Charles Allen Gallery: Paul Newman; Shelley and Howie Lubin. Henri Bendell Studio 57th Street; Valpolicello happenings; the first target Tom Websleman. Earl Randolf Michaelson and his harpsichord, friend of Jimmy Mathis; Leonard Bernstein. Later: Kipps Bay Plaza, East 33rd Street, gimme Pall Mall! Introduced to Eppie in a gay bar by PB; going down in a lift with BE – 'What's a beer' please? (I'D AVOID EYE CONTACT.) Alright, you've caught me out, I'll have milk.' Eggs Benedict at PJ Clarke's – 'Fucking long-haired faggot! Listen, buddy, this is a tough town and if I were you I'd leave.'

'Oh pretty woman' – Roy Orbison.

Route 66 – driving along it, listening to England's latest hit makers 'The Rolling Stones'. Disneyland – mistaken for a Beatle on a trip to the moon to escape the excitement of the Beatles at the Hollywood Bowl. Betty Davis in the flesh; Mrs Dennis Hopper; Beach Boys, Surf City; art hype; Nick Wilder; The Tumble Inn Motel, Santa Monica; Hard Day's Night – 6 no. 1 hits, The Beatles.

Fall: 1st time stoned listening to Dion Warwick with Celia, St Quentin Avenue. She first smoked with R in bed. JM thought they were lesbian because they were giggling guiltily.

1964

Jose meets Peke D'Oslo in Chelsea Kitchen with John Myer and April Ashley.

Noticed by Jainey. The drunken doctor with the bandaged nurse.

Worked in a shoe factory in Banbury in County Downe, Ireland, with Hilary Smith of Lawrence of Arabia.

Met Charlie Watts in the college bar through Shirley – Jagger wouldn't let him marry.

Ossie at a Patrick Procktor exhibition c.1968; his jacket is cut from a William Morris furnishing print in blue/green, blue, rust and lime green.

Paris with Celia. Mistaken for clients at Chanel, see her reflected mirrored spiral staircase, staring like a hunched-up crow; Maria Callas.

DH teaching summer semester in Iowa.

Won £150 shoe bursary – Moya Bowler.

Box basket fanny, cruising gasoline alley. Randy seeing MM incognito, sick on clam chowder and gin. First met Nicholas Haslam – parties, parties, parties. Klossowski & Brandouski on the apt bell – happenings.

First trip to New York: Diana Vreeland, Andy Warhol, The Velvet Underground. First target John Kloss. Robert Indiana gave me op art prints. Met Brian Epstien, gave me tickets for Beatles Hollywood concert. LA met DH, first experience San Franscico gay bars, bathhouse, terrified of the clanking leather queens.

Celia, you came to live with me after you got back from America, moved in together 8A St Quentin Avenue W10 – Jennifer Green commission; Blanche the cat; Beulah the poodle from Pam Procter; Anne Upton's shoes; the all-nighter in Wardour St, Georgie Fame and the Blue Flames.

Christmas in Rome with Celia. ZR; furcoats; Alek McKintee – 'We're not going to make it,' as we went through the St Bernardo Pass.

Met Alice Pollock at the opening of Quorum furnishings and fashion, Ansdell St, off Kensington Square. Tuffin there with John Kloss and Michael White. AP pregnant, Nick Pollock tries to pull Celia.

1965

Carol came to London.

Transferred from atomic energy to BOAC.

John Dunbar opens Indica, meets Robert Fraser, Jimmy following year.

1966

Started on Saturday only in Radnor. Vicky Wise on Saturday, AP to show off minis.

1968

Fired for telling a jealous rival to fuck off because Celia wailing on the phone.

Quorum in Ansdell St: Cleo Lane; Candida Lycett-Green; Kari-anne; Kathleen's story show at a night-club in Paris. Quorum employed Dave Gilmour – delivery, popping the leather jackets. Eddie de Vere Hunt driving first day to another leather warehouse, the first big rip off. The little leather jacket we sold for 15 guineas copied many times straight off by the outmaker, soon lined in Oxford St – everyone wore it. The first Quorum uniform – snakeskin waistcoat, Mr Kent.

Working full time.

Eric Clapton; Jimi Hendrix – 'all you English girls are so gorgeous', daughter of Claire Bloom, criss-cross lace showing cleavage; Natalie Wood; Picasso for coffee; Beatrice Wells; Dorrit Zarak; Gill Goldsmith.

1965

Graduated RCA

David Bailey photo in *Vogue*. Freelancing for Quorum met lots of new people, from Alice, Jane Rainey.

Sandra Keenan goes to work in Oregon.

Woolland's rip off – met Zelda, Marit Leiberson. *Vogue* spread.

First commission: *2001*. Arthur Clarke hires me, Stanley Kubrick shows me over the sets. Feel like the Rumplestiltskin's princess, drawing in a room at Elstree.

Record collection, one a week: Motown; Stax; Wilson Picket; Willy Mitchell.

Moved into Blenheim Crescent with Celia, overlooking a Carmelite nunnery, £10 a week rent. Tried to buy a house for £7,200 – John Lafflin, Roy Risdale.

New York: Harlem; Marvin Gaye; Martha and the Vandela's; silver zippos; cuff-links; Chuck Berry; Bo Diddley at a cinema near Broadway – live show; Del Shannon – 'My little runaway, run, run, runaway'; Lauren Bacall, 'My God, this pasta's good'; Maxime de la Falaise.

The Animals, fresh washed shine on their hair, shaking their heads like the mop tops. 'The House of the Rising Sun' in New Orleans, escaped the heat in a cinema. Marguerite Littman and Tennessee Williams party – 'My God , it's Anorexia Nervosa', 'My dear, you're so smart, you know everybody's name.' Drive in at Monterey, Michael Caine – 'Zulu'.

1964

While I was in the USA Kay meets Earl Van Dyke and whole Motown in Cumberland Hotel. 13-year-old Stevie Wonder sits on her lap, strokes her hair, even then Diana Ross abstained.

Ronnie Scott at Sutherland Avenue.

1966

Michael Fish opened Mr Fish, 17 Clifford St, in time for the Christmas. New and lingwood. Turnbull and Asser: Tara Brown; Chrissie Gibbs; Twiggy aristocracy. Hung on You – just opened before, granny takes a trip before that.

Douglas Cooper came to shop, Nimes, Picasso, Billy McCarthy? – Groomed for aristocracy, like a racehorse in a stable.

What year was Mr Chow opening? Take-aways from Queensway.

September: Jose Fonseca entered my life; Amanda fell in love, through the twins she met Dali; Milano with AP, guest of Fiorucci, flashbulbs popping; Max born?; Fellini, the elephant-hide luggage.

Verushka comes to my studio in Radnor Walk, towers in 6" taller than the door to be photographed for *Telegraph* magazine.

Spring: First fashion show for buyers on a barge in Little Venice. Sell to Henri Bendle in NY having realised no backing forthcoming. I went with the best offer, purposefully avoiding the Jewish rag trade.

'We must get an overlooker, make clothes properly, have a show,' – Penny Graham.

Celestia Sporborg – which magazine did she work on? With LouLou.

Met Prudence Glynn, Jackie Modlinger on the *Jewish Chronicle*, Molly Parkin – *Nova*.

DH later regrets giving so many drawings, getting ever famous, taken up by Tony Richardson.

AP worked for *Woodfall Films* – exotic birds, Gemini, Jean Moreau.

Jeremy Fry – trips abroad.

Loulou de la Falaise in chiffon with a dog in Marrakesh – marriage to an Irish lord?

Le Nid du Duc near Grimaux, above St Tropez – the Hollywood Pool in the mountains always kept 100 degrees; Paris art.

New York – meet Brian Godbold; met Colette, 1st groupie.

Lakis the Greek, Provanes restaurant – the opening. PP ordering 'hot prick on toast'.

Kiki Burn; Faye Dunaway; Sean; Kenny; Salvation night-club.

1st New York Christmas, 1st show with Jimi Hendrix.

Tennesse Williams lived in El Farra when he wrote *Suddenly Last Summer*, the football player who walked up the mountain and up the William Morris stairs. Tangier Kiffi the old boyfriend, now the gardener. El Farra on the old mountain. Rex Nankeville; Margaret Machey – the feast of the throne.

Tazi Hotel, Marrakech, by car. Coloured fields; the feast of the sheep, everywhere dead, being dragged back by one leg.

Stern Magazine, Bailey photos, Marissa Berenson. Jill Bennett finding the first snakeskin was no accident in the dark cavernous warehouse. Dickensian. 'What's that?' I asked, touching the gentlest touch to the skin of a 26" python lain rolled 20 years. Sprang back to life and opened before me. 'How much?' I asked, but matter-of-fact hiding my enthusiasm. 'Let's see, er, I can do that for thirty bob a foot,' glad to get shut. It was so wide I made it into a suit and Linda Keith modelled it.

Sandy Boyle weekend: Kasmin's new girlfriend; Dufferin and Ava, Linda and Sheridan.

Ossie wearing a Celia Birtwell scarf sits between Alice Pollock and Chelita Secunda.

1967

NY fall: Met Dick Polak in the Trencherman after the opening, freeze-dried mescaline from F, like chewing rubber.

Gervase sulky, we all wanted to go out from John's chrome and mirror expensive black apartment into Central Park.

Delivering a boaconstrictor coat to Star and Garter, first met Andrew Oldham who tried to freak me out.

LATE 1966

Move to Radnor Walk off Kings Road. First collection sent up in the press.

1967

Nova; the paper dress; Jane Asher; Marianne Faithfull and Twiggy; David Frost; Morocco with Tony Page, PP, Michael Duff; moved into Linden Gardens; long skirts, python; first car; LouLou's mail-order; Cathy McGowan; driving licence auto; grass joint from the bird Trisha Lock.

June: Marbella with Celia. The Littles, Micha, Suki, and Gavin Hodge. Portugal; Saville. Scala: Bob Ho – big tragedy there; the silver bus, 2nd car.

Doors at the Roundhouse; Jefferson Airplane; Jimmy Vomit; Barney Broadbent.

Eartha Kitt: python-skin dresses, photo session with live pythons.

Edina Ronay and Dick – tables outside Radnor Walk.

To New York on a ship with PP and Gervase: Sweeney Todds; Gary Craze; Anthony; Colette Mimran; Stella buying for a shop; The Doors – 'Come on baby light my fire'; Vietnam; second New York Christmas; first Barmitzvah – the Jew got rich making Mrs Robert Kennedy's pregnant dresses; stranded in deep snow in Philadelphia.

1969

Chelsea Town Hall Show: Gala Mitchell; Eka; lilies – 'Sorry! Good luck, hope it goes well. Lots of love, John and Yoko'; Marge Bev in the Buick, biggest bunch of flowers, lilies, 30 bouquets; 'If we don't go on soon the birds will get too hot.'

1968

Always crashing the same car – silver Buick Riviera. Crashed 3 minutes after being covered by insurance first day. Jesse Downe found it in Kilburn, ankles like glass.

Spring: Le Nid du Duc, met Melissa North.

[Earlier: Mark Palmer and Jose opened Models One with April Ducksbury.

9 June: B'day. AP hires Albert Hall – 'take a box'.

1967 – 68
The peak of the Speakeasy, Brian Jones bouncing.

1967
TC, £40 for a gig at the Blazes – cheques. When Brian Jones and Keith took to wearing the silks and satins printed by Celia and the skin-tight jewel coloured trousers from a stash of pre-war corset satin AP found. I made men's shirts with frills in chiffon, in crepe, with a one-sided collar, a leather jacket metallic with blue snake.

Marianne bought a suede suit trimmed in python with a fluted peplum and never asked the price.

Weekend in a rented country house, SS Mustang, shooting star.

1968
'Revolution Number 9'. Pattie Boyd models show at the Revolution and in the press.

'Come on, mother! We're late,' – John Lennon with Yoko looking like a porcelain doll. Kay, Carol tells, a light fell over the stage, like fell over, and he steadied the chair she stepped on, JL. Doctor John, the night tripper.

John Kloss had lent me his apartment while he went to Florida. The ice-skaters below in Central Park. Colette brought Jimi and Sandra, he whispered in my ear, 'I believe I am a prophet from outer space, a prophet, and I won't be here very long.' It's 1968, everyone, cheers! Crashed in a white jag on the Phili turnpike.

Prudence Glynn, dress of the year, Bath museum.

Peter Langan and Odins the artists café, mum's pullovers for everyone.

Marianne brings Jagger to Radnor Walk: first stage costumes fitting his crotch in gold leather. Revolving stage and *Top of the Pops*; Amanda Lear and Alice Pollock, Montreau Pop Festival.

1966
Brian Jones moves in above shop with Suki and smoke joints with him of an afternoon.

English Boy Mark Palmer.

Gave Paul Getty a belt, he never forgotten. Rosetti's house, Tahlita Getty in NY. Bill Willis. Maurice Hagenboom staying in YSL's house; Macy's with Chris McDowne, policeman with guns; recording studios, Jimi Hendrix – 'Electric Ladyland'; Tommy Nutter; Peter Brown (met 1964) apartment next to decota.

The Stones, she comes in colours.

Beatles come to a fashion Revolution club. George Harrison made a fuss about Patti going braless.

Ossie poses in a Celia Birtwell scarf in crêpe de chine and his favourite patchwork belt, 1968.

1968
NY Christmas party, Central Pk South – Jimi Hendrix and cocaine.

Visit to Brian Jones' house of AA Milne. Mini automatic, wouldn't let him drive.

Moved to 55 Linden Gardens with Celia. Where was I?

1967
Willy Daly; William; Michael. Pious John, we ran away to Ireland – romantic, he and the brown automatic mini.

Paris fleamarket: Jean Leger and Alexis; LouLou de la Falaise; Fernando Sanchez; Place de Fursteinborg – flat hash and mint tea.

1971
Early spring: Burnsall St SW3, Jagger brings Bianca. First meet, to make her wedding dress, forgets to tell me she's pregnant.

Suki Poitier (second from right) and two other models browse with Ossie through Celia's designs. The model on the right is wearing an Ossie Clark snakeskin jacket.

1969

Marbella with Suki – a bullfight on acid. Hugh Hefner and the bunny jet – menchu, a ride to Portugal. Two very near misses in the Buick. AP, Micha, and Celia. Saville, the Alphonso gypsies.

August: Suki and Roman Polanski – honeymoon with another woman. Stunned Sharron Tate murder, hear of in Bermuda. Trinidad in the rainy season, what a dump. Chelita's mother; instant coffee; Spice Island Inn, Grenada; Tony Howard; Norman Parkinson; the plague of snakes across the road, a bad omen; the yacht club.

September: Vichy by train from Paris. PS reading Proust in 17th Century opulence, delicious food and walks. Cut off my hair in Paris, vinq sept Rue de Seine.

1968

Ulla moved to Hesker Street with Eric Smith, opposite Charlotte Rumplery, Tom Weaver, and Petrovna.

1969

13 January: Ulla Larson marries Alan Styles. Flowers; best man; Florentine papist; hash; Picasso reception.

Cheyne Walk – Chrissie Gibbs and Marianne. Cocaine on the Georgian mantle piece in Jagger's house, first time.

Shaved off my beard in Harrods barber shop.

Bianca and the Buick. Roger delivered it Marbella flat first.

Morocco: Paul Getty, Aunt Krupp, Chrissie Gibbs, Jesse Downe, Oliver Musker etc. 'Shhh! Don't tell Belinda.'

Celia pregnant. PP paints silks. Left Celia, went to live in Battersea, kept first diary later destroyed.

Married Celia. Tears. 'Tell me what you want, I'll get you whatever you want,' – Hockney, Kay a witness. DH promised Kay an etching she never got. Indian music, the woman who sang with her hands. DH gave picture for wedding present – Mr and Mrs Clark and Percy, later sold to pay deposit on house, £7,250, brought by the Friends of the Tate for £7000.

22 October : I received the news of Albert's birth about four in the afternoon in my studio, 6 Burnsall Street. Celia had a difficult pregnancy, she slept in all eight beds of a ward at Queen Charlotte's because of high blood pressure. Over the last three months occasional weekend forays out.

1972

Le Grande Banc Provence: Lakis, 'I am Greek, I can not keep it all inside of me'. Drama, duty-free liquor, glass smashed everywhere. I knock myself out

At work in his Radnor Walk, Chelsea, studio. In the background excellent and loyal machinist Kathleen Coleman sews Celia's 'Lily' print on crêpe de chine, 1969.

running to get Valium would help that crash. The fields of lavender, the Belgian sex bomb suprise, reading the whole of *Albertine Retrouve* in 18 hours. Keep your electric eye on me.

Radley, metro dry cleaners.

1969 – 70

Michelle Breton filming *Performance*: first met John Dunbar; Anita Pallenberg and Brian Jones fighting on stairs of Cheyne Walk, real fisticuffs.

OCTOBER 1970

Kari-Anne Moller marries Rufus Dawson in a red lace wedding dress boned to hide her pregnancy, Paddington registry.

Models Mendes show with Gala, cobwebs of chiffon. Kari-Anne Moller infuriates me, painting her toenails on the floor in a silk suit.

Acid. 'Hey, man, where can I live?' – Morag. My love of Persian Carpets, mescaline – Redcliffe Square, Edina and Dick.

Isle of Wight with Roger, pissing in a beer pot. Bob Dylan.

1970

28 June, Widcome Manor, Bath: Mike Fish; Barney Wan; Suki; Kate Abrahams; Jack Bond – shadows of the Sharron Tate murder; Geoffrey Ross; Sabrina Carver. LouLou, Jeremy Fry. He changed his clothes for every meal and even to visit the rosegarden, she went somewhere with Barney Scott and Lakis driving. Jack Bond had crashed his motorbike last night having got bored at the Bath Pop Festival – Pink Floyd and Led Zeppelin. We got pissed, retired after midnight, I with Suki, the four-post Chinese drape.

Salt on Weetabix, 'Hey man, you wanna buy some good acid?' He posed about the window, sold cocaine. Kate Abraham lived in the same block as Carina en suite. California sunshine.

11 May, Mike Fish wonderful B'day party – Burkes; Proctor and Gamble; Clive Makey Kemp; Keith Wallis; Barry Krost; Cat Stevens; Diamond Lil; Robert Shaw; David; May West film; something about vodka this time of night slips down so easily – Donovan.

Jimi Hendrix at the Albert Hall – the yellow tartan coat; Jimi Hendrix at the Saville Theatre with Arthur Brown, Suzi Bell, Deborah and Clair.

Au Jardin des Gourmets – dinner in Soho with Mick Jagger – amazed at his knowledge of back alleys and short cuts.

SS in Cromwell Road, Tony Secunda a whiter shade of pale – she completely straight then.

Carlotta, the Italian waiter at the Aretusa – 'I cannotta eatta withoutta bread.' Mandrax – pulled over by the police. I switched drinking Dom

Perignon when it topped six quid a bottle. Drank Creme de Menthe with champagne and John Chrille in Aretusa.

David Litmanoff – the horror Kray twins.

Later: Samuel the jeweller's daughter, already over 1st marriage, Nikki Waymouth – Nigel. Taking Albert to visit her house.

1969

Mr WJ Hill. York Rd, Wandsworth. Mark Burns gives Hettie the white light ADDRESS.

The Tumbler of Brandy – Tony Howard, Arthur Max, Pink Floyd.

Kit Lambert, Egerton Crescent, The Who. The unused Rolls Royce, the Spanish waiters at the Yours or Mine.

Quidjeta's story: Paul Getty and Tahlita, Robert Fraser flat, Warhol's entourage wearing T's mother's clothes.

Walking round the round pond with Albert in a pram while Celia's Sunday house clean. Watched swans mating. Was there when mommy swan proudly led her brood, daddy swan bringing up the rear.

1970

Jimmy married Ronnie, August.

'Our Raymond knows that squirrel,' Wayne Sleep dancing in the Tales of Beatrix Potter.

First Mendes collection, Rue d'Uzes. Near miss driving the Buick from Paris to catch the hovercraft. Alice, Kathleen the machinist – 'What about bleeding us!' My one night at the Ritz and I hardly got to bed. 'I've just found this pill in my pocket, shall we take half each?' Amanda Lear took me to tea to meet Salvador Dali.

Carol married. Aretusa, June wedding.

I went to work in Paris, made a huge success and another smash in my Buick showing off to Alexis, why should I bother with traffic lights?

Meeting Paul Getty in Cheyne Walk, his rage and Parkinson's disease masked behind cordiality.

Kellie got married, 5 July, Bob Mayo photographer.

Sid meets Pam above Lens the Cleans. Hali a babe in her arms – she into quick romance on a tab of acid, Old Brompton next to the Drayton Arms.

The ride to Toulon to buy sailor trousers and exotic birds for Tony Richardson.

1968

The Citroen driver who longed for a laser beam; St Tropez deserted in spring. DH and PS. Met Jagger there being wooed by TR to play Ned Kelly.

With model and friend Agnes Kostrowski and surrounded by his own garments, c.1970

1969

Powis Terrace tea parties – EVERYBODY THERE.

1971

Tangier on a two-week package tour, Celia pregnant.

Carenac – electric storm, God taking flash photos, four windows from the turret, negative ions. Live trout delivered gleaming, gourmet food, oil of walnut. A ride to see Douglas Cooper's paintings.

Cadaquez – Catherine Guinness; Jasper; Mark Lancaster; Marcel Duchamp studio; Natalie Delon naked riding pillion on Bobby Key's motorbike; brother Sammy killed mysteriously; dinner with the Stones in Monte Carlo.

Ahmet Ertegun takes Catherine G. off to Turkey, showers caftans.

In Scotland with Roger Dixon, Caithness.

September: Antibes, France. Smoking opium with Anita Pallenberg – 'It tastes like poppies.'

November: Acapulco. Robert Seligman, Leslie Spitz and Alice; Audine Honey; Peao Ruban; Nikki Williams overtaking a bus on a bend on a mountain road, I photo?

November: birth of Shebah Polak. Went to see first in Redcliffe Square.

Met Brookie in Tramp with Willy Fielding and Michael Pearson. Minah Bird, John Bentley.

Jagger's wedding, St Tropez – Warhol dinner club.

'I know how to spell Warwick Gardens' – premonition of Tahlita's death in Rosetti's garden.

Jerry Hall – Bryan Ferry's house in Ladbroke Rd.

September: Nico smashing glass, 'Careful of the broken glass'. AW working in Radnor Walk, Minah Bird without knickers.

1973

All-black model show at Arctusa.

Jack Hazan filming *Bigger Splash*, unsuccessfully waiting hours in Radnor Walk to film Bianca. Kasmin's Jewish intuition – changing $ into Yen.

Blue Bentley, continental flying spur, Celia pregnant, romantic journey to Carenac – the shit-house chateau. Conran's; Hodgkin's; Kas-Jane, casaulet dinner. DH and PS split – Eric Borman dropped off at the railway station after TB said EB can't stay.

Brother's death, Bastille du Roi, Jagger's. *Exile on Main Street* – mobile recording studio.

Birth of George Igor, November 26. Mexico, 'Let's Stay Together' – Al Green.

Royal Court Theatre, Black Magic show. Terry Stamp, my Lady D'arbanville; Cat Stevens. Michelle, the black model from Mendes, in a cloud of pinks, floating on mescaline. Alice – please can wear it off the shoulder? Tony Howard did the music, Pattie Harrison twirling; Kellie, Gala.

1969

Quidjeta came to work for me in Bursall St. Back to RW when SHACK came on the back.

Summer beautiful summer – the Yours or Mine. Vikki de Lambray, the beautiful boy.

1973

Randolph Dean Cole, I met again back home in LA.

1974

Dinner with Bailey and Penny Tree, Widcome Manor, Bath.

1972

July: Drawing Ruth, Jeremy Fry's original, WM Bath, whippet. Garth Bardell, broken Bentley, taken away in a shroud, rescued by Lakis next morning. Visit to a beautiful garden, second Duchess of Westminster, P.M. connection – a party.

SS acquires Warwick Gardens. Opera to see *Carmen* – when? With Violet Wyndham? 'You know I once sat through a whole opera very bored because of the person I was with' – 'What are they saying, Dee-ah, dee-ah?' Suddenly becoming deaf, eating smoked salmon sandwiches belonging to red-faced ladies from Golders Green, dripping diamonds which flashed in their rage.

September: Ossie again Widcombe, Roger never signed the book.

Michael Rainey and Fish's wager in The Casserole.

Sex Symbols should never marry! Marianne Faithfull – the Tudor garden at Stargroves, lay-lines crossing, combe jibbet, hangman.

1972, OR WAS THAT 1971?

Australia – parades; George's of Melbourne; Adie Hunter; Lady Carina Fitzalan-Howard. Hawaii; Manilla; Sydney; David Litvinoff; Hong Kong; India.

1973

Minah Bird filming *Vampira* with David Niven.

Lindos: Bob Marley; Frou Clou; the children; the storykitten who gobbled the head of a cigarda.

Kari-Anne Jagger, gowned and photographed by Ossie Clark; the photograph became a postcard.

1972

The magic flute I never saw.

Munchen with DH to see the Olympic Games. Mark Spitz's; opera's; mad Ludvig's castles; Burt Lancaster. Met up with Jagger, watched the games on TV in the Hilton. Panic feeling, escape via Dortmund to Linden Gardens and the children in front of Beethoven funeral, on the telly the arena I'd just stepped out of.

1973

On my B'day at AD 8. I tell someone I've got an identity crisis.

DH rents Lee Marvin's house on Malibu Beach. Celia goes to join him there taking Albert and George. Palm Springs – Pam and Sid, Randy the donkey, Christopher Isherwood and Don Bacardi. Ahmet Ertegun flies us back to NY in the Atlantic Records private jet, gives us a lift. DH won't come, then wished that he had.

April: Jamaica to hear 'Sticky Fingers'. Keith rolling joints 10" long made from newspaper skins, 'Der's soul in the air man'.

1972

Trick or Treat – Bianca filming.

Trip to Leckslip Castle, Dublin, for fitting. Desmond Guinness; Marina on horseback; King John's bed and bath. Bianca rejecting bottle after bottle of perfectly good chateau wine, 'Madame is being very difficult today' – me to BJ.

Dancing with Ryan O'Neal and Bianca in the Your's and Mine. Barbara Striesand's ex, Jesse, helping Beaton with the sets. Helmut Berger. 'The Needle and the Damage Done', Neil Young. Mo's designer basement – Tchaik Chassey. Francis Lynn. DH living in TR's Paris flat.

Invitation for Mallard Street show. Very late because Rikki Burns draws Celia and Bianca for *Vogue*, cut off her hair like a boy's, all those dark tresses gone. Nikki Waymouth flaunting her mammories – 'Well, that's it, you can all F.O. now.'

Buying Cambridge Gardens with Brian Shack. 'It's quite simple, you just take a huge snort before you go and then keeping putting your hand up until it's yours' – C G on buying at an auction. Belle Jackson, Sheridan Barnett etc.

1972 is the drug year. Mo on heroin living in the basement of 17 Powis Terrace. Mangy Mick. AG connection; Marinka; Francis Lynn.

1973

Feb: Watching John Betjeman on TV with my new friend Randall Dean from Kansas, we met in the Yours or Mine.

July: Jagger's 30th birthday, Madison Square Gardens. Truman Capote; Lee Katzwell; Andy Warhol. Top of the sixties. Mayor of New York signs my back stage pass which Jesse still has. Pure hydrochloric merc, produce West Germany.

Model Sue Worth at Ossie's studio in Burnsall Street, Chelsea, wearing an Ossie Clark crêpe jacket, adorned with cock's feathers and appliqué studded stars, 1971.

Late summer, Lord Lambton's house, Hamilton Terrace, with Johnny Dewe Matthews. Albert and George swimming in a pool. Maybe later.

SS stealing at parties.

A party for Andy Warhol – Bindi on the stairs staggering, Jesse Downe necking. 'Fack off y'ol cunt! If I'm introduced to you one more time and you ignore me, I'll spit in your face.' – me to Lucien Freud.

DH in Powis Terrace and with Celia to Las Vegas to see Elvis. This big slob turned magically into the Elvis of old, had all the old matrons crying.

Ossie with Bianca Jagger, one of the muses for whom he created many opulent garments, 1972.

March: Agnes Mugambo comes to work for Alice. With Minah, Brookie's 40th B'day ball at The Cafe Royal – Lou Reed and David Bowie.

May to June: Tangier.

August: On a yacht to Turkey for the weekend with Polly Hope from Rhodos.

'I feel as though there is a great big drama going on and we just sat here in the wings' – me to Katie Windson-Lewis.

'If you can't dress out of Woolworth's you haven't got style' – Brian Jones. 'Divine! I'll have it in both colours.'

Jesse – 'What a class bird, she's got ankles like glass.'

Hockney teas – Joe de Lasandre.

Where did Rainey come from?

What date Victoria O-G wedding? Jesse had to drive Kenneth Anger home next morn, lost tie, first meet.

St James billboards – the Ossie Clark show.

Contract for cosmetics, party in Belgravia – Jeremy Thorpe, Joan Collins, Dandy Kim, Diana Dors. Jimmy Douglas penthouse, heroin and cocaine at each end of a mirror, inadvertently taken, vomit. Somebody jumped out the window – Gill Bobroff. Florence Flood actually butted her in the head.

Driving Celia to the Seven Sisters. I didn't drive for you until you got the Bentley. I came in the morning and rolled the first joint, part of my job.

Blow-up party, Gibbs party – shrimp, Palmer rolling joints.

Performance.

Martin Wilkinson – Astor girls wedding; Linda Keith and Shiela Oldham link; Julian O-G blew his brain out.

John Binden.

Vicky Hodge, yes she was definitely about.

Robert Fraser – a costume drama.

Duncan the van driver. He a scene with AP. The local yellow milk bottles at her Georgian front door on a Saturday night because she was living in sin. Portrait of Shakespeare in the kitchen.

1970

Glastonbury or Bath pop festival – Frank Zappa.

Marsha Hunt employed first as a nanny, later she sub-let from Brian Godbold's seat where Jagger used to visit' – remembers getting me the Buick.

John and Yoko at the Inn on the Park – The Rolling Stones concert with butterflies after Brian Jones' death. Like going into the jaws of hell for the first time, I experience the security procedure. Alan the driver. Wembley back stage with the wives and girlfriends. Bianca unhurried in Cheyne Walk making Mick furious, her immaculate timing.

'You've just acquired a millstone' – Wayne. We met in Odin's. 'I love tomatoes but I can only eat them when they are cut across.' He remembers DH drawing PS in the garden.

The Who – broke a lot of new ground; Townshend conception; Union Jack jacket.

September – Trinidad, Who's wedding party. Celebrity star guest caked out asleep and huge watermelon grin.

The Diaries 1974-1996

A Note on the Text

Ossie Clark's Diaries comprise thirty-eight diaries, notebooks and sketchbooks in which Ossie wrote, drew, doodled and noted appointments between 1974 and his death in 1996. The diaries are large-format page-a-day diaries, some of which, such as 1974 and 1989, are packed full with closely-written handwriting; others are less dense; and a few have many blank pages. Some of the diaries contain Ossie's engagements and lists of things he had to do mingled with his retrospective accounts of what had happened. In some years Ossie wrote in large, hardback notebooks as well as in his diaries; there are years in which he kept a diary and two journals simultaneously rather than consecutively.

Selecting from this mass of material has not been easy. The guiding principle has been to include Ossie's records of the most important events in his life alongside the most colourful and informative passages, while selecting enough from every year to make the whole into a rounded picture of Ossie's life in his own inimitable words. Some small details have been removed and some names have been abbreviated to a single capital letter for legal reasons, but at various points in the diaries Ossie proclaims his desire to tell the truth and this wish has been honoured as far as possible.

Each year has a short scene-setting introduction. Italic text in square brackets between diary entries are the editor's notes intended to elucidate the next diary entry, or sequence of entries, for the reader. Text in square brackets within diary entries is used by the editor to indicate time lapses, words or information missed out by Ossie and, on occasion, to indicate that the words are in someone else's handwriting. (Ossie quite often asked or allowed others to write in his diaries, and frequently carried them with him and read them out loud to friends.)

Footnotes are used throughout to explain who people are or were and to provide information that may help the reader's understanding. The footnotes are grouped by year and appear at the end of each year's diary. Individuals receive a brief explanatory footnote the first time they appear in the diaries as a whole; when they appear in subsequent years they are only footnoted on the first occasion that their first name only appears in the text for that year and the footnote simply gives their full name (they are not footnoted in subsequent years if Ossie gives their full name on their first appearance in that year). Footnotes are also included when two people of the same first name appear in close proximity. A bold numeral in the index at the back of the book indicates the first, which is also the main, footnote on an individual.

Ossie's spelling has been corrected to avoid confusion, and his punctuation has been altered in places for the sake of clarity.

1974

This diary is beautifully written in several different coloured inks. They might even be a code that explains Ossie's frequent mood swings: red, anger; blue, depressive; brown and mauve, in between. His handwriting varies throughout the diaries. This year's suggests a fast-paced life, full of frenetic activity often drug induced. His mood swings from excitement, wonder and wide-eyed enthusiasm to cynicism and, at the end of the year, despair at the loss of his wife and sons.

The year is a turning point in Ossie's life; the 1970s began well for him. He had made his reputation in the previous decade, and had become as famous as those he so elegantly dressed. It seemed that this would continue. But the problems that caused him to lose so much, drugs, drink, his lack of financial acumen and, above all, his careless attitude towards those who loved him – especially his wife, Celia Birtwell – are already looming. Yet, to outsiders, Ossie, still only 32, was riding high. As part of the 'jet set', he travels to New York. There, he takes a reckless dive into the drug-fuelled night-club scene. He parties with Andy Warhol, heiress Nikki Waymouth, Paloma Picasso, Loulou de la Falaise and Mick Jagger. He encounters the 'Biba' face model Ingrid Boulting and lunches with lengendary high priestess of fashion, Diana Vreeland, before dancing the night in Club 82 with Brian Ferry and Gary Glitter.

His hedonistic impulses are not conducive to domestic harmony. The drugs, selfishness and intense creativity, Celia could endure, but his relationship with Johnny Dewe Matthews, whom he had met in the late sixties, was ever more undermining to her. Ossie had had love affairs before, and never sought to conceal his extramarital flings with men and women, but this liaison pushes Celia to the edge. 'They were constantly coming round to borrow pots and pans to make meals in Powis Terrace,' she says.

Often abandoned by Ossie, Celia begins a physical relationship with Adrian George, a painter. Ossie was devastated. The diaries chart the final throes of the marriage which Ossie felt was hastened by the intervention of his friend David Hockney, who himself had been heartbroken when his relationship with Peter Schlesinger ended in 1971. Hockney had turned to Celia for comfort. Emotionally he seduces Celia from Ossie, believing Ossie's violence towards her is a sign of his frustration with his marriage. Hockney's caring for Celia perhaps hastens the divorce which took place in October 1974, leaving Ossie incredulous and in deep despair. Not only had he lost his emotional anchor, but he had also lost a vital and brilliant creative partnership. He felt deep bitterness towards Hockney, a long-time friend for whom, in 1971, he had modelled for one of his most celebrated works, *Mr and Mrs Clark and Percy.*

Throughout this turbulent year Ossie continued to lead the fashion world, staging a brilliantly received show at the King's Road Theatre on March 25. This *tour de force* was partly financed by one of his most ardent fans, Mick Jagger, for whom he had made one of his most famous creations, the jumpsuit that unzipped on stage at the Hyde Park concert in 1969.

Although, Ossie was making money, his lack of business sense was rebounding on him. He owed his bank £10,000 despite earning more than twice that amount, £23,000, in 1973. Even his backer, Al Radley, who had brought his couture clothes to a wider commercial market, despaired of his temperament. Ossie resented the restrictions imposed on him by Radley, and Radley became increasingly exasperated by Ossie's erractic working methods.

However, amidst all this financial and emotional turmoil Ossie paints a vivid portrait of London in that era, inhabited by a cast of beautiful models, rock stars and aristocrats. In London he can be found at the most fashionable society parties, night-clubbing at Tramp and attending Mick Jagger's thirtieth birthday party. He knows and dresses the most famous models of the day. One of his favourites is Patti Harrison, the wife of Beatle George Harrison, who 'cut glass ankles' enthral him. He captures the zeitgeist of 1970s New York with precision, but despite hanging out with Paul Getty and Paloma Picasso, he concludes cattily that the 'whole Warhol thing is a bore'.

We find him at peace in Ireland, where he spends his time collecting minnows with his son at the country estate of the Marquess of Dufferin and Ava. Although touchingly hopeful of making amends in his marriage – in New York he records his love for Celia and his boys, Albert and George – Ossie simply cannot alter his compulsive behaviour. He courts glamour. Sometimes up all night, he sleeps all day, yet he produces thirty outfits for Al Radley within his October deadline. At the end of the year Radley takes him to Hong Kong in the hope that he will extend his business there. Radley recalls with affectionate resignation that Ossie simply stayed in bed and failed to meet his appointment.

At the end of the year Ossie is in the throes of romantic despair, yearning for what he realises he ultimately prizes most, Celia and the boys; but he has stepped too far and spends a miserable Christmas on his own in Cambridge Gardens, tracing the movement of the sun across his room.

10 JANUARY

Moved into Powis Terrace.

Dinner with Mick[1] and Bianca[2]. Took Mo[3] to cheer him up. After, Paul Getty Jr[4] with Nikki Waymouth[5], Chrissy[6], Robert Fraser[7] and fantastic books that drove me away after a while.

27 JANUARY

Very violent visit. Celia[8] nag nag nag. Felt very bad afterwards.

9 FEBRUARY

Spent the afternoon sorting out fabrics and toiles. Scored more C[9]. Stayed up all night drawing.

10 FEBRUARY

Must make at least seven garments this week beginning with a dress and coat today. Must see the Munch[10] exhibition. Must see Patrick[11] before he goes away and not forget Valentine's Day on Thursday.

12 FEBRUARY

Munch exhibition with staff[12].

Confirm dinner with Merton[13] 8.30. I knew it would be a vile evening – no communication with Celia. She really is twisted like her sister. Merton is very sweet but after a very nice dinner and trying very hard to get through to Celia I ended up very emotional, walking out, apologising to him and hating her.

Felt a strong association with Munch and his work. Might try painting myself.

14 FEBRUARY

St Valentine's Day indeed – no nagging Celia but I miss her and especially the children.

16 FEBRUARY

Breakfast alone. Miss the children increasingly.

Andy Warhol[14] opening in Paris, Friday.

17 FEBRUARY

Went to visit Linden Gardens[15] to collect some shirts, passport, papers, etc. – saw my beautiful children. Celia cold but bid me goodbye.

22 FEBRUARY

PARIS PARIS PARIS. Please be a nice moon. Missed my plane.

Dinner with Andy Warhol with David. Buffet rather a fizzle. Johnny[16] was the hit. Paloma Picasso[17] in an 'after Schiaparelli[18]' dress. Yves[19], Loulou[20], Nikki, Lagerfeld[21]. Drank too much champagne – David[22] happy.

23 FEBRUARY

PARIS PARIS DEMONSTRATION.

Think lace dresses, think about drawing everything so far. Four weeks from Monday is the 25th[23]. Think Celia's new prints for Radley.

Warhol opening. Usual following.

La Flore for coffee – violent demonstration – police in masks and machine guns – a bomb went off four feet away from me – Johnny took a picture – confiscated by police – S H O C K – and sadness because there were pictures of Jean[24] in drag. Broke my sandal. Mandrax[25] didn't help. Masks and shields and tear-gas.

Jean Leger and Gregory[26] to a drag dinner – very amusing, didn't recognise Jean. Johnny slayed. Broken shoe is really a drag.

Should I put a lock on this diary, Mo? [Mo's writing] Yes.

'Paris would be beautiful if only the English lived there,' David said.

24 FEBRUARY

Think next week's clothes – last week's aren't finished. I'm sat at the airport longing to get home.

[Later] So glad to be back – the whole Warhol thing was a bore.

Sat up coked till after five.

28 FEBRUARY

Bathed, shaved, weighed myself – 8st 8lb again, what shall I do? Bad stars. Voted Liberal. Michael White[27] is in agreement and willing to put *The Rocky Horror Show* on early, March 25th, so as to accommodate my show[28]. 10 for 10.30 – all sounds marvellous.

Lady Rose[29] sick from smack[30] – but only a little.

2 MARCH

Cilla Black[31] in a copy of my dress on TV – I'm furious. Copyist John Bates.

I think Kit Lambert[32] is a pain in the arse.

6 MARCH

David to draw John Gielgud[33].

3 o'clock Warhol's new film – absolute waste of time and completely revolting – furious with myself for going.

Must work out tomorrow how to cut the two blouses, polka-dot black suit, white coat. Can't seem to do the invitations[34].

9 o'clock Dinner Alain Merton. Altogether a dreadful dreadful evening – boring people, delicious dinner. Pierro de Monzi[35] high-power, string-pulling press – Mr *Harpers and Queen*. Tasteful rich by no means – no style, no glamour, ponces all of them. I was very rude to the host Alain.

8 MARCH

MY GOD, WHAT A TRAUMATIC DAY. Full Moon rises at last.

Daily Express phoned to ask if it's true I'm divorcing Celia – fucking amazing.

Jack Hazan phoned arranging David's film[36]. Slammed the phone down on Shack[37] – TEMPER – phoned Radley[38] and told him direct that the show is off if Quorum is mentioned on the invitation. They are not running the show anymore – from now on I'm making the decisions – 'I am my own fairy godmother.' This year I'm definitely on top.

Radley and Shack appeared at six and I put it straight to them and they freaked completely – I became a bit shaky myself. They went away very glum and I phoned Merton who reassured me that I'm shaping up, everything is OK – that there will be traumas. Drinking too much whisky.

9 MARCH

Phoned David who burst into tears on the phone – the train was five hours late and the Gielgud drawing is getting him down. Then we drove to Friars Park, saw George[39] and Pattie[40] – the house is completely together and very beautiful. She is coming to see me next week.

10 MARCH

Phoned David who is much happier, getting the drawing done.

The people in this area have a fondness for Alsatian dogs. Consequently the street is always full of dog shit.

Finally got Jagger on the phone – arranged to pick up two dresses tomorrow – also recapped the financial backing situation[41] and he agreed on £5,000 which is wonderful news.

Happier about the situation with Celia whom I love dearly – still miss my mites.

11 MARCH

Radley phoned – I found out the invitation is NOT as I want it. Enjoyed talking to him with an audience – power. Put the phone down on both Radley and Celia – both negative vibe-givers.

12 MARCH

Celia round trying to design for jacket – wool embroidery. Didn't bring the children – really mean. Feeling very down about not seeing the children.

'Ossie Clark Originals' idea for new labels. Merton here filling me in on the situation – said they[42] want me at any price.

14 MARCH

OC in Chinese means Shit.

15 MARCH

Making boned bodice and green lace – designing in my mind. Pattie 2 o'clock. Ravishing beauty – fitted bodice on her. She said how secure it made her feel.

Seven o'clock Catherine Tennant[43] – toile fitted perfectly – vibed her brother – wonderful turn-on – gave them charlie – very happy.

17 MARCH

Kari Anne[44] has got a broken jaw – in hospital for three weeks so must send flowers and find another MODEL.

22 MARCH

Mirrors ready, champagne ordered.

Merton on the phone again with the New Quorum Deal: minimum of 30 designs per year increases in royalty to 6% guarantees £7,500 per year – hand over collection, production and handlings to me/Radley who will use Shack and Quorum. Separate showings in UK and abroad – future – Radley will organise separate methods of selling – separate showroom – separate label – if not they will go to court. (Bluff – I will call it.) FANTASTIC.

23 MARCH

Catherine Tennant's Ball. Very happy with her dress, just the most beautiful she ever saw. Divine dinner – Lady Rose, Michael Wishart[45] very amusing. His new painting might be exhibited in the RA. Then the BALL. Kasmin[46] called me a silly Cuss – we had words – I set Marianne[47] on him re David's drawings of Celia. I was very drunk – danced divinely with Vivienne[48]. Eric Clapton[49] completely out of it. Kari Anne looking like she's been bitten by Dracula, Amanda[50] looked like a rich Jewess from Golders Green.

24 MARCH
Mother's Day – sent her a telegram.
David returns from Paris.
Overflowed the bath – David very pissed off. Adie[51] marvellous – she stayed until four. Running-order and creds OK. Absolutely dead – lots more to do but I've got it in the whatever.

25 MARCH
[Ossie's 1974 show was a great success, attended by many leading names in the fashion world and a host of stars including Britt Ekland[52], Ringo Starr[53], Paul[54] and Linda[55] McCartney, Bryan Ferry[56], Rod Stewart[57] and Marianne Faithfull.]

THE DAY.
Uptight.
David confused, uptight, silly, spiteful, ratty, Celia helpful, Mo v. helpful – now it's all over so I can't remember all of it. Pattie in a pink chiffon dress – party after at Chris Stamp[58]'s – Sally[59] freaked – lots of coke, champagne, people. I'm very hungry, no dinner this evening.
I'm as famous as Egg Fo Yung. I'm a legend in my own time.
Spent till three doing lots – rehearsal – went, went – got the film together, I hope – rushes on Wednesday – Tony[60], Kath[61], fantastic, working like mad – loving it – K had half a PP[62]. Birds twittering, beautiful spring day today – like late summer – miss my babies – I enjoyed the show and want to draw everything I made – Valium! Work on – tired.
Fiona[63] just left Johnny asleep, also someone asleep in the tiny loo – Pauline Fordham[64]. Sally Stamp suicidal on the telephone.
Pattie sick immediately after the show.
Celia didn't like it but I think it went well.
Must tidy tomorrow. Bed after sunrise.
Chris beat up Sally – she very sad – he so misunderstands her.
First time no clean sheets on David's bed – I've really upset him on top of overflowing the bath, wrecking his trendy jacket and flooding Mo's basement.
The next will have sable and suede and EVERYTHING.

26 MARCH
David extremely miserable – woke me early, nagging about his jacket. The truth is Jack Hazan's film has completely depressed him. He thinks Peter[65] a little shit and completely insensitive, so I got the brunt of it. He's going over the edge.

Went to see the house[66] – work progressing. With Celia and the children to the park. Magnolia and yellow daffs. Albert and George[67] and a real policeman. Blackbirds singing, babies happy.

Bad vibes last night – Chris clouting Sally.

Long talk with Mo re David/Celia.

27 MARCH

Flowers from Linda and Paul McCartney.

Went to Kate[68]'s, got extremely stoned and we watched the Pink Floyd film again and went to the Casserole[69]. Mike Fish[70] and Rainey[71] streaked. R first, quickly, then Fish slowly – 'That'll pay for dinner,' he said and Michael Rainey waved a £20 note at me whilst Jenny[72], who paid, put her blouse back on.

28 MARCH

2.30 to Kate's for u know what, then to see *The Bigger Splash*. Actually v. good – more true than the truth – and a bit frightening to see oneself so big on the screen.

Visit Celia – parted with words and SMASHED GLASS. It was very nice to see the children. Continued to read *The Water-Babies*[73], feeling a bit down and mad with myself for getting so mad at Celia. Very violently sick. Vomited and felt awful. Must have been bacon fat or the milk, trying to put on weight – poor me.

29 MARCH

6.30 Drinks, Marilyn Quennell[74]. Alcoholic heap. 'Kiss my back,' she said as I left. I did, saying, 'It's better than kiss my arse, I suppose.' She was a bore, telling me how good my dresses are and showing me someone else's.

On the way home I thought I saw a drag queen, who turned out to be David Lindell[75] who gave me a sweet present – scored from a taxi window.

Saw the new moon, goodie goodie.

30 MARCH

Peter talking about Jack's film: 'I came out like a mysterious god and Ossie like a queenie dress designer,' when in fact I mostly noticed his knock-knees, funny feet and running eye make-up. Kasmin has been very heavy with Jack and wants to stop the film being shown – Merton to see it this week.

'Save your bad breath' – gypsy on TV.

31 MARCH

Kew Gardens is divine. Great big magnolia trees and the true spring weather.

However, there were far too many people so we drove very fast to Henley-on-Thames to visit Mr and Mrs Harrison – the whole day seemed very trippy, and that's what George said to me. We went for a walk by the lake and snorted the last – afterwards I ate a pancake, a toasted cheese sandwich, an orange, an avocado pear and an apple.

Very stoned and tired and headachey when I got back to London. Have just walked home puking every 10 yards – everything I ate today came up. I overdid it a bit, though.

Can definitely feel the effect of the moon getting fatter.

So now the Valium. Must get myself together for the morning in this fallen apart flat – pangs all day about Celia. Missing sons very very and Celia – so love that mother.

4 APRIL

1.15 Bailey[76] shoots *Vogue* cover – green chiffon dress. 'Posh birds at *Vogue* are whores at heart,' said Bailey.

5 APRIL

David and Celia on the phone together.

Dreadful, boring party – people fuck-ups. Got smacked in the jaw at Yours or Mine[77]. Very drunk. Slept in a basement opposite Celia in Linden Gardens.

6 APRIL

David on the phone re film and Hazan. Yack Yack – I'm sick of everyone yacking.

Good write-up in a trade newspaper: 'Ossie's solo hit.'

7 APRIL

Reread David's letter[78] – if I go to Paris I must talk to him.

[Later] Looks like I'm going to Paris. The next moon is for travelling – New York, Chicago, Dallas, LA. Come on, baby, it's not *Easy Rider*, is it!

9 APRIL

PARIS PARIS PARIS PARIS PARIS.

PIAF PIAF PIAF PIAF PIAF PIAF PIAF PIAF.

VODKA. TEARS. EXCITEMENT. PROUST[79]. SUNSHINE.

3.00 BA flight to Paris – very full plane with hot Indian salesman. Straight to David at La Flore where I met a beautiful French boy with yellow eyes like a cat and spilt vodka/lemon juice all over my purple suit. Then had very emotional conversation with David – cried and let everything I felt hurt about and resented come up. I think I shocked David.

We went to the St Regis and drank champagne. Back to a joint and bed with David.
Après moi means you love him after me, after me, after me.

10 APRIL
David really wants to sell Powis Terrace.
Cafe La Flore – Claude Picasso[80], Fred Hughs[81] looking at David's picture of Andy Warhol. A whorish boy smacking his lips at me. Fell asleep in the St Regis and then made a complete fool of myself in a restaurant by throwing a plate at somebody.
'Have you had sex in Paris?' 'Well, I haven't come yet.' So I ended up in some poove handbag designer's hideous dream-palace in Rue l'Alcion falling asleep all the time – went to bed around 4 o'clock. Slept badly until seven and got myself together.

12 APRIL
[Ossie, Celia and the children are invited to stay at Clandeboyne near Belfast in Northern Ireland on the Dufferin[82] estate.]

To Ireland with the Dufferins.
Lots of gossip after a wonderful divine dinner of beetroot soup and lamb. Children happy – weather very cold. A full house including:
Kasmin and his girlfriend wearing an old lady's dress
Toby something: attractive but uninteresting
Giles Eyre[83]: oldish bore but very sweet
Tchaik[84] and girlfriend: same as usual
Nicolette[85]: divine divine divine divine divine divine divine
Annette Bradshaw[86]: lovely lady from three years ago

13 APRIL
We made breakfast at ten to ten. SILENCE, the breakfast table like the reading room of a library – everyone grumpy.
11 o'clock Albert, Nicolette and I went fishing on the lake. Too much wine – after a futile search for fish at the wrong time of day, and rowing, and swans swimming, and a neurotic duck swimming round in circles to decoy us from its nest (which we were really not interested in).
3.00 Croquet on the lawn, football after tea and art talk with Lindy[87]. SUNSHINE DIVINE SUNSHINE DIVINE.
BITCHY dinner – Kasmin talking nonsense – Lindy intrigued. Conversation about female castration. If you get him warmed up he'd break the sound barrier. Sat next to the horrid Lindy. Couldn't get a word in between Kas

Nicolette Meeres in an Ossie Clark bustier at Cambridge Gardens, 1973.

and Lindy both talking crap – I also saw him on the floor massaging Annette – paralytic drunk.

14 APRIL

CLEAR BLUE SKY. WONDERFUL WALK. We saw 46 dead birds on barbed wire and two dead stoats – very strange. Beautiful trees and flowers and a water garden. Ann found a perfect blue egg fallen from a nest and still warm – translucent in the sunlight. Saw a beautiful yellow lily gigantic and a kind of rhododendron with red flowers like plastic.

Open-day at the house and croquet on the lawn – lovely noise it makes – beautiful perfect day. Now I'm ANACONDA CLARK sleeping off a great big lunch.

Sat next to Giles at dinner and talked of Paris, Coco Chanel[88], and his father. We had the remains of the turkey and a ton of chocolate cake. Afterwards we stayed in the dining room whilst the women powdered their noses and Celia bitched about me to Nicolette. We were left talking politics (Kas on about the Israeli war again). Giles and I had a homosexual conversation and he promised to give me an amber RING. Then we played cards – Canasta, Cheat, Chase the Lady and Sevens.

15 APRIL

Nicolette is really a nose freak.

Mariga Guinness[89] to lunch – minus her bustle (I can see now why she always wears one) – very affected under a sun-shade – very squashed into her roll-on and brassier.

Lunch rushed, and quickly packed, tipped the maid and butler, bid everyone goodbye and split to the airport to be searched. 16.35 back to LONDON. *Yellow Submarine*[90] on television.

18 APRIL

2.00 Radley. HEAVY HEAVY HEAVY.

Shack, Radley and Monty White[91] – Uptight Meeting with a complete breakdown. Have I burnt my boats? No, it's cool.

6.30 Nikki Waymouth here for clothes. She has bought C. Gibbs' flat.

19 APRIL
Up all night. Very tired today.
I love Celia – she understands more, more.
Mr Lamb[92] extended my credit. Bit heavy.
Spoke with Paul McCartney.
Nikki Waymouth off to New York.
Divine sunglasses from Mick[93].
Love future plans – confidence.

20 APRIL
3.00 Pattie Harrison – talk shop, take pants and John[94].
We are going to the country – space for confidence. My artworks can be my security.
8.10 Pattie very pleased but sad we arrived late – missed the light which wasn't very good today anyway. Tomorrow, maybe.
George H playing guitar by the fire, Indian food and Celia at Mo's avec le babies asleep.
[Later] So now I'm completely smashed – gobbing up blood.

22 APRIL
[Ossie goes to the USA, on business but primarily for pleasure. His first stop is in New York, where he seems very much at home in the company of his many friends and associates there – including some from London who are also visiting at this time, such as Mick Jagger, Nikki Waymouth and Christopher Gibbs.]

Travelling moon.
To NEW YORK.
Sat here watching airplanes take off. Why do Indian men always wear tight pants?
5.00 Flying over Newfoundland eating lamb curry at 31,000 feet. Ice wastelands below. Landed 7.34 excited but pooped. To the Stanhope Hotel. My eyes are green in this bathroom mirror. This room is all red which doesn't become me.
The night is warm and lots of people are in town, like Bowie[95]. Found Sandra and Mick[96] – back to their place, got smashed – and blew the whole night away.

23 APRIL
Downtown to see Colette[97] and met her friend Cindy Coope. Lots of good coke and swallowed some opium – talk, talk, very tired, bed, very zonked.

Colette very sweet, gave me some charlie. Loved Alice Cooper[98]'s girlfriend Mary. Strong jays[99] and good vibes.

24 APRIL

I went to see a Bowie movie and after had dinner with him.

25 APRIL

NO Alcohol Today, PLEASE.

Shall I come to live in N. York? or Paris?

Realised Nikki here as an ambassador for Chrissy, Paul Getty Jnr, as well as me and the rest.

Took off my mirrored shades to see the new moon above 10th Street – felt happy.

Scored from Colette – she served me melon and grapes and good hash. ½ Valium. Am I going to Woodstock?

26 APRIL

I slept on to 12.25 – my how those Valium work – must try no alcohol again – feeling very shivery.

Meeting at 3.00 – bang goes the no alcohol. Vodka and lemon.

Rag-trade couture: Halston[100], Givenchy[101], Balenciaga[102], Jean Muir[103], Didier Grumbach[104], ultra suede. Science fiction. I think they will discover the entire brain when they discover the entire universe.

Took too much everything – except dinner. The high life.

TV. Load of old shit. Zonked out.

27 APRIL

Sunshine, Headache, Too Much Everything. Must eat lunch – get myself together – make some decisions – decide what to do.

Everyone in New York is a philosopher – especially the taxi drivers.

28 APRIL

I'm reading book reviews in *Esquire* by Malcolm Muggeridge after being bored with cocks in *Playgirl*. Pooped, pissed, passed out in the sunshine.

Colette left a message telling me where to go and there I went: found all these pop stars and went to CLUB 82. Lots of heavy drag.

John and Yoko[105] together again – really. Nilsson[106] adores Laurel and Hardy movies – turned much fatter and seems much happier.

After, we had a great Chinese dinner. Told Alice the two tramps joke – she loved it. John Lennon didn't come to the club *après* – wonder what is going on?

Chicago tomorrow.
Sunburnt red face.
Nilsson: 'Two little grey heads on a pillow at 70.' Whew!

29 APRIL
Chicago – Hot Day. To the airport. 5.45 TWA Ambassador Service Chicago. AM I REALLY FLYING HIGH OVER AMERICA?
'Cool it on these joints, honey, the captain's on his way down here and he'll bust you once we reach Chicago' – Pat, the air hostess. Suddenly 6.30 Chicago time and I'm six nouns beyond reality already.
No more little white powder – in fact, someone hold me.

1 MAY
[Back in New York.]

Dinner Le Même Choix – it could be Ladbroke Grove outside.
Missed Bowie last night as well as lots of charlie.
At the first Alice Cooper do I met a man freaked by the transvestites who said, 'I knew the world was coming to an end but I didn't think it would finish up like this.'
Is it too early to drink? Of course not.
Phoned Andy – got Fred – tea tomorrow.
I love dancing on edges.

2 MAY
Bianca's Birthday.
NO ALCOHOL TODAY FOR SURE – feeling dead.
Mad extravagance at Tiffany's – $621: a ring, cuff-links and chain. Cab-ride along Park Avenue – distortion from heat, feeling BLUE and a LITTLE SICK.
4.00 Tea with Andy. It's very calm here. AW sat quietly drawing flowers on tracing paper. Everytime we answer the phone we have to say, 'Oh, bye, Andy! Hello?'
Red wine, champagne, vodka. SICK.

6 MAY
On the full moon we fuck.
Jagger party, maybe? Another Glitter[107] party – Club Cara Lero. Boring after the St Regis – pathetic hookers summoned to his presence indeed. Lost Tony[108] and Mickey[109] and Bowie and Marc[110]. Sandra gone. Michael said, 'Who's Gary Glitter?' I just couldn't cope.

7 MAY

EXIT EXCITE EXCITEMENT FLYING home – home to my babies and Celia and work, and the new me is ready.

[Despite his optimism regarding his domestic situation, on returning to London Ossie immediately crosses swords with Celia and David Hockney.]

11 MAY

Cindy Shirley[111]'s Wedding. Lots of Drugs.

Steve O'Rourke picking me up at 11/11.30 – only he didn't 'cos Linda[112]'s got mumps.

A full day starting with the good stuff and Keith Richards[113]. To Portobello on angel dust after being up all night. Alice[114] freaked – home to Linden Gardens. Spoke with David – freaked.

Collected the children and went to Cindy's wedding in the country with a friend of Dave Gilmour[115]'s. Slept in car, Children divine. Lovely old church – took me back to being a choirboy. A perfect day for a wedding – SUNSHINE.

The dresses looked beautiful, the children were a joy to be with and the reception was held in a really beautiful house with no sign of 'today' anywhere about. More angel dust, cocaine and lots of old friends – accidentally burnt George's eye. The children really enjoyed themselves – played the drums.

9.30 Back to boring David in his usual depressed London mood. Alice freaked him out as well as everything else – so he came on very heavy and says I have to leave Powis Terrace. HEAVY. Boring DOWNER David. WE HAD WORDS.

12 MAY

DAVID THE DOWNER DAY.

Had dinner with Al Radley – repeated myself over and over. Good vibe, rapport.

David at Celia's – where else? Futile conversation with him and Celia – everything I said was wrong with him, he said was wrong with me.

13 MAY

David woke me with a gas bill. DON'T GET DEPRESSED, OSSIE – come on. Celia yacking on the phone.

14 MAY

David to get his Honours degree. Found him with a bag on his head bleaching his hair.

Lord David Brooks[116]'s Ball 8.15, Café Royal. So many people very stoned and drunk. Catherine Tennant, Mick and Bianca, Robert Fraser, Mark Palmer[117], Ahmet[118] and Prince Rupert[119].

16 MAY

Radley letter – what should I do next? 5% is not good enough.

3.00 Claudia Naydler[120] wedding dress toile – perfect fit, but couldn't face shopping for lace so I shelved it. Pinched lovely flowers from Holland Park – had to climb in. Bacon and eggs and sleep with another Valium.

17 MAY

[Ossie helps to write an article for Woman's Own *magazine on George Harrison's famous home in Henley-on-Thames; Pattie, George's wife, has recently left him for Eric Clapton and the article provokes a negative response from George, who is unhappy with Ossie about his involvement.]*

Slept through this whole day in Mo's basement. Sleep, slept, sleep, hidden, hide, hide, avoid, avoid, avoid, Avoid.

David asked, 'Who's Keith Richard?'

Speaking with Pattie Harrison on the phone; likes the piece but thinks it should be rewritten. Talking business, offered me a week in a health farm. Seriously thinking about her offer.

18 MAY

No sleep at night, down the Portobello – divine lamp (£16) and blouse for Celia (£15.50). Suddenly five to twelve. Adie on the phone, and Pierre[121] on the phone, and here they are. Chelita[122] on the phone. Rushed over, giving Celia in her ratty mood her presents and collecting the children. Lent Chelita a silk trouser sample. Back to the make-up session. Johnny phoned – over for tickets for THE WHO.

The Pierre Laroche Number[123] was a bore. Willy whatshisname and Mo rushing. I freaked out, Marianne cool. A strange boy in drag thrilled with his face in the mirror scratched the big table with his high-heeled shoes.

Johnny arrived. Oliver[124] arrived. Rainy Monday. Spoke with Chris, now off to tea with Fiona, and THE WHO – left tickets here – vodka/lemon to go with ice in a flash – Michelle[125] bumped her wing (my fault – freaked her completely later), we had fish and chips on the way and lots of hassle to get in, despite hand-written notes. THE WHO are really on form – and who wouldn't be with 60,000 faces out in front and lots of madness on stage. I didn't make the backstage party. The O'Rourkes, Chelita. I drove the Rolls back through lots of violent scenes – they threw beer cans and vodka bottles on to the stage at the end. Savoury Church of St Temporary. Temporary Church of St Saviour. 1/2 oz of coke. Refined. Johnny phoned from Woody[126]'s. Lady Rose pissed off. Sally spent the night in jail – sprained shoulder. Sad that I've lost my American sunglasses again already. Michelle said that I'm evil. Am I?

19 MAY

Feeling Very Fragile.

Celia phoned at six o'clock – had taken acid and said I should be with the children. Slept away beautiful sunny day – what am I doing?

Sally Stamp in a bad way – says her old man is going to get her committed to a loony bin and has a court appearance at ten in the morning.

20 MAY

Apparently Amanda's had her face done and looks wonderful. 'Oooo, he's a darlin', Dali,' she said.

Mo on Mr Magoo[127]: 'Just carry on ripping him off like we've always done.' Have I always ripped him off?

21 MAY

Organisation, Moon.

Get Yourself Together, Ossie.

Off to get lace. Still haven't got the pure silk duchess satin. Went to visit Celia – usual row. Beautiful sunset. Alone, suddenly.

22 MAY

Another wedding – June 7th – Stella and Martin[128]. Spent morning designing Stella's wedding dress – fitting a week on Thursday.

The usual threats from Celia, nag nag, divorce divorce divorce.

Robbery attempt here at Powis Terrace. Phew! Hole in window.

Bianca coming. [In Bianca's writing] 'And she waited one hour. But she forgives, this time around. You can be anyone, you can do anything, this time round – because you are my most beloved one. Bianca.'

To Mick's – he wants clothes for a week on Saturday, so does Bianca – in love with Claudia's lace.

Going to bed at dawn again, after amusing evening – usual state. Birds singing.

23 MAY

Mick phoned and I met him very late. San Lorenzo[129] for dinner. Afterwards to boring Tramps[130] and back to Cheyne Walk to listen to his new song, watching Bianca changing – beautiful silver and purple Poiret-ish dress. What to make Mick?

So I flaked out there and had a really nice drug-free sleep, after phoning Mo (none left) and Danny Secunda[131] (asleep).

Mick said if he were American the mafia would own 15% of him. Mara said he had everything. 'I haven't got a son or a yacht,' he replied.

24 MAY

Bianca would like to adopt a three-year-old already.

26 MAY

Johnny here with neurotic Sally Stamp on the phone crying about her babies to Chris – HEAVY, HEAVY, HEAVY.

Extra piece of hash cake – nearly freaked. Getting rid of Sally was very heavy.

27 MAY

Too much sleep and too much worry day, but working too.

Handstitching, watching TV. Over to the Duchess[132] – scored a gram on tick. Johnny came too. Sally appeared at the door before I sent her away.

More handstitching. More blow. Van Morrison on TV. Everyone very manic and down.

Missing Albert and George desperately. Everything seems to be at stake tonight and there's always a wedding involved somewhere.

It seems to have become a habit – staying up all night – I worked on the lace dress, snorting. The night rushes by: Kenny Everett[133] on Capital Radio, eggs from the shop, feeling jittery and nervous.

29 MAY

Celia's first entry [in this diary], typical: 'It's a pity you cannot find more thoughts for your friends and talent, and less about moon and stars "crap".' Dangerous Diary. She gave me five pink pills – very nice indeed – we talked a lot.

30 MAY

Vikki de Lambray[134] jailed for two years – poor queen.

31 MAY

Anne Chubb[135] re Marianne Faithfull[136] wedding.

Claudia phoned. Loves her dress – and so she should, too.

Only two more wedding dresses to make and then I'm not making any more. I must get the selling range together, especially the blouses. I just love fitting and making boned bodices. Fitting Stella – very nice it's going to be, very nice. I like her great big tits.

1 JUNE

Merton's daughter Claudia marries. Didn't make it so Mick[137] woke me at 2.20, after I had crashed at 9.30.

Ronnie Wood phoned to invite me to his birthday party.

Picked up Celia, drove to the park rowing.

David phoned and spoke to Celia – hopes it's all right that we didn't go to Claudia's wedding, but it was too late and we couldn't of taken the children. I put all my effort into her dress and I'm very exhausted.

Took Albert to Ronnie's birthday party at Rose Lambton's. Met Chelita on the doorstep and she had brought stuff for Ronnie – even that didn't help – still extremely tired. Few new faces: Eric Clapton, Rod Stewart and Paula Boyd[138] with an eight-month son called William. Albert loved the garden. We left before eleven o'clock and came straight here to sleep – but of course I can't so I made eggs and tea and watched a boring late-night movie on TV.

2 JUNE

Slept right through to three o'clock – headache.

Sally Stamp cut her arm. The wounds looked self-inflicted to me. Ratty vibes, with lots of cocaine and a yapping, horrid dog. Everyone a bit freaked, especially Mo with Sally arriving, bloody dress etc. She very happy, gushing tea round in a circle.

4 JUNE

My saving angel Michelle back from Ibiza. [Michelle's handwriting] 'And decided that one could only visit Ossie with "hours to live" not "hours to kill".'

Ballet with the hoorays – the ballet was divine. I closed my eyes and imagined Nijinski[139].

7 JUNE

Stella Astor marries in the country somewhere. Bad aspect from Jupiter for Gemini so I'm not going to risk a wedding.

Naughty Marianne Snorting Smack. Missing hash terribly – oh, dear.

9 JUNE

My birthday again already – I expect they will come faster.

David[140] sewing a chiffon hem badly with a friend of Minah[141]'s. David stayed

Ossie and model Sue Worth study a new design in David Hockney's flat in Powis Terrace, 1974. Behind them stand tree sculptures made by Mo McDermott.

till he completely botched the hem AND I had to give him £1 for the taxi.
I did a gram and a half[142] myself. Very methodically I put the whole dress together, cut another skirt, made it, finished the bodice beautifully and made the top with long, flowing sleeves. By 8.45 it was almost complete when I phoned Helen Messenger[143] who appeared at 10ish and stab-stitched the finishing touches with her heavy hands.

10 JUNE

JH marries. Reception at the Ritz. Dramatic scene cutting the cake – the groom collapsed and had to be taken to the Brompton Road chest hospital because he's only got one lung and always overdoes it with alcohol. Sue Worth[144] and her husband drove me to a cold house in Battersea all beautifully prepared for a party, with lovely flowers, wine, food, etc., which was cancelled, and told me for sure he will be dead in two years. All a bit heavy. It seemed to me he should just sleep after crashing out, but I didn't know the complications and his family and all. So we went for a walk in Battersea Park at sundown and into a pub for a drink and caught an amateur drag show which was pathetic.

11 JUNE

David whining on the phone at me from Paris – I put it down on him. The Shit – he's ever so boring. Went back to sleep and didn't answer the phone which rang continuously.
Bianca phoned later – she wants fifties clothes for a ball on Thursday.

12 JUNE

No cocaine today. Feeling lost day. Chelita busted for coke. Marianne did a wonderful act like an eight-year-old girl, stamping her foot for smack.

13 JUNE

Still no charlie day. Rachel[145] played the piano, and we sang 'I Want to be Happy', which we all do. Liz[146] would like to turn her house into a drug-free nursing home – and would like me to stay a week.
I went home with Celia and we made a silent pact. I slept badly but woke to the children I have missed so.

14 JUNE

Letter from bank saying I'm now well overdrawn by £10,000-plus!

15 JUNE

Loved putting the children to bed – burnt Albert's arm with a cigarette.

The Yours or Mine for cheap champagne and lots of hot bodies including a George Barber who came back to Hamilton Terrace[147] for a swim but that was all, unfortunately.

17 JUNE

Spoke with Amanda – full of news – made a single in the USA.
Bolshoi Ballet: wonderful young dancers but a bit 'tacky' first act and costumes.

18 JUNE

Broke my fast day – Danny had heard I like drugs, money and young boys in that order.

19 JUNE

Dreadful letter from the bank. Mr Lamb is a Wolf in Sheep's Clothes showing his claws.

22 JUNE

Gala[148] pregnant again. How wonderful, darling! 'I don't know, it might be a black baby!' she said.

23 JUNE

Acid. Took a trip and walked to Linden Gardens. Graffiti on Colville Terrace: 'God won't fuck you if you're all fucked up. Fuck him.' New Moon with Celia is something to work for. Yes, New Moon with Celia is something to work for indeedy.
Bryan with a completely made-up Anthony Price[149] drove me and Keith[150] from one club to another – all closed but we heard his new album which is terrific, can't wait till it's released. They came back here for a jay and split after a while.
The walk to Linden Gardens, especially along Pembroke Place, was like a time-trip. It felt like 80 years ago. Beethoven on the radio.

24 JUNE

Me and Mick Jagger on the 'out' list of *Women's Wear Daily*.
A Chris T. here for a jay. He says he's 20 years old, with blond hair and blue eyes – a Mandrax a day keeps the bogey-man away – he has his own style of walking and a drawl to his speech, his clothes have a fifties influence and he insists on smoking Pall Mall Filter – even though it means a trip to Earls Court – he has a very sweet nature but we can't be sure if he tells the truth or not.

28 JUNE
Happy to be with Keith again, who takes the hump far too easily – I am very very fond of him.

29 JUNE
I was really sure somebody would break into Powis Terrace, as I'd left open the master bedroom window to remove the stale odour of sex.

1 JULY
I was so zonked I stayed in bed till 2.15. David has been asked to design the sets for Glyndebourne[151].

7.15 Hermione Baddeley[152] party. All cool. Strange mixture of people. Keith came with me. Catherine Tennant, Mark Palmer, Nikki Haslam[153]. Lots of old hoorays and a bunch of Californian fags. Got extremely drunk and went to a dreadful German-run club called Napoleon. Michael Wishart, Penelope Tree[154] and a bearded guy I met in New York ages ago – I kept pulling his beard. We had a dreadful scene in the Krout Klub and split to Yours or Mine where an old fag fell for me. Too much champagne. Saw the moon at last.

2 JULY
Sweet letter from my mother who is a little worried, to put it mildly. I think David isn't my friend anymore.

Celia on about separating again. 'You really like the gay life, don't you, Ossie?' she said. But do I? I don't know, I really don't know. All I know is that I miss Keith.

So we are off to see David's drawing exhibition with the beautiful pictures of Celia in it. Lots of faces – Patrick Procktor, Robert Mapplethorpe[155], Celia, Mo, usual entourage. Sheridan, Kas[156] and others who only crawl out of their holes for this sort of occasion.

4 JULY
Collect your debts together, Os.

Soon Hockney, £40,000 a canvas, leaves England for Paris.

Catherine Guinness[157] came by and I lent her a pink chiffon.

Johnny and Lady Rose here. Are having an affair. [Crossed out – new handwriting] 'We don't like the word affair – A ROMANCE, signed Johnny.' OK, so they are having a romance, and are very fond of reading other people's diaries.

Teddy Millington-Drake[158]'s party. Catherine looking divine, Nikki Waymouth looking terrible. Customs confiscated lots of her belongings.

5 JULY

Another dreadful letter from the bank.

Mr Magoo whining from Bradford[159] – mad-house noises in the background – move out by the end of this month etc.

7 JULY

It's a lovely day but at 11.30 David (David's been reading this diary) came in on the war path and played all his old songs again including two new ones: he's going to store the furniture and cut off the telephone.

8 JULY

Jenny Little told me that Nikki Haslam and Michael Wishart used to have an affair years ago, and were called Washout and Hasbeen.

9 JULY

3.10 Denis[160] phoned and I'm going to see him after the dentist – he will give me a cheque for £5,000 yippee yippee yippee yippee yippee yippee yippee yippee. Rang Mr Lamb, NatWest, and told him the news.

Sheridan's party. Divine Cindy Lang[161], with Eric gushing in her ear. Really warm beautiful evening. Too many people. Marianne fell madly in love with Cindy – I did all Jenny's charlie and Keith turned up obviously Mandraxed out. Usual mixture of lords, fashion whores, beauties, bores; fucking in the bushes; gossip; intrigue; champagne; strawberries; balmy weather; swirling upstairs, downstairs.

Home to Mo typing with one finger. Earlier he had said to Lambton, 'It's so marvellous you're wearing dark glasses because they're the ultimate gadget in vice.'

10 JULY

James Whittaker rang from the *Daily Express*. 'Are you getting a divorce from Celia?'

Keith phoned – he's going to Mayfair to hustle – 'If looks could kill, I'd be dead,' he said. He really likes me but I freak him out.

11 JULY

Got a lift in Westbourne Grove from Dave Gilmour to Marble Arch where a teacher demonstration was going on. I had to walk through Hyde Park to Denis O'Brien where the cheque was waiting – Hooray. Then to Keith for a haircut as I figured it to be a new start. A taxi to Celia's who was in a very bad mood trying to work. I split – fish and chips becoming my staple diet. Feeling blue. How far is £5,000 going to go, I wonder? – not very far.

Kari-Anne arrived looking very well indeed. She's enjoying the country – found a new girlfriend whose mother sends charlie from South America. I learnt the truth about the broken jaw incident – wasn't a car crash.

Altogether a very strange evening with an even stranger ending – poor Kari-Anne very sick and has to get up at 6 o'clock to do an all-day modelling job for chocolates.

12 JULY

'How The Ossie Clarks Try To Fashion Out A Married Life Together' – *DAILY EXPRESS* DRAMA – Celia on the phone – slammed it down and left it off the hook, only to catch her rushing round with it. We had WORDS.

Rushed to the bank to put in the George Harrison cheque. Must pay some bills now that I can at last.

13 JULY

Spent the day with Mo's help making a black suede cock-feather penis-envy jacket for Ronnie Wood – came out really divine. We are to meet in the King and Queen pub, Marble Arch. Mick[162] took us and we had a few drinks with Roddie Stewart and the roadies until he showed up with Keith Richards and a few other blasts from the past. Lots of hangers-on and drug-pushers. Good vibes and a really nice time was had by all, especially me. 'Are you from Mars?' asked Cathie Simmons[163] – there with George Harrison so I was able to thank him personally. The music is terrific. They really have been rehearsing and already it's in the can. When it was all over I lost Mo who had my snake jacket, and I was transferred to Richmond with three ecstatic pop stars.

14 JULY

David actually spoke to me, sympathising about the *Express* article. Sounds cool. Then a walk to Celia to babysit. George already asleep, she feeling a bit strange after taking some blue powder off Sid[164] at teatime. Anyway I had to persuade her to go and off she went – and I had a lovely time with Albert watching a nature program on TV. Made some dinner from a can and put him to bed after reading him *Pinocchio*. I love my son so much, I wish we could get our shit together. It's so wonderful when he calls me dadda and looks at me with his big beautiful eyes.

16 JULY

Up late and straight over to Denis – everything seems to be coming round to being resolved. I am to give the first twelve [designs] to Radley, and sixteen (actually more now) to Shack and design 30 more for the end of next month. I have got a lot of work to do, but they will employ Adie and Tony AND advance another £10,000.

Over to Quorum. Al phoned and immediately asked me to design a new knitwear line which I did later.

[Ossie begins work on the designs almost immediately. However, it is not until October that he eventually completes the task.]

19 JULY

From here it's all go – but where to? I ask myself.

Lady Rose phoned inviting me to a Guinness party – but I don't think so.

How are Celia and my babes? How am I?

Mouse in the kitchen.

22 JULY

I'm so sleepy but I did manage to get the drop-shoulder dress together – looks very different.

I've caught the mouse. What shall I do with it? 'Keep him for Albert,' said Celia, so I put him under glass with air and food.

23 JULY

Mr Mouse is quite happy.

My head is full of dresses, but I can't decide which.

Took Mr Mouse to the children, they called him Paul.

24 JULY

Celia phoned to say that Mr Mouse has got to go.

Somehow I lost my last snort which really was a bore – but I found a yellow pill in my pocket and took it, like Alice, wondering would I grow as big as a house or small as a mouse? – too late. It was a downer, and I began to fall asleep in my hamburger.

I cancelled everything and I went back to sleep, which was the best thing I could do. (Apparently, Lady Rose told me later, it was a hayfever pill.)

25 JULY

Mo outside with an armful of flowers, bringing me eggs, cheese and bread in exchange for you know what, a razor blade and a Valium. They had been raving at the Yours and Mine.

Mick[165] phoned, said he had to personally invite me to his party on Saturday.

Mr Mouse escaped.

Ossie fitting model 'Gala'. The dress is cream with tan trim; a complicated, bias cut-design.

26 JULY

Hettie[166] almost finished yesterday's dress which has come out like a Chinese vase and looked good on Celia.

'I want a new boyfriend or my old one back,' I said to Lady Rose. No sign of Keith since Yours or Mine on Tuesday.

Celia came and criticised my clothes but I could tell she liked them. To Regent's Park with Albert and George. 'Daddy, we forgot the scissors,' said Albert as we passed some beautiful roses.

27 JULY

Suki[167] phoned from Hong Kong wanting to know of doctors and hospitals in Switzerland – for a heroin cure, no doubt.

Jagger's party. He in yellow, she in peach, Jade[168] with honeysuckle in her hair. Celia already there. The house beautifully decorated with huge bouquets of sweet smelling flowers. Bouncers on the door, delicious spread, and tables in the garden. The occasional snort. Charlie and Shirley[169] (might stay with them in September), Keith[170] and Anita[171], Woody[172], Monster[173] absent. Chrissy Gibbs, Manolo[174], Bryan Ferry, Anthony Price, Mama Cass[175], Debbie Reynolds[176], Pete Townshend[177], Rod Stewart – phew! Of course, Gala's baby would have to shit and wipe it on the TV. 'I didn't mind,' said Mo, 'until I put my hand in it.'

28 JULY

The idea of this book in the hands of the police is terrifying.

29 JULY

No Hettie today and no work done either. I'm turning into one of the living dead, as Anita calls them – living as Dracula, wakening with the sun down and crashing after dawn. So easy to fall into.

30 JULY

I'm never going to get up in the morning again, and I didn't until four.

Very freaked by the death of Mama Cass[178]. Evening papers are full of it – I only just met her on Saturday night at Mick's party.

Touch wood this dump won't be sold for a couple of years or so.

Did you know it takes three weeks to digest a pepper?

1 AUGUST

Albert divine, full of chatter. We walked and watched the ducks being fed.

Letter from Mr Lamb at Linden Gardens like one old lady to another – such moaning.

Michelle phoned asking me over but I couldn't face another sleepless night on charlie.

19 AUGUST

David Chambers round and we worked on a dress. Hockney crept in – he's perfected the art of the soft-shoe shuffle. 'It's not fair,' etc. I told him I understand his feelings and want to move out as soon as possible. He's a bit sad, really. Celia seems to have the upper hand again.

21 AUGUST

I popped down to Mo who's low[179]. He entered, 'Love and friendship have flown' into his diary. He also thinks Celia might go away with the children at the weekend at Mr Magoo's expense – meddling again.

24 AUGUST

Hockney back to Paris. 'Do make sure he doesn't pinch anything,' he said to Mo about me.

25 AUGUST

CARNIVAL[180] today – a sea of black faces with occasional peroxide blonde whores. The children splashing in the bath for an hour while I prepared a chicken for dinner – I don't know how Celia manages every day. I dressed them and walked to the Jamboree – bit heavy, really. I drank a Guinness and the children ate an ice cream each and unfortunately Jimmy[181], Ronnie, Mo and Mick turned up – bit rowdy. Poor Albert banged his head.

28 AUGUST

4.30 Dentist, who did fuck all except look into my mouth and make another appointment – so back to Mish for more snorts. 'If I give you an extra snort will it cheer you up?' asked Michelle. I don't know why I feel so BLUE.

29 AUGUST

11 o'clock the big move to Cambridge Gardens.

Ordered a telephone to be installed. The beasts won't put in the pink thirties phones. Dare I take them from Big Brother Hockney?

30 AUGUST

Mother's birthday.

I slept all day whilst the movers moved everything. Very hard-faced about a tip so I had no choice except a cheque for £10.

Roddy Stewart wants some clothes. My horoscope for today said whatever is attempted will be futile so I didn't attempt anything, but I feel a bit groggy now.

I went to Cambridge Gardens to see my bed which looks quite disappointing – no mattress.

2 SEPTEMBER

Organise my bed, work-room, laundry and final exit from 'Doomsville' Powis Terrace.

5 SEPTEMBER

Woken early by the kids. The rain is so depressing all night long. Nag nag from Celia – 'You're really in a mess,' 'It's over,' etc.

6 SEPTEMBER

Celia angry because I took the children last night and they didn't wake until 10.30. So what? Much better, I'd say.

To Powis Terrace to find David, Celia and Mo there so I left – but came back to watch *King Kong Versus Godzilla* – my 'cultural intake for the evening', as David put it. He's taking Mo and Celia out. David's going to buy Celia a £10,000 diamond ring.

10 SEPTEMBER

First day back at work – up early. First remake the blouse – I did, and then down the Grove[182] for breakfast and the *Daily Mail*. Made a dress pattern from the blouse, and it's still only 1 o'clock!

10.30 Lee Yuan Chinese Restaurant. Saki and cocaine – delicious. Hope the saki doesn't give me a hangover.

12 SEPTEMBER

Marianne said of Bianca last night, 'She's a great beauty, but I'm a great actress,' as we went in the back of the Roller for a snort.

I stayed up drawing four very nice dresses and flaked out at five o'clock.

13 SEPTEMBER

I went to a secret place where I met Kenneth of Belsize Park Road and we did secret things, and stayed the night.

15 SEPTEMBER

I'm overweight – 9st 4lbs – from all the starchy and fried food I'm eating.

Ten-year anniversary of the beginning of my final term at the Royal College of Art. Pop art and diploma time. St Quintins Avenue[183] and fresh love with Celia. We got Blanche[184] at that time and I was full of burning ambition – rather burnt out now, I'd say.

16 SEPTEMBER

This must be the moon to get me together – oh, please, let it be so. I've certainly got to work very hard.

So I made a drop-shoulder block and now for a jay. This silence is killing me. I wish Mish would come – there is so much to do and I have no heart to do it. I wish Hettie would come. I cut the sleeves and a toile and made a pattern and Hettie came.

It's the Biba[185] fancy-dress do tonight. So now I've changed completely twice and still feel uncomfortable – toying with the idea of going in drag, but no, I think the white boiler-suit.

Pauline Fordham and Leslie Poole[186] were at Chelita's and we waited till gone midnight before she was ready. It was a bit of a drag and David, Celia and Mo were there. Adie, Bill Gibb[187], Hylan Booker[188] with a white face and Rickie Burns[189] as a gypsy queen. I drank half a pint of vodka and left to find petrol with Chelita.

17 SEPTEMBER

I think I have got a crank living next door – she dropped a ridiculous note on my doormat. I'm furious with the stupid old trout. I shall ignore her, I think. So ridiculous, preposterous and silly.

I think I shall go to sleep for a while when Hettie has gone. The satin and crêpe dress is finished.

Just woken up after a strange dream demanding I get off a bus with a woman driver, arguing all the time with Celia. This was a premonition: the bus was obviously my marriage.

That's seven dresses done[190].

18 SEPTEMBER

I really miss my children – can't say the same about Celia. I have never been so broke since I was a student living on two shillings a day. Thank God for my fantasies.

So now for a cup of tea, half a Mandrax and a joint. Into bed and out, can't sleep – my head full of dresses.

19 SEPTEMBER

The postman woke me up at 8 with The Who's new record. Wonder how Albert enjoyed his first day at school. I've neglected the goldfish so I'm afraid one is going to die. It's very sad. I must get them some food.

20 SEPTEMBER
Sunshine and Cloudy. Drama and Depression.

The little goldfish is slowly ebbing its life away. I'll go up the road and buy some food for him – I must. Well, I got it, but I think it's too late – poor tiny thing – it's very depressing and sad.

To collect Albert from school. Albert learning to write. We went to Shepherd's Bush market and bought three goldfish.

I got drunk and tried to phone Michelle and after a depressing walk, went back to Linden Gardens where I gave way to my temper and smashed a window after I had fallen asleep on Albert's bed. I can see now I was too heavy, perhaps, but I couldn't see what else to do, as the Rat[191] is threatening my marriage and Celia is very flattered by his attention. E.g.: it was his idea to get David to buy the diamond and between them they have poisoned Celia completely against me to such an extent she really believes I will beat her to death. Well, I refused to move, indirectly threatening to destroy the flat, saying I didn't realise (which is true) that matters had gone so far that I might lose her, and I would do anything . . .

21 SEPTEMBER
Rain and Heavy.

. . . but anything to try and save our marriage for the sake of the children – going so far as to threaten suicide because I can't see any point in continuing life with my financial millstones and the future not being as I planned it. I tried to talk to Celia, but she wouldn't listen or hear what I had to say, so I crashed out at 6 in the morning when George woke up.

Celia, went to go to bed and I only just got up in time to snatch Albert from her. I was so depressed by that time I even phoned her mother to see if that would do any good. She tried to sneak out to Stevie[192]'s in the country – I snatched her handbag and almost broke down in tears saying to Albert, who was hysterical, that Mummy was trying to take him away from me. It seemed so then. She said she would go to the police and would be back for Albert.

Meanwhile Radley phoned and came to take us to lunch and to see the clothes, which they were very pleased with. Back to Linden Gardens just in time to see Celia disappear with Rat and Georgie – I presumed to Stevie's.

I phoned Stevie, but Celia wasn't there, so where is she? With baby George and Rat. I put Albert to bed and lay in a coma when Doctor Gallway phoned saying Celia had phoned him and could he come and see me in the morning? I said yes and figured she must be in London. My mind is forming vicious patterns of revenge including Alice Pollock's gun, and beating up Rat, or me shooting my brains out. Instead I went to sleep with Albert in my arms and a very heavy heart indeed. Wind and storm raged through the night.

24 SEPTEMBER

I've just noticed another mad neighbour, out the back this time.

The sixteenth dress is almost made.

Celia hard again. I phoned Michelle earlier and she sounded emotional, so I rang again to see if she would come to Kasmin's 40th Birthday Party, but she wouldn't, so I took a taxi to Regent's Park and the first person I saw was Peter (Celia gossip – she's a blabbermouth). Jeremy Fry[193], the Hodgkinson[194], MacCormac crowd and Patrick. Spacey. Lots of champagne but no food. Very drunk, feeling nice. Catherine Tennant then Marianne, Oliver and Chelita arrived which was nice – fortunately there were no drugs or I would have succumbed as I haven't had any since the little I had on the 16th with Chelita, Emma Soames[195], and Nikki Waymouth.

25 SEPTEMBER

A quick drawing session produced number 19.

Celia came home and changed her mind about dinner and I knew she had been talking to the Rat and planned to split while I would be involved in putting the children to sleep, which is very difficult as they sense what is going on so George clings to Celia and Albert to me. So I confiscated her keys and was too heavy again, but it worked – I'm afraid I can't trust her and I know when she is lying . . . All I can see is gloom and the possibility of taking drugs again. Without her and the children life is meaningless. The house has no point, and there really doesn't seem any point in continuing.

26 SEPTEMBER

Number 20 is designed and number 19 off the machine. I'm off to have some breakfast.

Then to Powis Terrace to wait for David – then they all set on me and I have never talked so much in my whole life. Celia came back on her word yet again – after saying I can stay in Linden Gardens, now she insists I forced her into it. I still feel it is something for Celia and me to work out ourselves. David, no matter what he says (and he was very sweet last night), has got a biased opinion because of his feelings for Celia.

[Following this visit David Hockney returns to Paris to prepare for an exhibition of his work; Mo McDermott accompanies him.]

27 SEPTEMBER

Rain Rain Rain, depression creeping in. Come on, Ossie, don't get depressed – accept it, you've been beastly and must now take the consequences.

I've half cut number 22 but I'm not sure about it. I just might have gone haywire – I can't get Celia off my brain.

When I returned to Linden Gardens Celia gone to Manchester to see her parents and get away from me.

Very subdued evening – it seems obvious to me now I have to win Celia's heart back and play my cards right. Take David's advice and be calm, and carry on working at the rate I am. I feel so much better, it is two weeks since I had any coke. I'm getting up early and, if I get on with the house, maybe I can manage without Celia if I have to – but I don't know about Albert and George. I would battle in court for them if I have to, but they should have a mother.

28 SEPTEMBER

Bought an air pump for the glass tank I found on the Lane. The goldfish love it and I love the goldfish.

30 SEPTEMBER

I rang Celia and then her lawyer – said I would agree to leave Celia alone providing she lets me see the children and stops seeing the Rat. Spoke with David and sent Celia a flower.

George Harrison wants me to make him some clothes for his tour in America.

OCTOBER

Cut out dress number 25.

I arrived back just in time to receive a letter delivered by taxi from Stephanie Crossling[196]. A bit snotty – saying Celia wants me to have the children once or twice a week etc. – so I composed a reply. Let's hope it works. Meanwhile Hettie had finished number 25, so I composed number 26.

Albert behaved badly 'cos he's so freaked – Celia is very ratty and does nothing but shriek at me and him.

3 OCTOBER

Four more dresses to go.

A nosy man from the council came snooping. Oh, dear.

I had a conversation with Albert and asked him, if it came to it, who he would choose and without hesitation he said, 'I'd choose you.' How I love him.

4 OCTOBER
Over to Michelle with the excuse of getting some tapes back – stink of dogs and cocaine (which I refused). I feel so strong and good about it.

5 OCTOBER
Al Radley 1 o'clock. They weren't so ecstatic as I had hoped about the dresses. Al very interested about David's show, and whether I am going to Paris or not. Celia is.
I didn't go to bed until 2 o'clock – it's the latest I've been up in ages.

7 OCTOBER
Now come on, crêpe dresses, please. Got 29 – making the pattern now.
I persevered with Celia – kind of two steps forward and three steps back. She actually said I could have the children provided I was proved fit to – bit odd, I thought. Anyway it seemed a bit better even though she hasn't altered her mind. I've got a feeling I'm getting through to her.

8 OCTOBER
Have decided on dress number 30 but the machine is playing up.
Changed the fish water instead, but I know exactly how I shall do it – or do I? Well I've made the pattern, now what shall I do? Go to visit George Harrison – maybe? Yes.
Something told me to go there and it's a good job I did because the article I wrote has just come out in *Woman's Own*. What a shit that woman is – of all times to print it, and it is altered. 'Their friend explains why' etc., *and* it said I took the photographs. Naturally he gave me a really cold reception but forgave me when I explained – played some of his new album, talked of Pattie and his forthcoming tour. He seems in very good spirits and his new songs are divine, very happy sound. He told me of his version of 'Bye Bye Love' which he has rewritten as a parody of Pattie and 'Clappers', as he calls him. Thank god I went to Friar Park. I couldn't have coped with heavies. He explained about Cathie Simmons, the press, his feelings for Pattie, what he thought of Clapton, and we parted friends.

George Harrison, close friend of Ossie's and often a source of good advice in the 1970s.

9 OCTOBER

Saw a copy of my Bianca coat on Westbourne Grove – really brought me down.

Celia goes to Paris tomorrow and I thought of going myself – but got very negative vibes from Mo who I spoke to on the phone – David is very off me (I hope he doesn't brainwash Celia too much).

10 OCTOBER

General Election – I didn't vote because I couldn't be bothered and it all seems so pointless. I thought a lot about Celia and only hope she won't have her head bent by Hockney. Why can't David be satisfied with his genius instead of meddling in my life? Mo told me over the phone that he's angry with Celia for changing her mind – what has it got to do with him, I should like to know? Celia, can't you see I'm sincere? I don't want to throw away our life together, and what of the babies? Won't they be happier with us together? We can make it, I'm sure, because we are meant for each other.

11 OCTOBER

To the Casserole. Afterwards, in my drunken haze, I decided to go to that place I daren't even write, and I did things I'm sure I won't forget – but who knows, maybe I will. It doesn't seem to matter anymore. Maybe Celia is right, but I don't think so. All I know is she is making my life a misery – I wish she would change her mind and help me to get this house together. I'm sure it would work if only she could see the possibilities and have a try at it. I wouldn't have any need of the Jekyll and Hyde personality which every so often appears in me – god help me.

13 OCTOBER

Celia remains firm – she rubbed it in about Paris: wonderful party, photos with St Laurent, etc. Said all her friends are laughing at me and I should apologise to David. I left Linden Gardens in tears. 'What shall we do?' I asked Albert. 'Go to the zoo,' he said. I feel very down indeed.

I must work as hard as before but I find it hard without Hettie. I'm feeling good and proud about abstaining from cocaine – four weeks today, and not even wanting it.

14 OCTOBER

DOOM GLOOM STUPIDITY BLOOD TEARS.

The police drove me away then breathalysed me and took a blood test at Notting Hill police station after I collected Albert from school.

I took him round to Celia and she was extremely heavy about me seeing them every day – twice a week and weekends only, please. She seemed to enjoy goading me, liked the power she had over me. So I rang Alice and arranged to see her and a lawyer at 6.30. I filled in time by drinking vodka which was my first mistake.

The lawyer explained how the law sees it, over more drinks. Sad guy – he had lived with Pru Pratt, a model who had died in the Turkish air disaster, which brought tears to my eyes. I finally, like a bull with a red flag, learnt something I hadn't known about Celia and the past. So I split to Linden Gardens and was so furious I beat her and kicked her and her nose was a bloody mess – then I forced her to speak to her lawyer lady and it was she who sent the police round, who told me to leave, but I went back and collected my sound-system and they followed me, warning me not to drive.

15 OCTOBER

I slept badly and spent from 7.30 till 11.30 on the telephone. Stephanie Crossling rang to say they were going to court at 2 o'clock – so now there is a court injunction to stop me going round to Linden Gardens and my babes are harder to see. I went to get my car back from the police station and went to work at Quorum, making the quickest chiffon dress I've ever done.

The NatWest phoned to say the Harrison cheque had bounced which, on top of everything else, completely freaked me. I've arranged to go to Paris by car with Al very early Thursday morning. It was that damn article in *Woman's Own* which was the cause of the cheque bouncing. I had a real telling off from Richard and had to sign a paper promising not to tell any more secrets of George Harrison's personal life – phew!

17 OCTOBER

Long drive to Paris. Overcast all day.

Read *Tender is the Night*[197] which just matches my mood.

To Claude Bernard[198] where the first person I recognised was Loulou de la Falaise and her mother. Pink champagne and lots of food – amazing apartment, beautiful chairs – two with lions from the Brighton Pavilion. Lots of people I knew – Jack Hazan, Mo, Gregory, John Stephanidis[199], big-mouth Shirley Goldfarb[200], who said to me, at the top of her voice so everyone could hear, 'You can break your wife's nose but you're still very sexy to me.' I had a long chat with Mo who's pretty bored with the whole situation – we phoned Mick who was told off for letting me into Powis Terrace the other night. Then Fred and Andy Warhol arrived and Manolo and Paloma Picasso and everyone got completely drunk and I pinched some sea shells from the bathroom. Alexis[201] took me to the Bronx which was like a huge cocktail of groping people. I felt like a cherry being swished around – I don't think I want to go there again.

Ossie's old friend Mo McDermott in drag, 1974.

18 OCTOBER

I began a long letter to Celia. Broke off to meet Mo at La Flore, where we had breakfast, then over to see David's exhibition which is absolutely beautiful – the drawings of Celia pulled at my heart. How can I have done what I did to her?

Went to Angelo's for lunch where Andy and co. were. Afterwards Mo and I came back here and finished the letter. Said goodbye to Mo with a kiss as he's off to London at 6 o'clock.

19 OCTOBER

I really dread being alone with my thoughts at the moment, so I'm very pleased Alexis has just phoned up and will accompany me to La Coupole where I have arranged to meet Al's party for dinner.

Loulou, Didier Grumbach – who looked straight through me – and later John Laflin[202]. We walked home in the rain. Jean and her friend were playing Motown records. I'm still feeling sad and the book I'm reading is a great consolation – so I disappeared into it and couldn't sleep so carried on reading until it must have been after 5 o'clock.

20 OCTOBER

Long bath and read *Tender* and listened to Wagner. We walked in the wet to see the Impressionists and I loved the Van Goghs especially. Took a taxi back and finished listening to Valkary and finished the F. Scott Fitzgerald and had a little sleep.

I drank whisky and thought of Celia all the time – Jean gave me a sleeping pill and disappeared into the bedroom for yet more sex with the Iranian manic depressive who he feels sorry for.

Jean Leger says I must register my name before anyone else does . . . Ossie Clark, OssieClark, OZ, OC, Aussi, OH SI, Ozzie, O'zee.

22 OCTOBER

Albert's Birthday and Celia's divorce.

'Help me, Lord, to rise above this feeling,' sings George Harrison. Today is the beginning of my bachelorhood and I must do lots of things like get a telephone and buy a dog and get the kitchen together. I've just made scrambled eggs and taken a Valium.

Law Courts in the Strand 1.30. So now I'm ready to face the ordeal – I'm very apprehensive – I don't know what will happen. Will I be able to see the babies after? Well, NO. I arrived on time but had to wait ages while they explained the situation to me. Ironically we both wore the same colour and the barrister was to-ing and fro-ing for about 1½ hours. She refuses to let me have the children except for Sundays and bonfire night until the next hearing on the 11th – I am now instructed to countercharge and write my side of the story. We slipped in between cases and it was all over – I've agreed I won't molest her and not to visit either Linden Gardens or Powis Terrace. I think it's terribly mean of her and the barrister agreed. I'm afraid I hate her at the moment and wish she were DEAD but I hope that will soon pass.

So I went to buy a dog and found one in Shepherd's Bush market – absolutely divine and very friendly, and full of worms and fleas. I've called her EVE. It's my companion. I took her to the vet and defleed her and gave her a worm pill and she has really taken to me. Don't forget the judge picking his nose.

It's going to be a long time till Sunday.

Eve in the basement – she woke me at 4, howling in the top of the house. Shit everywhere. I had to take a Valium to go back to sleep. I don't know what I've let myself in for.

23 OCTOBER

Disinfectant, fed her on cereal and banned her to the garden. Howling ceasing, but feeling very wretched and miserable. Little weep. 3.45 – left the dog in the garden and over to Michelle and Chelita in a bad way after smack binge.

A better day with Eve but I hear her weeping. I must make her a proper bed. So I put some wool offcuts in a box and locked her in the basement. I'll put newspaper down and hope that works. I can do without all that shit and howling. She will JUST HAVE TO GET USED TO IT and so will I.

24 OCTOBER

Extraordinary day. Invited Paul to lunch at the Casserole. Arrived simultaneously with Pattie, Terry Doran[203] and Eric Clapton – very drunk, real vibe. I said we'd talk later and sat separately with Paul. Oliver Musker feeling very sorry for himself, said Marianne is devouring him – she at that very moment lunching with Chelita. Oliver told me lots of news and then went to cry on Pattie's shoulder. Eric pulled my leg about the *Woman's Own* article – Pattie not looking so good but finally realised it wasn't my fault.

Missing my babies very much.

25 OCTOBER

39th day without cocaine.

To Hard Rock Cafe for hamburgers – Vivienne working there. Some boy came and gave us some opium to eat, and off to meet Robert Fraser and Bill Willis[204]. Drank beer and felt ill. Robert told of Paul Getty's penis affliction.

Later we went to San Lorenzo for dinner. Bailey was there with Helmut Berger[205], and guess who at the next table hanging on to every word? Yes, Ponsonby Hasbeen[206].

26 OCTOBER

Back home to find no Eve. What a downer. Poor little Eve. Why didn't I leave her inside? Went to the police station.

28 OCTOBER

Lovely sunshine in the morning, more divorce papers in the post. So now I'm trying to write a short history of my marriage – very bitter it is, too. OH, if only a miracle would happen because that's what I am afraid it would take to alter Celia's mind. My heart is completely broken and if it weren't for my beautiful children Albert and George I'd kill myself, I think I really would.

An ad in the *Evening Standard* said, 'Make your friends envious – spend a night on the town with Ossie and Charlie.' My god, if only they knew . . .

29 OCTOBER

Decided to take a sauna bath and drove to St Martin's Lane and relaxed in the heat and anonymity until I met two ballet dancer friends of Wayne[207]'s – one called Paul Clark who I saw dance 'the witch boy' at the Coliseum.

31 OCTOBER

I went to Battersea Dogs Home, but no Eve and no record either – so to Notting Hill tube police station. Had to wait to see PC 134 Jessop. He said, 'I did something fatal – I took him home and the children love him, will you sell him to me?' So I did, for £27. Bye bye, Eve. I'm sure you'll be happy.

Drove to Chislehurst Caves for the Led Zeppelin Halloween party which turned out to be a drag. Saw one or two nice people: Steve O'Rourke, Phil[208] from The Pretty Things – but we decided to leave quite early.

1 NOVEMBER

My first thoughts every morning are of Celia and the babes.

At Cambridge Gardens I found two letters – one with tickets for Pink Floyd at Wembley on the 15th and one from the Metropolitan Police.

1.00 Lunch with Radley – gave me £500, £100 in cash. Wants me to do more designs and knitwear. The collection sold well in Paris, especially a skirt I did in about ½ an hour – sold about 1500 – so he's very pleased but so he should be.

3 NOVEMBER

Freedom with the children from 4 till 7.

The day went so quickly. Albert slept in the car and there were tears when I left him. Georgie was cool. I carried them upstairs, left the bag outside the door, and crept away like a leper – can she know what it's like for me? Surely it's worse than anything I've done to her.

Linda McCartney has been looking for me – wanting clothes, no doubt.

4 NOVEMBER

I phoned Celia to see if I could collect George first and Albert from school but she wouldn't hear of it – apparently there is a letter at the school banning me from picking him up.

5 NOVEMBER

50th jour sans coca.

Thank god it's a Tuesday. I can take the children to Maureen[209]'s bonfire party. I arrived early outside Powis Terrace. Celia came over and actually spoke to me. WOW. She asked where I would bring the children back to. So I followed wonderful directions and seemed to be the first to arrive – much preparation going on – Ringo playing his new album, Maureen making a punch from brandy, red wine and honey, a huge fire ready to be lit at 6.30 in the garden and lots of huge fireworks. Pattie arrived but Eric in Japan hating it. My children happy and enjoying it – suddenly lots of people arrived. Cilla Black, Twiggy[210], Bryan Ferry, Amanda, Kenny Everett, Maggie Bell[211], Neil Aspinall[212], Ronnie Wood (still owes me £100 but I didn't mention it!). He was snorting coke with the spade dealer and said to keep in touch.

7 NOVEMBER

It's very cold in my house. I found a letter from the bank – my overdraft up to £6,000 again.

I don't ever want to see David again.

8 NOVEMBER

I think it was very courageous of Julian[213] to put a bullet in his brain.

11 NOVEMBER

Rush rush to another court hearing, where I gained no ground at all. Complete bring-down and waste of time. I can go to Linden Gardens, but not in – also I've got the children on George's birthday for four and a half hours. And I thought she was feeling sorry for me.

15 NOVEMBER

Pink Floyd. Seven o'clock suddenly loomed up and we were ready and dressed in furs to go to Wembley – arrived exactly on time. The show was good but not as good as the last. The crowd certainly really dug it – and afterwards we went backstage for drinks. John Cale[214] very heavy, nasty roadies and lots of people I knew, then we went to Gilmour's new house behind Westbourne Park Road to watch a pornographic movie and Monty Pythons[215] on video tape.

16 NOVEMBER

I woke up feeling so down that I had to phone Celia. I sobbed hysterically and she offered to let me have the children for the day. So I dressed and rushed round and helped dress them (as they were in the bath when I arrived). It turned out to be the happiest day I've spent with them in ages.

I took the opportunity of talking with Celia – she 'sort of' sees my point and we got on quite well. I asked Celia if I could stay – she was reluctant at first but finally gave in, though I watched a boring midnight movie until she fell asleep.

17 NOVEMBER

Celia phoned to say she would pick them up – which she did, but they wouldn't go with her. Instead I took them and she grew ratty with me and we rowed. I cut the phone off, immediately freaked, and regretted it. Wrote 'When I left here in January' on the kitchen wall as it seemed to be Celia's key phrase. We argued about the RAT who's obviously still on the scene – she actually buying him underwear, which I took. I told her everything over again, including the fact that I was prepared to prove my love for her physically – she wouldn't hear of it and I was forced to leave after insisting she doesn't mention the phone-cutting to her DAMN Stephanie Crossling, the SHIT.

18 NOVEMBER

Shack was very cool, saying, 'The trouble is, Ossie, the shoulder-line has changed so much,' but he agreed to look at the clothes again on Friday.

Danny Secunda invited us to go to Paris in connection with the Jimi Hendrix[216] estate and the tapes, which he is very excited about.

20 NOVEMBER

To Paris.

With difficulty Chelita penetrated my deep sleep, but it took an hour to come back to reality. She hadn't slept at all, and methodically got herself together while I bathed, dressed and fretted. We arrived at the gate in time to see the aeroplane slowly backing away. Standby breakfast, jumbo crash in the newspapers and AF 12.30 flight to the horrid new Charles de Gaulle airport and drove to the city, stimulants on the way. Hanging about at CBS and feeling tired, finally we heard the Jimi Hendrix tapes, then Chelita and I split to Grumbach's house to bath and cool out. It was such a happy domestic scene with a three-year-old that I couldn't help comparing it with my own mess and got brought down, especially as the original plan to go back tonight was impossible and we had nowhere to stay.

Jagger and Nureyev[217] were in town.

I took a 10-milligram Valium and faded into the waiting arms of Morpheus in a room where Nancy Mitford[218] used to sleep.

22 NOVEMBER

[Back in London.]

To Linden Gardens, instinctively knowing Celia was with Rat. Sure enough, after ten minutes on the corner they drove by. I rushed to a telephone, begging her to get him out of my flat where my babes lay sleeping – no go. I got desperate, phoned Jimmy, she wouldn't let him in but did let Ronnie in – so I went with Jimmy to Ladbroke Grove and just couldn't resist kicking Rat's door in. Jimmy dropped me at Chelita's, collected Ronnie, and the Rat walked home to a smashed television set.

23 NOVEMBER

Jimmy helped me to make a room to live in at Cambridge Gardens. We set up the bed, swept the floor, laid the Persian carpets and I made a curtain.

In the end it looked quite cosy. I fell asleep in front of the television, woke at three cramped and shivery – I crept to bed miserable and feeling very alone, my head full of hatred for Celia and the Rat.

26 NOVEMBER

George's birthday – three years old. I wonder shall I see him today or will I be excluded again, as with Albert?

28 NOVEMBER

Utterly depressed and weeping. Listening to George Harrison records: 'Isn't it a pity/How we break each other's hearts?'

30 NOVEMBER

[Ossie goes to Hong Kong with Al Radley who has arranged a number of appointments for him with fashion buyers there, many of which Ossie unfortunately does not attend. The trip is not a great success.]

Celia and children drove me to the airport. No wedding ring on her finger.

1 DECEMBER

Arrived in Hong Kong utterly depressed, wondering why I came. Taken to the Hong Kong Hotel. Very modern, doomy and plastic.

4 DECEMBER

I think of nothing but Celia and my babes. Everywhere I go there are mothers with children in their arms. I feel like going home but can I consider Cambridge Gardens a home?

7 DECEMBER

My mind just put the clock back to London time and imagined Celia and the children getting up and beginning the day. I keep praying and hoping she will have changed her mind, or writing mental suicide notes, or trying to figure out my life when I get back to London. For two pins I'd go back immediately except I'm afraid to – as I'm half sure it won't have changed – and there's nothing to go back for except that big empty house and maybe a real suicide. I don't really want to die – but I can't see any point in living without her and just seeing my beautiful Albert and George occasionally. Listening to the radio, almost every song reflecting my feelings for Celia, wondering, dare I phone her up? Or could I write her a letter to express my feelings in a way she would understand? But then you're not Marcel Proust, Os, so take your Valium and go to sleep.

8 DECEMBER

I phoned Celia and wept from the depths of sadness and pleaded with her to try and understand my point, begging for a few days together at Christmas. She told me my beautiful RCA dress was stolen and that Albert has measles and hung up. I cried my heart out – then suddenly produced multi-coloured knitwear designs at her suggestion, though the scarf I brought with me was also inspiration.

9 DECEMBER

I finally got up at 4.20 and I'm utterly utterly depressed – my fake suicide notes becoming more real than mental.

10 DECEMBER

The Great Gatsby[219] proved to be so fascinating I read it all. The book is divine, on the same theme as Celia and my fracas but more dramatic and of course less real. Or was it, I wonder later.

13 DECEMBER

I'm so looking forward to going home. I bought (rather Suki bought for me) another jacket for Albert and a blue blouse and a night-dress for Celia and a Mickey Mouse watch for Albert for 21 Hong Kong Dollars – then I couldn't resist going back to buy some waistcoats I saw: cerise for Georgie, jade-green for Albert.

14 DECEMBER

Write up in *Hong Kong Standard* (very excited).

Chewed up my long nails. I just hope I hope I hope I pray I pray and I pray to god to forgive me and give me another chance at my marriage which I so stupidly fucked up. Please god give Celia back to me, I love her so much, I really do.

16 DECEMBER

[Back in London.]

Now that I've realised I love Celia so completely and entirely, I grovelled on the floor to be taken back. It's a case of after she got what she wanted, she doesn't want it anymore.

I had to wait until Celia arrived – she was very cold with me but let me in to see the children who were happy to see me. Poor George – in the agony of measles. How I love them. I showed them their presents and Celia too – I begged and pleaded with her to forgive my stupidity and wrong behaviour in the past saying couldn't I stay till the end of the year? No, No, No. I got on my knees, lay on the floor, cried on her shoulder, all to no avail. So I got myself together, read the children three stories and left, stealing the keys which was madness.

17 DECEMBER

Phoned Chelita and went over and fuddled my brain with cocaine. Feeling better, then down, then up, then down. Chelita is marvellous to me – but I can't help wallowing in self-pity. I can't see any way round my problems.

A terribly inaccurate report of my dilemma: 'Ossie Clark's wife Celia has left him for David Hockney, £10,000 ring etc.' It's all so horrible.

The way I feel at the moment is that I've just made one mistake after another all year, walking around with my eyes closed to what was really going on. And I've lost Celia. I must face the fact. I've lost her but my brain won't think of anything else, nor can it.

24 DECEMBER

Card from my mother full of hope that Celia and the children will join me in my new home. 'Without children Christmas is nothing,' she wrote.

25 DECEMBER

CHRISTMAS DAY.

I woke up to the rain outside and sorrow inside. I listened to classical music for hours smoking cigarettes – the tears came eventually and I'm as low as ever.

29 DECEMBER

Everyone seems to be affected by my misery and I seem to be helpless to do anything about it.

30 DECEMBER

Sat grieving in bed smoking cigarettes – not even the energy to dress myself. I've got stomach ache again. I've had it every night for a week – I'm not eating properly though I sleep very (too) well. Valium, I'm sure, but even after I wake (early) I stay in bed watching the sunshine trace its way across the room. (I can tell the time by it.) I feel very fragile and unable to do anything mentally and physically. I've stopped ticking over, and it's going to take a big push to get me going again. Is there any hope? Without it there is nothing. I must hope, and I pray (which she despises).

31 DECEMBER

And so the old year ended, lying on Jimmy's bed, watching a horror movie on TV. At midnight we all embraced, a tear in my eye. What will 1975 bring? Surely the worst is over?

1 Mick Jagger, lead-singer of The Rolling Stones. Jagger was one of the few men for whom Ossie designed clothes, his flamboyant creations a vital component of Jagger's androgynous stage-image of the late sixties and early seventies.
2 Bianca Jagger, model and actress. Ossie designed her wedding dress when she married Mick Jagger in 1971 and became her close friend and personal designer.
3 Mo McDermott, artist who also modelled for and assisted David Hockney. McDermott introduced Ossie to both Celia Birtwell and Hockney and remained a life-long friend of the three.
4 Paul Getty Jr, American oil executive and art collector; the multi-millionaire son of Jean Paul Getty.
5 Nikki Waymouth, née Samuel, heiress who was formerly married to painter Nigel Waymouth.
6 Christopher Gibbs, society antiquary; friend of Paul Getty and Mick Jagger.
7 Robert Fraser, art dealer and gallery owner.
8 Celia Birtwell, textile designer and muse of David Hockney; Ossie's wife. (Unless stated otherwise, all allusions to 'Celia' made throughout the text refer to her.)
9 Cocaine – also referred to as 'charlie', 'coke', 'toot' and 'snort'.
10 Edward Munch, Norwegian Expressionist painter, most famously of *The Scream*.
11 Patrick Procktor, successful British painter and illustrator; a close friend of David Hockney. In many ways Procktor was a mentor to Ossie, particularly in the later years of Ossie's life.
12 The staff at Radley Fashions/Quorum.
13 Alain Merton, lawyer introduced to Ossie by John Kasmin (see note 46).
14 Andy Warhol, American Pop Artist and film-maker who worked from the Factory studio in New York; friend of David Hockney.
15 Family home of Ossie and Celia.
16 Johnny Dewe Mathews, painter and photographer for whom Ossie had a great fondness. Dewe Mathews later married the writer Marina Warner.
17 Paloma Picasso, Spanish jewellery designer; daughter of Pablo Picasso.
18 Elsa Schiaparelli, Italian couturier of the twenties and thirties who commissioned fabric designs from Surrealist painter Salvador Dali, among others.
19 Yves Saint Laurent, Algerian fashion designer who was instrumental to the fifties movement to rethink fashion without couture. It is said that Ossie's first spread of pictures in *Vogue* inspired Saint Laurent's own collection of culottes and bomber jackets.
20 Loulou de la Falaise, model, muse of Yves Saint Laurent; daughter of French fashion icon Maxime de la Falaise.
21 Karl Lagerfeld, German couturier who attributes his influence 'le flou' to the long, fluid, high-waisted line that Ossie put on the catwalks during the seventies.
22 David Hockney, iconoclastic British artist. He was heralded as a star of British Pop Art in the early sixties and has since achieved significant international renown. (Unless stated otherwise, all allusions to 'David' made throughout the text refer to him.)
23 The day of Ossie's show.

24 Jean Leger, worked for designer Helena Rubenstein. Leger was part of an entourage of admirers of David Hockney in Paris at this time.
25 Mandrax is a brand-name sedative.
26 Gregory Evans, a boyfriend of David Hockney; he was also his model and later became his personal assistant.
27 Michael White, theatre and film producer.
28 Ossie's show was to be held at the Kings Road Theatre, where Michael White's production of *The Rocky Horror Show* was playing.
29 Lady Rose Lambton, daughter of former Conservative junior minister Lord Lambton.
30 Heroin.
31 Cilla Black, singer and TV personality.
32 Kit Lambert, manager of The Who; son of composer Constant Lambert.
33 Sir John Gielgud, actor and writer.
34 For his show.
35 Pierro de Monzi, fashion designer who owned the Monzi boutique in Chelsea.
36 *The Bigger Splash*. Directed by Jack Hazan. Film which documents David Hockney's life between 1971 and 1973 and in which Ossie, Celia and Mo McDermott all featured.
37 Brian Shack, accountant for Radley with whom Ossie shared a somewhat turbulent professional involvement.
38 Alfred Radley, owner of Radley Fashions. He was apparently 'mesmerised' by Ossie and worshipped him as a designer – despite the difficulties in their working relationship it is generally thought that they were mutually amicable.
39 George Harrison, guitarist and singer/songwriter, formerly with The Beatles. Ossie attended a 1964 Beatles concert in New York at the invitation of their manager, Brian Epstein, and was mistaken for George Harrison and besieged by fans.
40 Pattie Harrison, née Boyd, actress and one of Ossie's favourite models (though her only experience on the catwalk was in his shows); she was at this time married to George Harrison.
41 For Ossie's show.
42 Radley Fashions.
43 Catherine Tennant, society hostess; she would later become Lady Palmer following her marriage to Sir Mark.
44 Kari Anne Jagger, model; wife of Chris Jagger.
45 Michael Wishart, painter and writer.
46 John Kasmin, art dealer who gave David Hockney his first one-man show in 1963 and nurtured his success.
47 Marianne Faithfull, model, actress and singer. She was 'discovered' at a party by Rolling Stones manager Andrew Loog Oldham and subsequently had a well-publicised relationship with Mick Jagger.
48 Vivienne Jagger, ex-common-law wife of Chris Jagger with whom she had a child, Dimitri.
49 Eric Clapton, guitarist and singer/songwriter, formerly with Cream and The Yardbirds.
50 Amanda Lear, muse of Salvador Dali.
51 Adie Hunter, Ossie's PR manager from 1969 to 1974.
52 Britt Ekland, actress; second wife of Peter Sellers. She was a constant client of Ossie's.

53 Ringo Starr, drummer, formerly with The Beatles.
54 Sir Paul McCartney, singer/songwriter, formerly with The Beatles (he was recently knighted for his contribution to popular music).
55 Linda McCartney, née Eastman, photographer and animal rights campaigner; the recently deceased wife of Paul McCartney.
56 Bryan Ferry, singer/songwriter, formerly with Roxy Music.
57 Rod Stewart, singer/songwriter, formerly with The Faces.
58 Chris Stamp, manager of The Who; brother of actor Terence Stamp.
59 Sally Stamp, model; wife of Chris Stamp.
60 Tony Howard, manager of T-Rex, later agent for Pink Floyd. Howard often organised the music for Ossie's shows.
61 Kathleen Coleman, Quorum machinist who worked for Ossie for 17 years.
62 Pink pills (also blue pills) – it is presumed that these were tablets containing amphetamine, or speed.
63 Fiona Montague, wealthy, well-connected former débutante.
64 Pauline Fordham lived with RCA painter Derek Boshier in the early sixties and worked for Tuffin and Foule, RCA contemporaries of Ossie's who were producing collections for Woollands at the same time as he.
65 Peter Schlesinger, painter whom David Hockney met while teaching at UCLA in the late sixties – they became lovers and Hockney was reportedly devastated by the break-up of their relationship in 1971. It was through Schlesinger that Hockney became close friends with Celia Birtwell.
66 The house Ossie bought in Cambridge Gardens.
67 Albert and George Clark, Ossie and Celia's sons. (Unless stated otherwise, all allusions to Albert and George made throughout the text refer to them.)
68 Kate Abrahams, friend of Ossie's from his time at Manchester College.
69 The Casserole was a restaurant in Chelsea owned by Keith Lichenstein, run by Dickie Kriess and frequented by the 'in-crowd' of the period.
70 Michael Fish, fashion designer who made his name in particular for designing Kipper ties and radical menswear.
71 Michael Rainey, worked with Ossie and Alice Pollock (see note 114) and was well known in the rag-trade; husband of Jane Ormsby-Gore.
72 Jenny Little, wife of Anthony Little who, with Peter Osborne, runs wallpaper and fabric designers Osborne and Little.
73 By Charles Kingsley. This 19th-century fairytale is often cited as being full of opportunities for psychoanalytic interpretation.
74 Marilyn Quennell, wife of Peter Quennell. The notorious misogynist Cyril Connolly was a close friend of the couple and apparently only ever complimented Marilyn when she was wearing an Ossie Clark dress.
75 David Lindell owned a fashionable shop in World's End selling kelims and carpets.
76 David Bailey, internationally renowned photographer who photographed many of Ossie's early designs for, among others, *Vogue*. A notorious womaniser, Bailey has been married several times and romantically linked with many models and actresses.
77 The Yours or Mine was a gay night-club in Kensington High Street.
78 There is no previous mention of this letter in the diaries and no indication of its contents, though it appears to have provoked a significant conversation between Ossie and David Hockney (see entry for 9 April).
79 Marcel Proust, French author, most famously of *Rememberance of Things Past*, of

whom Ossie was a great admirer, often reading his work when reflecting on his own past.

80 Claude Picasso, son of Pablo Picasso.

81 Fred Hughs was Andy Warhol's assistant and ran *Andy Warhol's Interview* magazine.

82 Sheridan Dufferin, the Marquis of Dufferin, art dealer; business partner of John Kasmin.

83 Giles Eyre, in oriental art dealer.

84 Tchaik Chassai, architect who co-founded Soho's Groucho Club and the 192 restaurant in Notting Hill.

85 Nicolette Meeres, Slade painter and former employee of Paul Getty Jr. She met Ossie during his time at the RCA and later modelled for him.

86 Annette Bradshaw worked for the ICA.

87 Lindy Dufferin, painter; wife of Sheridan Dufferin.

88 Coco Chanel, French couturier who revolutionised women's fashion in the twenties; her personal life, in particular her friendship with the Duke of Westminster, gained her notoriety.

89 Mariga Guinness, first wife of the Honourable Desmond Guinness.

90 Film inspired by and featuring animated versions of The Beatles.

91 Monty White, chairman of Radley.

92 Richard Lamb, Ossie's bank manager at NatWest at this time.

93 Mick Sida, Mo McDermott's boyfriend at this time.

94 John Hammond, photographer married to Ossie's niece Carol.

95 David Bowie, singer and actor who created the androgynous alter ego Ziggy Stardust in the early seventies.

96 Sandra Kamen, an RCA friend of Ossie's whom he met on the way to his interview there, having noticed her wearing a red leather coat on the Underground. She is the wife of Michael Kamen, successful film- and pop-music composer.

97 Colette Mimran, French–American friend of Ossie's whom he met in New York in the late sixties.

98 Alice Cooper, American singer/songwriter, leader of a band with the same name.

99 Joints, cigarettes containing marijuana or hashish – also referred to as 'spliffs'.

100 Roy Halston, American designer who initially made his name as a milliner – designing hats for Jacqueline Onassis, among others – but by the sixties was known for designing clothes, in particular eveningwear.

101 Hubert de Givenchy, French couturier; particularly notable for the clothes he designed for actress Audrey Hepburn in the fifties.

102 Cristobal Balenciaga, Spanish couturier; most predominant in the thirties, though in the sixties famously became one of the first designers to dress models in body-stockings.

103 Jean Muir, British fashion designer and contemporary of Ossie's. Muir gained significant international reputation during the sixties.

104 Didier Grumbach, President of the Chambre Syndicale de la Couture. Didier represented Mèndes, a French manufacturer who also produced off-the-peg couture for Yves Saint Laurent, and organised Ossie's 1971 show in Paris.

105 John Lennon, singer/songwriter, formerly with The Beatles, who was shot dead by a 'fan' in New York in 1980, and his wife, Yoko Ono.

106 Harry Nilsson, singer/songwriter of numerous hits including 'Everybody's Talking', the theme from *Midnight Cowboy*. Nilsson and John Lennon were well-known drink-

ing partners, most famously during what is now referred to as Lennon's 'Lost Weekend' – a period of in fact nearly a year, beginning in 1973 and ending at around this time, spent drinking in Hollywood and New York while Lennon was experiencing marital difficulties.

107 Gary Glitter, British glam-rock singer/songwriter. On this visit Glitter signed Ossie's diary, 'This is the first autograph to be written in the famous memoir of my dear friend The Wizard of Oz.'

108 Howard (see note 60).

109 Kamen (see note 96).

110 Marc Bolan, singer, formerly with T-Rex.

111 Cindy Shirley, worked for fashion designer Rifat Ozbeck.

112 Steve O'Rourke, manager of Pink Floyd and his wife, Linda.

113 Keith Richards, guitarist with The Rolling Stones.

114 Alice Pollock, founder of Quorum and estranged business partner of Ossie's.

115 David Gilmour, guitarist with Pink Floyd. Gilmour became a close friend of Ossie during the sixties when he occasionally helped out at Quorum as their van-driver and provided music for the shows.

116 Lord David Brooks – 'Brookie' – of Warwick Castle, who sold his estate and went to live in Paris where he 'came out' as a homosexual and eventually died of AIDS.

117 Sir Mark Palmer, with Jose Fonseca (see note 00), founded the English Boy modelling agency which operated from above the Quorum shop. Palmer later drove to India on a motorbike, taking with him a range of Ossie's shirts which he eventually sold on the beach in Goa.

118 Ahmet Ertegun, founded Atlantic Records in 1948 and is still president of the company.

119 Prince Rupert Lowenstein, business manager of The Rolling Stones.

120 Claudia Naydler, daughter of Alain Merton (see note 13).

121 Pierre Laroche, make-up artist, most famously for David Bowie as Ziggy Stardust.

122 Chelita Secunda, former fashion editor for *Nova*. In a 1966 collection Ossie combined blue and green – a radical breakthrough which was the cause of a stand-up row with Margaret Buchanan, then editor of *Harpers Bazaar*; Secunda dyed her hair blue to celebrate and became his PR.

123 Laroche was employed to work on a photo-shoot of Ossie's clothes; Marianne Faithfull was modelling.

124 Oliver Musker, interior designer; former boyfriend of Marianne Faithfull.

125 Michelle Wilde, friend of Ossie's who would often take him partying in her Rolls Royce.

126 Ronnie Wood, guitarist with The Rolling Stones, formerly with The Faces.

127 'Mr Magoo' was Ossie's nickname for David Hockney, after a clumsy, myopic cartoon character.

128 Stella Astor, grandaughter of Britain's first female MP, Nancy Astor, was to marry Martin Wilkinson.

129 San Lorenzo is a restaurant in Beauchamp Place, run by Mara and Lorenzo Berni and popular with the glitterati.

130 Tramp is a night-club in Piccadilly.

131 Danny Secunda, brother of Chelita Secunda (see note 122).

132 Chelita Secunda thinks that this is her.

133 Kenny Everett, radio disc-jockey and comedian.

134 Vikki de Lambray, born David Gibbon, had a sex-change and famously boasted that she was a regular visitor to royal country home Fort Belvedere. At this time she was also using the name 'Le Viscount de Rothschild' and was jailed for stealing fur coats.
135 Anne Chubb, then fashion correspondent for the *Daily Express*. She has remained a firm advocate of Ossie's work.
136 Oliver Musker had asked Marianne to marry him; she initially accepted his proposal but later changed her mind and the couple split.
137 Sida (see note 93).
138 Paula Boyd, sister of Pattie Harrison.
139 Vaslav Nijinski, Russian ballet dancer on whom Ossie wrote his thesis at Manchester College. Nijinski died in 1950, having been declared clinically insane in 1917.
140 David Chambers, fashion designer and tailor, formerly Ossie's assistant. Now designs for, among others, David Bowie.
141 Minah Bird, model.
142 Of cocaine.
143 Helen Messenger was a third-year student at the RCA whom Ossie befriended during his first year there.
144 Sue Worth, model.
145 Rachel Wyndham, musician; daughter of Liz and Hugh Wyndham.
146 Liz Wyndham, wife of Hugh Wyndham who is the brother of writer Francis Wyndham.
147 Lord Lambton's London house.
148 Gala Mitchell, flamboyant, henna-haired model of whom Ossie was particularly fond.
149 A friend of Bryan Ferry.
150 Ossie's boyfriend at this time.
151 Glyndebourne, prestigous opera venue in Sussex. Hockney designed the sets for John Cox's production of Stravinsky's *The Rake's Progress*
152 Hermione Baddeley, actress.
153 Nikki Haslam, society interior designer.
154 Penelope Tree, model. The daughter of social diplomat Marietta Tree and erstwhile girlfriend of David Bailey, with whom she lived for eight years.
155 Robert Mapplethorpe, American photographer who built his name out of controversy – most notably with masochistic self-portraits and studies of genitalia.
156 John Kasmin (see note 46).
157 Catherine Guinness worked for *Andy Warhol's Interview*.
158 Teddy Millington-Drake, society painter.
159 David Hockney is visiting his family in Yorkshire.
160 Denis O'Brien, accountant at Radley. George Harrison has agreed to lend Ossie £5,000 to put into his business.
161 Cindy Lang, model.
162 Mick Sida (see note 93).
163 Cathie Simmons, model.
164 Sid Rotbart, entrepreneur; common-law husband of Pam Procter.
165 Mick Jagger (see note 1).
166 Hettie Quidejeta, one of Ossie's favoured machinists.
167 Suki Poitier, model. She lived above Quorum with Brian Jones (guitarist with The Rolling Stones until just prior to his death in 1969) and drove their delivery van for a time.

168 Jade Jagger, daughter of Mick and Bianca Jagger.
169 Charlie Watts, drummer with The Rolling Stones, and his girlfriend.
170 Richards (see note 113).
171 Anita Pallenberg was pivotal to the coming together of the aristocracy and pop stars that comprised the group with whom Ossie fraternised at this time. Through her estranged husband, painter Mario Schifano, Pallenberg was introduced to a group of friends which included Sir Mark Palmer, Christopher Gibbs and Robert Fraser. Modelling in Germany in 1965, she went to a Stones concert, met Brian Jones and subsequently became a 'communal' girlfriend of the group (most significantly of Keith Richards). Inevitably, the two worlds integrated. Pallenberg also starred in the 1968 film *Performance* (filmed at Hockney's house in Powis Terrace) with Mick Jagger – out-takes of the pair won an award at a pornographic film festival in Amersterdam.
172 Ronnie Wood (see note 126).
173 David Mlinaric, aesthete and society interior decorator (employed by, among others, Mick Jagger), was nicknamed 'Monster'.
174 Manolo Blahnik, shoe designer to whom Ossie gave his first show in 1972; Blahnik has since contributed to collections of many couturiers and costumiers.
175 Cass Elliot, singer with sixties folk-rock group The Mamas & The Papas.
176 Debbie Reynolds, actress and singer; first wife of popular fifties singer Eddie Fisher and mother of actress Carrie.
177 Pete Townshend, singer, formerly with The Who.
178 Seriously overweight, Mama Cass died of a heart attack at the age of 30 on 29 July.
179 Mo's relationship with Mick Sida was deteriorating at this point.
180 Notting Hill Carnival, held every year over the August Bank Holiday weekend.
181 Jimmy Melia, Ossie's nephew, sister of Carol Hammond; they are the children of Ossie's sister Kay from her first marriage.
182 Ladbroke Grove.
183 The house in which Ossie and Celia first lived together in 1964.
184 Blanche was the cat whom David Hockney named Percy in 'Mr and Mrs Clark and Percy'.
185 Biba, Kensington boutique owned and run by Barbara Hulanicki. The Biba name became synonymous with the louche style of the sixties, when the shop attracted visitors from all over the world who bought and copied the clothes and accessories available there.
186 Leslie Poole, designer; professional admirer of Ossie's.
187 Bill Gibb, designer; RCA contemporary of Ossie's.
188 Hylan Booker, designer; RCA contemporary of Ossie's.
189 Rickie Burns, hairdresser and owner of a popular salon of the same name in W1.
190 Seven of the 30 designs for Radley agreed on 16 July.
191 The Rat – Adrian George, illustrative painter with whom Celia was having an affair.
192 Stevie Buckley, girlfriend of Ossie's at the RCA and close friend of Celia.
193 Jeremy Fry, inventor, designer and engineer; owner of Rotork.
194 Howard Hodgkin, British painter.
195 Emma Soames, great-grandaughter of Sir Winston Churchill; later editor of the *Sunday Telegraph Magazine*.
196 Stephanie Crossling, Celia's solicitor.
197 By F. Scott Fitzgerald. Recounts the saga of a couple's troubled marriage and the

maelstrom of interpersonal conflict within their circle of friends; based on the author's personal experiences.
198 Claude Bernard, French art dealer who exhibited David Hockney in Paris.
199 John Stephanidis, society interior designer.
200 Shirley Goldfarb, wealthy American art collector.
201 Alexis was a friend of Jean Leger (see note 24) who also worked for Rubenstein.
202 John Laflin worked for Liberty and was Ossie and Celia's landlord when they lived in Blenheim Crescent in 1965.
203 Terry Doran, personal assistant to George Harrison.
204 Bill Willis, American aesthete and architect.
205 Helmut Berger, German actor.
206 Nikki Haslam (see note 153).
207 Wayne Sleep, popular British dancer and choreographer. Friend of David Hockney and former boyfriend of George Lawson.
208 Phil May, singer; husband of sculptor Electra Nemon.
209 Maureen Starkey, wife of Ringo Starr.
210 Leslie Hornby, model and actress. Dubbed as the 'Face of 1966', she became a symbol of the decade; she was a great fan of Ossie's clothes in the sixties.
211 Maggie Bell, singer with Stone the Crows.
212 Neil Aspinall, roadie for The Beatles.
213 Julian Ormsby-Gore, model for Quorum; brother of Victoria and Janey (now Rainey) Ormsby-Gore, all children of Lord Harlech. He committed suicide.
214 John Cale, singer, formerly with Velvet Underground, a band created by Andy Warhol.
215 Monty Python's Flying Circus, anarchic British television comedy team comprising John Cleese, Graham Chapman, Terry Jones, Michael Palin, Eric Idle and American Terry Gilliam.
216 Jimi Hendrix, American singer/guitarist whom Ossie befriended in the sixties. In 1968 Hendrix apparently told Ossie, 'I believe I am a prophet from outer space and I won't be here very long' – he died at the age of 28 in 1970.
217 Rudolf Nureyev, Russian ballet dancer at the height of his fame in the sixties, often appearing with Margot Fonteyn.
218 Nancy Mitford, British novelist.
219 By F. Scott Fitzgerald. The story's narrator befriends Gatsby, an enigmatic millionaire who throws fashionable parties of dancing, drugs and sex, and unravels the secrets of his personality. The book ends with the narrator reflecting on the emptiness of the lives he has just described.

1975

If Ossie's journal for 1974 reads rather like a record of one great extended party – littered as it is with glamorous events, legendary faces, insouciant drug-taking and family feuds – then 1975's diary documents a somewhat protracted morning after. Ossie seems to be calmer – the tone of his writing is more subdued and introspective. The diary is mostly written in blue ink, reflecting his mood, a sombre contrast to the colours and calligraphy, reminiscent of Apollinaire, which express his exuberant moods in 1974. Whereas last year' diary was filled with gossip an dreportage, this year's is marked by contemplation: regret, financial conern and a determination to start afresh predominate.

The change in tone owes much to the fact that in Cambridge Gardens Ossie has found his first stable base since leaving Linden Gardens at the beginning of 1974. He now has a space of his own in which he can think. At the end of 1974's diary he had great hopes for the new year, 'Surely the worst is over.' In some respects it is. His relationship wtih Celia improves on the surface druing 1975, particularly when they are working together. Their encounters are often fiery, but this year there are no recorded episodes of violence. Indeed, at times, such as in May when Ossie and Celia meet up and 'bitch' David Hockney, or when they spend the odd evening together, they appear to get along rather well.

Ossie seems prepared to be optimistic. Creative in his domesticity, he goes with Pam Procter to Syon House to find plants for his garden; later in the year he takes steps to refine his culinary skills with the help of friend who is a skilled cook. During his time at Cambridge Gardens, which extends beyond this year into the next period (for which his diaries have tragically gone missing), his skills as a host, his delicious and colourful dinner parties – always ten people – become renowned: his party recipes – such as baked salmon with courgette and new potatoes with mayonnaise, veal with peppers and cream – were published in a glossy magazine.

Whether it be looking to the future through the I-Ching, attempting to 'get high' on his work, or even having a brief heterosexual affair with one of his models, Sally Stamp, he is exploring new areas of inspiration inthe wake of his divorce. Driven partly by financial concerns, Ossie begins to discover the more simple pleasures in life. He takes weekend breaks in the country and a quiet holiday on the Greek island of Rhodes. Literature and his garden also provide Ossie with much needed escape routes from his family crisis this year; and with only his own well-being to think on a day-to-day basis he makes efforts to organise his financial affairs, selling his beloved Bentley and negotiating a new contract with Radley.

However, 1975's diary can be misleading with regard to Ossie's true state of mind. In an entry in 1988's journal, dated 9 September, Ossie looks back to 1975 and paints a picture of his own utter loneliness and despair. He describes his home in Cambridge Gardens as a place that 'only a few times...rang with laughter...', that would only 'come to life' with the fortnightly access to his children. He pictures himself 'alone in a mansion with tears trickling down my cheeks', drinking the 'bitter dregs of remorse' over his split from Celia. In his 1975 diary Ossie records a great deal of the sorrow he feels, but with nothing approaching the bitterness with which he describes this time when recalling it thirteen years later. Whether he was concealing his true feelings, even from himself, at the time, or whether the hurt and resentment grew within him over the intervening thirteen years, is impossible to say.

In many ways 1975's diary can be seen to document the beginnings of a great struggle for Ossie, the attempt to prevent the consequences of the events of 1974 from leaking into and dominating his future. The diary is dominated by a bitter custody battle for Albert and George, a battle that widens the emotional gap between Ossie and Celia and splits their friends into rival camps as affidavits are called for to prove each parent's worth. Every part of his life this year is permeated by the family split and, despite his efforts to begin a new phase in his life, he is preoccupied with thoughts of Celia and 'getting her back'. His efforts to reorganise his life are largely made for Celia's benefit and he seemingly finds it impossible to accept the inevitable – Celia's decision to divorce him.

5 JANUARY

Woke at 7.15 out of another 'happy ending' dream which are so terrible – gloomy thoughts immediately. I did my best to push them away and dozed, alternating between the two till after 10. Dressed and to Carol[1]'s for coffee and to phone Celia after two o'clock. Al Radley lunching with David in Paris, she told me – the children weren't ready – and again an entry in her diary concerning, 'A[2] stayed, we had a really nice time.' Completely brought me down. To the park where I met Rick[3] and Juliette[4] (who have been on my mind for some time now). Swings and to Carol's for lunch.

Tony Howard's. I got quite stoned and happy for a change. Tony is quite nice and I really like him and we made all kind of plans.

7 JANUARY

I woke early, packed a few things, collected the children in a taxi and went to Kings Cross – where the luggage and two children (especially George who misses his mamma already) were such a handful. I promptly took the wrong train and arrived at Herts North – so I took a mini cab which cost £5.60 to 'Therfield' to spend a few days with Rick and Juliette and their children Gala and Jamie.

11 JANUARY

Slept very well until 9ish when the roadies arrived as Rick and the Floyd are recording next week. Unusual for him to be home so much, said Juliette. He's a lucky guy, this house is really nice and his wife and kids adore him.

16 JANUARY

[Back in London.]

I saw Celia and the children in her car out of Jimmy[5]'s window at 10 to 4. I waved, she phoned half an hour later worried about the rent for Linden Gardens. I was so upset I hung up but of course she phoned back. She went on and on about money and said she will get really heavy. My weakness seems to give her strength. Can she know what she is doing?

18 JANUARY

Horrible dreams. The first I was with Tony Howard and we went somewhere where there was a great pit of water near a car park and somebody drowned in it. The second I've just woken out of and I'm shocked to discover it's 12.45 and horrible rain outside and more bills in the post.

24 JANUARY

Good day.

Slept badly so I got up very early at seven and after a cup of tea decided to see Celia. Miraculously, the front door opened and, as I thought, Adrian was in my bed. I told her I refused to let this situation go on anymore, either I move back into Linden Gardens or she hands the children over to me and they live with me in Cambridge Gardens. She finally gave in, saying she promised one or the other after thoughts at the weekend.

1 FEBRUARY

Celia came with George and I ended up pleading as usual. She hasn't given an inch, the divorce is still on and she won't give up.

5 FEBRUARY

Celia came round and we talked for ages, no children. The TV was installed. I feel so much better after spending the evening with Celia – very calm – but her drawings were not so spectacular as I expected. I read stories for Albert and George, David phoned from Paris; such a lovely evening – I had forgotten the stillness and quiet – Celia drawing, talking about fashion and Nikki Waymouth marriage[6] – I promised to take Celia – how divine it would be to live there again.

8 FEBRUARY

A horrid letter from the mortgage people.

12 FEBRUARY

In the afternoon I went to see Monty White and he gave me £50 and maybe will pay £500 to Celia. We will work something out when Al Radley comes back tonight. Jeff Banks has gone broke.

17 FEBRUARY

Nikki Waymouth marries Kenneth Lane. She's a true English Rose, he said – well fertilised but very rosy. She looked like a frump to me. So many people – all the English hoorays and an American entourage too. I talked to Jane Rainey, Peter[7] and Eric[8], Violet Wyndham[9], Fiona Montague, Sue Guinness[10] etc. Earlier I had promised to start work on a new Radley Collection.

23 FEBRUARY

Spent the day at Steve and Linda[11]'s – we went to Chessington Zoo. Celia was quite horrible about taking the children. She actually thought I didn't know she was in Paris and insisted the children be home by eight, which they were but she wasn't. So I brought them here and phoned and got nowhere and had to hang up when she said, 'Listen, you were just a frantic queen.'

3 MARCH

Got up late and in desperation I snorted some sulphate to try to get some work together. But it didn't really help. Carol came round and we made an attempt at sorting the fabrics. A VAT man came to the door and I got

John[12] to send him away – I phoned Monty about it who has promised to put him off. In the evening Carol cooked dinner and after taking her home I went round to Kay[13]'s and took her for a drink.

4 MARCH

I phoned Monty about the Radley cloth and Merton[14] phoned me about the contract. I took the speed and it seems to have helped a little. Ken, the driver from Quorum, came for the fabrics and now a big clear table awaits me.

Two of my dresses were featured in *The Times* today.

5 MARCH

Another wasted day – I feel really sad tonight – my head feels fit to burst. I woke early but didn't get up till 10.30.

I spent the day waiting for Radley cloth and making another version of the dress I made already. Minah Bird phoned, wants a dress for her birthday next week. I watched a play about two boys during the First World War – that is what made me so sad. I miss my children so much and I can't seem to get anything together or go right. I took more speed today but it doesn't seem to have done much.

8 MARCH

Thinking about my children.

9 MARCH

I must get myself together TOMORROW. I tried to phone Doctor Gallaway, no answer. I hope, just hope I can get some work done.

10 MARCH

Surprise party for Minah's birthday 11.30, Tramps. George Best[15], Parkinson[16], Amanda[17] fresh from NY.

11 MARCH

I rang Tony Howard for speed and got going at last to The Ideal Home Exhibition. Just awful – suburban fantasies. I worked all evening on my new dress and it's wonderful, marvellous – I'm happy for the first time in ages. Stayed up till 5 o'clock finishing it. Minah had phoned and I said I'd take her to dinner and her friend Tulla – but I chickened out – Tulla is nice and we like each other – but can I be heterosexual? I wonder.

I read the Radley contract – very heavy and binding.

Now the birds have begun to sing and I must go to sleep.

12 MARCH

Sandra Kamen arrived, first by phone then by taxi. She had come from NY. I was busy making a dress – looking awful in my dressing gown, I think she was a bit shocked at my appearance.

13 MARCH

Letter from Celia's lawyer saying the divorce case is due for hearing on April 21st. No hope now – but I pray still every night.

17 MARCH

Beautiful sunshine. Took speed and made a beautiful dress.

26 MARCH

I keep thinking I should write Celia a letter. The truth is I love her desperately, Albert and George too. She knows I can't manage alone. Sometimes I think I will boil over – I took a very hot bath to get myself out of the depths.

I'm still hoping and after Cary Grant remarrying Katharine Hepburn in the movie[18]. I just wish it could be the same way. My curtain and rail fell down a few days ago and the moon is getting fuller – everything changing and yet just the same.

I'm taking two little pills every night.

2 APRIL

I looked at Celia's work, it's beautiful, very like David's love pictures but I don't know what to make them into. Tried to work but can't. Wish I hadn't taken any coke yesterday, it really has brought me down and confused me. I've been taking some tablets but I missed two nights – noticeably – I wish I had some Valium.

4 APRIL

I decided to cut a chiffon dress and it worked beautifully indeed. Sandra tried it on later. Also had some coke, which I had snorted all day actually. Sandra and Michael organised a delicious dinner.

12 APRIL

[Ossie goes to visit David Hockney in Paris.]

Arrived at David's to find Henry Geldzahler[19]. Looked at David's exhibition – beautiful drawings of Celia naked. Dinner with a whole party of people including Peter and a Swedish school-friend.

14 APRIL

Dinner at the house of gallery owner Claude Bernard with George Lawson[20] (drunk) and Mick Jagger – excellent food but boring really. Club Sept afterwards. Mick asked me to make him some clothes for his next American tour in June[21].

15 APRIL

David's opening. Alexis said I looked straight out of Wagner. Lots of people – Patrick[22], Peter Langan[23]. Spoke to Celia – no good. Afterwards a big party in Montmarte, we left to find Mick and I stayed up with stimulants.

17 APRIL

[Ossie returns to London.]

Back to reality and depression, lots of bills and phone-calls. Kay phoned to say mother has found a flat and everyone is happy about it.

22 APRIL

Woke early feeling much better – I've decided to get the house together in six weeks if possible. I want to get blinds but they don't make the right size so I decided to look in antique shops – the prices amazed me! It was a beautiful afternoon with strong, hot sunshine – smoked on the lawn afterwards and watched the planes.

Later I got frantic about Celia – she was nowhere to be found. I even went round to Linden Gardens and her car was outside. Not knowing what to do I went to Pam[24]'s and fretted. Dinner was cocaine provided by Chris T.

26 APRIL

Went to Germaine Greer[25]'s house which Tchaik[26] has done and he was there, Melissa[27] too – has been to Afghanistan – her house is divine, he's done it really well. Went back to Steve's, David H was there – I got drunk.

29 APRIL

Had to go and see Radley's lawyers like I promised. All so stupid – legal ways are so stupid – like the divorce. I excused myself and stopped off for a hamburger at the Hard Rock[28]. Met Chris, Vivienne[29] and child. Took him home and heard his music.

1 MAY

Nasty Hockney phoned and ordered me to pay the money I borrowed from him in Paris to Mo[30].

5 MAY

'Tight Yorkshire monster' – Celia on David on the telephone – 'A tight-arsed cunt'.

6 MAY

I took the children to visit Pam while Celia bitched David (as she put it) to his brother Paul[31] re accounts. Spent the evening with Celia – I took a Valium to sleep.

7 MAY

Early to work, got straight into a chiffon pattern which has turned out absolutely beautiful – a tape which Jimmy made is also right on and I was so pleased and happy I danced around to it.

9 MAY

Paid a telephone bill: £5.48.

12 MAY

Paid an electric bill, too: £4.48.

14 MAY

Up early and to work – I had spoken to Lynne Franks[32] and she invited me to a shop opening of her husband's so I went at 6.30. The opening was very amusing – Amanda and Bryan Ferry complaining about everybody saying England is dead. I saw Tommy Nutter[33] and apologised for not paying my bill. Steve O'Rourke was funny – he spent a whole evening chatting up a spade girl beauty in LA who turned out to be a guy.

15 MAY

I told Monty I want seven and a half-grand retainer and he said he would talk to Al. 'I want to sign a contract,' I said.

I dressed up and went to a charity ball, got drunk on champagne and vodka. Afterwards the Yours and Mine, talked with Robert Fraser bitching David.

16 MAY

Felt terrible. Hangover. Phoned Celia – angry and threatening – she is just stupid now. I told her to fuck off and took a bath. Went to Pam and Sid[34] who had both taken acid, and spent the night there.

18 MAY

Slept late collected the children. Celia has been on the phone to David in his usual underhand way – I just don't want to know. I took the children to Kensington Gardens and had them in bed asleep by 9 o'clock.

5 JUNE

I'm really sorry about the gap[35]. Went to Germaine's house. Gave dresses to Vanessa Redgrave[36] for charity – Corin[37] keeps chasing me for a cheque for £25. Pam told me about Mo being sacked by David.

6 JUNE

I wasted the afternoon – really beautiful sunny day. I miss the kids terribly. Mo came over and told me about David's beastly behaviour – he has taken back the pyramid picture[38].

11 JUNE

Still avoiding Corin Redgrave – Sid gave me some bad news: A, is back from NY – he had seen him leaving Mo's, it really brought me down.

14 JUNE

I almost bumped into A as I left Mo's. So shitface Hockney must have let him stay upstairs for spite[39] – how I hate him. Still at least Celia's not going round there as Mo tells me she's very off him (Hockney) too. Half a Valium soon put me out.

16 JUNE

To Quorum early – more chiffon and organised finishing the pink evening dress, which is divine, and added another frill to the jacket. I rang Monty and tried to organise signing the contract and cheque for Corin Redgrave.

After work I went to see Mo and unfortunately saw David – I was just polite to him.

20 JUNE

I phoned Mick[40] and he tells me Mo has gone off to Glyndebourne and made it up with Hockney.

22 JUNE

Up early – George and Albert crept into my bed for a cuddle. I dressed them and bathed while they played. Gave them breakfast and took them to the park. Home to watch *Jason and the Argonauts* – good, with marvellous monsters that the children loved. Celia phoned – she just had to spoil it. Afterwards I took them to the cinema – once inside everything was OK – wonderful thirties cartoons.

29 JUNE
All day with the solicitor.

30 JUNE
All day with the solicitor.

2 JULY
I think the tide is turning – I'll see the children on Sunday. Tramps with Adie[41], Jose[42], and Bill Gibb.

4 JULY
Pink Floyd backstage passes for tomorrow, spoke to Rick re affidavit[43]. £500 cash from Monty.

5 JULY
I shall never forget today – speedy drive and lots of old friends. Showed Mo the art of the groupie. Smashed.

7 JULY
Overslept till 12, got Rick together and scored.

14 JULY
Off to dinner with lots of people, very drunk. Rupert Lowenstein said Bianca is in the White House[44].

18 JULY
The Wailers[45] at the Lyceum Ballroom were marvellous – but it was so hot. I danced as they sang all the songs I knew so well. Afterwards we went to the Casserole for dinner – spoke with Tim Curry[46] who has a new Germanic look, very Christopher Isherwood[47]. 'Everything's gonna be all right'.

I went to bed early but couldn't sleep, woke at four. It's getting light and Celia's on my mind.

24 JULY
Mike Douglas[48] at Carter's has received more affidavits from Albert and George's teachers and the nasty doctor – very heavy. So I went over to collect them and re-read them.

Phoned Melissa who told me David H has been on the phone about 'Poor Celia and nasty Ossie,' wanting to take the children away. Also, I discovered that A is living with her – what to do?

27 JULY

[Ossie again visits Therfield, home of Rick and Juliette Wright.]

Rick is in the country, so would I like to come here? Yes, please. We had a lovely day swimming and dined on the meat I took along. Rick agreed to swear an affidavit, so that's good – it's just a question of organising it now.

30 JULY

[The day of the custody hearing.]

Weepy, emotional day, hottest day in 20 years. Court hearing – what is going to happen?

[Later] Well, it was just the most awful day I think I've spent – I arrived at Carter's at 9.30 after collecting Pam's affidavit. We were due in court 31 at 10.30 but we hung around, my stomach churning, Celia laughing, me in agony – at lunchtime I rushed over to Al Radley for a quick drink and a cry and then back to court. At 2.30 we were put in court 44, a different judge – and he came down the other way[49] – alternative weekend-access and 10 days in September. I was so completely brought down – I drove home in tears after meeting the welfare officer assigned to my case.

I took a valium slept for two hours, Jimmy came round, Kay phoned, I phoned Rick and Juliette, went round to see Pam and Sid – quite calm now. I must rise above it all and get high on my work. I came home at 11 and crashed out on another Valium – sorting plans in my head.

1 AUGUST

End of moon.

SHOCK NEWS. Brian Shack is leaving Quorum after an argument – one too many – with Radley.

I set off to meet Tony at Tramps but instead to Powis Terrace – Mo on the phone to David in Paris at that very moment talking about me, the reverse of Celia's bitch-bitch-bitching. Then a trip to a very down Marianne[50] and a listen to her new album, 'Not bad'. I had to sneak away and leave them all yearning for the 'brown stuff[51]', as Mo puts it. So I crept into bed with my babies and slept for a few hours.

2 AUGUST

'Ossie, I think you should come home,' – Celia's voice on Capital Radio advertising *The Bigger Splash*.

[After the stress of the custody battle Ossie is invited by his good friend David

Gilmour to spend some time at his home on the Greek island of Rhodes. Tony Howard and Rick and Juliette Wright are also on the island.]

8 AUGUST

I woke at dawn and slept on till nine then did an hour on the beach. After lunch out to snorkel with Tony, Dave and Ginger[52]. Shower and a joint and back here to read and fall asleep.

13 AUGUST

Spent the day on La Scala. More snorkeling – Dave Gilmour speared a big fish but couldn't retrieve it.

Dave and Ginger married in secret and now they are on their honeymoon.

19 AUGUST

Dinner at the Wright's – weepy and depressed, missing my children incredibly. I took a Mandrax and staggered home to try to phone Celia. No good – I couldn't find the code – so to bed.

21 AUGUST

[Ossie returns to London.]

2.30 Taxi to the airport. Back home to an empty house – lots of mail including VAT, lawyer's divorce and a drag police-summons re drink and driving.

7 SEPTEMBER

[For the past week Albert and George have been staying with Ossie at his house in Cambridge Gardens. Such visits were allowed under the conditions of the custody settlement reached in July.]

George got into bed with me at about 8 o'clock. We all got up and dressed before nine. I sent Albert for the papers while I made breakfast, which we all ate with a good appetite. They played for a time and at 12 we watched a marvellous cartoon. Afterwards we went to the Cartoon Cinema in Victoria and visited the Albert Memorial. On the way back stopped for a drink – the children very excited. George fell over – bloody lip. At home they settled down but I had to cook more sausages before they would go to bed around nine.

I feel very bored now and have taken a Valium.

A lovely month here.

Only three more days with my babies, then what?

12 SEPTEMBER
Portobello[53] early – saw Celia who ignored me. I began singing, 'I saw her today. I saw her face. It was the face I loved.' At least she was alone.

23 SEPTEMBER
I spent the morning watching ballet dancers training and decided it would be impossible to use them as models as the very pretty ones are too thin.

24 SEPTEMBER
Jose rang and said she is marrying today at 1.30.

Tramps – I saw Minah Bird and decided to split when George Harrison arrived[54].

29 SEPTEMBER
Thoughts of suicide again and this awful rain – I should be designing black crepe dresses but I just can't – I love Celia so much and I want her back. But what of her? What is she thinking? What of the children? I look forward so much to seeing them and it's so soon over – oh, god, for a miracle.

6 OCTOBER
Saw Marc Bolan in the Kings Road on the way to Victoria Hall, Bloomsbury Square – Quorum show.

10 OCTOBER
Bianca fitting.
Red roses from Bianca.

13 OCTOBER
Sent flowers to Celia with an invitation to Roxy Music on Friday. Came home at three after cutting a chiffon dress for Bianca. £25 off Monty. I went to Mo's – he tells me David is back[55].
Bianca interview in the White House.

14 OCTOBER
Telephone bill. Cut Bianca's cape – yards of pink chiffon.

15 OCTOBER
Everything is OK at work – all the Radley crepes for Paris are ready so I finished off Bianca's chiffon cape. At 5 o'clock I went over to Radley to get some new Celia fabrics from India – very nice. I drank whisky.

17 OCTOBER
Roxy Music with Mo but no Celia – but a sweet note.

18 OCTOBER
Fittings with Bianca, Blake's Hotel. Took Jimmy, everything fine. Paul Getty's after – he was quite horrible to me and snatched a book from me as I was just going to read a passage 'Love is…'. Strong vodka.

19 OCTOBER
Fear eats the soul. Watched it while Margaret[56] got Jade[57] to sleep.

20 OCTOBER
Lots of work. Made the most beautiful white dress. Tony Howard married Nancy[58] in Kensington Registry Office – I couldn't go to the reception as I was so into work.

24 OCTOBER
[Ossie flies to Dublin to continue fitting Bianca for various outfits.]

11 o'clock plane to Dublin – castle Mick and Bianca – bed late.

Andy Warhol and Ossie sip wine together.

25 OCTOBER
Slept late so missed Mick who left for America. Jade[59] divine riding bareback on a pony.

1 NOVEMBER
[Back in London.]

I have worked out several beautiful dresses in my head – red silk organza, boned chiffon frills and an ultra-suede coat for Catherine[60] and a polkadot outfit for someone.
Over for a disappointing fitting with Mick.

2 NOVEMBER
Bianca due to arrive tonight, I'm working out what to do.

4 NOVEMBER
Party for Andy Warhol – very drunk, stayed ages and ages and saw lots of people I hadn't seen in ages.

10 NOVEMBER
Bianca came round to fit the jumpsuit I stayed up all night making. It fitted perfectly and she looked wonderful – a terrific working day.

11 NOVEMBER
[Ossie has a show for Radley and Quorum; another is scheduled for 21 November.]

6.30 prompt my show – a success – lots of people turned away really sad. Big party at San Lorenzo after, even Celia and the children came – I don't know what to make of the situation but I made it clear to her I think she is behaving ridiculously and if she intends to carry on the same way I'd rather not see her.

12 NOVEMBER
Bianca still in London – two jumpsuits, one cashmere black gala suit, green gala suit, black velvet suit, all for Friday at 4 o'clock.
Jade in bed like a little lady. Fitting with Bianca, she finally off to Rome at 7 o'clock. –
[Later]Bianca still here, just phoned me.
Mick brought nice records, including Pink Floyd, and is making a tape for Celia.

13 NOVEMBER

Bianca *still* here, leaving at 5.20. So I fitted her and we went to lunch at San Lorenzo – too much to drink and a little sleep.

She's finally gone to Rome – 5.20 flight.

16 NOVEMBER

Article by Michael Roberts in *The Times*[61]; don't know what to make of it at all – though it's definitely not bad – I wish he could have been more enthusiastic about my clothes.

The Bianca drama and my children's normal sad exit has quite brought me down.

I phoned Mo (again) but he was no help – sounded smacked out. By now I'm really depressed – I suppose it could be a delayed reaction from the Durofat[62] – haven't taken it since Monday.

17 NOVEMBER

GARDENING GARDENING.

Well, fuck madam[63] and back to money-making work – Bert the gardener woke me 8.45 so, as I was still very tired, I took a lovely hot bath and thought about my garden.

I went to Rassell's in Earls Court and spent £25 on TULIPS, CROCUSES, DAFFODILLS, SNOWDROPS, etc. – Bert is planting IRIS now. I also got two amaryllis to flower for Christmas.

19 NOVEMBER

Wayne[64] came over and we had coffee. Suzie Menkes[65] phoned re JL's death. Apparently he thought he was possessed by the devil, poured petrol over himself on a building site after saying there was no love in the world, and burnt to death.

20 NOVEMBER

Miss Germany borrowed a dress to wear to the Miss World competition.

21 NOVEMBER

Fiorucci[66] shop opening 10–12.30, Brompton Road. I scored a beautiful sweater and invited the Italian press and television to my show tonight. Enter Sally Stamp.

Had a row with Monty over my sound-system and Miss Germany's dress. San Lorenzo for dinner with models – Sally very amusing – and free Fiorucci dinner party. Celia drama over the telephone – completely lost my cool. I was so furious with her screaming.

22 NOVEMBER
Mo behaving ridiculously – all kinds of junkies at his place.

24 NOVEMBER
Oh! That magic feeling, 'Nowhere to go' – Paul McCartney.
I ended up in bed with Sally and there we fucked and I quite enjoyed it and she certainly did. First time in ages – thoughts of Celia.

25 NOVEMBER
Celia said, 'Go around with Sally Stamp and you'll end up in the gutter.' Chris[67] asked her, 'Has he asked you if he can borrow any money yet?' Crashed out from drinking all day. Celia thanked me on the phone for the flowers[68] so I said, 'didn't you get the perfume?' She said, 'Oh, yes, David once brought me some.' 'I brought you an ounce once,' I said. It's really brought me down, the moment I smelled it yesterday it reminded me of her – did it really remind her of Mr Magoo?

27 NOVEMBER
Sally just phoned from Geneva – or was she? Giggly and incoherent. I'm making myself dinner, broccoli, garlic prawns, tomatoes and a whisky sour and olive oil, it's going to be delicious and new Grande Champagne des Heritiers, 1906 – thanks, Sally.

[The following passage is a letter to Celia. There is no indication as to whether or not it was ever copied and posted.]

Celia – I haven't smelt 'Joy' perfume since I brought you an ounce in Paris when I worked at Moldes and Albert was a baby. Did it really remind you of David Hockney? I smelt it again the other day and it reminded me of what I miss about you most – where has the Celia I know gone? Anyway I hoped that the smell of the sweet perfume would anger me – but it didn't. How long can I go on hoping you will come to your senses and see that what you are doing is wrong, that I've learned my lesson?
The Celia in Burnsall Street and at dinner in San Lorenzo wasn't my Celia. I've done everything you asked of me – I've got over it – I'm my old self and the house is comfortable and warm – my work is together and the Radley crowd seem happy and are paying the mortgage. I've planted spring flowers in the garden and indoors for Christmas – it's all ready and waiting. I bought this to bring up our family. You and me to grow up with Albert and George.

5 DECEMBER
Celia phoned me to nag about work so I hung up.
My picture in the *Standard*.
Steve O'Rourke invited me to his place for Christmas day – he's back with Linda and I'm so happy for him.

[It seems Ossie is now continuing his letter of 27 November.]

You can't stop me waiting, Beakie[69] – that's really what you are trying to do. Well I won't give up, Beakie – I still love you and my sons and I hope that one day you will come here and live with me. I won't stop wanting and hoping, and I am not a pig. You are the one living a bad life now but underneath, somewhere, is still my Beakie, my love, my children's mother – I've waited a year already and I can wait until spring. We'll see how the land lies when my garden is full of flowers.

14 DECEMBER
Celia came round for lunch. We talked she gave me a hug (I asked) and a kiss when she left.

31 DECEMBER
I phoned David Chambers about my tweed suit and he told me Mo is in a clinic for a heroin cure.
Party at Hurtwood Edge, Pattie Boyd[70] and Eric Clapton, Ringo, Twiggy, Keith Moon[71], Dick[72] and Edina[73]. I made the mistake of phoning Celia.

Christmas card from Ossie Clark Limited, c.1975. The photograph shows Ossie and models - including Jerry Hall, Marie Helvin and Nikki Lane - on stage at the end of a show.

[The following three entries appear at the end of the 1975 diary.]

1976

1 JANUARY

Very depressed after last night. Pam phoned to wish me a happy New Year.

6 JANUARY

I left David[74] making my tweed suit and came home on a bus. Went out and brought the new Dylan[75] album listened to it and then walked to the Gate[76], met Germaine Greer and popped into Jimmy's for a valium.

15 JANUARY

'Busted'. This diary has been in police custody. Guilty of possessing 72 milligrams of cannabis and amphetamine sulphate and fined £70.

1 Carol Hammond.
2 Adrian George.
3 Rick Wright, keyboardist with Pink Floyd.
4 Juliette Wright, wife of Rick Wright.
5 Jimmy Melia.
6 Nikki Waymouth was to marry jeweller Kenneth Lane.
7 Peter Schlesinger.
8 Eric Boman, the *Vogue* photographer for whom Peter Schlesinger left David Hockney.
9 Violet Wyndham, mother of Hugh Wyndham.
10 Sue Guinness, wife of Jonathan Guinness who is now Lord Moyne.
11 Steve and Linda O'Rourke.
12 John Hammond.
13 Kay Melia.
14 Alain Merton, gallery owner.
15 George Best, footballer, most famously for Manchester United in the early seventies.
16 Michael Parkinson, TV personality and chat-show host.
17 Amanda Lear.
18 *Bringing Up Baby*, 1938.
19 Henry Geldzahler, curator of the Metropolitan Museum in New York; has been painted by David Hockney of whom he is a close friend.
20 George Lawson, antiquarian book dealer; close friend of David Hockney.
21 The 'Exile in Main Street' tour.
22 Patrick Procktor.
23 Peter Langan, owner of Langan's Brasserie who famously allowed Hockney to exchange drawings for food early on in his career.
24 Pam Procter, RCA contemporary of Ossie with whom he formed a close friendship. Having been introduced to David Hockney's set, she attended salons at Powis

Terrace and subsequently became good friends with Celia (the two became pregnant at the same time).
25 Germaine Greer, radical Australian feminist, author of *The Female Eunuch*. Later became a Cambridge lecturer.
26 Tchaik Chassai.
27 Melissa North, Chassai's girlfriend – they would later marry.
28 The Hard Rock Café, theme restaurant in Piccadilly.
29 Chris and Vivienne Jagger.
30 Mo McDermott.
31 Paul Hockney, accountant, brother of David Hockney.
32 Lynne Franks, fashion PR 'guru'.
33 Tommy Nutter, high-class men's tailor whose suits Ossie favoured.
34 Sid Rotbart.
35 The gap in the diary entries – there are none whatsoever between 19 May and 4 June.
36 Vanessa Redgrave, actress and writer, supporter of communist causes, in particular the Worker's Revolutionary Party, a British Trostskyist Party formed in 1973.
37 Corin Redgrave, actor; brother of Vanessa Redgrave.
38 Mo McDermott had hung one of David Hockney's paintings in his flat. Hockney temporarily threw Mo out of Powis Terrace.
39 David Hockney was allowing Adrian George to work at Powis Terrace.
40 Mick Sida.
41 Adie Hunter.
42 Jose Fonseca, set up the English Boy modelling agency with Sir Mark Palmer; now runs Models One.
43 Ossie has asked Rick Wright to provide an affidavit in his favour for the custody battle.
44 Bianca Jagger. She had become politically active on behalf of her native Nicaragua and other troubled countries and was at this time visiting US President Ford in the hope of promoting peace in Nicaragua.
45 Reggae band led by singer Bob Marley.
46 Tim Curry, actor, most famous for his role in *The Rocky Horror Show*.
47 Christopher Isherwood, writer; close friend of David Hockney. Like Ossie, later in life Isherwood became interested in Eastern philosophy.
48 Mike Douglas, Ossie's solicitor.
49 In favour of Celia.
50 Marianne Faithfull.
51 Heroin.
52 Ginger Gilmour, first wife of David Gilmour.
53 Portobello Antiques Market.
54 Ossie still owed Harrison the £15,000 he borrowed in July 1974.
55 From Glyndebourne.
56 Margaret Clementson, Beryl Westell's daughters, Ossie's niece.
57 Jade Clementson, Margaret's daughter.
58 Nancy Howard, née Petit, ran the child modelling agency Little Boats.
59 Jade Jagger.
60 Catherine Tennant.
61 Concerning Ossie's show.

62 Durofat was a brand-name amphetamine appetite suppressant taken in capsule form, since discontinued.
63 Celia.
64 Wayne Sleep.
65 Suzie Menkes, fashion correspondent for the *Herald Tribune* who was a great fan of Ossie's work.
66 Elio Fiorucci, Italian designer. In the sixties he began travelling to London to bring fashionable clothes back to his store in Milan; then in the mid-seventies became internationally famous, collecting ideas and items which he passed on to a team of designers and opening shops all over the world.
67 Chris Stamp.
68 Ossie sent Celia flowers and perfume by way of an apology for their 20 November argument.
69 Beakie is a nickname Ossie had for Celia.
70 Pattie Harrison had at this time reverted to her maiden name, Boyd, following the break up of her marriage to George Harrison.
71 Keith Moon, drummer with The Who. Later died of an overdose of drugs he was taking to control alcoholism.
72 Dick Polak, photographer and fashion designer.
73 Edina Ronay, Hungarian knitwear designer of the firm Edina and Lena; daughter of Egon Ronay, wife of Dick Polak.
74 David Chambers.
75 Bob Dylan, American singer/songwriter. The album Ossie is referring to here is *Desire*.
76 Notting Hill Gate.

Blanche the cat, also known as Percy, curls up with Celia Birtwell in Linden Gardens, 1978.

1979

The jump from 1975 to 1979 (the diaries for 1976, 77 and 78 are sadly lost) is disorientating. There are new people in Ossie's life and they contribute to the radically changed tone of his journal. He has a new business partner, Peter Lee, a new boyfriend, Nick Balaban, and a new home.

In the three years since 1975 Ossie's business affairs have been extremely erratic. After his divorce his business went into a decline as he neglected work and suffered from inertia and depression. In 1977, however, at the end of the four-year contract he had signed with Quorum and Radley in 1973, Ossie acquired a business manager, Tony Calder. Calder – who had worked for Andrew Oldham, the discoverer of the Rolling Stones – set up Ossie Clark Ltd and in July 1977 to separate Ossie from Radley, informing him that Ossie now wished to produce his own separate couture collection under his own name. Later in 1977 Calder and another backer, Peter Lee (who was appointed managing director of Ossie Clark Ltd), put their own money – £8,000 and £10,000 respectively – into Ossie Clark, a retail outlet at 117a Fulham Road. Inspired by this reinvention of his business name, Ossie spent 1977 and 1978 enjoying a revival, commercial success, hugely successful shows and rave reviews. In 1978 the fashion writer Ann Chubb wrote, 'It is great to see him right back on form again after a few years in the doldrums.'

After suffering periods of severe depression in 1975 and 1976, Ossie seemed to be recovering in 1977 and early 1978, both professionally and in his personal life. In an interview he gave in 1978 to Andy Warhol's *Interview*, Ossie spoke of his marriage to Celia and remarked, 'Really, I did give her a bad time. I couldn't see it. I mean, I was an egomaniac.' He also recounted how Sheila Oldham – the manager of the Ossie Clark shop and former wife of Andrew Oldham – had come to his rescue in 1977, sending him to an acupuncturist for four months. 'Through this,' he remembered, 'I rose from the bottom of the pit; it was like climbing and getting out. I'm now so happy to be alive, after wanting to kill myself.'

However, despite his renewed *joie de vivre* and the apparent resurgence of his business, by the end of 1978 Ossie was once again in a financial and emotional tangle. Despite its apparently high profile, Ossie Clark Ltd did not appear to be making any money and by August 1978 Ossie could not afford his mortgage payments and his house in Cambridge

Gardens was repossessed. Ossie and Celia, with whom he was still working, found it difficult to comprehend the failure of Ossie's business in the light of its critical success, and their working relationship with Lee became difficult. Although he is mentioned in Ossie's 1979 diary, Lee is almost conspicuous by his absence.

Ossie was hit very hard by the repossession of Cambridge Gardens, watching the receivers taking 'everything I had fought so hard to earn, paintings by David Hockney, furniture etc...' After fighting for almost four years to overcome the upset of his divorce, Ossie's financial ruin brought back his great feelings of loneliness. Even when his business had been going well during 1977 and 78, Ossie had shown many times that he was feeling very needy. On a trip to New York early in 1978 Percy Savage remembers him behaving intolerably, demanding attention from everyone he met, insisting that he be centre-stage, telling people to 'fuck off' and sulking if he did not get what he wanted. As Marie Helvin, who met Ossie around this time has said, 'Ossie had at this point a grandiose idea as to how people should treat him and as a result many people began to think of him as a pain in the ass.' Ossie craved the spotlight that had fallen on him during the first decade of his working life, but his emotional needs were met when he was knocked sideways by, and fell hopelessly in love with, a nineteen-year-old waiter, Nick Balaban. His love for Nick existed despite his testimony in Andy Warhol's *Interview* that, 'although I'm divorced from Celia, we're still in my view meant for each other and I'm hoping she'll eventually see it that way.' Although they were later to separate, Ossie remained in love with Nick until Nick's death from AIDS in 1994.

Ossie met Nick who was working at the El Sombrero, a gay club on Kensington High Street, in January 1978 and over the ensuing months began to see him regularly. Before meeting Ossie, Nick had fallen for the painting *Mr and Mrs Clark and Percy;* he was undoubtedly in awe of Ossie and the glamour that still attached to him. Ossie, meanwhile, convinced himself that he saw a great talent in Nick; he was interested in painting and fashion, and Ossie urged him to go to art school. In early 1979 Ossie eventually invites Nick to move in with him, into the basement flat he is temporarily renting from his friend Marianne Faithfull in her house in Danvers Street, Chelsea.

Marianne is at this time recording a new album and living with her boyfriend – later husband – punk musician Ben Brierly. She remembers the time Ossie and Nick lived with her as 'terribly squalid but kind of wonderful'. The atmosphere within her house most definitely contributes to a great change of tone in Ossie's 1979 diary compared with the diary for 1975. Her house, unlike Ossie's in Cambridge Gardens, is seemingly filled with sex, drugs and rock 'n' roll or, as Ossie puts it, 'bad behaviour'. This change of scene gives 1979's diary a lighter feel, a more colourful and humorous tone than that found in 1974 and 1975, with Marianne as undoubtedly one of its highlights.

Ossie seems to find it easier to enjoy himself this year, whether it be while judging the Miss St Martin's pageant with Marie Helvin or at home. There is certainly a mutual fascination between him and Marianne. 'I contemplated a threesome,' she says, 'but I knew what heartache it could bring. He was dangerously attractive at the time. Indeed, Marianne remembers Ossie in much the same way as he portrays her in his diary, as 'incredibly naughty, endlessly so'.

It is not only the tone of Ossie's life that changes radically in this year's diary, the social firmament too is now greatly altered. In 1975 it was Bianca Jagger and the Walters who were all the rage; this year it is Marie Helvin, Jerry Hall and Roxy Music who are the people to be seen with. Ossie himself is still a 'name' but no longer quite the name he was. He is still meeting the stars of the day (stars such as Derek Jarman) but not perhaps in quite the glamorous surroundings that he is used to. He is still a vital and loved component of glamorous social events, notsbly Patti Boyd's and Eric Clapton's wedding to which he drove down with Chelita Secunda in his blue Bentley and touches Patti by giving her a kitten as a wedding present. Chelita remembers this as 'the greatest line up of rock musicians ever'.

Ossie's life this year is, however, dominated by the state of his finances and by the fact that at this rather unstable period he seems to be surrounded with people who do not quite meet his needs. While his business is failing him financially, Nick Balaban does not seem sure enough of his own emotional requirements to become the stabilising influence Ossie needs at this point in his life; ultimately Nick, young and needing to become his own man, wanted to be something more than a catamite following in Ossie's turbulent wake. If anything, Ossie's relationship with Nick seems only to sharpen the pain he is feeling over Celia's continuing relationship with David Hockney. Nick, who throughout the year becomes ever more dissatisfied with Ossie sexually, only serves to make

Ossie very conscious of the fact that he is not getting any younger. Poignantly, while Celia and his children – under the full spotlight of the press – are being wooed by Hockney and his millions, Ossie is spending lonely nights, searching for adventure through various sexual liaisons on Hampstead Heath.

Ossie is forced to move house twice in 1979 and is forced to rely on friends to provide him with accommodation, and his finance are so precarious that he cannot afford to buy presents for his children or wine at the annual Red Cross ball. He is also in an unstable love affair, so it is hardly surprising that he finds it almost impossible to relax in 1979. When he does finally find some peace it is on Christmas day, 'The most beautiful blue day, cloudless and peaceful, almost perfect' and it is then that he seems happiest. After the frantic emotions of the past five years, Ossie appears to be enormously grateful to find even the smallest moment of tranquillity, moments when he is able to forget his emotional and financial problems, when he can stop thinking and – as George Harrison suggests to him – 'breathe out'.

26 MARCH

Don't tell the press, Celia is going to America[1] for a week, her mother will look after the children. She was offered £10,000 cash for her story[2] and has gone to Barbados.

Nadia[3] is making Carrie Fisher's clothes for *Star Wars 2*.

27 MARCH

I woke at 7.30 and got up and bathed and was at work by nine just before Peter[4]. Things are looking good and Peter seems pleased. I worked until 7.30 then home. Must tidy, for Marianne returns tomorrow[5].

29 MARCH

Celia came in, I've promised to make a dress for her American trip. Home to find Marianne and two cronies. Marianne was up late, she was about to ask me to get out of bed so she could have a threesome but I refused and they slept on the sofa.

30 MARCH

Got up at nine, cut wrap trousers and a wonderful red wool dress, cut a wonderful shirt and later a wonderful T-shirt. Everything is going wonderfully

– today's pieces are fabulous, divine and easily made. Party upstairs Angie[6] and Marianne. 'I hate sequins,' said Marianne, but she loves black net and lace. What a night, bed after three.

5 APRIL

We have just returned from seeing *The Deer Hunter*[7] which was horribly depressing. At home we found the electric fire on and all the plugs moved about – the clock fucked up at 5.40. Is it the poltergeist again[8]? No, Marianne, her behaviour the equivalent to Herod[9]'s crapping in corners – because we weren't home when she got back she has tonight gone on a bender which has resulted in a spot on her chin.

Penniless, I phoned Nadia and Swami, we went to Spaghetti, drank, smoked and talked of LA where they are going on Sunday as the guest of Diane Keaton[10] who sounds wonderful.

[Ossie goes on holiday to Tunisia with Peter Lee.]

12 APRIL

Air France flight 811 to Paris at 11.30. A beautiful sunshiny day. Lunch in a snack bar, then Tunis Air flight 723 to Tunis. We were met at the airport and taken to the hotel Mirimar where I now write. A very badly organised journey ending typically with the slowest taxi driver in Tunis. Peter is already in bed and we are looking forward to sunshine in the morning.

13 APRIL

We woke at eight to brilliant sunshine, overlooking an overgrown garden of poppies and wildflowers. We had breakfast and discovered a swimming pool surrounded by many Germans and French. Few English. So we flopped out and toasted. After lunch I went to bed to read *Mary Barton* by Elizabeth Gaskell, which I began last night. Peter had a little walk but discovered nothing. I've had too much sun – later I bathed to take the sting out of my back. We dressed and walked into Hammamet where we had a look round and ate dinner. We were too late for the souk but it looked the usual tourist crap anyway. So home in a cab. A quiet, brisk walk and back to bed to carry on reading.

Peter woke me in the night. He barked like a dog twice.

20 APRIL

[Back in London.]

Met Mrs Clark[11] on the way to work and she let me in to collect some mail –

which threw me into a gloom all day. Bills Bills. A tax demand for six thousand. Home at six to find Nick[12] waiting – we had a quiet evening at home watching television. Early to bed but the tax bill worry kept us awake – maybe I should ask John Kloss?

23 APRIL

Spent all day composing a begging letter to John Kloss. Well, not really – I offered my remaining Hockneys for sale and talked with Celia on the phone – she wanted the children's school-fees. A man called Peach of Orchard Avenue was murdered at an NF demo.

7 MAY

Marianne back. I made dinner and we ate watching *The Dirty Dozen* on television. She has been at Angie's snorting coke for three days.

9 MAY

Oversleeping has become a habit. It seems fate is against me, for I was determined to get up early today – but Marianne up all night with some loud-mouthed friend.

In the evening to the West End to see *The Lady Vanishes*[13] which was extremely exciting. A credit, 'Furs by Ossie Clark'. It had a starring role and looked wonderful.

Home to find Marianne upstairs out of her mind on Mandrax. We took half each and soon crashed out after making wondrous love.

10 MAY

Forced myself out of bed at nine. Found a strange man but no Marianne. At work I cut some lingerie and made a nightdress for Marianne. Home early with Nick. Angie stayed in Marianne's bed – she is a junkie who was in Jimi Hendrix's dressing room so long ago. 'She's a wonderful fuck,' said Marianne the following day.

11 MAY

Very good news, the lingerie[14] has sold more than 10,000 pieces and they reckon they will sell 16,000 by the end of the season – was funny though to see what my exquisite design was turned into.

14 MAY

Pattie Clapton[15] phoned inviting me to a wedding party on Saturday. Home to the usual crowd. Angie and co. Marianne and Ben[16] off to the smack dealer. Nick has found a job in a pub.

15 MAY

Marianne made a pathetic dinner and I went to collect Nick – home to Ben giving us marching orders, the pair of shits say they are getting married – as an excuse, maybe, or perhaps they really are.

16 MAY

Marianne must be feeling guilty because she rushed upstairs as soon as I arrived home – there was a message from Chelita[17] when I arrived at work this morning so I rang her back and she invited me to see Roxy Music. I went to her place at 7.30 and over a drink I told her of my accommodation troubles and bitched Marianne and Ben. Chelita to the rescue – she says we can live in her flat, in the basement, that is, then in September I can move upstairs for six months while she is in Trinidad (escaping the smack stigma and setting up a small hotel). At 8.30 we went to the Hammersmith Odeon and saw Roxy Music, very nice. Minah Bird was there.

17 MAY

I woke early to find one of last nights' crowd on the day-bed with his wife. Later he said, 'This flat is like an Alan Bennett[18] play: Ossie and his boyfriend in the bath, Ben pissing, us on the sofa and Marianne in bed smoking and coughing her guts out.'

Went to Quaglino's[19] – Nick in my green linen suit – to a party for Roxy Music, lots of friends and a conversation with the Irish writer Edna O'Brien.

18 MAY

I didn't get into work until midday, hungover a little bit from last night's champagne. Marie Helvin[20] and Fiona Montague came in, she tried things on and loved the dress I had made for Minah Bird – wants me to make her one – she also brought a beautiful sample slip, she is so wonderful and looks great in everything.

22 MAY

'There's only one thing about coke, one snort makes me into a new man and that new man wants two snorts…'

4 JUNE

Marianne is getting married on Friday[21].

8 JUNE

The marriage – we were late. Marianne looking radiant, nervous, wonderful – her voice carried better than his and when she was told Nicholas[22] was too young to sign as witness she said, 'Never mind, darling, next time I get married.' I wish them luck.

18 JUNE

A picture of me in *Ritz* taken at the Roxy party. Jenny[23] told me someone was asked to leave after trying to film Brian Ferry.

24 JUNE

Rain to dampen the spirits. Guy[24], Ben and Marianne arrived for lunch – she in a temper spoke of divorce, in a tantrum until J arrived with cocaine which spoilt eveybody's appetite.

26 JUNE

Esther Ranzen[26] came in – I'm going to make her three pieces, she's pregnant again and it's a secret but she likes to gossip.

'We are using all our energy in the wrong direction' – Nick.

7 JULY

We[27] have just had a beautiful ride in the sunset to Hemel Hempstead and are in the Watermill Hotel going to the 25th anniversary party for *Playboy* magazine. I arrived very early amazed to see a complete funfair and everything one could want. Fireworks, drinks, a dip in the Jacuzzi, lots of friends and even a snort. I spoke to Celia and maybe the children will come by train tomorrow.

8 JULY

Celia promised to bring the children by train, she tells me they are all going to LA at DH's expense.

The children loved every minute, went for a helicopter ride and everything. I, of course, had to have a go on the roller disco and did my leg in. It got worse all night and by the time I had driven home I couldn't walk.

10 JULY

I had a very weird dream about a visit to Paris to see DH. Girls in midnight blue with feathered stockings, a mad man with a bomb and DH leaving me. He went back to London; I had only been in Paris two hours.

13 JULY

I cut a beautiful black silk nightdress, backless. Celia came in, descending on cloth for the next collection. I picked up the children then Nick, we had dinner and spent the rest of the evening with Celia – who is very friendly lately. She goes to LA on the 24th and is staying with Michael Caine[28]'s wife Celia showed me a photo of Mo looking about 50.

16 JULY
No Peter at work, I suspect he's off on holiday again.
I'm a bit worried about Nick – he seems very frustrated so he went out for a walk and found sex in Hyde Park. Fucked an American with a knapsack by the Serpentine[29], naughty boy.

10 AUGUST
Nick has got the clap[30].

14 AUGUST
Back to work to find a write up in the *Standard*: 'The Past Masters'. Had a drink in a drag pub and saw a boy with a bleached cropped head with 'Sid Vicious 1957–1979'[30] written on it.
Read about 20 sixties magazines and went to bed at 11.

20 AUGUST
Peter has dug up a Jew who might back me. His name is Monty Beverman.

24 SEPTEMBER
I was interviewed for *Time Out* magazine.
Alistair Derbyshire[31] phoned inviting me to dinner tomorrow.
Made a dress and jacket, not very good.

25 SEPTEMBER
Celia phoned this morning complaining about Peter and I must say I agree with her.
Went with Alistair to see a pop group, The Rent Boys, at the Rock Garden, afterwards dinner at Legends.

27 SEPTEMBER
Hangover. Meeting with accountant Maureen Anger then back to bed cause I feel so ghastly.

22 OCTOBER
Spent the day in bed reading a Harold Robbins book, *Stiletto.*
At six I went to Celia's to wish Albert a happy birthday.
At 7.30 I went to visit Mick[32] and Jerry[33], found Woodie[34] there. Spent the evening with them, coke, telly, later dinner – he played some of their new

songs, did a funny impression of DH on telly drawing Celia (that I missed yesterday).

3 NOVEMBER

Slept late and shopped down Portobello. Dropped Nick home (his tolerance of the children becoming less and less) and on to the West End for hamburgers.

6 NOVEMBER

I went to visit Marianne, she wasn't home but on TV – I just missed it. She and Ben have been in NY where Anita Pallenberg was staying and visited Mick in the Electric Ladyland studios – also stayed in Chris Blackwell[36]'s house in the Bahamas.

Unfortunately went to HH[37]. Cold and damp and none to fuck.

16 NOVEMBER

I only went into work to collect money. After we had collected Nick's dole (we felt quite rich) we went to buy some model cars for the children, only I didn't 'cos I they were too expensive.

19 NOVEMBER

10st 10lbs.

20 NOVEMBER

I met Peter on HH where I fucked a young nigger with a very large cock. 'That was nice,' he said, rushing away. The whole thing over in three minutes.

17 DECEMBER

At work I found my ticket for the Red Cross Ball[38] at the Hilton. I had to leave, the usual embarrassment – no money for the five-pound raffle and to pay for wine.

1 To spend time with David Hockney.
2 The story of her affair with David Hockney.
3 Nadia La Valée, designer; wife of photographer Swami La Vallée with whom she co-owned the Spaghetti boutique. Both were friends of Ossie's since the sixties.
4 Peter Lee, Ossie's new business adviser and backer. Following his unsuccessful involvement with Ossie, he became an estate agent.
5 Marianne Faithfull. She had been in Holland.
6 Angie was a friend of Marianne Faithfull. She is neither Angie Best nor Angie Bowie.

7 Vietnam War-movie starring Robert De Niro and Meryl Streep.
8 Ossie has believed for some time that Marianne's house is haunted by a poltergeist.
9 Herod was someone's dog.
10 Diane Keaton, American actress; girlfriend for many years of Woody Allen in whose films she made her name.
11 Celia.
12 Nick Balaban, Ossie's boyfriend since January 1978.
13 A stage version of the 1938 Alfred Hitchcock film of the same name for which Ossie had provided some of the costumes.
14 Ossie designed a bra for lingerie manufacturer Charnos.
15 Pattie Boyd has now married Eric Clapton.
16 Ben Brierly, punk musician; boyfriend of Marianne Faithfull whom she met through her heroin addiction – although he was not a dealer, he helped her to obtain it. Their subsequent involvement, both romantically and musically, was said to have been a strong influence on her musical career.
17 Chelita Secunda.
18 Alan Bennett, dramatist and actor.
19 Quaglino's was a popular four-star restaurant in St James's.
20 Marie Helvin, model whom Ossie frequently employed early in her career; she became a constant client of his. Helvin was married to David Bailey (see note 00) – they apparently lived in a house with 100 parrots until he caught psittacosis.
21 To Ben Brierly.
22 Nicholas Dunbar, Marianne's son by John Dunbar.
23 Jenny Dearden, friend of Ossie's since his days at Manchester College. She was married first to guitarist/singer Steve Marriott of Small Faces and later to screenwriter James Deardon.
24 Guy Burch, artist and writer, journalist for the *Gay Times*; close friend of Nick Balaban.
26 Esther Rantzen, TV personality.
27 Ossie and Nick.
28 Shakira Caine, actress and model, former Miss Guyana finalist; wife of Michael Caine.
29 The river that runs through Hyde Park.
30 Sid Vicious, bassist with The Sex Pistols. He died of a heroin overdose in February 1979.
31 Alistair Derbyshire, marine engineer. He would later lodge with Ossie in Chelita Secunda's house in Warwick Gardens.
32 Mick Jagger.
33 Jerry Hall, American model; wife of Mick Jagger since his split from Bianca.
34 Ronnie Wood.
36 Chris Blackwell, founder of Island Records.
37 Hampstead Heath.
38 Red Cross Ball, held annually to raise funds for the English Red Cross; this year Ossie had donated a dress.

1980

This diary and the three that follow are written in a beautiful script, tiny and meticulous, producing a woven tapestry on the page. Sometimes Ossie writes in rhythms, or waves, with the precision of a medieval manuscript. The inks used change from blue to pink to purple and the whole is far more ordered than the frenetic, highly charged look of the 1974 diary.

In 1980 Ossie no longer owns or rents a home and has to rely on his friends' hospitality. Although he can stay with Chelita Secunda in Warwick Gardens or sometimes with his nephew, Jimmy Melia, he does not feel secure and is constantly seeking - through his friends, in particular Cosmo Fry and Jose Fonseca - alternative accomodation. His boyfriend, Nick Balaban, is with him but, it appears, Ossie is not as obsessive about this relationship as he will be in later years. However, there are signs of possessiveness and the occasional tender not to Nick.

Despite the fact that Ossie is on pills, he is very active designing. He is self-aware and honest as always, saying, 'I must pull myself together and get on with my very important work.' Meanwhile his social life is still flamboyant and refined. He parties both with the upper crust and with the aristocracy of the pop world. He stays with Jeremy Fry, the brilliant engineer, architect and founder of Rotork, at his home in Bath's Royal Crescent. A great friend at this time is Marie Helvin; Ossie extols her beauty and she admires his artistry Other friends include the society model Chessie, also known as Franscesca Thyssen, daughter of the steel magnate and art collector, model Patti Clapton, designer Edina Ronay, Jose Fonseca of Models One, and Melissa and Tchaik Chassai, fashionable hosts who along with Melissa's sister Mary owned two beautiful houses in Lindos. He encounters Vanessa Redgrave fund-raising for the Workers Revolutionary Party and shows an awareness of politics although it is never central to his thoughts, and parties with the Pink Floyd.

In the spring Ossie takes a holiday in Lindos accompanied by his sons, Albert and George, as well as by Nick Balaban. There are different impressions of this holiday. Dave Gilmour of the Pink Floyd whom Ossie visits saw him as a marvellous and devoted father. However, Albert and George saw it differently, resenting Nick's presence. However, later in the year Ossie thrills his sons by taking them to the lavish and exciting *Playboy* party at Stocks.

Ossie spends two glamorous weekends in the country: the first with Candida and Rupert Lycett Green at Blacklands, near Marlborough in Wiltshire, where he enjoys the fineries and comfort of the house and the delightful mother-in-law, Lady Grimthorpe; the other is spent with the Littles, he delights in gossip which ranges from the Marquis of Bath's son Christopher to Lady Diana Cooper.

Despite the disorganisation of his own life, Ossie moves around London at speed, is razor sharp and in with the rag trade gossip, 'the backers have decided to drop Thea Porter, poor dear'. He makes a breakthrough in his own work with 'the black dress' - 'I have been waiting for this, and I shall call it my off-the-shoulder line.'

In April Ossie Clark Ltd is bought from Peter Lee by a company called MAK, headed by Noel van den Berg and Hans Hogben, for £80,000. Van den Berg and Hogben have big plans which include organising a show in New York. Ossie travels there to promote it, but the show never materialises and Ossie is constantly at loggerheads with his new bosses. Revealingly he trusts Celia sufficiently to consult her and once again she proves to be a mainstay of sound sense in his life. When he visits Hockney's exhibition in July, he is only aware of Celia's overpowering perfume, suggesting his continuing emotional involvement with her. In September Ossie jets to New York and spends a glamorous week visiting the Met. and lunching and dining with Mick Jagger, Jerry Hall and their entourage.

Despite his business worries, Ossie is still coveted as a wedding dress designer, creating a sensation with his design for Susan Watts, daughter of Pete Watts, roadie for Pink Floyd. He makes dresses for Gill Goldsmith who will be entertaining both Princess Margaret and the Jaggers on Mustique, the West Indian island owned by Colin Tennant, now Lord Glenconner.

Ossie flies to New York again in December and after an evening of excessive behaviour with Mick Jagger misses his plane for Barbados where he is awaited by his hosts, Sandra and Michael Kamen; he reads Nancy Mitford for consolation on the next flight and is forgiven by the Kamens who are always tolerant and understanding of their friend. At the Kamens' home which is poised romantically on a cliff over the sea, Ossie relaxes and finds his imagination excited by the constant crashing of the sea against the cliff. Such exotic places are fundamental to Ossie's quest for escape, romance and glamour and, like family and friends, recur as a leitmotif throughout the diaries.

His delight in his work is apparent as he enthuses about chiffon, seams, fronts, silk and the paraphernalia of his trade, despite his business worries. He is observant and touchingly loving about people - trying, for example, to help Molly Balaban, Nick's mother, with land problems in Turkey - but this does not hinder his forays into the lowlife to which he seems compelled.

8 JANUARY

At last a wonderful day at work. I produced cami-knickers, a knicker and slip. Up at nine and a whole pink pill which I'm sure is responsible. Peter[1] saw Monty White yesterday for 24 designs, end of Feb. They will cancel the 25 grand debt and pay 7% – a way out but such a lot of work. Carla[2] came in, we smoked, she took some work home – I'm not being especially friendly with Hettie[3], but she can't see.

9 JANUARY

A friendly letter from Chelita[4]. A loss in weight at last. I worked on a dress but didn't get on until the afternoon, using a cheap fabric and French underwear (intending it for the Radley collection, though I didn't tell Peter). Drama on the way home as a wheel almost came off the car. Peter is looking for new premises – the rent in Fulham Road has gone beyond £10,000 so it is ridiculous to stay there.

10 JANUARY

Slept until 10.20. Pushkin[5] is so sweet. Every morning he comes to my bath and drinks from my hand.

I finished yesterday's dress. Just OK. And went to visit Nadia and Swami[6]. Busy with the sale so I read *Ritz* from cover to cover and home to an empty house – Nick visiting friends. I stayed in till 10 then went to visit Kay[7] – who told me all her problems with Joe[8]. He really thinks he is going to die – wants Kay to marry him to inherit the house (so snubbing the other) bought with money made from the sale of a lorry stolen at the end of the last war. She doesn't want to know. Also he is impotent, but since he has stopped taking painkillers (his back was broken in two places) he thinks he can do it. Unfortunately Kay doesn't fancy him physically, so Tuesday after mum left they had a fight till three in the morning – at least it's taking her mind off Jimmy[9]'s problem.

Let's not talk about Peter. Let's not talk about money. Let's see what's on the telly.

12 JANUARY

Slept late, breakfast and began a letter to Chelita. We went shopping on Portobello in the freezing cold – later Jimmy came round with Sam[10], and Nick[11] played Monopoly. Jim told me all his troubles – he has got a stall in Kensington market and I warned him of the danger of ignoring the tax man.

14 JANUARY

Late to work where all I did was finish the long letter to Chelita, which turned out to be depressing.

16 JANUARY

I've been taking ½ a blue per day and when I get home in the evening I'm exhausted – I have to lay down on the sofa for an hour. I'm having difficulty sleeping at night so I've been reading short stories of Truman Capote[12] – very slight about nothing with no endings.

Paul McCartney busted with half pound of grass.

18 JANUARY

Made two slips, both nice, yesterday. Particularly good cut on the straight with a sexy slit – still worried about being overweight but was so hungry I couldn't resist lunch – bought meat for dinner. At four o'clock the sad news that Cecil Beaton[13] has popped off. I rang Johnny[14] with the news – he was terribly upset. I left work early – worried about all the work I've got to do next week – there is a show on the 28th and I've got to produce six pieces for it.

19 JANUARY

At last Nick heard he's got an interview for art school.

20 JANUARY

Our[15] first anniversary. We celebrated with lunch. Carla came with a bottle of tequila, Johnny dear, Alistair[16] and Guy[17], who stupidly had eaten at the Colony already and were booted out anyway. We watched James Bond on TV and I made cocktails with the tequila. Last night I was up re-reading last year's diary.

22 JANUARY

In bed I'm reading scary stories but sleeping better, thanks to the little white pills. When I came out of work tonight I saw a beautiful crisp new moon – smiling and bright stars, a good omen?

23 JANUARY

A photo and a write-up in the *Guardian* and a picture of Pushkin and me in *Vogue*. At home no Nick – I'm sat here in agony with my back aching – I took a very hot bath, shouted at Nick, had a very strange dream in a huge house/ship with Mo[18]. I lost my hat overboard.

24 JANUARY

Carla rang at nine and I went with her to visit her punk friend Gash to score a smoke – he wasn't there but we went later and got some. Had words with Hettie about dress lengths – lovely Marie[19] came in and the underwear and new black boned number looks divine.

25 JANUARY

As arranged to Glebe Place and Alistair's farewell dinner at the Colony. I arranged the placement and sat next to Tommy Nutter, talked and drank too much. Ended up all four in bed.

28 JANUARY

Celia phoned. Albert needs to go to a dentist and she wondered which one. Late to work but full of wonderful ideas. Marianne[20] came by with some cocaine and wanting a slip 'cos she is to appear on an American Saturday night TV spot – I worked on a beautiful pattern. Then went to the Old Rainbow Room to see the mid-season collections except we arrived so late I only saw my own. Afterwards went to have a drink with Thea Porter[21], who tells me she is having an affair with Peter Langan. She has got a wonderful pad but her business is in a worse state than mine. Peter talked with her manager then to dinner at Langan's. Peter bought us a drink. I went to Danvers Street for another toot – only a rather pissed-off Ben[22] – so we went to one of his dealers who obliged. Bed at three with a quarter of a Mandrax.

1 FEBRUARY

I've got a 31-inch waist back. Wore white sailor pants.

9 FEBRUARY

Saw my name being painted in gold on Crocodile[23] shop windows. Talked to the woman inside. Bought some flowers, intending to give them to Marie Helvin in the Nuffield Clinic, instead decided to give them to Molly[24].

21 FEBRUARY

There is a lot of argy-bargying around who, when and what happens to the children. Celia is a very protective and conscientious mother.

25 FEBRUARY

I am sat in S.S. Travel making out my trip to Greece – 'cos Celia phoned this morning and the children would rather go to Greece with me than LA with her – Yippee!

I organised the trip and rushed back a minute before Edina[25] arrived looking for a jumpsuit, in the meanwhile Kathleen[26] put together the second backless plunge and divine divine Marie Helvin, more exquisite than ever. I took pix and Marianne I kept waiting. She was a bit pissed off but I stopped her disappearing – Marie told me that Jerry[27] is cross she didn't get her dress and at my show had to go up to Marianne and say how much she liked her record. M snubbed her and J was upset – I took a couple of pix of Marie and celebrated with a small Wyborawa[28].

27 FEBRUARY

Must buy books, especially the *Book of Thoth*, Aleister Crowley[29]. George Lawson says it's a 'load of old rubbish'.

12 MARCH

DRAMA. The bailiffs at David Chambers. So I went over and lent him my £180 air-ticket deposit.

13 MARCH

I wore a towel to receive my guests. First Minah[30] in her mink bubbling, then Melissa[31], Tchaik[32] and Mary[33]. Peter came with ice for the Stolichnaya and more wine. So we were seven to dinner – perfect company. The dinner was delicious, the conversation interesting. Everyone got on well together. Melissa looking seven months pregnant. Just as she was leaving, Mary told me she is pregnant too, which amazed me as it hardly shows. She is really pleased and says they will almost be twins.

14 MARCH

[*Ossie goes to visit Rupert Lycett-Green and his wife Candida*[34].]

We arrived at a little after nine to find them watching ice-skating on TV. I walked dog shit into the hall. Two dogs who growled at Pushkin. Soup for dinner and the most divine and comfy red bedroom with four poster, fresh linen and bathroom *en suite*. This house is absolutely wonderful, warm, pretty fires, marvellous garden, water at the edge of the lawn, stables with horses, a pregnant mare called Nushka. Everything has its place and the children have a set of rules. They call their parents Mama and Papa. I love the loo off the stone hall, smells of horse shit.

15 MARCH

I drank too many vodka tonics and smoked a lot of hash. I took Marianne's record. C likes it, tells me she writes lyrics for Georgy Fame[35].

Lady Grinthorpe is sweet. We had a conversation after dinner 'cos the rest are *Dallas* freaks. We talked of grandchildren and the war.

16 MARCH

Woke in the night and pissed on my socks.

18 MARCH

[Back in London.]

'Is there life before death?' – graffiti on corrugated iron. 'Speed kills,' I read daily on my way to work.

19 MARCH

The blue pill situation is desperate – only one left.

21 MARCH

My cousin Ron Clark is here in London. He told me the history of the Clark family. Quite extraordinary. My uncle Maty the seventh son of a seventh son etc. Grandma Clark, a six-foot, money-lending school teacher who liked gin – grandad a donkey man on the ships. Lots of bizarre deaths.

26 MARCH

Ben phoned as I was leaving work so I went round to see him and Marianne. She has got to have three pieces for the *Sunday Telegraph* magazine who are writing an article on her.

More coke and more coke when Ben came round after we had decided on three dresses, so I didn't get to Jimmy's till ten o'clock.

28 MARCH

[Ossie goes to stay in Polly Hope[36]'s house in Lindhos on the Greek Island of Rhodes with George, Albert and Nick. David Gilmour also owns a house on the island and is staying there at this time.]

Just landed on Ródhos. A nice taxi man drove us the odd way round to Lindhos. Went to Polly's house: no answer. So I found the key and went in. The cat, Dracula, gave us a warm welcome, which is more than we got from the Carsleys[37], who were there when we got back with the luggage. Maybe they had been there all the time. Anyway, he especially is typical of the uptight, expatriate American writer, a snotty arsehole. 'There is no stove, don't disturb us, we don't want to know, etc., etc.'

29 MARCH

I woke at seven, uncomfortable but rested. The view from the window made up for all last night's bring down, the bay so beautiful and bright sunshine. The whole village is full of life, school kids and women in black. I can see now through the window as I write, the children showing Nick the beach.

31 MARCH

Dave Gilmour came by and invited us over. The holiday has really taken off. We saw the full moon from his roof as we kissed Alice[38] night and stayed to dinner. What a divine house and how quickly they have done it. I helped design Alice's wardrobe as we smoked delicious Lebanese hash. He must be a millionaire now, the house must have cost a packet. *The Wall*[39] is still the number-one-selling album in America.

Of Ossie's many rock star friends, David Gilmour of Pink Floyd proved most enduring, putting up money for a new business venture long after Ossie's star had begun to wane and several times inviting an impecunious Ossie to holiday at his house in Lindos.

2 APRIL

Woke before seven. Slept without tranquillisers.

5 APRIL

Blissful day. We spent four hours on rocks, swam before nine. The children made friends with a family from Surrey – we all got lots of sun and very pink – the children so excited with their new friends, rushed off back to the rocks. I grabbed the moment alone to read more and make love to Nick – blissful, I love him, so love him.

8 APRIL

George is unwell. I sent Albert off to get a thermometer. He came back empty-handed with lots of stupid advice like, 'Give him a bath in vinegar,' from Ginger[40].

10 APRIL

A perfectly divine day indeed. I spent the morning sunbathing and listening to Beethoven until the power suddenly went. Nick and the children went to the rocks. I masturbated over a very old fantasy going back to the swimming baths in Warrington. I felt very happy today, inexplicably. I suppose it must be today's sunshine and that we are going back quite soon – I know Nick is looking forward to dear Old Blighty.

13 APRIL

[Back in England. Chelita has returned to London so Ossie and Nick go to stay in Jimmy Melia's house.]

A sumptuous sleep on Valium in my own bed. Went to my studio and showed Chelita the clothes, Peter filling me in. The showroom looking divine.

15 APRIL

DAY OF PHOTOGRAPHING GIRLS. Chessie[41] doing wonderful high kicks. Twirling scarlet, red shoes. 25 rolls of film, the fat make-up artist, the little queenie French hairdresser, the Devil is a Woman dress. Marianne falling over Chelita. My head banging in the car on the way home, my cough hacking, a real drag, Greek tranks and bed and Nick saying, 'you must see a doctor, you must see a doctor . . .'

18 APRIL

Dinner with Ben and Marianne. Ben very amusing telling stories of his coke-dealing days. Peter Grant[42] who dropped an ounce down the loo, snorting with a teaspoon, had infra-red cameras set up to look for ghosts at night around his house, and Jimmy Page[43] who is always so stoned. 'He just has a stupid grin on his face,' said Marianne.

23 APRIL

Delivered a jump-suit for Astrid Wyman[44] to the Stones' office.

Nick is being very difficult. I know it's not very nice staying in Jim's house but what can we do? So it's untidy and it smells a bit. At least it's cheap, warm and there's hot water. He is being too moody and won't let me touch him and sex is out of the question. Still, I love him passionately and hate him like this.

24 APRIL

So here I am in the dressing room at the London Clinic waiting apprehensively. I was shown to a tiny windowless changing room, put on a blue gown and x-rayed. Then I was taken to a room with an Irish nurse and friendly doctor who gave me sherbet powder, a tiny drink of water and an injection to stop me burping then barium, a foul, thick black liquid – I had to roll around (which made me feel sick) and be x-rayed about 20 or 25 times. Another little wait and OK. No ulcer. No rupture. So I dressed and rushed away feeling dreadful.

Spoke with Hogben and van den Berg[45] about Jerry Hall's dress and going to NY maybe. I was determined to see Mick Jagger so after a couple of joints and pills I went round. Oh, joy, there he was, beardless on the phone to Charlie[46] in France. I packed Jerry's white ball dress for him to take. He's going to the Loire Valley tomorrow to look at town houses to buy with Chrissie Gibbs.

25 APRIL

Visit to Celia. As usual snotty at first. Francis Lynne[47] came by and we both listened to her (Celia's) Hollywood stories. Billy Wilder[48] told her funny stories. He's David's best friend. Some 76-year-old man who wrote 'Hi Lili Hi Lili Hi Lo' who thought she looked Polish and fell for her. The cocaine evening with William Burroughs[49]. David jealous. 'You had to pick your nose for a week after,' she said.

29 APRIL

I've finished reading the Joe Orton book[50], I skipped through the last chapters as they were so boring – poor guy, what a sad ending to his short life.

30 APRIL

Woke early with a terrible hangover. Decided not to show up for the Charnos meeting and get my car mended instead.

Last night at Langan's I met Jeremy Fry's boyfriend and asked to stay a weekend in Bath.

5 MAY

7.30ish Bombs going off in the Iranian Embassy. We watch on TV. One man shot dead. Embassy on fire. Nick saw the smoke from the top of the house.

6 MAY

'He used to be famous in the sixties,' said the boy at the garage.

Nadia and Swami seem despondent about the future. Third world war etc. I said no point in working, enjoy yourself.

The car is really working properly. Thank god it was the air filter clogged up with carbon.

But there is no coloured silk organza anywhere in this city . . .

On the way home Nick told me that on the day we met he had been to the Tate Gallery and fallen in love with my portrait in the Hockney picture 'Mr and Mrs Clark and Percy'.

15 MAY

I suppose the high point of Mr Fish[51]'s party was Bubbles[52] and Diana Dors[53] sat talking at the same table.

Also, when I walked over to Mike with a joint he said, 'There are three policemen here.' He passed it on to June Churchill[54] who made a fuss of Pushkin.

Poor June is not long for this world. She's living on morphine.

Later went to the heath, driving past the window of Crocodile. Met a wonderfully muscular guy in ripped vest and peaked cap called Dennis, a banker from Victoria.

17 MAY

In the Colony restaurant someone has just been telling me of Elton John[55]'s little kinks – the socks stuffed up his bum and the attempted fuck on the winter lawn after strip-backgammon.

20 MAY

Nadia full of gossip from Manolo[56] re Bianca[57]. She hates New York and her last film isn't going to be released. One of the Sunday papers says she looks like Carmen Miranda[58]. Poor B. And Manolo has got a broken neck. He fell down the spiral steps in Old Church Street.

Phoned Dennis. Arrived at Carlyle Place at 6.30. A huge, austere mansion block. He was living in a tiny room with frilly opera shirts fresh-washed on the back of the door – lots of invitations from members of the Royal Family, some dating back to 1974 for a buffet at Windsor or a garden party at the Palace. As I suspected, he is older – and horror! Worst of all, a hairy back. He is weird and insular, taking his pleasure in wanking, opera and the Queen mum. It was a mistake to have gone. I was glad to escape into the damp Victoria night . . .

23 MAY

Weekend with the Littles[59].

Over dinner a lot of society bitching: R has his nipples electrocuted regularly by H. But worst still is the fact that Andrew Fraser[60] shoots 'Anything that moves,' as Amanda put it. So proud of killing peacocks and a tiger. Such a conceited prig: a honeymoon tale of waiting three hours for some animal to appear and instead singing 'Three Blind Mice'. Jenny has been here all day. The house is very suburban inside with all mod cons. Dinner: spinach soup – 'To make you fart,' she said and told the story of Diana Cooper[61] falling down stairs completely naked, demanding breakfast after crashing out on sleepers.

26 MAY

Went with Jenny in her car to the most beautiful house belonging to Simon Elliot who is married to Mark Shand's sister Annabelle[62]. I got on very well with her. We arrived in a sort of farmyard to be greeted by children and two dogs, a black retriever and a bearded collie who at first freaked Pushkin out but they were soon romping playfully on the lawn. The children are sweet. Their father was a bit snotty at first but OK later. We had Pimms and the Lichfield's[63] arrived from viewing Cecil's house with Haslem – a Nigel Waymouth portrait of Annabelle on the wall. After a walk round the kitchen garden, she sat me next to her for lunch and asked about my divorce etc.

27 MAY

Picked Nick up on the way and the children. *The Empire Strikes Back*[64] at the Odeon, Leicester Square. It was very, very exciting, full of action and fast-moving. The ending wasn't too hot, obviously to leave some for volume three. Celia wasn't home when I dropped the children. At a nearby pub we had a half and walked in the park while they rode their bicycles. She had taken Pushkin so we had to wait for her return. She was horrible on entry and the third time she said Pushkin was neurotic, I smashed a cup of tea in the sink and left.

30 MAY

At work a message to ring a man at the Customs and Excise. Yuck, what next?

Susan Watts[65] 2.30. I was late and in my haste cut the front toile from the wrong block, so I scrapped that and the second was much better – but still not perfect. She has a difficult figure to fit. A very round back with very small tits, though she looks OK. I remember her mother saying, 'Now, looking at Susan's problems, what do you think?' I thought she was being very hard, but now I'm not so sure.

2 JUNE

Met Divine[66]. 'You're one of the greats,' he said. 'So am I.'

3 JUNE

Mr Allsopp, Customs and Excise. It is to do with VAT and he is a sweet man, even dictated a note to himself saying I've ceased trading etc.

Nick has gone out with his friend Peter who likes prepubescent boys – or is that a story? We had a mild argument over money. I haven't got any. Though the real issue wasn't really discussed – I tell him I love him a hundred times a day, but do I?

6 JUNE

A shitty letter from Radley solicitors claiming four grand.

Kari-Anne[67] phoned up and came over with Chris[68] – a night out for them – she said they had Jade stay who was very bitchy about Bianca, who has asked after me.

10 JUNE

Went to the Playboy club. Tessa Dahl[69] was there. Bill Gibb has gone bust again and Tessa tells me that he just wanders round saying, 'What am I going to do, what am I going to do next?'

16 JUNE

Jerry Hall came by to borrow a red dress to wear to a ball in Paris on Wednesday, staying only a minute – promised to bring it back on Thursday.

18 JUNE

Billy[70] came in. 'God, you are thin,' he said.

20 JUNE

Frustrating day indeed. Noel van den Berg is back from NY. I overheard Hogben's heated words as I arrived in my room. 'I'm experienced and I'm not aggressive,' he complained. I quickly turned on the Velvet Underground and Noel came and gave me a pep talk re America and the future and plans and dates.

I've spent another very frustrating day at the drawing-board – the blockage continues.

24 JUNE

June Churchill's funeral. Bye bye, June. I knew her death was imminent but she was so riddled with cancer she topped herself.

25 JUNE

RCA fashion show – Pushkin was bored and so was I. Met David Hockney[71], was nice.

29 JUNE

Playboy party at Stocks[72]. Flat party despite the non-stop champagne, food and old friends with toot. Lionel Bart[73] after a two-week stint of drying out – helicopter, hot air balloons and an aerial display – a new outdoor pool, the children disappeared for hours playing space invaders.

1 JULY

Hockney at the Tate. The first person I saw was his brother Joel gobbling the hors-d'œuvres non-stop. In fact, quite a family gathering and Celia's overpowering perfume. I had seen most of the work before, like most of the people viewing – a very nice big picture of a lot more of Anne Upton – the three big Celia's.

4 JULY

Edina was very intrigued to hear of Shakira[74]. 'What's she like?' she asked. Michael Caine was her first major affair and it lasted three years – before Bianca, who she had met in a gym recently.

9 JULY

Nick's 25th Birthday.

As I got out of the bath I noticed a huge crack in the ceiling. 'That's going to fall,' I thought ominously and, sure enough, Nick phoned me at work at eleven. 'Darling, the most awful thing has happened. The bathroom ceiling has fallen down.'

10 JULY

Patrick Lichfield photos with Susan Watts. The whole trip including him was a bring down. First of all he complained it was too long then shot it against a black background. 'Do you actually think black is the right colour to photograph it against?' I asked tactfully. So he did change it to white but only photographed it in one position and close-ups on a stool – complaining he had to spend the evening with Princess Anne. It took him half an hour and he was off at six on the dot – what an arsehole!

18 JULY

Moya Bowler[75]'s 40th Birthday party. 'Like a whist drive,' said David. 'And isn't that your friend Andrew Logan[76]?' There were lots of old friends from the sixties, some I haven't seen for ages, lots of fashion people and a movie in the background but it was very flat and we left before the cabaret – I refusing the invitation to go to Heaven[77] with Hockney and Gregory[78].

21 JULY

I've had two visits from Peter Watts, the bride's father – re photos. As I suspected, Patrick Lichfield's were no good except for one close-up.

22 JULY

I've been suffering from inertia – I've been very freaked about work and not doing anything – hating it there. Hogben has destroyed the whole ambience. I went into work full of good intentions but each time as soon as I got there Hogben's silly laugh and the destroyed ambience drove me away. I've tried everything, the coke is destructive – one morning determined to get something together, anything together, I snorted and snorted but to no avail. My head whizzing and nothing. Just frustration and feeling ill – and no hash.

28 JULY

Marie Helvin came to visit with Fiona Montague (such an odd combination). She is so brown after a trip to Hawaii and bubbling with good health and enthusiasm. She tried things on and looked wonderful. Was very pleased with her black lace dress which I had almost forgotten about. I apologised about not having repaid her £200 I borrowed for the Greek holiday. She suggested I make another dress.

29 JULY

I met Vanessa Redgrave on her way to visit me, begging funds for her Workers Revolutionary Party.

2 AUGUST

I met Christine Hargreaves in the street – just on her way to see Maureen Starky – she tells me Ringo has no intention of marrying Barbara Bach[79].

5 AUGUST

Richard[80] phoned. 'Come downstairs, there's someone very special to see you!' he said, and there was Marsha Hunt and Karis[81]. 'I had such a crush on this one,' she said and we talked over old flames.

7 AUGUST

I said I'd take Tessa to the Pink Floyd Party. Nick very unhappy not knowing anybody, pleaded to go home – I couldn't stop yawning but was determined to get a smoke before leaving – I danced with Nancy in a cute fifties hounds-tooth suit with tight skirt and velvet collar and Tony[82] provided a small piece of hash. A small crowd gathered and Tessa disappeared to go to the loo after searching for her basket. 'Here's God,' said Leslie as Roger Waters[83] arrived. I'd said hello to Juliette and Rick[84] but no sign of the Gilmours – I said hello to Jane Asher[85]'s pale freckled beauty. Chessie's creepy ex sucking up to Steve O'Rourke. Linda calm and lovely in an antique beaded dress, the elder daughter very grown up – the little one divine, dancing in red satin pants and top – but it was all too flat and obviously on for the night so we split at 2.15, pleased only to have seen Pattie[86].

11 AUGUST

Jill Goldsmith[87] first thing. She came to the door in her nightie and was very sweet and understanding. Immediately wrote a cheque. She has been in Mustique.

On Friday waiting for Mick[88] in Le Suquet[89]. Jerry filled me in the details of the Marsha Hunt saga – I had mentioned her to him – he pulled a face and later said, 'Every time I see her she slaps another writ or sues me.' Apparently Marsha invited him to see Karis, and Jerry (having met and been enchanted by her) persuaded him to go. Unfortunately for him, going was what completed her case – publicly recognising her as his daughter clinched it – also he has got a sixteen-year-old son somewhere in England. Ronnie Wood spends $200,000 a year on cocaine.

13 AUGUST

Dinner at Langan's. Marie Helvin's birthday. The champagne flowed. Bruce Oldfield[90] had asked to sit near me. Questioned me about business and got very uptight when Swami and I threw champagne over each other. 'Uptight English queen,' said Nadia.

Marie Helvin, the top model and former wife of David Bailey, modelled Ossie's clothes and became a close friend and supporter.

Marie looked very beautiful. At 29 she is as ravishing as ever – there were an awful lot of cameras and photographers – Terry Donovan[91], John Swannell[92]. Richard Young[93] always on the ball, snapped Sean Connery[94] and Donald Sutherland[95] at a nearby table.

I gave Mick a joint and sat between Marie and Jerry and asked about my New York show. 'Why don't you give Ossie a big party?' asked Marie, and Jerry loved the idea. 'We've never given a big party.' She said she would talk to Mick about it – he was a bit pissed off with the flashbulbs popping – complained about his retinas and we left together, only I stupidly went to HH[96] where I got an excellent blow-job but we didn't get home until 3 o'clock and I got horrible itchy bites on my feet.

15 AUGUST

Rushed off to meet Mick at Le Suquet. He was late so we drank pink champagne till he arrived. Then we sat outside – he has promised to give me a big party in NY and talked of the models – then they ran away to look at a flat and I was left with an almost full bottle of pink champagne which I took – a small crowd in the street. 'You've just missed Mick Jagger,' said one to another in disbelief.

25 AUGUST

Went to the heath. 'Be quick, darling,' I said to Nick, and fifteen minutes later I was back in the car after being sucked and arse-licked by a guy who finished up sitting on my cock – I sat in the car for more than an hour waiting apprehensively for Nick, at one point a crowd left *en masse* and I thought maybe the police were raiding so I went back and met him on the hill. I soon found another guy with marvellous chest and nipples and a beard – we kissed and hugged, his not unpleasant body-odour vaguely familiar, reminded me of Harry Clark, now a street trader on Portobello, who I bought wonderful linen sheets from.

26 AUGUST

Lunch with Jackie Modlinger[97] at Meridiana. They wouldn't let Pushkin in. We drank champagne and she took notes – tells me Suzie Menkes is going to *The Times*. The pictures are wonderful, Jerry Hall is divine. 'The wonderful wizardry of Oz' is the headline.

1 SEPTEMBER

Excellent. Mick Jagger phoned, Jerry has gone away – shall we have dinner tonight? He'll collect me at nine – so home with Nick to tidy.

'Have I been here before?' he asked on arrival after passing Richard's basement bell – there were two movies on the telly so we stayed at home and I cooked dinner and watched them both. 'You can watch three at once in America,' he said. Alistair phoned – would we go out with him and Tommy?

11 SEPTEMBER

Jerry Hall phoned – decided I should go to New York with them next week – it seems the obvious thing to do.

16 SEPTEMBER

[Ossie goes to New York to stay with Mick Jagger and Jerry Hall and to prepare for the show planned for the beginning of 1981 by seeing some buyers and giving interviews to the US media.]

I read finishing Somerset Maugham[98] and the book on Marilyn[99] – I felt homesick almost before we left and the first book really depressed me as I could so easily see myself turning into the same sort of crotchety old man, screaming at Nick and lost without him.

We arrived about 9.30 NY time and outside I soon found Mick and a huge limousine quickly zoomed us into Manhattan and to Jerry.

18 SEPTEMBER

At 11.30 walked with Mick to 53rd Street to the Museum of Modern Art to see the Picasso exhibition. The reaction of people in the street was amazing. We were met and ushered straight in to avoid the crowds and crowds there were. Still, the pictures amazing.

I walked home through Central Park in beautiful sunshine and found Mick in further movie discussions. I left him to it and took a nap between answering the phone – Jerry's sisters mostly. She didn't get back till eight when Mick's cheerful mood suddenly changed violently. Mick was cross because Jerry mentioned a story in the news he obviously wants to forget.

19 SEPTEMBER

A write-up in *Women's Wear Daily* and very friendly people but MY GOD what an exhausting day – so tiring and my bloody back, such pains. By three I was totally pooped and aching all over. The model business was very disorganised. I wasn't pleased with the story that I'm making a special line for the US – also the guy wasn't very nice – though the photographer was sweet. *Harpers* came and looked and were enthusiastic.

Mick was in conference with movie writers and Jerry met with Rosie her sister and a Californian full of confidence who knows David Hockney. Jerry is incredibly organised, she possesses a remarkable down-to-earth sense of reality – when I said Mick is such a dealer, after he told me of a house in France with acres and two studios he is after, she said, 'I've learned such a lot from him. He really is like a king with magic at his fingertips.'

3 OCTOBER

[Back in London.]

At work got called upstairs to van den Berg who gave me another ultimatum – even heavier than before. 'I'm going to stop paying your rent and payments to Celia etc. – one week to pull your socks up.'

So utterly depressing, then Vikki de Lambray suddenly appeared so I went off to a drinking club in the West End and drank champagne all afternoon.

8 OCTOBER

Back at work, I was summoned upstairs and van den Berg was all smiles and about turn. 'I'll cancel the NY show if necessary,' he said.

9 OCTOBER

Sandra the machinist came in and asked, 'What's going on?' She took my number and will ring later. Sandra phoned and says VDB and Hans are plotting. Hans is horrible about me behind my back – so I phoned Peter Lee. 'My hands are tied,' he said. I am becoming increasingly worried – I phoned Celia and went over to see her.

[Ossie returns to New York, from where he intends to fly to Barbados to join Sandra and Michael Kamen at their invitation to spend Christmas with them.]

20 DECEMBER

Went to the plaza to cut A's coke and get stoned. In the taxi on the way I noticed a Christmas tree in Mick's apartment so I phoned him. Come and have a drink. I did. Dom Perignon and lots of it. Mick set the table for dinner and picked his nose through too much toot. Without realising what time it was I left, took a taxi to the St Marks baths and spent the rest of the night making love.

21 DECEMBER

Realised too late I had fucked up completely and missed the plane to Barbados.

1 Peter Lee.
2 Carla Ames, machinist and assistant to Ossie who became a life-long friend. She was married to journalist Kenneth Ames.
3 Hettie Quidejeta.
4 Chelita Secunda.
5 Ossie's dog.
6 Nadia and Swami La Vallée.
7 Kay Melia.
8 Joe was Kay's boyfriend at this time.
9 Jimmy Melia.
10 Sam Melia, son of Jimmy Melia and his wife Veronica.
11 Nick Balaban.
12 Truman Capote, American writer.
13 Sir Cecil Beaton, British photographer and designer.
14 Dewe Mathews.
15 Ossie and Nick's.
16 Alistair Derbyshire.
17 Guy Burch.
18 Mo McDermott.
19 Marie Helvin.
20 Marianne Faithfull.
21 Thea Porter, designer specialising in chiffon and silk eveningwear. Until her bankruptcy in the eighties, Porter had shops in London, New York and Paris; she has since started business again, selling mainly in the Middle East.

22 Ben Brierly.
23 The Crocodile boutique on Bond Street was part of a small, quality chain run by Peter Davis. Davis had commissioned Ossie to provide a few small collections. While some thought the venture a come-back for Ossie's career, the relationship did not last long – Davis eventually sacked Ossie because he simply 'did not produce'.
24 Molly Balaban, hypnotherapist, healer and student counsellor; Nick Balaban's mother.
25 Edina Ronay.
26 Kathleen Coleman.
27 Jerry Hall.
28 Wyborawa is a Polish vodka.
29 Aleister Crowley (in fact called Edward Alexander) was a diabolist and prolific poet who claimed to be the Beast from the Book of Revelation. His work demonstrated a preoccupation with the occult and often reflected upon the torments of drug addiction.
30 Minah Bird.
31 Melissa North.
32 Tchaik Chassai.
33 Mary North, founded Looms of Lindhos; sister of Melissa North.
34 Rupert Lycett-Green founded gentlemen's outfitters Blades; son of Lady Grinthorpe. His wife, Candida, is a writer; she is the daughter of John Betjeman. The couple were known as 'Tailor and Cutter' – she the 'Cutter' for her notoriously sharp wit.
35 Georgy Fame, British R&B singer/pianist.
36 Polly Hope, artist; wife of Lord Hope at this time, she later married Theo Crosby who founded Pentagram Records.
37 The Carsleys were friends of the Hopes and staying in their house.
38 Alice Gilmour, daughter of Dave Gilmour.
39 A Pink Floyd album released in 1979.
40 Ginger Gilmour.
41 Francesca Thyssen Bornemisza, model; daughter of steel baron and art collector Henry Thyssen.
42 Peter Grant, legendary gun-toting manager of Led Zeppelin.
43 Jimmy Page, guitarist, Led Zeppelin.
44 Astrid Wyman, former wife of bassist Bill Wyman of The Rolling Stones.
45 Hans Hogben and Noel van den Berg of MAK bought Ossie Clark Ltd from Ossie and Peter Lee for £80,000. They planned a New York show for buyers for the beginning of 1981 which was eventually cancelled, and later put the business into bankruptcy.
46 Charlie Watts.
47 Francis Lynne, film columnist for *Ritz* magazine; close friend of Celia.
48 Billy Wilder, film director and producer and screenwriter.
49 William Burroughs, American writer and artist.
50 *Prick Up Your Ears*, by John Lahr. In 1967, at the age of 34, playwright Orton was beaten to death by his lover, who then killed himself. At that time, Orton's death was more famous than his plays – they later achieved the status many thought they deserved.
51 Michael Fish.
52 Patricia Beverley, former wife of the third Viscount Rothermere, was nicknamed

'Bubbles' after the delight she took in drinking champagne.
53 Diana Dors, actress, rather unsuccessfully groomed as the British answer to Marilyn Monroe.
54 June Churchill, wife of Randolph Churchill, son of Sir Winston. She had cancer of the pancreas.
55 Elton John, British singer/songwriter and pianist.
56 Manolo Blahnik.
57 Bianca Jagger.
58 Carmen Miranda, Portugese singer, dancer and actress of the forties.
59 Jenny and Anthony Little.
60 Andrew Fraser, son of the 17th Lord Lovett, eventually died in Africa having been charged by a rhino.
61 Diana Cooper, society hostess married to Duff Cooper.
62 Annabelle Elliot, sister of Camilla Parker-Bowles.
63 Lord Patrick Lichfield, photographer, cousin of the Queen, and his wife, Lady Leonora.
64 The sequel to *Star Wars*.
65 Susan Watts, daughter of Pink Floyd roadie Pete Watts.
66 Divine, notorious gay personality and drag-artist.
67 Kari-Anne Jagger.
68 Chris Jagger.
69 Tessa Dahl, writer; daughter of Roald Dahl, mother of model Sophie.
70 Billy Henry, Glaswegian friend of Ossie notorious for his wild behaviour.
71 David Hockney is back in England to attend the opening of his show at the Tate Gallery.
72 Stocks was a night-club in Chelsea.
73 Lionel Bart, songwriter, composer of the musical *Oliver*.
74 Shakira Caine.
75 Moya Bowler, shoe designer.
76 Andrew Logan, designer.
77 Heaven is a night-club in Charing Cross.
78 Gregory Evans.
79 Barbara Bach, American actress, Bond girl in *The Spy Who Loved Me*. Ringo Starr, by this time divorced from Maureen, did eventually marry Bach.
80 Richard was Ossie's neighbour.
81 Marsha Hunt, actress who danced naked in the original stage version of *Hair*, and her daughter Karis. Hunt claimed Mick Jagger to be Karis' father; Jagger initially denied the allegation – though later accepted it to be true – and a complicated paternity suit ensued.
82 Nancy and Tony Howard.
83 Roger Waters, bassist and singer/songwriter with Pink Floyd until 1985.
84 Juliette and Rick Wright.
85 Jane Asher, British actress who modelled a paper dress for Ossie at the RCA – the first design Ossie and Celia produced together. Asher is married to cartoonist Gerald Scarfe who has worked periodically with Pink Floyd since the mid-seventies.
86 Pattie Clapton.
87 Jill Goldsmith, wife of ecologist Terry Goldsmith who is the brother of the late Sir James. Ossie had been commissioned to make her some dresses for a trip to Mustique

and asked for money in advance in view of his increasingly difficult financial situation.
88 Mick Jagger.
89 A popular restaurant in South Kensington.
90 Bruce Oldfield, British couturier who made his name in the mid-seventies; he famously designed many clothes for Diana, Princess of Wales.
91 Terence Donovan, fashion photographer.
92 John Swannell, fashion photographer.
93 Richard Young, successful paparazzo who uses a Harley Davidson as his transport for work.
94 Sean Connery, British actor, famous for his portrayal of James Bond in many of the films.
95 Donald Sutherland, Canadian actor, starred in *M.A.S.H.* and *The Dirty Dozen*; father of actor Kiefer Sutherland.
96 Hampstead Heath.
97 Jackie Modlinger, fashion journalist whom Ossie met in the mid-sixties when she was working for the *Jewish Chronicle*.
98 Somerset Maugham, British novelist and playwright, author of *Of Human Bondage* among others.
99 Marilyn Monroe, legendary American fifties film icon.

1982

Money is Ossie's greatest concern this year. He spends a great deal of time either worrying about it, waiting for it, looking for it or pleading for it. Indeed his financial situation is so bad that it seems to dictate his every move, and he is forced to begin what will become a long and drawn out battle with the DHSS for financial aid. Because of his lack of funds Ossie spends a great proportion of 1982 indoors and alone, and his impoverishment affects his work, his health and even his appearance. Most importantly, however, it affects his relationships with those around him.

1982's diary begins with a violent episode between Ossie and his boyfriend, Nick Balaban, both of whom are finding sexual partners outside of their relationship at this time. As well as financial ruin, Ossie has to deal with a wayward lover, considerably younger than him, who cannot cope with his possessiveness. According to Molly Balaban, Nick's mother, Ossie could be cruel and demanding, and occasionally even locked Nick in the attic at Warwick Gardens. As Ossie's glamour waned, Nick, who, friends testify, did love him and continued to love him, left him to establish himself in his own right. Years later, the same friends say, Nick, having proved himself as an entrepreneur, still loved Ossie but found his negativity hard to take. When Nick left, he set up a company with Mo Yusef called Balaban & Co. marketing tee shirts of his own design. Years later Ossie attended one of their Christmas parties.

When friends such as Sandra and Michael Kamen are prepared to listen to his problems this year, they give Ossie great heart, but separated from most of his friends by his inability to afford to venture even out of the house, he finds himself most of the time seeking solace alone and this greatly affects his confidence.

Ossie was not alone in his predicament. Thea Porter and Yuki (?) and Bill Gibb had also suffered severe financial difficulties, and Ossie's empathy with others suffering from his now increasingly familiar predicament is illustrated on 19 November when he points to 'signs of poverty everywhere'. To his credit he is able to appreciate that he is better off than some. He is still working, making one-off dresses for private clients including Shakira Caine, Angie Bowie and Jenny Little; he is still making *some* money and he still has his indisputable talent. His wit and sense of humour are also very much intact and he remains able to fill his diary with wonderfully lyrical and entertaining prose, and writes one of this diary's most entertaining passages while mourning the death of his friend Fiona Montague.

The tragedy of Byron Upton's death has a devastating effect on Ossie's and Celia's circle. Anne Upton, Byron's mother, never recovered and remains a close friend of Hockney's and Celia's.

Socially, despite going out very little, Ossie's life has vivid moments; he becomes friendly with Muriel Belcher, the Queen of Soho's Colony Club, frequented by Francis Bacon, Lucien Freud and other artists and writers. Throughout the year there is a feeling of life's simpler pleasures being enjoyed: meals cooked at home, walks in the park, evenings watching television. A telling reminder of Ossie's continually straitened circumstances comes when Sandra and Michael Kamen are flying to Barbados and Ossie realises he hasn't repaid last year's airfare.

However, the combination of Nick's rejection of his love with constant reminders of financial ruin frequently leaves Ossie lethargic and depressed. Although Celia and Alice Pollock remain supportive, Ossie's characteristic lack of self discipline afflicts him more than ever and he is left feeling extremely lonely, producing a sparse journal with long, unexplained gaps, swathed in a tone of nervous – perhaps even desperate – tension.

4/5 FEBRUARY

Nick[1] and I went to eat a hamburger. I dropped him at Subway[2] and drove to the wilds of Finsbury where a grotesque Frenchman sucked my cock painfully for ages – I was stopped by the police on the way home – went to bed feeling shitty. A little after four I woke and, going downstairs for a drink, found Nick in the kitchen with Steve Swindles[3]. We had tea. I was very X[4] and went back to bed in a rage of jealousy – couldn't help it – while he took S upstairs to show him the paintings. I phoned upstairs and told him to come to bed which he didn't want to do but said he would. I waited five minutes then got very angry – ended up sat on his knee in the kitchen while S took the hint and departed. 'I suppose you want to go with him,' I said and he began to put his boots on – I really saw red and snatched them out of his hands. We carried on arguing until 5 o'clock; suddenly the boots were in my hand. I acted insanely as though I had stepped out of my body, I watched myself smash the boots full-force into his face – complete madness – he screamed and screamed and fell to the floor. I had to gag him, fearing the police etc. When I saw what I had done I was shocked and begged him to forgive me and finally got him to bed. He invented falling downstairs to explain the wound.

10 FEBRUARY

Very depressed to read that Fiona Montague was found dead, overdosed because her Lebanese lover wouldn't marry her. Jose[5] has organised a memorial service for Friday morning.

The money situation is really getting to me – I haven't got any. I decided I had better sign on without any more delay.

12 FEBRUARY

Woke at 7.25 and out to a church on Fulham Road for Fiona's Memorial Service. I soon found the church, a few people cheered by a few glowing candles. However we were ushered out into the street and into another ghastly room by a sort of Irish woman, a cross between a nun and a cleaning lady. Salmon-pink room, neon strip-lighting and plastic flowers, half-asleep chrones blinking in the viscous light, a fatuous priest, Irish with a phoney accent. Two ridiculous texts: the first about a man cured of a speech impediment by Christ's spittle. What they had to do with poor Fiona's suicide was beyond me. I had never taken communion in a Catholic Church so I watched the priest with revulsion and fascination as he poured the wine from a half-pint beer glass, adding a tot of pure spirit. The blood-sweet white wine given by the Irish cleaning lady, he glugged what was left.

15 FEBRUARY

Woke early but felt terribly low, no cat and no heart to do anything. Straight back home to bed with the Beatles book[6] which is becoming more fascinating. I know whatever I put my hand to will go wrong so I've fallen into the trap of escaping into literature. The Gas Board want the standing order increased from £52 to £58 a month. How? I don't know.

God, I so hate being alone.

11.45 Sandra invited me to smoke. Michael[7] still can't roll a proper joint. I drank brandy and opened my heart. They were very receptive, concerned and I feel a little better and more determined to get myself together.

16 FEBRUARY

Noel Coward[8]'s diaries to be published soon and being serialised in the *Daily Mail*. How different to mine they are, although there are no new revelations as I've read Coley[9]'s book which is much more interesting and I'm sure Sheridan Morley, a real hack writer, has censored anything interesting out of them.

I feel really nervous about everything and at the point where I really dread the jarring ring of the telephone.

17 FEBRUARY

I got my P45 form and went to the unemployment in Hammersmith, filled in the forms and have to go back there at 9.45. Behold a minor miracle – found £8 in the front pocket of my cashmere suit.

I spent the evening at Nick's flat watching television and groping him, much to his annoyance. I do love him so and I know I'm only making it more difficult for myself as he feels trapped. He begins work tomorrow and is looking forward to it if only to be away from me for part of the time.

18 FEBRUARY

Gerald Scarfe has been told to cool it on the *Wall* movie after Alan Parker walked off the movie for a week.[10]

19 FEBRUARY

Nick got me £50 from the bank so he's overdrawn again. Made tinned rubbish for dinner and Nick went off to Subway leaving me to cope alone.

22 FEBRUARY

Signed on at 9.30. Passing a 'right to work' demonstration on the green, poor sods.

23 FEBRUARY

Appointment with the SS[11]. I went over to Kay[12]'s to borrow a fiver. Nick is feeling so bad I took him to a doctor in Scarsdale Villas recommended by St Stephen's hospital. He has got influenza and a temperature of 101. Ordered to bed for a week and given a sick note.

24 FEBRUARY

The promised Giro for £42.30 arrived from the SS so I rushed to Safeway and bought chicken, veg and a bottle of wine to celebrate. John[13] phoned – he's had a small windfall and is off to Clapham to score – do I want any? I told him I would go a fiver. Afghan hash absolutely the genuine thing. Carla[14] helped to tidy up a bit – we had a very pleasant evening for a change.

25 FEBRUARY

Ben phoned, hanging about the joint before finally coming out with the fact that it was sold – the Hockney drawing he had restored. I blew my top but there doesn't seem to be anything I can do about it. Bloody Ben Brierly.

26 FEBRUARY

How perfectly beautiful the amaryllis was last night. The peak from today is downhill, and yet I can only marvel at nature while I loathe it, I wouldn't have it any other way.

How on earth will I cope with the children without any money for food? I did phone Linda O'Rourke but she has gone to the coast for the weekend. The lump where I clouted Nick has disappeared; he complains of headaches and pains everywhere. 'I'm not staying here if you've ruined my health,' he threatened. I'm sure our precarious situation is really what is making him sick. I can't help but see the black side of everything but what I should do if he walks out of my life I don't know.

27 FEBRUARY

I didn't do any work today, just watched endless TV. A good program about WH Auden the poet with lots of Stephen Spender and Christopher Isherwood[15] – quite interesting. In many ways he must have been like DH – a Yorkshire man, difficult, bloated ego.

I've got one week's supply of pills left and mounting debts. I've got almost a fully-grown beard. Look dreadful. First bath in a week. Letter informing me I'm not entitled to Unemployment Benefit.

1 MARCH

Chris Jagger came round, told us about an interview he had just attended for a telly commercial – he goes on a bit – went back to my sewing and showed it to him. As he said, a real work of art.

2 MARCH

David Bowie in a play on telly was just a bore. I went to see Carla at 10.30, really to pluck the wretched annoying hairs from my nose. I washed my cock and went to the heath in the rain – a fine beginning but no, nothing. I hung around shivering and than home listening to Grace Jones[16] singing 'I want a man.'

3 MARCH

It was three before I went upstairs and soon lost heart with the amount of work to do. Nick came home from school, we went to see *Death Wish 2* which only managed to stop me thinking for ninety minutes. Michael K is back, jetted over on Concorde – he's bought Sasha[17] a Malaysian turtle and she has lost a tooth. Angie Bowie[18] had stayed in his apartment while they were here, behaved badly and run up a huge telephone bill.

5 MARCH
'Do you photograph everything you do?' asked the psychiatrist[19]. 'Well, I do intend to,' I replied, 'but it doesn't always work out.' 'Yes,' he said, 'I have the same problem with my transsexuals.'

7 MARCH
Ned Sherrin[20] told me of the first time he picked up a guardsman who he paid with ten shillings and a squeaky toy.

11 MARCH
I've been taking Valium as I'm afraid of another night of pain – I have got a pain more or less constantly on my chest.
My beard is fully-grown now and I don't like it very much but I have received a few compliments, the fact is it certainly isn't attractive under the trees on Hampstead Heath.

12 MARCH
Waking earlier and earlier. At midday I went to collect a bunch of pink blossom, which has suddenly appeared in the garden – so pretty the blossom.

14 MARCH
A beautiful sunny day – I think – but I didn't go out because I'm definitely unwell and also missing Pushkin incredibly. It seems just about everything has gone wrong since his death and I find myself imagining him excitedly begging for walks. Oh how I miss him. So I carried on reading Balzac[21] and watching television.

15 MARCH
Round to Gregory[22] and bummed a fiver, which was torn so I sellotaped it together, and went to buy food. Nick was very unhappy about my state when he got home and who can blame him. However I was too engrossed in *Old Goriot*, I couldn't put it down until I had finished it and very depressing it was too. I don't see it as one of his finest – rather a farce – but certainly the tragic ending is very powerful and too true to life.

5 APRIL
I phoned Shakira[23]. She will see me on Thurs. Said how useful the simple black dress I'd sold her is and definitely wants more – yippee.

I wrote eight letters, mainly apologising for unpaid bills.

I'd phoned Pete Townshend to return my tarot pack and he came at three with a smoke and some painted goose eggs.

Nancy Howard phoned – can I make a beaded twenties dress for a girl marrying the actor Bob Hoskins.

6 APRIL

A woman phoned researching the sixties for Channel Four breakfast TV. I said I'd see her on Thursday.

7 APRIL

The girl Nancy mentioned arrived – a sweet mousy little thing, a sociology teacher who had met Bob Hoskins avoiding the Royal Wedding. Over tea we agreed the fabric and the style. Then went to Harrods where I haggled and paid £50 for two and a half metres of lace. Then went to find mother-of-pearl beads.

I went to the heath and picked up an antique dealer from Cambridge and brought him home to spend the night here. Retaliation for Nick staying out. Fucked all night. Finally came in the morning.

8 APRIL

Breakfast TV interview girl I'd forgotten about arrived.

Angie Bowie. I went over and Michael was there too, as well as champagne and red Leb[24] – it's two years since I saw Angie. I asked to see her baby.

16 APRIL

Even though I'm doing hardly anything at the moment time flashes by – and at what cost.

17 APRIL

Michael K arrived with a bag full of change and two cakes, enough hash for one joint. 'There, you can go to college on the bus after all,' I said to Nick and off he went.

I felt horny all day but missed the sex cinemas – instead to Kings Cross to unsuccessfully search for the HH guy who keeps leaving notes in my pocket. Shoplifted at Safeway for pork chops and went to Carla's and then on to the heath early, where I fucked a guy mechanically with no relief whatsoever.

19 APRIL

I'm beginning to fear for my sanity after writing up this diary. I decided to bathe and fantasised. 'This is Roger[25] rogering me,' I thought as I bought myself to a climax with difficulty, doing something very obscene with a lubricant – almost ashamed to write it down. The line of a Bob song going through my head, 'I can't get no relief[26]'.

24 APRIL
Angie Bowie fitting.

26 APRIL
Cut off my beard and hair shorter, immediately felt much better and the sun shone, real spring in the air, feeling much more optimistic about everything. Poor Chelita is desperate for money and sounds very depressed – she has been busted[27] yet again and over there it can't be any joke.
Finished Angie's dress, Michael came over with champagne.

27 APRIL
Angie Bowie's number – got £250 cash.

28 APRIL
Ordered a foreign draft for £250 for Chelita.

29 APRIL
Argentina invaded the Falkland Islands – big, boring drama, the press love it and we are sending an army.

1 MAY
A cheque from the SS for £113 – Hooray!

2 MAY
Marianne[28] on the telephone – she had seen Kasmin[29] the night before, boasting all over of his sexual conquests. The youngest he has had is a twelve-year-old girl, the oldest a 70-year-old woman – what a disgusting person he is.

[Here there is a five-month gap between diary entries – they resume on 2 November.]

2 NOVEMBER
Letter from Chelita saying she is coming home at Christmas or the New Year.
I went to see a preview: *The Best Little Whorehouse In Texas*[30], Francis Lynn sent me a ticket. Then worked 'till about four when I stopped off to drink some red wine and my thoughts turned immediately to sex. I went to

Kilburn and scored a half hair[31]. Back home we had one big snort.

Celia came home with the most terrible, terrible news – Byron Upton[32] dead. I spoke to Anne and went over to Linden Gardens, gave her the last of the coke. Poor Anne said, 'I just hope some good will come of it.'

5 NOVEMBER

Home to a steak but no Nick. He was working and went to some nigger usher's party in Putney. 'Why didn't you come to Subway?' he asked me in the morning after creeping into bed around 3.30.

6 NOVEMBER

Nick didn't come home all night. I'm sleeping well – despite the pills.

9 NOVEMBER

Wrote a letter to Chelita telling her to come home and we love her. More importantly, sent her £50. Scored another half, then to Jenny Little and drinks. And then on to old faces, Muriel Belcher[33] paintings exhibition given by Molly Parkins[34].

Watched a stupid TV play and missed a play by Joe Orton. I sat up 'till 1.30 reading *Gay News* and waiting for Nick, who came in through the window just as I'd given up. Couldn't sleep.

11 NOVEMBER

[*The day of Byron Upton's funeral.*]

At 3.30 drove to Kensal Green cemetery. Cold damp day, muddy underfoot. Bit of sunshine. Quite a crowd of sombre people gathered. I shuffled into church. Stood at the side. Saw Hockney and Mike Upton arrive. Felt terribly sad, everyone so quiet. A priest said how popular etc. Reggae music and prayers. I threw earth on the coffin and walked away crying. Home, tea and sympathy with Anne and on to drinks at James Kirkman[35]'s. I hovered around a bit pissed and went to the sex cinema where I met a young black man, tall, with roller skates and a huge cock. I had to do it but stayed less time than usual.

12 NOVEMBER

I went to see David to give him my address. He's been here since Sunday and takes the 11 o'clock flight to LA. Talked of Byron. Celia arrived looking daggers and then left. Met Carla selling her wedding ring for five pounds. Collected Nick from the Coleherne[36], he is being difficult and says he wants to leave me – he went off to Subway, while I watched television with Alistair.

16 NOVEMBER

Worked till 5.30 and then rushed to Channel Four to see the sixties program, expecting to see my little bit in it. No – just a mishmash. Light-hearted at first, then pessimistically depressing and when Bertrand Russell[37] talked about CND realised absolutely nothing has changed at all despite the colour and permissiveness. Drank red wine.

17 NOVEMBER

Went to see Carla and we worked on Edina[38]'s jacket until 2.30 when we drove to SW14 to visit Roger Waters and Carolyne[39] who is very pleased with the red leather jacket – gave me a cheque for £600 and wants me to make her a green silk taffeta top and pants to wear underneath it. Beautiful house, immaculate. Marvellous pre-Raphaelite paintings and drawings. Made Carla a delicious steak dinner. Watched TV and took her home then on to the heath where I fucked a guy against a tree. Butch in leather but passive. Last night, drunk, I phoned Roger[40] and told him I loved him. Coming Monday.

18 NOVEMBER

I watched *Miss World* alone by the fire. Nick, I discovered later, had been at college till 8.30 then in the Coleherne, met his rubber man and gone to do naughties.

19 NOVEMBER

Signs of poverty everywhere. Walking along Golborne Road we saw an old man pushing a barrow towards the market with a wardrobe in it. He looked so sad.

Crisp sunshine day. Woke at five to discover Nick hasn't come home. Felt sad. I must say I can't help feeling jealous pangs. I do love him so.

Went to see *Fantasia*[41] at the Odeon. Albert fell asleep. Lovely film. Brought back memories of my school days and my art teacher Roy Thomas.

20 NOVEMBER

Saw the new moon. Ended up drunk in Seven Sisters with a boy called Paul. Stayed the night.

21 NOVEMBER

Fish for breakfast and then bed to recuperate. An hour or so later Pete Townshend and family arrived. We had coffee and I put on dinner after a trip to find coal. Offered to take them to dinner. He had already dished out 10-mil Valium but I refused to babysit and sent them packing in the rain.

22 NOVEMBER

Discovered a discharge from my penis so felt very pissed off indeed. Nick came home after eleven and we went to bed early after listening to divorced couples complaining on *Claire Rayner's Casebook.*

23 NOVEMBER

Celia phoned and came over with some black fabric she has printed and wants me to make up for her. I tried things on her and measured her up. She is very big but still beautiful.

Celia told of a dinner in Mr Chow[42] – £160 for three with Gregory's best friend Anthony and boyfriend Scott who broke down and cried at the end of the evening. Repeated her theory that I've taken too much acid in my time, etc. but actually she was very sweet.

I slept badly, took Valium and had a weird dream that I murdered someone.

24 NOVEMBER

Dreadful letter from the Inland Revenue. Bankruptcy. So I phoned the lawyer and sent it on to them.

Went to Subway. Stopped in my car by very polite police in Leicester Square. Incredibly they let me go. It was Oscar[43] on my lap that saved me, I'm sure.

25 NOVEMBER

Anne Upton has gone to Los Angeles. She phoned later and wept when she heard of George's birthday party[44]. I do feel for her so much.

A wretched gas bill for £400 and two electricity bills. So I got on the phone to sell the Hockney etchings. I spoke to Kasmin who said I'd be lucky to get £2,000.

26 NOVEMBER

George's eleventh birthday.

I promised to take Sandra to Portobello but I felt a visit to the clap-clinic more important so I went, which took up the whole morning, but thank god that's all over. Gonorrhoea, as I thought. How many times this year?

Actually working and enjoying it. I got on the machine and began sewing organza and taffeta together. I went to meet Nick at the Coleherne. Drank lager, home to dinner and to Subway. £10 from the cashpoint and a funny incident: we saw a policeman arrest a man running with a cooked turkey under his arm, partially eaten.

27 NOVEMBER

Sweet letter from the lawyer about the income tax.

2 DECEMBER
Depressing fitting with Carolyne Waters.

5 DECEMBER
Pills have run out so slept late and felt ghastly all day.

8 DECEMBER
Had a perfect fitting with Carolyne Waters and she said, 'Now, we haven't said a word about money. How much?' I replied, 'Well, I usually charge £500 plus fabric. Is that OK?' She didn't bat an eyelid.

10 DECEMBER
At Subway I picked up a delicious bearded boy, social worker, and went back to his piss elegant basement in Shepherd's Bush for wonderful sex. Poppers and three fingers up his arse but I didn't come. Though I did really fuck him.

13 DECEMBER
Doctor examined me again. Heart beat OK. Blood-pressure exactly right and repeated he didn't see anything wrong with certain people being prescribed, which he did, 100 Dexedrine[45] and 50 Valium.

16 DECEMBER
Delivered green silk to Carolyne Waters, £370. Then went over to say goodbye to Sandra and Michael who are going to Barbados tomorrow. How I wish I were going with them but it's out of the question since I still owe them for last year's air fares.

They were quite upset I didn't stay for dinner but I had arranged for the boy[46] to come to dinner so I rushed home to organise it. He never turned up.

25 DECEMBER
Christmas with Nick's mother in Egham. The exhaust dropped off the car on the way but Nick managed to fix it with a key-ring. Thank god no rain and mild weather.

1 Nick Balaban.
2 A gay club in Piccadilly.
3 Steve Swindles, club promoter at this time working for Subway.
4 Cross, angry.
5 Jose Fonseca.
6 *Shout!*, a biography of The Beatles by Philip Norman.

7 Sandra and Michael Kamen.
8 Noel Coward, British actor, playwright, director and composer. His work often reflected his notorious arrogance and apparent view of human beings as the dupes of Divine irony, characteristics of both the dandyish twenties and the cynical thirties.
9 Lesley Cole, *The Life of Noel Coward.*
10 Gerald Scarfe had designed the sets and puppets for Pink Floyd's *The Wall*, a theatrical performance of the music from the album, which the band toured internationally. British director Alan Parker was brought in to work on a film adaptation of the stage-show and arguments ensued over the amount of Scarfe's original material to be used – the film eventually contained only 20 minutes of his animation.
11 Social Security.
12 Kay Melia.
13 John Hammond.
14 Carla Ames.
15 WH Auden, poet. Auden was part of a group of writers including Stephen Spender and Christopher Isherwood (with whom he was good friends and frequently collaborated) who responded to the political chaos of the thirties with left-wing near-Marxism.
16 Grace Jones, singer and actress; gay icon.
17 Sasha Kamen, daughter of Sandra and Michael Kamen.
18 Angie Bowie, ex-wife of David Bowie.
19 Ossie had been seeing a Harley Street doctor named Randell who supplied him with numerous drugs to counteract his depression.
20 Ned Sherrin, humorous writer, lyricist and broadcaster.
21 Honoré de Balzac, 19th-century French realist novelist who drew material from his personal experiences of unhappy love affairs, debts, defeats, ruinations and unsuccessful enterprises for his books. Ossie is reading *Old Goriot*.
22 Gregory Evans.
23 Shakira Caine.
24 Red Lebanese – hashish.
25 Apparently Ossie invented names for his lovers, including 'Roger' and 'John', to preserve their anonymity.
26 Bob Dylan's 'All Along the Watchtower'.
27 Chelita Secunda. She was arrested in Trinidad for possession of cocaine.
28 Marianne Faithfull.
29 John Kasmin.
30 A play based on the novel of the same name by Tom Robbins.
31 A half-ounce of hashish.
32 Byron Upton, son of Anne Upton. He died after falling under a train while high on drugs.
33 Muriel Belcher, founder of the Colony Club, a haunt of Soho's literati.
34 Molly Parkin, former editor of *Nova* magazine; painter and designer for whom Ossie and Celia produced the paper dress at the RCA. She was married to art dealer Michael Parkin.
35 James Kirkman, art dealer who worked on behalf of, among others, Francis Bacon and Lucien Freud.
36 The Coleherne was a gay pub in Earl's Court.
37 Bertrand Russell, philosopher and social reformer who died in 1970.

38 Edina Ronay.
39 Carolyne Waters, wife of Roger Waters.
40 See note 25. This is *not* Roger Waters.
41 A Walt Disney animated film.
42 Mr Chow was a fashionable Chinese restaurant in Knightsbridge owned by Tina and Michael Chow, both great admirers of Ossie's work.
43 Oscar is Ossie's new dog.
44 The next day.
45 Dexedrine was a brand-name amphetamine, since discontinued.
46 The boy Ossie met at Subway.

1983

1983 is a year of increasing indignity for Ossie, another turning point in his life and again for the worse. Though he is still very much the star, he is beginning to feel that his life has become a nightmare and out of control.

At the beginning of the year, he and Nick are still staying with Chelita Secunda in Warwick Gardens, but by April Chelita, who is struggling to cure herself of a heroin addiction, has had enough. In the past Ossie had managed to pay the rent, but now he owes her £2000. Chelita made concessions for Ossie because she had worked for him since the sixties, adored him and believed totally in his talent, but now the boiler needs mending and she is furious that the house has deteriorated into a state of squalor: 'It was like a junkies' crash pad. I had to repaint the walls and there were knickers in the loo. I loved that house; it was my home.' In his embarrassed situation Ossie cannot appreciate Chelita's largesse and turns on her.

The biggest trauma for Ossie, however, is that the male love of his life, Nick Balaban, seems to be slipping away from him. This anxiety, indeed obsession, runs like a thread through the year. Nick has started to take other lovers an finally seduces the dreaded Robert. Those close to Ossie were unsurprised by Nick's infidelity, since they say he dominated Nick too much and was cruel to him. Throughout 1983 Nick successfully plays one lover off against the other, while Ossie – despite the acknowledged emergence of AIDS, from which one of David Hockney's close friends, Joe MacDonald, dies in New York – comforts himself with a number of fleeting encounters.

Ossie's third trauma is bankruptcy. His business was put into bankruptcy in 1981, but this year he is personally bankrupted over 14 years' unpaid tax, a sum reported to be £14,000. This bankruptcy will affect the rest of his life, involving him in legal complications that will disable his future activity to a large degree, but for now it is just another weight on his shoulders in a year filled with traumas.

Early in the year David Hockney arranges for Ossie to design the costumes for Sir Frederick Ashton's new ballet *Varii Capiricci.* Although he is frequently annoyed by Ossie's lax time-keeping, Sir Frederick is delighted with his work and Ossie joins him and Hockney to see the ballet performed at the Metropolitan Opera in New York. On this trip Ossie is also invited to join David Hockney in Los Angeles and there he plays the wild child, fills his hair with flowers and buys, or is given, many pairs of zany shades, most of which he promptly loses.

However, after the glamour of this American jaunt, Ossie returns for his Kafkaesque bankruptcy hearing to find that Chelita has finally had enough. She orders him out of her home and, in bitter fury, he cuts all the electrical wires in the house. After this climactic incident, which Ossie neglects to mention in his diary, there was acrimony between the former close friends for many years.

Homeless, Ossie finds refuge with his old college friends, Sandra and Michael Kamen, who rent a beautiful house in Melbury Road called The Tower House. It doesn't take long, however, for Ossie's demanding ego to overpower his hosts and again he has to leave. His sister Kay looks after him for a while but becomes infuriated by his lack of domesticity. A friend eventually finds him a pretty basement flat in Redcliffe Road, owned by Antony MacKay, but this does little to cheer him; he is used to better things, is lonely and missing Nick.

He relies on other friends, who feel very much for his plight and depression, but nobody seems to able to offer concrete solutions to his problems. He does, however, become particularly close to Brian Clarke, also from the north, who commissions him to design a dress for his new wife Liz.

Throughout 1983, Ossie is still invited to glamorous events, including the society highlight of the year, the wedding of Catherine Guinness to Lord Neidpath, an occasion attended by the Guinness clan and by Earl Spencer, father of the Princess of Wales, who spent much of the evening hiding behind a tree to avoid the attention of the press. Ossie also weekends with his old friend Jennifer Little, of Osborne and Little, where he is tracked down and interviewed by the *Daily Mail* and talks without bitterness of his glory days in the sixties and of that era's obsession with youth. He is an enchanting guest at Sheldon Manor, near Chippenham in Wiltshire, where the Catholic hostess, Elsie Gibbs, compliments him and surprisingly admits that even she, despite her ample girth, had been a fan of his and had worn his dresses.

Despite these short bouts of escape, Ossie's practical and emotional situation continue to cause him despair, and even the Buddhism, to which his friend Ulla Larson introduces him in an attempt to give him strength, helps little at this stage – not until the late eighties will he gain a positive spiritual life. Towards the end of the year, impelled by Nick, he goes back to work at Radley's and designs a selection of black cocktail dresses; but, since his depression, he finds it hard to concentrate.

5 FEBRUARY

Nick[1] woke me as he crept in during the night after picking up someone on Holland Walk and going to Pimlico for a fuck – 'Put it back,' he cried after Nick had withdrawn and come.

Carla[2] came over and we went to the park. Nick and I marched briskly all round. He lit a wonderful fire later, insisting I get out of bed – he's so sweet and I adore him.

7 FEBRUARY

How sweet tastes water after the horrid pile of puke. Dreamt of Chelita[3] in a nasty frame of mind. I'd taken Valium in the night after I was so sick. Nick woke first, made coffee and went to get the papers. I had to get up for the laundry man and complained about my lost pants, felt dreadful. Coffee and cigs didn't help and I had to sign on, so was really pissed off to find no hot water – boiled some and bathed, signed on and went to bed. I lay in bed dozing and watching TV . . . But when a movie starring the dreadful Hayley Mills came on, I decided I could lay there no longer.

I was feeding the animals when David Chambers came back for a left bag – Bosie[4] grabbed the opportunity to gobble Oscar's dinner – and I'm afraid I lost my temper and belted him and threw him out of doors – did he yelp? And guilty I felt, too, but he makes me so angry and I'm afraid I cannot control my tempers – I brought him in limping and trembling – how I hate myself yet he still comes to me and I hugged him to me, crying for his forgiveness . . . Nick came home. We watched Marsha Hunt in an appalling film *Dracula* AD *1972*. God, I bet if she was watching she was embarrassed.

8 FEBRUARY

I am determined to work today. I took Alistair[5] coffee early for him and he was snotty about a book I asked to look at, so when I returned it and he trilled, 'Good morning, darling,' I told him to go fuck himself and started work, seething over his meanness. I began marking out Shakira[6]'s suit . . . The money order from Shakira arrived from LA. $296 is £200, which is quite ridiculous. At home a woman I'd met at Cosmo Fry[7]'s wedding phoned inviting me to the country next week[8] – I should very much like to go.

9 FEBRUARY

Slept badly until I took a Valium in the night. I crept into the bathroom to take it and wank at the same time. Up at eight. I had just returned back to bed to read when Pattie Clapton arrived. She had tried to phone but I'd take it off the hook while out. What joy to see her again. I made tea and we chatted round the kitchen table about keep-fit, horse riding and Peter Asher[9] (Eric[10] is going to play on Roger's album[11] but doesn't like Asher who is somehow involved). We went upstairs and Pattie tried on the white silk dress made for Carol White[12]. It fitted but won't do. She wants a maroon dress. We looked over old photos and on the radio 'While My Guitar Gently Weeps[13]' came on, ex- and present husbands performing together.

10 FEBRUARY

Decided to go to the Tate Gallery. Had coffee and a croissant before viewing the art. David's 'Mr and Mrs Clark and Percy' in a prominent position just outside, complete with drawings and photos – nobody recognised me.

The first snow of winter already thawing on the heath today. Grizzly human remains found in a drain in Muswell Hill – parts of three males, they suspect there are 13 more – a former policeman[14] is helping the police with their enquiries.

On *Russell Harty* – Edna O'Brien talking about her drawings, full of self-pity – I know exactly what she means.

17 FEBRUARY

[Ossie visits Lady Henrietta Rous in Clovelly, a privately-owned estate and village in North Devon.]

I phoned Nick from Clovelly and interrupted a dinner party he was giving. He was also entertaining a new pick-up – Robert. Twenty-five mutual complaints from their respective lovers, i.e., his, who won't even kiss him, and me. They fucked in my bed – he confessed later, making light of it – I know it's wrong, but I am deeply jealous.

'What's an anomaly?' asked Carol[15] to someone who said they'd just seen one. 'Come on,' he said, taking her by the hand and dragging her to a sleazy pub nearby. She described the inside, 'Like the bar-scene in *Star Wars*,' smoke-filled atmosphere and weird characters and there on the wall above them all a reproduction of 'Mr and Mrs Clark and Percy'. '*That's* an anomaly,' he said.

22 FEBRUARY

[Back in London. David Hockney has arranged for Ossie to design the costumes

for Sir Fredrick Ashton[16]'s new production, Varii Capiri, *which is to play at the Metropolitan Opera House in New York.]*

12.00 Sir Frederick Ashton.

Fifteen minutes late to Sir Fred in Baron's Court – I was ushered into a tiny mirrored room. He remembered me. How could I forget him? I shall always see him as one of the ugly sisters from *Cinderella*, peeved (by my interruption at that point? My lateness? I think not – rather the expression on his face reflects a lifetime of stamping his foot. I remember when Wayne Sleep danced for the children at Albert's third birthday party – he put his hand on my shoulder. I had interrupted choreography). He introduced me to two dancers, Antoinette Sibley and Anthony Dowell[17] – both friendly. They finished the passage they were working on, then, for my benefit, took it from the top. I must say he (Sir Fred) is very clever indeed, inventing movement on the spot even, at his great age, making the movement himself.

23 FEBRUARY

After yesterday's long walk from Oxford Circus home through the park I notice I've worn a hole in my down-at-heel brogues – it's times like this I realise that some things are now impossible – my hands are tied, so to speak. Shakira's skirt is unfinished and, even though I know it has to go before the crack of dawn, no way can I bring myself to complete it. Nick came home a little after eleven and we were very ratty to each other – I put the machine needle through my right index finger.

25 FEBRUARY

Found an extraordinary chrome fork, with a plunger like a hypodermic needle, for pickled onions – the perfect gift for David Hockney – a slightly sinister, intriguing implement.

3 MARCH

Went to Celia, bathed and talked shop. As I was dressing she said, 'You look better without clothes on you – you wear clothes that make you look like an old man.'

4 MARCH

Slept till after nine because of the late night and ratty with Nick's constant physical rejection – I suppose I am really repulsive to him and that's hard to take. I love him passionately and tell him so all the time. 'I love you Nick,' I'll say. 'I know, darling. Now leave me alone, you old fart,' is a typical exchange.

3.15 Royal Ballet Practice School.

Sir Fred was furious that I wasn't punctual – I fell on my knees. 'I am so sorry,' I said, producing the drawing, 'but I was carried away with inspiration.' 'What?' he said, fumbling for his spectacles. I'd noticed Antoinette and a little group around her as I slipped out of my coat. I realised she was actually in a mock-up of my design – the pleated godets being joined to the side-seams of her leotard – she pirouetted – well, I clocked that and was thrilled. She was thrilled. Sir Fred was thrilled, deciding who should wear which design. 'Pink for her,' he said. Which one is Chesney? This jade green? Yes. He got quite carried away.

5 MARCH

In the press a picture of the Queen looking like a china teapot and Nancy Reagan like a badly mended broken vase. Nick phoned his friend and went off to bathe. He got waylaid by pornographic magazines and of course ended up in the pub until closing time. Was absolutely furious when Robert phoned for Nick. I answered and he didn't acknowledge me. I just boiled over in anger as they connived their secret plans – the outcome was a blast aimed at Robert's ear straight down the phone-line, a sulk from Nick and a repeat argument, as last Saturday.

8 MARCH

Royal Ballet practice school 2 o'clock.

Joined Sir Fred for tea – he has got the finest feet and is so alive for his age – he has no style, dresses more for comfort in comfy cardigans and slacks, mostly dark. Then we went to meet the cast and principals. What ravishing grace and beauty – lithe, long-backed girls giggling, some breathless from the dance. One dressed in raspberry – my god, what a bum – another with leaping legs like scissors, another high-kicking perfectly like a showgirl.

9 MARCH

A dreadful letter with summons to court for the rates outstanding.

16 MARCH

I didn't get to sleep until it was light – no Valium so didn't surface till about nine – Nick phoned at 9.30. 'Hello, darling – I spent the night with Robert.' 'Come home,' I demanded. 'Come home now or don't bother.' 'I'll come back later and pack my bags.'

Gregory[18] phoned to beg a pill – I'm so glad I went round because he was throwing out David's entire wardrobe so I grabbed all the wonderful Nutter[19] suits and jackets – like Christmas.

17 MARCH

A long, boring ride and taxi to a pretty Georgian square – Lucy Fry greeted us and then Craigie[20] was there with his two white dogs he dotes on. Cosmo and Cosima came – she had a tantrum after drinking some whisky: flicking her hair, she cracked her head open on a low beam. Henri[21] sat next to me and I thought it odd she had her back to me most of the time so we hardly spoke. Instead I had a long conversation with Sabrina[22] tut-tutting in our old age – 'we didn't behave like that when *we* were nineteen,' she said as she was splashed with wine.

21 MARCH

Nick came home early but again had to go to work. I walked him there with the dogs – we discussed the situation – it's definitely getting worse, but he said, 'Never mind, darling, everything will turn out OK.' But I don't know, I'm torn between screaming at him – 'Fuck off, get out of my life' – and saying, 'Please don't leave me, darling, I'll die without you.' Certainly without him I am very miserable.

22 MARCH

Jimmy[23] came round and Chelita said, 'You're the only person in here that looks worse than I do. You're a perfect example of sex and drugs and rock and roll.'

25 MARCH

We went to the Coleherne. 'I like your hat,' said the queen with the high thighs who had squealed like a stuck pig when I fucked him. And Nick kept saying, 'I feel like picking up a man, darling,' – 'Just do whatever you like, darling,' I replied. 'Why are you being so nice to me?' he said, 'I much prefer you when you are worried.'

27 MARCH

Robert phoned from Amsterdam and I told him Nick wasn't here, only Nick heard. 'Who was that?' he asked. 'Wrong number,' I replied but I didn't fool him and I confessed when he asked me again.

28 MARCH

Tim Curry said that once on a trip he made love to a woman who said, 'At first I thought he was a bear, then he turned into my father and I settled for that.'

I had just got stuck in when Gregory came round. He told me he's leaving for NY tomorrow because Joe Macdonald[24] is in hospital and 'Somehow I don't think he will come out alive.' Poor, beautiful man is dying from a sexually transmitted disease, AIDS, which breaks down the body's natural defence system. It's too sad and apparently quite ghastly.

29 MARCH

I forced Carla to drive me to Hampstead. She dropped me before the heath . . . tried to talk me out of going, but I was determined to have sex – I turned my collar against the wind and crept stealthily down the familiar slopes. 'Why have I bothered?' flashed through my brain, but the thought of Nick and Robert making love drove me on.

30 MARCH

Chelita told Carla she needs clothes like a hole in the head. It's cash she wants.

Later I phoned David Hockney in LA. When David got on the phone I said, 'What's the matter? You sound distant.' He answered, 'Do I?' He has got to go to NY tomorrow to see Joe Macdonald, who is definitely near death, in hospital and he's not looking forward to it at all – 'I think it will be pretty awful', he said.

1 APRIL

Nick arrived at 4.30 – I confessed I missed him terribly. I asked him would he rather be with Robert or me and he assured me that he was torn between the two but said he loved him. 'I am allowed to love more than one person,' he half joked.

7 APRIL

Joe Macdonald died.

8 APRIL

Pattie Clapton at 11.25 – told her Michael Kamen mad about her and she said she had dreamt of him.

18 APRIL

[*Ossie goes to the States for the opening of* Varii Capiri.]

Collected my Bankruptcy Petition from Inland Revenue solicitors, SW1. Celia came round and said my mother was worried about me. 'I'm an old woman. I look into his eyes and know something is wrong.' So I gave a solid oath I wouldn't take any drugs for two weeks. 'The women-folk gathered to bid farewell to the conquering hero,' said Alistair before driving me to the airport. George came for the ride and it was a tight squeeze time-wise. Jose[25] smiling in the corner of a completely packed plane. I was put to sit between two babies, given the oddest looks. So eventually I moved into the smoking section and wrote a letter to Nick.

'John Lennon,' muttered a woman after I finally cleared customs at JFK Airport. Jose and I both laughed.

19 APRIL

David always cupping his ear. 'Sorry, luv, I can't hear.' I kissed him on the shoulder and told him I was sorry to disturb him. David very morose about the Joe Macdonald memorial service.

Was late for the dress rehearsal at the Metropolitan Opera House. 'Well, you've missed it,' said David in a fury. 'Where were you? Just tell me what period this is supposed to be?' I felt very hurt with David's non-appreciation but shrugged it off when Sir Fred came over, obviously very pleased. I told him DH wasn't thrilled with my costumes and he just shrugged his shoulders as though to say, 'Well, I'm very happy and that's all that matters.' Fuck her dear, which is just what I thought – poor David had made a little speech at Joe's memorial and was choked up. At the Algonquin[26] I thanked Sir Fred for showing me the beauty of the male body (I said David had shown me how to see in the first place).

20 APRIL

David brought me tea in bed at eight. Breakfast with three beautiful boys. David took photographs.

David said British Airways had offered him a three-year first-class ticket in exchange for being filmed simply buying a ticket and boarding a plane in LA. He turned it down.

22 APRIL

Woke to DH laughter. He on the phone to Celia.

28 APRIL

I just have a feeling everything is going to be all right.

8 MAY

Back to London. 'I shall miss you,' said David Hockney. As soon as I got back to England I missed Nick terribly. I love him so much, will I ever see him again?

9 MAY

10.15 Met Kenneth Woolfson outside Royal Court of Justice, the Strand.

10.45 Bankruptcy Hearing. What a dreadful time. Like a Kafka[27] novel. Go to Room This, Room That – filled in a 30-page booklet of questions. Didn't get away until 1.15.

11 MAY

At last a meeting with Nick. We embraced and I taped the conversation. 'Let's walk round the block,' I said, my heart pounding. 'Have you forgiven me?' I asked. 'I suppose so,' he replied. In the pub I kissed him and we held hands. He smiled a lot. He was initially reluctant to look me in the eye but did eventually and smiled a bemused smile. I put it to him to come to America with me in September and asked his first impression. 'Let's just see what happens,' he said.

18 MAY

Jimmy Page busted in his Windsor house. Hope they don't come here.

Well, it's ten past eleven and I'm feeling utterly miserable. A cup of tea and salt for herpes on my cock. Met Nick outside school and immediately brought down by him in Robert's clothes. I still love him and I still haven't given up hope. But almost.

20 MAY

I began to read *Funeral Games* by Mary Pienault and became quite engrossed in it, missing Nick. When I got to the part where Roxanne poisons his other wife and her sister a real feeling of melancholia came over me. I grew very sad and with tears in my eyes wondered if in a similar position I would actually do away with Robert[28] in the same way. But I know that it's morally wrong to even think it – instead I imagine what it would be like to fuck him and masturbated fantasising that he's got Nick's cock in his mouth and mine up his arse. I think the only way I could come to terms with my jealousy would be to have him and I'm sure Nick wouldn't like that – I'm sure his feelings for Robert go deeper and that saddens me.

25 MAY

Henrietta had called. I called her back, inviting her to dinner, and made a reservation in Lorenzo. I dressed in my yellow suit and she kept me waiting. After HH. Why, I wonder, do I gamble with death? There was absolutely no way I could resist going up that hill – and what for? At least I took the precaution of wearing boots and changing out of the yellow silk suit.

1 JUNE

[*Chelita has asked him to move out of her house so Ossie is staying with Kay*[29].]

DRAMA DRAMA DRAMA DRAMA DRAMA. We were watching television and listening to David Bowie – suddenly Kay blew her top. 'I can see my cooker's going to be in the same state as Chelita's,' she started as the coffee pot hissed and splattered – it seemed to me afterwards she was just determined to have an argument. She went on about all her grievances. 'You think you're a special person. Well, you're not. I'm not going to be your drudge,' etc., etc. 'Shut up.' I shouted. 'Shut up!' 'I won't.' 'Shut up!' 'I won't.' Nag nag nag nag nag nag. In desperation I put the bench over my head, not knowing what to do really. I accidentally smashed the lampshade and she called the police to have me arrested.

8 JUNE

Jose came round just after ten. 'What's the matter,' she said as I burst into tears. 'I'm so alone,' I said. 'Well, cheer up,' she said, 'TV AM' are on the phone. They want to wish you happy birthday on telly . . .'

13 JUNE

I found a letter from Henrietta inviting me to Brian Clarke[30]'s opening. It was very nice with lots of old faces like a sixties bash – passed Chelita on her way in with a very made-up Duggie Field[31]. Everyone was there. Manolo[32]. Bailey[33]. Paul and Linda McCartney – Nick insisted I go search out Chelita, which I did. Gave her a big hug and told her I was in a mess. She was very warm from being inside. 'Much better to be friends,' she said.

15 JUNE

Drunken day with Henrietta. Talk with Anthony McKay[34] re Social Security. He called me a star. Talks in such a long-winded way. Said I should say I'm his 'house guest'.

Dancing at Tramps with Carol Edge[35]. A very sad looking Angie Best.

17 JUNE

Met Nick in the Coleherne. He said, 'I don't think it will last long with Robert. He is so annoying. He's got no taste.' Well, that was good news to my ears but when I begged him to come home with me he said, 'Not yet darling, maybe in a year. What would happen, when I meet somebody else? I don't want to hurt you.'

20 JUNE

David Hockney's back. I spoke to him on the telephone. 3.30. Jimmy came round with a message from a very irate Kay. Al Radley's been in touch with her so I phoned him and he tells me that the press are hounding him, looking for me and again asked me to do a dozen pieces for him for spring. 'I'm a pest, aren't I?' he said.

DH seems very relaxed and happy to be painting. He even suggested he paint me next week. He goes to Hamburg on Wednesday to collect the Shakespeare Prize. He talked about the by now usual subjects – AIDS and Cubism and Picasso.

22 JUNE

Drove to Oakley Street to visit Isobel Strachey[36] for drinks. Mostly old codgers, except for Andrew Barrow, who has just written a book called *International Gossip*. It was held in a pretty garden, and although the people were a boring lot, there was an out-house covered with ivy and it held two birds' nests – a robin's and a blackbird's. I could hear the young calling and watched in fascination as the mothers to-ed and fro-ed with food – just as we were going to leave Rose and Oliver Musker[37] arrived with Desmond Guinness and mistress. Rose was very warm and they invited me to stay in their house at the end of July. 'You have always been so generous in your hospitality to me. I should like to repay it,' she said.

23 JUNE

Walked to the Coleherne to see Nick with a feeling of apprehension, slightly depressed he was there with Mike[38]. Then a friend he works with came in and he turned his back, in conversation with him. So I turned my attention to Mike and received warm body-language. If only Nick would respond so. I fucked him in the toilet and Nick didn't even notice. He joked about picking up a man, saying, 'You silly darling, if I did, Robert would be so jealous he wouldn't see me again.' 'What difference would that make to me?' I asked. 'I'm only joking,' he said. But is he? I love him so, why do I keep on tormenting myself. I went to the loo and a leather queen creamed on me. I left to go to a party with Henri, but met him again, took him home and creamed on him. A taxi to Pamela Glenconner[39]'s washout party. No sign of Henri. Another sad encounter, Holland Park.

25 JUNE

To the country by train[40]. Had to stand till Reading. By taxi to Sheldon Manor – a stately home open to the public. Had snapped at Henrietta and was full of remorse and so pleased to see her I bought a bottle of gin and was given the priest's room to sleep in, the oldest (12th century) in the house. We drank wine and medieval Ribena out of doors – lunch of homemade paté and ham – dogs and ducks and their little ones and noisy guinea fowl on the lawn, all so charming. Later an engaged couple called Buchanan[41] arrived, sweet and giggly and so in love. Everyone dressed up to go to the wedding party. I made three joints and a huge gin cocktail. Henri looked splendid in a hired dress Faye Dunaway[42] might have worn in the *Three Musketeers*. I wore my yellow suit and off to The Ivy, a beautiful house in the middle of Chippenham. We made quite an entrance, drank lots of champagne but I was bored. Thought only of Nick as the full moon rose.

30 JUNE

A phone call from the famous Mick Jagger office about an interview for his autobiography.

3 JULY

Plucked up courage to ring Nick at Robert's and he answered the phone. Nothing has changed and when I got to DH he could see I was down and he asked me what was wrong and put his arm around me and held my hand while I wept at 4.30.

4 JULY

11 o'clock. Jane McKay[43] to go over fabric. We went to a pub for lunch. Lasagne and bloody Mary's and she gossiping about Bryan Ferry, his rudeness and disenchantment. How they laughed at his predicament when Jerry ran off with Mick[44] – I told them Mick's story about Bryan stamping on his foot when their paths crossed at a New York party.

6 JULY

Went to see *King of Comedy*. Afterwards, talking outside with Tchaik[45] and Melissa[46], I was pushed aside by someone barging me on purpose. 'Wouldn't you know, it's fucking Lucien Freud[47]!' I shouted after him. Melissa was quite shocked and I explained being introduced to him sixteen times before I said, 'If I'm introduced to you one more time and you ignore me, I'll spit in your face.'

8 JULY

I rang Sandra[48] and told her I was lonely so she invited me over to dinner – I walked home with a futile hope of picking up somebody I could sleep with, I so hate sleeping alone.

11 JULY

Three months parted from Nick. Woke at half past five, dammit, to the sound of dustbins and once my eyes were open I couldn't go back to sleep.

I felt pretty miserable and determined to accomplish something today, what with the new moon and all, so I made coffee, wrote and went to see DH. Arrived at five past nine and blurted out my tearful story.

Collected Shakira's bodice to deliver it to her at Arlington House. Michael Caine answered the door and wouldn't you know, it was too big. Michael in high spirits having just bought three of David's photographs – he's keen now to get DH to photograph Shakira and child who's desperate to see little Oscar. Michael told me he has introduced David to Steven Spielberg[49], and said he has the same photographic eye as Hockney but no colour sense, having been brought up on black and white movies. I was quite excited about that and when I told Celia she said, 'I met him too.' Shakira had been to lunch with Tessa Kennedy[50] and said Tessa should have a suit made too. I hung around and drank long vodkas, talking to Michael about the movie he made in Rio with a seventeen-year-old – a cross between Brooke Shields and Marilyn Monroe with perfect tits who's got a crush on him.

13 JULY

David did a drawing of me in the nude.

17 JULY

Francis Lynn tells me that James Dean was receiving a blow-job when he crashed his Porsche.

21 JULY

I love you, Nick, so much and miss you even more. I hope you are having a nice time in Greece with your mother and I hope you will come back to me.

22 JULY

The official receiver's meeting. 11.30. Room 410, Thomas Moore Building. I went off to the law court in the Strand to be confronted by a Mr Magison who had unearthed two companies I had shares in and bearing my name, Celia's and John Kasmin's. He wants a copy of my divorce certificate and Kasmin's address and seemed to think they can go after Celia's flat. Gloom and again like Kafka, down to Room 410 for nothing and as I was leaving a wretched woman reporter said with great sympathy, 'I had some of your dresses.' I was pretty choked up and taken unawares.

23 JULY

Instead of Nick being my first thought, it is now Robert followed by Nick. Eventually phoned him at 10.30. 'I'd like you to sleep with me,' I said. 'I know.' 'I just wish Nick was here.' 'That's silly. If Nick were here, we wouldn't be speaking to each other.'

'I know Nick better than you,' I argued, 'And I'm sure he wouldn't mind. You see it as a threat and I as a bond.'

Henri phoned almost as soon as I'd hung up. Caught the 11.45 to Exeter. It was well after five when we drove into the grounds of Clovelly Court. Round full circle I couldn't help thinking. My last visit was the beginning of Nick's affair with Robert. OH! If only I hadn't gone, how different things might have been.

26 JULY

To Cork Street, where there was an artists and galleries street party. Spent most of the time leaning against a car watching the throng go by – John Dunbar[51] had very encouraging things to say about going bankrupt. Patrick[52] in town with a young photographer who wants to take my picture – told funny stories about Cecil Beaton. He has got the job of designing *Turandot* for Los Angeles and has asked for my help.

I can hardly bear to write down what happened next. Why, on top of everything else, should I behave so stupidly? We drank in the pub till 11 and I chose to drive Henri's car and got breathalysed and over-the-top – hideous, horrible, misery – and I lied to them, saying my name was Oswald Clark with no previous convictions. I don't think I will ever forget the procedure – the vile police like gleeful school bullies – oh, so hateful.

27 JULY

Stories in the wretched press. Why can't they leave me alone? Caught unawares, I had put the blame on my marriage break-up with Celia, which is pretty true anyway. Celia's mother being very upset doesn't help matters between us, either.

29 JULY

My life is so empty. The problems seem insurmountable and I feel as though suicide is the only way out. I can't work. It's just impossible. I toyed with the idea of writing to David, but what can I say to him? Do I actually want to run away to LA?

3 AUGUST

I rand Nick at Robert's – said he loves R and wants to live with him. R still not sure. Nick says R loves him ¾ths and is determined to have his way. All this very depressing for me to hear. 'I've got nothing to offer you except my love, please come and live with me, darling,' I said. 'Everything would be OK if only Robert would say that,' he replied. And he's not even that good looking – it's his rabbit teeth.

4 AUGUST

I phoned Robert and asked him of his intentions re Nick. He was surly, said, 'You know Nick,' and that he would give in to whatever he wanted. 'You wouldn't give him up?' I asked – no, he wouldn't give him up.

Nick again at ten to eleven. 'How's Robert?' I asked 'Oh, fine,' he replied. 'Everything OK?' 'Yes, I'm going to live with him.' It wasn't a shock yet I lay on my bed and tried to cry. However, I found strength in George Harrison's 'Breath in, Breath Out' – and you're another person. I do it and a sort of relief washes over me like warm sea – at least it's all over now, surely I can accept it for the best.

10 AUGUST

Went to Covent Garden – on the way met Derek Jarman[53], who's in the same boat. Depressed about his no-go film but better able than I to cope with being alone.

13 AUGUST

Perhaps the hardest part was seeing Nick with Robert. The children were looking at bicycles and I was looking at second-hand books, avoiding seeing Chelita who walked by. I spotted R first, then Nick. My heart leapt. I walked slowly towards them, wondering what I'd say – they were looking at carpeting, setting up home together. I just stood there watching and they walked by without seeing me – I touched Nick, forced a feeble smile and hung my head. I told him I was OK, though it's very apparent I'm not. The children appeared. 'Oh, hello,' said George to Nick. I watched as he looked from him to R and without saying anything saw how he understood the situation. 'Well, goodbye,' said Nick rather curtly. Maybe he was as embarrassed as I.

I walked away in the opposite direction, wondering if I am ever going to get over him. He has dismissed me from his life and I love him more than life itself.

23 AUGUST

Ulla[54] asked if I want to go to a Buddhism meeting tomorrow. I said, 'Why not? I'll try anything once.'

8 o'clock. With Ulla to party. Lots of literary people and a television crew with Peter York[55]. Peter was very sympathetic about the bankruptcy, saying people he knew who had been through it just wanted to sleep all day.

'And read,' I added. He asked me if I'd be interested in writing an article for *Harper's Bazaar*. I said I would but was in a void at the moment.

24 AUGUST

My first meeting of Lotus Sutra Buddhism. Practice chanting. Nam myoho renge kyo, which is sort of hypnotic. Then the Gongyo Gohonzoh. Such weird words. Means: 'I devote myself to the inexpressibly profound and wonderful truth, the law of life, expounded in the Lotus Sutra, which embodies the loftiest teachings of Buddhism.' It acts like a magnet to attract happiness.

29 AUGUST

I was almost happy. I smiled at a young black man and he returned it and a wave – he was pretty and I think I am regaining the power to attract.

1 SEPTEMBER

Met Nadia[56] who heard I've taken up Buddhism. News certainly travels fast.

8 SEPTEMBER

Nick at half past six. What a darling he is – so cheerful and smiling – I fell on his neck and told him I love him and he stayed only a moment and didn't even come indoors.

9 SEPTEMBER

Lunch with Baroness Thyssen[57] and Mrs Branch Clarke[58]. They want my help to dress for a party on the 17th. I drew a quick doodle and off in a taxi to De Paris for the cloth. To Ruskin Flint[59]'s to check with Brian. 'My wife's got an annoying habit of stealing my boyfriends,' he complained. They seem to have a wonderfully open, loving relationship. He had been to New York recently, had sex once, got a sore throat and was convinced he had AIDS.

13 SEPTEMBER

Nick briefly at 6.30. I wept. I had asked Jimmy earlier for some privacy, so when there was a rapping at the front door about twelve thirty I assumed it was him. But it was Vanessa[60], drunk. She was very persistent and insisted on staying the night and we made love – first time with a female for years – since Nikki Waymouth[61], I think. Actually I quite enjoyed it. Left everything up to her, playing hard to get.

23 SEPTEMBER

The drink-driving charge[62] arrived from the police. Saw Nick at 6.30. He says he does miss me and we do suit each other but he won't come back to me while I'm in this state. I said I didn't feel in charge of my own destiny and he surprised me by saying he felt the same way too and he hasn't been well for a while. He really does miss me – we sat on the sofa, my arm around him, my nose buried in his hair at the top of his head.

I went back to a very drunk Jane McKay. 'Will you give me a fuck?' she asked. I ended up staying the night on the sofa.

28 SEPTEMBER

This morning buying a newspaper, a woman smiled at me with capped upper teeth, so white against her real ones on the bottom. 'Ossie, you don't recognise me.' But I did. It was Anita Pallenberg.

30 SEPTEMBER

The longest day, but with unforeseen outcome. Please, god, let Nick come back to me.

Since I last saw him I've had the feeling that all is not well between him and Robert. Tonight he told me he is fed up with him and is going to leave him. He said he loves me more than Robert. My heart is overflowing, I simply couldn't believe it.

3 OCTOBER

Nick phoned – will be here in half an hour. And when he arrived he said he will come and live with me – he has talked it over with Robert who agrees it is for the best. (In fact Robert has suggested they try a separation.)

4 OCTOBER

Nick phoned – we were supposed to meet at one but he had forgotten a previous appointment with Guy[63].

5 OCTOBER

Perhaps the longest day waiting by the telephone.

6 OCTOBER

Nick moved in. We are together again. He has shaved off his moustache. The new moon. A new beginning.

Oh, the joy of Nick in my arms. I had forgotten how wonderfully smooth his skin is.

7 OCTOBER

Horrible letter from Chelita with a veiled blackmail threat[64].

9 OCTOBER

In bed last night Nick said he missed Robert so I was apprehensive he might not come home tonight. I couldn't bear the day without him – and he didn't want me to go with him – I can see I'm being too possessive.

11 OCTOBER

Met Guy in the Black Cap. 'I told you everything would turn out all right for you,' said Robert as we danced embracing each other. Nick was confused and went off to get another pint and there was terrible drama later. Nick said, 'I want to stay with Robert tonight,' but he didn't – a hollow victory for me. I begged and pleaded – almost let him.

12 OCTOBER

Robert has turned up again and Nick is going to stay with him tonight.

18 OCTOBER

We met Robert Mapplethorpe – he asked about clubs where he could find blacks – Nick told him of a new club in Brixton called the Fridge.

1 Nick Balaban.
2 Carla Ames.
3 Chelita Secunda.
4 David Chambers' dog.
5 Alistair Derbyshire.
6 Shakira Caine.
9 Cosmo Fry, son of Jeremy Fry. He married Cosima Vane-Tempest-Stewart, daughter of the Marquis of Londonderry, in November 1982.
8 This is Lady Henrietta Rous.
9 Peter Asher, former pop star, now US-based manager/producer.
10 Eric Clapton.
11 Roger Waters' solo album *The Pros and Cons of Hitch-Hiking*.
12 Carol White, actress.
13 A George Harrison song on which Eric Clapton played guitar.
14 Denis Nilson was later convicted of the murders.
15 Carol Hammond.
16 Sir Frederick Ashton, choreographer at the Royal Ballet School.
17 Antoinette Sibley and Anthony Dowell, principal dancers for the Royal Ballet.
18 Gregory Evans.
19 Tommy Nutter.
20 Craigie Aitchison, Scottish painter.
21 Henrietta Rous.
22 Sabrina Carver, girlfriend of painter Tony Fry.
23 Jimmy Melia.
24 Joe Macdonald, close friend of David Hockney.

25 Jose Fonseca.
26 The Algonquin Hotel, New York.
27 Franz Kafka, Czech Jewish novelist. His work is often filled with proliferating beaurocracy, tyranny, computers and the lies of politicians; and deals primarily with the question of the meaning of existence – his characters progress, or fail to progress, because they are beset with uncertainty. Ossie adopts such terms as 'Kafkaland' and applies them to situations in which he himself feels confronted by an increasingly unpredictable world.
28 Robert is Nick's new lover, for whom he left Ossie.
29 Kay Melia.
30 Brian Clarke, stained-glass artist.
31 Duggie Field, British Pop-Artist.
32 Manolo Blahnik.
33 David Bailey.
34 Anthony McKay, landlord of a property in Redcliffe Road in Fulham into which Ossie moves.
35 Carol Edge, former wife of Terence Stamp.
36 Isobel Strachey, writer and painter.
37 Lady Rose Lambton had by now married Oliver Musker.
38 A friend of Nick's.
39 Lady Pamela Glenconner, née Paget, mother of Catherine and Colin Tennant.
40 To accompany Henrietta Rous to a wedding.
41 Hugh Buchanan and Princess Ann de Rohan.
42 Faye Dunaway, American film-actress.
43 Jane McKay, wife of Andrew McKay of Roxy Music.
44 Jerry Hall and Mick Jagger.
45 Tchaik Chassai.
46 Melissa North.
47 Lucien Freud, British painter; son of Sigmund and father of Bella.
48 Sandra Kamen.
49 Steven Spielberg, American film director and producer.
50 Tessa Kennedy, interior designer.
51 John Dunbar, painter; former husband of Marianne Faithfull.
52 Patrick Procktor.
53 Derek Jarman, outspoken British painter and film-maker whose homosexuality was central to his work.
54 Ulla Larson, Swedish casting director and former model.
55 Peter York, journalist who popularised the term 'Sloane Ranger'.
56 Nadia La Vallée.
57 Baroness Fiona Thyssen, former model; mother of Francesca Thyssen.
58 Wife of Brian Clarke.
59 Ruskin Flint, artist whose studio Brian Clarke lived in at this time.
60 This is an unknown Vanessa. It is neither Vanessa Denza nor Vanessa de Lisle.
61 It is not known when this was.
62 From the night of 26 July when Ossie lied to the police about his name.
63 Guy Burch.
64 Ossie still owed Chelita Secunda rent.

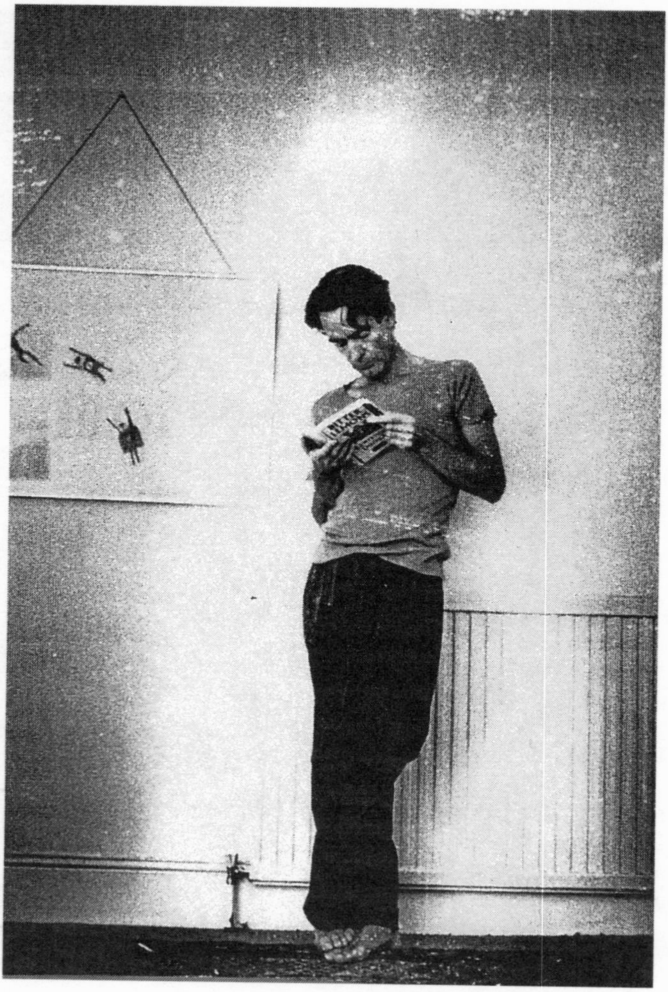

Reading Lawrence Durrell's *Bitter Lemons*, Ossie stands in his flat in Redcliffe Road, 1984.

March 1974

MARCH					
Monday		4	11	18	2
Tuesday		5	12	19	2
Wednesday		6	13	20	2
Thursday		7	14	21	2
Friday	1	8	15	22	2
Saturday	2	9	16	23	3
Sunday	3	10	17	24	3

29 Friday

WEEK 13·88·277 Shark to Paris new collection? no

must repair the frock for Rosemary. Helen Messinger • long rap.
ringing B Miller re Britt Ekland. photo 3rd 4th April
• paid her £15 cash £38 cheque 379994 + 3 yards Celia fabric
£12 cheque Meg Cooper 379995 — Johnny phoned
Marilyn Quinell Mini documents from Alice Pollock.
Fillongley Service Station on the M.1.
Britt Ekland between 2 & 3. adi still in hospital 825
→ no sign of her and it's way ringing now to check on h
past 4. DRAG condition Peter popped Round.
lovely pictures from John Hammond mick Rock re Nino Inc 837
Peter Warner rang — I gave him
a press release for an international
Catherine Tennant re Peter Cyke 12 South Terr. SW7 will phone
£150 cash hopefully Rang Nilfisk will repair vacuum cleaner next
went for a walk to see my house and bought a persian carpet and so
new pens and this beautiful Osmiroid pen which writes too thickly — needs blotting
2-30 Sarah Drummond 36 Winchester St SW1.
3-14 she arrived raved about and quickly split
Cancelled Pam coming to measure up fabric cheek Bloody cheek also
Tony is coming back Monday because he hasn't finished pattern mak
Drinks Marilyn Quinell 6.30 7.0 26 Cheyne Row
Tried Ian Harris not home must phone him about position of sinks
ring Alice in Cumberland 8-0
Felix Garth & Eric dinner 8-oclock Mo too if he can hobble
alcoholic heap "Kiss my back" she said as we left (I took
Chris's bike) I did saying "it's better than kiss my arse I supp
she was a bore telling me how good my dresses are and showing m
someone else's — Sorted out Ian Harris and the kitchen [illegible] Gam
made a delicious dinner and upset Mo, by insulting mick trying to ge
him to understand tomorrow — phoned David — at Douglas Cooper
Tony Page to see it — on the way home I thought I saw a drag Queen in a ta
who turned out to be David Lindo who gave me a sweet present - screwed
a taxi window — Max Gordon boring party — frustration with Garth Yours and mine Peter [illegible]

Above: David Bailey's photograph of Ossie with Chrissy Shrimpton in 1967. She is wearing an Ossie Clark design made from an op art print on silk satin, quilted fabric which Ossie obtained in the United States.
Right: The setting is thought to be the Chelsea Arts Club in 1970. The man wears a scarf in fabric designed by Celia Birtwell. The woman's dress is designed by Ossie and made from a Celia Birtwell print inspired by medieval manuscript illumination.

April 1974

COLOUFUL DAY

APRIL		
Monday	1	8
Tuesday	2	9
Wednesday	3	10
Thursday	4	11
Friday	5	12
Saturday	6	13
Sunday	7	14

8 Monday

WEEK 15-98-267

must get the libruary window secure + change combinatio
Shirley Beaney on the phone re playboy and the Jaggers.
11-0 Ring Mrs Smith she will phone back.
Kieth Milan Louis Bunt Cockfeathers
Paul + Brigitte on the phone coming over later. phoned Merton
12-0 Heather Kirby re photos re Patti Harrison
She came to collect them and seems quite happy Maurice of the phone
returned from Paris — tried to phone David no answer — phoned Mrs Lamb re
phoned Mick Rock he's sending a sheet of contacts in the post
Gregory off to felicity to collect money sent him to Louis Bunt to get fe
gave him £20 note — Paid £60 to Tony £42 to Kathleen Marilyn Chi
3.0. Merton to see the Hazan movie Stitching Weekend Telegraph M de P
Johnny on telephone here 500 francs cheque going to Paris tomorrow
Spoke to Kieth Milan he's coming thursday. £1 for stamps
4-0 Claudia Naydler measured her — Sent mo of
express tax demand from postoffice — Breda here sewing on
David Still not home Spoke with Tony Howard. £1 for hook & eye to
Spoke with Nikkie Weymouth ring later — she's going to ceylon
shoulders wednesday tea — Mrs Smith phoned is coming thursday
£16-48 for Coq feathers — mustn't forget Mikslava / or Oxana
trying for the cash from Christa Peters re Britt Ekland cancelled
Celia at home with a streaming cold — Ami Petersburg press. Spoke to
DAVID SECRETLY IN LONDON TO SEE HIS MOVIE —
6-0 Monday Britt Ekland re white three piece
after Merton at Robuses — vib celia. What Merton thought of
phoned put off till later Nothing offensive and nothing
Must Ring Tony Howard. interest with one exception —
Sinister Celia and Peter Hazan // Merton wants meeting with W
Bahamas accounts — soon as poss — ring tony then Radley
terrific vib with Merton £2 taxis phoned Tony — Merton thinks
go after Harrison Money talking with Celia on the phone to Mo
She rang up spend £85 on booze about — Quorum show tonight
Gregory Score half a Gee don't talk about Gas leaks to me have realized
David was here all the time talking with Mo seed of doubt but NO! I know W

paid Ossi £5 expenses

he thinks Mrs Bunt, needs fucking with a swastika and i think Claudia needs to loose her moustashe

THINKS MINSENSATIVE

Enjoyable night realise 3/4 had gone by

	6	13	20	27
	7	14	21	28
1	8	15	22	29
2	9	16	23	30
3	10	17	24	31
4	11	18	25	
5	12	19	26	

1974 April

13 Saturday

Easter Eve SR 0610 ☼ SS 1953 WEEK 15·103-262

children slept well and woke early Gish though we thought it
y in fact we made breakfast at 10to10 SILENCE SILENCE
Breakfast table like the reading room of a Libruary everyone grumpy
ORGE HAS GOT A SORE EAR Celia looking after
SHING FISHING FISHING FISHING him
work We, Albert Nicholetta and I went fishing on the lake in
we caught nowt be it was very enjoyable and gave us a
ific appetite for lunch which was delicious and I eat like mad.
much wine — after a futile search for fish at the wrong time of
+ Rowing Swans swimming + a neurotic duck swimming
in circles to decoy us from its nest which we really were
interested in VERY EVER SO COLD on the lake
between Tchicke and Annette Bradshaw
Thiacke
I slept through a 1936 Gary Cooper movie I really wanted to see
at last the sun is shining divinely here hoping tomorrow it will carry
CROQUET ON THE LAWN FOOTBALL
TER TEA AND ART TALK WITH LINDY
NSHINE DEVINE SUNSHINE DEVINE
and warm now the children are eating scrambled eggs Albert has bathed
ge is a little more difficult because of his ear however this fresh country
shoved knock them both out. Celia in her rollers
ert is behaving wonderfully so obedient went to bed before 8 after doing
rounds biding everyone goodnite so I had a cold bath washed my
and Celia is taking a well earned rest
TCHIE dinner Kasmin talking nonsense. Lindi intrigued
ell over twice playing Freda — Sheridan won twice — Conversation about
ail Castration — Vodka lemon/orange juice
you got him warmed up, he'd break the sound barrier
ger Ryger I found myself shuffling him backwards
ding the fridge — cold Turkey and chocolate cake.
next to the horrid Linda couldn't get a word in between
s and Lindi both talking crap — later saw him on the floor
ssaging Annette — paralytic drunk

April 1974

APRIL			
Monday	1	8	15
Tuesday	2	9	16
Wednesday	3	10	17
Thursday	4	11	18
Friday	5	12	19
Saturday	6	13	20
Sunday	7	14	21

14 Sunday

WEEK 15·104-261 **Easter Sunday** CLEAR BLUE SKY

wonderful walk we saw 46 dead birds on beachead wi
and two dead stoats very strange beautiful trees and flower
a water garden Albert and Nicolette eat a great big lunch
Linda Gave everyone a present for Easter the children behaving
OPEN DAY AT THE HOUSE well – George a bit b
but Albert walked with us all the way around walk – saw amazin
plants and flowers – a beautiful yellow lily Gigantic and a kind
Rhododendron with red flowers like plastic CROQUET O
THE LAWN lovely noise it makes – beautiful perfect da
Albert was devine at lunch sat next to him and Linda
Kasmin in Tennis rig Anyone for Tennis – how didn't he have a h
Toby did Too much whisky ITS SUCH A PERFECT DAY
ANACONDA CLARK Sleeping off a great big lunch.
FISHING FISHING FISHING FISHING
I fell asleep after tea really tired after fishing for Albert and a
audience of day trippers – was lovely being patient – Celia N
Tchick and Anne who caught one also afterwards we went to look at the
Sat next to Gilles at dinner and talked of Paris Coco Channel
his father very nice and dummey – some boring Irish labour
We had the remains of the Turkey we stole for dinner and a t
the Chocolate cake – Linda and Sheridan are devine afterwards we
stayed in the dining room whilst the women powdered their noses
Celia bitched me to Nicolette – we were left talking politics (Kas on
the Israeli war again) Gilles and I had a homosexual conversation
and he promised to give me an amber RING the we played Cards
Canasta Cheat Chase the lady and Sevens – not a murmur fr
the babes – not a very nice dinner – I must have put on wieght
my purple suit is too tight for me – but goody because I must
put on wieght – Also in 5 minutes I had to dress and
be at the dining room between Gilles and Nicolette – so that h
nice – he had a perfect Edwardian upbringing served army time in Ind
had a scene with an indian tank driver etc etc. Met Chanel Sciaparelli
Paris Parties

7 magpies
blackbirds
Ravens
stoats
seagull
chiack

ook
photographs

n found
perfect
ne egg
len from
nest and
ll warm

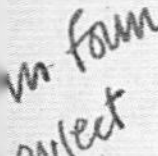

ns cut sent
the
insight
he fish
littles
ckie were
Chanssies
home
ignwent
Gon Hands
Georgy played a talcum powder trick on Mo

	6	13	20	27
	7	14	21	28
1	8	15	22	29
2	9	16	23	30
3	10	17	24	31
4	11	18	25	
5	12	19	26	

1974 April

15

Monday

SUNSHINE

Easter Monday Bank holiday, England, Ireland & Wales WEEK 16-105-260

n or Quater to Twelve" that's real Irish said the maid
d and washed Albert's hair – really overslept – So missed out the
to bath in. Decided with Nicolette it has really been a laws
trip ALICE IN WONDERLAND Nicolette is really a nose frick,
inda and C° Scrabbling on the gravel Sheridan asleep no sign of lunch
iga Guiness to lunch – minus her bustle (I can see now why she
ups wears one) very affected under a Sun shade – very
ashed into her roll-on and brassiere – lunch rushed by Albert
vine and beautiful George not so well behaved – squirming on Celia's
banging a fork – quickly packed tipped the maid and butler
goodbye and Split to the airport to be searched and tried to read
EWIS book Giles e Nickerleg suddenly 6-15 motorway George/Giles
D I SPENT IT WITH YOU asleep in the back of Celia's fiat
kache bathed Celia took Giles to Jermyn St and Came back with Nicolette
pies school grown bean plants 2 inches taller watercress in an eggshell
mistaken for Elton John Several times on Bricks lane' Mo yesterday hissing.

speak with La Weymouth Trying to get Tony Howard.
FIRST LINDEN TREE IS GREEN ALREADY
– 35 back to London LONDON LONDON
w Submarine on television Percy and Blanche happy to see
Percy doing his catching silver paper trick – Spoke with Mo
Gregory re. Patti Harrison Spoke with Kathleen's son on telephone
borrowed original one and her rust thing \ coming tomorrow
produced the biggest chocolate Easter egg with Gold paper
rown Satin and a chocolate bunny Rabbit for Albert the egg is for herself
is terrace – Mo still uptight £60 blown on Charlie – Spoke with David in
– he has drawn divine Jaque with green eyes – Gregory lonely
with Getty Weymouth Jagger Maxim McEnery Rose is putting on her
ng shoes Yours or mine / Talking With PATTIE 8 Stone 11 lbs
5 lbs on

Model 'Gala' wears a crêpe dress designed by Ossie for Radley, 1973.

Right and below: The Chelsea Town Hall in 1971. In the photograph below Amanda Lear wears a cream chiffon, wrap-around dress, printed in charcoal and pale pink.

AY					
onday		6	13	20	27
esday		7	14	21	28
ednesday	1	8	15	22	29
ursday	2	9	16	23	30
iday	3	10	17	24	31
iturday	4	11	18	25	
inday	5	12	19	26	

everything crosses today
on my biograph

1974 April

CHICARGO HOT DAY

WEEK 18·119-246

29 Monday

king Paul Mc'cartney's father-in-law. Today is bad for discussions
Paul woke me at 10 oclock and again and again I dont know whats
next. Spoke with Peter Brown - Gary comes in tonight will bring my
forgotten stuff. Tony Howard phoned from London is coming Wednesday.
I'm looking forward to it Beautiful day again Sunshine and a Breeze.
Ben Shaw meeting 1-oclock. 86% riding through the park.
everyone in N.Y. is a philosopher — especially last nights taxi driv
221 4252 Ben Shaw in N.Y. will ring wednesday
TOO HOT TOO HOT TOO HOT 86 TOO HOT 86 degrees in
C.B.S. May is Monument Month Don Ellis in a room full of gold
discs and photographs Glitter party in L.A. 500 beautiful girls
who came out wearing virtually nothing plenty of exposure AHMET
henry called driving round manhatten very hot
Bloomingdales Nice Sunglasses underwear Calling Colette busy again Peter Brown
Mr Ertigun phoned 484 8133 going to ring back tomorrow maybe MIAM
alet been and gone Mrs Weymouth 419 will leave her a note
the regency Gary 89% in Manhatten to the airport 5.45 T.W.A. ambassad
Chicargo? AM I REALLY FLYING HIGH OVER AMERICA servi
doing biocharts high over the clouds dropped your Zig
cool it on those joints honey "the captains on his way down here and
uste you one we reach Chicargo Pat air hostess T.W.A.
suddenly 6·30 chicargo time ASHA PUNGHI LIES LIES LIES
ow we are inside pauls brain up over a lake very unreal devine deja vu I've be
toward Mendlesohn hes a great lo young in head TOO ALCHOL Much
GLITTER I think Chicargo is the heart of America I think it must
is the centre of America I've decided DANA GILLESPI ANDY WARHOL
this is the first autograph to be written in the
famous memoirs of my friend "the wizard of oz".
SS OR IS IT the coffee
achine dispressed
but to for good she's in there
e are in a mist. I'm 6 hours beyond reality already
more magic white powder infact some one
ette Alan stroh
3030 I could write I'd just

fire has gi my mother posed at MGM Studio – Sounds like an insurance job to m Tony

May 1974

cuban breakfast

Full Moon

missed a John Kloss fashion Show

MAY				
Monday	6	13	20	27
Tuesday	7	14	21	28
Wednesday	1 8	15	22	29
Thursday	2 9	16	23	30
Friday	3 10	17	24	31
Saturday	4 11	18	25	
Sunday	5 12	19	26	

WEEK 19·126-239 ○ **Bank holiday, Scotland**

on the full moon we fuck Tiffanies please

Call ~~2-0~~ 1-30 Ben Shaw SALEMADERSALEMADER

Eric phoned going away to Bermuda Gloria phoned speaking with M.B. Back

then to Regency to see Tony eating his breakfast phoned Ben Shaw postponed

Returned the ~~money~~ but didn't get my salamandre Regency Tony Marek Mickey Glori

Sandra MU3 4980 Called. Shopping more sunglasses and Earthshoes

Jamiela coming to meet here looked up at Bloomingdales Bangles for Celia from Tiffan

miss phoned 11 past 5 54% Larissa spoke with Cofrano

Vodka lemon juice fix the pusher Call heroin hot line Washing ma

FOR YOU Mickey Finn almost materialised driving morning feeling

horoscope OBLITERATED MICKEY GEMINI FACES Blazing Saddles I OWE TONY $100 LOVE Tony howard sandy outside

all space nietheri! I'm sorry mickey missed Peter M

Drag music to the folks whores Fuck it I owe Tony £40 or $100 I couldn't bear looking at it 117lbs today.

this was Mickey Finn's signiture and also a mess Joy Samara comme

HOT DOGS Squatting times or fast Tony back 122

my father he was a sinner Just got into bed and @ TONY howard

Nikki on the phone demanding me to go

wearing the same suit again ossie what are you talking about I dont even know wher

Straight skins grass roll Mickey keep back on ice on the telephone

Right now I'd like to close my eyes and wake up in los angelis Tony

Tony is Mad about Devorah – Putting my fur coat on inside out

~~Jagger Party~~ maybe: another Glitter Party Club Caballero

2045 Air India 102 JFK 45 E 58th St 6-83

boring after in the St regis Pathetic Hookers Was Summoned to h

presence indeed lost Tony and Mickey and Bowie and Marek Sandra Gone Mick

said "Who's Gerry Glitter I just couldn't cope. O.C. HAS 4 NOSTRILS +

MARC CALLED HIM DOZEY – SO THERE! he's got a fucking nerve if I've got 4 he's got 20

and he oozed into my ears much longer than I oozed into his ONAMATAPOEIA

words which sound what they mean It sunk in at school but I must look it up in the dictio

palindrome ROTOR embire Cinema 42nd Street finished though and coul

get in so we went to the Stage Deli, pastrami and I saw the full m

afterward Boring 82 and I fell asleep in the car collected

my stuff from Tony's Hotel Lowel Almost left it in a taxi

I got you babe

make

MIRR
MPA

A scene staged by Ossie on 7 September 1967, then in his 'Bonnie and Clyde period', just off the Fulham Road. At the left, model 'Kellie' is wearing 'Tour d'Argent', a green Giselle silk, long Grecian dress. The models came from the English Boy model agency whose offices were behind the Quorum shop. Standing to Kellie's left is Sir Mark Palmer, co-founder of English Boy.

Above: Flowers in many colours on cream chiffon for a wrap-around dress designed by Ossie, 1972.
Left: Soft, cream chiffon, full-length dress with moss crêpe neck in Celia Birtwell's 'Floating Daisy' fabric, 1968.
Right: Model Karrianne Jagger wears a dress in white silk georgette fabric with Celia Birtwell's 'Lapis Lazuli' print. The fabric was 'pigment printed', a process that created a crisper texture to the cloth.

March—April 1980

woke about seven according to nicks watch. I'm beginning to really hate the Greeks - always trying to fiddle - no eggs no bread for a hour so home to wake everyone and make tea. the ska music that Jimmy lent us now always remind me of this holiday!

slept heavily on valium woke groggy at eight to grey skies and rain oh dear what a drag. we had scrambled eggs for breakfast and couldn't get through to Celia on the phone so we have decided to go to Rhodos on the ten thirty

woke before seven slept ... tranquillisers the Sun's back but a lot of cloud at 9.16 again its complet... and Thunder. I wish it ... storm then maybe the s... retur...

31 Monday

Week No. 14 ○ 15.14

sent Albert off for the bread nick cont. his drawing A reported veg for sale so we rushed off to buy eggs toms cucumber lettuce pots spring onion and more bread so at least we have got breakfast for a few days I'm so pleased with the wild flowers I picked the first day here so beautiful how they come to life with the first sun we changed money phoned chelita the cats are O.K. she fine I'm glad I spoke to her she loves nicks painting Albert ratty 'cos I couldn't get through to Celia we celebrated with a drink coffee fix coke and bought post cards to sent to Alistair and candida and on to the rocks leaving nick to finish his courtyard drawing and post cards. I plunged into the sea again nick joined us to sun then home to lunch boiled eggs cheese and salade was fun to prepare and quickly ate then we went to mary's house to sun bathe and nick began another drawing I slept and woke cold we rushed off to phone celia but only got the hired help it cost 11 dracs to say I'd call tomorrow the noise on the phones here is exactly like Ipcress file we bought tin foil to bake pots mustn't forget the cat piss in the little room the post cards to Ben Celia molly C.Ltd chelita etc and a whole salami for dinner and went to mary house for hot bath Dave Gilmore came by and invited us over The holiday has really taken off we saw the full moon from his roof as we kissed Alice 'nite and stayed to dinner vegetarian pie and wonderful electronic toys what a divine house and how quickly they are done it the Kukladia looks as though it was always there I helped design Alices wardrobe as we smoked delicious lebanese hash. Be[ing] a millionaire now they had forgotten it was there and the house must have cost a packet. The wall is still the no one selling album in America and he has been here since March 1st. Ginger told me they have been out of England for more than a year and will live in house six miles from George Harrison found by Perry Press of Perods in ...

08.00 09.00 10.00 11.00 12.00 13.00 14.00 15.00 16.00 17.00 18.00

Memoranda

1 Tuesday

it was quite nice the journey took a hour and a half and when we got there we wandered around the market and bought mincemeat and stolichnya which is very cheap we ate lamb for lunch and then looked around the battlements and old city - the last bus back is at three so we had to rush just enough time to pee in a local cottage and buy George a sheath knife for 100 dracmas

one the otherhand the journey back was a nightmare a fight to get on and full to the brim with horride gold toothed greeks who crossed themselves each time we passed a church or a cemetry and there equally nasty childing one distroying carnations another occupying a seat he wasn't even sat in while weary pack laden hikers and old lady german tourists had to stand - George with his charm squashed next to two german girls I stood with Albert and immeadiately opened two windows - as they were quickly shut I asked nick standing two rows in front to open the ones near him - one quickly got slammed shut by the conductor so I tapped his shoulder and pointed at Albert he opened it an inch - I tapped again and the gentle breeze of spring blew in - yesterday I counted three sweaters on a young manuel worker and it was really hot the last of March Back at the studio we had a snack and a nap then the children with such enthusiasm climbed through the window to collect and saw up olive branches to light a fire how the dry leaves crackle and how warm we all are

nick is drawing Albert and George a view of today's journey bob marley on the tape deck hot water for us all to bathe George and I are going over to the museum for more wood. "isn't it fun" said nick as he stepped into the too hot bath and it is one could so easily get used to this primative way of life I'm sure - meanwhile somebody must go to get the coke because I'm longing for another vodka - "stick your bum in" "I'll boil my balls off" he replied - George has got pencils from Harrods with his name on them and cigarette papers are illegal in Gr...

2 Wednesday

we found two books on medi... and european flowers which I ... and then picked an enormou... in a down pour for mary and ... arrival - the children helped ... all got soaked - so we changed and went to the museum, George found a vase for the flowers ... a fire for thier arrival. and to... wood to light a fire in the stud... Alberts shoes - it rained inter... all day but somehow it doesn't and otherwise I would never h... coved the names of all those ... flowers - lunch was ham bre... tomatoes and a siesta - Al... crashed out and dear nick fe... so off we went again to light welcome fire we found Ginger soup a girl from England calle... with a boy called desmond with news that mary isn't coming she has the flu and melis wi... in two hours - Dave had gone to ... Lea is here on her way to Patm... Luigi with girl friend we cho... Andoni was Bill clay's teleph... age 14 - they arrived just ... were leaving clutching a fe... logs for the fire we stayed ... come: then home where n... done a beautiful drawing asleep then I discovered the on... drac note gone so back to the ... where I found it and melis w... message from Celia nice we ... for take away chicken and ... dinner - nick came too I told ... that the house we first stayed ... an olympic villa - hers too she had spent nine summers ... is very sad about that - but ... is so lucky the museum is a house (Luigi had made a st... the A.A. and says it really is special) and it seems to c... life when full of people we all sat around the very ... and I longed for a joint which was refused - The children ... beautifully and brought in ... dry. - we talked of the far... fairy stories of drugs of easter and plans to ... Desmond had met Aleist...

day over
Alistair went to china 5 days ago
Waterloo Stn
928 5100
April 1980
back to work

up at 10 to 7 breakfast and quickly to white knight laundry for a white shirt for nicks court appearance to the butcher and called on Pam e Sid who weren't home now at chelitas with cat food. arranged to pick up chessie order loin of Pig for friday

slept till 8.30
Jims phone cut off
1st shopping trip in Harlesden

14 Monday

k No. 16 Woke early up at seven
fasted and bathed got ?nny up
the bank where he cashed mariannes
o hrs. i gave him two weeks in Advance
and
or 90 gave 10 to nick its a beautiful
I walked into the park where I now write
lected the crisallis and pills from Al
d news at work re my car ready 3.30
t the morning making trousers
yself blue a practice for the silk
tch the David chambers jacket
have come out very nice and
they are blue I phoned nadia
ook lunch with Vanderberg
hats O.K. I've arranged to meet
n wednesday but what a night
they have laid on me – model
g – a shoot tomorrow etc.
total confusion I phoned marie
hose three models Scarlette a
ead lily I've used before and
blonde called Deborah hope
ent. goofed Ilkhoff the Ger
clients came in and lily
ed for them she's too short
eter but she seemed absolutely
me to me
anola and met his sister
m with marianne she has
songs and divine hash
ng singing with Joe on guitar
as dissapeared. and the car
ady and waiting in Egham hi
sat in a train at Stains Station
se delayed through a suiside
gham Stn so phoned Molly
came to collect me and worried
was one of her students maybe
my lovely mini back
nick at Jims so I drove to the
for the car documents for
ordeal tomorrow and
to make dinner – I phoned
lita earlier and arranged to
her up tomorrow morning
has cost £157-78 to repair
emoranda but I dont care
Cecil Beatons will in the news
a Single Red Rose for Garbo

15 Tuesday

03.46

Loretta Shapiro 2 oclock cancelled
which I did after collecting a new parking permit
Colin Thomas
26 Searla St.
nick's case was adjourned till 10th of June "day after your birthday"
Kathleen came to do all the ironing
popped into Locks.
at chessie later we had a joint with emma and Roy both high on heroin
Berwick Street
Grey mullet
THE DAY OF PHOTOGRAPHING GIRLS
Chessie doing wonderful high kicks
Lily looking like cleopatra and twirling Scarlet in red shoes 25 rolls of film replacing the white the vodka. Roy flustering and signing all the chits. the fat make up artiste the little queenie french hairdresser
The devil is a woman dress could have been made for deborah
Johnnie dewe mathews came to dinner has seen patrick returned from china and had been to a nigel Weymouth opening saw the crowd
Marianne falling over chelita
we went to see Ash who had nothing so we went to see Ben John Porter and ex wife who cooked a trout Marianne had been to dinner with the Von Furstenberg man and millermundi re the movie
Watched television first time for ages the acadami awards
PHOTOGRAPHING GIRLS IS TIRING
my head banging in the car on the way home my cough racking
a real drag greek franks and bed
and nicola saying you must see a doctor you must see a doctor

16 Wednesday

In work not feeling so good so I've phoned Patrick woodcock and I'm trying desperately to get Desr the homipathic doctor phoned sid
21 Albion St Dr Trevor Smith
he went on and on o[?]sid bout hom
spoke to Albert pintwell hot water problem concerned about celias return
Chelita 12.30 I collected her and she dropped in in hans Crescent
lunch cancelled by secretary at 12
1 oclock lunch with Vandenberg
I told her I want to speak to him before he goes to Dusseldorf so I rang
Colin Thomas and arranged to see the photographs at 50 Hans Cre
rang Jenny little and arranging to see her tomorrow
chessie came in with steve stran with very wierd contact lenses in
I chose the pictures at 50 hans cresent Vanderburg was there and the pictures are divine
nadia and suami for a joint
Patrick Woodcock 4.15 who gave me four kinds of medication sai I dont have a stomache ulser or need to see a specialist then back to the office and on to ba and suntan at chelita's then back to work where I finish the blue trousers with a red zip and they are divine so I rushed off to Pam – Sid at work the have got thier shop now and showed me the plans and her garden coming to life
saw carla had a glass of w
collected the washed track su
home to a boring tele and de
dinner veal and vegetables

Celia said Rachael Welsh loved the dress Ms Cain wore to the academy awards and she wants another two

woke 8 30 ish groggy but no hangover
beautiful Sunshine day

May 1980

So I lay in the garden for a while

Band 14th Mercury and Uranus badly aspected
79°/o Farienheit Hot Day
Got up richish divine again so after
coffee and a bath operation to get
brown legs in the sunshine

14th Venus and Jupiter good a
up at seven thirty Sammy tol
horrid Kitty. had yesterday
black bird another brilliant

12 Monday

reakfast for the deli in Elgin Cres

Week No. 20 then we went to see Carla
nd smoked a couple of joints she's
ut of work now but in good spirits
08.00 hrs.
uckie sleeping after a night on the mini cab
ot to work before midday a new cutter
elping tony – the back converted into
very hot stockroom Richard wasn't
09.00
ere but the repeat slip made – Mrs
arker talking about American express
o Ruth. I made a long discriptive entry
ito my other diary – and may chelitas
10.00 red waistcoat more comfortable
ft Mariannes jacket to be lined by Rich
nd went to Warwick gardens to take
e wonderful sunshine the australian
oy is painting marie helvin as cleo
11.00
atra a catalogue of Alma Tadama
recognised her breasts – he's getting
grand from Bailey then we drove to
ampstead a pint of largre and lime
12.00 there at 4 oclock to view the
ampstead crocodile talked to Peter
avies on the phone and his son in the
flesh its next to Woolworth by the
orge IV in the high St. Hogben & Ruth
13.00
e shall put a blow up in the window
nd my name on it / then we drove to
ffridges for a piece of very expensive
alibut we went to chelita and there
14.00
as some talk of going to a movie
ut nothing came of it – instead we just
opped in front of the telly and later
15.00 on & made dinner with a
ottle of white wine: it was delicious
atch 22 was on the T.V. and a
program about Roche valium and
16.00 a poor shmuck whose lost
everything. Earlier I got so excited
writing in my other secret diary
had to go to the loo to masterbate. I
17.00
shall write more in the same vien
after Joe Orton – the thing is that
he truth comes out better and is
often funny as well as ironic
18.00

Memoranda at Mariannes party
Ben was very angry with me about
The Hockney pictures which have
surfaced again – We shall take down
The Doggie field and hang it in
chelitas living Room

13 Tuesday

a postcard from Albert in Belgium – one
for Sam and one at work for me and nick

I stayed in the sun till the laundryman
came £25.50p then quickly dressed in shorts
and to the Elgin Cres deli for breakfast
and Kingsley for meat for the cats which
I dropped in at chelitas just about
to sun herself in the garden Nick has
gone to the clap clinic and now at work
Richard is making camiknickers after
putting in Mariannes jacket lining.
Hogben asked me to design some Ascot
dresses. I told him I don't work like that and
went off to chelitas garden to sun before
he thought up any more bright ideas
Actually I stopped off to see Nadia and
Swami for a couple of joints He is very
down – with a septic foot from roller
skating – says he feels trapped in
England wants to open a restaurant
Chelita was in her garden with Richard
and a very pale blonde boy she made a tea
and more hash Richard provided a whisky
and I ended up on the sofa feeling very
wierd indeed I must not smoke so much
I couldn't even lay in the hot sunshine
nick arrived with the news that hes
got non specific urithitis. Chelita bathed
and Richard overdid her face but she
was very pleased and was going to see
a pop group with Kevin Whitney We
went to eat a hamberger and I left my
dorothy bag in the restaurant stupidly.
we drove to the ICA. to see a gay movie
but it wasn't on tonight so after a
quick Pushkin walk in St James Parks
we drove to the Screen on the Hill to
see first, Marianne in Broken English
Three songs with her mooning round
on top of multi layer images and the
"Tempest" of Derek Jarmin: to me a
Fat Queens Dream some nice visual
images but so many candles tinsle.
flowers and Yolande Sonabend design
just doesn't make it we stopped off to
see Carla on the way back. she was drunk
but made me tea and carried on cooking
complaining she misses Alice and the
boys at flip

I suppose the high spot of Mr Fish's party
was bubbles and Diana Dors sat talking
at the same table. Also when I walked
to mike with a joint he said "there
are three policemen here" he passed
it on to Jane Churchill who made a
fuss of Pushkin saying / this is
... must be able

14 Wednesday

● 12.00

So odd to be at work at 9.30 yest
cami knicker is divine Kate Fran
here at ten o'clock and lau-ri-
I phoned peter Ruth and Hogben ha
stocking hampstead crocodile s
the camiknicker is divine on Aut
now quickly a french knicker and a
slip to design we managed to get news
from manchester (day of Action T.U.C.)
while eating a greasy breakfast and I
some fresh fish for supper. then we we
chelita to sunbathe in her garden –
Richards painting whilst drinking
and then chelitas mother Connie d
came by while I was reading a
erotic book written from the woman
that Chelita had lent me written b
at four oclock we all drove back to fr
and connie tried on clothes for about
and a half. "Good P.R. on mummy" s
who rumaged through my sample
found three things to try on at h
Ruth tried on the french knicker Rich
managed to get wrong but not serio
smoked we went home shopping o
over tea in Warwick gdns Chelita
over a legal document from hugh
father who is offering £15000 for her
of the mewshouse her father left the
watched Layna Lovitch on T.V. and I
luxurious long bath and delicious h
baked with lemon and Black pepper
and mushrooms fu had been maki
walking trumpet noises all day
I Rang Albert back from school
liked the first world war Hill 60 a
best! Rang Brit Ekland to get Chelit
waxed – I dressed in my new blue
I'd just sewn buttons on to wear
braces and we went to Mariannes
was in a very peculiar mood pret
to be sick on the After 8 dinner w
we brought when really she must h
at the other a lot of people there i
porter and a man from the m
eating American hot pizzas: Ir
it is thier wedding aniverser
we smoked the end of C's hash
Tony Secunda arrived thier
meeting for years his childr
5 and 3½ from his second ma
I gave him a lift home tea a
and bed at one

... Jane is not long for This World

Ossie at Quorum Studio to meet Sonia Rykiel in 1969. One of his snakeskin jackets hangs behind him.

Above: Painting from one of Ossie's numerous sketchbooks.
Right: Dress designed by Ossie in 1971 and made up in silk crêpe de chine. Celia's print, with its bold chevrons, is in charcoal, pink, rose and blue.

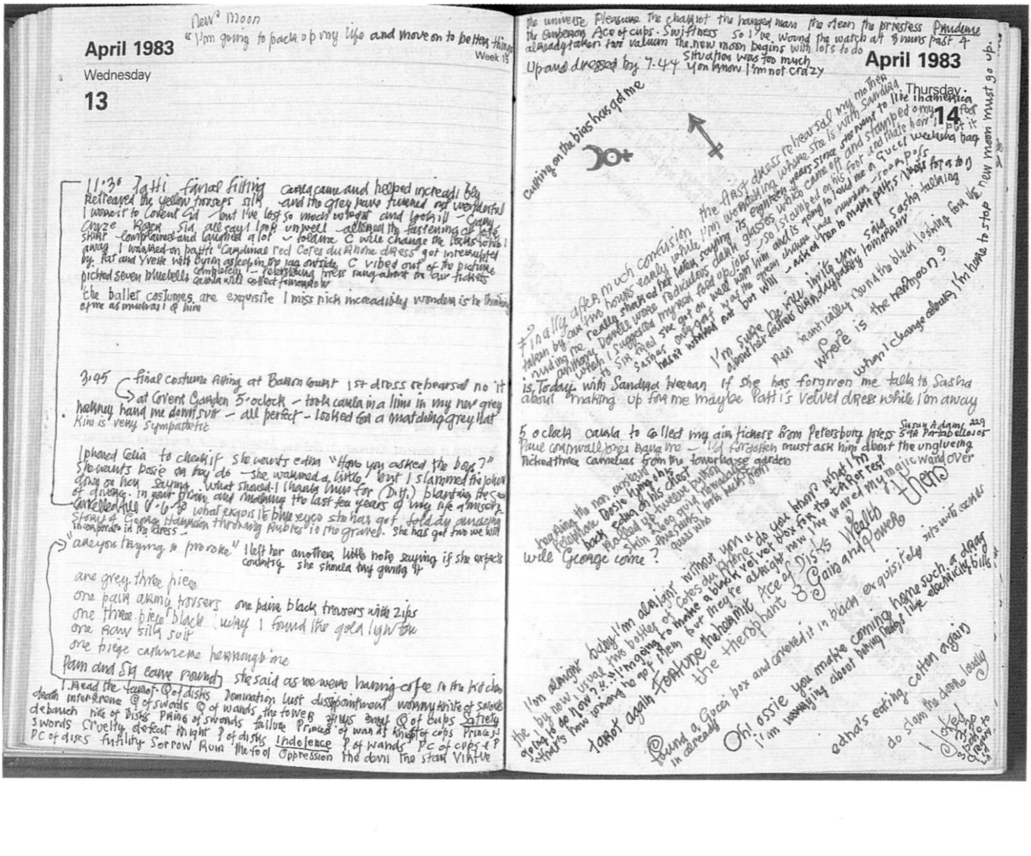

April 1983
Week 15
Wednesday
13

New Moon
"I'm going to pack up my life and move on to better things"

11.30 Patti final fitting

the ballet costumes are exquisite

3.45 Final costume fitting at Barons Court 1st dress rehearsal
at Covent Garden 5 o'clock

Kim is very sympathetic

I phoned Celia to check if she wants

"are you trying to provoke"

one grey three piece
one pair army trousers one pair black trousers with zips
one three piece black
one raw silk suit
one beige cashmere herringbone
Pam and Sid came round

April 1983
Thursday
14

the universe Pleasure the chariot the hanged man the Aeon the priestess Prudence
Ace of cups. Swiftness
Up and dressed by 7.44
you know I'm not crazy

Cutting on the bias has got me

where is the new moon?

5 o'clock carla to collect my air tickets from Petersburg press

will George come?

I'm alright baby I'm alright without you

tarot again Fortune the hermit Ace of Disks Wealth

Found a Gucci box and covered it in black exquisitely

Oh! Ossie you maybe coming home such a drag

edna's eating cotton again

do slam the door loudly

April 1983

Wednesday

27

...p
...sain
...rela waldela gone anthem...
...autiful sunshine day
Phone Shatung Cameo answer...
— david was heavy cheerful at breakfast pheme...
...noned Carola who follow me nicke has mended
...ne box The copelating dogs in the bushes toy
...what a freelancing fight arose "i am very angry she...
...art the suit is costing her $1275 and she insists on having
...man to the alteration — and i must admit it needs re doing
...nicke david chambers did i dont know — her house is fabulous — coll...
...alique Le Salle tiffany panoramic view. lunches beyond belief
...carola is staying with her — I sat waiting this as I wait to be collected
...Generally this Hotel — the taxi here costs $11 and David Graves again to the
...leaving out foramed volvo — drum is cooking supper tonight she abandoned...
...leaving — I had to sneak back the white shoes I paid $120 to Gregory for left...
...anniver... anthony his very gay friend gave david a haircut told me of his plans to
...Peter and the frame Emperor extremes for the studio people no crash helm...
5 o'clock post party with champagne last look at that woman he said that is Rita...
...etlef is driving me we are almost ... $358 8 une et A...
...o SL in evac I rang nina her long red hair in a plait " I said as I got out of the car
...heaven with two sitting tonights & likeyou Detlef I commented to him on the telephone
...in Detlef I was in the other day " said Richard grumpy after he'd moved out with Jenny
...old Detlef of bad stewarts graffiti in 125 Ladbroke Grove I dont know ev...
I saw some scarlet flowers 6 45 now talking with Richard
...ell pauleny

James I wrote on a card for the one who finally painted the photo of the
...and is heaven in the leopard and leather quite refused to take it off — he's strai...
...moon tonight
been running around all day and I've got diape...
...is quite niere blonde and extremely desirable
...shall I take Ernst I wonder
we got pretty ripped last...
...lef or shall I take Bin...
...en just swam in the po...
...full moon
...I shenoo...
...fond ca...

r only

Detlef called up

illing
ashed his car

the way home

were prepared for Gregory and said

above anything and he thinks we will be

great friends

spot from davids embassy picture

almost seven ian here showing david his canvases - an old woman two

homo erotic boys and anne - its the month that really difficult said D.H.

its hard to get him to keep it still said ian

Shaindy Fenton is a heaven

burger 817 429 0161 fort

worth Texas her son is

17 with 28" waist 46

deliver on the dot

said Paul

actually

friendl

do you finally think we have lift off

no! Just a bloody hangover and a very Ratty.

p very early - jetlag - some notes - 5 mil val - only six left - zon

I just have a feeling everything is going

alright

8.15 - first up - grey day pool 10% down - made coffee shivering

Saw the Poster for langans brasserie on the way to pay

cash shaigias cheque - In rain trip with sorely

ugk surfaced - smelt the coffee - we lit the fire - David appeared

Richard on the telephone suggesting I make designs for a Broadw

Sh

emed cheerful but didn't say much till ian phoned got

bout extentions with mark - I reading L.A times not a peep fro

e miracle maid arrived when she

May 1983

Wednesday

11

Bring mo at 8.15

Sandra cabbage white buttery

Bring Mark Burns

drove the children to school collected [illegible]

dentist Sandra pick up at the bank no that was yes

take some coffee to Sahara said Michael

phoned the Byam Shaw got him who told me

I'm trembling as I wait

Nick is probably at Robert's I'm so nervous I went off with

At last a meeting with Nicholas Satan in his leather jacket

keys to the [illegible] and dressed like so filled with trepidation and very

and earphones listening to David Bowie the bus and into a taxi

arrived at the Cock late because of the key jumped off the bus

1.43 maybe at first I thought he wasn't going to come / climb a large Bl[illegible]

and gave up at two o'clock - but walking toward this school there he was rushing

me we embraced and I taped the conversation / tell me all about your trip

so cheerful and excited and full of questions - lets walk round the block

my heart pounding - I told him about the hair and he told me about Chelita and the soc[illegible]

[illegible]ciality which won't help matters "Have you forgiven me?" I asked "I suppose so" he

I paid him a month's rent but has spent most of his time with Robert "occasionally"

answered to my question "have you been letting him fuck you" and I shall have to

"He won't like that" he said He's rehearsing tonight has got a job in God[illegible]

what about Robert I've grown quite fond of him or I get on quite well with him

the bomb I kissed him and held hands he smiled a lot and only occasionally

huge bloody relief he was reluctant to look me in the eye but did eventually and smiled

pursed smile I put it to him to come to America with me in September and asked his

[illegible]ssion "lets just see what happens between" he said "when will I see you again"

how about Saturday? he asked him what about tomorrow so I shall take

wedding and he says he is going to stay with his mother tonight forced

[illegible] but I'm not so sure he will certainly be living there! kisses

by taxi to Chelsea where I discovered T.C. gone all his

we Bluebonnet and Suntan were being moved out then

Ami Nadia in Dubie arabia phoned [illegible]

extremely sweet and divine excited about

I'll see her tomorrow

Nick has got NS is another

was not drink it seems to give it

passion for supper Something

spent time with in

and Daisy

...ent ...
...ro at 5 ...
...n here waiting ...
six with a cup of co...
...ed from head to foot in ...
...move to Covent Garden and the reduce...
lots of lilies wedding ...
...s of all the staggering and cat calls ...
wonderful having a big beautiful ...
zoomed around all morning food for ...
children to school and suit pressed etc Collected ...
come traip to collect sounds from Celia her toy boy jittery ...
a cup of tea geisage in bed unwell Albert arrived as I was ...
... had worked into the night was surfaced and cheerful when I got ...
I was at a loss as to what to do — I set carala on the cloth for Zoe and she ...
chaos with Albert who wouldn't relinquish the lead for the tape machine so we had a brandy
took a walk — Kay here and getting on very well with plain Ray complain the
made coffee — I suggested carala go to chelita shrieking over the telephone! its my bloody house
what about me! "you're a coward" said carala and its true I simply dont want a confrontation with h...
however she has gone off and will get what belongs to me — the dole cheque and I'm
a fresh shirt for Adi's wedding I'm a bit nervous of seeing nick I love him so and
worried I overdid it yesterday at our first meeting in 30 days in fact chelita
threatened to reclaim the giro so carala had to hand over a 20quid note I ge...
her to pay for the Laundiay which turned out to be mostly Allsorts towel
him as we parted

I went to went to pick up darling nick
the lift in grey and pink. I waited all anxious few minutes drawing a girl and walked
the pavement he came smiling at 6.15 dropped the bombshell "well I'd forgotten I'...
and I'm going to see Robert at ten" I was crazy downcast and silently all over to the
...lehman and begged his forgiveness and said Ray to understand I don't want to
see him "do whatever you want darling" and wheeled to the Tower house
he didn't want to change out of his wreathed trousers cellar until Sandra insisted
...h came on" she said Kay tantrum as I opened a bottle of champagne
...ade up and mad" she said to carala Vida was very cheerful and optimistic
...cked me off saying "Dont! what's the matter" agreed Sandra and I said through
...e out too — I insisted on driving and collected a camellia from Holland Pk
...s wedding
...ind black and it was a very nice champagne affair lots of old friends like fish
...aghasted Jenny pink boots thrilled with my for giving Vera long toot etc I've
been very good indeed refusing a sister numerous occasions I see you got your suit
case back said Jose her sister so sweet Jenny I said I was calderon
was great fun and we had dinner in Lancaster's ... quite a hit but not a
...tler table ... Roger etc Oliver Tobias was quite a bit after and it was
... when nick collected his clothes from the car and went off
... a morose after too much everything in the taxi to Cel...
there I walked Holland Pk and all ... maybe ... she was ...
... comprende? "Capriccio" every ... stop ...
... alright if I were to just ... I s...
... hands on you ... would ... it?
... answered ye...
... ing ...

Left: Model Celia Hammond wears a fake-fur coat designed by Ossie, c.1968.
Right: A hurel jersey trouser suit with a real fur coat; Ossie's amazing cutting technique is evident in this garment, c.1975.
Below: Dress designed by Alice Pollock.

Right: Ossie used Celia's print with pink flowers and stripes to make this full-length dress, bias cut with a fabulously complicated bodice; there are draw-strings on the sleeves and neck, c.1970.
Below: Model Penelope Tree wears a moss crêpe fringed suit. Celia's green, yellow and charcoal print was inspired by Nijinsky. c.1971.
Below right: One of Ossie's versions of the 'little black dress'.

May 1983

Friday

27

Three seven

3 o7 and i'm in the process of ad[...]

moving out of this wonderful Jack and I [...]

and I don't know where I shall sleep tonight Sandra says I'm

difficult person to live with one day I'm an angel I'm ten percent mad

everything was late this morning and michael batty we went do[wn]

portabello and had a greasy breakfast with zoe who had missed an[...]

it was all very odd a wind down day Sandra did her bes[t]

explain it was really michaels decision he felt I had moved in on

lock stock and barrel but he hadn't got the balls to tell me himsel[f]

he left that to dear Sandra " If it was up to me.." she said a[...]

apparently I'm still welcome for a weekend in fact I had a brain[...]

while I cleared out and hoovered I rang Joe Goldsmith but [...]

was after Kay said where are you going to stay tonight" "I don't [...]

well you had better stay at my place so I dug out the yellow [...]

dress I'd given Sandra and had to interrupt her explanation "I [...]

understand perfectly" and was very graceful as the I ching sa[ys]

I went in at a[...] to Fulanshaw

interrupted Alexa[...] A level history cra[m]

and she alarmed Bubb[...]

nicholette and wendy off

I had to persuade her into t[...]

on the yellow dress and cut

hem with nail scissors

it suit her what a magnificent [...] .and w[...]

I drank an awful lot of alcohol [...]

might four fingers of vodka with pinapp[le]

Julie to hile Sandra gently nagged me

I even went out I drank two gins and

bourbon at Jills with a cheque for a hun[dred]

pounds made out to Nick Balaban I left elated

I staggered away down

field road and dropped

in to see Jane Rasmin in her

chatty kitchen with children and

friends preparing dinner she offered

glass of wine and a girl called

a father said she had a room to let

James house but she phoned the

and cancelled without any reason

[...]ed into see Tony and Nancy Howard smoke[...]

[...]en took another gin in the new revamped

[...]dious obviously trying to copy harpo[...]

[...]ed leather queens looked out o[...]

I took the joy to celia later

instead of [...]

* the movie ... olivier age 25 with music called nick

We got to the expensive end
stile rain and leaking shoes we ...
at stalls and I went back to Portob...
s fags past one and there he was "I the...
not wearing anything of his no more ta...
he seemed pleased I was there and I too w...
relieved we walked to get money at the g...
and for a drink in the champion I'd given
the cheque in the stall "That's good darling
as I explained how I got it. he complained a b...
Kim and is glad to be moving out - has got ...
four days next week - we went to get a greasy ...

Nick had arranged to meet mike at six and
said he would like to sleep so I
made another trip with carla to
take my clock and more stuff at kar...
we smoked and drank whisky till she
arrived to prepare dinner she told Car...
She doesn't want nick here while she is at
I showered and washed my hair and wal...
Oscar to the crown and Septre half an hour lat...
than I'd said "it must be six months since I've seen ...
said mike "I've got a present for you" I said producing ...
dildoe Gala Mitchell left in my house so long ago. Kay! ...
told a funny story - Pete King in the BBC. thinking it a cle...
part, I drank more whisky and while nick put money in
jukebox I told mike I would like to make love to him tonight
Nick was quite cross at first when I told him - I've had enou...
he told mike when he asked why nick would let me make
to him - I had to return oscar to the tower house and collect
wrapping a dinner party Tim Curry and Janice looking tir...
Micheal over-friendly put his arm round me and fed me cake
... nick dressed as ...

six grey days I moved 7.15 ...
and noted ...
...sed portabello at ladbroke ...
stupidly no money not ...
for cigs got soaked and ...
we walked the market together ...
to get Dukie up and tea and to alter ...
phone sitting think seriously of a home ...
ping to everyone
Carla in a foul
but we parted
and after she took
to Tower house to collect some
longing Georgie there goofed
a new stand in waiting Sandra
Micheal came soon after she furious he
embarrassingly kissy kissy. I got a key from
and we took suitcases and toiletry to her little where
, scored dope and back to the tower house
She was hung up babysitting while they were shopping

Trinity Sunday

Sunday

29

... we raced ... kissing openly ... would respond, ... thought I spent the ... roommate I'd only ... buy hash ... to nick couldn't ... in bed where I ... proper "which way ... front or back? ... already he had ... openly in the club ... with a very sore cock, nick ... walk for tea "stop it ossie" he pleaded ... and caresses we walked round the ... miles and left them at the gate ... and breakfast was very ... quite phrase is "fucking ... treating me like a ... earlier with mu...

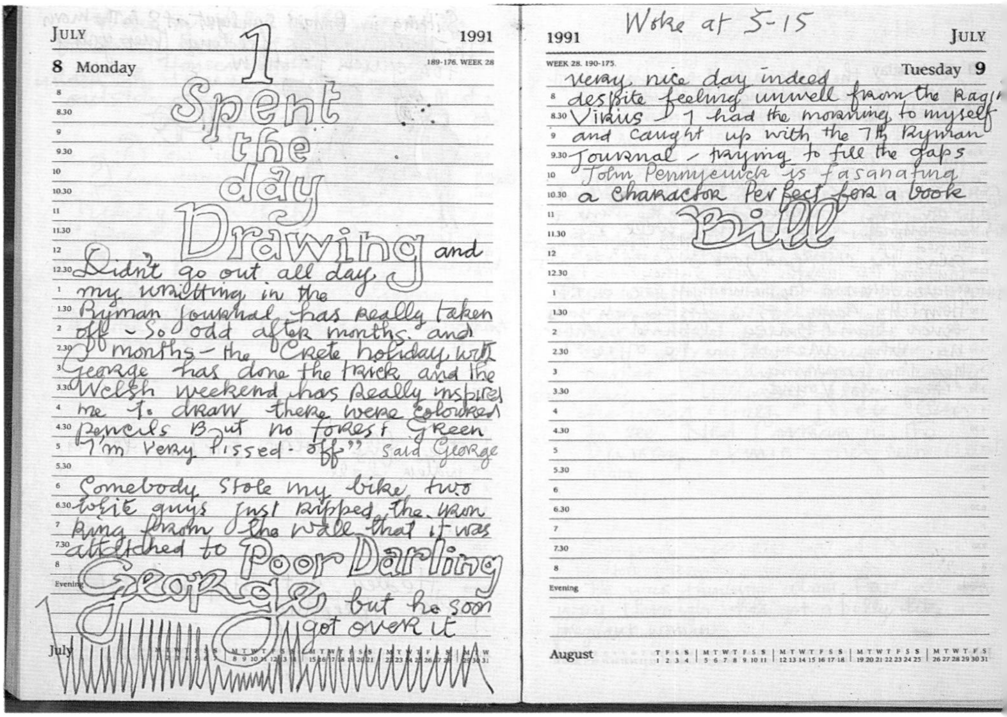

JULY 1991

8 Monday

189-176. WEEK 28

1 Spent the day Drawing and Didn't go out all day, my writting in the Ryman Journal has really taken off - So odd after months and months - the Crete holiday with George has done the trick and the Welsh weekend has really inspired me to draw there were coloured pencils But no forest Green "I'm very pissed off" said George

Somebody stole my bike two white guys just ripped the iron ring from the wall that it was attached to Poor Darling George but he soon got over it

Woke at 5-15

1991 JULY

WEEK 28. 190-175.

Tuesday 9

very nice day indeed despite feeling unwell from the Ragi Virus I had the morning to myself and caught up with the 7th Ryman Journal - trying to fill the gaps John Pennycuick is fasanating a charactor Perfect for a book

Bill

Left and below: In the mid-1970s Ossie created some less feminine, overtly vampish dresses.

Left: A page from one of Ossie's sketchbooks.

SEPTEMBER 1991

6 Friday

the funny sensation in my ears before sleep after 1 a.m. the Symiter end of the moon as Mary rang 4.20 we left 4.45 Hedley in a towel searching for escape
7.30 ferry to Calais Mary's got shares in P. and O they hadn't told me we weren't booked but got on anyway The Pride of Kent – breakfast powdered eggs blotting paper mushrooms – instant coffee
the channel smooth as a mill pond
10 I could have had a kilo of hashish no customs
M gave me the window seat and we set off along the nearly complete high speed rail link
11.30 1st stop for coffee – beatiful day triangular overpass cabbage whites rose hips
Betty's Bedford midi van wont do more than 55 mph – its 5 years old and done 100 000 miles – John Major's got big hairy hands & big feet
2 Paris "No! its not a pollution haze"
Night mare traffic – "just follow the signs for Bordeau Betty"! John could drive from Paris door to front door in 6 hours
4 Lunch egg mayonaise hamburger and chips real coffee 3 pills for my headache I began to wonder if I've made a mistake in coming
I miss Oscar desperately
6 Stop for tea – in a lay by beside slender silver birch Betty brewed up – she'd bought biscuits which tasted like soggy spong fingers – I was sick – up came the apple from her garden along with the undercooked red meat I foolishly ate at lunch. ½ naked drivers returned to their lorries to drive to IRUN and Valencia, we chug slowly on everything passes us

Europe Endless

1991 SEPTEMBER

Saturday 7

I saw the sun arise over the Loire Valley shrouded in mist
a drawing a swim
M. on the phone the day begins – Now everything is wonderful and I'm so glad I came. Indeed it is a magically beautiful place – spectacular views idillic tranquillity – no wonder Mary loves it
Betty said He's as happy as a sandpiper and I am
a glass of champagne every day is essential
You get a straight answer here
confit de Canard salade
Legumes Vapeur maison
Salade Verte
what it actually is is left – ov
2.20 by the pool 3rd swim I was going to write flies too quick to catch but I caught one and drowned it
4 o clock "any chance or if this friend of mine comes down that you will stay on for another week?"
Salade de Tomates. Melon st directe des champ
fromages Chèvre brie & frais
Alors les rognons blancs
des Raisins
accompagné du bon côtes du Rhône

SEPTEMBER 1991

8 Sunday

Up at 8
Gunshot and dogs bark the start of the shooting season no longer can I make it through the night without emptying my bladder. unfortunately there is only one toilet on the ground floor and the stair creak like hell "what you need is une petite pot de chambre" said M. of course she always travels with one
Jane Cooke Steel has always called Henrietta Hettie
Stung by a wasp
were going for a excursion explore and we'll probably have supper by the river are you interested?
Yes – So we went looking for antiques with Mary pointing out all the churches chateaus and castles – Sarlat Montford and Benac where we had dinner by the river.
Crudite
Trout
Red wine

1991 SEPTEMBER

Monday 9

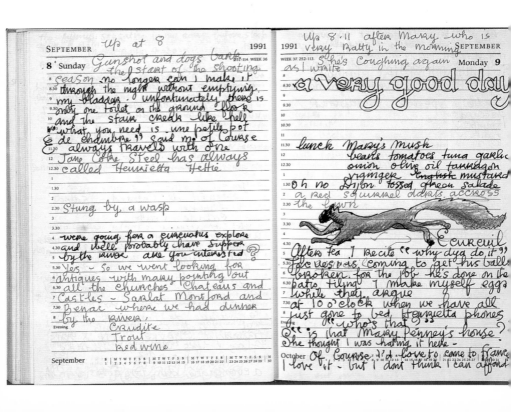

Up 8.11 after Mary who is very Ratty in the morning She's coughing again as I write

a very good day

lunch Mary's mush
beans tomatoes tuna garlic
onion olive oil tarragon
vinegar ~~English~~ mustard
Oh no Dijon ~~tossed~~ green salade
a red squirrel darts across the lawn

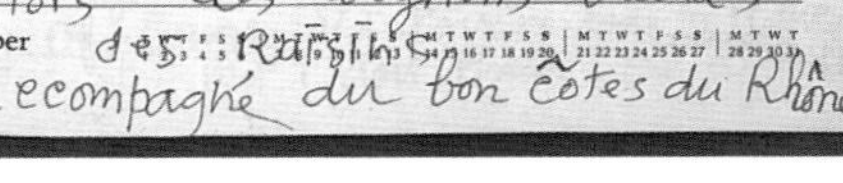

Ecureuil
After tea I recite "why dya do it" Jacques is coming to get his balls broken. for the job he's done on the patio tiling I make myself eggs while they argue
at 10 o'clock when we have all just gone to bed Henrietta phones "who's that?" "is that Mary Penney's house?" She thought I was having it here –
Of course I'd love to come to France I love it – but I dont think I can afford

1984

The diary for 1984 is extremely short. Early in the year Nick has once again grown dissatisfied with his relationship with Ossie, and has spent time going between him and Robert, playing one off against the other. The pain of this may explain why Ossie did not write in his journal in the early months of the year. Even in the later months he is reserved about his feelings for Nick, leaving only clipped, muted clues. What he does write, however, is in fierce block capitals: 'SO MANY MEMORIES', 'MUST ELIMINATE ALL REMINDERS'.

Ossie begins this year's diary with the revelation that he has been sacked by Radley. It was Nick who inspired Ossie to go back to work with Radley and Ossie had a show at the Rainbow Room early in the spring. The 'little black dresses' were celebrated by Liz Smith in the *Evening Standard,* but the show did not take off and, according to Radley, afterwards Ossie just drifted away; later Ossie was to tell the DHSS that he got the sack.

This is another low year for Ossie. He attacks Celia bitterly for being 'selfish' and seems rather desperate, but his priorities and need for escapism are again revealed when the money he has made from a dress designed for Jennifer Marriott is spent on a flight to Barbados. The break gives him an important psychological boost; it does him good to escape from London at this time and he returns revitalised in 1985. In contrast to this year's diary, he fills 1985's to the brim.

19 OCTOBER

Note to the DHSS:

I did not leave my position as a dress designer with Firwool of my own accord, as stated overleaf. It was put to me that as my designs weren't selling they couldn't continue to invest in me and I was given two weeks notice on the 19th October 1984. I wasn't offered a choice of continuing to work or not – I was fired.

Radley fired me, which absolutely stunned me. The collection hasn't sold. Do you think it's evil or good – cunning.

23 OCTOBER

Wilf[1]'s birthday. Selima[2] anorexia.

27 OCTOBER

Nick phoned – 'I'm staying with my mother, OK?' I went to Hampstead Heath.

30 OCTOBER

Rang lots of art schools, polys and colleges[3]. Rang George, Celia.

1 NOVEMBER

Daphne Teggue, London College of Fashion – said she had made some enquires on my behalf and someone said whoever got me would be lucky.

18 NOVEMBER

[*Celia travels to America to visit David Hockney.*]

Celia to America. Selfish cunt.

20 NOVEMBER

Didn't buy newspapers after yesterday's *Standard* cost 20p.

'I feel like a fireman – don't be ridiculous, where can I get a fireman this time of night.'

21 NOVEMBER

Jennifer Marriot fitting. The bluish colour of the inside of her bodice is exactly that of the butterfly's wings which make the Rio picture that Robbie Brook-Howard gave me so long ago.

22 NOVEMBER

Carina[4] told me the builder had said, 'Was that really *the* Ossie Clark?'

23 NOVEMBER

Portobello for bargains. Bought lillies and hyacinths in bulb.

Trip to Radley. Frowda[5] has made up the beaded velvets. Took an iron and ballet drawing to frame. On the bus home a robbery committed with a rivet gun through plate-glass for diamonds.

Guy[6] came over for supper. I spent the evening drinking brandy and making a pair of braces from purple taffeta and gold leather. George came over and he was so sweet.

24 NOVEMBER

Up early, ten to nine Portobello. At least I found a pair of old riding-boots, lovely trousers and a pink vase.

Tim Curry phoned at two – talked of Marie Helvin, Eddie Grant[7] and his new love of opera and Pavarotti who wants to be a superstar (he earned $50,000 per night in the US. Phew!!!) Also said Pattie[8] having an affair.

25 NOVEMBER

Up at 9.30 – tea and a walk round the Serpentine in bright sunshine before the pouring rain. A mention in the *Times* supplement.

At 4.13 I saw the finest new moon. No money in my pocket to turn over but thoughts of Nick.

I tried to phone Guy but got an answerphone. Even plucked up courage to phone Robert's number – got an answerphone. Thinking malicious thoughts . . . Meanwhile the bodice is in one piece.

Now at ten to five the sky is pink. How clever Diana Vreeland[9] was to call pink the navy blue of India.

26 NOVEMBER

Must buy ink for the three pens I nicked from Hockney last year. Rang George – happy birthday, now he's a teenager.

Couldn't stand it anymore without a smoke so rang Carla to get a 10 quid deal.

Julian came by. Although it's quite nice to see him and the attention he pays me, I can't help feeling he's using me. Drank vodka and feeling blue phoned Roger[10].

27 NOVEMBER

Oscar barking furiously, very annoying, up at 7.10.

Roger coming? No, but hopefully . . .

Carina phoned, voiceless – sounds sinister.

Got a flight to Barbados[11], December 26th till 18th January.

28 NOVEMBER

Fresh sheets for Roger.

Rang Gillian Bobroff[12] for news of Ulla[13] and to tell her I was chanting.

Today Roger coming. No, not today but maybe tomorrow – I spoke to him 5.45.

Guy phoned, will come later.

SO MANY MEMORIES.

Ulla being difficult.

29 NOVEMBER

Roger met me at Euston.

30 NOVEMBER
Phoned Jenny re cash for air ticket.
More antibiotics, Dr King.
Portobello with Roger – bargains.
Anthony McKay, fucking ARSEHOLE[14].
Paid £440 cash for my flight to Barbados.

2 DECEMBER
Up at 9.30. Felt blue – rain outside – until I remember my bambino.
MUST ELIMINATE ALL REMINDERS.
Keep busy. Work. Keep tidy. Exercise. Stretch. Stop smoking so much. Never drink in the day.

3 DECEMBER
Dr King refused me antibiotics.
Roger phoned and will come and stay again.

4 DECEMBER
I made a sort of shrine from a photo of silk and six Kari Anne[15] postcards, which came out like a Brian Clarke.
At some point I carefully put away the miniature tape cassette that was in the machine, found another I assumed to be BLANK. Recorded over the conversation after he first left me[16]. No coincidence in Buddhism.
Simon[17] at seven. Sex and all it entails with Simon. He really is very sweet.

5 DECEMBER
Struggling with the blue silk.

6 DECEMBER
7.30 That time of day. Finished the last of the vodka – resisted the temptation to go to HH. Went to get some more. Jose[18] gone to India.

7 DECEMBER
Is Nick really coming to visit me? Yes and he misses me and I miss him – he really loves me.

11 DECEMBER
Jenny thrilled with her dress and gave me a grand in cash. It's on the stand, only side seams neck and hem.
I fucked Simon while Carla[19] was changing the machine to white for the lingerie.

14 DECEMBER

Jumped on a bus smoking a joint. Collected my car from the back of Jack Straw's Castle[20] – freaked to find the huge plant pot I nicked from Chelita[21]'s garden last night.

Spoke to George – suggested *Dune*[22] on Sunday.

15 DECEMBER

Dashed off to the West End for cinema tickets then home to a rather down evening alone. Frankie[23] on *Terry Wogan* said less than a year ago he was signing on the dole – his song 'The Power of Love' always makes me think of Nick.

18 DECEMBER

Hockney in town.

1.30 Nick arrived looking terrible. Gone to the dentist.

3.10 Sent Robbie[24] away.

5.20 Robbie at the door again as Nick arrived. I had to give him £5 to get rid of him.

Agnes and Andi[25] dinner – 'What's a Polish gesture? – To buy three bags of potatoes.' Wonderful sex with Keith[26] after – he left a pullover behind.

22 DECEMBER

3 o'clock Pattie[27] coming. Nick arrived instead.

Wonderful evening with Chessie[28] trying on clothes being photographed. Drove absolutely drunk to a non-existent party at Henri[29]'s.

26 DECEMBER

[*Ossie flies to Barbados to stay with Eddie Grant. Bryan Ferry and Tim Curry are also on the island.*]

BARBADOS. Wonderful new moon.

29 DECEMBER

At ten past nine I returned to the house to shower after swimming and sunbathing – signs of life but I get the feeling I'm not liked here.

Phoned Bryan Ferry, went to have dinner. On the way ran out of petrol – got aggression because I had no shirt.

Tim Curry – fun.

31 DECEMBER

Conversation with Eddie and watching video of Mohammed Ali. After dinner Tim Curry was very funny talking about a couple from Birmingham he met in Jamaica – proud to say I refused a toot of cocaine. In the afternoon I said I'd like to wear horns shaped like a leaf of aloe. Tim said, 'That's what I wear in my late movie, *Legends*. I kept putting people's eyes out because I forgot they were there.'

1 Wilf Butler, actor; old friend of Ossie's.
2 Selima Guirey, painter and photographer, descendant of Genghis Khan; girlfriend of Wilf Butler.
3 To inquire about vacancies to lecture.
4 Carina Frost, née Fitzalan-Howard, former model whom Alice Pollock 'discovered' in the street; daughter of the Duke of Norfolk and wife of Sir David Frost.
5 A machinist at Radley.
6 Guy Burch.
7 Eddie Grant, reggae singer/songwriter.
8 Pattie Clapton.
9 Diana Vreeland, former editor of American *Vogue*.
10 Julian and Roger were lovers of Ossie's.
11 Ossie has been invited by Eddie Grant to holiday at his home on Barbados.
12 Gillian Bobroff, former model; had recently converted to Buddhism.
13 Ulla Larson.
14 Anthony McKay is complaining about unpaid rent for Redcliffe Road.
15 Kari Anne Jagger.
16 Ossie is referring to his conversation with Nick Balaban which he recorded on 11 May 1983.
17 A lover of Ossie's.
18 Jose Fonseca.
19 Carla Ames.
20 Jack Straw's Castle is a pub in Highgate.
21 Chelita Secunda.
22 A science-fiction film starring Sting.
23 Holly Johnson of Frankie Goes to Hollywood.
24 An ex-lover of Ossie's.
25 Agnes Kostrowski, former model with whom Ossie intends to start up a lingerie company, and her husband Andi.
26 A lover of Ossie's.
27 Pattie Clapton.
28 Francesca Thyssen.
29 Henrietta Rous.

1985

The year begins exotically with Ossie's holiday in Barbados as the guest of Eddie Grant, the reggae singer. His writing is alive with description – conch shells, rum, private swimming pools, a spoiled child – and he is soothed and inspired by the sun, the sea and the colours. He is, however, taking Mogadon to sleep and enjoyably smoking a great deal of hashish. He overturns Eddie's moke on a steep cliff path and the lives of the occupants are miraculously saved. Superstitiously, he credits his survival to his 'long black, cashmere scarf'. One evening he goes drunkenly too far and is asked to leave after embracing Eddie's wife in too intimate a manner. Luckily, he can stay with his old friend Vicki Hodge.

The holiday re-energises him and helps him face increasing vicissitudes in London. He gets teaching jobs in Manchester and at St Martin's College of Art in London and uses the extra money to revive his social life. He keeps up with old friends such as Ulla Larson and Jose Fonseca; and even Chelita comes to supper, as does Lady Carina Frost, the former model married to Sir David Frost. Later in the year the models Marie Helvin, Patti Boyd and Jane Mackay are all mentioned.

However, Ossie is emotionally lonely without Nick and tormented by the fact that his former lover is still linked with Robert while he, Ossie, is not meant to mind. About this he is miserable and says, 'I keep having hateful thoughts which I have to shoo from my brain.'

Halfway through the year he has to move from his little flat in Redcliffe Road. Friends try to reassure and comfort him, but finally it is Nick, Robert and Guy Burch who come to his rescue and invite him to stay at their council flat in Islington. Nick stays with Robert in Ealing and it is Guy who provides companionship. Ossie notes that this is his eighth move in the eleven years since his break-up with Celia and it is salutary for the reader to reflect that of the eight residences, only one has been his own.

1985 is a year, as always, of extremes. He is kind to a demanding young artist, Selima Guirey, who is a little dependent on him, and spends much time with Pauline Fordham, an old friend from the sixties who is now a heroin addict and later goes to prison. But, despite his feeling for youth, his teaching does not go well; he is disenchanted by his students' lack of inspiration, becomes impatient with them and soon realises that this is not his metier. He approaches a literary agent with a view to writing a book, which he describes as 'Waspish and name droppy'; the agent takes him to a publisher but nothing comes of it. However, his approaching the agent is significant because from here on it seems likely that Ossie is aware that his diaries might one day be published.

Ossie's family - sister Kay, niece Carol and nephew Jimmy – provide him with humour and support, and an extraordinary character from his past reappears: Vicki de Lambray, formerly a man. She hosts a joint in Soho, La Valbonne, with showy largesse and Ossie is courted as a celebrity and allowed to invite 100 guests; he writes vividly about these strange evenings.

Ossie has a series of small setbacks. Sometimes he goes round with flowers for Celia, hoping for a reconciliation, but this is not to be. David Hockney appears not to return his calls, although he had invited him to Los Angeles in the spring. Most seriously he is banned from driving for three years after an incident in his car while driving Pauline Fordham. However, his friend, Pam Procter, has bought a house with four acres at Monkleigh in North Devon and this proves to be a haven for Ossie.

After his move to Islington something decent and humble emerges in him; at this time an old friend found him, 'very appealing and a far cry from the arrogance of his earlier days'. He finds solace in reading the novels of Marcel Proust and, more than ever before, in writing his diaries. 'Are you living to write, or writing to live?' Carla asks him on 17 April.

2 JANUARY

Bryan Ferry rang. Will come tomorrow.

3 JANUARY

Went to collect Bryan Ferry. Told me about his record, his father's death.

4 JANUARY

Long conversation with Eddie[1]. He is such a nice guy. Talked of Bryan Ferry, how he feels on the edge of a precipice and could either fall or fly. Watching the end of a video, he said when he first planned to move here his wife asked, 'Whatever will I do without a television?'

11 JANUARY

Was the dead bird under the hanging tree an evil omen? I did see half a rainbow. Went through the usual routine when, laying in the sun after my first swim, Eddie came by and said, 'Bad news, old boy. You were inordinately drunk last night and insulted the Mrs.' At first I couldn't understand what he was talking about but then I figured it must have been my putting my arms around her and being shocked to find her wearing a roll-on panty-girdle. The Bajans are odd in that they don't like to be touched. I apologised profusely and told him I would move on.

[*Ossie contacts Vicki Hodge*[2] *who is also on Barbados and agrees to Ossie staying with her.*]

Vicki is an angel and made me feel most welcome. I encamped at the end of her bed and told her about my goof.

14 JANUARY

Vicki said of Prince Andrew, 'He was just a cunt. He sussed I was the best fuck, fucked me rotten for three days and then fucked off.'

16 JANUARY

Kent Proverbs is a 23-year-old Bajan Vicki thinks I might get on with. He's here now. Must be the only gay on the island. I behaved outrageously with him.

19 JANUARY

[*Ossie returns to London.*]

Woken by a nudge. In my hat the hibiscus I took last night before I boarded the plane. I'm wondering what horrors are in store for me at home.

12.30 landed. Snow about. God, how I miss the sea, the sun, the colour.

21 JANUARY

Al Radley phoned, 'Where yer bin?'

26 JANUARY

So stiff in my ribcage.

Scene with Celia.

Had a long conversation with Guy[3] about publishing, journalism, my future and Nick.

Completely freaked out by a police car which turned in the Fulham Road to take another look. Passed me and turned left – am I paranoid? I don't think so. I dived into the Post Office, stashed my hash in my underpants – my heart pounding – met Guy, couldn't eat, very tense.

31 JANUARY

Pauline[4] phoned at 1.20 and took me for a delicious lunch. On the way I related the true version of the Chelita[5] soap opera[6]. P had seen Jose[7] lunching with Keith Lichenstein – I told her they are secretly married. 'They are not like married people.' Jose so glamorous. We were laughing so much. She said she had had a premonition of my death. 'I must buy some contraceptives, then,' I said as we were leaving. She filled me in on her life. So much I must talk to her more. She went to NY. Jasper Johns[8] fell in love with her. 'It was just after I'd made a lot of money with Chelita selling coke,' she said.

2 FEBRUARY

I heard that Kenny Everett is left at weekends chained and handcuffed to scream and scream.

4 FEBRUARY

At the Hippodrome Peter Stringfellow[9] said, 'You don't know what it means to me to meet you.' And, 'You'll be amazed at the speed I organise your celebrity membership.'

Home at five to four, Pauline gave me a snort of heroin.

6 FEBRUARY

Took Kay[10] for a drink in the Coleherne and after to Tony Howard's. Charles[11] there, told me he used to drive Brian Jones to gigs, even shared a flat in Chester, something about he kept a locked cupboard with a loaf of bread and HP Sauce.

8 FEBRUARY

Celia being freaked out about AIDS – the comic aspect of the latest victim, a prison chaplain, good as gold with the boys but went to London gay clubs – his corpse cremated at twice the normal temperature, five times longer.

9 FEBRUARY

On the way to the bus I was snowballed and a black nearby said, 'We don't want your kind here: homosexuals bringing AIDS and herpes into the country.' Huh, that's *your* lot, Haitians,' I sneered back at him. He menacingly said, 'You obviously don't read the *Guardian*.' I refused to be intimidated, called him 'arsehole'.

10 FEBRUARY

Tea at Ulla[12]'s. April[13] in the kitchen – told me about an incident with

Schiaparelli[15] when she worked in Paris. Apparently S had come to her club with a silly rose sticking two inches out of the top of her head and all the artists took the piss and appeared wearing a flower in the same ridiculous way – Schiaparelli was furious, demanded each one apologise. But someone refused so they all had to refuse and there was all hell to pay. 'Oh, they all came,' she said. 'Marlene[15] and Noel Coward who said (at the end of his life), 'I always get up for a lady,' struggling to stand, and his entire head and face a mass of blackheads.

11 FEBRUARY

Celia called. She filling in a form for Albert's passport – he is going to Vichy on an exchange system – later she will put up a French boy. 'Any news of DH?' I asked. She said she is just relieved not to be with him – and that he is in Mustique. With Jagger[16]? On Mustique there is only Jagger and royalty.

Seven to ten, I'm on my third large brandy. Feeling much better, more awake – am I becoming an alcoholic?

12 FEBRUARY

TVS, Southern TV, want me on a program called *Regrets*. Am I interested?

14 FEBRUARY

Headline in the *Islington Gazette* – 'AIDS scare in Highbury'.

15 FEBRUARY

At last the celebrity invitation from Peter Stringfellow.

Paranoia is a lawyer.

16 FEBRUARY

Phoned Guy, got him to phone Robert[17]. Nick[18] is there, so fuck him – I shan't phone again.

19 FEBRUARY

Feeling great, afraid I'm missing out, writing it all.

20 FEBRUARY

I always fall in love with the waiters.

21 FEBRUARY

Sign on. I walked there. A grey, damp day, Surely there will be a Giro for me this week, I thought confidently, but there was not. I dropped in on

Nancy[19] and the kids for a cup of tea and a moan about my plight. Lovely pictures of Felix[20] scowling in *Face* magazine – I am trembling as I write. Now in the wine gallery with Pauline. Oliver Musker here. Pauline tells me Oliver and Lady Rose[21] have split up, banned from driving for three years. Hot, red-faced and fat, someone had said.

Every day a hassle to find cash.

22 FEBRUARY

Terrified of seeing the new moon through glass.

Teaching in Manchester.

23 FEBRUARY

I began to drink whisky at ten in the morning and continued all day.

24 FEBRUARY

Brought the newspapers and another story about AIDS, all the usual crap.

25 FEBRUARY

The laundry man arrived at 10.35 but refused to leave the fresh laundry unless I paid, so no shirts – so I jumped into the bath.

Pauline was very cross when she discovered she'd left her smack at home, so we went there and off in a taxi to The Night of a Thousand Frocks[22] where I judged the competition and I met Adam, a 21-year-old wearing a blond wig and a white dress and rouged cheeks – it was fun and he came home with me and we slept in each others arms.

26 FEBRUARY

Two years ago on Ilkley Moor with a guy I met on the Gay Pride march, I lay in a stream with water running through my hair. I fucked the guy I was with and a party of school children and two nuns walked by. All I could do was smile.

Dragged Adam out of bed, he is absolutely adorable – needs looking after. Listening to Lou Reed[23] and Prince[24]. Adam, 16" collar, size 12 feet, big heart, big cock – we finished screwing at half past six.

28 FEBRUARY

Graffiti on the wall, 'Thatcher's answer to unemployment – cheap heroin.'

Received an uncashable Giro for £128.75.

I rang Nick, 'I was just dreaming about you; we were in a garden, you were rolling a joint and my mother and my sister were there,' – he'll meet me tomorrow at Euston.

1 MARCH

Teaching in Manchester. I had arranged to meet Nick at Euston at seven o'clock – the train from Manchester was on time but he wasn't there so I began to chant[25]. He appeared just before 7.30 – he had been to King's Cross by mistake. He wouldn't come back to my flat saying he was expecting an important call at 8.30. I fell into a gloom. I should never have rung him. I persisted. Then he got angry and said he would go. I'd said OK, goodbye, but I couldn't bear to part that way . . . I didn't dare say anything – in a perverse way pleased I'd made him miserable too.

2 MARCH

Pauline phoned very concerned about Adam, thinks he might have AIDS.

Selima[26] spilt ink on the carpet and I went berserk, called her a stupid bitch and dragged her about by the hair. She had a nosebleed and also frisked. I scrubbed and scrubbed with a nailbrush. Anger and fury over Selima's stupidity, madness at myself.

3 MARCH

Grey and rainy day. The Valium really left me drugged, groggy and untogether. I shall never take Valium again.

4 MARCH

I'm fed up with you, Selima. I have finally got rid of her – I had to leave her bags on the roof of the car – I pleaded with her in the end. Poor sod, she really is in a sad state – cold and unhappy. I took pity on her and had to take her back indoors.

On the way to see Ben and his girlfriend [27]. Pauline told me Harriet had gone riding last week in Richmond Park and asked for a job looking after the horses. So now she lives in a tiny cottage, getting up at seven to muck-out – kicking her heroin habit. Meanwhile Ben says the *Daily Star* are interested in his story[28] and he should make £15,000. Pauline was keen to rave it up so we went to the Hippodrome to see Divine (Adam might be there) Kenny Everett drunk at the bar with his boyfriend, besotted. Divine was truly vulgar in a glittering dress.

5 MARCH

Whisky all day. Sunshine outside is wonderful. I haven't eaten anything and I've got to take the fucking carpet up tonight and all I want is sex.

6 MARCH

To Stanley Gardens. There was Colette[29], exactly the same after fifteen years.

So nice to see her. It turns out that she fucked Jimmy Page in my bed in Linden Gardens.

1.20 Anthony McKay on the phone threatening. Arsehole he is. Will I agree to move out on March 1st if I can't pay[30]? What a complete bore Anthony McKay is. What sort of fool does he think I am? Will I move out indeed.

7 MARCH

What a bloody bore the LEB is. The fucking electricity turned off and I need a hot bath and Nick is coming tonight. Why all this damn flak all the time. Pauline took Oscar off and bathed him. She was bored so came round to chat to me while I took a bath and dropped me in South Kensington to get the tube. I took a taxi from Russell Square to the British Museum, arriving after four. Late, but thank god Burnett[31] was waiting and we walked to Bedford Square to the publisher, Alan Brooke[32], who kept us waiting for an hour – he seemed genuinely interested and I left one of my diaries and promised to write a synopsis over the weekend.

Cashed my miserable 25 quid Giro then home to find the electricity turned off, what a drag. Rushed to LEB 1.20, it was closed till half past. Next door for a pils. Paid the £14 reconnection charge and they refused to put it on until tomorrow, so I bussed it home, brought fuse-wire and put it back on myself, so fuck 'em.

9.17 I'm waiting for Nick – he hasn't come as he promised – reluctant to admit it but it looks as though he has stood me up. Disappointed and time is going very slowly, I wonder where he is and why he treats me like this – I am so miserable and getting drunk.

8 MARCH

Teaching in Manchester – it is the most beautiful, warm, sunny spring day and I'm stuck in a great big studio. The students' work this week is a little disappointing – though they are still enthusiastic. Where is Nick, I wonder? Was he at R's last night when I rang?

Vikki de Lambray on television – very funny, name-dropping. Even me.

8.30 Henrietta[33] rang saying Anthony McKay had called saying he is so overdrawn that he is seriously thinking of renting his house and will have to live here.

10 MARCH

Charlie Tennant in the Sunday papers, busted with eight grams of opium at Heathrow. Vikki de Lambray phoned, has invited me to dinner on Tuesday and wants me to invite a hundred people to a party for his – birthday on April 2nd.

I phoned Nick but no answer so I plucked up courage and rang R's number, got someone else. 'Is Nick there?' 'No, they've gone out for the day.' 'Oh, well, tell him I called.'

11 MARCH

I can't cope with being an undischarged bankrupt.

Wrote a bit more of the synopsis. Burnett here at 20 to four. A very slow reader, he's taken it straight off to the publisher.

12 MARCH

'I don't need an excuse to be the woman in me' – Donna Summer[34].

I got to the pub and Nick was waiting for me there, smiling 'Hello, darling.' 'God, I hate this pub,' I said. 'No seats, cramped, lots of clones.' 'What shall we do, darling?' he asked. 'There's not much we can do,' I replied. 'Shall we go home?' he asked, but he wasn't serious, adding that he had to go home tonight. We walked to the bus stop. 'Talk to me,' he said and I replied that I would only say what he didn't want to hear. 'When shall we meet again?' he asked. 'Do you think we *should* meet again?' I replied. 'Whatever you want,' he began, his usual tone. 'OK, goodbye, darling,' I said and kissed him, a bus approaching. 'Shall I ring you?' a little panic in his voice. 'Yes,' I replied. 'When?' 'Whenever you like.' 'OK, I'll phone you tomorrow,' and he wobbled off on his new bicycle.

I got home at nine and waited until 9.30 to phone him, somehow I knew he had gone to R in Peckham, so got Carla[35] to phone him and he called me back. We had a few words and I hung up.

13 MARCH

Ben came to the door at 3.30 very freaked out after being with Pauline on the street outside her house. She had been busted by plain clothes policemen – poor Pauline, she doesn't stand much of a chance of escaping prison now – they took her upstairs and found two packets of heroin and a little hashish. I was on my back reading Proust.

8 o'clock. Guy said the CID had been on the phone looking for Ben – Pauline freaked and began to tremble, incensed with Guy. She became convinced he had set her up. Ben has got a dreadful criminal record. Pauline became convinced they were trying to set her up: she got very angry and wanted to beak Guy's knees.[36]

Tried to phone Nick, hoping against all the odds he'd be there – pissing in the wind. So phoned Adam and 15 minutes later he arrived – most unsatisfactory, he wouldn't allow me to screw him and I lay awake thinking of Nick before taking half a Valium and finally got to sleep at four.

14 MARCH

Pauline came round with an odd story – on the way passed a demented Emma Hunt[37] followed by ten pressmen with cameras and tape recorders. 'Fuck off and leave me alone,' she screamed as she disappeared into Finches. (I spoke to her mother later and asked her about it. She said, 'She's been a problem for 12 years and I've no idea what it's about. Goodbye.'

15 MARCH

In the *Daily Mail* a whole page on Emma Hunt giving evidence against two drug pushers in Knightsbridge Crown Court.

16 MARCH

Ben phoned. Says he misses Marianne. He says Chelita has sold her house for £50,000.00 so I phoned Chelita and left an answer on her machine saying I might go see her tomorrow.

17 MARCH

Through the I Ching got 'interference' but the reverse reading was wonderful, told me exactly what I wanted to hear. The superior man stands back to work out what to do and the grass bends before him in the wind, advising people what to do – well that's the gist of it. 'That's a good one,' said Sid[38], pointing it out to me.

18 MARCH

Set off for the Hippodrome to see the truly dreadful Angie Bowie.

Got collared by Peter Stringfellow – do I want to help in 'Fashion Aid', in the light of Live Aid's success, a charity to help the starving Ethiopians? Do I want him to sponsor me? I told Peter Stringfellow I don't really give a fuck about the starving in Ethiopia – I thought it part of the world's natural safety mechanism.

21 MARCH

The bloody teaching cheque wasn't in the post. Just finished talking to Burnett. I told him I was sick of being labelled unreliable and a junky – it's not true. I said I wanted to wait to write the book myself. I told him I think they are all shmucks when he asked what I thought of junkies.

Carol[39]'s 40th birthday. She very weepy on the phone when I rang to wish her all the best. 'Thanks for your card but I didn't get one from John and Jesse[40] was with him last night.

Rang David Hockney – talked to somebody there and got an idea of his movements. He's flying to Bradford from Milan on Saturday, will be in London on Sunday afternoon then on to San Francisco – I suddenly had a vision of myself as a tramp pitched outside Linden Gardens.

5.30ish Burnett called back and said he's to meet Alan Brooke tomorrow. Feels confident he can work something out.

At Carol's I tried to commiserate with her – she is still so completely – besotted with John but says she will get a lawyer.

22 MARCH

10 o'clock rang Sandra who told me off for calling Michael[41] a fat Jew. She was very offended with me, made me feel really bad.

23 MARCH

I had to face Chelita and she was monstrous. An ugly, sneering face at the door. 'You want?' she sneered. 'I want my money.' After I'd said she was just delaying it she asked, 'I thought you were trying to replace a broken friendship.' Bloody Chelita, she's such a bring-down. I don't know which way to turn. God, I mustn't get depressed. Did I take a pill last night? Well I've just taken two. I'm scared.

Phoned Burnett – who had 'forgotten' I need my transcript back and postponed his meeting till Monday. I called Anne Upton and I bumped into her on the corner of Warwick Gardens on my way to see Chelita – she commented on my short hair, couldn't remember Oscar's name. Earlier she had said it unlikely Hockney would come tomorrow. But I think Anne was just playing protective female – I told her I would visit DH in California. She said tritely, 'Well, you don't get on with Gregory[42]' so obviously he's still the dowager boyfriend.

I'm feeling very inert, I don't know what to do – I should work, work, work. I spent the whole day watching TV and listening to music, trying to decide what to do and not doing anything, and even when I managed to get outside to go and see Tony and Nancy I had to force myself to keep walking.

24 MARCH

Carla phoned me. 'Celia's just been on the phone to me.' Snooping about me, no doubt. 'She's worried about what you are doing and your finances. Did you know Hockney was in town?'

[Ossie takes George to visit David Hockney.]

David drew George and he said to me, '*La vie* goes on.' He asked after my mother. I saw my letter opened, and under a book on his table but I didn't say anything. Celia came and he showed us Polaroid photos of his paintings. It seemed impossible so I put my coat on and said goodbye to David in the kitchen.

25 MARCH

Evening with Peter[43], he left at 20 to 11 after abruptly, hurriedly, dressing. said he'd explain if I turned the music down. He said I looked battered. It was all so untidy and depressing, cigarette butts in the sink. I seem to represent a side of him he prefers to forget – it was my charm and big dick which brought him, his words. 'You don't eat properly.' And lots more complaints. It quite took me aback – 'I know I asked you what's wrong but I didn't expect the answer to be so heavy.' 'It's all so tacky,' he said.

26 MARCH

Can't help smarting over something Peter said last night – that he doesn't want to become like me. I am not a person to emulate. 'You could never be like me,' I began weakly. 'You could never have children.' If that is how I appear to someone slightly younger than me, how do I appear to the very young? I know my own children think I'm odd – George especially thinks I drink too much. 'You're drunk, dad,' he's said at least twice. 'You drink and smoke too much,' Peter had said. 'But we fuck so well,' I protested. 'Makes no difference. I'm not seeing you again.' Of course, the children have known me all their lives. Eccentric is what I am. Sex-mad eccentric? Or worse, as Peter thinks, tacky, battered and charming.

28 MARCH

Poor Pauline sat on the step at the corner of Redcliffe Road (as I have done on many occasions) 'I'm so hungry I must eat,' she said but wasn't fooling anybody. What she wants is a smoke of smack. She has been without for two days and after a delicious dinner she rang and some boy came over with some. She said, 'You see, it's psychological, as soon as I know there's a smoke on the way I feel all right. If this is what life is like without it, depression and pain, I might as well top myself.' And I know exactly what she means – adding that I don't particularly want to do myself in but there doesn't seem much alternative. Anyway, I had to lend her £25 to buy it and the boy who delivered it was beautiful but he had what I can only describe as 'slack' eyes. Heroin the very devil has got him in its grip. I went to bed and carried on reading Proust.

29 MARCH

To see Kay, much better after being ill with a virus for two weeks – she babbled on about a woman who lived above her in Sutherland Avenue who was regularly fucked by the local catholic priest. Originally she had been a virgin and engaged to be married to a sailor in Australia. The priest came to give her guidance, first once a month, then once a fortnight, then twice a week. Finally she fled to Kay, shaking with fear, while he was there. 'Tell him to fuck off,' advised Kay. 'Oh, I couldn't say that,' she said. 'OK, tell him to fig off!' and she did.

Carla rang and came over. Asked all the wrong questions. 'So, no desire to work? Any word from the police? Have you sorted out your situation with Radley?

30 MARCH

First day with Nick in ages. He was waiting for me outside the Venus cafe with a new very short haircut, like a Greek peasant boy. He came on his bicycle and looked tired with bags under his eyes and a sprinkling of grey in his too-short hair – dreadful jacket and jeans and horrible shoes his mother had given him.

He wanted £10 to go home in a taxi and I refused to give it to him (having bought another bottle of vodka and wanting him to stay anyway) saying, 'Get Robert to take you home.' 'He's gone to Bristol anyway. He's got a part in a film.' So that's it – Robert had phoned me earlier, very cheerful, asked me questions. I was as calm and polite as I could be under the circumstances – but when he asked, 'How are you?' I said, 'I'm fine, Robert. Goodbye,' and slammed down the receiver.

31 MARCH

'I could do anything. Sail a yacht. Walk around Land's End, or ballroom dance. Still, it's much nicer with a snort,' said Pauline, dying for heroin.

I walked Oscar around the Serpentine – beautiful day but again I felt very alone in the park with lots of people and dogs milling about. Young couples in love – how I wished I had somebody with me. Even George was too busy to see me. 'I finish school on Wednesday,' he said. 'See you then.' And Celia so hostile. I tried to phone David H – had to pluck up all my courage – and got a person who didn't seem to know the name and only spoke Spanish. Annoyed Nick by calling him again. 'I love you, darling,' I said. 'I know.' I had to say it three times before he said, 'I love you too.' Slept badly.

1 APRIL

Anthony McKay phoned while I was in the bath. Instant gloom. Finally got DH after calling at ten past every hour. He said he has no kitchen – has only just got back[44] himself. 'It's been five months.' 'Come in May.' I asked about a drawing and he said, 'Ring me back in a week.' Subconsciously I knew I wasn't going to go away just now so I'm not so disappointed – I just feel trapped, not knowing which way to turn.

Pauline decided to score. There was a slight argument over £10 Pauline insisted Ben owed her. I stayed out of it; I find the whole thing quite sordid, yet I do prefer her after she's had a little smoke of the dreaded gear – she is very thoughtful and considerate, without it she's short-tempered, even nasty at times.

2 APRIL

[Ossie goes to Vikki de Lambray's birthday party at Studio Valbonne.]

Phoned Vikki. 'My dear, you can invite hundreds of people.' Rang everyone I could think of, no reply from or Carla or Kay but I did speak to a few people. I arrived at the Valbonne to find Vikki outside shooing Cynthia Payne[45] away to the nearest pub. 'We had to send away a television crew already,' he said smugly. Inside a double photo of me and an invitation to spend an evening with Ossie Clark, internationally famous designer. As usual Vikki was being very bossy and ushered us here and there. I ordered a bottle of champagne – Dom Perignon – which I drank to myself throughout the evening. Richard Young asked, 'Who's going to be here tonight? Do you know Jagger's in town?' I did because I had spoken to Chris[46].

The lights went down and I faced the arrival of guests at nine o'clock. Nick behind me with Oscar at my shoulder with his front paws in the back of the sofa – I fed him champagne from the tips of my fingers. They all arrived. Minor pop stars, page-three girls, but no Ian Rush[47]. Angie Bowie in a maze of flash bulbs.

Ben and Harriet arrived. 'I don't look too scruffy?' asked Ben. I found myself drinking more and more glasses of champagne. Craigie[48] very silly – bought whiskies all night with Lord Patrick Conygham[49] who was extremely rude to Pauline. Almost bashed her over the head with an empty bottle.

Hat's story about Robert Fraser. Apparently he's lost a lot of weight – suffering from a rare blood-disease – had many tests – it's not AIDS. Or is it? Pauline thinks so.

3 APRIL

The Butterfly Ball at Stringfellow's with Henrietta. Janet Street Porter[50] very friendly. Angie Best coveting my jacket. Gary Crowley[51].

4 APRIL

In the local bookshop in a book on the male nude I found the Hockney drawing of me.

10 APRIL

Beautiful sunshine outside, dark in here.

12 APRIL

British baby dies of AIDS in a London hospital.

Lousy fuck with a gay marathon runner who put a contraceptive on me – soon over. Faked orgasm and later listened to him complaining of lack of action.

13 APRIL

I'm so lonely I could die. Oscar is being very compassionate and seems to understand how I am feeling. I tried to phone Nick. I miss him so much. I keep having hateful thoughts, which I have to shoo from my brain.

Reading Proust until after four last night. At last the introduction of Saint-Loupe[52] and his first name is Robert. Now I'm trying to keep *him* off my mind, too. I suppose they are together. I tried to phone Nick again at six and even phoned Robert's number – but just got the answering machine, which I listened to but didn't leave a message on it.

15 APRIL

Phone David Hockney in LA. He also incredibly depressed. Poor David H. Gregory drinking will just about finish him off – and he's got a bad eye as well – he sounded so low. 'Don't think of coming here just yet,' he moaned. 'Let me sort this lot out first.' I had no chance to say what I wanted to say. I did try. 'I can't even seem to see the children. Nick has been gone ages. I'm so alone.' 'Albert's in Vichy,' was all he seemed to hear and repeated it wistfully. 'You must try to work David,' I advised and again, 'I wish someone would give me a job or commission me to make a dress.' He didn't hear. Poor David. Despite all his riches he sounds worse off than I do even in this dreadful plight.

Told Pauline I was feeling suicidal. I am. I cannot deny it. I don't want to but I've almost accepted the fact that I will. My God. How terrifying to even write it. It's because I can't see any alternative. No money, and getting old. I just can't bear the idea. So I phoned Celia and had a 20-minute conversation. Told her about David H and actually got her sympathy. She said it's a case of 'over-talented and undereducated' and that I should talk to Liz Wyndham.

10.15. Rang David H again and got Gregory. He was very polite. Didn't sound drunk. He took my number but of course David didn't call me back.

16 APRIL

Burnett was sat at the table already when I arrived. The girl from Sidgwick & Jackson was 15 minutes late – they hadn't met and she knew nothing of me. They exchanged publishing stories. Burnett answering her questions, said he was at the lower end of the market. She's having difficulty with the forthcoming book on Boy George[53] – it has been postponed. I tried to give her an idea of what I wanted to do, with Burnett chipping in, exaggerating. He seems to think I'm making an effort to be more public – coming out more – and cited Vikki's party as an example. 'There was a lot of press there and they don't come for nothing.' He also told her I made the wedding dress for Mrs David Frost. (Where he got that from I don't know.) She said if they commission the book it should be name-droppy and waspish. 'Oh, I think it will be,' added Burnett. After my second trip to the loo I declared that I was bored. 'Does that mean you are going to leave now?' asked Burnett. I did, leaving behind the blue Perspex lighter Anita Pallenberg gave me.

17 APRIL

Burnett rang. Could we meet at one o'clock so he can collect the first draft? Spoke to Carla. 'Are you living to write, or writing to live?' she asked in her usual perceptible way. Burnett was late. He told me the scoop, 'Princess Michael's father was an SS Nazi,' was almost accidentally discovered by a *Daily Mirror* reporter. He told me Vicki Hodge is to be auditioned before Aaron Spelling of *Dynasty* fame – and she has applied for a gambling license to open a casino in Barbados.

18 APRIL

Rang Nick, 'Couldn't we have dinner before you go to work?' 'OK, darling.' So I'll see him after 16 days – I worked it out later and told him. Quite shocked by his appearance, very tight trousers, big feet, effeminate movements and hideous mirrored glasses hiding his beautiful eyes. 'Hello, darling, how are you?' he asked. 'I'm fine,' I said but was I? What do I see in him, I asked myself as he went off to buy a pint. No cigarettes so he went off to buy some and returned with a bunch of fresia – I was quite touched, so sweet like a child. 'I must see you more often, Nick. Don't abandon me,' I said. 'You abandoned *me* – you hung up,' he replied. 'What are you doing tonight?' I said.

19 APRIL

I asked Nick if we could go to Portobello tomorrow. 'No,' he said, 'it's too difficult – Robert will be there.' 'Shall we go together?' he said, knowing full well I'd say no. 'What about tonight? What about Sunday?' 'Darling, I've got to do my own thing.' He ran to get a number 9 bus. Now what to do? Feeling so alone and rejected and there isn't anyone I can turn to. I brought a can of Special Brew then spent 15 minutes in the tube station toilets waiting for pick-ups.

20 APRIL

Met Terry Donovan who asked what I was doing. Seemed a bit concerned, though I'm putting on a brave face. 'Do try to sort out a publisher,' he advised and introduced me to his handsome son.

I found two yellow roses decapitated on the wet road – perfumed.

22 APRIL

Been meaning to write to Hockney all day, yet I still put it off – what on earth can I say to him?

Carla got home before 8, 'What's the matter with you?' she asked. I gave her five reasons: I'm so lonely, I've got no money, I'm getting deeper into debt, I can't make clothes here, I don't know what to do. I could go on, I love Nick and miss him desperately being the main reason for my misery and he obviously doesn't want to know.

Carla says Celia doesn't look very happy, not sexually fulfilled. 'Why don't you write your own impressions?' 'That comes later,' I replied. 'She is a bitch,' she said of Celia, saying she had told me what to design in my heyday.

23 APRIL

Michael has got work in LA; it wouldn't bother me if they gave up living here.

Can I face another evening alone? – No, I can't.

24 APRIL

Jill Goldsmith rang so I pulled myself together and walked there. Such a pretty house. Such a pretty grandchild called Maxine. She adored Oscar and took him into the garden while I went upstairs to alter the green dress I made so lovingly. When? Two or three years ago.

Got to Studio Valbonne by 9.15, a bottle of champagne and Vikki as bossy as ever. The owner with a bald head and perfect teeth who asked me how I kept my figure and drank so much.

25 APRIL

Went to the Hippodrome in a bunch where Vikki and Mr Stringfellow had words. 'Eer, luv, I don't think that's very good for the image of the club,' said Peter, leading him out.

28 APRIL

I have just returned from Pauline in Oakley St – a junkie den with everyone waiting for the phone-call.

28 APRIL

Pauline called me – poor sod, now she's had a car crash. No insurance, no dope and I've given in to drinking whisky.

28 APRIL

[Ossie has been given a part-time teaching post at St Martins College of Art.]

Finally sent a letter express to David Hockney in California begging for funds – because I think Anthony McKay has been round this morning while I was out doing my first stint of teaching at St Martins. Miraculously Henrietta on the phone – has £400 for the leather suit, which I can give straight to Anthony.

I seem to be ageing extra quick – my hair is getting grizzled, I loathe my body, I'm slightly heavier. Don't know what I'm doing. Has David received my letter? Why doesn't anybody ring me?

Simon came before eight: 'Shall I make us a nice joint, darling?' 'No, I want to screw you,' I replied, even though I didn't feel like it – he stank to high heaven, everything he did seemed to annoy me. Afterwards the bedroom smelt awful.

30 APRIL

I wondered what to tell Sally[54] because I've no intention of making her a dress – so when she called I had my story ready. I could tell she was annoyed.

To a party in Studio Valbonne. I got photographed with the new page-three girl and even a Mafia boss. We saw Tony Curtis[55] and waiters made a fuss of us.

Carla here and Pauline, we are drinking Special Brew. 'All you've got to do is shed your laziness,' said Carla.

3 MAY

Henri phoned and invited me to lunch – she was entertaining a two-year-old child (her godchild) and a big Spanish girl looking after her (a Caledonian nanny). Henri gave me a huge whisky and reheated a lunch of liver – and later we went back to Alma Leather and bought red suede for her suit. We went back to Duke Street for a quick whisky before Hedley[56] came back.

4 MAY

To Pauline's. She explained she had to see J. 'It's business, luv, and I need it. (On Monday she was saying, 'I'll never speak to him again!') So we drove to Egerton Gardens where he lives and I waited in the car – she came back and said, 'He's got a gold American Express card. You can sign your own name and then there's no hassle with the signature etc.' I advised her not to do it – the plan being to go to off-licenses and get 20 quid's worth of alcohol. Pauline said, 'Guess who's going to do it?' (Meaning use the card to make money). 'I promised not to tell you,' she said.

11 MAY

Bombshell – Anthony McKay phoned, very heavy. 'I'm going to move in there in three weeks,' and Ben told me it's definite that Robert Fraser is a goner with perhaps a year to live – he had heard that Paul McCartney and Paul Getty offered to pay for him to live anywhere of his choice and he chose London.

Three weeks exactly is my 43rd birthday.

14 MAY

Met Danny Moynihan[57] in the corner shop. 'Have you seen Michael Wishart,' he asked, and proceeded to complain about him being drunk for three days after his exhibition while he was staying with him.

I went to the sauna in St Martins Lane – a guy jerked me off. Such a lot going on there – I'm beginning to recognise the regulars, but so difficult to do anything. I jealously watched other contacts being made – the furtive rustling behind newspapers, the erect cocks and give-away enthusiastic leg twitching, the mutual masturbation.

15 MAY

I woke at about 8 out of an extraordinary dream where I was at the bottom of a mine-shaft with Chanel and discovered a stash of her fabric and a silk flag to commemorate the end of the second world war – Alice Pollock was there and the other girl with big tits who used to work for us. I had to make an escape from a closing trap door under water like in a Stephen Speilberg movie. The velvet was exquisite, like petrol on water. Michael[58] had slept on the sofa (not very well) and had been up for two hours. Oscar had woken him – two exquisite drawings on my table. Michael was wonderfully amusing – even in the morning – said his son is bisexual (his wife is a dyke) and was a bit worried about AIDS because he had a scene with someone who's got it, poor sod.

18 MAY

Couldn't resist buying more Special Brew, Pauline didn't help saying 'Your liver must be in a hell of a state.' I realise I am just topping up the alcohol content of my body and I'm worried about it.

19 MAY

First day without alcohol. Anthony phoned with the demand, I move out in three weeks.

20 MAY

2nd day sans booze.

Phoned Henrietta and told her my predicament. 'Something will turn up,' she said. I phoned Pauline. She was very sympathetic, 'It's probably a blessing in disguise,' she said. 'You need light and that place is not conducive to where your head is at.' Which is true. But I feel like committing suicide. I am so low, unhappy, missing Nick. I wish I could get on with Henrietta's suede suit, occupy my mind somehow. I had to pluck up the courage to ring Sid and ask if he could help me find somewhere to live. I was hoping maybe somewhere in his new home there would be room. He took my number and said he would call, but of course he didn't. I read Proust until three and couldn't sleep still – until I realised it was because I hadn't taken a pill.

21 MAY

3rd day no drink.

Really heavy rain. I walked a reluctant Oscar through the park to Stanley gardens. Sandra answered the door and was very friendly. Her mother was there. We sat at the dining table talking while Michael[59] was next door with Terry Gilliam[60]. 'We had Pattie Clapton to dinner last night,' said Sandra. Michael, seeing Oscar, asked, 'Where's Ossie?' Came in and gave me a kiss. I was invited to eat with the children and stupidly refused even though I was very hungry.

I rang Henrietta who didn't know which of four invitations she was going to accept that evening, and Pauline who said, 'Are you going to buy food this evening, luv?' more or less a command.

22 MAY

I'm beginning to panic. What on earth am I going to do? Where can I go?

23 MAY

Champagne, I couldn't resist.

Henrietta phoned and said Selima had offered me her flat, so I went to see her after the dole – she her usual dithering state and made no mention of it. I went home. The phone rang; no one spoke when I picked it up. I rang Pauline to tell her and then Adam[61] arrived at the door. He's also looking for somewhere to live. He told us he is on a charge of indecent behaviour, having been arrested on Holland Walk by two policemen.

24 MAY

Friday was a weird day. Began in bed with a gardener in Putney, then dressing Henrietta for a wedding in Duke Street, and watching dealing in Pauline's junkie den. She'd offered to take me for the drive when she went to score somewhere near the airport. I refused the offer and got arrested instead. A single policewoman. I stunned, she very chatty. I took it very calmly – a nosy woman outside commented on the weather while we waited for transport. 'Are you the same Ossie Clark who was a famous dress designer?' she asked, and, 'What went wrong?' God. If only I knew.

To Kensington Police station where I was charged – emptied my pockets, was searched and put in a cell with a man I vaguely recognised on a charge of receiving stolen goods.

'I think you'll find this a nice clean cell,' said the jailer, opening the door with his great bunch of keys.

25 MAY

I was at Marlborough Street Magistrate's Court before it opened at 10, was quickly and surrealistically fined £110 and banned from driving for three years.

No drama, just loud feet belonging to the plain-clothed policeman in charge, questions and quickly on to a very irate judge. The same smarmy heavy-footed cop who charged me and really laboured the facts. 'He was better known as . . .' etc. 'His rent is paid by the DHSS.' Everything came out pat, a little bit mangled and of course two court reporters. The judge interrupted, 'Enough of that. Now, what has he got to say?' pointing at me with his head. 'I've got noth...' I began. 'Get up,' said the policeman behind me, so I stood up and said, 'I've got nothing to say, sir.' So he banned me for three years and fined me a hundred pounds on the first charge and 10 on the second and mumbled that's the minimum he could charge. I walked out free. I repeated, 'I have nothing to say,' to one of the court reporters who scurried behind me. Jimmy said he'd been offered 10 grand to tell all he knew about me.

26 MAY

Whisky and Special Brew. Yesterday afternoon, lying on my bed in the aftermath of the courtroom drama. The *Mail on Sunday* phoned. 'Look, I've got nothing to say.' *Sunday Telegraph* at the door – I didn't open it. Then a girl from the *Mail* outside in the rain – left a note inviting me to lunch. They came again at 4.30. Drank another can of Special Brew.

'How'd you get home from the heath?' asked Carla in front of Albert.

27 MAY

Woke at 7.30 but slept on till the wretched woman from the *Mail* knocked on the door at 9.30. 'Look, I'm not talking to anyone, please leave me alone,' I said through the door.

28 MAY

11.30. The *Sunday Mirror* at the door. Oscar barking.

29 MAY

9.15. 'Mr. Clar-ar-ar-k.' The *Daily Mirror* journalist at the door again and she was waiting outside when I went to get a newspaper and milk for tea – I still refused to talk to her.

30 MAY

Hashish and five cans of Special Brew.

1 JUNE

Champagne, wine and beer.

2 JUNE

Found a big black spider in the bath. Carla said it's unlucky. I don't need a spider to tell me.

3 JUNE

[*Ossie begins to organise his exit from Redcliffe Road.*]

Nick phoned me at 9.30 to say he can't get hold of the guy with the van. What a nice way to wake up, but how ghastly reality is and I've got cold sores on my top lip. 'Your phone's still on,' he said. I plucked up courage and rang British Telecom. Told a downright lie. They will expect payment on Friday. Called Sandra. Guy seems quite confident about being able to move everything at this moment. It is very daunting. I rang Pauline, who was a bit standoffish. She suggested I stay in Hat's flat with Ben. Thought of Selima.

4 JUNE

Anthony McKay on the phone and coming round. They were actually very understanding and sweet. 'Oh, we'll forget that,' he said of the telephone bill. He asked about the cooker. I confessed the waste-disposal broken – told of the nest of moths – the upstairs banging. He was very amicable. J, snorting heroin, said, 'Ahh, if only life was like that.'

5 JUNE

Now at 7.30 the room completely rearranged. Anthony came and took away the moth-eaten sofa. I've reduced paperwork and shifted furniture, books in piles and boxes. I rolled up the carpets and swept the floor. The room almost dismantled. Carla is coming over to help with the workroom. Poor Oscar knows something is wrong – he's just lying listlessly, on my bed as confused as I am. Pauline on leaving: 'You can't stay at Harriet's. She doesn't want you there.' A forgone conclusion. At quarter to 12 I called Nick. 'I can't get the guy but Robert says he will do it for you.' As I'd feared. 'Do you think we can get the bed in his van?' I asked, trying to hide my emotion. Dear god, can I cope? I'm afraid I'm hopelessly depressed, speeding. I don't know what to do.

6 JUNE

Is this my last night in Redcliffe Road? Last night I worked out (with Carla's prompting) this is the eighth move I've made since I left Celia and 23 years since I came to live in London. I hated beer then and alcohol didn't interest me. Life was so exciting then, so easy. Why didn't I think about now? Like I think about the next 20 years now. If I actually get through this present harassing eviction. Feeling suicidal. I called Guy, he suggested selling everything. I'll have to sell something – an etching.

7 JUNE

[*Nick, Robert and Guy come to Ossie's rescue and have invited him to stay at their council flat in Islington.*]

The move to Pondfield House. Guy arrived after one. He tackled the task with more enthusiasm than I could muster but the job has to be done. Oscar has nervously settled on my bag of expensive cloth as we reduce and sift through the remains of my life over the last two years. So many reminders of Nick. Nick arrived shortly afterwards. 'Don't worry, everything is going to be OK. Look at it this way, it can't get any worse.' I told him I was jealous of Robert and hated myself for it – that I'm dreading being with them together. He said, 'It's just easier living with him – he's happy because he's working' – actually, I worried unnecessarily. Robert was late. Perfectly sweet, obliging, strong. Guy had tidied up the flat – the little room for my bed smelt of roses – he had collected a mass of apricot roses. He's so sweet.

9 JUNE

My 43rd birthday, a horrible day indeed.

10 JUNE

I got Guy to store Nick's castration painting face to the ceiling – those scissors seem to symbolise too final a snip and tidying Nick's desk photos and reminders of he and Robert on occasions when I wasn't present. So happy together while I was so miserable. I put Albert's superman-in-flight drawing on the black wall. Walking through the hall to the kitchen I heard a dull crash behind me and saw the mirror shatter in pieces. I couldn't believe my eyes. Seven years' bad luck. I shrugged my shoulders and set about to find a box and clear up the mess. I told Kay when she phoned. She talked of our grandmother and her wise sayings. She insisted she treat me to dinner and listen to her sing at her regular gig at L'escargot. Henrietta phoned – so I invited her to come and listen to Kay also.

13 JUNE

Nick came here at 2 o'clock. I kissed his neck, meanwhile on the radio, 'You are my obsession, you are my obsession.'

22 JUNE

A View to a Kill[62], with George, Nick and Pauline, who couldn't even sit through it without smoking heroin. She went to the toilet twice.

25 JUNE

Stupid Carla phoned me at 7.15 to kindly tell me Zandra Rhodes[63] on television. Henrietta phoned while I was in the bath inviting me to a cocktail party for her sister-in-law tonight.

Got dressed and went to Henrietta's party for her Indian sister in law – I was the first to arrive, a huge bin of champagne on ice. Drank a lot and had to refrain from making an Air India joke – there were so many there. And afterwards pulled the taxi driver who brought me home. 'I've got a wife and a girlfriend, I'm not queer,' he said.

27 JUNE

Pauline came over in a state. She was busted yet again yesterday.

2 JULY

Talked to a drunken Irishman drinking cider. 'We built this country and we'll pull it down.' Poor guy, I could see myself in the same position – sympathised.

3 JULY

Went to Kari Anne and Chris Jagger's charity tea on the roof gardens in aid of Broadreach House. Kay singing, a beautifully sunshiny day. We are in the middle of a heat-wave. I sat and watched a poxy fashion show, enlivened only by Kari Anne modelling a thirties tea-gown.

4 JULY

Went for cocktails with Henri to another of her relations in Kensington Square Gardens. Met the Marquis of Queensbury who invited us to dinner at his house: a delicious salmon trout – I made the salad dressing – and was very rude about Fay Maschler[64] to her sister who he was with.

22 JULY

I phoned David Hockney[65] to ask if I might see him today – call again at three, he said – even though I knew he wouldn't be home. Nick phoned at twenty past five; Guy had left a message earlier about the phone bill – otherwise I don't suppose he would have. Everything so hopeless and so alone. I just couldn't hide it from Guy who was very sympathetic. 'You could be really close friends,' he said. But I can't see it. I'm so besotted with him. I can't bear to be alone, so I rang Sandra and Michael and went over there and put a brave face on it.

23 JULY

Went unwashed, without even a cup of tea, to see DH, using returning the Proust as an excuse. He sent me off to buy milk as soon as I arrived and we had tea and I sat reading in the garden, in beautiful sunlight, while he dealt with one or two visitors. We, or rather he, brought up the subject of AIDS. He asked me how I am but he is hardly interested and soon changed the subject to his own work (no mention of my letters) and how poor Gregory is having a hard time. He showed off his recent work of which he is very proud. How we need reverse perspective to put us back in the real world and in touch with god. Then he offered lunch in a local pub. I asked after his mother and he said she was fine, had recently visited him in LA, but that Celia's father is really ill. Before he left he said, 'Cheer up, Ossie, it could be worse.' 'I know,' I replied. 'I could have AIDS,' which made him laugh – or rather brought a smile to his lips. He seems quite happy. Pleased with his work, I expect. He said to meet him at Kasmin[66]'s at three.

I got there late, he surrounded by gushing sycophants – he was going to take me to see his other, much bigger, exhibition, at the Hayward Gallery, but dismissed me instead. Totally unaware of my lonely predicament and unthinking, though it was stupid of me to have gone in the first place. Home feeling filthy and exhausted to another evening alone and more thoughts of suicide.

24 JULY

On Radio 3 news of Rock Hudson[67] suffering from cancer of the liver in a Paris hospital and when Guy arrived he had the *Sun* or *Star* with the headline, 'Rock Hudson dying from AIDS.'

28 JULY

I stayed in bed all day and fantasised about travelling back in time.

29 JULY

Nick could see the state I was in and tried to cheer me up – he still has faith in me. While I have absolutely none in myself – more and more it seems like suicide is the only answer. I told him how I had dreamt of murdering Chelita and Robert and killing myself by shooting with a gun. I told him I wish Robert would find a new lover, 'Well, I don't' he replied, 'I'm very fond of him.' I told him I was important – said he was too.

31 JULY

Henrietta invited me for drinks for her brother's birthday. Later in Stocks, Hedley drunk and Henrietta fuming. I was dancing with her friend Clementine – she slapped us both round the face as we danced on the floor then went off in a huff and took Oscar and the car.

Hedley gave me a cheque for £110 for the police fine.

23 AUGUST

Anthony McKay phoned at 8.30. He has been robbed of a video today and of course was wondering if I could think of anybody who might have a key . . .

30 AUGUST

I'm not sure if it was last night but, anyway, whenever it was it was pretty humiliating: I picked a guy up – not young or handsome – and he asked if

I had a place. We were on our way home when he caught sight of me – full-face under a street lamp. 'I don't think I'll bother,' he said.

31 AUGUST

Called Alistair, he thinks I should go to a meeting of Narcotics Anonymous. 'You're an addict, just like me,' he said.

Met George with a crowd of teenage friends. 'How are you?' he asked – what answer is there to that? How can I tell him how I really feel?

4 SEPTEMBER

Henrietta invited me to lunch. She plonked a glass of gin in my hand and all my determination not to drink went out the window. I was soon drunk and only afterwards did I realise she had gathered a party of females to give me work. I stupidly left them talking over the lunch table and turned to whisky with the usual consequence – went to HH, gambling with death. Made love to a handsome young man and took home an 18-year-old called Peter.

10 SEPTEMBER

Saw Rachel Wyndham and that boss-eyed lump of lard Lord Hesketh[68] – all those millions, taking a tube.

13 SEPTEMBER

Spoke to Ben who told me Pauline got a 15-month prison sentence with nine months suspended which means she will actually do four months, poor thing.

14 SEPTEMBER

Had a really weird dream where people were jumping from great heights into pints of shit for sport.

19 SEPTEMBER

Teaching – I was on my fourth cup of coffee before I got to my class. Eleven girls and one beautiful boy. I waited for more coffee before addressing them from the window, smoking.

21 SEPTEMBER

DH phoned and I spoke to him. 'I'll do my best[69],' he said.

Anne[70] told me Gregory is in a bad way. 'I could never tell him', she said, meaning Hockney. Poor Gregory has been on a binge for 18 months – in a clinic.

23 SEPTEMBER

Buying hash certainly was a mistake. I spent the whole day not making a shirt, just fiddled around. I don't really know what I'm doing.

15 DECEMBER

I went to visit Pauline in prison at Bullwood Hall, Hockley, in Kent. Met Henrietta there and left Oscar with her. She, dizzy as usual, was waiting in the wrong place.

It was my second visit – last time a weekday, we had a solitary meeting in a room and then were moved to a small library mostly made up of Mills and Boon paperback romances. This time I was taken to a much larger communal room – full to the seams with prisoners and their families. I took her overcoat and two books. More red tape at the entrance. Soon over, I rushed to embrace her. She looks exactly the same – slight argument about visiting time and how long I was to stay. She was bubbling, very happy to see me. I made her laugh. At four o'clock she is locked up for 16 hours. She didn't seem to mind. 'I'd love to take a few cigarettes but I daren't.' That was how she lost her job as a screw's trustee. She couldn't even take the Kit Kat.

1 Eddie Grant.
2 Vicki Hodge, ex-lover of Prince Andrew; old friend of Ossie.
3 Guy Burch.
4 Pauline Fordham.
5 Chelita Secunda.
6 Ossie is referring to the occasion when Chelita asked him to move out of her house.
7 Jose Fonseca.
8 Jasper Johns, American painter, set and costume designer for the Merce Cunningham Dance Company, for whom he has been artistic adviser since the mid-sixties.
9 Peter Stringfellow, owner of several night-clubs in London, including the Hippodrome in Leicester Square and Stringfellows in Covent Garden.
10 Kay Melia.
11 The Hon. Charles Tennant, the eldest son of Lord Glenconner.
12 Ulla Larson.
13 April Ashley, restaurateur; notorious character-about-town.
14 Elsa Schiaparelli.
15 Marlene Dietrich, German actress.
16 Mick Jagger.
17 Nick Balaban's lover.
18 Nick Balaban.
19 Nancy Howard.
20 Felix Howard, child model used by Madonna in one of her pop-videos; son of Nancy Howard.

21 Lady Rose Lambton.
22 A gay fashion event run by Andrew Logan, jeweller and friend of Ossie, who also runs the Alternative Miss World competition.
23 Lou Reed, American singer/songwriter and guitarist formerly with Velvet Underground.
24 Prince, American singer/songwriter.
25 A Buddhist Mantra.
26 Selima Guirey. She has been staying with Ossie.
27 Ben Brierly, who has split from Marianne Faithfull, and his girlfriend Harriet.
28 The story of his split with Faithfull.
29 Colette Mimran.
30 Ossie is in huge rent arrears for Redcliffe Road with McKay.
31 Burnett Rigg, literary agent who is helping Ossie pursue publication of his diaries.
32 Alan Brooke of Michael Joseph.
33 Henrietta Rous.
34 Donna Summer, American pop-singer and gay icon.
35 Carla Ames.
36 Neither Guy Burch nor Ben Brierly set Pauline Fordham up with the police.
37 Emma de Vere-Hunt, sister of Eddie de Vere-Hunt who was a van-driver for Quorum.
38 Sid Rotbart.
39 Carol Hammond.
40 John Hammond, who by this time has separated from Carol, and Jesse, Carol and John's son.
41 Sandra and Michael Kamen.
42 Gregory Evans.
43 A lover of Ossie's.
44 To LA.
45 Cynthia Payne, celebrated madam who ran a brothel which accepted Luncheon Vouchers.
46 Chris Jagger.
47 Ian Rush, footballer, most famously for Liverpool FC and Wales in the eighties.
48 Craigie Aitchison.
49 Lord Patrick Conygham, Irish poet and painter.
50 Janet Street-Porter, TV producer and presenter.
51 Gary Crowley, British radio disc-jockey.
52 Character in Proust's *Rememberance of Things Past*. Robert Saint-Loupe is one of Proust's great portraits of the effects of sexual jealousy, jealousy which, according to Proust, prolongs the course of love.
53 George O'Dowd, British singer/songwriter, formerly with Culture Club.
54 Sally Stamp.
55 Tony Curtis, American actor.
56 Hedley Marten, chancery barrister, common-law husband of Henrietta Rous.
57 Danny Moynihan, painter; associate of Damien Hurst.
58 Michael is a man Ossie brought home on 14 May; he is neither Michael Wishart nor Michael Kamen.
59 Michael Kamen.
60 Terry Gilliam, American film director, ex-member of the Monty Python team.

61 Adam is the man Ossie met at The Night of a Thousand Frocks in February this year.
62 A James Bond film.
63 Zandra Rhodes, British fashion designer; RCA contemporary of Ossie.
64 Fay Maschler, food writer for the *Evening Standard*.
65 Hockney is in London for two exhibitions of his work.
66 John Kasmin.
67 Rock Hudson, American film actor.
68 Lord Hesketh, wealthy young aristocrat.
69 To help Ossie financially.
70 Anne Upton.

1986

Ossie begins the year at 4 Shrewsbury Mews in a flat that Bella Freud described as 'hideously modern and in Bayswater'. 1986 is a busy working year for Ossie. In May he is encouraged by Agnes Kostrowski, a friend and former model, to design a collection of lingerie under the name 'Rustle'. The deadline for the designs is 16 September. During the frenetic race against time to meet this date Ossie's diary entries provide a fascinating insight into his working practices.

When he is working Ossie seems highly energised by his task; indeed it seems to improve the quality of his life a great deal. On 7 September he exclaims, 'I am working again and indeed it does feel good. How I can have spent all those months, years even, doing nothing seems incredible to me now.' Indeed Ossie seems happiest when working and 'glad to be alive'. 'The time is flying and really goes fast when I'm at the sewing machine,' he declares. Throughout August Ossie seems to thrive on the pressure he is under, filling his diary with words, waking in the middle of the night to write it up, and becoming angry with himself if he does not make an extremely early start to his day – 'Up at five past eight. Thick head.' His lingerie designs are exquisite.

Inspired by this rediscovery of the pleasures of work, Ossie begins another job, working for Tanya Sarne at the Ghost design label. Despite the shock of working regular hours, Ossie at first seems to like this new challenge and he and Tanya rapidly become friends. This job and the friendship provided by Tanya help Ossie enormously this year, improving his quality of life a little and alleviating his money worries slightly.

A setback comes when the lingerie designs prove too delicate and complicated to be made up in a factory, and Ossie's susceptibility to mood swings resurfaces on his return from a trade fair in Harrogate: 'I know I'll lose if I don't produce.'

Ossie discovers another ally, Dr Michael A.F. a'Brook, who, as Ossie's pyschiatrist, gives him something he has been sorely missing since Nick left him in 1983, a sympathetic and understanding ear. Ossie, as usual, has much to talk to him about. He is still bitter about Celia's relationship with David Hockney, and is visibly in pain when he hears of Hockney's suggestion that Celia, Albert and George go to live with him. Ossie also needs to address his addiction to amphetamines which becomes more and more evident as the year wears on. Dr a'Brook encourages Ossie to face these things, and – as a friend, which he rapidly becomes – attempts throughout the year to find Ossie a business backer.

Neither of Ossie's new friends are able, however, to help with his biggest problem, his inability to find a stable and permanent home. Ossie moves again this year when Prudence Glynn, a former fashion editor at *The Times* and a great admirer of his work, offers him the chance to rent part of her house in Powis Terrace. Within six weeks of Ossie moving in, however, Prudence is dead and Ossie is forced to deal with her relatives over his right to continue living in her house. He tries to convince Paul Getty to buy Prudence's property, but by the end of the year is not having much luck.

17 MARCH

9.30. *Pebble Mill at One*[1].

19 MARCH

Cut off my beard.

21 MARCH

Woke at 7.49. Rang Carol[2] to wish her a happy birthday. She's very happy. I thought Kay[3] had been poisoning her against me, as I'm convinced she has with the Kamen[4]s, who are on holiday in Switzerland. Michael won a BAFTA award for *Edge of Darkness*.

Carla[5] here with a Special Brew at 3.30.

22 MARCH

Up before ten. A grey rainy day. I walked Oscar to Portobello and had a chat with Carol, who goes on about John[6]'s return. Of course I'm very pleased for her, but bored of hearing about him, and Celia (who has got four pages in *Harper's*), and Kay, who says I downed a bottle of brandy at the Kamens.

23 MARCH

Really had to force myself to cut the remainder of the negligée. I would rather do anything else. And no cigarettes until Carla came at about two o'clock. No money in a way would soon stop me smoking.

24 MARCH

Excited about seeing Nick[7]. He had suggested we go for a drink over the telephone, so we did.

He told me he felt claustrophobic, that he wants to be alone, to be by himself in the country. To my surprise he said he'd like to go away with me. I put records on the jukebox – Elton[8] and the like – the sentiment didn't go unnoticed. He didn't mention what's-his-name once – neither did I – I couldn't believe he'd suggested we go away together. So I asked if he really meant it – he said he did but time was the problem – we stayed till 3 and got slightly drunk. I embraced him – I didn't want to leave and when I got home I rang him to tell him I love him – 'You told me already,' he said.

12 MAY

I slept on the floor in a flat near Gower Street after an odd night with Ben[9]. Drinks in a Soho pub and back to his place where I made pasta. We played Trivial Pursuit and I won. Ben complained of pains in his kidney, a warning to me – struck home. No more drinking for a while. I am determined to do it. I find myself longing for booze. So far resisted. I am ashamed of my appearance – overweight.

Meanwhile the gas in 4 Shrewsbury Mews has been turned off. A real drag. It appears the garage door has been open all the time I've been here. They just walked in and took the meter away, disconnecting it. And I stupidly simply ignored the bills.

20 MAY

[Agnes Kostrowski is trying to get Ossie to work for her company Rustle, or at least to use his patterns. But Ossie can't see what's in it for him.]

I slept till after 10, phoned Agnes and went to the Barbican Centre to see the Cecil Beaton exhibition.

6 JUNE

I kicked a horrid dog that attacked Oscar so hard I've really banged my big toe.

9 JUNE

The bath overflowed.
The bailiffs. Yuck.

30 JUNE

Relapse on the fiftieth day without drink. I had two pints and a trip up the hill to rethink pent-up feelings.

20 JULY

Spent all day making Marie[10] bodice.

16 AUGUST
Officially moved into 26 Powis Terrace[11].

20 AUGUST
I gave Prudence £120 and complained about the smell of cat piss.

22 AUGUST
[*Ossie has to get a collection ready for Agnes by 16 September.*]

I'm very worried about all the work to be done.
12.30. Now sat here with Carla, trying to work up some enthusiasm. What a battle. Smoking a joint and feeling shivering and cold.

23 AUGUST
I went to my old cornershop, bought another Brew and took the tube to Hampstead. Just after dark when I got there. I fucked a moustached Scot and brought home a Mexican called David.

24 AUGUST
Carnival[12]. A spade friend of Ben's gave us tea and a line of speed – he plays a trumpet.
'Dogs are like video cameras,' he said, looking at Oscar. I was quite surprised when he accepted my offer to share my bed and we made love after a fashion. Lots of poppers left by the Mexican bandit.

25 AUGUST
The carnival music is getting louder and louder. Bob the busker stayed until after Guy[13] arrived at 1 o'clock. I had to give him £2 to get rid of him. Meanwhile pouring rain. I gave Guy a book to read while I finished the bodice pattern of the nightdress. Prudence had come down for her by now customary chat. I can't make any impression on her about the stench of cats or the daily fresh turds. I hate those cats. They are vile.

26 AUGUST
Carla came at five and Bella[14] went off to Morgans to buy cotton and a zip. We were upstairs while Bella tacked but I remember her sewing downstairs at my machine. 'That is the first time I have sewed anything like a straight line,' she said, and quite enjoying it. Carla chatted to Pru who is very impressed with her while Bella muttered under her breath she had given me £15 and we were now drinking Special Brew.
I took a taxi to Hampstead Heath and, despite the damp and muddy ground,

the usual gathering. Eventually I picked up an Italian waiter from Napoli who looked like Burt Reynolds[15] in miniature. He could only have been 5 foot tall but with a beautiful body, the outlines emphasised with black hair. He didn't say much and refused poppers.

27 AUGUST

It was after two when Agnes got here with Andi[16] and the velvet.

There is so much to do. I simply couldn't cope if Agnes failed me. I asked her about the Dexedrine I feel I need. Indeed, I've got to have them if I am going to pull off this miracle. She had already talked to one of the committee women who said she could help but couldn't. And so she phoned the other: 'What are amphetamines?' I heard Agnes asking. Anyway the outcome is I've got an appointment tomorrow with Keith Stoll, a psychiatrist.

28 AUGUST

At twenty to six I took a taxi to the psychiatrist who turned out to be a psychoanalyst who had worked with Selima[17]. It was a bit odd really. I explained what I needed and he set to asking me questions about my childhood and family. He couldn't prescribe amphetamines.

I was in there about 1½ hours – and at the end, 'Um, um, what shall we do about my fee?' So I filled in Agnes' cheque for £55 – but found a note saying David, my Mexican bandit, had phoned, so I called him back and arranged to meet at 9.30.

To kill time really I called Celia. 'Hello, darling,' she said. Apparently she had called me on Pru's number, and said Anthony Page[18] has suggested we design a theatre play for Lindsay Anderson[19] to be put on the West End with Malcolm McDowell[20]. She was full of news of Los Angeles. Mo[21] is thin and drinking again. A beautiful house with 5 cats and Lisa[22] not very nice. Ian[23] HIV positive. Jimmy Sweeney[24] took the children to Magic Mountain. They went to Utah and Mexican Hat. They really enjoyed themselves and she said she would like to spend more time there. Tonight she's off to meet Rupert[25] and looking forward to meeting Bob Dylan.

I met David[26] as arranged and had good sex. 'I want you to fuck me,' he said and I did. Lovely.

29 AUGUST

It turned out to be a wonderful day. I got lots done. Agnes a great help. We phoned lots of people and I began a very positive list.

George came round and helped me move the television up to my flat. George told me more about LA including DH having bought the house next door in LA and offering it to Celia if she goes to live there, and Albert and George. Selfish cunt.

30 AUGUST

After my bath I discovered three crabs in my pubic hair. Who left me that boring legacy and no money for the lotion? Today my mother would have been 80 years old. My thoughts are often with her.

Bella phoned soon after I got up about 10.10. She had got 3 pills for me and will come over 1.30ish.

2.00. I called Bella who, as she was just leaving to come and see me, discovered her brother had absconded from his drug clinic. So she was unable to move, keeping a tight reign on him.

[*Ossie collects the pills from the front desk of a strip club in Soho.*]

Now now, what did I do in the evening? I remember cutting the striped silk into skirt panels with Prudence hovering over me, and I cut the inner bodice (I'm writing this on Monday evening listening to Kraftwerk[27]) and of course I had the telly and *Twilight Zone*[28] and horror movies I can do without.

1 SEPTEMBER

I woke at ten to five, so got up and put laundry in the washing machine. Made tea without milk, read a little about jewellery, and went to bed to masturbate. Difficult to keep a hard-on.

At last a postcard from Nick in Greece. A naked man, what else? I knew he would send one. I'm so relieved, I dithered about taking the remaining speed pill but eventually did.

[*Ossie travels by train to Hayes in Kent to meet Michael a'Brook*[29]*. He describes it as a 'Hitchcockian adventure'.*]

Dr M.F. a'Brook was very sympathetic about the difficult journey but went through the usual regime. What was your relation with your family? Are your parents alive? Etc., etc.

2 SEPTEMBER

[*Back in London.*]

What a fantastic day. Carol came grumbling after ten (I had almost given her up) but she turned up trumps. She immediately suspected what the pills were I was collecting from Baker Street. I told her special vitamins and I had to eat one green vegetable a day and a piece of fruit.

Kay came at three to clean the kitchen. Carol said Kay doesn't get on with Pru who thinks she is a dirty bitch.

I'm really enjoying sewing again. The striped sequin and Devil-is-a-Woman bodices are going to be a treat. Both are going to be exquisite.

4 SEPTEMBER

Up at five past eight. Thick head. Trying not to be despondent. Thirteen working days left. Last night I pinned the black lace up on the wall and gave up trying to figure out how to cut it. This morning as the speed enters my bloodstream it all becomes clear. I shall simply put it on the net and make the bodice construction and lining separately.

I must not be disheartened by feelings of inadequacy. I will produce 12 white rabbits from this empty top hat empty top hat empty top hat empty top hat.

Carla spent the whole day hand-sewing the pink beaded bodice. Beautiful it looks too. Neither of us ate anything all day.

I went down to the basement to sew and Prudence appeared like an apparition. Was fascinated watching me sew. 'It would be nice to be doing something like this when Suzy Menkes comes to interview you.' She had better bring a gas mask, I thought to myself, if she is to visit this basement. Maybe I should ring and warn her.

5 SEPTEMBER

I spent the afternoon cutting the rest of the lace. The sleeves alone will be a work of art. I shall use every offcut. I was sorely attempted to machine them, but the cat stench has now reached the top of the stairs (I have to close the sliding door to my flat to keep it out of here) plus my time would be better employed cutting. I have so many ideas it's difficult to decide what to do first.

6 SEPTEMBER

Eventually I was forced to sew the skirt lining and patch the toile together downstairs in the cat's piss parlor. I have left the window open permanently so the smell not too intense but fresh turds right under the cutting table. Carla cleaned them up which was unfortunate because Prudence came down and, when I complained (saying what are the journalists going to think who are coming to interview me), she replied: 'If you don't like the heat stay out of the kitchen.' I had finished sewing so I said, 'It's none of my business so I'm going to make my pattern,' and left her to talk with

Carla. I was furious. The stench is much worse. It hits you the minute you open the front door.

7 SEPTEMBER

Again I got up in the night and wrote my diary.

I'm amazed that everyone is so thrilled that I am working again and indeed it does feel good. How I can have spent all those months, years even, doing nothing seems incredible to me now. There is no doubt speed has a marvellous effect on me. The work is really going a treat.

8 SEPTEMBER

The time is flying and really goes fast when I'm at the sewing machine.

9 SEPTEMBER

Up at 6.30. The velvet jacket on the stand is just fabulous.

11 SEPTEMBER

Trudy, the model, arrived at exactly the right moment so I could fit the bustle effect on the skirt. She stood patiently while I fiddled with the positioning. And how perfectly it worked – a perfect complement to the shapely bodice. She was looking amazing when Liz[30] arrived. Fortunately Prudence was out as Liz thinks she's mad and, I'm afraid, that's the general opinion in Fleet Street. Then we had a little fashion show. Trudy tried on everything I've made so far. Fabulous but still masses to do. Carol had arrived and made tea. And Ben was here. After Liz escaped Pru's imminent return, I rushed back to my machine and Ben left, taking Trudy with him. 'I don't think I can get it up,' he said. Well, the skirt surpassed all expectations, is absolutely fabulous and new, even though it's a Victorian concept.

12 SEPTEMBER

Poor Carol in a state arguing with Joe[31] over money. I suggested we go away on hols when this show is all over.

As I sat working on the coat pattern wearing a T-shirt, I felt that peculiar itch and on inspection pinpointed another horrible crab, which I cracked on the glass table. I must get some Quelada[32]. Obviously they won't just go away.

I met Derek Jarman in the street. He has been in New York for the opening of his movie *Caravaggio*. I didn't tell him I thought it a piece of shit and walked out after the close-up of Chelita[33]'s pock-marked face which no amount of plastered on make-up could disguise.

Prudence complained about owed rent and says she needs the basement.

13 SEPTEMBER

Alone for the first time in a while, I phoned David (the Mexican, now abroad on business)'s Scottish flatmate who I fancied over the phone. I invited him over for a drink and he said he would be here at nine. Neil (I think that's his name) came at 9.30. I finished cutting the purple bodice – with a mistake. Then we went to bed and fucked each other. I feel guilty about the, by now, very obvious crabs.

14 SEPTEMBER

Up at 7.30. My groin very itchy, which is extremely irritating. Neil up 15 mins later. I still couldn't bring myself to confess. I'll phone and pretend I've just discovered them while taking a bath. I applied the Quelada lotion. That'll put paid to the little buggers.

15 SEPTEMBER

I will have ten dresses if I cut the last black velvet. It all seems an impossible task as I counted only five pieces, some still only a bodice tacked together and ideas on paper.

I machined and machined, went into the street and vomited bile[34]. Again till the green spool ran out. Bed at five.

17 SEPTEMBER

Special Brew. Drinking hers caused Carla to fall apart – no more work from her, just giggling.

I lost my hat and sunglasses last night. My fingers are very sore from sewing.

I told Carol I felt, in kicking the dog which broke my right big toenail (now almost totally regrown), that it was since that act of frustration I felt a change, that everything from that moment would be all right, a definite change in my destiny. She understood. She talks constantly about money, can't understand the way I live.

18 SEPTEMBER

I spoke at length to Agnes. Again about money. She desperate. Andi's dole not through. I told her my idea of trying to raise money and, if I did, I wanted more control in the company's direction.

Guy arrived and made tea and drove me to Highbury through thick traffic. I collected a few things: diaries, pictures, my clock, a mirror. Nick wasn't there but arrived just as we were leaving – still looking gorgeous, fading tan. I saw the photo of the German boy[35] – very close receding hair, not handsome, not handsome. In a strange way I'm quite pleased about it, and I hope Robert[36] is going through what I felt. But I don't expect so.

19 SEPTEMBER

Isabel[37] and Carla worked like a dream today. But still I underestimate how long things take to get made to my exacting measure.

20 SEPTEMBER

Up at six-thirty. A huge moon still in the sky, the brightest of the year.

I went to see Carol at 10.40. She bitched Kay. And on to Highbury on the tube, and the train to Canonbury. I collected a few things. Couldn't find swim togs. I peeked again at the photos of Rudi and wonder what on earth he sees in him. 6'2" and a deep voice.

Guy at the Venus cafe. I didn't get there until 20 past 12. I'd told him last night I'd got two lovers, which is sort of true. John, whose pots I've got and haven't seen since I moved to Powis Terrace, and David, who is on his way back to Mexico. Not to mention Neil.

Nick is besotted with Rudi. Says he's going to learn German, maybe live there. Most intriguing of all, Robert doesn't know. He still loves Robert, but they don't have sex anymore. I look forward to further developments and hope Robert gets really hurt. I still love Nick but don't think of him so often.

After the 3rd Special Brew with Guy and Pauline Fordham I crashed out till 8. When I woke, dinner was ready and Guy had tidied up and rearranged the flat. He's so incredibly considerate. After dinner we did the tarot on Guy's suggestion. Pauline's first card was death. Obviously heroin, though she denied it. After she had gone I discovered her lighter and cigarettes and, inside, the foil tube she uses for smoking the evil vile drug.

21 SEPTEMBER

Poor Oscar's got a burst abscess on his anus.

While I was downstairs working on the green silk nightdress, Guy phoned to say he had found a small packet of brown powder in the packet of cigs he took last night. P's heroin. 'I feel like throwing it away,' he said. But instead I got him to bring it here and, when he arrived, got him to fix up two lights I'd retrieved from Highbury. It is still the most beautiful day outside. When Pauline came over we went to Hyde Park and walked around the Serpentine.

23 SEPTEMBER

Vanessa[38] called at 10.45. She's sending a car to collect four pieces plus the purple top – sent by cab at 11 o'clock.

This morning I spent a good two hours writing in my other journal, trying to catch up on the last two years. Fascinating reading it all makes. Bad news from *Vogue*, I'm afraid. Miss Nuclear War quite likes the striped purple/green bustier but that's all. Vanessa is sending them back in the morning. 'What can I do?' she asked. 'I did my best.'

I called L out of the blue. He was surprised to hear from me, asked what I'm doing on Thursday. I quite want him to fuck me but, like Oscar, my anus is sore.

24 SEPTEMBER

8.00 up. Grey morning. Feel terrible. I must stop drinking Special Brew completely.

Look at Robert. His claim to fame was that he'd slept with Rock Hudson. He (Hudson) was buried a fortnight ago. 'I love it when I'm stuffing 50 pound notes in my pockets.'

Prudence Glynn died at 2.30.

25 SEPTEMBER

I am very depressed about Pru's sudden death. At last Henrietta[39] is back. She phoned, has got her court appearance for drink driving at two o'clock.

Dr M.F. a'Brook phoned whilst I'm sat here with Agnes and Andi talking about our gloomy prospects. He said he has talked to the woman – a Mrs Susan Taylor – and she's very interested and I'm to phone her on Monday morning.

I heard noises downstairs, and in walked Angus and Pru's brother, John Glynn, obviously in a state of shock. I murmured my sympathy. 'It's a bore,' he said. The other twit seemed quite cheerful

8.35 L called from Euston. I played Prokofiev and we made love.

10.00 'You have one of the great cocks of all time,' he said, as he left.

26 SEPTEMBER

Pru's obituary in *The Times*. Last night I read what she had written about me in her book and started to read *The Irish R.M.*[40]

27 SEPTEMBER

Now at 10.30 I've blitzed the flat and await Richard Miller, a solicitor, and John Glynn, whose hands I'm in. They are joint executors of Pru's estate and are checking the valuables. I've offered to make coffee. In my nervous state I spilled both coffee and sugar. But I needn't have worried. Everything worked out OK.

Pierre la Roche coming for tea. He came early and gave me a book, *The Blissful Life* by Sri Nisargad Sita Maharaj. Pauline was here and we didn't have much persuading to get her to try on the clothes. And she was transformed into a Duchess. I sent her to buy vodka and she picked up Richard Vickers. He came 10 mins later with a half-bottle. He is the next door neighbour Pru referred to as her minder. Pierre and Pauline both fancied him. We were quite jolly and he said, 'I've never been in this room when it rang to such laughter.' Pru had been so heavy at times. He and his brother drew lots as to who would tolerate an hour wasted on her demented rantings. 'We knew it was just a question of time,' he said. 'She had a real drink problem.'

28 SEPTEMBER

I took two pills to cope with the move. To Highbury to sort out my remaining possessions. Nick arrived with Mo and Mandy, handsome and bearded, his hair longer, a few remaining streaks of henna. He helped me through the clothes and dirty laundry, told me more about Rudi. He's very excited about his forthcoming trip to München to see him. At 39 he really does think the German incredibly handsome, said he'd like to speak the language and maybe live there. He asked what he should see there, so I told him about my visit in 1972 when I went to the Olympic Games, about Ludwig's castles in Bavaria and the tiny Art Deco museum, the Dürers and the Cranachs. 'Does Robert know?' I asked innocently. 'Of course he doesn't. I am going to leave him. Anyway we don't have sex anymore.' He insists he spent a week cuddling with Rudi which I find hard to believe, but want to desperately. Everything fitted into the van wonderfully. Mo drove and Nick sat on my knee – no escape. I cuddled his torso all the way home, tweaking his nips and drinking in his peculiar odour, which I find so erotic.

29 SEPTEMBER

Ben called from a local pub at 8.30. The Warwick Castle on Portobello. I met him for a drink and we went to the British Oak. He's here now phoning his friend Herman whose house he's staying at. Now he's talking to Pauline. Carol asked her why she takes heroin. She replied, 'Because I was spoiled in the sixties.'

30 SEPTEMBER

On Pru's scales I weigh eleven stone.

2 OCTOBER

11.00 Dr M.F. a'Brook. As usual he is just marvellously understanding.

3 OCTOBER

A bill from Dr M.F. a'Brook in the post. £110 – phew! For two visits.

4 OCTOBER

Up at 8.40 out of a dream with Hockney – as usual DH making everyone's life miserable.

Carol whinged about John – last night drunk, menacing her with a baseball bat and taunting her about Joe. 'Whadda ya gonna du boutit?' Why she let him know, I can't understand. She's really fed up and talking of divorce.

5 OCTOBER

To the Two Brewers to meet Neil and eventually to see a male stripper. I peeled off the stripper's sock and he offered a kiss – instead I got the sock in the face.

6 OCTOBER

[Ossie has spent the weekend with Neil and his friend Michael near Clapham Common.]

Neil got up and went very early to work. Michael brought me coffee just before nine. I showed him my erection and he sucked it and jerked himself off. I'd sucked Neil when he came to bed. Even though he pretended to be asleep I made him come.

I phoned Agnes only to discover D was raped on Saturday night. She's not at home so I haven't spoken to her. I do hope she is OK.

1.55. Got D on the phone. She laughing, so OK. It was a boy, 18 or 19. Climbed in the window, saw nothing to steal, so knocked her to the floor and took his trousers down. He had tremendous strength. She screamed and eventually he fled with a huge erection, much to the amusement of the people responding to her cries. She's had the police all weekend.

I told Carol I'd spent the weekend with Henrietta.

I called Celia. She told me Mo's in a bad way. It's over with Lisa, and Hockney has offered Gregory $50,000 and a drawing which G has refused. He wants more and might get a lawyer. He wants to be Celia's agent in America.

D and Agnes turned up so they stayed for dinner – D a bit sour which, I suppose, is understandable. But what have I done? 'Always lived in a cloud of your own,' she says. She wanted to talk about her experience but nobody wanted to hear.

7 OCTOBER

Five past seven. Just had a nasty incident outside. I threw a glass of wine over a girl who seemed to be a psychopath – tried to steal Oscar then called me an AIDS carrier, which made me really angry. This while Carla buying

Special Brew at the corner off-license. The psycho came back more furious so I threw the other glass of wine over her. 'Don't, mummy, don't!' I heard her child cry as she repeatedly hurled herself at the front door as I escaped inside. 'Come on, Carla,' I'd said as she watched, resting on a parking meter. 'I don't want to get involved,' she replied. And when the psycho twigged we were together she attacked Carla, pulling her hair, throwing her to the ground and banging her head against a car. Poor Carla. Yet she holds me to blame.

8 OCTOBER

Violence in the very air. Agnes on the phone – Carla's got a broken hip and refuses to be operated on. She's in hospital. I feel really bad about it but refuse to accept guilt.

I collected my dinner suit in Golborne Road. 'Get yourself about,' advised the boy behind the counter, after asking did I design the shirt he was wearing. I looked at the label, which said, 'Clark. Made in Florence.'

Back via Tesco. I saw a horrible incident. Police brutality. Maybe 12 policemen dragging a mother and child apart. 'Can I have some police protection?' she wailed as local blacks threatened her. They took the child – maybe three years old – and left the mother hysterical on the ground screaming. 'I'll kill you,' she had sworn to the social worker. A great crowd had gathered, weren't pacified and went away grumbling and cursing.

Annual textile dinner. 7.15 in the City.

9 OCTOBER

More violence as a black man died in police custody. Riot at Notting Hill police station.

Dr a'Brook rang with another backer, Maggie Quinn, as Susan Taylor just doesn't have that kind of money – I remember the look in her eye as I left her. 'All part of the service,' said Michael a'Brook, and rang off after telling me to get in touch with Jilly Elliott.

The NA method – 12 steps. Ben explaining how Marianne six months cured. 'Don't you think you should try some work?' I asked – but apparently not, according to NA.

Julian rang at 7.35 and came at the end of 'Eastenders'. Not very good sex. I came too quick, due to his expert fellatio.

10 OCTOBER

Trying to raise money makes me feel sick in my stomach.

[To help him back into the 'rag trade', Ossie sees Jilly Elliott, Nadia and Swami La Vallée and Maggie Quinn.]

11 OCTOBER

Made coffee for Richard Miller and John Glynn. They think it extremely unlikely they will keep the house.

12 OCTOBER

Maggie Quinn has already checked out planning permission for a proposed outlet and reckons they would view it favourably. She loves the clothes and reckons they would walk out of the shop. But, like Sid, she's not too sure W11 is the right area.

16 OCTOBER

The four roses I stole with Ben on Saturday have opened perfectly.

Hillman, Detective Inspector, re Carla's assault. He rang just after ten to break our appointment because they have arrested the black man who attempted to rape Carla on Saturday the 4th. Poor sod.

Sid incredibly generous. Gave me £130. He was marvellous with Maggie. Put her straight and made complete sense. He is very keen we should take over his shop at 13 Marylebone Street. So we walked there to look it over.

Celia on the phone at 8.30, worried about Albert. He wants to change school and do a crammer, which is very expensive. He is also very keen to get a motor car.

17 OCTOBER

Made Pauline her black beatnik dress in 1 hour and ten minutes. She very pleased. So am I. It can be my first jersey number in the separates line.

I told Maggie Quinn to put Bernie Ozer's comment, 'Ossie Clark makes real dresses for real women with real money' in the program of the Gold Ball. And Rustle's phone number.

18 OCTOBER

Carol here ten to twelve. She stayed an hour. Has got John to agree to marriage guidance. A feeble sun is trying to get through the grey.

Phoned Neil, arranged to see him Thursday here. He filled me in on his sex life since his advert in the gay press.

20 OCTOBER

Woke very early, still dark, to incredibly heavy rain. No more alcohol for a while.

Last night was such fun. I so enjoy having the boys round, though I drank far too much vodka. I notice Albert likes alcohol much more than George.

10.15 I rang Sid[41] to say I think 'Jane Rustle' is a great idea for a label. Also begged him to talk to Agnes like he'd done with Maggie Quinn.

Took Oscar for a walk in Kensington Gardens. Lots of great fallen branches from last night's storm. Shopping on the way back. Tesco's plate glass smashed in riots last night. And outside now a police surveillance helicopter hovering menacingly.

Percy has got Montpellier to give us a free party on the 16th November. Who do I want to invite? Shall we invite Susan Taylor and Maggie? No, as I hope there won't be any need for their service by that time.

22 OCTOBER

Up at 8.30 Agnes coming over to collect the lingerie – let's hope she's got some cigarettes. Five past ten – where is she? Because I can't do anything without a cigarette.

23 OCTOBER

Up at 8 o'clock, drinking lots of Perrier to flush the alcohol out through my kidneys.

And a very beastly letter from Neil in the post. Sexually we are incompatible so he's not coming tonight. Disappointment at first. Now I don't care.

I'm actually pleased Neil isn't coming tonight as I have to confess impotence. I haven't had a hard-on for days.

Carol phoned just before 8, fed up because Jimmy is more and more demented.

24 OCTOBER

The downer day. I'm feeling washed-out and depressed. So alone.

25 OCTOBER

I realise I talk to the cats in Pru's voice. 'Hello, darlings,' she would say to them and to me too. I really miss her.

[Ossie goes to see Mona Lisa *with Alastair.]*

What a fine actor Bob Hoskins is. I remember making his second wife's wedding dress, and I also remember meeting Neil Jordan over dinner at Sandra and Michael's. I love his circus imagery – a white rabbit and dwarfs. It was very exciting. I had to hold on to Alastair's arm, and afterwards we drove to visit the Kamens. Michael says it was really Bob Hoskins' movie, as he wrote the script and showed Neil Jordan what to do.

26 OCTOBER

Lunch at Pauline's. She did me proud – a half-bottle of champagne and a delicious meal. Some excellent grass from New York. Openly she smoked her heroin under my nose. The pretence is over, which is just as well. Now it's just as it used to be – as though she had never gone to prison. 'I keep thinking about F,' she said. I'm afraid the truth is she's a much nicer person smoking that awful stuff and I half suspect she's dealing it as well. Colin the DJ came round to get some. He's going to try to get us into a Red Stripe Durex party on Wednesday in Heaven. Michael Clark is going to dance a durex dance and there's going to be a durex putting-on competition as to who can put it on most erotically. I had a coffee with Alastair on the way home. Contemplated walking the rest of the way, but didn't. What's the point? I see lots of people around I could easily fall in love with, but I seem to be invisible to everyone I fancy. So home alone again and thinking about Nick.

27 OCTOBER
[Ossie goes with Pauline to visit Pauline's mother.]

Pauline drove home very aggressively – keen to smoke, I soon realised. The phone rang as she reached for it. 'John? Yes.' So she prepared a sinister little envelope of the evil smack, now hidden in the basement, and delivered it from her car outside a church in Sydney Street. Driving me home she confessed she wished 'it' wasn't so addictive because she likes it so much. She has to find 1,100 quid by Thursday (actually 600 'cos she handed over 500 last night). Stupid bitch. It's much worse than I thought. She has got an ounce on tick and is doing most of it herself. Today she hadn't indulged until we got back, having glugged methadone before she left. Hence her aches, pains and bad temper all day. Oh, foolish Pauline. She thinks she can restrain herself to the occasional evening smoke and sell the rest, when we both know she can't resist. She will end in debt with a bigger habit. 'You talked yourself into that,' I said, after I'd asked to borrow a fiver for cigarettes and dogfood.

28 OCTOBER
Reluctantly I set to work marking out the red suede for Henri's jacket[42]. I was in the bath when Pauline arrived with her usual cry, 'Have you got any bread?' 'No, Pauline.' She's convinced she's about to win the lottery in the *Standard*.

29 OCTOBER
[*Ossie goes to the Kamens.*]

I pounced on a carton of Marlboro, stole a packet, drank coffee in the garden. I had intended to help myself to the change, usually in a bowl in the kitchen, but there was a man there. So I took a fiver from Sandra's pocket – I have to admit it – and bought copydex and vegetables and cigarettes. In one way I don't feel guilt. In another, what a little shit I am. Will she miss it, I wonder? Anyway, it's just a means to an end. At least I can glue the seams open of the suede jacket and eat supper.

At ten o'clock I arrived at Pauline's to go to the 'Cum to a Party' at Heaven. A vodka and a line of speed before we left. We were too early. A queue. Pauline made a fuss, loudly dropping my name. Inside quite a mix, mostly pretty and half my age. The show didn't go on till 2 o'clock and was a con.

30 OCTOBER

On the radio, 'Time keeps on slippin' into the future' – Steve Miller Band. Ten years ago I was doing jigsaw puzzles – at least I remember the big circular Chinese dragon – how foolish to have wasted all that time.

31 OCTOBER

9.40. I rang Paul Getty.

Lovely day. I'm rich and Pam gave me £100.

2 NOVEMBER

I bought the *News of the World* and, looking out of the window, saw a handsome roadsweeper. Walked past him and bought *The Times* just so I could have a closer look.

Arrived in Oakley Street at 2.30. Pauline very cheerful, fire glowing. 'Vodka or whisky?' she asked. Told me how she had scraped another £500 together for her dealer in Maida Vale, how he generously let her off the extra hundred she didn't have.

'I want Paul Getty to buy the house for me and I want Sid to run the business.'

4 NOVEMBER

Maggie Quinn on the phone again, fussing. 'I can't get hold of Agnes,' etc.

9.45 Sign on. I got there at ten, having bought a day pass at Westbourne Park tube station. How Joe Public, the average guy, manages it every day is beyond me. I certainly couldn't do it each day.

[*Ossie inserts 200 studs into the suede jacket he is making.*]

About five o'clock a ring on the doorbell and a man called Peter Webb writing a book on David Hockney[43]. 'Can he interview me? Tomorrow maybe? After he's seen Celia?'

5 NOVEMBER

At the London Clinic I told Paul Getty two stories about Cecil Beaton fucking Garbo after agreeing to have his hands tied. Paul said, 'She might as well have used a dildo.'

[*Afterwards Ossie goes round to the Kamens' and notes with relief they haven't noticed his theft of five pounds.*]

'A cross between Robin Hood and Sir Walter Raleigh' is how I described Henrietta's red suede jacket to Pauline on the phone. My fingers get more and more tender but the jacket looks better and better.

6 NOVEMBER

At eleven a reporter and photographer from the *Mail on Sunday*. I told them it wasn't convenient and they are coming back at 3. They said they want to write a story about the charity show, but it smelt a bit suspicious to me. Fucking press hounding me again. Who has got a vendetta against me? Out, damn Spot.

Pauline is so vulgar. All the heroin-smoking makes her nasal passages blocked so she coughs and flobs all the time. 'Ugh! An oyster,' she says gleefully, gobbing it out. It's quite horrible.

7 NOVEMBER

Bombshell. Just after I'd called Percy to warn him about the *Mail on Sunday* reporter, she, a Linda Doodley, phoned and said of course she'd agree to send me a list of questions etc., but there is just one other matter. 'Why am I living in Prudence Glynn's house?' 'I don't think that's any of your business,' I replied. 'Well, we hear from a cousin the family don't want you there.' 'But that's ridiculous. They are only too pleased I'm looking after her cats,' I said. I just knew instinctively something was up. And such a bitch from the tone of her voice. She continued, 'We hear you don't get on with the cats.' 'Who said all this?' I asked. 'We are not at liberty to reveal our source of information.' I phoned Pru's cousin in Bath and she was as flabbergasted as I. 'We are only too pleased you are there,' she said.

8 NOVEMBER

In the post a letter from the DHSS informing me a supplementary benefit officer will visit on Monday.

A beautiful sunny day with a blue sky but very cold. I spent a couple of hours writing, then bathed and walked to the market about 1.30. First I bought a rent book. Afterwards I gave up the idea of locking the ground floor. I think it's impossible but fortunately it looks locked when the door is closed. So now it's a question of removing all traces of opulence and earning power. The TV and video, the telephone, my work and stand, etc. Shall I even hide the vase of flowers? I'm beginning to wish I'd never applied for the paltry 30 quid per week rent. There are easier ways to get money.

TV was lousy all evening. How I hate all these quiz shows that entertain the general public so – Paul Daniels and Bruce Forsythe – UGH!

9 NOVEMBER

Up at 10 o'clock to a slow start. Remembrance Sunday on television. The Royal Family and other old farts laying wreaths of poppies when I would much rather have looked at the handsome soldiers.

Lunch at Pauline's. She was extremely stoned. Said she owed her dealer another £700 and only had 10 grams left to sell. She gave me a couple of snorts of sulphate. I left after six but it wasn't until I was in bed at 3.38 that I realised just how strong it was.

And despite all those pamphlets and the TV program warning of AIDS – strolled up and down Westbourne Grove. Almost picked up a drunk bit then lost him.

10 NOVEMBER

A visit from the DHSS. They, two Asian women, came at 11.30. One did the talking – got everything wrong. Gave me a pamphlet entitled, 'Living Together as Man and Wife'. No, dear. I explained my story – depressed in Highbury, difficult to find a job being an undischarged bankrupt, etc. No, dear. It's self-contained. I don't share my sitting room. 'If you've had no money for the last month,' she asked, how I'd managed? 'I've got a sister lives nearby and I've simply had to ponce off people,' I replied. I showed them my bedroom and bathroom. And downstairs the beautiful roadsweeper sweeping leaves outside my door. I actually spoke to him because somebody had dumped a pile of old clothes outside my house. I asked how I could get it removed. 'Maybe he'll take it away,' he said, pointing to his older companion with a mobile refuse cart. I grabbed the opportunity to just gaze at him. 'You've got a never-ending job,' I said. 'That's true, but only one more week and the leaves will be gone.' Beautiful mild sunny weather. So I took a delicious bath and put the video and telly back and settled down to altering the neckband on Pam's blue velvet dress.

11 NOVEMBER

I love the name 'Ghost'. A nest of vipers. All those Scorpios and Capricorns.

12 NOVEMBER

Pauline came over while I was making Pam[44]'s slip from a scrap of blue silk.

She very stoned. Immediately complained about owing her dealer 900 quid and she's only got 300. She really gets on my nerves.

13 NOVEMBER

Woke out of a dream. Nick was between me and Robert. I was between Nick and Carla. What on earth does it mean? It certainly quite upset me.

The roadsweeper at work outside my front door as I left. If only I could make contact. Instead I walked to the dentist's, dejected in drizzle, to have my teeth seen to.

14 NOVEMBER

[Ossie has been receiving threatening calls and borrows my answerphone to record them.]

15 NOVEMBER

A trip to the toilet, a glass of Perrier water, and my two magic pills. And back to bed to cuddle Oscar and masturbate.

Suddenly I remember ripping the etching above Celia's bed and feel a little guilty. It slipped from the frame so easily and I tore it apart with satisfaction. Perhaps she will just give up now trying to hang his pathetic efforts on her wall after all[45]. I must have destroyed ten or twelve of his so-called artworks, the most dramatic occasion being the nude Celia drawing at Philip Prowse, Christmas 1984.

Gazing out of the window at 10 o'clock I saw the roadsweeper. So rushed down to buy a newspaper and say good morning.

Agnes found out – (as I suspected) Carla is responsible for the press harassment. So I am completely finished with her.

16 NOVEMBER

Pauline came after two – very stoned, and drunk like a tornado. I was feeling so fragile. She intolerant and demanding my complete attention. Her constant coughing and gobbing up is particularly revolting. She's taking so much heroin it even affects the way she speaks.

18 NOVEMBER

The sudden realisation that I have to go to work at Ghost. I hate rushing and I'm not awake without my bath. I must stop smoking – I've got two years at most, otherwise I'm sure I'm not gonna live long.

I find Carla heavy on my mind and realise I miss her. Can I cut her off completely or should I forgive, if only to stop any more evil complications, like her ringing the DHSS. And what if she found out I've got a job etc?

[Ossie goes to my birthday lunch.]

I sat opposite Patrick[46]. He mentioned Joe Orton's diaries describing where he's crammed between visits to cottages on the Euston Road. He gets ragged by his son and school-friends who scream, 'pooves, pooves!'.

19 NOVEMBER

I noted the roadsweeper at work in a new blue uniform.

20 NOVEMBER

Although I really don't like going to work I enjoy it once I'm here, but oh! how many problems. Tanya[47] told me someone said, 'So long as you've got Ossie Clark, you'll be OK.'

21 NOVEMBER

Is it the spirit of Pru which causes me to sit up at night reading Chips'[48] wartime diaries and drink red wine?

Henrietta phoned early to say she had got off – her driving case thrown out of court. 'The police told such whoppers.' She is elated.

I returned to Chips' diaries. His exotic life just faded away. Why did he divorce, die so young? I have a feeling, despite all Chips' riches and social success, I am like him. Even the same hairstyle, till he lost it. I felt quite empty at the end of the book.

23 NOVEMBER

Quite a sad and lonely weekend. Mostly reading.

24 NOVEMBER

[Agnes tells him that Rustle is in financial trouble, so Ossie decides to make some clothes for Carolyne Waters and Marie Helvin, among others.]

25 NOVEMBER

I spent the whole morning writing a piece about Peter Lee in my journal with the use of *Roget's Thesaurus* for the first time.

Unscrupulous swindle, deception dastardly dishonest, prudence caution intuition foresight anticipatory.

27 NOVEMBER

Drunken Day. Disastrous Night. Lost my hat. 1.25 in Duke Street, drank three vodkas and was very amusing – I arrived at Ghost pissed, people staring at me on the way. Tanya gave me more vodka, a bloody Mary and a joint – then I worked on a trouser pattern and a waiter's jacket – all the time joking with the girls. The 20s dress went through the wash and came out an Ossie Clark.

9.30 The Special Brew had the usual disastrous effect. I fell in the mud, lost my hat, though I did find somebody to drive me home. If I'd known he wasn't going to stay, I'd have gone back to look for my headgear.

28 NOVEMBER

It was a wonderful day, that clear bright light like early spring – as though winter already over and summer to look forward to – I realise I must always have hated the cold winter. I put my trainers in the washing machine and hoped for the best. I realise I am glad to be Alive.

1 DECEMBER

The first of the month and another new moon and a Monday. It must be right to stop drinking for a while. But, of course, I had to finish the red wine and the white.

7 DECEMBER

Lionel Bart to lunch.

Except he did not come.

I'd spent a week organising my lovely late lunch. Went all wrong. The linen, the roses, the lamp with the patchwork silk, the rampant lion cushion. All beautiful.

8 DECEMBER

I phoned Carol who had just finished composing a very revealing letter to her lawyer re a defence divorce.

9 DECEMBER

It was 1.40 when I got to Sandra's. She was in a foul mood because of a £1,000 phone bill and having still not found a house to live in. They go to Barbados next Wednesday. She had to go out to the bank and search for a bra for Annie Lennox[49] who she adores.

10 DECEMBER

I'm going to organise the Balaban Xmas party which I only promised to do on the condition Robert wouldn't be there.

I was very late for Nick. 'For God's sake, take that hat off!' he said. I embarrassed him – 'You're just an old queen.' We saw a movie – I shouted at the man next to me because of the stench of his popcorn.

11 DECEMBER

I've made a plan to stop smoking cigarettes on my next birthday with the help of my camp-coloured cigarettes and my holder that's 'longer than Princess Margaret's', as Jane Rainey said.

Sandra was very negative on the phone about Carolyne Waters. 'I don't think she buys much eveningwear.'

12 DECEMBER

No humour, no sex.

13 DECEMBER

Up at five to nine. Oh dear, a hangover. Roger[50] gone at six. I just knew he wouldn't be back and was immediately guilt-ridden and sad. He hadn't wanted to sleep with me and did [so] very reluctantly and rejected my persistent desires.

I wrote a postcard to Molly Balaban saying, 'If I had a magic wand I know what I'd wish for.'

Ulla[51] came by – I told her I thought David Hockney a genius. We disagreed.

14 DECEMBER

Roger's birthday. Actually quite a nice day. Spoke to Roger at five past six. He not upset at all. He was merely tired and couldn't phone because my number was in the car.

Seven little goldfish I rescued. 'You're going to feed them to the cats,' said Tanya.

15 DECEMBER

Carol in the kitchen. 'Isn't it awful about Mo,' she said. 'He's in prison for beating up Lisa.'

16 DECEMBER

[*Ossie has been delaying for some weeks now a visit north to see Beryl.*[52]]

Carol said the reason Beryl wants to see me is to give me the £300 Mum left me. And, boy, can I really use it and how stupid to assume the worst.

17 DECEMBER

The day just flew by making Marie's dress.

18 DECEMBER

[*Ossie goes to Warrington to visit his family.*]

Disastrous beginning to my quick trip north, but lovely when I got there.

Bastard cunt hostess had me turfed off the coach. Objected to Oscar, even though the driver and everyone else didn't mind at all. I was seething with rage as I phoned Carol to inform Beryl. I walked in the spring-like sunshine and realised it was probably all for the best. The coach to Warrington with mindless people like sheep accepting anything without complaint. The whole journey a nightmare. The video blasting an incredibly loud black and white movie I'd seen. Nothing to do but sit back and watch it.

Beryl has knitted me a huge sweater but I'm not sure I like it. Outside like Siberia. Margaret and Bev came over with Jade[53]. I made delicious vodka, orange and Perrier. I felt in good form and made them laugh with anti-Semitic jokes and wisecracks.

19 DECEMBER

[*Ossie returns to London.*]

Up at 5.30. Very dark. Rain lashing at the windows as I made coffee in a jumper. Beryl up at six. Made me a bacon sandwich as I took a shower. Taxi ride too early and the coach late. Almost full of sleepy people. And outside and covered in snow, the sky the colour of lead. I slept a while. Dawn didn't come until 8.30, a dull blush on a range of distant hills. About an hour from London the black clouds opened to reveal a section of blue day.

3.00 Marie Helvin to fit. She came early and I was downstairs still sewing her skirt. She's going to do a TV show called 'Frocks on the Box' and says I must be her guest on it. She's so nice – loves the skirt.

'My mate says you're in *Emmerdale Farm*,' said a man in the pub next to Highbury tube station.

20 DECEMBER

I saw the dreaded Carla on crutches hobbling along Golborne Road. 'Hello, Carla' was out of my mouth before I realised it. 'That's the last word I'll ever speak to you,' I said straight into her ear as she drew level with my left shoulder. A sort of bemused look on her face.

22 DECEMBER

Time flies when I'm handstitching and I'm making this garment with love and beauty. It's going to be exquisite. I was very groggy from the two 2-mil Valium I took in the middle of the night to counter the extra yellow pill I took to get it together last night.

2.15 San Lorenzo. The Balaban Christmas Party. Guy was very sweet, gave everyone Xmas presents.

23 DECEMBER

Cramp in my leg. Horrible and cold when I awoke and pain in my innards. I am not going to drink at least until Xmas Day.

[*Ossie has to undergo another unpleasant visit to the dentist.*]

2.22 I rang Paul Getty and I'm trembling as I write. I'm going to see him for tea tomorrow. 'I've unearthed some photos of my stay in Marrakesh. Are you up to seeing them?'

Ten past ten. On the phone to Carol. More trouble with John who left the house drunk as she arrived.

24 DECEMBER

[*Ossie fails to find Paul Getty at the London Clinic but decides that 'psychologically I must have missed him on purpose'.*]

25 DECEMBER

Dreadful dream. Mocking teenage boys reading my diaries.

[*Ossie spends Christmas Day with Tanya Sarne and others. He goes down quite well with Tanya's father who Ossie describes as a 'great bear of a man who lay on his back to eat his Xmas dinner balanced on his great belly'.*]

26 DECEMBER

[*Ossie prepares a dinner for Nick, Albert and George. Everyone arrives late, but the meal is even later. Nick is in a bad mood and Ossie is upset Nick won't give him a 'proper Christmas kiss'. Ossie ends the evening by watching* Some Like It Hot.]

I watched that fabulous movie – Marilyn Monroe worked her magic charm – to cheer me out of my (I have to admit it) depression. I still love Nick with all my heart. Today's lunch, despite everything – the scented and coloured candles and delicious food – Nick was hardly there.

27 DECEMBER

Albert here talking about dear Mo. He's out of prison in a new flat overlooking the lake in Echo Park, working for DH. Wept on the phone to Celia on Christmas Day. Poor Mo. I was so looking forward to seeing him. He's really determined to stop drinking otherwise he will be dead in a year.

I went to Pauline's on the 31 bus. I could feel the tension between her and

Rocco as soon as I arrived. But I'd drunk a couple of large whiskies so, relating her tarot reading, I really put my foot in it by sending a glass of wine crashing over her precious stash. We are both afraid she is taking more and more dreadful heroin. She was really angry but managed to control it. It's true she never goes over the top, no matter how much or whatever she takes. Dinner was just delicious.

28 DECEMBER

Bleary-eyed, I began work handsewing Marie's bodice. It's looking really good. So simple from the outside, it belies the fantastic amount of work inside and all that construction.

29 DECEMBER

I scrubbed the kitchen floor. How I hate grease underfoot.

30 DECEMBER

[Ossie sends Marie Helvin her dress.]

Cottaging in Victoria Station. I picked up Ian with a black Scottie dog. I invited him back for a drink and fed his greedy dog (which cocked its leg as soon as it walked indoors) on chicken wings just going off. It had just crunched the last one when he discovered the bones and, freaking out, he made a hurried departure. He was hideous anyway. 39 and ugly teeth.

31 DECEMBER

Angry that Hockney hasn't even bothered to phone me. Angry that Nick hasn't answered my calls. And I seem to have mislaid my wand.

Congratulations from Marie. The dress a great success.

On the news. JP Getty has given £10,000 to restore somebody's birthplace.

Nick rang at 12.30. Could not say he loves me because Robert sat next to him.

1 Ossie was invited to the program to discuss fashion in the sixties and his clothes.

2 Carol Hammond.

3 Kay Melia.

4 Sandra and Michael Kamen.

5 Carla Ames.

6 John Hammond.

7 Nick Balaban.

8 Elton John.

9 Ben Brierly.
10 Marie Helvin.
11 The house owned by Prudence Glynn, former fashion editor for *The Times*. Prudence had a great affection for Ossie and admired his skill enough to allow him to move into her home so that he find his feet and once again put his talent to great use. Ossie was allowed to use her basement as a workroom.
12 Notting Hill Carnival.
13 Guy Burch.
14 Bella Freud, fashion designer; daughter of Lucien Freud. She was introduced to Ossie by Ben Brierly because she wanted help with some pattern cutting.
15 Burt Reynolds, American film actor.
16 Andi Kostrowski.
17 Selima Guirey.
18 Anthony Page, British film and theatre director; former director of the Royal Court Theatre.
19 Lindsay Anderson, British writer, critic, actor and film director.
20 Malcolm McDowell, British actor.
21 Mo McDermott.
22 Lisa Lombardi, Mo McDermott's new wife.
23 Ian Falconer, close friend of Celia's.
24 Jimmy Sweeney, costume designer; friend of and assistant to David Hockney.
25 Rupert Everett, British actor; friend of Celia's.
26 Ossie's new Mexican lover.
27 Kraftwerk, German synthesiser band.
28 *Twilight Zone*, spooky sixties American TV series.
29 Michael a'Brook, psychiatrist; became a close friend to Ossie.
30 Liz Smith, from the *Evening Standard.*
31 Joe was Carol Hammond's boyfriend at this time.
32 Quelada lotion, for the treatment of hair-lice.
33 Chelita Secunda.
34 Ossie had been smoking strong hashish earlier in the day.
35 Rudi, whom Nick met and fell in love with on Mykonos in Greece.
36 Nick Balaban's lover.
37 A machinist working for Ossie.
38 Vanessa de Lisle, Ossie's assistant in the sixties, then became editor of *Harpers and Queen* fashion pages.
39 Henrietta Rous.
40 *Some Experiences of an Irish R.M.*, a bestselling collection of stories by Somerville and Ross.
41 Sid Rotbart.
42 The jacket was part of an outfit commissioned to wear to the Wessex Party's region-

alist campaign for seats at the European elections, and supposed to be something simple in country colours – the result was a red suede jacket covered in studs.

43 A biography with Hockney's cooperation to be published at the time of his 1988 exhibition.

44 Pam Procter.

45 These etchings were by Adrian George.

46 Patrick Procktor.

47 Tanya Sarne, fashion designer, proprietor of Ghost.

48 Chips Channon. His diaries are a social and political record of his time.

49 Annie Lennox, British singer/songwriter, formerly with The Eurythmics.

50 A pseudonymous lover.

51 Ulla Larson.

52 Beryl Westell, Ossie's sister.

53 Margaret Clementson, Beryl's daughter; her husband Bev and their daughter Jade.

1987

Despite great attempts to convince Patti Harrison and Paul Getty to buy Prudence Glynn's house; despite trying to discourage the estate agents appointed by Prudence's family to sell the property; and despite attempting to ignore the various notices to quit the property that he receives; on 20 September Ossie is forced to move out of Powis Terrace after losing a court case against the executors of Prudence's estate.

Fortunately the DHSS find Ossie a small flat, in Penzance Street, Notting Hill, but once again, Ossie's confidence seems to take a great blow as yet another move awaits him. Indeed, towards the end of August, with the pressure of eviction bearing down on him, he seems more reliant than ever on amphetamine pills to get him through the day. 'Whatever would I do without them?' he declares. Of course, Ossie is candid about this throughout his journals and the reader is very aware that he is almost continually taking 'uppers' and 'downers'. This year, however, they seem ever more to dominate his life, as he himself realises when he writes: 'It suddenly occurs to me that the drawers on either side of my desk where I keep my pills – Valium on the left and Dexedrine on the right – are like the sides of the caterpillar's mushroom in *Alice in Wonderland* and in the same way I go up and down.'

Despite his eviction and his bouts of depression, Ossie is quite active. He spends a lot of time out on the town with his old friend Wayne Sleep and even more of his time, it would seem, on Hampstead Heath. Because of his increased sexual activity, he worries a great deal about AIDS and about the possibility of someone discovering his 'debauched sex life' by reading his diary. Ossie undeniably feels rather guilty and ashamed of his sexual habits and realises the danger inherent in them. However, in recording his exploits in his journal he also shows us that he sees no point in keeping what he does hidden or in denying his true feelings. 'I cannot tell a lie,' he states on 27 August. 'I must write true everything. I am ashamed to – again I went up to the wretched hill.' When on 27 March a friend suggests that he should consider editing some of the sex from his diaries if he is considering publishing them, he finds the suggestion 'rather prudish (especially after reading the Orton diaries).'

Despite a high profile in the press, with interviews in the *Sunday Times* and *Elle* magazine, Ossie is still broke and is becoming increasingly bored with and 'sick' of money and the necessity of continually thinking about it. His mood is not helped by the death of John Kloss and the deterioration of his friend Bill Gibb who has cancer. Still, he is able to help much more fortunate friends such as Tanya Sarne with their problems and, more importantly, has lost none of his wicked sense of humour. He is able to smile at the irony when on 7 April he reads a Samaritan poster which asks, 'Could you face Divorce, Eviction and Bankruptcy on a Monday morning?'

There are strains of sadness this year. In June Ossie reveals his anxieties about old age after being compared with Charles James. He imagines fearfully what life will be like in 1997 when his dog, Oscar, will reach the age of fifteen – a horrible portent: Oscar will die in 1992 aged ten, and Ossie's horrific killing will be only four years later.

1 JANUARY

Nick[1] at 7.30. I had to take a taxi because I was so late – he was on the corner with oiled hair in black. The pub closed so we walked to Soho – a rent-boy pub, just boring. I wore eye make-up, drank vodka – how I long for him, adore him, wanted him. 'I'm impotent,' I tried to explain as he rejected angrily my caress. 'I'll go home,' he threatened. Really it was a failure.

2 JANUARY

Celia's birthday. Another selfish cunt. Fuming with rage and a shout-up with my selfish cunt of an ex-wife – she has the green gabardine suit I made for Bianca[2]'s ill-fated movie *Trick or Treat*. 'What's all this queeny talk? Oh! Darling!' she mocked, knowing I hate to be called a queen. I'll never get it back, she said, when I asked her for the suit. 'Where are the boys' Christmas presents?' Anyway, fuck Celia. I can do without her slagging off. Fuck her.

3 JANUARY

Dinner with Tanya[3]. More delicious cocktails and Jackie[4] moody in bed.

4 JANUARY

'Thank you for cheering me up last night,' said Tanya. God, she saved my life.

6 JANUARY

So I went to see Ulla[5] in Zandra[6]'s smelly house. Really, she must be a creature of dirty personal habits. Ulla, on the other hand, was charming.

[*Ossie journeys north to see his family.*]

Carol[7] still irritable. 'Sometimes I think I must be part Jewish,' she said, 'because I'm so like them.' She certainly is tight. She even asked me for half the petrol money.

7 JANUARY

Day in Chester with Margaret[8], Beryl[9] and Carol. Got out as the cathedral bells struck 11 o'clock – the cathedral where I sang as a choirboy 31 years ago.

'I think it's disgusting you came without any money,' Carol said later. As though I had any choice. I took a hot bath and bitched about her to Beryl. Beryl made me laugh. On the news a vicar in a car crash – 'I was dragged out by the Balls,' referring to the misses Balls on their way to choir practice.

8 JANUARY

Edina[10]'s 44th birthday and officially 41.

Pattie[11] to lunch. I greeted her in the street and we walked and bought vodka. 'How is it with Eric[12]?' I asked. 'Or shouldn't I mention him?' 'No, it's OK, but I just can't be enthusiastic,' she replied. 'I've told him I want my own flat in London.' 'Darling, why don't you buy this house?' I said, and the idea went home.

14 JANUARY

To the Kamens[13]'. Sandra looking very healthy with her Caribbean suntan – Michael in LA working on the Mel Gibson movie. So she alone and driving the Mercedes (just expensively repaired after some uninsured cunt smashed into the back of it). Nervous, she asked me to accompany her to Harrods. She as expensively dressed in animal skins as the other shoppers. Fitted in perfectly – all the money it must have cost and they all looked identical. Fox, mink, badger, even sable – all pathetic and I'm sure just as bored with everything as she.

16 JANUARY

8 o'clock. Strand Theatre stage door to see Wayne Sleep. 'Give him a brandy,' he said as I was shown into his dressing room. He was on sparkling form and the show, *Cabaret*, was quite good. (The last time I saw him in *Dash* with Nick – a bit of a boring hotchpotch.) 'The whole of Kent has cancelled because of the weather.' The theatre wasn't even half full but it didn't dampen his enthusiasm – what a trooper he is. Course, I should have realised when he said, 'I've been doing this show eight times a week for

over a year,' that he must be using some stimulant. Before going out on the town we zoomed to some Iranian coke dealers in Finchley Road where he handed over 100 quid for two grams.

'You're an eccentric,' he said twice over dinner in Langan's Brasserie as he handed over snort wrapped in a five-pound note. We certainly went on a binge – he really is a star.

19 JANUARY

Neil[14] on the phone, morose and drunk – he has the AIDS virus. The Clapham roadsweeper is 'body positive' and can't handle it. 'They reckon I've got three years to live and that my liver will pack up first – I suppose that's why I'm drinking so much.' He thinks he got it from David the Mexican who seems to know all about it – all the other people he's fucked are clear. He said it is my duty to get the test. Somehow I'm very calm about it. I knew when I started taking speed I'd freak when I lost weight, and all the casual sex I've had – it's too late to bolt the stable door.

22 JANUARY

Lunch here for Pattie. Great success. She told me a very amusing story of how Eric proposed in America when she was accompanying him on tour. They had argued and she had gone off in a huff to stay with a mutual friend. Eric phoned the next morning and the friend told him she was still in bed. 'When she wakes up, can you ask her to marry me in three days in Tucson, Arizona, and if not then to forget it?' She laughed telling it and her giggle is infectious.

7 FEBRUARY

Ulla told me of R's gardener who wanks in her bedroom.

8 FEBRUARY

Wayne and his friend Tony arrived pissed and loud at 1 o'clock. Wayne was extremely generous – gave me ten quid for tin foil and £25 for a quarter of dope. Two Iranians brought a huge rock of very good coke.

14 FEBRUARY

Went to High Street Ken and shoplifted. I do hope it doesn't turn into a habit. But it's so easy and I just don't have the money.

16 FEBRUARY

NA[15] pamphlet entitled, 'Are you an addict?' 'Have you ever sharpened a needle on a matchbox?' 'Have you ever shot or snorted your best friend's morning (wake-up) high?' I answered yes to five questions. Ben[16] answered yes to them all. Henri[17] answered yes to three.

17 FEBRUARY

Woke at 7.30 to Piss, Pop and Put on the heating.

11.30 J.D. Warol Estate Agents. 'It's definitely going to be difficult to sell,' I stated emphatically as I let them out. 'It's right on frontline Mugsville – see, it's right down there (Powis Terrace), along Westbourne Park Road to All Saints Road and down there!' Yes, they agreed and rushed away.

Ossie's photograph, taken at his flat in 1987, of Lady Henrietta Rous in the rainbow dress he designed for her. The skirt is made from eighty-three panels.

22 FEBRUARY

Rang Wayne and was late to col lect £50 from the Strand Theatre, his dressing room. He fondled a pretty chorus boy I'd noticed.

23 FEBRUARY

Guy[18] tells me Andy Warhol dead this afternoon – so, another one bites the dust. Of course, Guy suspects AIDS but I'm not so sure. I rang Celia and told her – she was very shocked. 'What a beautiful man,' she said, even though she had only met him once.

3 MARCH

I rang Paul Getty – at last I am to see him. He sounded very reluctant, but maybe it's too early in the morning for him. I worked on his hat – fine pink binding, the pink lining already cut.

[Later] Well, I've finally done it – I asked Paul Getty to buy Powis Terrace. I certainly had his ear and he was bowled over by the hat – 'How did you know my size,' he asked. Grown fatter – I looked him over. Tubby belly, a grey, whiskery beard. Still lots of colour in his hair, but I noticed his legs all gone when he stood up. I could see he was all choked up looking at pictures of Tahlita[19] – I gave them to him and shook his hand and said something like, 'She's always alive so long as you think of her.'

8 MARCH

Celia said of Hockney, 'According to him, I'm the bitch.' But George told me that none of them are 'speakers' with Hockney.

11 MARCH

Photo exhibition of famous legs at the Hamilton Gallery. Marie[20] surrounded by who knows how to describe them, wearing a perfectly hideous dress. I was photographed as I arrived and each time I said hello to anybody of importance. David Bailey looked like he was up from the country in a heavy tweed overcoat and flat cap. 'I can just see the caption in the papers,' he said. 'Two relics from the sixties.' I left as Bruce Oldfield arrived. 'How are you?' he asked without any interest or waiting for a reply. I wish I could have thought of a sarcastic answer.

13 MARCH

Rchard Miller[21] on the phone and coming round with a formal letter – a notice to quit. He seriously expected me to sign an official notice, which I refused.

14 MARCH

Wayne Sleep is as paranoid about AIDS as I am. A crowd in his dressing room after the show – he was very on form. He told me a very funny story about Noel Coward – he had been to the first night of *Gone with the Wind* featuring an eight-year-old Bonny Langford[22]. When asked his advice, Noel replied, 'If I were you, I'd cut the first act and the little girl's throat.' Wayne took me out on the town. I almost left Oscar behind but he was a hit in Brown's champagne bar. Huge snorts upstairs in the office. Kevin (Wayne's boyfriend) was disapproving so we left him downstairs – he seems quite used to playing second fiddle.

19 MARCH

[Ossie has agreed to give an interview to Elle *magazine.]*

Mike Evans and Liz Leigh. I told her of course I recognised her (I didn't). She's a typical Jewess with bad skin and I suspect halitosis (though I never got close enough). He said he had once met me when he delivered a calendar of paintings of rock stars. I do remember. They asked specifically about 1967 – I told them I thought the period the last great flowering of the individual. Now it's all clones: Prince a clone of Little Richard, Blondie of Marilyn, Nick Kamen of Elvis – and in clothing, too.

23 MARCH

2 o'clock. Terry O'Neill to photograph me for *Elle* magazine. He was ten minutes early and I let him in wearing my bath towel. I explained my idea for the shoot and he complied, taking about as long to arrange the lights as I did to complete the picture – cloth on the walls, lots of little pictures, printed muslin at the window. The first lighting test was the best – I looked quite like my mother in the subsequent tests. Looking through the viewfinder he said, 'Cor, it's incredible – it's like the whole room's like this.' He didn't mention his wife Faye Dunaway and seemed a little depressed – and no wonder because in the Sunday newspapers a report of his divorce because of her unreasonable behavior. Poor sod.

24 MARCH

7.15 at George Lawson's. John Kasmin was there. I had a drink with them and stayed to ask George's advice about publishing my diaries – even allowed him to read a few extracts. He said the usual thing – get a good agent – which I am loath to do.

27 MARCH

I left Wilf[23] reading, engrossed in my journal begun in 1980. 'I'd edit some of the sex,' he said – rather prudishly, I thought (especially after reading the Orton diary).

I've perfected the art of shoplifting from Tesco.

30 MARCH

Cashed the Giro. Spent ten quid on essentials in Tesco and left with a fillet steak down my armhole.

1 APRIL

Richard Miller: 'You're being obstructive!' on the phone. 'You have no tenancy rights' – indeed. So he's finally shown his hand. 'I shall get very angry if you're being obstructive,' he threatened. He must have got my solicitor's letter by now – surely I am not being obstructive, I am being uncooperative.

3 APRIL

Sad news of John Kloss suicide. Sandra gave me the terrible news. My first friend in New York committed suicide last Sunday. Oh no, oh no, oh no, I wailed and it upset me for the whole day.

I went to the market despite the fact that my pockets were empty – I sympathised with Mrs Burnett[24] about her husband's death. I committed an act Joe Orton would have been proud of – with the same hand as I shook Ma Burnett's, I stole a pair of fingerless gloves off her stall.

4 APRIL

Feeling blue, I wrote a very bitter and sarcastic letter to Nick and sent it addressed to 'The Rt. Hon. Big Girl's Blouse' at his studio.

Spoke to Sandra. It's odd how the sudden death of a friend brings people together. I realised that when Byron[25] died. Last night she showed me a 1967 photo of herself with John Kloss – she so young and he so self-conscious.

7 APRIL

'Could you face Divorce, Eviction and Bankruptcy on a Monday morning?' asked a Samaritans poster on the tube.

To Michael and Sandra. I stole a bottle of vodka bottled with a herb beloved to the bison. I went to Pam and Sid[26], my timing spot on – I always enjoy making them laugh. Sid loved the vodka – it was new to him.

10 APRIL

It suddenly occurs to me that the drawers on either side of my desk where I keep my pills – Val on the left and Dex[27] on the right – are like the sides of the caterpillar's mushroom in *Alice in Wonderland*, and in the same way I go up or down.

14 APRIL

In the post a letter from Trespass[28]. Not helpful, in fact quite gloomy – their notice to quit is going to turn into a possession order – very downer.

[On 30 April Ossie has a show at a Mayfair salon; it is sponsored by Neil Zarach, who gave Ossie one of his first shows, and Jerry Hall, Marie Helvin and Francesca Thyssen all model for him.]

7 MAY

Albert moved in with me.

19 MAY

Georgina Howell re an article[29]. Georgina, it turns out, was always a fan. Said she felt she was at the fringe. She brought a tape-recorder and asked really interesting questions. I told her stories of The Rolling Stones – 'Slower, slower!' she squealed as she took notes.

23 MAY

Wayne Sleep dropped in out of the blue, very drunk, with George Lawson and another person who very reluctantly handed over £20 to get vodka and hash. Wayne called his friend Kevin, and Wilf came round. The plan was to go out to dinner but Kevin was in a very bad temper about being neglected overnight and he gave Wayne a clout – a lump like an egg on his forehead!

24 MAY

We went to Tramps last night after I bawled Kevin out. Stupid, he's just stupid and Wayne would be better off without him. Once again Wayne told me all sorts of extraordinary things about himself – how he used to stand in front of the Caravaggio painting in the National Gallery and ask God to make him grow up just like Bacchus. 'And he did and now I'm not sure I asked for the right thing!' he added with a laugh. Returned home to find Sid very excited, trying to get at something under the armchair – it turned out to be a young sparrow, which flew from my hand out the window, I hope to safety.

27 MAY

Slept with Wayne. Dinner with Tanya and Jackie – pinched her bath and interrupted a fuck about to take place. She was furious.

31 MAY

Rang Tanya to thank her for dinner. 'Well, I didn't finish it because you two pissed me off,' she said. 'I know, darling, but Wayne's something else – if you think I'm difficult he's ten times as bad. He's loony.' 'Yes, darling, he's loony, aren't we all?' 'I'm not giving back the watch until you return my tape,' (Mozart). I then went on about Aloe Vera until eventually, 'OK, Ossie, I've got the message. Now we are just going to finish making love.'

5 JUNE

'Listen, are you on speed? I'm worried about you,' said Jose[30].

10 JUNE

I was late for my own dinner with Tanya. Ulla was already very pissed – sang German songs and gave me roses. Edina told me Sandra's mother Elsie died. I sat next to Dick[31] and told him jokes. Tanya is quite a different person with people she doesn't know – puts on her little girl act. She had known Edina since they were children and played together in Campden Hill Tennis Club.

Percy[32] described Annette Worsley-Taylor[33] as 'someone you don't really get on with, you put up with' – rather like a bad case of piles.

11 JUNE

Whole day working on Gill Goldsmith's dress but didn't finish it in time for the ball – poor Cinderella.

12 JUNE

The *Sunday Times* article in which I appear today, 'Big Splash'. In one of the photos I look like a newly hatched owl.

Tanya phoned – sounds in a mess. Jackie has left her and she's very unhappy. Odd that one goldfish should have died as she's discovered a letter saying he feels terrible guilt at leaving his wife and child.

16 JUNE

It was Wilf Butler who first compared me with Charles James[34], though I'd already made the connection because he owned an old dog – I remember thinking, wondering, dreading how it will be when Oscar's old. And me. Now I will be left with him on his fifteenth birthday.

22 JUNE

A real Monday feeling. Quidejeta[35] difficult and I am ADAMANT she will make a shirt in the exact sequence and method I want. I demand perfection, as I said to her. 'I'll only make you unpick it if you do it wrong.'

Tanya called to wish me luck and tells me Jackie is coming back tonight – to work for Ghost. 'I'd rather have him back part-time than not at all.'

16 JULY

Amazing of Celia to say I am a genius and, what's more, that no one refutes it. Am I a genius? Certainly I've never thought so. Instinctive, extraordinary, imaginative, creative capacity.

19 JULY

Lunch at Sabrina and Tony Fry's. I sat next to Peter Maddox[36] who was prickly. He told me that last time he had seen me was on my 33rd birthday, when I'd told him I had got an identity crisis! I told him jokes and put him down. He told an amusing story of Robin Maugham[37] who had gone to visit Harold Nicolson[38], and in the rose garden Harold got down on his hands and knees and fiddled with Robin's flies. He was in a quandary as to what to do – in the end he decided not to spoil the moment for Harold (aged 81). Peter thought it an admirable thing to do and so do I.

28 JULY
Stupidly gave ten quid to the drunken woman in the launderette without giving her my address and, of course, no sign of her when I went to look for her at 3.

6 AUGUST
Five to twelve: 'Mr Getty is having breakfast.'
Five to one: 'Mr Getty says can you call him next week, please?'
Fuck Paul Getty. He is a cunt. However, life must go on and there's Chessie[39]'s tutu to finish.

8 AUGUST
Rang Albert from Tanya's. 'Your fucking friend Wayne Sleep is here and is driving everybody mad.' Wayne was very drunk, had been up all night and although he put on a very brave face, I could see he was very freaked out and a little sad. He is moving into a new flat and, 'Guess what, the mortgage is £500 per week and I don't give a fuck.' Kevin is still in the picture and he talked to him on the phone. Would I like to go to Freddie Mercury[40]'s birthday party in Ibiza on 24th September? Yes. 'I'll try and swing it.' FM is having some sort of horrific – cobalt, is it? – on his nose? Face? Not AIDS.

9 AUGUST
Nick in his studio – he was in a very happy mood, almost demanded lots of cuddles yet always pushing me away, which I always do.

14 AUGUST
I am sick of money and the effect it has on people. Where can I rustle up the necessary funds? It seems I need at least one hundred pounds a day.

15 AUGUST
I left this message on Fran's answermachine at ten past nine: 'I'd like you to know that I haven't got enough money to eat, even.'

18 AUGUST
Quijeta at the sewing machine, handstitching. She had tidied up the kitchen first and remembered to bring black plastic bags, for there is a stench, a stench which is revolting and I can't figure out where it comes from. Under my nose now even as I write.
Horrified to discover jumping fleas at my ankles by the bed. I remember Celia in a room at Ladbroke Grove, sat on a bed – 'Watch,' she demanded and,

putting her feet to the rush matting, half a dozen fleas jumped on to her already horribly bitten legs. 'My god!' I was appalled. 'You had better come and stay with me,' I said, and that was how we first came to live together.

19 AUGUST

One year ago today I moved into Powis Terrace. God, if only I had known what was in store for me. Prudence[41] was alive but only just – poor darling. She was so ill and lived only 36 more days. How those nurses could have let her get into that state, I'll never understand.

I was still friends with Carla[42], she was living on that hideous housing estate – with all the drunks and druggies and the alcoholic mute neighbour – helping me to get the show together. Little did I know that I would never see her again.

22 AUGUST

I rang Wayne. He full of nerves because he had given a drunken dance in Zanzibar[43] last night and is afraid someone might have taken a photo, which might just appear in the press.

Wayne Sleep, dancer and long-time friend of Ossie.

I took two Valium and slept until ten to ten. It must have continued to rain during the night, as I was immediately aware of the noise of traffic on wet roads. I went downstairs in the hope that there might be a Giro. No – instead just another wretched form. Gloom and grumbling and climbing wearily back upstairs, a dead frog sprawled on its back outside Pru's room. Back to bed utterly pissed off and quite prepared to fall into the gaping jaws of the black hole of depression. But meanwhile the sun peeped through the blanket of grey clouds and my pills began to work. Whatever would I do without them? But going back into the kitchen another frog, just alive. No. Two frogs mort. 'Fraid so.

24 AUGUST

Filled in the form for Rent Allowance for private tenants – my god, it's complicated. Kafkaland again. I can't cope with this. 'Yes, I can!' I said out loud, clenching my fist.

25 AUGUST

Great excitement. Four fire engines in Powis Terrace to put out a fire smouldering three doors down. I went outside to look – at the firemen, really. The chief they addressed as Col, short for Colin. He had beautiful teeth and a moustache. Two policemen came to turf out the guilty dosser who turns out to be the loony who walks around talking to himself and throwing his arms about.

26 AUGUST

Patrick[44] rang the doorbell around midnight and I let him in. 'Listen, man,' – he began undoing his trousers – 'I need to go home to Waltham Cross and I need the taxi fare so if you want a fuck, I've got a lovely arse' – indeed he has. 'Give me a smile,' he said at one point. Of course, I responded, but very sternly said, 'Come on, admit it, you like being fucked, you like cock up arse.' And he let slip his real feelings when putting on the contraceptive – he said, drooling, 'Cor, you've got a lovely cock.'

27 AUGUST

I cannot tell a lie. I must write true everything. I am ashamed to – again I went up to the wretched hill. It is like a magnet – the first time I went recently. I watched in horror, and repulsed by the smell of human shit, a drunk young man being savagely fucked. Thought of AIDS. Tonight I did the same – fucked a guy, snorted his poppers, thought of the dangers of AIDS.

30 AUGUST

CARNIVAL. Once I got outside with Oscar there were good vibes and food and drink stalls everywhere. We walked to Tanya, in a foul mood talking of Pauline Fordham. 'Let's give her credit for staying away,' she said. 'I thought I as going to have to look after her for the rest of my life.'

31 AUGUST

Albert was sick last night after yesterday's garbage food. Celia has forbidden Albert to come to this house.

Nick here with Graham[45] and Mo[46]. Graham very pissed – told me he hasn't asked Nick to come and live with him because of me. I told him I knew that (because in fact he did ask Nick, who then threw it in my face all the time). I think he thought he was being sincere.

I gave Nick huge hugs as he eagerly tried on his jacket. 'When are you going to finish it?' he howled. Mo and Graham were very impressed. Nick explained that I won't finish it until he comes back to me. I whispered to Nick to come back after. 'After what, Christmas?' he joked. After he got rid of him, I hissed, nodding to the drunken sop Graham. Nick laughed, but didn't come back.

7 SEPTEMBER

I got Albert up early and sent him off to enroll at Hammersmith and West London College. He came home around four and apologised that he hasn't yet moved into Celia's house. 'Did you get into college?' 'Of course,' he replied and later enthused to Guy about the computers and advanced technology.

8 SEPTEMBER

'I'm going to move to mum's house today,' Albert announced when he got up.

13 SEPTEMBER

In the supplement of the *News of the World* an article about PG[47] – really puts paid to any hope he might give me this house.

20 SEPTEMBER

[*Ossie begins to move out of 26 Powis Terrace after losing his battle against Prudence Glynn's family to stay, in Bloomsbury County Court. Fortunately the DSS have found him a very small flat in Penzance Street in Notting Hill.*]

The fourth trip. The fish, the carpets, more pots, the plants, mirrors, the cupboard for sewing thread, etc. On the way I met my neighbour who must be a single man also. Tells me my flat has been empty for about a year. I set up the fish in the kitchen and discussed ideas with Nick. Nick is so incredible. Fiddling about while I was deciding what the last load should be, he pressed 123 on the push-button and opened the front door. How ironic to discover the secret opening two days before I leave.

21 SEPTEMBER

John Glynn[48] phoned. Apologised for phoning and said I hope to out by tomorrow night.

Even a year after her death, Prudence Glynn still sending her encouragement – a piece in the *Telegraph* with a mention and the photograph of her choice: a 1969 chiffon and satin trouser-suit, garment of the year in the Bath Museum.

I have got the uncontrollable urge to find real love and I can't even get a hard-on. 1 o'clock, home with Steve – a lovely wide-boy, 31 years old, Scorpio, has been in prison under a masculine front, has a longing to get fucked which he only discovered 18 months ago. 'I love your cock,' he kept saying. He sucked it for hours and I fucked him proper, though I didn't come again (I'd come in his mouth on the heath). We smoked lots of dope and finished the vodka. Didn't get to bed until 5.15. He marries on Saturday.

22 SEPTEMBER

Mo phoned from LA[49]. Wouldn't stop talking about Hockney, an absolute stretch of venom – 'I hate him, surrounded by blue-rinsed AIDS victims and rent-a-death' – after he's thrown him out. Mo's back in his own little home. What Hockney must do, I don't understand! Mo sounds exactly like Gregory[50] had when he said, 'I'm on holiday and as far as I'm concerned that's anywhere away from him (DH).'

23 SEPTEMBER

Vile day – back to Powis Terrace to find the locks being changed and John Glynn and Richard Miller tut-tutting like a pair of old chickens.

Albert had promised to come and help at 3 o'clock. I found out later that he had taken an aeroplane to the south of France with Celia and George to stay with Rupert Everett on film location.

3 OCTOBER

Speaking to Beryl. Told me lots of family news: John[51]'s eldest son has emigrated to Australia. Ian, the second, handsome boy, is about to leave home; and his daughter Trace still overweight. His mother-in-law has put herself in Winnick to take a rest from her cantankerous husband Jimmy Tunstall who is demanding of her all the time, and pipe-dreams (what will he do when he wins the pools, though he never does them any more). 'I wish they were all like Margaret,' she said wistfully. Angel's husband, who's rather thick (can't even spell elephant), is going to university. Gladys[52] has been staying with Beryl. What a mad family I've got.

9 OCTOBER

Bombshell. When I called Nick after 3 he said, 'Where are you? You said you'd be an hour – I want to buy an overcoat and I'm going to stay with Robert[53] tonight.' 'Oh,' I said, sounding like his mother. Even as I muttered I realised how Celia must have felt when long ago I'd given her reasons why. The death of our physical passion was how I'd put it. 'Oh,' she'd said, and must have felt the hurt I was now feeling. He couldn't have hurt me more if he'd stuck a dagger in my ribs.

15 OCTOBER

Evening with Tanya and a visit to Lynn Franks, who was actually quite pleased to see me. She filled me in on all she's been doing – Coca-Cola, clothes, etc. – and told me the gossip of Jasper Conran and Galliano having an affair. 'He may have the talent but I have the money,' is apparently what Jasper said.

29 OCTOBER

Spoke to Nick.
'Hello, shit-face.'
'Hello, fart-face.'

4 NOVEMBER

Sick, hungry and alone. Inertia, too.

7 NOVEMBER

Jimmy and Christine[54]'s wedding. Tanya had organised the wedding feast in an Italian restaurant off Tottenham Court Road. I've learnt my lesson – where I would once have guzzled, I now sip and count the amount of alcohol I consume.

Later, under a canopy of trees, wondering why I bothered to go, one of my fantasies suddenly appeared before me. A kilted Scotsman, stumbling tall and broad-shouldered, lost yet by instinct in the right place. I moved square on him, our body-language spoke and we agreed. We fell into an embrace, locked together for a moment like two broken pieces that travel great distances to soundlessly click together and become whole and complete.

10 NOVEMBER

'Do you think it's time to approach PG Tips again?' asked Michael a'Brook. By PG Tips he meant Paul Getty.

14 NOVEMBER

Shout! Shout! Let it all out!

15 NOVEMBER

Dinner: Tanya, Alvin and Jill[55]. I told them the story of Tony Secunda[56] busted with a gram of coke in his knickers – on arrival at the police station he pulled a dramatic scene: opened his fly, pulled his trousers and underpants down to his ankles, then, unnoticed, deftly retrieved the illicit drug and swallowed it – packet and all – and began to scream, 'I know you lot are perverts! Go on, then, feel me up, I don't care, you're all puffs,' etc. Apparently Boy George always when being searched says, 'Careful, I might like it.'

18 NOVEMBER

Kings Cross tube a ball of fire. At 8 o'clock a wooden escalator I've used so often burst into flames. I had the horrors thinking Nick could so easily be passing through about then.

18 NOVEMBER

'Do you shoot to kill?' – graffiti on the condom machine in the toilet at the Coleherne.

2 DECEMBER

I'd just fallen asleep when the telephone rang. 'Ossie,' in a voice I immediately recognised and full of remorse. 'It's Carla.' I slammed the receiver back in its cradle. Damn! The last person I want to hear from. I do miss her but I cannot forgive her evil deed. George called. 'You hung up on her? You're silly.' But he didn't know she rang the *Daily Mail* claiming to be Prudence Glynn's cousin.

13 DECEMBER

Robert was asleep when I called just after 11. 'Have you seen Nick?' he asked innocently. 'I never see Nick nowadays, Robert – he's got a new boyfriend.' 'Yes, I know, have you met him?' 'No.' 'I wonder what he's like.'

19 DECEMBER

One day I felt very panicky that someone might [read] this diary without me knowing who might let it all out – expose my debauched sex-life. I have almost lost one or another several times. I don't think they can be published until I'm dead – don't see how. Even Jose was to mention when you can publish your diary – if only she knew what I was up to on Saturday night and Sunday night and Monday night, too, and several other nights lately.

22 DECEMBER

Saw Celia's red-painted room – was touched to find one of my drawings among the first collection of hung artwork.

23 DECEMBER

Bill Gibbs in hospital. I could hardly recognise him – he lay on his back without any Kyo, so weak and in pain constantly. Propped his head against pillows, only his arms with movement, so thin and drained of colour – like marble, even, with a tinge of blue. I didn't know what to expect. God, it was so sad. His eyes revealed some of the terrible pain he is suffering when they rolled to the back of his head and periods of lucidity then he got things wrong. He is drip-fed his painkiller which is morphine-based. He talked of my children. I could see sometimes that I wasn't getting through – though he made it clear that he remembers Mo so I told him all about Mo, how he was near his death. I didn't dare ask but I suppose the end is near for Bill. I can't imagine the pain he's in, I just can't.

25 DECEMBER

Christmas Day. On Celia's mantleshelf I recognised Sandra Kamen's handiwork amongst the greetings cards – peevishly I thought I must get all my belongings back because she didn't send me one.

1 Nick Balaban.
2 Bianca Jagger.
3 Tanya Sarne.
4 Jackie, friend of Tanya Sarne.
5 Ulla Larson.
6 Zandra Rhodes.
7 Carol Hammond.
8 Margaret Clementson.
9 Beryl Westell.
10 Edina Ronay.
11 Pattie Clapton.
12 Eric Clapton.
13 Sandra and Michael Kamen.
14 Neil was Ossie's lover in 1985.
15 Narcotics Anonymous.
16 Ben Brierly.
17 Henrietta Rous.
18 Guy Burch.
19 Tahlita Getty, model; wife of Sir Paul Getty until she died of a drug overdose in 1971.
20 Marie Helvin.
21 Richard Miller, Ossie's landlord.
22 Bonny Langford, British dancer and singer noted for her 'bubbly' personality.
23 Wilf Butler.
24 Mrs Burnett had a stall in Portobello Antiques Market.
25 Byron Upton.
26 Pam Procter and Sid Rotbart.
27 Valium and Dexedrine.
28 An organisation which advises on tenants' rights.
29 For the *Sunday Times*.
30 Jose Fonseca.
31 Dick Polak.
32 Percy Savage.
33 Annette Worsley-Taylor runs London Design Week.
34 Charles James, British designer. He showed his first collection in New York in 1928 at the age of 24 and had continued international success until his retirement in the late fifties. James apparently looked upon his timeless designs as works of art, as did many of his customers. He died in poverty with his old dog as his companion.
35 Hettie Quidejeta.
36 Peter Maddox, writer.
37 Robin Maugham, British novelist; nephew of W. Somerset Maugham.

38 Sir Harold Nicolson, British diplomat, writer and critic. He died in 1968 at the age of 82.
39 Francesca Thyssen.
40 Freddie Mercury, British singer/songwriter, of Queen.
41 Prudence Glynn.
42 Carla Ames.
43 Zanzibar Brasserie in Bromley.
44 A lover of Ossie's.
45 Graham is Nick Balaban's new boyfriend.
46 Mo McDermott.
47 Sir Paul Getty.
48 John Glynn, brother of Prudence Glynn.
49 Mo McDermott has gone back to the USA to work with David Hockney.
50 Gregory Evans.
51 John Clark, Ossie's brother.
52 Gladys English, Ossie's sister.
53 Nick Balaban's lover.
54 Friends of Tanya Sarne.
55 Friends of Tanya Sarne.
56 Tony Secunda, music PR manager; ex-husband of Chelita Secunda.

1988

Ossie spends a great deal of 1988 haunted by the spectre of his mortality. This is hardly surprising. Not only do four of his close friends die this year, but there are also disturbing rumours in the press of his own demise, which he finds highly disconcerting. Ossie begins the year mourning the death of his friend Bill Gibb, but it is the death of Mo McDermott which hits him hardest. Mo was one of his oldest friends; they had met at college in Manchester in 1964. It was Mo who had introduced Ossie to Celia, and Mo who had inspired Ossie in many of his earliest experiments with fashion. They had very similar backgrounds – both Ossie's and Mo's fathers were working class and worked at sea – and Ossie had identified greatly with Mo throughout his life. In losing him he feels as if he has lost a great part of himself, feels more detached from his childhood and the memories that only Mo and he share.

Driven by these factors, and also perhaps by his diaries seeming closer to publication this year than ever before, Ossie devotes much space in this diary to attempting to put his life into perspective. The entry for 9 September is the prime example. After an argument with his son Albert, Ossie turns to his diary to vent frustrations he seems to have had locked up inside himself for years. This is undoubtedly one of the most significant entries in the whole diary sequence, and definitely the most revealing concerning his relationship with Celia and David Hockney, their relationship with each other, Mo's life, and Ossie's marriage and his reasons for it. Written in a stream of anger, it is by Ossie's own admission 'a powerful piece, a raging complaint against both Celia and DH, in which DH comes off worse'.

Ossie uses his diary this year more than ever for release and to face his past. By deciding to publish his diaries, he is aware that he will be releasing his feelings about the past into the open, and that he will be resurrecting events that will cause many of his friends great pain. On 11 September Ossie copies in his diary a letter to David Reynolds at Bloomsbury Publishing informing him of the 'flak' he is receiving from friends about his decision to publish: 'Certain people are not going to be too pleased, are they, nudge, nudge, wink, wink.' However, it is highly important to him that he does not shut away and ignore his past – an attitude not shared by some of his friends. Perhaps inspired by his new interest in Buddhism, Ossie believes that making his personal history public will enable him to release himself from its grasp.

After his entry for 9 September Ossie feels 'washed clean' and in many ways this year's diary does convey a sense of healing. On holiday in Marbella he becomes fascinated with the healing qualities of the aloe plant and seems determined to spread the word to others. Within Buddhism Ossie finds friends who are prepared to provide him with escape routes from the depression which has dogged him for so many years. Through them he finds tranquil moments and healing spaces away from his usual concerns. This is particularly true of Pam Procter and the weekends she offers Ossie at her house in Devon. In her Ossie finds a great ally in his fight against his various problems.

For a man who is so poor at the beginning of the year that he must raid his ex-wife's fridge for food, Ossie seems throughout 1988 to be amazingly resilient and is consistently ready to be inspired. He reads a great deal and, perhaps inspired by James Joyce's *Ulysses* and what he describes as its 'beautiful language', writes some wonderfully lyrical passages while visiting Madrid and when he returns home. He seems at times to be experimenting with Joyce's stream-of-consciousness: on 22 August he describes 'a policeman with a sneer – I see the look of sheer hatred from behind his shades as he checks me out over the faint muscles in his neck turned robot automatic rage, stamping, ceased frozen posture for a split second direct eye contact (the face can give 2500 signals a minute).' He writes some thirty pages, reproduced earlier in this book, about his early life in a form of stream-of-consciousness. Ossie has always been a great reader but this year he begins to cross-reference his life to various works of literature.

In Marbella Ossie is greatly struck by the amount of money his friends waste: '10,000 pst notes are frittered away like nothing.' Back in England he comments that he is able to have 'a perfect day' on what is the equivalent of '2000 pst', recognising his ability to live very simply and to be just as happy as the friends he used to believe were better off than him.

Ossie spends 1988 surrounded by old friends and new, takes three holidays and still has a job working for Tanya Sarne of ghost, yet he is still very lonely. He remembers Nick on the tenth anniversary of their meeting and spends more time on Hampstead Heath. Ossie's desperation for love is heartrendingly demonstrated when he takes in Martin, a homeless person on whom he takes pity and with whom he has a brief affair. Having cut down on his drinking, he is smoking a lot of hashish – occasionally seeming unable to function without it. However, he seems better off than he has for some time; his problems are not over but he is emerging from the depths.

PASSAGE UNDATED.
Life is like an express train. It begins with a long wait in the station. How do you arrive there? Do you notice the slow chugg off? You don't always see what is apparent as the journey begins – preoccupied with taking account of where to sit. Did you rush to get on? Are you asleep? Who bothers to look out the window at sleepy suburbia or Battersea Power Station or what went just before you settle down? How long is the journey? What shall you do? Read – you should read a book if you're lucky enough to have a book – or look out the window, peer into other people's lives. Or see nothing as you go through blackness – a tunnel – perhaps you stop – click your heels – sometimes you see beauty – sometimes ugliness – always different – maybe a fog. What's happening out there beyond the swirling mist?

1 JANUARY
Hangover and so the New Year begins with grey skies. A stranger in my bed – a real cocksucker who fortunately has scarpered without even drinking his coffee. An untidy flat like an obstacle course. But at least my bedroom is sorted and the annoying split in my mahogany bed superglued back together.

2 JANUARY
Michael Fish is stuck in Trinidad. 'I'm here because I'm not there, if you know what I mean.'

3 JANUARY
Edina[1] was the bearer of Bad News, the death of Bill Gibb. Ulla[2] phoned and I arranged to pick her up and collected George on the way. We walked in St James' Park. So mild, such a lot of birds, especially beautiful the black swans, like exquisite orchids with deep pink beaks. Tourist London so beautiful – I realise I hardly know that park. We walked round the lake, Ulla taking photographs – and after to a very crowded Tate Gallery where we looked at the pre-Raphaelites and Dali.

4 JANUARY
Horrible front page headline in the *Sun* newspaper. Di's Dress man dies in AIDS clinic.

The flat was very untidy when Ulla and George were round last night. Before she left she said, 'You're getting like Quentin Crisp[3].' Not true, said I. Nevertheless, I went through all the precious mess of boxes of photos and patterns. I ripped into Celia's cloth and covered one of the three cushions on the sofa.

6 JANUARY

Sunshine, clear in blue church sky, goodbye, Billy. Memory, tears and overcome with emotion at a service of Thanksgiving for the life of Bill Gibb – in a sunlit Church of Scotland, packed. 'Maybe he's the lucky one,' I said to Ulla in Joe's Café once we had escaped the photographers. Poor Tessa Dahl very distressed getting into her car as we drove by – the fashion press out in force.

8 JANUARY

Woke at 8 to find my new Japanese carp committed suicide.

10 JANUARY

Horizontal cold, chilled to the bone; a night of pain, hot sweats, fear; icy sheets.

13 JANUARY

I stole the first camellia in Holland Park.

15 JANUARY

Jenny Dearden[4] rang at six while I was in the bath. She had tried to get hold of me three weeks ago to see a preview of *Fatal Attraction* but was ringing my old number. Do I want to go to the opening tonight at the Plaza, Lower Regent Street? Yes, I do. As I bathed I wondered who I should take. Nick[5] said he was too exhausted and would fall asleep. Albert said what's it about, then refused, so I took Henrietta[6] who said, 'Why did you bring me to see such a horrid film?' at the top of her voice, and insisted on taking me to a Yuppie Party in Knightsbridge afterwards. I escaped and went to see Tanya[7].

16 JANUARY

I met Boy George. My hat drew him like a magnet. He looked dreadful. 'Don't get me wrong, I still long to take heroin but I realise it's no good,' he said.

18 JANUARY

[*Ossie accompanies Wayne Sleep to the theatre in which he is playing the Geni in* Aladdin and the Lamp.]

Wilf[8] rang early, came round, read my diaries and said, 'I hope you're using condoms.'

I recognised Wayne's car, the chauffeur told me he was in the pub, and parked my car in a company space. I had a drink. Wayne was nudgy and the traffic hell all the way out of London and even in the middle of nowhere. I got out to piss with Oscar. I played tapes I'd brought. Wayne told me he was doing the panto for the money to pay the mortgage. They have made £90,000 per week. We went straight to the theatre then had tea – a toasted sandwich. An idiot next to me spilt milk on my hat – poor Oscar (not allowed in) could never be so clumsy. He was with the sweet old man who looks after everything in his tiny dressing room. I was quite fascinated with the stuff he puts on what little hair he's got – 'Here watch this,' he giggled, spraying hair extension like brown spider threads, 'but you have to hold it with ordinary lacquer or it just blows off.' So with another can he sprayed glue, then another to hide the grey of his side hair. 'Takes years off!' he laughed.

22 JANUARY

Spoke to Nick. Got a good sense of timing, haven't I? It's 10 years today since we met.

23 JANUARY

Ben Brierly rang, told me Eric Clapton has been going to AA[9] meetings then going home and getting pissed.

27 JANUARY

I rang about the hot water and waited all day for a plumber to come round, reading about Oscar and waiting. Rain outside and no word from Quidejeta[10]. Obviously she is waiting to hear from me. Albert rang at 5.00 – will I pick him up from Holland Park tube in ten mins? So I ventured out into the wet. The Rock and Roll Years 1957. What memories it brought back – 'That's the first record I ever bought,' I told Albert, 'Bye-bye Love' by the Everley Brothers, there on the TV screen in black and white.

28 JANUARY

Woke at 9.15 – intending to work. Instead I fell on the book on Oscar Wilde at page 170 and read on. Poor Oscar Wilde how glorious his youth. Long walk in the rain on the heath in Hampstead. Still light, cold and grey. A meal in the Venus had put me right – it was simply hunger of another kind that forced me to squelch through mud in the twilight heavy downpour.

Only when Oscar began to whimper from the cold and wet did I reluctantly return home to bathe him and continue to read. The facts are riveting. Oscar Wilde.

30 JANUARY

Got Nick on the phone – met him at 1.15 in the Venus cafe. So handsome he looked. We were both 15 mins late and arrived simultaneously. He bought two eggs, bacon, tomatoes and sausages twice. 'I'll have to learn Portuguese next,' he said, when I asked about his German. Ten years ago he loved me – we were so happy together living in Bramerton St.

Did I fuck the leatherman with the naked buttocks and did he leave me panting?

3 FEBRUARY

I rang Liz Wyndham. Andrew Golden had made a visit to see Celia who wasn't there. He told Liz he had heard I was in hospital and VERY ill – 'Absolute nonsense,' she said. He's from the *Sunday Mirror*. I eventually learnt the hideous implication of this persistent Reporter – indeed there is a CLARK (without an E) admitted into St Stephen's hospital on the 6th floor.

5 FEBRUARY

[*On 31 January Ossie had picked up a homeless man, Martin, on Hampstead Heath; he has been living with him ever since.*]

It was almost 10 o'clock when I woke to find Martin looking very uncomfortable – asleep and uncovered on the sofa. I decided, enough, he must go, and told him. He took it very bad: 'You should have told me last night,' he said, 'before I spent all that money.' I resisted the feeling of pity and said that he was disrupting my life, that I can't continue to look after him. 'Give it two weeks,' he suggested, but I was determined, asked where he'd lived before, discovered he needed £20. I'll give you £20, I promised, and tried to cheer him up, insisted he took a bath because he didn't yesterday. Once it was run I got in first. Walked down to the market and had breakfast in the Venus Cafe – he had little appetite, fed his bacon to Oscar. Martin said, 'I don't feel very well' when we got back home. 'Don't get into my bed. If you get into my bed I'll only want to fuck you.' He looked at me with his sad blue eyes. 'I know,' he replied. I relented and put him to bed. 'Look, you can stay one more night but first thing in the morning I'll take you to, where is it? Old Street.' He got into bed relieved, fully clothed, exhausted – but I couldn't resist getting in with him – nor his huge cock, nor having my way with him.

6 FEBRUARY

Back to Normal.

I woke Martin at twenty to ten. Sheepishly he bathed after I made him tea and bathed myself. His eyes showed just how hurt he was, how I betrayed his trust – so fragile.

Great sadness. He asked for my phone number. Why was I so reluctant to give it? 'Will I see you again?' he asked quietly looking at me from downcast eyes which couldn't disguise his hopeless plight. I'd handed him his backpack, the car door already open – I could so easily have said get back in – it crossed my mind – but instead replied, 'Of course,' and smiled and kissed him goodbye. At the time I felt relieved – I'm free, I thought, as I drove away – but I looked back and felt remorse as he walked dejected in the opposite direction.

7 FEBRUARY

Coming across chocolate bars in the fridge later almost broke my heart. Do I miss him? Certainly I worry what will become of him.

9 FEBRUARY

I took a long walk on the heath – I felt like a detective. There were certainly lots of clues as to the nocturnal practices that go on. There are the muddy footpaths leading to secluded and sheltered places where tracks cross and footprints make plain the frenzied and frantic dances that are going on every night – hundreds of spent proplactics form swirling patterns of silver and pink. So obvious to me – do they go unnoticed by everyone else?

Impotence – powerless, helpless, decrepit – a complete inability to work or even tidy the flat – no, I've got to have an orgasm . . . The more I tried, the more impossible it became.

12 FEBRUARY

It was a filthy day, raining and very cold so I didn't go out until six o'clock when Martin phoned. 'Where are you?' I asked. 'Kings Cross,' he replied. I told him to take the tube to Latimer Road and phone again. I ran out in my slippers but the car died as I tried to start it. Typical, I thought, as the last of the electrical power failed to ignite the engine – so I had to dash back indoors and dress properly (as well as slippers I was wearing only my overcoat and my cashmere over a vest) to walk to the tube station. 'Sorry I took so long,' I said, 'the wretched car won't start.' 'Where's Oscar?' was all he asked and we walked back in silence. At least he had a few cigarettes – I without and completely penniless.

Martin's back and so is my libido. He was wearing the same clothes as when

I left him last Saturday and he smelt like a trooper – his pheromones produce the magic effect. I put my nose to his unwashed hair and a beard almost formed – I insisted he cultivate it but made him take a bath. He's been fighting again, fresh wounds and his nose bashed again. I found him fresh underwear and a shirt but he put back on his green trousers. 'Did you miss me?' he asked, once I'd put Oscar on his lap, all fresh from the bath.

13 FEBRUARY

A complaint letter from the stupid black woman below accusing me of racial harassment because Oscar shits on her doorstep occasionally.

Raided Celia's kitchen for food.

25 FEBRUARY

Swirling flakes of snow suddenly as I gaze out of the window at ten past one – I shudder wondering where Martin might be and hope he's somewhere warm. He had called me once more: 'I dunno what to do – you're not like everybody else, you were nice to me.'

28 FEBRUARY

No money, no food. Quite by chance I got a delicious lunch at the Kamens[11]'.

1 MARCH

PP[12] was in fine form: 'I was reading Derek Jarman's book, it's all lies, isn't it,' he said and found a passage where he jumped into Jagger[13]'s unmade bed saying, 'You needn't change the sheets' – obviously untrue.

2 MARCH

Martin rang at 2.45 while I was in the bath. I must admit he has been on my mind, he's still living on the street – just 'wandering around' – as he puts it. I told him I'd meet him on Ladbroke Grove tube at 4.30. In freezing cold I waited till six on Ladbroke Grove tube station. He rang soon after I got back home – found his way over – once he was here, sat smiling and coy – I forced him to bathe, brought milk for his tea, undressed him, first the filthy Aran sweater (potent stink), dragged him to bed after painful penetration on this sofa where I now write. I was gentler in bed at first. I dressed choosing a fresh shirt and went to the Buddhist meeting.

3 MARCH

A French photographer, Jean Cassel, tall handsome and polished: 'How did you let yourself get in this state?' he asked. 'You were so Big.'

6 MARCH
I took Oscar to walk rather than watch Cilla Black on TV.

7 MARCH
[*This entry refers to the death of the great gay personality Divine.*]

Another death – men are men but Divine man is woman.

14 MARCH
Celia had heard the rumour again that I'm dead – this time the source being BQ. Always a little jealous shit – and been dead himself for years.

23 MARCH
Jose[14] woke me at 8.15. Jenny Dearden has been trying to get me to make her a dress for the Oscar award ceremony in Los Angeles.

4 APRIL
Brazil, the Terry Gilliam movie – Michael did the score, quite good but too many bangs.

5 APRIL
I rang Tanya. 'I thought I'd walk the dogs. What do you think?' So quickly to pick up Wuffy and a half-hour in Holland Park. When I returned Tanya was completely alone. She gave me £20, and I bought two bottles of red wine, Orangina, 2 packets of Marlboro and my Sobrani cocktail. I opened the wine while she smoked at the kitchen table.

She confided in me, a real heart-to-heart.

She is an 'only child' which explains a lot. She confessed she always thought the female form more aesthetically beautiful. (I think the opposite but kept mum). 'I don't want to hear any of this,' I told her. 'You know I'll only write it down in my diary.'

8 APRIL
I walked Oscar in Hyde Park – a sea of golden daffs and more to come, it blossoming the colour of old ladies' hats and veils. The azaleas beginning. My only answer to my plight – what to do is just do nothing except climb into bed with Oscar.

9 APRIL
Ulla rang fresh from swimming and says we are definitely going to Madrid next Sunday[15].

13 APRIL

Electricity turned off so quickly. To Tanya in desperation – she very kindly gave me a cheque for half the £200 I've got to find. Fiona Thyssen to the rescue – she's giving me a cheque for the other £100.

16 APRIL

Tanya gave me two £50 notes – 'You knew I would and it's only because you need a break – but what am I going to do while you are away? – Jackie[16] goes to Paris on Wednesday and you going for the weekend.'

17 APRIL

[*Ossie goes to Madrid.*]

New moon and a night in an aeroplane.

I went to bed at six in the morning – still unpacked but everything sorted and ready to go, I laundered shirts – the green dress – my dinner black tie. Ulla rang at 8 and 9 and 9.30 before leaving to take the tube. My car started straight away. I put the keys through Kay[17]'s letterbox and phoned Pam[18] from the airport once I'd struggled to the tube – met Ulla and checked in – we got the last two seats in the last row of the Iberian tristar, drank champagne and laughed all the way – it dawned on me an hour before we landed – 'I think I must know Sylvia Polakov' – and, sure enough, the moment I set eyes on her I recognised her: she had modelled in the 1974 show – from there met Bryan Ferry etc.

Madrid is on a Grand Scale: she lives on a wonderful tree-lined street in a high old-fashioned apartment in a Belle Epoch building with round turrets, opposite a beautiful park full of fountains and giant monuments, chestnuts all in blossom.

18 APRIL

We took a long walk to an Egyptian temple from Aswan, which would have been underwater. Beautiful, elegant, extensively restored, well-positioned, high up on inclined plinth – had a soothing effect on Ulla. We took photographs. She put on high heels. 'Me Spanish no good,' said Ulla.

19 APRIL

The cut of the policeman's trousers is late seventies and a most hideous colour, low-waisted and still the hint of a flare.

Museo Prado. Bosch, Velasquez, Durer, Rubens.

We saw the new moon as we went to steal greenery from the park opposite at 8.30.

20 APRIL

We went to a cocktail party, arriving late, just in time to see the food taken away. Sylvia introduced a half-caste model girl called Dolores who will try on the green dress and Ulla chatted up a beautiful boy called Bernard from Belgium with eyes like Nick's which made me think of him and I feel sad and very old and ugly.

21 APRIL

I miss Oscar and feel trapped.

22 APRIL

I woke at 7:30 groggy but awake so I ate Cornflakes and read for half an hour or so then I fell asleep till 11.45. We didn't go out all day. 'I find it hard to do nothing,' Ulla said, which she really believes yet she quite happily paints her face for an hour. I found *Ulysses* of James Joyce[19] and began to read it – incredibly beautiful writing. Ulla really getting on my nerves. We fall out over a cigarette – having smoked all her own, she wants mine.

23 APRIL

'He used to fuck whilst driving. I was terrified,' says Sylvia as we drove out of the city, surrounded by mountains at least 500 miles every way around, the most beautiful clear light which one never gets in England. After an hour or so we drove up to Plateau – a huge monastery. Grey, undecorated, incredibly carved rock, lined with marble ruby-red and charcoal-black. Bleak Pias. Weird – in the middle of nowhere, a round room of gilded coffers. Valle de los Caidos – COR that was incredible, wasn't it! A huge cross – and inside carved out like Ming's palace in *Flash Gordon*, the angel of Death always hooded. Puncture driving back – 1st time I changed a wheel, ever.

Saturday night in Madrid and we stayed indoors, played gin rummy, and muchos laughter. Sylvia and Ulla drank a bottle of vodka; I drank whisky; we dined on trout at 5 o'clock. I walked to Retiko park opposite – I knew it would be cruisy – behind a tree a wide-eyed boy: 'Este una Condom?' taking my cock in his hand.

28 APRIL

[Ossie returns to London.]

And home with new sunglasses. The plane was overbooked in Economy so we were put in Club Class – got my poncy fags in Duty Free – Ulla bought 400 more. Very cool reception from Oscar.

6 MAY

Mo[20]'s Dead.

George came round. 'Dad, I've got some really bad news.' I knew from his faltering voice immediately he said Da'ad. 'Mo's dead!' 'Ohhh,' as though I knew already – he has been so on my mind. So many people loved him. Although it was still a shock, I accepted it – no tears: 'Well, we must drink to dear Mo,' but my voice cracked and I said no more, washed a glass and drank a sip of clear vodka.

7 MAY

Up at nine – I phoned Michael[21] early, begged to borrow his Merc and zoomed off to get my pills from the chemist in Paddington Street and took the opportunity to visit Patrick. 'I know,' he said, 'I know,' as I fell into his arms. He had heard from George Lawson. Gave me a cup of coffee and said he would ring DH in California later today and he suggested a wake when David is in London. I had to return the car so I rang him later from Tanya's. DH is coming on June 8th and Peter Langan (who was there with Patrick) offered to do the catering.

15 MAY

I keep looking at that sunshine and feel I should go outside, instead I'm trying to write it all down.

19 MAY

Albert rang and came round in mum's car – more talk of America – where can he stay in New York? He's going to travel across in a greyhound bus, wants to visit Chicago.

22 MAY

Woke hungry, early in brilliant sunshine and out early to walk Oscar in Holland Park and buy my poncy cigarettes (the duty free all smoked) and the *News of the World*. The yellow roses are just beginning – I stole four buds, put them beside my bed.

23 MAY

[Ossie goes to the Ritz Hotel to meet David Reynolds, Publishing Director at Bloomsbury Publishing, to discuss possible publication of his diaries. Ossie was introduced to David by Michael a'Brook.]

Meeting the publisher (David Reynolds). My vow not to drink went out the window as soon as I arrived late to find them drinking champagne.

25 MAY

Ulla tells me Chelita[22] is in a clinic called 'Clouds' to withdraw from heroin addiction.

29 MAY

I woke at nine, hungry. Hunger I'm getting used to, but no cigarettes I simply can't do without, and I do like milk in my coffee. I walked out and it began to rain.

Got Sam[23] out of bed – I was drenched, and Oscar too. Smelly room – his only chance of a lie-in. An unopened packet of Bensons in the kitchen drawer, boiled eggs and toast, the *News of the World* (Jade Jagger in trouble). The rain won't let UP.

30 MAY

Another AIDS death, Sheridan Duffrin yesterday in Clandyboyne.

31 MAY

At last something to do, a dress for Tanya.

Spoke to George Lawson about Sheridan. Told me the details, how he couldn't ride because no flesh on his backside – then he couldn't drive because he couldn't feel his feet then his legs – so he went to Clandyboyne, fell into a coma – occasionally waking and lucid. Fortunately no pain.

I took three bodices and Gill Goldsmith's bodice pattern, the black moiré seven-piece block closed at her waist. I had to cut the shoulders at the seam – the cloth still undecided. I cut mauve moiré. 'Where's me dress, Oz?' she joked.

'I'm just cutting it now, Tanya, you know that's the hard part.'

1 JUNE

I'd cut the bodice from Gill Goldsmith's block, adding length – an inch more – her nape-to-waist an incredible 17". Reshaping the back waist, hollowing out a lower back, the emphasis on her derrière – so I began before lunch and finished by 4. She kept me waiting – Wuffy to the vet – it was 5.30 by the time she put it on. Perfect after I'd reduced the front side by 1/2 an inch, lopped 3" off a swan waist and tits on a shelf. The stomach held flat and firmly in place. She was amazed and thrilled. 'I've never had a dress I could wear without a bra before,' she said.

Rude awakening by two of Maggie's thugs at 10.15 to turn off the gas – a smarmy black man and a giant lout with a beer gut. I managed to stop them on a technical point. 'I'm not Mr C. Raymond.' I found my passport in my proper name, Mr R. Clark.

6 JUNE

'You should enjoy restriction,' said Anthony Price, very impressed with the fit of Tanya's dress. He ran his fingers over the fabric and along the boundary to the huge bosom, heaving. 'Incredible! Not a wrinkle in sight.' 'And no fittings, either,' I boasted. The British Designers award dinner with Tanya. Her dress is a big success.

8 JUNE

It's my Birthday tomorrow, Henrietta, and if you don't give me a brand new telephone answering machine, I won't even be bothered to talk to you again.

9 JUNE

My 46th Birthday. 'It's my Birthday today,' I said softly about 7.30 in the kitchen over the road. 'OH! Ossie, you should have told me.'

13 JUNE

Ron originally from Birmingham – Pisces, 38, works in the rag trade, gone home to West Hampstead on the 31 bus. Drinks too much, terrible skin, wonderful fuck.

14 JUNE

I really wanted to write, but as I had no skins, I dressed without bathing and caught a 52 on Ladbroke Grove. I was incensed to find my neatly prepared dresses I'd so carefully left wrapped in a roll of pink card, placed on a chair by my machine. So I blew my top. 'Jesus Christ, is it not possible to have a little fucking space on one of these huge tables?' I asked loudly to no one and all present as I placed the roll of card back on the table where I'd left it last night – removing a pot of black plastic tulips and hurling it out of the open door where it smashed – and ignored all cries of protest. 'There was no need for that, you have broken Tanya's vase.' I did reply to Therese[24] that she was a fine one to talk of making a bad atmosphere. That really shut her up.

15 JUNE

At Tanya's suggestion, I took a great big beautiful Cabbage Rose, completely open, from the modern churchyard in Kensal Road and gave it to Therese.

16 JUNE

John Swannell rang early to ask if I'll be on the Bill Gibb Committee and the memorial show is November eleventh. Patrick tells me DH been and gone and very depressed. Still no clue to the circumstances surrounding Mo's death. As I write this, in my bed there sleeps another bearded stranger.

20 JUNE

I woke at ten past six, no doubt nervous about the meeting at 10 o'clock. I took my pills and went back to bed – didn't get up till 7.30 despite a seven o'clock alarm call.

David Reynolds. It was after 10 before I even left home – after sorting out what to take, making a huge tip of my flat. I was very apprehensive but cool and calm from the outside. I took a taxi and got there at 10.30.

24 JUNE

[*Ossie has been invited to stay in Marbella by Micha, an admirer and friend from the sixties.*]

Distracted by my forthcoming trip to Spain and only sixty quid to hand. I was considering asking Pam for money for Pattie Boyd[25]'s cockfeather jacket.

Micha called: 'What time do you arrive?' Afternoon. 'Come to the house of Jackie Pressman where I'll be having lunch. You should be in Puerto about 4.'

25 JUNE

Tanya suddenly got very serious about work and said she could offer me a room downstairs, which is currently full of old stock, insisting I must pay my way. We went outside to look at it – its own entrance and a shop front – couldn't be better – my silence[26] has paid off. Lynn Franks can be the first customer.

26 JUNE

[*Ossie goes to Marbella.*]

Alarm call at 5.30 but I was already up at ten past. Which clothes should I take? The suitcase slowly filled up. I put in the linen sheets first, black trousers, a pair of boots, lots of fresh shirts, T-shirts, my supernatural hat and black cashmere. I had to rush my bath, though I took the usual care shaving. At 7.45 completely ready, photos, pills, hash all stashed. Found the cab outside. Had to ring and ring and bang the front door to wake Tanya who opened her bedroom window and blinked in the sunlight – though in fact the morning was iron-grey and drizzling rain. A £50 note came floating down in an old Christmas card and envelope. 'I couldn't wake up,' she gushed twice, 'have a nice holiday,' and with a wave was gone back to her bed. I unzipped my flying-suit pocket on my right calf and took out my passport and counted the cash. Three 50s, three 20s and two 10s, one for the taxi, one for a return ticket to Gatwick. I ran to jump on the 8.15, sank into a seat with my back to the engine, as Battersea Power Station's impressive bulk came into view and disappeared to be replaced by endless monstrous suburbia.

[*In Marbella.*] I slept OK with two Valium and was first up. Micha and Leo[27] sleep very late. At 12.30 Micha appeared. 'Do you want to come to the bank with me?' Yes, so off we went leaving Leo to let in the maid. We walk along the Pemato – millions of pounds worth of boats and yachts all neatly moored. Looked at the helicopters about to take off from Kashoggi's yacht, parked beyond the harbour, BMWs, Jaguars, Rollers, Porches, all neatly parked. Then we walked to a restaurant bar. He pointed out a building with domes, iridescent in the weak sunlight flashing lilac, blue and purple. The Great Albion, a new Arab apartment block. I said it was like *Doctor Who*. An avenue of palms just planted, their fronds bound together until they have properly taken, each one cost £250, Micha informed me. Nothing is older than 20 years. Quite unbelievable. I soon realised that this is Micha's normal routine. Coffee at 2.30 in a bar called Windsor, followed by a Gin and Tonic. I drank Campari Soda. Later Micha prepared a chicken with mushrooms and a childhood friend called Ghicka came to dinner.

The Oasis club is seven kilometres beyond Marbella. Jackie Pressman turns out to be a vivacious blonde with an ample figure about my age. The door was opened by Leo, a handsome young Spaniard with quite good English who is Micha's current boyfriend. They were all drunk, having consumed bloody Marys, and holding lunch until I arrived. Micha was bearded, overweight and laughing – I'd wondered how he would look and he wasn't so different to what I'd imagined – he definitely drinks too much and still chainsmokes, but he wasn't clutching four packets of cigarettes as he always used to. There were two houseguests – a couple, Jackie's doctor and wife – he with cancer, she posh.

27 JUNE

Micha's apartment, a penthouse with a harbour view, is a kitsch nightmare. I've got a little suite at the back, so recently vacated by his mummy. I slept in her sheets – OK, as it happens. There is nowhere to put my clothes – the whole place and every surface is crammed with knick-knacks. There's a Dali bronze horse, an ARAM lamp which cost £1,000 20 years ago, Picasso plates, a Magritte drawing bought from his widow, a beautiful Goya drawing in red chalk of a man on horseback prancing, and a lovely

Rosemary Strachey painting of Sidney, the wonderful dog I remember so well, who makes me think of Oscar whom I miss so much. Maria, who has married a Catholic Syrian, has three daughters and lives in Washington, and is tired of being put on a pedestal, thought I was a very sensitive person. She asked what I did for a living. Micha enthusiastically explained how I was king of fashion in the sixties. 'Have you still got the snakeskin coat[28]?' I asked. He sent Leo off to find it from a closet somewhere. 'Le-Oh!' he shouts, then makes his demand. Leo returned, struggling to put it on. 'You could get a lot of money for it in America,' I told him, half under my breath. Then he went in to his bedroom and returned with a cream silk shirt printed with one of Celia's first designs from a wall painting in Crete. After Maria had gone he asked how much I thought he could get for the jacket. $5,000, I said. 'That's exactly what I thought,' he said, very pleased.

28 JUNE

I slept very badly in pink synthetic sheets and a saggy double bed. I must have dozed on and off but it seemed like I lay awake all night. Reluctantly I took two Valium at seven o'clock and at last fell into a deep sleep, only to be woken at 11 by somebody hammering. I woke up Micha, early for him because he has to go somewhere and pay the taxes. He wasn't keen to get up. 'I'll get up in ½ hour,' he said, but after 35 minutes no sign of him, so I went to wake him. Oh dear, I found him being buggered by Leo, two wriggling figures humping cocooned in a pink blanket. I don't think they noticed me, being so occupied – but I was flabbergasted and for a second riveted to the spot, just long enough to etch the vision into my memory. For some reason I was shocked having wrongly assumed Leo to be the passive partner, yet I didn't turn back. I crept past to listen to the heavy panting and quickening rhythm. Fortunately I was bare-footed, wrapped in my cashmere. Quietly I stole away as they groaned in orgasmic union, back to write in this journal laid open on my bed where I'd left it to innocently remind Micha of the time. He appeared five minutes later dressed and (was there a knowing look in his eye?) enquired, would I like to go wherever he was going to do whatever he had to do. Having regained my composure, I replied as the sun had come out at last I thought I'd go to the beach.

29 JUNE

Last night Jackie Pressman came home to have supper – she looked quite stunning dressed all in red. I recognised Manolo Blahnik shoes. She goes to London tomorrow to see *Aida*.

'Do you like steak tartar? Good.' Leo does all the preparation, Micha the rest. We ate indoors. I've never known it so cold in June, she says. I played The Doors, one of the three tapes I've brought with me.

30 JUNE

I seem to have lost my ruby pin last night. I've looked everywhere and can't find it. I wonder if it's a bad omen? Yesterday I pinched Micha's sun oil so today I bought some of my own and although I didn't get to the beach until three, I had a really long blast. A German businessman cruised me then went off with another prettier boy which made me quite jealous. I followed to see where they had gone, and then had to retrace my footsteps to find my cigarette holder which I'd lost. Fortunately I found it and when I got to Micha's shop – 'Good news, Frank has found your pin.'

2 JULY

Today, before going to the beach, I decided to explore the outer sea wall of the harbour where fishermen cast their lines and English tourists comment on the state of the sea. In the evening: Jo's party. Jo arrived in Marbella nine years ago playing a guitar in the street. Now he's sold his half share in his bar for £40,000 and he's going home to San Diego – hence the goodbye party in an awful little bungalow. The garden unlit, and a motley bunch sitting round in the darkness. On the beach they were barbecuing sardines: Micha made off with a bottle of whisky. Jo took over the microphone to say thank you to everyone for making him so welcome in Spain and then told some hopeless jokes. Fortunately Maria arrived and we left on foot to a restaurant half a mile nearer Puerto Banus. Micha continued drinking the whisky and threw up the lot, blaming the Gazpacho (which was delicious). Then Maria invited us to drink in the Marbella Club. She hung her dress in her little room, which costs £150 a day at least – it's easily the smartest club in Marbella. It consists of a covered dancefloor with twinkling lights and French windows all round, with ridiculous little stools arranged in little groups like at Tramps. Reserve cards on most of the tables, full of hookers in short skirts keeping an eye out for the rich punter. The waning moon rose out of the Mediterranean, and I wondered what I was doing there and how much my glass of Perrier cost.

3 JULY

One more week will be quite enough,
I've overdone exposure to the sun maybe.

When Micha woke, being Sunday it was decided we would all go to the beach. 'Are you making coffee?' asked Leo, still in bed, watching pop videos on TV, the thin curtains drawn against the blazing sunlight. As a surprise I gave him one of Nick's T-shirts, new and still wrapped in polythene. And with the coffee I treated them to one of my Dexedrine pills each. Leo was a bit suspicious and a little reluctant to take it. After eyeing the jumbo shrimp gambas and ladybird lobster, so temptingly displayed outside the restaurants on the front, I suggested lunch and forced the £50 note on them, saying I felt I must contribute something to the housekeeping.

Plans to go to the beach went out the window when Frank Phillips invited us to swim in his pool. What luxury to swim in his beautiful swimming pool surrounded with lush greenery. Frank told me he had bought an Alma Tadema for £1,500, which he sold six months later for five and a half grand. One of his biggest regrets was not buying another big one on the toss of a coin for £20,000, which is now worth at least £150,000. Three more people arrived – a real-life princess! – the Austrian Princess Bea of Augersberg – somehow related to the Von Bulow scandal in NY. She looked the worst Swedish blonde tart, and was very sceptical of the healing power of Aloe – until I rubbed some on her arm. Later Micha told me that he's thinking of closing up his shop – clients are coming running and ordering direct. His sense of humour (through his alcoholic haze) is his most endearing attribute and quite contagious – he has a bold, deep, ha ha ha which immediately triggers me off, and anyone else within hearing. Real scandal and salacious stories are his speciality.

4 JULY

I woke before seven and was smoking a cigarette when Micha staggered into my bedroom to get water from the kitchen. 'What are you doing awake?' he asked. I could hardly tell him I was feeling very bored, missing Oscar and in need of sex even though I'm feeling hopelessly impotent.

We went to the beach. I stayed till six thinking maybe I'm overdoing the ultra violet, but no, it's amazing how the skin toughens up and how magically the Aloe combats the redness. I bathed and Aloed and carefully dressed myself in grey, even wore a tie for a long and delicious dinner at the Greek restaurant next door to his Micha's shop called Black Pepper. Taramasalata and huge fresh prawns.

5 JULY

I couldn't help thinking I should be signing-on today and how absolutely ridiculously bizarre I'm here in the sunshine living in the lap of luxury, which Micha takes completely for granted. 10,000 pta. notes are frittered away like so much monopoly money.

'I'm going to do a Gigot for dinner tonight,' Micha promised. At last I feel I can say I've got a suntan and feel elated because I feel so healthy and happy. Feeling happy.

I took a long walk along the beach collecting pretty stones and bits of shell and glass worn smooth by the sea. Also walked to the end of the man-made pier. Micha's Gigot a feast.

6 JULY

To the beach with Micha. It was crowded and very hot. We drank a beer which, on my empty stomach, made me feel sick. We talked about local gossip, Tanya, Micha's drink problem, dogs. We were just about to go for a swim when four police cars zoomed along the pier. 'Do not enter the water. All people in the water get out.' Boomed out over a microphone. No reason given, so we went to have a look at the sea and found it the colour of red wine – contaminated.

8 JULY

I woke at 7.45 and walked down to the beach and found two girls chanting. It was 11.15 when I got back home and they were all still in the arms of Morpheus so I left a note saying I'd gone to Jackie's house at the Oasis Club. She hadn't yet surfaced, but was about to and gave me beach towels and coffee and I greased up again for the sun was completely overhead and the hottest I've taken so far. Tommy Steele[29]'s daughter came over from next door dressed for water-skiing and complaining about her sunburn. I had collected a huge horn of Aloe and quickly applied the soothing goo from inside the leaf. The Jacuzzi is not working properly and I could hear the whines of mosquitoes. 'I'm not getting in there – it's the perfect breeding ground for bacteria,' I said, remembering the attack of Gungas Revenge I suffered from Hockney's overheated pool in 1983. Micha and Leo arrived and prepared a pitcher of delicious bloody Marys.

Finally on the 12th day I succumbed to alcohol. Barbecue lunch, but it never happened because too many people turned up. It was at this point of being drunk that things started to go wrong. I remember making a big hit – applying Aloe to the whole of the Steele's next door and the sister-in-law (who still gets a good price for my dresses – in fact more than I did in the first place).

9 JULY

Nick's Birthday.

Funny last day.

Wounded and in shock[30], I eventually got to bed around 2 o'clock. 'I'll make dinner in half an hour,' Micha kept saying. I kept waking in the night and took Valium three or four times. 'Is fantastico,' said the doctor at

12 o'clock after he had removed the dressing and stitches from my collar bone. 'Is completely healed.' He told me I was lucky the dog had missed my jugular vein and how he must see the vaccination certificates. A really gentle man blinking brown eyes magnified through the pebble lenses of his glasses. The bill was 12,000 potatoes.

Micha and Leo still in bed. I said I'd go to K at the Oasis Club but she was so heavily tranquillised I spent the whole afternoon alone. At six she surfaced, looking very pale and half-mad. She had taken hash cake and had a very bad trip last night. 'Are you really here now?' she asked. Her face relaxed as I took her hands in mine. She made boiled eggs and toast and I planted three Aloe in her garden.

It was late when I got back. The beach was deserted except for two men returning their horses to the stable. The sun out of sight and the sky a soft, clear violet and peach. Ghicha was there; in my honour he had scored again and was preparing another Gigot. I felt very relaxed.

10 JULY

[Ossie returns to London.]

Another blazing white-hot day begins. The sky is a brilliant intense blue, but after today I'm getting off this carousel and going back to London. First my last blast on the beach . . .

Spoke to Nick to wish him Happy Birthday and told him, unlike Christ, I didn't think he would die at 33. He excitedly told me he's paying half the rent on a flat in Paris. 'You must come,' he insists. I haven't yet met Claudio[31]. 'You'd love him.' 'I'm sure I would, darling, if he loves you he must be nice.' I feel like a hypocrite. 'That's wonderful,' I'd enthused at first. 'What do you mean?' he asked suspiciously. 'Well, you go to Paris whenever you like. He comes here whenever he likes.' What I actually meant was – I think you're being taken for a ride again, Nick Balaban, and secretly I hope it's the thin end of the wedge which will eventually split you apart.

Back to London Rain. Darling George picked me up at Victoria.

11 JULY

Back to Kafkaville walkies in Holland Park, signed on, and a delicious Sauna. Summer rainshowers.

13 JULY

Tanya has lost weight – one of the few advantages of being absolutely miserable and totally fucked up, is not feeling like eating food.

14 JULY
Sunshine feeling fine.
Johnnie Rozza[32] says Lynn Franks has sold her business for £3 million but will still preside over it for five years, then she will devote her life to Kozen Rufu. (Actually he said £10 mil[lion].)
I'm staying with Charlie Tennant at the moment. I went to the Spanish Dali on Portobello Road for Colombian Coffee and found the wine Carte de Plate that I drank with Micha in Spain. Then I found Prosciutto, and bought 1/2lb cut so thin. I realised I had bought lunch for Tanya without realising it. Between her bouts of bursting into tears, her mind went over and over: 'I'm a horrible mother, I scream at everyone around me, I'm a woman and I need sex and a man to be happy, I haven't felt like this since mother died.' Eat the Prosciutto, have you tasted the wine?

17 JULY
I have been doing such a lot of shouting recently. Lynn Franks is supposed to be a Buddhist. 'Stop that!' she shouted. 'You're not to take even one of my flowers. I pay a lot of money for my flowers!' 'But I only want one.' I was flabbergasted. She was dead serious, and Tanya agreed with her. 'Just drive me to the nearest tube,' Tanya had the nerve to ask. 'Listen, Tanya. LF wouldn't give me one tiny blossom which she'd never miss and whose exquisite perfume would carry me through the day; she wouldn't give me that one flower because she's a Jewess. And you agree with her because you're a Jewess, too. And if that sounds anti-Semitic, Tanya, I'm sorry.' 'There's a tube station right there, Ossie, good-bye.'

18 JULY
Chanted for an hour. Pam said that maybe I can have a studio in Marylebone Street.
Tanya, grey and puffy eyes avoid contact. I photocopy the synopsis of my book. 'You might at least have the decency to ASK,' she screams at me.
The publisher reluctant to let me upstairs at first. I charmed him into a Buck's Fizz.
Exhaustion. Bed before 9, only to be woken by Albert, full of enthusiasm. Somehow he's managed to get an international driving licence, aged 22.

21 JULY
There's more out there than we can see.

23 JULY
George gone off to Spain without saying goodbye.

27 JULY

Really weird day. S snarly. 'You shouldn't smoke hash first thing in the morning. You should take cocaine. Smoking hash destroys your memory.' Definitely not true. Cocaine destroys your brain cells as they are formed. I rang Sid but no answer – beautiful sunshine but I lay down, confused.

28 JULY

Beryl tells me mum miscarried before she was born. Four years between B and Sam[33] so I'm the seventh child.

Pam was just finishing morning Gongyo. 'It's so weird, when I chant now I see my mother and other departed souls all happy and dancing in a meadow . . . Mo hasn't come through yet, though.' 'No, I'm afraid Mo has to spend some time in purgatory.' I told her about being the seventh child. 'Yes, I can see all those abortions as well.'

29 JULY

[*Ossie goes to stay for the weekend at Pam Procter's Devon home.*]

Full Moon. Pam was waiting with the roof down. I ran indoors and grabbed some clothes, forgot even a cigarette holder and took nothing to read. 'Mo came through today,' said Pam. We were both in a good mood – zoomed off listening to Prince: 'You need another lover like you need a hole in the head.' On the M4 we ran into traffic. We opened the roof and did five mins *dymoku*. I slept for an hour. The full moon rose. We got to Bristol at 7.15. 'Something about Bristol makes me vomit.' Pam bought pizzas and we drove to Devon – a long, uncomfortable ride and a pain in my chest. I woke at first light to find the Dower house shrouded with mist. I made coffee and a fire in the dining room, then looked over the garden. Peas, garlic, beans, strawberries, are laid out in neat beds where last time I came here an asphalt tennis court was being dug up by a mechanical digger. Now snails and slugs and caterpillars dine lazily on the lettuce and rabbits munch the cabbage where once mixed doubles was played. The Aga isn't working – so we breakfasted on toast and eggs boiled in the electric kettle.

3 AUGUST

Half an hour late for the meeting with David Reynolds at Bloomsbury. I told him my ego was as big as the moon. He wrote down (at my insistence) the offer and conditions. I got him up from 10 grand to 17 and a half. Still not enough.

Gatwick train from Victoria.

Ossie photographed with his most flamboyant cigarette holder; the collage at his side includes a newspaper cutting from his very early days, Nikki Lane (top right) and water-baby, George.

4 AUGUST

[*Ossie returns to Marbella to stay once again with Micha and with Jackie Pressman.*]

A very weird first day. I walked along the surf from Jackie's to Micha's, to Puerto Banus. In August it's quite strikingly different – different class of people and the boats now like sardines. The beach and sea is filthy with seaweed and garbage. Even the Aloe seems to be drying up. Micha looking grey in blue Kaftan. Gin and tonic in hand. 'How are you my sweet?' NK is living with a 16-year-old gypsy boy – he needs £10,000.

5 AUGUST

The art of telling jokes is a form of currency. A sense of humour is the first essential. Victor's beach begins to resemble a garden party. Naked flesh, windsurf sails, motor boats and jet skiers. Jackie tells me more of her marital history and me mine. I recognise the same pattern: the child as bargaining power. I make a comparison between she and Celia and me and Ronnie. They are still at loggerheads, like distant thunder rumbles before a storm, each pulling to go in opposite ways, like two donkeys tethered to a post. A stalemate threatens to disrupt the holiday – I bend over backwards to keep the peace, and play soother, my usual role and one I am well versed in.

7 AUGUST

I took the car and went off to look for the Buddhists, leaving a note for Jackie still in bed. Puerto Banus very busy, no sign of chanting so I drove on and found Frank Phillips' house, the two girls just leaving to get Sunday papers, he already at the pool. We argued: 'Just because you've had dogs all your life doesn't mean you know anything about them.' I was furious. He had replied 'No' when I politely asked if he had the facility to transfer LP discs to cassette, when he knows I know quite well that he does. At least Tanya with clenched teeth had offered me a drink – fresh orange juice downed in one. Also, the 'Of course, I always said that about Aloe,' when he had accused me of insanity last time. I downed my drink and left, wondering why I'd bothered, reeling from his prudery and meanness.

9 AUGUST

I shall miss La Conche. Swimming with Jackie the sea is like silk – she complains of the debris. 'Better than the Kensington New Pool,' I repeat. A jellyfish like a great stomach floating, a translucent bag grey and dirty ochre round with jagged tentacles to ensnare fish like Quatermass dragged to the pebbly shore, struggles and finally makes off back into the deep.

Jackie asked about my sexuality. 'I don't know, it's a chemical thing, isn't it? My preference is for men but some women turn me on – very few.'

11 AUGUST
[*Ossie returns to London.*]

I stood up in the train all the way to Victoria, reading about the controversy of a new book on John Lennon in the *Daily Mail* over the shoulder of a boy. I staggered to a taxi and I was in my flat by 9 o'clock. I spoke to Michael Kamen and I spoke to George and I finally evacuated my colon – the longed-for bigged ones.

I must confess: even in the luxury of Jackie's Jacuzzi I was looking forward to Sauna in St Martin's Lane. Aching and exhausted as I was – I knew I should have gone to bed – instead I took the tube. I was given key number nine. I lay in the steam and relaxed, the crick in my neck slowly unknotted. I felt very glamorous next to the only other occupant – an old man who looked very grey in comparison. After the cold plunge, my penis is the Greek ideal. More steam, more cold water and upstairs mattresses. I chose one isolated, aware of other eyes ogling my firm tanned body. No one caught my eye. I slept for an hour.

Downstairs back in the steam more people had arrived in the hotter sauna. I sit next to a young man whose skin I touch. 'We are the same colour,' I comment. I follow a man with a very hairy body whose short legs don't matter as he lies on his back fingering his genitals. He's not drawn but another comes over – motions my complicity, wanks as I bite his right nipple too hard. He comes on the floor and winks with a smile and hurries away. More cat and mouse activity until a clone arrives as my erection beckons. I follow him upstairs. We lay on adjoining beds. 'You've got a beautiful cock,' he whispers before using his mouth for a better purpose. Still only 5.30. I slosh off in the shower and take my book upstairs. In the back room a guy I'd clocked earlier writhes on his stomach lifting a perfectly beautiful arse, round and firm. 'You really wanna get fucked, don't you?' Yes. 'It's very dangerous here, do you want to come home with me?' Yes. Outside I ask his name. Francis.

13 AUGUST
Ulla phoned after I'd just gotten into bed knowing the phone would ring. 'Can I get some hashish?' She came over, and looked like a limp rag.

14 AUGUST
Night of sex.

16 AUGUST

Sat in the cruisy meadow in Hyde Park in brilliant sunshine after my visit to Michael a'Brook. Surrounded by queer men lying about transmitting through body language. A butch black just arrived, fingering his genitals towards a responsive Japanese.

Before Michael a'Brook at 3.30, lost my temper at Ulla. Sat in her garden nursing my bruised foot while she painted the deformed nails on her ugly feet.

If only I'd brought a piece of Aloe Vera with me. Michael was quite amazed, I think, by my healthy appearance and my progress, both. As I split partridge-breasted Aloe and applied it, I explained how Aristotle had advised Alexander to capture Socotra (an island off East Africa rich in Aloe) to heal his warriors wounds, and how Cleopatra attributed her beauty and irresistible charm to the use of its gel, and that it's mentioned in the Ebers Papyrus and that Dioscoridies made a lengthy report on it and how it's mentioned in the bible as part of the mixture used to anoint Christ's corpse. He missed the point entirely by offering me a waste-paper basket to throw it away.

I showed him David Reynolds' letter and asked if he would like to read my synopsis. Yes, he said. I said I would like to go into a trance to write when I've got all the gaps and missing information back. He offers hypnotic recall.

17 AUGUST

Nick, smiling, embarrassed, looking tired. No colour, a zit on his cheek. 'So this must be Claudio?' his arms round Nick's shoulders making no pretence of his adoration and physical contact for the person I still love. I cannot deny it. Oh dear, poor Nick. Clearly ill at ease – neither responding nor rejecting the strong arms and thick neck pressed so close. Claudio either choosing to ignore or smothering.

Later – Kay at loggerheads with Jimmy. So I drove to pick her up and gave her an Aloe treatment. Bad News. Beryl has skin cancer.

19 AUGUST

Julian[34] invited me to hear his new band launch at 6.15 in Ronnie Scott's – they are called STRESS, a good title after this week. So now it must be 6.45 and I'm sat in Ronnie Scott's listening to Stress. The handsome black young man sings. Now I understand why he's so fascinated by Jimi Hendrix. Sat next to Tanya with a glass of champagne, Oscar on Ty's lap. I give Tanya a kiss and tell Julian I should dress him in spangles – he should show his pubic hair. 'I'm into that,' he agrees.

20 AUGUST

It was quite painful to write up my visit to Balaban on Wednesday (17th). I'm in turmoil about my feelings, so I ring Robert and of course he feels the same way. I told him I thought Nick looked grey and unhappy, that he hates to be continuously fondled, and that there's no sparkle in his work. I remember Red Nose day and Robert's song for some charity. Nick calmly announcing that he had a new boyfriend. 'Do you mind if I bring him?' Well, yes, said Robert. 'Either I come with him or I don't come.' I can still hear Nick saying it in his 'I don't give a fuck' voice, knowing Robert would agree all along because he, in his vanity, wanted to be photographed. 'It won't last with Claudio,' Robert states. Is he ignorant or smart? I ask. (I still don't know.) 'I hate to say it but I think Nick's being taken for a ride again.' I called out from the bath, 'Don't you go repeating our conversation to Nick. I'm passing your way. Shall I call in tomorrow night?' It occurred to me then that I would sleep with Robert the following night, and I was right.

21 AUGUST

The Roof Garden, a new gay venue, with Mike Fish. Such a lot of pretty moustached Arab boys – one giving me the eye. I stroke his buns as he passes, he responds with a smile and touches gently the sleeve of my yellow jacket. The pretty Arab boy walked by and I took his hand in mine – we dance and make a date to meet next week.

22 AUGUST

It was one o'clock when I drove along Bayswater Road feeling like shit. What a time to get home. Yet still I fumble around inventing chores to delay taking my prescription pills – my subconscious is telling me I don't really need them, and lately I am consciously aware of their over-effectiveness – like I suddenly hear myself talking too quickly or dogmatically.

A walk in the park, deserted because of the weather – only very little sun interspersed with long bouts of grey clouds bearing summer rain. A policeman with a sneer – I see the look of sheer hatred from behind his shades as he checks me out over the faint muscles in his neck turned robot automatic rage, stamping, ceased frozen posture for a split second direct eye contact (the face can give 2,500 signals a minute?). Thank God I was actually passing water – no matter how you shake your leg, the last few drops run down your leg. He fell in step with a woman outside similarly garbed, so unattractive on a female. They are really on a mission – the same vile force drives them impatiently. He stops her from going into the ladies and points towards Queen Mary's garden. Why don't lesbians cottage, I wonder, as I call Oscar to heel. Sid[35] was in quite a good mood. 'Well, actually I've been taking too many drugs . . .' Got any hash? I interrupt.

23 AUGUST

I rang Penny[36] at Bloomsbury. 'If there's a choice, can we go to Lorenzo's?' but of course, it's closed in August so I booked a table at Langan's Brasserie, then settled down to a really productive bout of writing, which turned out to be very expensive – when I went out at five past one, no car. I simply couldn't believe it.

'Well I hope we are going to thrash out a deal,' she began. I had chanted in the taxi to regain my composure (15 mins late). The staff fussed. She couldn't wait to unburden her boyfriend problems. Ex-junkie etc. The food was awful. She returned my 1974 diary, and asked my advice. I am aware I am playing a role of mystic. I asked for £17,500 non-returnable and went through David's letter point by point. She was defenceless, in my pocket. I want I want I want an answerphone, hi-fi, laundry bills paid, or I want to live in the Ritz Hotel in Madrid and you take care of the bills. Are you serious, she asks? Yes, absolutely. What happens if it doesn't sell? It will sell barring a holocaust. Can we put that in the contract? Of course. Whatever argument you put forward I'll smash down. I know my worth and I'm not asking too much. She was much happier talking about her emotional life and asked questions you might ask a guru. I answered with jokes and made her laugh.

24 AUGUST

I bathed and aloed and Suzie Menkes phoned, very gushy and helpful about press association. Made a new plan with Minah[37]. Minah is on the straight wave-length – produces a jacket from 1974. 'Isn't it wonderful I've still got my figure? I'm not being big-headed, but when I think what I did for Jerry Hall, when I see those black girls modelling, its all off my own back because, believe me etc.' She was looking at one of my design books, heaping praise and compliments. She tells me she's got even more of my clothes stashed away in a trunk in Nigeria. She had complained the other day that I kept nicking back a python coat she tried repeatedly to steal. I'd apologise, but realise now that she must have quite a number of original samples, which is actually good news. 'You crafty cunt,' she laughs.

25 AUGUST

Driving to the factory I notice boardings going up to protect against carnival this weekend. Nobody is looking forward to it after murder and crime of last year. In 26 Powis Terrace the walls vibrated to three different rhythms. At the factory I bum another two quid from Jimmy to achieve the £7.50 needed to get into the sauna and assure him I'll go to Agnes for the Golden Lebanese if Alvin doesn't turn up. I thought of George Lawson and Wayne[38] as I parked in Long Acre, and stayed at the Sauna till 9.30.

26 AUGUST

Murder already – 15-year-old boy stabbed on the canal fishing. Stymied in every attempt to discover the whereabouts of Norman Steven[39]'s funeral at 11.45. When I gave up I cupped my hands at the small of my neck and curved my spine backwards becoming very aware of blood pumping through my veins into each arm. 'Thank you, Lord,' I said out loud. What should I do? Shall I change my ways, the homosexual treadmill plotting its revenge? Putting stolen rose petals in my bath as Norman's coffin is put in the ground.

'Acid House.' That's the third time I've heard that phrase today – apparently the words on any invite ensure a sell-out.

27 AUGUST

At home, writing. Opposite a pretty naked boy leans out of the windows to catch some keys thrown up at him. He succeeds second time. Wayne is the name of the beautiful black boy who sings with 'Stress', but I didn't know that when he said, 'Ossie, just the man I'm looking for.'

28 AUGUST

Two hours writing already done. No cigarettes. In desperation I smoke Ulla's dreadful menthol. Today is 17 years since my brother Sammy died. I was staying with Mick Jagger in Bastille du Roi; no, I was still in Cadaquez.

30 AUGUST

The bank was full of cranks – an oldish woman talked to Oscar about her cat, while another shouted her own story for all to hear. I drummed my fingers laden with my three rings while the cashier went through a ridiculous procedure. It must have distracted her because she gave me a pound too much. £9.84. I bought a packet of my poncy cigarettes. By 5 I'd filled my allotted space in the red diary, and was in Edina's workroom, with only one cigarette left.

Ed has got thrush giving her sinus trouble – refuses antibiotics – so is on a diet. She doesn't mind giving up cheese, pasta, oil and bread, but longs for a glass of wine. She had met Bernard Neville over the weekend and thought him wonderful – his Gothic folly in the country. 'Three days in

Wiltshire is more stimulating than 3 weeks in Sardinia with Lynn Franks' (which cost 3 grand including air fares). Edina finds me 'stimulating'. That's her new word, says Tanya.

31 AUGUST

Spoke to Pattie – she invited me to lunch and will help with reminiscences. What a darling she is. Kay was in a FURY– such a state, a screaming rage. I don't know what to do, she wailed, ranted, cried. I felt helpless, made camomile tea, gave sympathy, left her smoking a joint, listing PRIORITIES. She lent me £20 for petrol and cigs.

9.50. 'Tanya's so mean she won't even let me chop the onions.' Tanya has decided she is going to be mean. We are arguing – I insist she takes back her statement. I did not call her a 'mean Jewish cunt'. I'm just giving tit for tat, Madam.

1 SEPTEMBER

Stopped by the bloody police and I have to show my documents. Now I have to get my driving license and insurance together. What a bleeding bore. Showing off on the way back from Heaven, where I saw Stress the group. What a drag. Where am I going to get the money?

2 SEPTEMBER

Pattie phoned me 12.20. I was bathing, having accomplished all the driving bumf. 'Listen, is it a drag? We are invited to an all girls' lunch.' 'Have you got transport?' No, she's banned till December. 'I love your hair like that,' gushed Pat Booth[40]. Over lunch she talked to Pattie about a lawyer because the divorce settlement is getting très compliqué with Eric Clapton. George Harrison playing tennis with two wives. Maureen Cleave[41] had an affair with John Lennon.

3 SEPTEMBER

I rang Mo Yusef[42] and asked for £100 to buy the second-hand Polaroid I spotted yesterday in Hammersmith. He sounded pretty miserable and obviously hasn't got it. I said, if you're really serious about me designing for you, I cost five grand.

4 SEPTEMBER

I spent the afternoon with Ulla – refused to be wound up by her demands. 'I need ten minutes to make-up.' At least she was dressed. I told her I'd smoke a joint, then I'm going, ready or not. Her dog is a problem. Wuffy hates it and so do I. She calls him Wolfie which infuriates me – so today, realising he is going to be around, I decided to try and make friends with him, only to have him growl and snap at me. After the dog-biting incident on the beach in Spain, I simply kick him out of the way – a black Scottish Carie with a bloody big head like a Great Dane and 4" long legs – no wonder he's neurotic.

I was sat writing in my underpants as George let himself in with his keys. I'd already taken my Valium when I discovered no cigs, and I was hungry so I drove up the hill as well, and the perfect fuck at last. Just delicious – a young German staying in Stoke Newington. Relief at last, and on the way home a huge bunch of pink roses.

6 SEPTEMBER

Celia's mixing calculated lies and barbs, thrown on target, aimed perfectly to explode in my ear.

Migraine and tears in disappointment and impotent fury like before, when I was forced to give up my role of father, swimming exhausted against a whole ocean of opposition. Why should a boy of 18, with his head screwed on properly, with the world at his feet, handsome and solar-kissed from six weeks in the California sunshine, bother to see his father? Why should I be so hurt that I bother to cry out in tears of rage? He knows I'm always here should he fuck up. Now this. How can he understand Celia still extricating revenge for dues long paid? I wonder if she really cares for her new boyfriend, whatever he's called. Will he still be there when the house is finished? Has she become so brittle that she can now just use him, just as she herself was used by AG[43] to get another step up the ladder? What price success? Like a dog always sniffing around. The RAT, the little cock crowing, basking in a usurped barnyard, smirking at my hopeless plight, whilst with stolen paper and pen and another man's wife he draws sick copies of a true artist's work, safe behind police protection, for as well as being banned from the matrimonial home (Linden Gardens), I am also banned (on threat of prison) from Powis Terrace too. Whilst David Hockney is IGNORANT, thinking she was actually working there on her textile designs. Surely he would never knowingly have allowed a known plagiarist access to his studio and personal effects? David, who was the one to suggest DIVORCE in the first place, is away round the world with Mark Lancaster to get over Peter Schlesinger. The true artist is ignorant of what is really going on. BOO hoo hoo, poor Mr Magoo has enough problems, with Mo addicted to heroin in the basement, who is also laughing at me as I drink the bitter dregs of remorse, alone in a mansion with tears trickling down my cheeks.

I peered out of the front window to see the little Basset House uniformed schoolboys on their way to swim or sport, walking two by two along Cambridge Gardens, one of whom is completely unaware that his father's heart is breaking on the other side of the street behind the purple curtains of number 86, a house bought on borrowed money, a millstone round my neck which only came to life with the fortnightly access when Albert and Georgie Porgie played with the electric trains, and I learnt the art of cooking. Only the few times when it rang with laughter.

And what of the true Artist? Now world famous and a reputed millionaire, Albert has just spent six weeks with him. He, who calls me 'a little fucker'. The dye is cast; a role model based on that of the interloper. His successes include breaking up Nick Wilder[44] and Gregory[45] (who he stole, but my, has he paid for that) and Ossie and Celia. But Celia is female, and his love for her apparently overrides his misogyny, because perhaps she is exactly like his mother was. But he can't keep her no matter what riches are offered her or heaped on her, unless he can find a replacement for me. Hence his consideration and complicity. In 1973 on Malibu she shared Lee Marvin[46]'s ten-foot bed with David Hockney. Afterwards he told me, 'I would have if I could have.' I'm not suggesting he went out of his way to find AG. The RUNT (always sniffing) was in the picture from early college days at RCA when he worked in the style of Milton Whatsisname, who's work appeared regularly in *Esquire* magazine. Nor am I shirking any blame. Undoubtedly, as with everything else, my immediate success and following was handed to me on a plate. I took Celia's love for granted and abused that gift. On the other hand, I refuse to accept 100% blame. How could Albert know all this? That he wouldn't even exist if Celia hadn't chosen to become pregnant when she did? At the time I was besotted by somebody else. I admit to being utterly incredibly stupid – nevertheless Celia has admitted to Carol that she knew what she was doing at the time and chose to get pregnant to keep me – I was so miserable and unhappy I stopped smoking HASHISH. In doze days it cost five or six quid an ounce and we, Celia and I, went through an ounce a week. Too late I realised my mistake, too late – because, according to Doctor Patrick Woodcock, this was the beginning of my clinical depression, 'the final straw that broke the camel's back,' as he put it. It's not something you just get, but many little hurts over the years, like a tap drip dripping little tears of misery into a barrel. Slower than is noticeable, the barrel fills up and when it's full there is nowhere else for the pain to go. The hidden emotion burst over the surface, the little jibes I pretended not to notice all my life joined hands and I fell into a deep black pit of despair. Even as the embryo grew in Celia's womb I left her alone and went to live in Battersea and take the pills prescribed. Like an automaton I continued to work and live, but the spark had gone. In the morning I took Parstelyn (an anti-depressant) which made me vomit if I ate cheese, and at night I took Mandrax to switch off. I functioned like a robot – I was in a similar state to Brian Jones, but his pain was worse and he killed himself. He tried to reach me on the telephone a few hours before he was gone – and I couldn't be bothered to call back. How could I have been so BLIND? That (even now) I am blessed by God? We both are. With Albert's birth I regained my sanity or rather I regained a will to live – a life force and marriage. How could Albert know I married his mother because that was what she wanted? He knows how sharp her tongue feels. He's experienced her nag nag nagging. He doesn't know of the jealousy of two other women, that I was fought over like a prize fighter, that I stepped over women who fell at my feet, that there was no need to marry, that I loved Celia all the time with all my heart, that marriages are made in heaven. How could he possibly comprehend that in 1969 I married his mother against my will, because his namesake and grandfather wrote me a letter and told me to do so? A long nasty letter in spidery illegible scribble saying what a shit I was – in other words, I wed to stop the nagging and keep the peace. For the same precise reason it was a secret ceremony, only DH and Aunty Kay knew and were present – I cried tears on that day too. Was it some premonition of the misery to come? David, in sympathy and exasperation said, 'What is it Ossie? Tell me what you want and I'll get it for you.' How could he understand that I didn't know what I wanted – although I could have given him a list of things I didn't want? Things like responsibility, commitment, mortgage repayments and life insurance. More drops fell into the overflowing barrel of tears as David put his arm round my shoulder and Celia drank champagne.

With the birth of my son, however, I saw through another pair of eyes that life could still be beautiful. Celia, too, suddenly understood that her selfish act had a meaning far greater than she had anticipated. Mother Nature, in whichever devious ploy, wins out. We both understood simultaneously that the purpose of life is to reproduce. The helpless bundle of joy is given in trust to point the direction towards TRUTH. The blinkers fall away. The conditioning and propaganda both parents accepted unquestioningly from birth disappear like a fog lifted suddenly. For the first time you see what was always there, but not apparent – like the inevitable fact that you will die . . . But now it doesn't matter any more. And as the babe grows, you re-live what you thought you had forgotten as the child experiences for the first time the power of gravity, the taste of champagne, the wetness of water, the size of the sea. And you make sure he doesn't feel the strap or go hungry as you did.

8 SEPTEMBER

Dinner with Sid in the wine gallery on Westbourne Grove. He told me he's back to normal. 'I lost my ego for a while there, been taking acid for a while.' He was pleased to see me, full of ideas for furniture again. My timing spot on – I had no hash, so I decided on Sid, even risked leaving my car in a resident's permit space. He gave me hash and tab of acid.

9 SEPTEMBER

No room beyond colour and shape. The spiritual is beyond DH's wit. An edition of plastic ugly-shaped screens by Hockney. IDM guessed the price exactly right: $200,000.

11 SEPTEMBER

I write an open letter to David Reynolds whom I like too much to bullshit: Dear David, such a lot of flak I'm receiving from certain quarters, concerning the idea that I should even see the truth so clearly in hindsight, let alone write it all down, and dare we even consider publishing it? Rites and rituals, and what is right and what is. And of course certain people aren't going to be too pleased are they, nudge nudge, wink wink, know what? Right ho, David, my innermost thoughts . . .

Albert just dropped round, sort of apologising and is now filling me in on the LA scene. Do you know how rich DH is? 'I already knew he was rich, that he's worth millions, but I didn't know how many millions. He could give a million to each person he's wronged over the last 25 years and still have millions left.' I told Albert of course I knew of his love of money, and how he's shuttered himself off from the real world.

I tried to explain to Albert what it was like when he was born, and read the beginnings of this piece (written September 6) to him. I couldn't have got it down on paper unless I had been so angry, so impotent. It's a powerful piece, a raging complaint against both Celia and DH (who comes off worst). He listened attentively without interruption as I struggled with emotion. Finally getting the rhythm of it, I had to swallow and pause to stop the tears, which I knew would come. Unstoppable. Inevitable. But I was determined to finish it. I was facing away from him, but could feel his sympathy rapt in silence. His presence so solid, so eager to listen as I took the final deep breath and fought to keep my voice reading out the words which cracked up – and for a moment we were transported through time and space to that unhappy period twelve years ago – tears to exorcise that unfair guilt all laid on my shoulders, already crushed submissive, helpless, shackled with the millstone mortgage inertia. 'Ah, Dad, don't,' he began, and taking my body (slumped in the misery of memory), wrapped his strong arms around me in an awkward bear hug. It brought us both back to reality. 'I'm all right, Albert,' I said, wiping away the tears and just lay back while he put the kettle on and complained about the poncy cups. 'What are you afraid of, Dad?' He made a cup of tea and I felt washed clean and the bond between us is stronger than ever.

I took Sid's bitter acid. Determined to move out of my trap – no space, no money, no power, why can't I have a miserable face, tantrums, demand things?

Sigmund Freud. Id, ego, superego. Fascinating program on TV on psychoanalysis. He saw what I have only just discovered, the importance of the joke.

12 SEPTEMBER

Headache, shits and not able to stand until after 11.

Forced periods of abstinence (a whole day, or three, a week even) are essential to maintain the difference between reality and 'drugs real' (which is about six foot off the ground). Wondering was the little bit of euphoria worth all the physical discomfort . . . Oh, but the euphoric feelings of yesteryear, so immediately conjured up by the Beatles' *Help* album. (I heard it the other day in a Soho pub.) So I was feeling very mellow and relaxed when suddenly Albert appeared. It was perfect. He barged in wearing a new jacket and trousers, saying, 'Look, I'm sorry about shouting on the phone the other night, but I'm sick of being screamed at from both sides.' It's all right, Albert, I said, it doesn't matter now, but at the time I was very hurt, hearing your mother's words in your own mouth. Don't you think I missed you at all in the last six weeks? Anyway, how was it? He knows the score. DH had tried to Big Daddy them.

13 SEPTEMBER

Bored at a Buddhist meeting. Lessening the Karmic Retribution, the speaker fumbles and the Paki picks his nose. Eradicate sins from previous life times . . . Boring, boring, boring.

I'm just longing for the Gigot in Pam's Aga.

14 SEPTEMBER

I rang Johnny Dewe Mathews and told him what Albert had told me of Mo being dumped on, expected to perform. It is definitely a court, and Mo is the court jester.

16 SEPTEMBER

Tanya relayed a message from Lynn Franks. 'Is she going to appear in your book?' 'Tell her, she should be so lucky,' I replied sarcastically. 'Right, that's what I'll tell her.'

17 SEPTEMBER

'I don't like your fashion business, mister, I don't like the drugs that keep you thin' – L. Cohen[47].

'Always favours you want,' Celia on the phone when I threatened to go round if I can't speak to George who is quite obliging and will feed the fish. Only five of the 17 tropical fish I bought are left.

To Devon. There was a lot of traffic. Pam zoomed at 110 mph. Oscar couldn't get comfortable. The sun came out as we bypassed Bristol. When we did stop the crowds were queuing 50-deep for the lavatories. It was like Blackpool on a bank holiday.

18 SEPTEMBER

I got up at ten past seven. The roses wafted a delicious perfume which set the day pleasant, and fresh coffee, Aga warmth, the kittens at home, Oscar out on the lawn doing pee pees. I settled down to write in my new notebook, for Pam fast asleep till 10.45. Out in the garden everything so tranquil, beauty everywhere, Mother Nature in her prime. Pam in a white towelling-dressing gown makes more coffee, which she drinks, on the bench under the mimosa tree with the kittens playing at her feet. In silent reverie I made scrambled eggs which made me full up and feel ill.

In the late afternoon we prepared a Gigot, stuffed as much herbs and garlic into it as possible. We went for a drink and cigarettes in the local, a hotel Pam knows the owners of, to catch up on the gossip. They busy making plans for a wedding – she has never been further than Barnstaple and collects cheese dishes.

19 SEPTEMBER

Sunshine. Oscar being bothered by the kittens who have made their home behind the sink. They only come out to hiss and intimidate with sideways walk and toilet-brush tails. He distracts me as I concentrate on writing and drawings, so I put him to bed with Pam which backfires – I hear his sharp bark – just one, saying I'm trapped, please release me.

20 SEPTEMBER

[*Ossie returns to London.*]

Home to a Dump at 8.30. 'Oh goodie, you're home,' said George on the telephone.

21 SEPTEMBER

I woke at 7.20 in my own bed. Scarlatti on Radio 3 brought the irate niggress neighbour stamping upstairs from the ground floor, heavy rapping at my front door (which I ignored). I do hope there won't be repercussions.

22 SEPTEMBER

Kay rang yesterday. I'd put Aloe on the nape of her neck, taped across. She kept it on all night. She marvels at the effect – another complete convert.

Albert came round about 1 o'clock, I was just out of the bath. He was ratty and seemed out of sorts. He flopped on my day-bed while I made more coffee. As I attempted to rescue the papers he was sprawled on, I came across Mo's last postcard. 'Look, it's of a great tomb.' 'I'm sick of Death!' Albert said. 'Every time I come round here there's talk of Death,' and he went off to try to find George in Holland Park.

I had this idea to be photographed with DH's drawing of Albert as a child. But they're all locked up because this house is so easy to break into. ''Ere, d'you ever worry about AIDS?' asked Sid as I arrived a little late at Coleville Terrace. He was all spruced up and ready to go out. A very empty feeling and bright clear light, trippy vibrations. I am immediately aware of enough black hash to make three joints. I'd grabbed it and begun to skin up, not properly aware of myself – non compos mentis.

23 SEPTEMBER

'I hate her!' said Pattie's niece. 'There are some people you hate instinctively when you first meet them and she's one of them.' She is the 17-year-old daughter of Jenny Boyd and Mick Fleetwood[48]. Amy Fleetwood has given up trying to be a model and wants to act. She hated Lynn Franks on sight. The dinner wasn't a success – awful Indian chicken tough as old boots, too spicy. I drank wine which I shouldn't have (driving). I took some notes, gave a reading or two, made them laugh. I quoted the Capote[49] biography Patrick Procktor had lent me, and gleaned a little more from Pattie re her bust when they put hash in her car and in George[50]'s boot. It was the wedding day of Paul and Linda[51], and when she saw five cars arriving in their driveway at their house in Esher, she thought it was the party arriving, not the fuzz.

28 SEPTEMBER

I came across Mo's last letter sent in June 87. Darling Mo – it hasn't sunk in yet that we won't meet in this lifetime. Of course all the clues are there – he mentions his teeth, and how Arnold Schwarzenegger[52]'s gap had inspired him, so he'd been making a montage of his smile clipped out of old magazines and pasted on to his own in photographs. He calls AG 'piggy'. 'Kill him for me if you see him.' I didn't notice the portentous amount of praise heaped on me. 'Oh talented one,' he began. Tells it like it is. I floored Patrick Procktor on Thursday when he obsequiously talked of DH's drawings of his daschund. 'Hideous dogs, impossible to house-train,' I spat out, remembering the filthy little beast AP[53] had when she lived in the house in Cambridge Gardens, that I actually booted out the front door, after it excreted everywhere – on my pink carpet, in the bathroom, on the stairs. And I remember going, cap in hand, to visit DH during the short period he lived on the top floor of 17 Powis Terrace in his £200,000 studio with the proper north light, when I took Dodie Dodie. In vain I tried to make reconciliation, because the first words he said to me were, 'D'you know your dog's just pissed on my chair?' I wonder why Dodie Dodie did. So uncharacteristic.

29 SEPTEMBER

Lunch with Pattie, but I wasn't feeling at all well. The truth is I've had the shits since I took the LSD. As a matter of fact, I wish I hadn't taken the wretched hallucinogenic. I don't think it achieved anything, much to Sid's chagrin – he actually thought I would stop taking my daily pills, just thought I'd have one or two low days. I put him right, saying he didn't understand that if the chasm opens before me, I run in the opposite direction in my red boots. If I actually were to fall, I'd go headfirst downwards, a long way into the blackness.

I couldn't help but notice the effect of age on her face. Still beautiful, her figure still stunning, her giggle so infectious. Even irate and foot stamping. 'I so hate being without a telephone,' she says in exasperation. She is less than two years younger than I. She has always been interested in beauty. Her father remarried and in classic wicked-stepmother style, she had an expensive education, all in boarding schools. Cherry Marshal became her agent and Dick Lester figured early on. When she was up for the movie (*Hard Day's Night*) he was directing. She thought it was for another TV commercial (having done one with him for Smith's Crisps, and also the dog shampoo, before that first Beatles film). She had told me long ago how she met them, how at first she refused his offer, and a near summons from one of the fab four tried to procure her services as a bimbo. 'Tell her to come to my caravan after filming,' was the message she received, or words to that effect[54].

I dropped in on Johnnie Rozza watching Olympics on TV. Poor Daley Thompson[55], bandaged one leg and broke the pole vault as he jumped. 'I'd love him to fuck me, wouldn't you?' he asked.

Doctor 3.30. I told him Celia still getting at me and I hate to feel vulnerable – I thought none could hurt me anymore. I asked if he would read the piece I wrote in anger about Celia.

30 SEPTEMBER

A beautiful day, clear, crisp and cold, but I felt unwell. After a simple lunch of trout and salad – packed full of all the right seeds, pulses, nuts and garlic – I got out my notebook and read a few pieces out loud.

2 OCTOBER

No hash, no car, no money, no word from Albert. A hard combination. I found myself in an absent state, non-functioning.

I felt very alone and as I walked through happy crowds in Holland Park, I began to feel very low indeed. I thought I might eat so I walked home and cooked bacon and eggs and went to bed for an hour, waking even more miserable. The combination of no hash, no car and a deep hurt thinking of Albert, and the bottomless pit opens before me. I quake, I totter, knowing if I fall I'll go headfirst into that black abyss – and that really scares me on top of everything else.

3 OCTOBER

Today I had better tuning, but still I missed David Reynolds. Instead to Ghost with Oscar. 'My brain ceases to function without hashish.'

4 OCTOBER

Modern life is rubbish.

5 OCTOBER

Life is a merry-go-round but you might fall off at any moment.

Sheridan's Memorial Service, St Margaret's, Westminster.

Patrick sat with Mike Fish, DH with Celia. Late, I stood at the back of full pews with Jonathan Guinness. In my ginger tweed suit and sunlight on my head through stained glass windows, I remembered happier times, joined in singing the hymns and listened enthralled.

7 OCTOBER

I feel so old. DH here. I asked George when next he sees DH to find out if I am invited to his reception at the Tate.

The autumn leaves fall to the ground, swept off the tree by gales all around.

In agony. Cold, aching tired muscles, headache, bunged up.

Night of passion with an insatiable Scorpio I've renamed Vincenti. Real name

Francis. An orphan with a very peculiar accent. Very forward – he did all the talking and led the dance.

8 OCTOBER

I was at Ghost early. I photocopy and make coffee. A sweet Greek-Cypriot girl standing. Vaguely Indian design in gold on hideous stiletto-heeled shoes – sherbet pink and rust. 'Don't you love them?' They may well have looked glamorous in 1957 but many a beautiful inlaid wooden floor ruined.

Albert's got a pager, so I rang him to tell him I've got an answerphone. 'Still, not as good as my pager,' he said. 'It will stop mum being hassled: she freaks out for five days every time you come round.'

9 OCTOBER

The Ghost show in the Pillar Hall at Olympia – packed. A success. I took my notebook and bitched, but really it was OK for this day and age. Tanya unapproachable, spinning like a top. We watched *The Clothes Show*, which reported on the designer collections. Ghost got a mention and so did I as Jeff Banks made this year's choice for the costume museum in Bath. He chose Gaultier[56]. My 1968 Chiffon and Satin two-piece chosen by Pru Glynn flashed on the screen. I was stunned by its beauty, never realised the print red. I left Tanya crying on her bed after putting a little hash in her hand.

10 OCTOBER

'I think you were a schmuck to choose that Gaultier rubbish,' I told Jeff after the show. He squirmed a bit and said, 'Well, call it a political move.' 'You should have had the balls to say so.' I always thought he was a bit of a creep; I'd said so to Jackie yesterday. Dinner at Groucho's, but I had to beg for it.

11 OCTOBER

Bernard Neville[57] is always so indiscreet with me – he's found his fantasy: a hairless Chinese boy who lives in a council flat in Peckham with his mother who's interested in fashion. 'I want to get him into college, educate him, promote him,' he said. 'I haven't fucked him yet, but I think he's queer. He's got no girlfriends. I gave him a massage and he was terribly embarrassed. How's your love life?' he asked. Non-existent really, I replied. I still love Nick, I suppose.

He hadn't heard about Mo's death, but wasn't surprised, just simply dismissed him. He was amazed DH hadn't paid for Albert's recent US trip, or got in touch with me (but actually I'm quite proud of the fact that Albert paid his own way).

Gill Goldsmith. Salvation: at last some cash. £100 quid.

12 OCTOBER

After Bernard's comments last night I decided I had to write DH a letter which I did as soon as I got up.

Madame Pressman blows 15 Grand on a mink coat in the basement of 162 Bond Street. Revillion Furs, run by Bernadette Bishop. Of course she chose the most expensive mahogany female strands to be made into full sleeves and 2' longer. She dithered on one at £13,000 which was so long, and because of the Tudor cut made her look like Henry VIII. I gave loud hints that I would love to borrow her silver Merc convertible as she drove me home, but she didn't hear.

Wrote a letter to David Hockney:

'David' – I can hardly write dear – 'It no longer surprises me that you're never in touch; though sometimes I wonder why. I did think I might receive an invite, this time, to your Reception at the Tate, but not so far which just proves how right my mother's advice was, never expect anything and you'll never be disappointed.'

With Best Wishes, Ossie.

PP[58] tells me he's in Florence, anyway.

16 OCTOBER

The grey blanket covers the sky; still no sign of the new moon. I went to Holland Park on the off-chance that I might just see it peeping through. Darkness and the car park empty. I took seven deep pink roses for Pam.

18 OCTOBER

Called in to see Brian Clarke – he is also troubled by the press and the AIDS rumour – really doesn't like Hockney – 'He's not very intelligent, is he?'

20 OCTOBER

At last the not-so-new moon sighted.

22 OCTOBER

Albert's 19th Birthday. A rather miserable day alone without hash, without cigarettes even.

23 OCTOBER

No car is really a drag. I can manage no money and no hash but not all three simultaneously. Johnnie Rozza provided cigarettes. Very thrilled to find a buff envelope delivered by hand, foolscap and folded, addressed to Mr Ossie Clark. I recognised Hockney's style, realised it was the invitation at last. I was so excited I delayed opening it, hoping there might be a note inside. Instead two openings. I was so disappointed I didn't notice the different dates.

24 OCTOBER

Woke early feeling DREADFUL.

The Hockney opening at the Tate is tonight. Slight panic as I rang Jackie and she had to rearrange everything. Lindy Dufferin was so sweet, 'Oh here's Ossie, I'm sure he's on the list.' 'I don't think so,' I told her, but if Kas[59] had been there I might have gone – she gave a dinner for 40 people. Instead we joined PP and Anthony Page for parsnip soup.

25 OCTOBER

PP gave me an M&S lunch. Tells me he's only got $^1/_3$ of his stomach left and even though he only ate a spoonful he felt very queasy. He gave me a £10 note to give to Albert for his Birthday. I used it to pay for my prescription while he prepared lunch. He tells me Peter Langan is in a coma and having skin graft operations on his head.

26 OCTOBER

To the factory. I found a sewing machine that worked (not very well) and made the alterations to Gill's black silk satin bodice that Quidjta has made quite well, though the ends of the bone casing tape not at 45 degrees which is so important. Nevertheless, the cloth is exquisite and already its going to be a fabulous dress. I fitted it on Monday – she's lost weight. 'I do want my waist back, as it must be 25",' which is amusing as she's past 60.

28 OCTOBER

Minah Bird rang 10.35. It's 26 days since I promised to take a walk with her. She spoke as though it were the day before yesterday – 'You didn't turn up, do you remember? I was worried about you.' Actually Minah, I don't know where I've been. We talked shop, literally. 'If you really want a shop we've got to find out how much it will cost.'

Angry and irritated. The complaining neighbour knocking at my door as I listen to *Carmen* – Bizet's composer of the week on Radio 3. She started banging before nine, so I turned the volume up full-blast and now I'm a bit freaked – I'd listened to the whole opera on CD with Nick in Ponfield House. I tried to phone him again and realised he must be away.

29 OCTOBER
Driving back to Penzance Street, an old car and a camera set up on a tripod. An autumn marriage. As I got closer, the bride appeared on the porch, a bow low down below her bum. Too big a train, and I recognise a well-made dress when I see one.

30 OCTOBER
Yesterday I blew all my money on a tweed suit and a pair of brown lace-up boots. On Thursday I had over £200 and now I've less than £20.

31 OCTOBER
The gasman cometh – the first of a deluge of problems. Didn't answer the door.

2 NOVEMBER
Gill gave me a cheque to pay the Gas Bill. Thank God. The clouds dispersed and gave way to sunshine.

'I'm not a charity,' said Tanya when I beg funds for petrol, yet she gave me a fiver eventually after fumbling in her bag. She was snappy and demanding, insisting I accompany her down the road to pay a bill for last night's festivities. She became quite demented because I let the dog out. In an attempt to stop him barking she puts a hairband round his jaws.

Illicit sex with the leatherman Maurice Pickering. Two ancient hideous dogs and a very twee flat. Awful, I couldn't perform – no element of fantasy (so essential). When I got home I discovered I'd got crabs. Ugh.

4 NOVEMBER
Word reached me there was one of my old chiffon dresses on a stall under the fly-over. Looking at jodhpurs on a fine cold morning. Muchos sunshine.

5 NOVEMBER
In Cleveland Square with a dreadful cold. I met John Dunbar with his young son. 'Until a couple of years ago the young female residents of this area were very suspect.'

8 NOVEMBER
Ghost for a day of work. Tanya rang at 11.15, the Polish prick Theresa not in work today.

9 NOVEMBER
Strange dream of DH – 'You're not going to have Mo, you fucker.'
Enjoyed work.

11 NOVEMBER
Jackie Pressman's red dress, unlike Gill's black silk, was doomed from the moment I started cutting a length short of cerise moiré. What I hadn't also realised was Madame Pressman's gain in weight, that it would be 4" too small across the back and short over her ample shoulders. Madame has grown plump and I hadn't noticed.
Sadness. *The Bigger Splash* on TV. I'd forgotten it opens on Mo, sat at the art deco table, and the story unfolds all through his recollection.
I've had enough of Tanya.

14 NOVEMBER
I was engrossed in preparing the back opening on Gill's black satin dress.

15 NOVEMBER
You see, to do the writing I need the hash.

20 NOVEMBER
Up at first light. Snowflakes swirling against a grey mist. The loving couple opposite peering out at the weather in amazement.

22 NOVEMBER
Oscar's got the same sheen on him as the black satin of Gill's dress. Yesterday she rang – 'If I can't have my dress today I don't want it,' she threatened. She came for a fitting at teatime and it is perfect with the bow on the bum. I set to and made the net sleeve padding and attached the bow and started hand-sewing, working my fingers to the bone.

23 NOVEMBER
In a taxi, delivering Gill's dress. I told her it's the first time I've sewn a dress including the buttons from beginning to end since I was a student. Got £50.

25 NOVEMBER
Depressed and ratty with little Oscar who is the joy of my life. Usually I don't mind him hogging my bed but today he got kicked to the bottom.

28 NOVEMBER
Low.

5 DECEMBER
My car has been towed away, gone, and hardly any coffee. I'm quite freaked

out, I really am. I did have brilliant sex in the sauna with a very handsome chap. We noticed each other in the steam – I'd made another come by sucking his nipple, something I'd done before. The other took his place and waited patiently until we were alone. 'Stand up', he ordered in a whisper, and blew me.

8 DECEMBER

I set off early to walk to my appointment with Michael a'Brook through Kensington Gardens and was very depressed to read that Peter Langan Dead. After six and a half weeks in a coma his kidneys gave up.

13 DECEMBER

I've put on weight with bread and garbage food – 9st, 12lbs. I took a long walk with Oscar beyond the Albert Memorial then along High St Ken where I ate a bologna in Holland Park, listening to foul-mouthed schoolchildren. Really obnoxious – 'fuck you, got my fackin' hash.' I eavesdropped in shocked silence, newspaper in front of me until the food arrived. Oscar tucked beside me. Mild, crisp weather, alone with Oscar.

17 DECEMBER

Carla brought bottle whisky round and drank most of it sitting on my bed complaining, 'You're still young, wait until you're sixty – the most ghastly things begin to happen like you can't walk and your skin gets all loose and wrinkly.' She spent all her time obsessed with cleaning and 'hygiene'-cleaning with a toothbrush around the taps on the bathroom sink.

When Albert was six or seven and George maybe four years old, I managed to get them into an X-rated movie called *Phantom of Paradise*, having already seen it but wanting to see it again. I took them because I thought they'd enjoy it. George asked if I'd seen it (it was on television), saying how he remembered seeing it.

18 DECEMBER

George told me on the way back to his house that he had set up the electric train set. It was understood between us that there was no question of me seeing the train and engines set up inside Westbourne Park Road even though he longed to show it to me and I would love to see it. I don't ask, and we both know why.

20 DECEMBER

10.30 p.m. A man my age or older bought me a second whisky – he'd come up to me the other day at the same bar (the Champion) and said he remembered me from the Kings Road. 'They said you were the best, how are you getting on now?' He'd offered to buy me a drink then, but I'd refused. This time I was glad to accept. He was maudlin and talked of old times. Then I spotted the guy I'd noticed at the sauna who runs a stall on Portobello. I went over unhesitatingly. He asks if I know Hockney, what the scare was along his lower spine. He's called Kevin, and he's going to Istanbul for Christmas.

22 DECEMBER

No pills. It was after two in the afternoon when I finally staggered home resisting my own wise counsel to buy provisions. I climbed into bed with Oscar, drunk. I slept for two hours for I had consumed enough bloody Marys and vodkas and a bottle of water on Paddington Station where I said good-bye to last night's grotesquery in the daylight, feeding his dogs from packet sandwiches.

23 DECEMBER

At last I got hold of David Reynolds at Bloomsbury. 'The problem is they can't sign a contract with you because you are an undischarged bankrupt.' Well I knew that, didn't I! 'But there is a way around the problem – I can sign as your agent. Come for a drink at 12 on Boxing Day.'

25 DECEMBER

Xmas Lunch. I waited until Pam called before I actually decided I was going. 4.30, she said. I was surprised to find Sid first on arriving. I suppose I was hoping he wouldn't be there. I sat with Pam's dad. Delicious food – the turkey cooked in the Aga.

Albert brought me a bottle of champagne. 'You should be very proud of him, he's a lovely boy,' said Billy[60] after Albert had left to rescue the turkey breasts, and sweetly saying, 'I'm sorry you can't be there with us, but you know mum.' It was nice to drink champagne, and very potent marijuana. Billy made us laugh.

1 Edina Ronay.

2 Ulla Larson.

3 Quentin Crisp, eccentric gay icon, famous 'Englishman in New York'; was incredibly poor and lived in squalor, famously noted as saying, 'If you don't clean anything for four years it doesn't get any dirtier.'

4 Jenny Dearden, formerly Jenny Marriot – since her divorce from Steve Marriot she has married screenwriter James Dearden, who wrote the script for *Fatal Attraction*.

5 Nick Balaban.
6 Henrietta Rous.
7 Tanya Sarne.
8 Wilf Butler.
9 Alcoholics Anonymous.
10 Hettie Quidejeta.
11 Sandra and Michael Kamen.
12 Patrick Procktor.
13 Mick Jagger.
14 Jose Fonseca.
15 Ulla had invited Ossie to go to Madrid with her friend Sylvia Polakov, a former model.
16 Jackie, friend of Tanya Sarne.
17 Kay Melia.
18 Pam Procter.
19 Joyce's groundbreaking novel for which he famously invented the 'stream-of-consciousness' style of prose. (It is interesting to consider the effect Joyce's 'beautiful writing' may have had on Ossie's entry for 23 April and subsequent entries in a similar vein; it almost certainly influenced the chronology found at the beginning of this book, which he began on 15 July 1988, shortly after finishing *Ulysses*.)
20 Mo McDermott. He died of liver failure.
21 Michael Kamen.
22 Chelita Secunda.
23 Sam Melia.
24 An employee at Ghost.
25 Pattie Boyd has by now divorced Eric Clapton.
26 Keeping calm when annoyed with Tanya.
27 Micha's boyfriend.
28 A present from Ossie in the '60s.
29 Tommy Steele, popular British singer and actor.
30 Ossie was bitten by a dog that morning.
31 Nick's new lover, with whom he is living in Paris.
32 Johnnie Rozza, photographer friend whom Ossie has made through his Buddhist practice.
33 Sam Clark, Ossie's brother who died in 1971.
34 Lover of Ossie's.
35 Sid Rotbart.
36 Penny Phillips, editor who worked with David Reynolds.
37 Minah Bird.
38 Wayne Sleep.
39 Norman Stevens, painter; close friend, from the north, of Ossie, Hockney and Celia.

40 Pat Booth, writer.
41 Maureen Cleave, journalist, one of the first people to write about The Beatles.
42 Mo Yusef, Nick Balaban's business partner at this time.
43 Adrian George.
44 Nick Wilder, dealer in contemporary art with whom Hockney lived for part of 1966.
45 Gregory Evans.
46 Lee Marvin, American actor; friend of David Hockney.
47 Leonard Cohen, Canadian singer/songwriter and poet; these lyrics are from 'First We Take Manhattan'.
48 Mick Fleetwood, British drummer with Fleetwood Mac.
49 Truman Capote.
50 George Harrison.
51 Paul and Linda McCartney.
52 Arnold Schwarzenegger, Austrian actor; former Mr Universe.
53 Alice Pollock.
54 This was how Pattie Boyd first met George Harrison.
55 Daley Thompson, British athlete.
56 Jean-Paul Gaultier, French fashion designer. Fun-loving and witty, Gaultier's designs have their origins in the London street-styles of the seventies; his clients include Madonna, who wore his outfits on many of her tours in the eighties and early nineties.
57 Bernard Neville, textile designer; one of Ossie's tutors at the RCA.
58 Patrick Procktor.
59 John Kasmin.
60 Billy Henry.

1989

Ossie begins his third year in Penzance Street with a very powerful outpouring of emotion inspired by his son Albert. 'I'm sorry for the things I've done. I've shamed myself with lies. I was manipulated too by flattering words, glamour…' The entry is in much the same tone as that of 9 September 1988 and contains the same need to release his past that dominated 1988's diary. However, this year all Ossie's attempts to 'unscramble' his past, to make a fresh start, are inextricably linked to his continuing interest in Buddhism. 'Daimoku is a great clearing house. It unscrambles the brain, all the trivia melts into a proper perspective.'

Ossie pursues his Buddhist beliefs and, as his son George comments, they undoubtedly help him a lot. However, despite the force of his new beliefs, in 1989 Ossie is still not able to rid himself of his love for Nick or the jealousy he feels towards his new lover, Claudio. Buddhism has not yet taught him about forgiveness. He is still finding it very hard to talk to Celia or to forgive Tanya Sarne who has fallen out with him, and he can be uncharitable, to say the least, to those he dislikes.

Ossie seems at times to be concerned that he may be turning into an invalid, emotionally as well as physically. He reads and identifies greatly with Denton Welch, who wrote extensively about his own exposure to poverty and isolation, impelled by a physical disability sustained early in life. Although Ossie is feeling rather physically immobile, it is undoubtedly the metaphorical implications of Welch's writing that he identifies with most.

When Ossie meets a woman in a wheelchair, he is surely thinking of Welch and of his own troubles when he records how inspired he was by her resilience to her condition. 'I walked away with a spring in my stride,' he says. 'Even the grotesque deformed ankles splayed like ancient gnarled tree roots did not detract from the radiance of her smile.' An ability to carry on and to smile in the face of what seem like impossible odds is bound to appeal to Ossie at this point in his life.

Ossie does try - apart from his usual trips to the sauna - to follow a healthier lifestyle this year. However, when he congratulates himself one night for walking to Hampstead Heath, a little irony emerges considering his willingness to gamble with his own life through the risk of AIDS once he gets there.

In 1989, once again Ossie is haunted from afar by the figure of David Hockney. When Celia, Albert and George again go to visit the painter in Los Angeles, Ossie at first seems annoyed that it is Hockney and not he who can entertain his family at huge expense. However, soon afterwards the reader is reminded through a poem Ossie composes of another possible reason for Ossie's obsession with the painter. The initial letters of each line of the poem spell out the line, 'Oswald loves David'. It is a reminder of another angle from which the Celia, David and Ossie dynamic can be viewed, an angle that has not been hinted at for many years.

The paradoxical nature of Ossie's existence in his later years is nowhere shown more clearly than in 1989. While on some days he is without food or battling with the DHSS over his entitlement to £40 a week living allowance, he is still very much in touch, and great friends, with the super rich. His trip to Tangier at the invitation of Nadia and Swami La Valle, and his holiday in Marrakesh at the home of Bill Willis are poignant examples; indeed the atmosphere inside and around Willis's home is so exotic and louche compared to Ossie's life at home in his council flat in Notting Hill that he exclaims to himself, 'This is what immortality must be like.'

Suzy Menkes, the respected fashion correspondent and old friend and admirer of Ossie, also remains loyal. When she threw a dinner party for Christian La Croix, who regarded Ossie as one of his heroes, she went further than just inviting Ossie. Aware of his plight, she wanted him to feel a star again, and accordingly sent a car round to collect him. 'We hoped to give Ossie a little revival. We got out *his* clothes and Pucci clothes.' However, the memory that haunted her was of 'Ossie in the garden tucking into plateful after plateful of food'. 'It is such a sad story, but the temperaments of artists mean that often they do suffer,' she reflected.

1 JANUARY

I didn't wake until almost eleven and I'd promised Pam[1] I'd be there for Gongyo at 10.30. Surprised to find Sandie Shaw[2] there. I'd seen her on TV in *25 Years of Top of the Pops*. 'Do you ever cry?' she asked. I confessed that I did.

So the year began – on my feet, putting fresh linen on the bed I got out of and have spent so much time in, in a state of indecision.

[Following an argument, Ossie writes the following passage to Albert – a confession perhaps inspired by the Buddhist ethos of truth.]

I'm sorry for the thing I've done. I've shamed myself with lies[3]. I was manipulated by flattering words, glamour and greedy people and ragtrade Jews, jealous interlopers, impotent and powerful, by sycophants, by envious thieves who stole all they could lay their hands on. I think I've paid my pound of flesh and I regret nothing. What good would that do? I can live with it because I didn't do anything truly evil. Sure, I committed adultery, but I didn't steal another's wife or lover – ever. I did what millions did and still do – but I never stole – I gave and gave willingly.

3 JANUARY

What words, I wonder, did he[4] choose to scheme his dastardly deed, garbled what I said. 'What I choose to do is none of your affair,' is all I'd said and when he scurried up the stairs muttering, 'I think I'd better just let Celia know you're here,' I thought perhaps she was in the bedroom having a nap.

Do you think perhaps he's so insecure because he knows eventually she will tire of him? He's much younger – it's on the cards. Perhaps when the housework is complete. Or do you think he'd like to marry her? Or maybe he feels threatened, as though just as love turns to hate and then indifference, that by some miracle Celia will stop hating me – which seems unlikely to me. However, the Celia I loved exists only in my memory. Hate me she does, whereas I don't give a fig except for Oscar, after my sons.

6 JANUARY

Is it true Pauline Fordham's going to prison[5]? I have no idea but I wouldn't be suprised.

7 JANUARY

Walked in Ken Gdns – Lloyd Honegan bounced by. Not just another jogger but a famous boxer and he was absolutely tiny. Charismatic and instantly recognisable. We were all quite amazed. Back home George said, 'I wish your TV was colour.' So do I. Climbed back into bed to watch it till the small hours then I got up and took Oscar for nocturnal walkies, or maybe I didn't. Yes I did. It takes an hour and forty minutes to walk back from Hampstead Heath.

13 JANUARY

I woke at first light out of a strange dream. At night I met up with Ben[6] somewhere and brought him home to see Mo[7]'s murals – clouds painted on walls, billowing muslin curtains. Albert was living with me and on the first floor we walked into a party. In horror I watched a boy inject himself as he sat on a bed surrounded by others. I made a scene by throwing out the junkie and all the others with track marks. Upstairs on the top floor a plague of kittens. One Burmese Tom spraying . . .

16 JANUARY

I met Bella Freud on my way to Carla[8]. She surprised, pleased, but looking awful – pale, face tense, a huge zit blotching her cheek.

18 JANUARY

More weird dreams. Another empty day and not wanting to write it down doesn't help.

On Friday Guy[9] is going to Paris for three days with Nick[10] to stay in his little flat. Then Claudio[11] comes back to set up a gay contact agency-line on the French telephone – my heart sank, it all sounds so lovey dovey and sordid at the same time.

19 JANUARY

Giro in the post so money in my pocket and a trip to the sauna – on the tube going I had a feeling it would be more expensive and it was – £8. The steam works wonders on my morale and on my aching limbs and back. My stiff neck eases up and becomes supple. Today more young men than usual – not so many ogres. Upstairs, lying on one of the cots, relaxing smoking a cigarette, surrounded by the furtive movements and body signals – some subtle, others just blatant. I turn my eyes closed to the wall and repeat, 'Go away – go away,' under my breath to combat the come-on directed at me from the balding, pot-bellied occupant of the next bed whose heavy-breathing and genital-fingering sicken me. Sadder because my own precious time wasted. Will I end up such a heap? The revolting ones wear their towels folded in such a way as to expose their wares. But then the beds change their occupants and the same signals from Charles (a student nurse, young and Johnny Dewe Mathews-shaped) produce a response, which makes it all seem worthwhile. We wank and the orgasm is marred by a spoilsport attendant who kicks my bed as my jism spurts.

20 JANUARY

In a dream I introduce Salvador Dali to George. As we looked on he changed from an old man into the young and handsome one he once was. And when I woke, news of another relapse. Apparently he hasn't eaten for five years – he's been fed by tube.

Patrick Procktor has been blowing his trumpet all day. Had Stephen[12] the Buddhist with him who is going to write Patrick's biography. Asked if he could interview me. I was reluctant, but agreed. After all, we did go to Morocco for the first time together in 1967.

23 JANUARY
Salvador Dali dead.

24 JANUARY
Woken at 4 something choking on my own vomit. Staggered to the bathroom and threw up.
Trip up north with George. 'Where did he get his full lips? asked Beryl[13].

25 JANUARY
[*Ossie returns to London.*]

Straight back to the sauna. Wayne Sleep was there.

26 JANUARY
Ian[14] again. Shitty sheets.

31 JANUARY
Day with Carla. I left a sarcastic message on my answerphone: 'Should anybody, by any chance, phone me, well I'm sorry I'm not here.' I related to Carla an incident where DH's with Billy Wilder[15] in some smart restaurant in Los Angeles. Jack Lemmon[16] stopped to say hello on his way to the mensroom and said, rounding off the chat, 'Well, I must shake the dew from my lily.' Carla laughed, but asked, 'What kind of Jew would he be shaking from his penis?' She thought it was one of my anti-Semitic jokes.

6 FEBRUARY
No more sleep and manic thoughts. After nine days without, I take two pills and start to write again. And a new moon fired me to try again. I had a real fear of abandoning jotting down the sequence of daily events – and even now there is much left out and gaps to fill in.
The weather so beautiful, like April. A perfectly clear blue sky. I set off for Kensington Gardens, pushing a lady in a wheelchair to Westbourne Grove Post Office. 'You're my fourth pusher today. It has only taken forty mins from Shepherd's Bush. I work in the theatre – I've got four jobs.' She is having a running battle with London Underground. I left her feeling quite elated, not only made suddenly aware of what I've always taken for granted, i.e., sound limbs and good health, but also admiration for her amazing pluck and cheerful acceptance of what fate had laid for her. 'Well,

what else can I do?' she asked philosophically, and answered her own question: 'Lay down and wait for death or make the most of it and get on with life.' I walked away with an extra spring in my stride. Even the grotesque deformed ankles splayed like ancient gnarled tree roots didn't detract from the radiance of her smile.

15 FEBRUARY

I went with Billy[17] to Highbury Lloyds bank and he gave me 20 quid and dropped me at the sauna. Again I was caught as I orgasmed. It's just as well I had to leave early to go for dinner with Ben and Emily[18].

16 FEBRUARY

Michael a'Brook had a nosebleed when I told him I suspected DH guilty of *schadenfreude*[19]. He knew the word and said, 'I wouldn't be surprised,' taking the bloodied handkerchief from his nose to do so.

18 FEBRUARY

Carried on reading *Maiden Voyage*[20] until about six when I went to St Martin's Lane sauna. In the steamroom Wayne Sleep came in – 'I thought you would be here,' he said. 'I just had a feeling I'd see you as I came here in the taxi.'

20 FEBRUARY

I finished reading *Maiden Voyage* and quite enjoyed it. I suppose if I'd had a public school education, come from an aristocratic family, become motherless at the age of nine and been in China at the beginning of this century, I might have picked up pen and paper sooner. In many ways I felt a strong kinship with him – we are so alike in many ways. Even things I dislike in my own character he owns up to and writes about, with an admired honesty I find difficult to muster. So I returned to the library and was pleased to find they had got *A Voice Through a Cloud*[21] sent over from Chelsea as promised. But, as soon as I read the first sentence, a cloud of despair settled over my head – no way could I snap the book shut and avoid it, as I would have liked to do. No way at all. I was forced to relive all his pain and agony, his slow partial recovery. He brought it so vividly back: after fifty years I saw everything through his eyes. I took his first faltering steps. Instead of morphine I drank two pints of beer as I quaffed the first seven chapters in the Champion on Notting Hill Gate.

21 FEBRUARY

On Portobello I came across Wayne, the black singer, who asked if I was

going to see Tanya. 'No,' I replied 'I haven't seen her for more than three months.' 'Well, I think you are both being very silly,' he said.
The static ping of lead pellets on glass[22].

22 FEBRUARY
Bad vibes. Last night Ian phoned and I went to meet him in the Champion and escape the persecution of the sniper at my bedroom window. It was unusually crowded for a Tuesday, and he was there already, drunk. It took ages to get a pint. My nerves, already on edge from the shooting, made worse by the hostility of a tall ugly queen chatting up a peroxide young rent boy, who thought I was treading on his patch. Nothing was further from my mind. I merely put Oscar in a window bay for fear of him being trodden on. And then a too-pretty, over-concerned handsome smarmy ordered me to 'Come here'. Accused me of neglect and said I'd put Oscar's tail in an ashtray with a lit cigar in it, which I knew I clearly had not. The outcome being forced to stand in an uncomfortable position with my back to both of them and Oscar looking fretful with pleading eyes. With the smug seated do-gooder complaining in a loud voice to his cronies, 'Well, he shouldn't bring a dog into a crowded pub.' Actually his little circle gave sympathetic nods when I asked, 'Do you think he looks unhappy?' But he answered 'Yes' emphatically, making a fuss of Oscar. Stupid, indignant, self-righteous . . . My temper finally snapped with the first ugly busybody who pushed me. 'Do you want this beer in your face?' I spat out, looking daggers of hate.

23 FEBRUARY
On the telephone Albert tells me he is going to LA in a month to work for six months in a restaurant. 'I'll get a flat, dad, then you can come and stay with me,' he said sweetly.

25 FEBRUARY
I have been taking too much Valium – eight milligrams, even ten. I sleep well but hate waking. It's a no man's land between the two. My brain starts churning so I take my pills. Then there is a gentle tug-of-war between the chemicals which lasts about an hour – sometimes sinking, floating, loop the loops. Usually it's very pleasant tingling, warm like being back in my mother's womb or able to breathe in a warm sea of tranquillity or like a rocket flying then exploding, and sparks and melting colours. Then I slowly realise I am conscious and I've no milk for morning coffee. I reluctantly get out of bed, face the drab reality, my surroundings, my cramped untidy dishevelled shoebox and Oscar's delight and wagging tail beating the carpet as he sits patiently by the front door.

26 FEBRUARY

A dreary day. I slept so late I decided to go without pills. I didn't bathe. Nor could I muster the energy to dress even though I was without cigarettes. I went back to sleep until about two o'clock, Then, as much to appease Oscar's patience, walked through Holland Park. I slept again fully clothed and when I woke at seven o'clock to rain lashing at the window, to make another cup of coffee. Oscar crept under the duvet to lay his little head between my chest and upper arm and was content while I lay in a trance watching the black and white TV flickering.

2 MARCH

'I've been away' – said Minah[23]. A lame excuse and invented. She told me she had been to San Francisco for the weekend. I gave her 50 quid and encouraged her to bitch about Ulla[24] etc. – she is dropping them, cutting out the dead wood. She wants to open an orchid shop with clothes on the side.

5 MARCH

'Did you hear the one about Imelda Marcos? She had to go into hospital for a cholostomy but she was dead pissed off because she couldn't find a pair of shoes to match.'

6 MARCH

The mild afternoon of perfect spring – Carla came to collect me and I write at her glass table facing open windows. A bottle of wine is placed in front of me to be opened. I removed the cork saying to Carla, 'You are not having a drink until the Gigot is stuffed with garlic – J'insiste!' She eyes the full bottle of Johnnie Walker's Black Label and reluctantly brings a glass circle with a frosted edge and a small sharp knife and l'ail on it. 'How much shall I prepare?' she asks.

7 MARCH

I'd put Carla through hell yesterday. Her voice sounded weary when I rang her as promised. 'Don't put me through that again.'

I left home intending to go to the Kamens[25]', walked towards Pam instead. She was in the shower. 'I've got exams all week – that means early nights and no boogying.' Giggles.

8 MARCH

Minah Bird is really hassling me. Almost 3 and she's still at it – she must be fuming with rage. Wilf[26] came round at my bidding with 10 cigarettes. I played back her outburst yesterday morning. 'Do I have to buy your drugs?' 'If you want me to make you a dress you do.' She hung up. I rang straight back. Suprised to hear a deep male voice. 'Yes, you can give her a message.' He relayed the message out loud then listened as she said, 'Fine. Tell him to return the fabric and forget it.' She's so stupid, she keeps ringing, determined to shout at me.

9 MARCH

Listening to Mozart having just made a recording of news of IRA bombing and putting it on my outgoing message tape, which caught Minah, and then started pulling her lavatory chain – she's furious, I've beaten her at her own game.

13 MARCH

Robert Mapplethorpe snuffed it. Blew out the candle with his bad breath.

19 MARCH

Depressed.
No motivation.
Can't get out of
Lack of concern.
No life force.

21 MARCH

I should be machining Emily's dress. Instead I'm filling in the gaps in this diary. Still incidents missing. Like jigsaw pieces they only fit into the correct slot.

Carol[27]'s birthday, she in tears. 'I think she'd find your place very depressing, depressed me,' said Kay[28]. Cheeky cunt.

22 MARCH

Ben's joke: 'Have you heard about Salman Rushdie's new book? It's called 'Buddha, the Fat Cunt'.'

29 MARCH

[*Ossie goes to Tangier for Nadia La Vallée's forty-third birthday party, which is being thrown for her by Princess Fatima al Sabah.*]

Where am I? At first so confused I wondered if I was dreaming. But the excruciating pain in my head was real enough and it took an effort to raise my head. I managed to hold it up for about 30 seconds before it dawned on me that I am in North Africa; I put my head back on the pillow.

30 MARCH

'If it weren't for the fact that you are a friend of a friend I'd have thrown you out last night,' said Mercedes[29] in her voiceless rasping croak.

6 APRIL

[*Back in London. Not only has Ossie's telephone been cut off by British Telecom for non-payment of his bill, but also the letter he sent to the DHSS, informing them that he would be unable to pick up his benefit because he would be on holiday, did not arrive. Now Ossie must begin a new claim for benefit.*]

No telephone is really a drag. But worse the discovery, after an amusing visit to JR[30], that my claim closed down. All the Kafka nightmare released again.

All those forms to fill in again. I told the woman at reception in the new claims office I'd be sick if I had to wait to be seen when they could fit me in. Overheated in my country squire green wellies.

I walked later to see Henrietta[31], my only hope of paying the telephone bill, but she wasn't home. And so by chance got dinner with Dave Gilmour at the Kamens'. 'So did you have a good time in Morocco with no money?' asked Sandra sarcastically.

15 APRIL

Explosion at Carla's. A broken mirror. Big drama. She called me a back-stabber and I really laid into her, called her a stupid cunt – she is too. She willed it on herself because she doesn't like my writing.

18 APRIL

Suzy Menkes phoned again from Paris to make sure I'm able to go to her dinner for Christian Lacroix, because he asked especially for me. I am his hero.

19 APRIL

George said, 'I think the Buddhism is really good for you, you must continue doing it – it really works for you.' He's very supportive.

I'd read him some poems of Denton Welch's (about death, very moving). I said I knew Albert found my constant preoccupation with Mort too heavy, but that I'm quite freaked out by all the people who have popped off over the last two years. The list continues to grow, I think he felt the shiver of having to come to terms for the first time with his own father's eventual death. I'm quite prepared for my own death and it could happen at any moment.

23 APRIL

I rang PP[32] and he burst into tears – 'Dick's dead, my brother, last Friday night.' He consoles himself that there was no pain, a heart attack aged 55. Inside must have been turmoil. Poor Patrick.

24 APRIL

UGH! – The triple horror of a hangover, Kafkaville in the form of filling in a lost form at the DHSS and wet feet trudging through icy wet weather to Ken Library to pick up the last Denton Welsh book, *Brave and Cruel.*

'Hello this is Celia Birtwell's,' said the voice of Andy on her answerphone so I hung up without leaving a message.

25 APRIL

9 $^1/_2$ stone.

'Awareness Day'. I went as a condition of making my claim on the DHSS or income support, and I must admit I learnt a lot of facts about red tape, form-filling, setting up in business etc. Caught the lecturer out several times and knew before I went that I am not eligible for this scheme because I haven't got a bank account, which is essential. Nor have I got a thousand pounds.

Albert is taking the blue 1956 suit to LA – he rang and came round at two o'clock to say goodbye.

30 APRIL

A walk early in Holland Park wearing wellies and my gamekeeper's suit – so perfect for stealing a nice bunch of camellias. A handsome keeper feeding the birdlife told me to put Oscar on a lead – fortunately didn't notice my pockets full of flora.

I decided to visit the Kamens. They were pleased to see me and readily agreed to my suggestion of walking Sasha[33] round the Serpentine. At 13 she is going through a rebellious phase. I've witnessed her being beastly to her mother, who, to be honest, has laid herself down as a doormat. I'd thought I'd have a quiet word, offer a few pointers as we walked in Kensington Gardens. In fact I showed her how to train Kier the dog and she did very well. I couldn't help but admire Sasha's pert breasts – so perfect under a charcoal sweatshirt – nor ignore the attention she drew and the leering, longing glances and staring of old men drooling – I felt very protective toward her and offered Sandra and Michael a warning when we got back.

1 MAY

ONE YEAR TO GO until I'm discharged from my bankruptcy and a plan is forming in my head.

[*Albert, George and Celia have gone to stay with DH in Los Angeles. David hopes to set up work for Albert in a restaurant, a scheme which does not work out.*]

A holiday and the realisation that Albert and George are 6,000 miles away brought on a feeling of loneliness.

2 MAY

Called to see Johnnie Rozza. 'Just look at this weather. Can't you just feel everybody's sperm count rising,' he said with excitement.

11 MAY

I phoned Hockney and asked if I could borrow some money for a car. I gave him really good reasons and excuses. Said he was going to send the money in two days. Wonder if he will.

13 MAY

At Agnes and Andi[34]'s in Camberwell after a sauna in St Martin's Lane full of ogres. The typical and a mutual wank.

17 MAY

Day without food. Black tea with honey, a lot of sleep, and worked on my python-skin reveres.

23 MAY

[*After a week in which he was unable to afford to eat, Ossie attends a dinner given by Suzi Menkes for the designer Christian Lacroix.*]

After 8 in a taxi going to a buffet dinner for Christian Lacroix given by Suzy Menkes. I'm barefoot dressed in white – the Pierre Cardin tie with a silver cross in it. Such luxury to travel in a taxi – £8.80 on the clock and Zandra[35] on the doorstep.

1 JUNE

Cash cheered me up no end – the fact that the DHSS is sorted out. I phoned this morning and they at last tell me the good news.

3.30 Dr M.F. a'Brook. He was immediately concerned, sympathetic, and compliant though he had no idea and couldn't really grasp the pittance I exist on. In a lowered voice out came a torrent of self-pity. It hasn't been a good month. I miss the children terribly, feeling inadequate. 'What time of day is the worst?' a question he's asked before. I suppose it's the morning, I answered, and he set to writing a new prescription[36].

I phoned Julian Bicknell. 'Is it *the* Ossie Clark, they ask?' He was pleased to hear from me. Took my number and said he would give me a ring, which I'm sure he will.

Back to Paddington Street in the drizzle at four in the afternoon. Decided not to fill my script in the chemist even though I had 70 quid or so dans ma poche because I had plans – ambitious plans – to score hash, and in fact achieved later. But I didn't get to the sauna because once again fate intervened.

Suddenly on the phone to David Hockney. Early morning in his (really just a shack, said PP later) Malibu beach house. Albert and George are asleep. Dogs barking.

'Hello, David,' I said, trying to sound cheerful.

'Just a minute. Just a minute.'

'Ha ha ha. The dogs are barking. Shut up.' I thought of him on TV saying everyone knows of Harold Wilson and his pipe – it's just a device to give him time to think over the answer while he lights it.

'How are you?'

'Well, I've just been in New York. You know Nick's dead? And Nathan. That's why I was in New York. I hate New York.'

'I'm sorry David. How long ago?'

'Two weeks ago.'

I feel no remorse over the death of either Nick Wilder or Nathan Kolod.

2 JUNE

A good sleep and a good shit. FLOATERS. Albert rang at 8.20. I try to sound cheerful but my true feelings must have been so obvious and I soon tell him I'm broke, miserable, lonely.

3 JUNE

'I look like Pope John the 23rd risen from his coffin,' PP said.

9 JUNE

Ha Ha Happy Birthday[37]. And I made it to deliver the forms to begin to claim sickness benefit. And in the press an inquest of a 19-yr-old actor who threw himself off Beachy Head – CLINICAL DEPRESSION.

13 JUNE

I walked to Manchester Street through the park filled with near-naked beauties in the sweltering heat, through crowds of tourists on Oxford Street, past pints of lager on pub tables, to the tranquillity of Patrick's dressing room.

I told Patrick what Albert had said – 'I'm sick of death. Every time I come round here it's talk of death.'

How odd we had talked so much about death before Langan[38] and Mo died – now his brother gone. 'But don't you see, Ossie, that's the extraordinary thing about life.'

18 JUNE

Billy stayed the night and got up before me. He knows I find him annoying and yet he's doing thoughtless actions like filling the flat with the smell of bacon.

19 JUNE

Patrick is giving a barbecue and I'm invited. 'It's just a sausage in the garden.'

He read out very inappropriate prayers for his brother's memorial. 'Well, I can't read THAT!' from *The Tibetan Book of the Dead*. Nor Milton's *Paradise Regained* – all about 'supping up your brains and all your bones yet still shall ye not die.'

22 JUNE

I rang Carol for news of Beryl. Not good, I'm afraid. They found and removed a tumour 'as big as a head'.

24 JUNE

I phoned Margaret for news of Beryl, and it's worse than I imagined. Again the metaphor 'as big as a head' – the tumour they cut away (as much as they could), they found six more.

28 JUNE

Billy's really proud of his horrible big belly. He opens his shirt and he's back-stroking it, a self-satisfied smirk on his face. It's quite revolting.

3 JULY

Sleep isn't the answer.

4 JULY

I took the last (of 20) pills and I'm not taking any more.

9 JULY

I miss Albert and George incredibly – more than I anticipated or they know, or Celia or DH whose enjoying their company. I bet he's unaware of my dire misery.

22 JULY
Lost Oscar, so engrossed in composing a poem:
Only secret words
Anonymous lexigram
Denote laconical oblate.
Vizards euphoric,
Sensation, desire, audacious;
Very illogically dared.[39]

25 JULY
[*Ossie travels north to visit his sister Beryl who is by now dying of cancer.*]

Ever since I got back from Tangier in April I've been in a quandary, existing on tiny amounts of money I've had to battle constantly for with the DHSS. So poor I've even been days without food, too proud to beg (except once from Kay). Oscar has gone hungry, even snatching titbits from the pavement. I've been merely existing on string coffee with honey, chocolate, cheap pies or the occasional fillet steak, chicken, etc. I went through 20 hellish days on some pills a'Brook prescribed.

Things I'd looked forward to fizzle out into disappointment. Minah has persistently harassed me – I've sat there listening to the phone ring, smug when no answer left – vile insult from the first; angry, petulant demands from the second.

I went to visit Beryl twice in Margaret's lovely garden, enjoying the dogs and the birds.

9 AUGUST
[*Back in London.*]

Albert on the phone at 9.30 – bad news. 'Dad, we are in serious trouble.' Rupert's been killed – DH's favourite daschund – got out through a hole in the kitchen. Albert saw it which must have been horrible. 'I could've swerved the car,' he said, sorrow and regret in his voice. 'We're shitting ourselves. What are we going to do?'

14 AUGUST
Albert woke me at 8 o'clock. Midnight in LA and he was still fuming with rage at Hockney after a fierce argument. 'I've got all the power and I'm going to crush you. You should learn by your father's mistakes.' Hockney seems to want him out immediately and has even banned him from driving the car. How petty!

29 AUGUST
At PP's.
'Derek Jarman – you do love him, don't you? He did seduce me on a little bed on the trip to Egypt that never happened.'

11 SEPTEMBER

[*Ossie has flown to Marrakesh to stay with the Texan architect and aesthete Bill Willis who lives there and is at this time designing a palace for the Saudi Arabian Prince Nashour.*]

In Fernando[40]'s Marrakesh house.
I was writing a note on the back of a photograph with Tahlita[41], me and Fernando in 1970 when we picnicked in the Eureka Valley. When he walked in the doorway with Quintin[42] wearing a Batman T-shirt and mauve pants rolled inside black sandals. He photographs us. They had just returned from swimming in Saint Laurent's new house. This house used to be Saint Laurent's. Nicolette[43] switched personality as soon as we arrived in Morocco. Miss Bossy Boots was giving a present of a Mars's tin to the eternally grateful servant.
A chubby black boyfriend, New York smart, noticing the silver ring with a turquoise on my finger. 'That's a beautiful ring,' said Quintin. 'It's a Buddhist ring,' Fernando informed him. I've made up a story – the crack in the stone represents the way into Buddhism.
'This is the only girl I've ever asked to marry me,' said Bill sitting next to Nicolette, 'and she refused,' putting his arm around her shoulder. 'No, I didn't refuse you – I was menstruating at the time.'

12 SEPTEMBER
I miss Oscar, his warmth on my lap. It's impossible to look at any passing beauty without receiving lowered luscious lashes in acquiescent cow eyes. Responsive, inviting, sultry. The young men walk by in couples holding hands or alone smoking, genital fingering. Slouching in threes, they argue, gesticulating.
I write lying on Bill's bed. He has trouble with his back, so this is the hardest you can get. I drink vodka with lemon juice. Karim sits next to me. Of all the boys (though I have not met them all yet) I find him the most attractive.

13 SEPTEMBER
Sick of the Kasbah.

Christopher Wanklyn[44], very quiet and 62–3. Looks older, obviously not a heavy shagger – got two regulars. He has proper relationships. 'How long have you lived in Morocco?' '35 years.'

14 SEPTEMBER

When I returned to my bedroom, all tidy because the maid had done it, Karim was replacing the bulb by my bedside so I can read. It was a complete surprise to find him there. I felt awkward. 'Monsieur Osi.'

6.45 On the roof terrace. Wonderful fading light. Evening prayers. The full moon risen. I lay on my back a while absorbing the atmosphere.

17 SEPTEMBER

I must have a little read and a lie down before the next bout of dipsomania.

I must get Rashid to teach me how to say Stupid Bitch in Arabic.

18 SEPTEMBER

Surrounded by palms. Waiting for fresh-baked bread at a picnic table outside. Verdi and Mozart opera floating angelically over and around us. I feel detached and almost weightless. This is what immortality must really be like.

A battle through the Souk – the sales pitch revs up. I was so totally exhausted and aching by the time we got back to Sidi bel Abbes I didn't recover all evening.

'I never take drugs except for fun. I don't believe in crutches,' said Nicolette over coffee in the drinks salon after I had suggested a Valium. But I slept badly after a horrible dream about driving through the desert without water.

19 SEPTEMBER

When Rashid talks to Bill he curls his second toes on to his big ones.

20 SEPTEMBER

The best thing about the day was the boy on the way to the Souk.

21 SEPTEMBER

'This dinner has cost more than you'll ever know.' In Yacoubi, for Harry Bailey[45] and his German friend. 'I think he's kinda cute, don't you?' 29 years old, from München, with good English, he blushed every time he spoke.

It was good you were late, the view is so breathtaking. And it was. But the stairs spiralled up like Holland Park tube station. I drank a beer.

Bill stayed in his car to hear the end of some opera. You philistines.

22 SEPTEMBER

Preston[46] is a monster teasing Rashid. So much has happened. A new ice machine. My back aches from all the concentrating. Preston's irate telephone voice. Masses of drawings, which look better at night. Bill's house is so inspirational.

23 SEPTEMBER

I'd slept a second night with a piece of Aloe taped over the nasty recurring zit. 'Ah, let's see. Show us,' demanded Nicolette.

A nasty man, Brion Gysin[47], William Burroughs' sidekick. He got so sick of drawing bicycles he had a stamp made. And nipples like cigarette butts. I discover my room is called 'The Cock Room'.

25 SEPTEMBER

[*Ossie returns to London.*]

Yesterday I returned from Marrakesh chez Willis. 'I think I'm going to stay in a den of iniquity,' I'd said to Pam[48]. It was certainly that, and much more.

I discover in the sauna I have lost eight pounds in weight. The sound was quieter than usual, the same eyes flashing predatory looks.

27 SEPTEMBER

'Listen. I owe you some money,' said Jane Rainey[49]. 'Can you come round tonight?'

And Albert was cross in his chef's whites, chickpeas in his big hands. 'Whatya doinere, Dad? I'll get in real trouble.'

Jasper Conran overweight. Looking like an expensive pudding.

30 SEPTEMBER

Flashback. The arrival at Bill's house in agony of backache. About 15 mins dusty road. The ancient walls Sienna red. A gate. A twinge of memory. Entering narrower and penetrating deeper the Medina. Suddenly the excitement. More voices. 'Do make sure you've got all your luggage.' A dark door ajar, darker than night, and darker still inside. And dogs excited. Up a flight of stairs. 'My de-ah, at last, we were getting quite worried.' Bill already roaring drunk, our host. I dropped into a chair draped with embroidered cushions in a room with no edges, dried blood-red. Above – unfathomable octagonal designs painted on an 18th-century wooden dome.

Later Bill told me a story (but insisted I shouldn't write it down) about a time he was watching TV (a video movie – horror) with PG Tips[50] deep in the night. 'Look, Bill! Whadda ya think of that?' Turning his attention from the screen he saw in profile a hypodermic needle sticking out at a right angle from between the eyebrows of the person addressing him. 'The police would never think of looking for tracks there . . . huh?'

That first night I made a connection between the beautiful roses and Bill's boys glowing like jewels, whose dark eyes look at nothing and see everything, whose lips curl carmine and ruby like the edges of rose petals. One glance speaks volumes.

[*Ossie attends the wedding reception of Rachel Wyndham to Andrew Drake on the first floor of a club overlooking the river in Putney. He writes twenty pages in his notebook about the evening, most of which is unintelligible.*]

My back is giving me constant pain.

Celia sweating, mopping her brow, makes me dance, stopping me writing.

Surprise request from George: 'Dada, I want to ask you something . . . Will you do me a favour . . .? Will you grow your sideburns down to here?' Putting the knuckle of his index finger to the base of his ear.

To recap – my arrival at Rachel's. I was reluctant to go. It was twenty to nine when I arrived, the party in full swing. A reggae band, dancing, a buffet, maybe 10 or 12 round tables. Eating just over, everybody in good spirits. Beam me up, Scottie. It was [as if] I hadn't walked into a wedding party, more like I'd just appeared there. Confusion. I saw Celia as she looked at me. I'd taken in the scene in one optical arch, recognising faces and resting on Patrick Procktor. My first impulse to join him, but no place. And placement. All eyes on me. I wasn't expected. They didn't think I'd come, even though I'd RSVP'd.

1 OCTOBER

I'd dialled and Hali[51] answered. 'Got you at last! If you come and take this fucking Hoover away I'll give you a spliff,' I said. I gave her explicit instructions and she arrived in seven minutes.

George came over to be drawn at teatime – he was so sweet and attentive last night. I captured a perfect likeness – he is so beautiful.

2 OCTOBER

I'm going to do ever such a good picture of you, I tell Oscar.

Walking back from the shops I just kept saying I want 50 quid a day, I want a car, I want to plant bulbs in the spring. I want so many things. I repeat, JR is a Jew first, with all that a Jew represents, and a Buddhist second.

[*Ossie rings Michael Kamen and demands back his wooden pillar, kilns and vases. He is insistent, feeling the 'power of nam myoho rengi kyo'.*]

3 OCTOBER

The DHSS building in Elephant and Castle has got to be one of the most hideous buildings in London. You've never seen anything like it. It's fucking horrible but has got listed status. preservation order on it. I can't believe anyone wanting to keep it as it is.

Patrick took his time answering the front door. For a moment I thought he wasn't going to. I couldn't wait to show him my Marrakesh notebook, but first claimed his seat on the bed where he siestas. 'But, my dear, these are the best drawings of OC I've seen. In fact, you should put them on canvas.'

4 OCTOBER

Visit to Carla. I didn't get there until 4 o'clock, having spent the day sewing the last big cushion, which I'm leaning on as I write in bed to prop up my aching back. Machining all day I forget my posture with the concentration and pay for it later.

5 OCTOBER

10.54 Smoking my last joint, the third this morning, and drinking my third cup of coffee. And suddenly it was one o'clock.

Guy came at four, bringing flowers – yellow chrysanthemums and a ginger flower. So sweet. I had become engrossed in covering my ginger suit waistcoat with badges and bits of leopardskin and a black triangle, a silver whistle, a miniature gun, stars, letters, the Lenin badge from Patrick's visit to Russia, two horse shoes and some studs. Looks pretty effective.

6.34 The twilight bathed my room in a peach glow. Now smoke blue, azure to lavender and still pink, peachy, fading before my eyes. Three trees not quite black, like shadow under a deep forest.

6 OCTOBER

3.20 Went for a walk to Portobello and bought a tiny eucalyptus. I have started asking for receipts. Nick and I weren't very impressed with Kevin Whitney's paintings. We stayed only 10 minutes.

Home visit. Henry Tennant 9.25. So tall. Stooping, looks so ill, his head draped in a scarf – muffling out the cold and partly obscuring the terrible ravages. A Tibetan hat to cover his hairless head. His blonde mane gone, caused by chemotherapy. What should be pink is puce in the corner of his eyes. Putrefaction visible under the flesh manifests itself in yellowish green and bruised blue blotches. Yet his spirit glows with radiance.

17 OCTOBER

[*Ossie has decided to perform a million daimokus and has constructed a chart consisting of boxes to be shaded in to help him with the undertaking. The performance of a million daimokus will entitle him to a Gohonzon.*]

Suddenly I've run out of money. It dawns on me one million daimokus is an awful lot of chanting. Henrietta rang while I was in the park with Oscar. A beautiful day. She seriously expects me to start making over her pink suit, which is in shreds.

30 OCTOBER

Dust everywhere. I want the diamond sparkle. Dust offends me. I hate dust. All I see is dust on the outside wall. Clean, and cover, perhaps, with the faded dusky pink cotton floor covering from 26 Powis Terrace, which has been outside flapping in the wind for two years.

31 OCTOBER

On Saturday I was so depressed. At 4 I wanted to pack it in, but I stuck it out until 1/4 to 5. I made three sales to Belgians. I owe the bank 15 grand and want to borrow £20,000 to just get straightened out.

3 NOVEMBER

I did Gongyo twice this morning and have filled three boxes already.

4 NOVEMBER

First joint listening to Beethoven on Nick's borrowed radio. Rain. But at 9.28 the first blue drifts into the sky. In two mins it's blended in. Thank you, I address my amber holder, as I look for the palest grey pencil again.

I rang the number John Maybury[52] gave me. 'You have 60 seconds to leave a message.' So I chant for a minute.

5.20 Walked home concentrating only on the skies. Feeling tired, longing for my hot water-bottle and a lie down. I intended to siesta. A vague longing for sex, some passes. I am feeling quite content and very happy doing two hours daimoku a day.

8 o'clock in the evening and I'm wondering if George will show up. My friends are gone and my hair is grey. Albert has given up his job.

6 NOVEMBER

6.45 I must stop working on the picture of Karim. I've put gold in his eyes, silver in his hair and roses surround him.

I walked home from Sandra's chanting and filled in another box – I have developed a rhythm as I walk and divide 1000 x 20. I realise I must say *nam myoho rengi kyo* 50 times every minute.

8 NOVEMBER

Daimoku is a great clearing house. It unscrambles the brain, all the trivial melts into proper perspective. Creation of an impenetrable circle around me. I am protected; a force field holds back all the flack. Perfect tranquillity.

Another little box. Another tiny step nearer.

9 NOVEMBER

8.03 I've filled 4 boxes.

8.54 2 more boxes filled.

10 NOVEMBER

Nicolette rang at 7.15. Got back yesterday. Got photos of Karim, she just had time to tell me. Never mind you didn't get the trousers made. Karim was sacked and then reinstated. Beware of well-diggers – they beat Bill's door down, stole Nicolette's painting.

11 NOVEMBER

Daimoku, and fill four boxes in red.

18 NOVEMBER

My posture's gone. My back aches as I colour in the boxes of my one million daimoku chart.

2 DECEMBER

I had a bit of a relapse. Nick cancelled lunch – threw me. I've been taking four mils of Valium to sleep so stayed abed all morning.

14 DECEMBER

My whole body aches like a runner after a marathon.

1 Pam Procter.
2 Sandie Shaw, British singer; former Eurovision Song Contest winner.
3 These words quoting Neil Young's song 'Round and Round'.
4 Andy, Celia's boyfriend at this time.
5 Once again for drugs offences.
6 Ben Brierly.
7 Mo McDermott.
8 Carla Ames.
9 Guy Burch.
10 Nick Balaban.
11 Friend of Nick Balaban.
12 Stephen Barnham, writer.

13 Beryl Westell.
14 A lover of Ossie's.
15 Billy Wilder, American film director.
16 Jack Lemmon, American actor.
17 Billy Henry.
18 Emily was to marry Ben Brierly; Ossie was asked to make her dress.
19 Taking pleasure in another's misfortunes.
20 By Denton Welch, writer and painter.
21 By Denton Welch. Posthumously published, it deals with the aftermath of Welch's bicycle accident in 1935 which rendered the author an invalid for the rest of his life.
22 It appears that one of Ossie's neighbours had taken to shooting an air-rifle at his window.
23 Minah Bird.
24 Ulla Larson.
25 Sandra and Michael Kamen.
26 Wilf Butler.
27 Carol Hammond.
28 Kay Melia.
29 Mercedes Guiffa, ran a colonial-style pension in Tangier.
30 Johnnie Rozza.
31 Henrietta Rous.
32 Patrick Prockter.
33 Sasha Kamen, daughter of Sandra and Michael.
34 Agnes and Andi Kostrowski.
35 Zandra Rhodes.
36 For 20 75mg Prothiaden tablets.
37 9 June was Ossie's birthday.
38 Peter Langan.
39 When read together, the initial letters of each word in this poem spell 'Oswald Loves David'.
40 Fernando Sanchez, knitwear designer; childhood friend of Yves Saint Laurent.
41 Tahlita Getty.
42 Quintin Yealby, painter.
43 Nicolette Meeres.
44 Christopher Wanklyn, Canadian painter.
45 Harry Bailey, American anitques dealer.
46 Preston Smith, painter; childhood friend of Bill Willis.
47 Brion Gysin, artist; childhood friend of Bill Willis.
48 Pam Procter.
49 For an outfit Ossie had made her.
50 Sir Paul Getty.
51 Hali Rotbart, daughter of Pam Procter and Sid Rotbart.
52 John Maybury, film director; friend of Derek Jarman.

1990

Ossie begins this year like he did last, in front of his friend Pam Procter's Buddhist Gohonzon shrine. He has, it seems, after many years of searching found something solid, stabilising and relatively permanent in his life. Throughout this year his dedication to Buddhism is unwavering, and inspired by the increasing strength of this dedication, he goes for months without amphetamine pills, taking vitamins and guarana tablets instead; he even gives up coffee, an amazing testament to the power of his religion. Spurred on by news of David Hockney's heart attack, Ossie becomes increasingly conscious of his health this year, weighing himself regularly and continually attempting to give up alcohol. As a result 1990's diary is perhaps the least introspective of all Ossie's journals as with a clearer head he seems less inclined to wallow in his own emotions and begins to become ever more aware of the world around him. When Ossie meets Nick this year in Hyde Park, rather than give us a page of emotional heartache, he writes instead a wonderful description of a pike being caught in the Serpentine, using his powers of observation – rather than introspection – to the full.

Ossie also becomes deeply interested in current events this year, reporting them in his diary as he sees them on the television. Inspired by this, he also begins to record the current events of his own life in bulletin fashion – the diary is full of short, sharp and pointed entries. Of course, Ossie was never, if he could help it, the kind of diarist who liked to write up his journal at the end of the day – that would not have been in line with his spontaneous and vibrant character. Rather he attempted whenever he could to record the moment *at* the moment – a very 'sixties' way of doing things – to record it like television, in mutlicolour as it happens, and the increase in 'as it happens' entries this year contributes to the effect of his writing.

Thanks to his Buddhism, Ossie is more relaxed this year. He also seems inspired by a new confidence. Before the end of the year he has completed wonderful dresses for Gill and Cleo Goldsmith and Candida Lycett-Green for the Chatsworth Ball (the society event of the decade), and has had a rave review in the December issue of *Elle.* Despite the odd hiccup, such as a possession order for his flat for non payment of rent, he seems to be firing on all cylinders.

However, despite the surface appearance of this year's diary there is an undertone of emptiness to Ossie's writing this year. Its short, clipped entries and its dwelling on the depressing nature of current events give it a hollow feel. Ossie seems unable to record much to do with himself this year, perhaps because he feels like there is nothing much of any substance to record. Does he record the voice of the television because he has no faith in his own? The pain that he feels when informed of his sister Beryl's cancer is muted, hardly expressed, but this only serves to make us even more aware of the effect this news has upon him.

1 JANUARY

I began the New Year on my knees in front of Pam[1]'s Gohonzon with her and Lynn Stone[2] up from Bristol. Sid[3] didn't join in, he stayed downstairs.

10 JANUARY

Sara[4] came at 11 o'clock in a smart grey Prince of Wales check. Straight and smart. Just back from Florida. We did a rambling Gongyo before going to Henry Tennant's cremation at Kensal Cemetery. I wore yellow and green wellies and took Oscar. It was cold and I should have worn my hat. There were a lot of people there even though we were early. A mixture of aristocrats and Buddhists. 'I must just go and kiss a few old trouts,' said Christopher Gibbs.

14 JANUARY

[*At the bottom of this entry in Ossie's diary is pasted a newspaper clipping reporting the funeral of Henry Tennant, 'who died of AIDS aged 29'.*]

Nick[5] woke me at eleven. What about our walk. Meet you at 12.30 at Notting Hill Gate tube. I was ten minutes late. He wore snow boots from Denver, Colorado, guaranteed good up to below minus 40 degrees. We walked slowly through Kensington Gardens and round the Serpentine. When we got to the Knightsbridge end, one of the anglers had landed a huge pike. He was gingerly holding it in the pale sunlight, its camouflage markings glistened, darker on his back, brownish gold and finally urine-coloured on his belly. He had a great big jaw and teeth like an alligator, and must have put up quite a fight because the boy was holding him firmly behind the gills, expert but apprehensive.

17 JANUARY

By hand a letter from the Director of Housing and Property Services. A

Notice Seeking Possession is enclosed, which threw me into a furtive gloom.

18 JANUARY

Giro in post, £48.35. A bright day. After cashing it I walked to Ken Gardens to walk.

20 JANUARY

Guy[6] in the Venus. Walking back along Portobello I met Duggie Field who looked as though he was wearing make-up. And I met the boy who is a friend of Ulla[7]'s who is trying to borrow money to go to Berlin. We looked at rubbish art in the new galleries.

22 JANUARY

Really longing for a cup of coffee. It's eleven days since I drank coffee and fifteen since I began taking the vitamins, guarana de amazon and five spigaric drops three times a day. I do feel different.

23 JANUARY

I chanted and bathed and walked Oscar through rain and blustering wind in Holland Park after talking to Ulla on the phone. She is very depressed, in bed, her flat a mess. Another death. A girlfriend called Sara Jenkins. Ulla is devastated.

26 JANUARY

New Moon.

A plane from Columbia crashed in Cove Neck, they think it ran out of fuel approaching Kennedy Airport. 60 people dead.

Seven – rang Patrick[8], he said I must write to Pauline Fordham[9], so I did, sending her a Buddhist booklet and a postcard of Ron Masa[10]. 'We are well and happy watching an amaryllis grow.'

30 JANUARY

I heard the postman and Pauline's letter plop through my letterbox. A gushy, newsy letter filled me in. I suppose I must write back to her.

Gill Goldsmith wants a ball dress. Salvation – I searched out her toile pattern, dithered about what cloth to cut the toile in, as I've no calico, so I ripped a length of shantung from the roll. Chose Celia's trellis red on white, cut out on my carpet and put it together, bone casing et al.

31 JANUARY
9st 9lbs.

9 FEBRUARY
Eclipse of the full moon.

21 FEBRUARY
Henrietta[11] rang early to tell me she met Boy George last night at the Trocadero, he's a dog lover and didn't approve of the suede jacket she was wearing.
My tarot at midnight. Devil 5 Worry Discs Princess Wands Queen Wands Victory Wands Prince Disks Knight Wands Change Discs The Priestess 4 Power Discs Prince Wands 2 Wands Domination 8 Indolence Cups 3 Works Discs The Universe No Swords. That's good.

27 FEBRUARY
Woke from a funny dream where Oscar had no back feet, but was just as frisky. Gill's fitting. Albert back working at 192.

6 MARCH
I finally cut the skirt and sent the letter to Pauline Fordham in Bullwood Prison.

7 MARCH
[*Ossie is visited by Mahendra Patel, a Buddhist leader in Kensington and Chelsea and a friend of Pam Proctor's.*]

Blitzed my flat. Threw everything on to my bed and was surprised by the amount of space I achieved.
Mahendra and Pam home visit. 'Do you want a cup of tea or shall we start straight away?' 'I'm OK,' said Pam. He [Mahendra] had removed his shoes in the hall, I'd offered the only chair, 'There, that's for you, Mahendra.' I realised I was nervous, wanted everything proper. I overheard Pam say, 'They're Ossie's wife's. Ossie's wife designs them.' He stood up again and admired my batsuma putsadam, I think he was amazed and a tiny bit envious. I whisked his folded jacket from under Oscar who had just settled on it.

8 MARCH
Candida Lycett-Green. 'You wouldn't make me a dress, would you?'

9 MARCH

8.30 news: Poll tax riots in Hackney, Swindon. West Midlands. $1/3$ higher than Government estimate. Iran Contra Affair with Ollie North. Cuba will continue in economic isolation after the fall of Communism.

11 MARCH

Well, it began very sunny, darling, but now it's greyed over. I turn off the radio, just can't bear to hear of the tragedy again. Three boys, aged three, four and six suffocated in an abandoned freezer. And instead I fold silk, zigzag along the bias and make an incision with the pinking shears, which aren't sharp enough, but the coupe is achieved to cut through layers. My mother's method. A crêpe paper Christmas rose transformed into a pink silk peony perfectly. Thank you, Mum.

15 MARCH

Pauline Fordham rang, got out of prison at 9 o'clock this morning.

16 MARCH

The dress is finished off.
Gill thrilled and so am I.

17 MARCH

[*Ossie has been asked to design a wedding dress for Cleo Goldsmith*[12].]

The iron blew. My scissors are blunt. My favourite carp finally expired. I tried to revive it, first with an air pump.

A very pleasant fitting with Cleo who breezed fresh into my flat at 5 mins past eleven while I was in the bath. 'Isn't it a beautiful day. Where are you?'

Her beauty glitters like a jewel. The sun she adores, lived in Mexico and Guatemala for three years.

Her seven-year-old daughter speaks with a deep Italian accent. 'Mama, you are-a naughty, where-a RU?'

19 MARCH

Cleo to India.

23 MARCH

I met Carla[13] again on Portobello. She was buying fruit and told me she had seen the Kamens[14]. Michael said I've been avoiding them. He hasn't been round for months. They are off to New York next week.

Drove to Hampstead for nocturnal walkies.

24 MARCH

10 stone. 3 pounds.

Carol[15] rang while I was in the bath.

'What are you doing tonight?' All chirpy. I had already decided I must wash my hair and weigh myself in the sauna.

'Well, you're coming to my birthday party.'

27 MARCH

Carefully prepared the toile and marked out the bridal bodice using pink and green pencils and juggling case to make a 23" waist, made the final marks with an ordinary soft HB.

Dr M. F. a'Brook – 'For a moment you looked unhappy in your face. How long is it now till your bankruptcy's over?'

'The day is May Day.'

'What's your favourite champagne, we'll drink a glass to your freedom.'

28 MARCH

I rang Nick and offered steamed fish for lunch and then we walked in Hyde Park. Suddenly the rhododendrons are in blossom. One near the peacocks unfolding with tambourine shake is so unreal, like flowers daubed with fresh blood.

29 MARCH

Not a good second fit with Cleo. The grain, the opening, the back all wrong – saw the new moon over my left shoulder as I set off for a drink in the Champion.

31 MARCH

Chanted for forty minutes for success with the wedding gown.

1 APRIL

I put off cutting the third calico until almost midnight, it was such a beautiful day, I walked in both parks.

3 APRIL

Henry Tennant's memorial service. I always think Princess Margaret looks sad. 'I'm not wearing black,' she'd said to Lord Glenconner – I thought she dressed like a peep show.

6 APRIL

The bloody *Sunday Mirror* rears its ugly head, a reporter at Celia's shop.

9 APRIL
Cut the wedding bodice in exquisite silk.

15 APRIL
Garbo dead.

16 APRIL
At last they have planted the irises round the pond, on which swam Mummy duck and her six ducklings which must be only a few weeks old. Dad guarding.

28 APRIL
Cleo's wedding.

4 MAY
Sat on my balcony early. A whole week of sunshine has disappeared and I've hardly written a line. I'm surprised this is Friday. The roof obliterating my view is half done, a stolen lily bulb stands a foot tall like a miniature palm growing at an angle at the edge of the sea.

31 MAY
Candida – 15 metres red organza, 5 mts crêpe satin. This is going to be a real Tart's dress. 'S'wha we want, isn't it?'

18 JUNE
The sun has come out again in a clear blue sky. I cut up the red net and sewed it into a huge underskirt edged with a two-cotton bias.
Candida was early, the fitting was perfect.

9 JULY
Happy Birthday, Nick

14 JULY
Jerry Hall and Mick Jagger in the park[16].

27 JULY
Pam asked me to be Man's unit chapter chief. I've said yes.

2 AUGUST
Sunny and very hot.
Bill Weston came to Gongyo and brought a compass. I've been facing the

wrong direction all the time.

4 AUGUST
Nick on the phone sounding very cheerful: 'Come here and see my butsadan.'

5 AUGUST
Couch potato. The unbearable heat continues. I lay in bed all day without energy or the enthusiasm to do anything.

The television is full of programs about the dwindling Earth's resources, the slaughter of wildlife, news of bush fires, pollution, water shortage and the real threat of war in the Arab world. Discontent everywhere.

Sometime after ten I woke out of a dose to the noise of confusion outside. Bright lights flashing, a crowd gathering. Shouts, doors slamming, machines vibrating. From my balcony I saw three fire-engines but not a fire. Looking down I noticed the lights rippling a reflection in a veritable lake of water. Another flood, so out to look with Oscar. A river of water gushing down the street and the basement's seven foot deep in water.

Posing for Lorenzo Poccianti, c.1990.

8 AUGUST
US nuclear sub with 60 planes down the Suez Canal.

9 AUGUST
Arab leaders in Cairo. King Khalid pleading.

US build-up continues in Saudi Arabia. Turkey airforce on standby. Alert decision.

Gongyo with Sara.

15 SEPTEMBER
Cut two pairs of boxer shorts. Electric blue silk satin, backed crêpe de Chine.

18 SEPTEMBER

Madame Jean Baptiste de Montpezat[17] phoned early hoping to catch me off-guard; she was very irate.

24 SEPTEMBER

Don't overlook the unforeseen.

9 OCTOBER

I did a very quick drawing of Ulla without her realising, just a series of curves. The last one, her tit, I got wrong. 'Now how did I get in that position?' At first I didn't realise. She loathed it on sight.

22 OCTOBER

ALBERT 21 TODAY.

1 NOVEMBER

[Ossie has been to Crete on holiday; though he wrote very little in his diary during his time there.]

Yesterday arriving back in London after a week in Crete was like that part in *Star Wars* when they are escaping in the spaceship to a little moon that Frankenstein (Peter Cushing) has just blown away from the Death Star where he holds Princess Leia prisoner. As they come out of hyperspeed they hit a lot of turbulence and debris flying around. 'It's not there,' says Harrison Ford/Han Solo.

I notice an expensive crocodile handbag on the floor. Angela heard the key in the lock. She was very pleased to see me and we had a cup of tea while she told me of her travels. 'Since I saw you when last we met I've been in Japan and across Russia.' Steve Miller Band on *Top of the Pops*; 'The Joker' revived by an advertisement for Levi's on the television.

3 NOVEMBER

My enshrinement at 10 o'clock on Saturday night. With pomegranates in a pyramid, athanatus leaves, olive branches, epkanithos oil from Crete and roses from over the road. JR[18], which was nice, and George came ten minutes early. Pam, Rosita, Yarbora, Angie Clarke, David Phillips, Justine Silver, Sara Lamb, James Noons[19] just in time. He told a silly joke: two cows in a field chewing on the cud.

6 NOVEMBER

Blow job in *The Times* crossword – the clue, deceiving flattery.

13 NOVEMBER

Today is the fourteenth without pills. It seems impossible that only two weeks ago I was swimming in the sea.

18 NOVEMBER

Sunshine. A walk with George. All his beautiful hair cut off. He looks like I did when I was 19 except his hair is the most wonderful colour. He absolutely shocked me telling me that DH had a heart attack.

22 NOVEMBER

On the telephone Carla tells me Thatcher has resigned.

1 DECEMBER

World AIDS Day.

24 DECEMBER

Christmas Eve

New pens from Rymans. Light golden trail of the sun and a diamond-bright half-moon in an azure sky.

1 Pam Procter.
2 Lynn Stone worked for Ghost and was a Buddhist friend of Pam Procter.
3 Sid Rotbart.
4 Sara Lamb, British TV actress.
5 Nick Balaban.
6 Guy Burch.
7 Ulla Larson.
8 Patrick Procktor.
9 Pauline Fordham was in prison for drugs offences.
10 One of Ossie's dog Oscar's ancestors.
11 Henrietta Rous.
12 Cleo Goldsmith, daughter of Gill. She was to marry Mark Shand.
13 Carla Ames.
14 Sandra and Michael Kamen.
15 Carol Hammond.
16 This was Mick Jagger's fiftieth birthday party, held in the Serpentine Gallery.
17 Madame Jean Baptiste de Montpezat was formerly Jill Goldsmith. Ossie has written to her demanding more money for the work he has undertaken for her and her daughter Cleo.
18 Johnnie Rozza.
19 All Buddhist friends of Ossie.

1991

Although this year Ossie presents a veneer of cheerfulness, deep down the diary suggests that he is haunted by despair and vulnerability. He begins the year very depressed, lethargic, indecisive and wallowing in 'a sea of sadness'. He declares that he has 'nothing to get up for', seems to stay indoors a great deal and begins to use his diary mainly to record his answerphone messages. Although these messages read rather humorously, portraying each character in a different way than any description could, Ossie seems, by filling his diary with other peoples voices in this way, to have willfully given up on his ability to be creative, to write, and to observe the world around him. Rather, he absents himself from these entries, puntuating them only with the dead sound of the 'clunk' of a receiver being put down at the end of a call.

Depressed by the condition of his sister, Beryl, who is dying of cancer, Ossie is almost unable, at the beginning of this year, to find any point in keeping a diary at all. Indeed, when Beryl's condition does begin to seriously deteriorate Ossie stops his diary altogether. For three months there is nothing, and then an extremely heartrending entry on 15 June: 'Three months have passed since I wrote in this book. Beryl died on a Saturday, the thirteenth of April...Wanted to write it all down but just couldn't.' Ossie uses his diaries as confessional texts; he writes down what he wants to release, but as we see here is unable to write down what he does not want to face. Recording an event in his diary for Ossie meant accepting it as true, and in the case of Beryl's death that is something which took him a great deal of time. Even when Ossie has accepted the event and begun to keep his diary again he is still in the depths of depression. He reverts to taking amphetamine pills again and, as a result, begins to feel like a failure, decrepit and imprisoned in himself. He is concerned for his own health, consults his shrink, Michael a'Brook, and has a test for thyroid. In Greece, on holiday with his son George, he becomes aware of being old and worries about becoming a burden to his children, as he had felt his father was in old age. He is touched by George's loving attentiveness. He arranges his room and organises his room so immaculately, 'so like Celia'. He also has flashbacks of days of former glory.

However, by 2 July Ossie has recovered somewhat. He is helped greatly by his friend Henrietta Rous and her offers of weekend breaks in the country at her family's North Devon estate, and also by the offer of a holiday in France from a new friend, Mary Penney. Ossie called the van they drove down in a bone rattler and compared this trip unflatteringly to his previous trip to France with Celia in 1971 when they were in his blue Bentley. These holidays give Ossie time to get over his sister's death and also contribute enormously to this diary's rather subdued tone. In the closing months of 1991 Ossie seems more or less back to his normal self. He is, for instance, again determined once more to pursue his Buddhist practices, which he does, rigorously. However, Ossie has absorbed yet another blow this year and it is not one he will find easy to forget.

5 JANUARY

Hi, Dad, it's George. Ringing sort of to confirm that you left your glasses at my house and I'll bring them round tomorrow with the money I owe you. See you soon.

Hi, Ossie, erm, it's Hali[1]. You're invited to my 21st birthday party on Wednesday. Erm, it's going to be at the Walmer Castle which is on Ledbury Road and it starts at 8. Give me a ring to tell me if you can make it.

15 JANUARY

Beep.

Hello, Ossie, oh darling look, erm, I was just with Mary Penney[2] and, oh, I think she'd love you to do something for her. Um, I haven't got her number, erm, but why don't you just drop round sometime? She's 38, as you know, and um, um, um, you know you can work out what sort of material. She says she hasn't got lots of money at the moment, of course she'll pay and she's terribly generous so you know you can get going and think of ideas together and erm, type of dress. So just get in touch with her, drop her a line or drop round, I think she's in today. Love, Henri[3]. I'm coming and going, bye bye.

Clunk.

Beep.

Gone for a walk, I've left the bottom door open – Hedley[4] will be there by six, but anyway, lots of love, it will be great if you can come, bye bye.

Clunk.

17 JANUARY

78th day without pills. I slept till ten to twelve. Tranquil in a warm sea of sadness, inert and overweight. I curled up with Oscar on my pillow and a full belly. After Operation Desert Shield, interrupted a Richard Burton movie where he plays a homosexual villain.

I woke while it was still dark but had no trouble going back to sleep – I don't like waking up and there is nothing to get up for anyway.

During Gongyo I thought of Beryl[5] – she's in Ward 35 of the Borough General Hospital in Lovely Lane. 'She's on slow-release morphine, I haven't told Kay[6],' said Gladys[7]. So that made me feel sadder. I can't decide what to do and I don't do anything. It took three days to write this page.

I wanted to write about James Joyce. 50 years dead and hearing him read from *Finnegans Wake* on the radio . . .

19 JANUARY

After morning Gongyo with JR[8]. The sun is shining outside in a blue sky. I am unshaven with dirty hair which needs cutting. He gave me two candles, present and a paw-paw and I started reading *The Temple* by Stephen Spender – reluctantly he lent it.

Home to a message.

Carla[9] is very depressed by the outbreak of the Gulf War. She stayed up all night watching television for news of it – I suppose anyone who remembers the last one would.

3 FEBRUARY

Beep.

Hi, Ossie, it's Nick[10] here, erm, I'll call you another time about arranging morning Gongyo with you sometime, all right? Speak to you soon, hope you had a nice weekend. Bye.

Clunk.

12 FEBRUARY

There was no tea after Gongyo at Pam[11]'s. I sat at the back. 'Are you all right, you're eating and everything?' she'd said on the phone when I rang from Patrick[12]'s yesterday. Tonight she told me Oscar's breath smelt. And Carla was in a funny mood – drunk and ready to argue but pleased to see me at the same time – she gave me a glass of wine and chicken soup (which was not up to her usual standard – a thick layer of grease on the top) and even a joint, but she didn't want to make me a cup of tea which was all I really wanted. She talked all through a TV programme about an artistic boy who draws buildings. So I rang Ulla[13] when I got home at ten past midnight – she had seen Anita Pallenburg who is having trouble with her teeth – she's got a swollen throat like a bird, you know. Ulla still cherishes hope to have a mouth job – 'I want teeth like Yoanna Yumley[14],' she says in all seriousness, then joins in my laughter when she realises how funny it sounds. Yoanna Yumley indeed.

18 FEBRUARY

While I was swimming in the Kensington new pool:

Beep.

Hello, Dad, it's Albert. Just called to say hello, erm, amongst the chaos in London I missed the bomb by five minutes. I'll speak to you later, bye bye.

Clunk.

And later, after a meeting at Pam's and a cup of tea and two potato pancakes at Carla's, even a joint.

Beep.

Hello, sexy darling, this is Ulla here (breathless), er, I'm home so please give me a ring when you get in if it's not after one o'clock. OK, bye.

24 FEBRUARY

I registered with a local GP yesterday and today I wrote a letter to Michael a'Brook . . . so that he can arrange blood tests. Michael thinks that my thyroid gland is working properly. On Friday I weighed myself after swimming in the new pool of the leisure centre. I weigh eleven and a half stone and today it's the 118th since I took any medication.

2 MARCH

Three messages while I was with Billy[15] watching a movie. I'd rung George begging him to dogsit Oscar.

Beep.

Hello, Dad, it's Albert. What's the whinging voice for? I'll speak to you later.

Clunk.

Beep.

Dad, I'm sorry. You know I'm grumpy in the morning.

Clunk.

Beep.

Ossie, it's Henri . . . Look, erm, some silly girl ripped my dress with her stupid hoof at that ball. It's all rather dreadful, erm, I'm back in London briefly give me a ring. It's Saturday.

Bye bye.

Clunk.

13/14 MARCH

About two o'clock in the afternoon – writing sat on a great log from a fallen tree in Hampstead Heath. I've got Ziggy[16] and the car. Henrietta is at work on the *Standard* Diary – writing a piece on John Major's dress sense. She met him over the weekend and asked for names and quotes.

It's a beautiful spring day, warm sunshine, all the birds singing. I asked Carla to come but she wouldn't: 'Daaaarlink, I've got so much to dooo!' she said – so I left her to do it and took the ball dress she has patched the skirt of. 'Honestly, how does Henrietta get into these scrapes?' she complained yesterday when I took it to her but she gave me dinner later so I mustn't complain about her – she would have loved it here. I'd woken at first light, did an early morning Gongyo, determined to break this block. My flat is such a mess – so much to write, so much I'm missing.

Henri rang early and the car was good incentive as is the brilliant weather. I'd woken at first light. Walked down the Portobello Road to Carla's flat – she was very nosey, asking, 'Do you still enjoy working?' and 'How much do you earn?' 'How much do you have in your bank account?' I asked, never expecting an answer, so I was surprised when she replied, 'One thousand six hundred pounds. Just exactly enough to bury myself.' I tried to make light of it, saying, 'Oh! You're mad – you should buy a little car,' but I knew she was dead serious.

[*Ossie remembers an episode two weeks previously.*]

Henrietta had rung about her dress so I left a message on my answerphone that I'd be there, but when I got to Sutherland Place, Carol[17] had rung. The news of Beryl isn't good; do I want to go up to see her with Carol and Kay? Yes, of course – two Saturdays ago. I took the Denton Welch Journals and sat behind Carol as she drove. 7/3/91 the last time I saw Beryl. Kay sat beside me and Oscar slept on the front seat. It was a beautiful day but in the north it was raining. This was the 1st time in Carol's car since I got out of it in Camberwell, screaming at each other – when was that? – I knew Kay felt the same way. But all that was forgotten in the deep sadness we all share of Beryl's deteriorating condition. But it was Carol, so calm and collected it appeared, who broke down on seeing Beryl after I had realised she lay asleep downstairs next to the kitchen partition, zonked out on morphine – they had just got her down. Gladys very cheerful, down to earth, laughing and joking. 'Accept the unacceptable.' She's going to die very soon.

15 JUNE

Three months have passed since I wrote in this book. Beryl died on a Saturday, the thirteenth of April – the following Friday Albert drove me to the funeral with George where I did my back in. Sat in the back behind him, listening. Wanted to write it all down but just couldn't.

18 JUNE
[*Ossie holidays on Crete with his son George.*]

This is the fourth day on Crete. I'm here with George, who is not well – reading indoors while I write outside on the shaded balcony. It's too hot for either of us to go into the sunshine.

It's about three o'clock in the afternoon and we have settled into a routine, though it is thrown off course today because we had planned to go to Knossos but as George so unwell he stayed in bed all morning and only got out for the maid to tidy the room – I've got clean sheets, he hasn't.

19 JUNE
'So what are those other pills then?' asked George. I owned up and confessed. Tried to explain saying Doctor a'Brook thinks I should take them again – how they give me a feeling of optimism for the future – that I'm aware I'm wasting my talent, afraid of becoming decrepit and a bit afraid of becoming a liability to him and his brother. Remembering when I was his age how I thought my own father to be just a drag and how sad I felt thinking about it now – how I'd hate it if they were to feel the same. I just couldn't cope with that . . . How I feel that my life is imprisoned in those four walls – How Beryl's death seemed to stop any flow of work. How pointless it made everything seem. How I understand Celia's action in the past and bitterly regret my own foolish deeds.

25 JUNE
We rode to a beach through Hersonissos. I wore rolled-up grey Y-fronts for the first time to swim in – a handsome German with tattooed shoulders and chrome yellow trunks with his pale topless girlfriend who retrieved her wrap from a hole in the rock just next to where I lay. The rest of the bathers were recent arrivals, English, pale, two boys swam in protective wet T-shirts – two women exposed enormous mammaries. 'Huh!' said George pointing them out. 'The Fat Slags – you know like in *Viz* magazine. You must have seen them.' 'No. Only Johnny Fartpants.'

28 JUNE
I got terribly sad thinking what to write on a postcard. Choked-up, couldn't speak. It returned like a sledge-hammer blow, Beryl is dead, gone in that box into the ground next to Winrick Church.

29 JUNE
[*Back in London.*]

I'd thought of Billy while we were away. 'If only I could fly I'd have come with you,' he'd said. I imagined him swaggering round and staring at all the exposed female flesh. 'Cor, look at the tits on that one. I'd shag her.' The fat slags would have loved it, too.

30 JUNE

Ugh! Grey outside and been raining. I miss the light. I miss the sea to swim in. My arms ache from the exercise and I've lost weight from chest – I'm firmer, my feet a fraction smaller. The weightlifter's belt fits around my waist one eyelet hole tighter. My toenails shine, but my bloody back still aches just carrying apple juice and milk.

JR introduced me to his sister Eve. 'Is it the sister who had the face lift?' I enquired, expecting someone who looked like Phyllis Diller[18].

1 JULY

9 a.m. 'Sorry I am not here to answer your call. Please leave a message and I'll get back to you. Or could you try me on my friend Henrietta's number. Please speak after the music.'

No replies.

2 p.m. 'Sorry etc. I'm just going to walk in Holland Park; I should be back by three. Please speak etc.'

Beep.

Hello, Dad, it's George. Erm, if you're gonna be in when I've finished work I'll come round and say hello.

Clunk.

Beep.

Ossie, darling, it's Henri. Sorry to have missed you. I'd better dash, it's time for my weekend thing down the river. Help! Help! Bye bye.

Clunk.

After a miserable start to the day – grey sky, rain in the night, backache and so much to catch up on – I read over my written efforts, then to my prayers to make determination for the day.

I refuse to continue living as an untidy, lazy, bored slob. Clean bath, sheets and clothes shall be the order of the day from now on – is the advice I heed from my Butsadan. I have been praying for guidance and this is the answer.

2 JULY

By tube at three to see Michael a'Brook – he could see the improvement and I told him all about my holiday and how wonderful George is. I opened this book at the mosaic drawing and said finally that I'm over Beryl's death. The writing is flowing again and how I'd like to spend three months in the Greek Isles and really write the book. Her illness had caused a block and I had to grieve but now I think it's in the past. He said that was really important otherwise it could come out later with complications.

6 JULY

11.25 on Saturday morning in Wales. Hedley's house CWMR UCHAF in Powis. The village PEN Y BONT FAWR. Outside the sun has broken through on to a valley with sheep bleating. Yellow and pink roses climb up – the yellow rose only flowers three weeks in the year. I write in the kitchen with a black slate floor and a fire in the grate. I think lighting a fire is one of the great joys in life. Hedley in bed reading *Tintin in Tibet* – had been up till dawn seeing to fresh roses in a vase.

15 JULY

Henrietta gave me a fifty pound note as an incentive to make her a blue silk suit by August for a wedding.

So I was on my way to Pongee in Hedley's Sierra with Henrietta by my side: 'Do be careful,' and I handle the gear-stick gingerly since I snapped it off after a day out with Ulla when we went to the new wing of the National Gallery and I saw some of my old favourite pictures rehoused and some restored. Exhausting and futile excursion in an attempt to get Ulla to chant. 'No, I'm finished. It's not for me any more,' she said in Holland Park yesterday. I, on the contrary, am practising every day.

16 JULY

Yesterday George brought a pair of trousers to take in. He paid £25 for secondhand Ralph Lauren – crap made – seams overstitched and top stitched down.

21 JULY

[*At Clovelly, North Devon*]

After lunch we lay in the sun in a trap outside the dining room. Henrietta read the *Sunday Telegraph* which I later rescued just as the wind was about to take it. I refused to walk down to the sea. Instead took a key and drove to Mouthmill to swim over slippery rocks in the sphincter-tightening cold water – not enjoyable after the sea in Crete – even Highgate Pond is warmer.

22 JULY

Seagulls call. Almost noon. Henrietta's gone to Mouthmill. She has just returned from a cruise around the coast of Turkey. Two days ago she was wearing a white smocked dress. Henrietta got a huge atlas and we saw where she sailed in a yacht which is owned by the man who also runs the Orient Express. Henrietta was very interested in the crew: 'Come on! All the nice girls love a sailor.' The cabin boy was dishy, the food was over the top – vegetables tied up in bows made from onion skins etc.

Lunch is over and we are also being shooed out. Henrietta's picking flowers. 'Oh, please, Ossie,' wailed her mother, 'don't let her be too long.' I collected my books and pens and moved to the car. So now I'm sat in the Sierra waiting. It's ten past two. Then Henri decided to wash the windscreen. 'You know your own daughter, Mary,' I answered with humour in my voice but also firmly showing her the car ashtray which I was ordered to empty.

23 JULY

Next day in London I got up at 6.15 and spent about 3 hours colouring in the few lines I'd drawn sat in the pavilion. It was like doing a jigsaw puzzle and got easier the more I worked on it.

28 JULY

There was a massive traffic jam on the M4, driving a new route to Taplow Court. Sat and listened to Mozart Requiem, waiting for CT[19] as he slowly made his way down the steps of Hill Lodge, commissioned by his arch-enemy.

At Taplow I managed to get a conversation with Christopher Tennant: 'Do you ever go fox-hunting?' he asked. 'No, but I've raced with Bianca[20] in Jamaica.' 'Who's Bianca? A horse?'

7 AUGUST

Marianne Faithfull was a good customer – she bought everything without even trying them on – all the lovely chiffons and the silk blouse which became pin-holed with hash burns. She bought more – she was very generous.

10 AUGUST

Today is the New Moon. I always fear I will see it through glass. My mother used to say, 'When you see a new moon turn the money in your pocket and make a wish.'

Turn the coins in your pocket. Turn your luck for the better. Cut your nails and your hair and plant before the moon is full but not before you've seen it and make a wish.

FLASHBACK – on my 27th birthday I was living in a room on Prince of

Wales Drive in Battersea and very unhappy over a man, which seems impossible now as I write over 22 years later. Celia was pregnant with Albert and I was crying over the phone to Amanda Lear who said, 'Never mind Ossie – lots of people are 27 years old.'

10 AUGUST
[*Ossie has crashed my car.*]

Henrietta was quite brilliant about the car! I had expected to be screamed at but when I told her she was calm and kind. Huge relief.

12 AUGUST
Henri's taken Oscar to Cambridge by train, recovered the Sierra and driven back with the recovery man while I went to the psychiatrist – Michael a'Brook very smart and tanned.

6 SEPTEMBER
[*Ossie has been invited to stay with Mary Penney at her house in the Dordogne.*]

Paris: Ten past two in a traffic-jam on the E15 to Bordeaux – ugly buildings and pollution haze – hideous urban sprawl – accident. Betty[21]'s driving us in her Bedford van to Mary Penney's house in the Dordogne. She's got flu. Five to four – stopped for food and diesel and took the A10 to Tours past fields of sunflowers. The trees are beginning to turn. VERY LONG DRIVE. Five to six – we pull off the motorway and Betty brews a cup of tea – at last I manage a bowel movement and then throw up – immediately I felt better. They didn't even notice and were very concerned, offering to make space in the back but I couldn't have laid down. MP is an incredible woman – we have diametrically opposite views – we argued about the sunset but agreed about the stupidity of the French farmers with hedges ripped out and nitrates ploughed in. Ominous absence of birds. The lorries thundered past as the hours dragged on. At 12.30 I was so uncomfortable – back aching and dying for a ciggie – not smoking in the van because of Mary's flu. Somehow ate a packet of biscuits then chanted for the destination to arrive. Finally arrived 11.15. I'm afraid I couldn't muster any enthusiasm.

7 SEPTEMBER
In the kitchen after breakfast I lay down some rules:
Stop bitching the guests who have just departed.
No drinking until after six except perhaps for a glass of champagne.

Sometime after two. Sunshine, swimming, surrounded by green hills. Silence except for flying insects buzzing and a magpie jabbering in the woods. Butterflies pirouette. Occasionally a breeze rustles through the leaves of the aspen. Wasps drinking. A huge bee plops on to the surface of the pool. Mary's cough, but I hear an improvement in her voice and her temperature is down – as is her tirade against the guest who just left.

8 SEPTEMBER

We raced back from Lot where I'd failed to find the shit-house Château – I'd bought postcards and was thinking maybe I'd send one addressed 'David Hockney – LA – California.'

I was terrified of unleashing Mary's fury if we didn't get back in time to take her to tea but I insisted that we stop at the antique shop we'd spotted on the way. She bought an old enamel set and I found an amber cigarette holder. We rushed on laughing all the way along the twisting road. She actually overtook three vehicles – I chanted all the way.

9 SEPTEMBER

'Do you want to have lunch with us or not?' Mary's rude summons disturbed me from my drawing. 'Does it not occur to you that I might actually be doing something?' I thought I might say but I didn't.

Talking to Elizabeth[22] about Rothschild houses – Exbury in Hampshire – unbelievable colour – just rhododendrons – a tower from which you can see seven counties. I longed to swim. Read an article about Derek Jarman. Over bean salad and lettuce I questioned Elizabeth about food. She says she should write a cookbook because in S. America she had rustled up delicious food for up to 40 often at a moment's notice.

11 SEPTEMBER

I changed my mind about accompanying M to some antiques fair in Lalande. They set off before 8 with M grumbling about everything: 'Really, when they can put a man on the moon, why can't they produce a liquid to wash colours and whites together?' She had accidentally put the wrong stuff in the washing machine – I stayed out of the kitchen that morning!

I was sunbathing by the pool and drawing when I recognised the put-put-put of the white whale chugging up the hill in first gear – the end of my deliciously productive first day alone which was blissful. I was lying on a towel on my belly with my drawing stuff scattered all around me – books, pencils and postcards – listening to *The Magic Flute* loud enough to reach across the lawn. Happy and content – just bored enough to welcome their return – it was 4.45.

Elizabeth was first, M having stopped off to talk to Jeannot the neighbour. 'Let me just turn down the music,' I said, having gathered my things into a jumble. 'Do you like Mozart?' 'Don't know a thing about him – it's all above my head.' Self-deprecating as is her way. 'Well, this is *The Magic Flute*, which was his undoing. After writing it he fell from grace because the Freemasons said he gave away too many of their secrets.' 'Oh really – my husband is a Freemason.' My already-formed impression of David Fuller fell even lower. 'Oh dear, I don't like Freemasons,' I said.

Big storm arriving – very frightening. I felt charged after prayers with the lightning flashing and the thunder rumbling in the valley.

So much achieved today. Before storm drawing on the terrace – insects, buildings and a jet from Toulouse that flew over. Sunbathed and swam – listened to Neil Young, Jimi Hendrix and Prince FULL BLAST – I'M SO HAPPY. This location is, as Mary says, pure magic, therapeutic and conducive to work as though it's managed to avoid all the horrors of the 20th century. Nothing offends the eye – no plastic, no advertisements – the harshest colour is the orange of the hawthorn by the pool and even that only jars slightly before the sun goes down over the forest-green hill at the magic hour.

15 SEPTEMBER

Last day – and bliss. Betty went to another fair and Mary accompanied her. I stayed out of the way. 'Not coming with us, Oz?' No! Firm answer. I must do my prayers and I want to write. It was grey and overcast. The field mice had departed and were gone all day. I bathed and swam in the pool and settled on the terrace.

23 SEPTEMBER

[*Back in London.*]

I think of Brian Jones and remember being driven in his chauffeured silver Roller to Hammersmith where we park outside a recording studio and smoke dope which makes no effect on his melancholia and megalomania. God knows what cocktail of drugs he'd already consumed just to get out of bed – where he'd been sleeping all day above my workroom in Radnor Walk while the sun shone – now with a three-day beard and dirty blond hair in crumpled clothes, a pin-striped jacket and one of Suki[23]'s satin blouses. He wails, 'It's not fair. That's my band in there recording and I'm being kept out here.' Poor Brian – neither of us knew it then but he only had a few months to live at the time . . .

. . . My mind went back to 26 Mallard St when Nikki Samuels[24] lived there in splendour with Kita, her maid . . . Chrissie Gibbs decorated it for Nikki and between marriages she gave opulent soirées in the big plum studio. I remember one with a choice of joints rolled – 70 red Leb and 70 Kashmir – and favoured guests doled out the snort from her huge high bed where she held court, often in a nightdress or one of my chiffon wraps.

Outside a squirrel scampers under the walnut tree and George sprays his bicycle with foul-smelling lacquer. Celia snipes at me for writing. 'Shall I give you a reading?' 'No,' she says.

24 SEPTEMBER

I must go home to ring Derek Jarman. Outside a policeman. Overweight beer gut in a white shirt while a shrieking siren goes down Ladbroke Grove. Carla is sewing a cream shirtfront. Downstairs the mains are still not properly positioned. The sweaty policeman swaggers off having spoilt the day for three bikers on their lovingly restored Harley's. Old ladies sit behind their curtains too afraid of the muggers to go out. Crack is sold openly on the street. The first time I walked down Ladbroke Grove more than 30 years ago it seemed smaller and more peaceful. A nostalgic view shared by many others.

11 OCTOBER

On Thursday I rang Derek – I'd written him a letter after I noticed that his film opens soon at the Gate cinema. He hadn't answered because he's so busy but was pleased to hear from me. I knew from Henrietta there was a party at Heaven. 'That's gone. That was last night.'

Oh God, I hate Heaven, which is a sewer under Charing Cross – homosexual dive.

17 OCTOBER

Met Derek Jarman in the foyer of the NFT[25]. He was very smart, very thin, very swarthy with suntan and great wide smile. He's been up and down the country previewing his film *Edward II* – they laughed at it in Newcastle. 'We'll meet up later,' he said. So I sat alone and saw his idea of queer Edward.

1 Hali Rotbart.
2 Mary Penney, friend of Henrietta Rous; world conference organiser and chief interpreter for the European Bank.
3 Henrietta Rous.
4 Hedley Marten, barrister.
5 Beryl Westell.
6 Kay Melia.

7 Gladys English.
8 Johnnie Rozza.
9 Carla Ames.
10 Nick Balaban.
11 Pam Procter.
12 Patrick Procktor.
13 Ulla Larson.
14 Joanna Lumley, British actress and former model.
15 Billy Henry.
16 Ziggy is Henrietta Rous' dog.
17 Carol Hammond.
18 Phyllis Diller, comedienne who also appeared in several films.
19 Christopher Tennant.
20 Bianca Jagger.
21 Betty Fuller, antiques dealer.
22 Elizabeth, friend of Mary Penney.
23 Suki Poitier.
24 Nikki Samuels became Nikki Waymouth.
25 National Film Theatre.

1992

The back pains Ossie has mentioned in previous years have only been indications of a potentially life-threatening condition from which he almost dies in August. He begins this diary complaining that all his days are the same, 'empty and bored'. This is a diary of illness and of fading hope. Nick Balaban has HIV, Oscar – Ossie's King Charles spaniel – dies, Ossie himself is hospitalised twice, his phone and electricity are cut off. He looks so thin, weary and generally 'rough' that many who know him suspect him to be HIV positive himself. It is hardly surprising that in the wake of these events Ossie's determination to give up his reliance on prescription pills and alcohol fails and that his Buddhist chanting is 'no help'.

There are bursts of optimism and excitement, however. He travels to Paris for the Comme des Garcons fashion show and meets old and new friends. At home he seems surrounded by people who care for him, but no amount of encouragement from friends, positive thinking or religious belief can help with his ulcer problem, which is serious. There are harrowing accounts of him vomiting blood and being rushed to hospital where eleven pints of blood are transfused, accounts that serve to remind us and him of his mortality and fragility. Years of exiguous living have contributed to this.

His taste of a champagne lifestyle when attending the Commes des Garcons is a welcome relief and glamorous reminder of his exotic past. But, how ironic that Ossie, the star who had put on the most coveted shows of his era, now consents to model as a 'Mature Rebel' for a Japanese company and is even appreciative. However, he tries to keep faith in himself and his ability to overcome his age; he even attempts to identify through the television with Christopher Columbus' perseverance and the seemingly insurmountable obstacles he had to climb before finding success in later life.

Despite excruciating physical pain, Ossie's concern for others is touching; his prayers are for the solutions to their problems and include 'all those suffering from HIV'. He also prays for 'Justine, Pam and Sid, Albert and George' and for 'guidance, courage, forgiveness, to be a good person, to improve my life'.

The impact of Oscar's death cannot be overestimated. Darko Luger, the manager of Ossie's local wine bar, just off Penzance Street, has testified that Ossie never recovered after he lost his most cherished companion, and, indeed, Ossie seems greatly affected throughout this year by Oscar's slow and painful demise. In fact, he records Oscar's death in much the same way as he does his sister Beryl's, long after the event because it is too painful to put in at the time. Oscar's death and Nick's illness leave Ossie bereft. By his last entry, he is unwell again and is too weakened and demoralised to chant any more.

11 JANUARY

After 5 o'clock – listening to jazz records requests after a crimson sunset and a beautiful day cold, but a clear blue sky. At last I found this cut-price diary, £2 on Portobello. Money is a problem – I'm very worried about telephone and gas bills – afraid I might get cut off. I even went to the Kamen[1]'s hoping Michael might pay the £61 phone bill – but they weren't home. So far this year I haven't missed a Gongyo and I haven't taken a pill, even a single Valium. I have to force myself to write. I'm drinking hot chocolate longing for a joint – it's days since I finished the ounce scored before Christmas – I'm really straight, sleeping too much. Walking a lot – the weather has been very mild after a cold snap at the beginning of December. But I seem to have made a determination to do without the pills, eleven days already but I don't know how long I can hold out. Oh, how a joint would help. The TV is dreadful – I woke at ten to six, turned off the news – so depressing: bombs, murders, job losses, recession – slept on till 11 o'clock – Morning Gongyo helps. I bathed, walked to Carla[2]'s, as I have done these last 3 days. She cooking Goulash for dinner. I've promised to take a bottle of wine.

12 JANUARY

Ten past one. I saw the new moon through glass on Wednesday, or maybe it was Thursday – all the days have been the same, empty and bored.

27 JANUARY

I slept till almost 12. Regretted sleeping so long into such a beautiful sunny day – I had to resist taking a pill. I still haven't but how long can I hold out?

28 JANUARY

Up at ten past ten. Henri[3] phoned while I was in the bath – Hedley[4] had seen me walking 'and shall I tell you what he said – he was struck by how painfully thin you looked – shall I leave you some money, it's your money anyway. I'll leave £10 by the side where I usually leave the key. I'll dole it out' – she was still there when I arrived – so I drove her to Kings Cross and kept the car for the day.

30 JANUARY

Guy Burch rang at 9 o'clock waking with bad news. ''Ere Oz, didn't you know someone called Tina Chow,' he began, 'she died on the 24th, there's an obituary in the *Independent*' – oh dear, another to add to my list for the 5th prayer.

31 JANUARY

The E generation call amphetamine WIZZ. I took half a pill reluctantly, after phoning Michael a'Brook about my sick note, which hasn't come in the post. 'I've already sent it,' he said.

5 FEBRUARY

Author death: Jane McKay.

It's impossible to write down every thought – yet I did think of Jane McKay about three weeks ago and that's when she died of a massive coronary. 'Can you imagine?' Mind you, she's a perfect example of the wrong lifestyle; too much drinking, smoking and a high cholesterol diet. But she was only 44. Bryan Ferry blamed her for the break-up of Roxy Music – always said she was a bad influence.

Dinner at Jenny Dearden's. A limo arrived simultaneously and disgorged Adie[5] and Spouse and Richard O'Brien[6] with a new wife, already drunk, all. 'You haven't met her – I must tell you, she's a wonderful cutter.' He said his joy in life is to have a major dump.

6 FEBRUARY

I was watching Derek Jarman being arrested on the 5.40 TV news when Albert rang. Still keen for me to make him a pair of leather jeans.

11 FEBRUARY

Crashed. The Buddhists say there is a reason for everything – why should I reverse into a car with a policeman in it – totally unreal experience[7].

12 FEBRUARY

I woke at 8.25, just in time for the Radio 3 news – but I couldn't get out of bed until almost eleven and Henrietta phoned before I even had a chance to make coffee. Depressed.

'God, you look rough,' said Henrietta. Leaving Oscar with her while I went to the sauna. Walked in the wet through a miserable day.

9 stone 12 pounds in the sauna. I check my belt, buckle up one notch wider on both belts and notice my belly bulging. Getting into the bath, I chanted for Billy[8] to ring leaving an urgent message on my answerphone.

Beep. Er, Raymond, it's me, Bill, er, I'm at work all day but I'll ring you at teatime tonight whatever tonight is, probably Wednesday, isn't it. OK, so I've spoken to Henrietta 'cos I thought you might be there so I'll just try and get in touch, erm, today or tonight. Bye. Clunk.

13 FEBRUARY

2.30ish Writing in Holland Park. Beautiful day – it has been spring for the last five days – the big grey clouds have blown away and the sun shines in an azure sky.

16 FEBRUARY

I put off confessing to Hedley until after 6 – I'd been there once and found the house empty and very tidy – so I walked on to Carla's who demanded to hear what's going on. 'Come on, I want the truth. Billy had let the cat out of the bag – so I told her – I backed Hedley's car into a police car and smashed his front head light and, worse, they might charge me with driving with undue care and attention. That's why I was desperate to get hold of Bill.

But worse when I told Hedley – he wasn't sure if he had an MOT.

19 MARCH

Psychiatrist – his hand trembled as he wrote out a different prescription.

25 MARCH

12.27 And am I feeling a little bit better? Certainly Hedley's call cheered me up. 'Oh, don't worry about it.'

29 MARCH

Errol[9] woke me at 9.30 out of a weird dream – I wanted to get back to it – all about escaping chemical war and green caterpillars which burst open and oozed poison – the location was the beach in LA and Hockney was there and somebody else. I did sleep again though and this time I was woken by the telephone: it was Bella Freud – could I possibly help her, she's having trouble with her patterns?

14 APRIL

10 stone 3 pounds in the sauna.

Ossie's friend, the painter Patrick Procktor.

24 APRIL

After yesterday's dream which was full of bickering where I was a pawn between PP[10] and DH, last night's was much more pleasant – I was in Japan and the first thing I did there was learn to make a hard bed, a do-it-yourself kit which cost 300 times £99. At dinner I was served an egg-shaped sort of steamed dumpling, which I deftly trimmed and cut in half, then watched amazed at my audience as the two halves expanded and grew, fluting into a perfectly matched pair of sleeves.

25 APRIL

Up at five past nine to beautiful sunshine – much later as I lay watching television Billy rang at last. 'Thank God, are you all right? Where are you? Raymond, if I die you'll know I haven't committed suicide. Vikki de Lambray was murdered.'

26 APRIL

George drove me to see Billy in the mental home, the Royal Bethnal.

28 APRIL

All my prayers are for Nick[11].

After Gongyo I rang Nick who's constantly on my mind. 'Hello, darling, I've been thinking about you. How are you?'

'Terrible, I'm feeling so weak.'

'Oh God, I wish there was something I could do.'

'It's worse. The HIV is getting worse.'

'Oh, I am so sorry.'

'I'm so depressed. All those fucking bills and the fucking mortgage, which I never wanted anyway. It was my mother insisting I should buy it, the broken toilet. I can't face it – I've no strength to go out.'

He began to sob.

'Shall I come and see you tomorrow?'

Like a sledgehammer, the inescapable fact slams into my consciousness. 'Is he going to – I can't write it – just fade away in a couple of years and be gone like Henry[12] and Tina Chow? 'It is a pity,' said Michael a'Brook, 'just when you were doing so well.' He's the only person I told. 'I don't like the sound of this cold,' he said. I'd confessed to feeling very low and resorting to 10-mil dexamphetamin. Carla knows something's wrong but I haven't told her.

29 APRIL

By chance I met Robert Yuen[13] at NHG[14] after buying an all-day pass. 'Hi,' he smiled after recognising Oscar. 'Hey, your friend's got AIDS, hasn't he?' he blurted out accusingly, completely unaware of what he was saying, with no compassion or change in the tone of his voice. I should have asked, 'Who told you so?' Why did I meet this person today? Instead I denied it. 'No, he's HIV+.' There was confusion, him realizing his lack of tact. 'Hey, listen, can you catch it from just kissing?' he asked. 'Don't be stupid. Look, I've got to go.'

I'm late on a 52 bus for Bella Freud, a new shop by the stop selling men's hairpieces, before and after photos. Half an hour to sort out a woman's waistcoat pattern, then on to the Central Line to Oxford Circus and the Victoria Line to Highbury where it was a beautiful day. But in my memory, it was raining.

30 APRIL

Tea with Patrick. He appeared at the door, beaming, bearing the tea tray. 'I'm in love with a gorgeous young man with the most beautiful young name in the English language. He's called Adam, he's divine. Only 20. I have just been to Paris with his mother. We went to look at an exhibition. The first day at lunch I asked her, do you like wine? And she said, 'Yes! It's that first sip.' He likes wine, too, and he lets me make love to him when he's drunk. He calls me a disgusting old man because I pour wine into his naval and drink it from his body – you know, I just sip it and it has the most wonderful taste. How's your love life?'

'Non-existent,' I lie, without thinking.

'How's the usherette? What's his name?'

'Nick, oh he's fine.' I couldn't tell him, he was in such mood.

6 MAY

At 4.15, I met Ulla[15] at South Ken Tube. She came on her bicycle and we went to look at Jade Jagger's paintings and then to the Tate to look at the seven Hockneys on show including 'Mr and Mrs Clark and Percy', which doesn't look any different. I had to leave Oscar outside, left all the admiring students and went back to him while she bought some postcards.

7 MAY

The weeks disappear so quickly and I achieve nothing. I have been back on 4mil Valium for a week, sleeping seep dreams, getting up earlier – still aching more, creaking like an old war-horse.

I went to Carla's where I read Marlene[16]'s obituary in yesterday's *Times*. Carla said she quite understood why she took to her bed and stopped looking into a mirror – 'watching all this loveliness just fade away.'

9 MAY

Last night in my clumsiness I knocked over and trod on a tube of copydex – I cleaned up the mess but forgot about the tiny piece of hash until I woke early this morning. I've searched and searched – I've looked high, I looked low. Eventually I found it, but it took Gongyo and two hours of looking.

11 MAY

[*Ossie goes to Pam Proctor's in Devon.*]

Devon – Yesterday I chanted for 20 minutes before Pam got up – she never even heard me. At 9, I decided to do MG. She joined me in three minutes and I led the prayers.

13 MAY

[Answerphone message.] Beep. Hi Ossie, it's Bella. It's Wednesday morning. Erm, could you give me a call as soon as you get back, erm, just a bit stuck on the collar of the dress, hope you're well, see you soon. Bye. Clunk.

18 MAY

Henrietta woke me at 7.30 all excited – she'd met Prince Edward ('he was rather nice') over the weekend at some tennis tournament. I met L at the flower stall on the corner of Elgin, I asked him if he could get me some hash. He said he might, he'd be there at teatime.

21 MAY

Oscar's birthday – 10 years old and suddenly since this July heat and the trip to Devon he isn't the same, he's getting old.

23 MAY

I phoned Nick and he came at one o'clock. We walked down Portobello and he bought me a box of Chinese water colours, an early birthday present. I had the car so we drove to Highgate and I threw Oscar into a pond because he was so hot and I thought it would refresh him, but it was ghastly. When he got out he keeled over and I thought he was going to die. I felt his heart, which felt very uneven.

28 MAY

'Ossie! You're much too thin,' declared Tanya Sarne in her studio in Kensal

Road where I'd gone in desperation to make a decent photocopy for the Buddhism monthly schedule.

[*It appears that after this meeting Ossie and Tanya have patched up their differences.*]

9 JUNE

My 50th birthday. Felt Oscar's heartbeat flittering, as he grows feebler. Last night I gave in to despair and had a little weep. How many times have I said, 'Oh Oscar, whatever would I do without you?' as I cradled him in my arms. 'You are my only friend, so faithful.' A complete stranger said, 'That dog really loves you,' in a pub. 'He hasn't taken his eyes off you since you came in here.'

Beep.

Happy Birthday, Dad, lots of love, George.

Clunk.

And later, after dinner, Carol[17]'s cheerful voice. Beep. Happy Birthday, Darling. I thought I'd see you soon but never mind. I've got a nice present for you. See you soon, goodbye.

22 JUNE

More bad news.

Beep.

Hello, lovey, it's Kay[18]. I'm just off to see Gladys[19] in Mablethorpe. She's had another heart attack and she's nobody with her this week so if you'd like to call her. Talk to you when I get back on Friday. Bye Bye

25 JUNE

Great improvement in Oscar's heart. Borrowed Justine[20]'s car to go the RCA fashion show, which was dreadful. Tanya was there, and afterwards to Patrick's. He'd been photographed for a Sunday supplement. We drank Martinis. I met Adam[21] – walked home collecting a little posie of sweet-smelling roses and eucalyptus.

26 JUNE

Hung over. So late to MG[22] at Justine's and tired all day. I really shouldn't drink alcohol.

30 JUNE

Nick is looking so much better. He was at Carla's when I got there at 3.30, after running around all morning fitting Jose[23] – was perfect, I needn't have worried. We swam in the rain in Highgate Pond – so refreshing. Nobody there except a few hideously hairy and very grotesque Jews and their equally overweight sons. He dropped me off at Bella Freud's. Her toiles are looking OK, just about.

1 JULY

[*Ossie has been invited to model in the Comme des Garçons show in Paris.*]

PARIS

12.20. I was in quite a sweat and ticked Yuki[24] off – for having me rush – as I stripped off my T-shirt to mop my brow. She was staggering under the weight of antique Japanese marble slabs, which she smuggled through customs. Once in the taxi, she informed she was travelling Club Class, which was OK. Yuki, like all the Japanese, is inscrutable, carefully imparting information only when necessary – in the taxi from Charles de Gaulle she informed me that John Hurt[25] ('do you know him?') also modelling, that she isn't staying in the same hotel – she dropped me outside Hotel St Romain in the Rue St Roch just off the Rue de Rivoli and seven minutes walk from the Comme des Garçons office in the Place Vendôme, promising to call within an hour – which she did – and I walked to be inspected by Rei Kawakubo – the designer – a little woman in black with a very severe style and, hidden under the fringe behind 50s shades, the expressionless grey face of a workaholic.

2 JULY

Hangover in Paris – threw up the second cup of coffee after breakfast. Last night was such fun. Dinner with Loulou de la Falaise, her husband Thadee Klossowski, her brother Alexei and a French woman whose name I didn't catch, at their local garish Brasserie Le Zeyer in Montparnasse. I really felt the need for MG but I didn't have the time to bring candles – so I went looking and found a wonderful selection in Galleries Lafayette. I chose deep red, 30 centimetres long.

As instructed, I was punctual arriving at C des G at 12.45. You are the first to arrive, said Yuki – who took me upstairs – a hospitality suite, chairs around the walls, an overweight photographer's assistant like a fish out of water, his boss German . . . I chose my position carefully, took out my 9th Journal and started writing.

Already tipsy, John Hurt, next to arrive, threw his arms round me, a long-lost friend, rather too much kid-gloved, as though I had returned from the dead or been insane. 'You'd better call me Vincent because there are so many Johns around.' I thought we met in 1961, but he corrected me, it was 1967.

The fitting was a nightmare army experience. The shoes did my right foot in, and after Yuki paid me. I was surprised by the amount, 5,000 francs. I told her I was very impressed with the organization. Everyone Polaroided, measured and shoed – even the clothes weren't bad, except for one sleeveless jacket made from horsehair which, had I let it come into contact with my skin, would have brought me out in a rash.

Lyle Lovett[26] – such blue eyes – 'no, I've never done it before.'

I walked to St Germain, bought coloured pencils in the little art shop on the Rue des Beaux-Arts.

3 JULY

The Comme des Garçons show – so I was up before seven and down to the basement where two black maids serve breakfast.

Today was the same procedure. But where are the shoes? In disbelief I looked around for the slip-ons I had almost worn in yesterday. 'Noh, 'tis dease,' said my Japanese dresser, squatting, holding open a shoe I'd never seen before with a worried look on his face.

'But where are the slip-ons I wore yesterday?'

'Please quickly put on these,' he pleaded. All around me were similar wails, moans, curses and grunts. The left shoe I got on OK. The right one was so rigid it could have been made out of Bakelite and designed as an instrument of torture. Angry, I snatched it out of the hands of the terrified boy. The unwielding object – it was leather all right – but it had the same dull gleam as plastic.

John hasn't been to bed. 'I can't be hurt anymore.'

Everyone sat round chatting, smoking, eating peaches and drinking cans of Heineken.

'Why are we waiting? It's half past one. We're late.'

The inscrutable Japanese dresser, all in sober navy, picks his nose after bowing as he passes.

'Everyone here?' One guy's getting his hair cut. There are now 25 people present.

'Still writing your diary?'

'It's a journal.'

'It's the same word in French.'

'It's the mature rebel look we're after. One by one keep your own pace. Think power and strength – at the end of the runway don't do anything fancy – just a natural turn.'

'Do we need someone to translate from the French?'

'Where's the talcum powder?'

'OK, Ossie.'

'Me now?'
'In a minute. We keep the best 'till last.'
'I cannot believe there is nobody here who smokes hashish.'
'I do.'
'You have?'
'Just a little piece.'
'Haven't you got any rolling papers?'
'I'll go and get you some.'
Tyrone goes for papers. He is 16 today.
Yuki is under pressure. She feels nervous. 'We're running a little late.'
'You should never start on time. Ten minutes late is fine,' I say.
'It will be half an hour late. If the *Daily Telegraph* don't turn up, it's OK but if *Vogue* don't turn up, we'll have to wait.'
Chanting Gongyo whilst having my hair cut.
Champagne at last.
It's quarter to nine. I want to be in an altered state.
Boy George is on stage at the Jean Paul Gautier party whilst the famous kiss between Burt Lancaster and Deborah Kerr[27] plays on the video screen. 'We're going to give you some live music, as live as you can get,' says Jean Paul.
'Do you really want to hurt me?
Do you really want to make me cry?'

4 JULY
The last day in Paris. So that's settled it.
I'd chanted to stay and will take up Alexie de la Falaise's offer made so spontaneously only last Wednesday night when we dined in Montmartre.
'Or stay here,' said Loulou. But Thadee has already told me that she has left the city.

6 JULY
[*Ossie has returned to London.*]

At Sandra and Michael's. It's the men's final at Wimbledon. Agassi[28] wins. He has a sexy body – a beautiful torso which shows now and again as he leaps around. Fashion is to wear two pairs of shorts – Sandra is mesmerised.

7 JULY
I am determined to make the pleated jacket and trousers for Jose. This is really the reason I came back from Paris. I need the money. I fancy a week in Crete.

Carla gets cross because of what I choose to write. 'It makes me paranoid when you write this stuff down.'

8 JULY

It's Nick's 37th birthday today. It's my sister's 50th today, and David Hockney's 55th.

A meeting with Rosita[29] to discuss her wedding gown. 'You know what I visualise, is one of your little sexy numbers with hardly anything there. The same duchess satin as Cleo Goldsmith's, maybe lace.'

'What colour?'

'Champagne.'

'D'you know, that's just what I was thinking.'

9 JULY

8.30 MG with Rosita – I got very choked up at the 5th prayer for the dead. Tears streamed down my cheeks for Beryl my sister.

News on Radio 3 that relatives of the Lockerbie victims are being persuaded to accept $1 million compensation by a business man, keen to end sanctions with Libya. So he can make millions more.

'I feel as if I've achieved lift off,' I told Pam on the phone today. I've just got to organize my thoughts. Bella Freud on the phone at 11 o'clock – plans, plans.

More bad news. Henrietta was mugged.

Tanya Sarne just told me that Lynn Franks has given it all up. She's not a Buddhist anymore. She's tired of giving everything out. 'Now she wants everything,' this said with a grabbing gesture.

10 JULY

I slept without Valium only because I haven't got any – but actually slept quite well. I rang Nick who sounded very faint when he answered the phone.

Waiting with Pam Procter at Cheyne Walk for Jose to fit her crocus-yellow silk jacket and trousers. But Jose's in a car returning from the airport with her aunt, who they are going on holiday with next week. She's probably forgotten and we were so prompt. 'Can you wait half an hour?' said her secretary from Models One.

Two hours later. 'Ossie, are you ever going to forgive me,' Jose shouted from the front door as I sat in the kitchen with her Welsh aunt – who, apart from the trouble with her legs and a slight deafness, has still got all her marbles – drinking tea and telling me about Jose's forgetfulness. There was Jose alongside her sleek gun-metal grey XJS. 'Aunt Edna, this is Ossie Clark, the famous fashion designer.'

'Have you seen Bianca[30]?' says Jose. 'She's a grandmother now. Looks good! How does she do it? That bitch! They're gonna make her President of Nicaragua! Thomas Akmon invested the paltry sum of money Mick gave her. He's so mean, he doesn't give any money to charity while I'm paying the hospital bill for three friends dying from AIDS. I hate dykes mind you, I hate faggots as well.'

In a sauna in Covent Garden, watching a video – 'Take a Chance on Me', an Abba song, and 'Voulez-Vous'.

11 JULY

I woke at six o'clock. My back still aching, pains in my chest. I attempt to do without medication. Fiddle with the radio and go back to bed until 7.30, then give into the pills and then lie down again until they start to work.

I must write a letter to Jose while she's away straightening out the payment of her yellow job.

Overheard on Portobello – a black youth being questioned by the police – he protests, 'That's my name on there, innit?'

'What's your name and date of birth?' says the sergeant holding, a credit card. Terror in his eyes, he doesn't know.

What am I going to do? No electricity over the weekend. It's getting dark already. Carla's unpicking a black bodice, which I fitted on Rosita, originally fitted on Marie Helvin. 'What do you think of a nice black and white movie on TV?' Carla asks. 'There's no electricity.'

She hands me the backside of the bodice. I rush to the iron, plug it in but there's no electriciteee!! Oh well, that definitely ends work for today.

In conversation with the London Electricity Board.

'It's worse than Russia. Tell me how many flats are affected because I seem to be the only one in this vicinity. Odd, isn't it?'

I think I'm going to get a bottle of wine and get pissed.

13 JULY

They can't arrest three million dope smokers.

It's on! It's on again! The electricity's back on! The orange light in the hall – Oh goody – the iron – racing on TV – Elvis on the radio. A knock at the door. It's a man from the LEB. 'It was a fuse in the distribution box,' he tells me. That was quite nice, just coming to make sure I was all right.

Watching a programme about Columbus.

Carla heard a medical clinic being advertised on the radio, 'From cosmetic surgery to piles. We do everything in half an hour.'

'A good cough after smoking hashish makes you stronger than twelve camels.' An Arab proverb.

14 JULY

At the bus stop I thought, if a 15 comes that would be great; if a 5a comes I'll go to Justine's; and if a 295 comes I'll do EG[31] at home.

15 JULY

Henri on the phone. 'Listen, Ossie, would you like to come to dinner tonight? Who shall I invite?'

'Bella Freud,' I suggest.

'Nick wants to meet you.'

'Who's he?' She tells me.

'Invite Bella's boyfriend. He looks nice. I've met him, tall, 30ish. Look, I've got to run to do my prayers with Justine in five minutes.'

At a quarter to twelve precisely I rattled the door of Telford House. 'I knew it!' came Carla's irate voice from behind the door. She opened the door with a stern look on her face which softened on noticing Oscar who bounded in. 'Knew what?' I asked calmly, collecting what I'd gone for – the yellow silk and the bag of ribbons and lace. 'That you could be punctual,' she said, adding, 'when it soots yoo.' An argument was brewing and I was hoping I could get out without a shout out. 'Oh!' I said, turning to the cassette player, thinking, 'shall I just take her scissors and cut off the plug?' Instead I just took the tapes and put them in my bag. A dramatic exit.

'Ossie, have you got any money for me?' Carla called out in a little girl voice from the window.

'Do you think you deserve any from the amount of work you did yesterday?'

'But I haven't got any. I need money. You promised to pay me on Wednesday.'

'I'm not giving you my dole money. Where's the shirt?'

'What shirt?'

'The shirt I'm gonna cut up for the psychiatrist.'

'I'm not going to give it to you until you pay me.'

'Look, I said I'd pay you fifty. I've given you thirty. I'll give you the other twenty when I get paid.'

'Listen, you've been here for ten days using my electricity, using my iron, using my tea.'

I stared at her in disbelief and she shut up. It reminded me of last week, handing Justine the car key. Snatching it, she snapped, 'Did you put any petrol in the tank?' like a Jewish harridan.

Mrs Roberts[32] left this note on my machine:

5 June 1992 – *New Statesman* Earth Rape. President Bush said he would not sign a treaty to protect natural species at the Earth Summit in Rio. Vice

President Dan Quayle claims it would 'restrict domestic and international trade'.

At Highgate Pond. A Rabbi parks behind us on the road off Highgate West. We swim in the gentle rain with a 'few Jews' and the park of resident swans. Nick is so thin and nervous of wetting his head – while I dive and swim. 'It's so cold,' Nick complained, standing on the ladder, only half in the water. He showed me the dark mark where the hypodermic needle had punctured the skin on the inside of his elbow. 'Do you think any bacteria will get in through here?'

'No, no,' I reassured him.

'I've got to be careful,' he said, but he was smiling.

17 JULY

I'm really sick, backache, vomiting, exhausted, afraid to stop taking the amphetamine. Hedley had told me about this man called Bendon in Elgin Crescent who just bashed my poor torso about. 'Oh! I've come across a back like this before' – in a horrible hot little basement he pummelled and crunched, and he was very tall which made the room seem smaller.

18 JULY

Albert's definitely leaving work at the end of the month – but there's good news. The Halcyon Hotel are interested in him. And he had lunch yesterday with David Hockney – they got on very well. 'He didn't talk down to me, like he usually does, like a little boy. He talked to me like a man – wants me to go to Los Angeles.' I told him what Michael had said about LA – how hideously polluted.

'I know, I don't want to go. I told him I want to go to Mexico and he said he knew the richest man in Mexico. Basically he just wants me to go away with him.'

19 JULY

I rang Nick who's bringing wine and Carol's bringing my present – a pearl pin with a diamond behind it – 'The man said the diamond is stronger than the pearl.' We all sat in the garden admiring it over a glass of delicious Sancerre. 'We all know he's the master, don't we.' They all nod in unison.

Nick has to lie down. He's not used to smoking hashish. 'He has that look,' Ulla had said.

I miss Mo[33], everybody misses Mo.

20 JULY

Albert phoned with good news. The Halcyon Hotel have offered him a job –

head chef in their very smart hotel. They want him to start straight away at the beginning of August.

21 JULY
My telephone cut off – what a bloody bore and how stupid of me.

I'm still doing my exercise to rap music. It's a different kind off rhythm. Henri chats away happily. Well, it's nice to have some nice people in the world.

23 JULY
9 stone 5 pounds in the sauna. Last time I came here I spent hours and I got told off. 'There's a four-hour limit,' said the nasty Chinese masseur. I've lost twelve pounds since June 5th.

'There's not a spare ounce of flesh on you,' said the man from Zimbabwe enviously. 'AIDS capital of the world,' I muttered. Ignoring my comment, he told me about the wonderful climate. Dry heat and no rain from March to September. 'You get used to it,' he said licking his lips and blatantly scrutinizing my naked body as I rose from my horizontal position to take a cold plunge.

Tea at Patrick's. 'D'you know, I've been staring out of this window for twenty-eight years,' he said from the kitchen where he was making tea. 'Come and have a look at these Moroccans, they're wearing jellabas.' But I was in agony, lying on my back on his ottoman.

24 JULY
I wanted to do so much – but the backache is terrible. I'm really a bit freaked.

26 JULY
Agony.

27 JULY
I set out early without doing Gongyo. Oscar collapsed in St James' Square though I didn't actually see – I'd reached St Anne's Villas and went back to find him panting in the shade under the trees. I was on my way to buy some more pharmacy specs – the weather is unbearably hot so I carried him – and by bus to find Tanya Sarne in a state as usual. She's got a new boyfriend.

I get back from Ghost. Usef,[34] who's got to sign on between two and three, tells me he's really getting pissed off – 'sit on my cock,' he said, which is a way of insulting amongst Arabs.

28 JULY
I have stopped taking my morning pills for four days and stopped writing. I

went to see the osteopath, paid with my dole money. Indeed he is very good – very gentle, young. It took him 40 minutes to unkink my body which is so wound up. He says for my age, I'm in good shape.

29 JULY

Rosita found me in tears for Oscar. 'Never mind, come on let's chant for him.' I lay in an agony of pain and sorrow – remembering the times we'd had together and praying for him to die – but his little heart beat on and he lay beside me terrified – the light in his eyes flickering off and on.

Yet when George rang the doorbell, Oscar knew it was him and that was the turning-point – he started to rally. I laid him in front of the Gohonzon and did a very tearful Gongyo.

30 JULY

I took him to the vet, who's not so mercenary after all. God forgive me for what I called him at the chemist's last Tuesday. In fact, Oscar's heart is still improving, it's now 51% efficient.

'So it's the weather that's against him.'

'Yep, you've hit the nail on the head, that's it,' he replied. 'Even my own dog,' looking down to the great white chow, 'who's only four, is having a very hard time.' One of God's great failures, the design of the heart.

3 AUGUST

[*Ossie writes to Michael a'Brook.*]

Dear Michael – Greetings. Another three months have flown by and again I need another sick note. I know I've asked before and been refused – but please could the sick note be for a period of six months instead of the usual three which passes so quickly. Just in case I do manage to get away – though to be honest, at this moment I'm feeling pretty low.

I've made a pact with Oscar to stay with him until the end – and to be cheerful. My back is so bad I simply can't carry him. Even the weight of this book is a drag to carry round. It's funny, when I began this series of journals I would only write outside – stopping in the street to complete something before going indoors. Now it's completely the opposite, but I find myself memorising turns of phrase and forming sentences which often don't even get written down. Some quotes stay in my head for months. All I'm afraid of is repeating myself, and yet some things must be said over and over in order to be heard once or to make something add up, or to give drama to a situation. Then I question my motives – Why am I writing? Writing when I can't even spell.

4 AUGUST

Chanting for my back to stop aching – a different ache today – deeper set, more scary – for Oscar, for Nick, for a cure for HIV, for Tommy Nutter, for Billy to appear, for money and other things like a fridge, for a beautiful yellow gown for Rosita, sincerely for Justine's happiness, for Albert and George, out of work, for order in my flat, for Pam and Sid, for Hedley and his financial crisis, for the weather to stay cool, for Steve O'Rourke to be amenable, for Jose to get in touch, for Gladys my sister, for guidance, courage, forgiveness, to be a good person – to improve my life.

Albert's gone to Los Angeles for a fortnight, George tells me. 'You've just missed him.' I wonder, am I hurt because he didn't ring to say goodbye?

Clapped out and penniless I prepared a hot water-bottle to relieve my aching back. Channel hopping, a Marilyn Monroe movie came on – *Gentlemen Prefer Blondes* – she was so gorgeous then – in comparison Jane Russell was vulgar and crude. I took 6 mil of Valium.

Nick came in the afternoon after a check-up at the hospital. The last time we went swimming on Sunday he'd suggested I take the test. 'Just think of the benefits,' he joked. 'Well, at least go and see a doctor. I refused. He is genuinely concerned about me and recognises his symptoms in me. The loss of weight is frightening. This feeling of a blockage between my rib cage drives away the desire for food.

John Hurt has done a voice-over on TV for a new razor, 'So powerful it has to be kept behind bars. ' I bought one this morning.

6 AUGUST

9 stone 2lbs in the sauna.

Judging a talent competition.

1st contestant, David Osbourne semi-pro, funny bugger, wants to be bigger than Madonna – dreadful clothes.

2nd contestant, greasy make-up, it's the blonde I couldn't help seeing in ten years time, dressed in op art.

Andy Raffles, no. 6 contestant – needs a dentist.

'I'm Roy,' says a guy wearing jeans, 'I've got a picture of you on my bedroom wall. What happened to the cat?'

7 AUGUST

I keep throwing up; I'm quite freaked actually. Oscar lies at my feet.

Sid told Pam he had accepted an offer on the house in Landsdowne Road. So that's it. It's over with Sid. She feels completely betrayed and so now it's divorce time – though how they can divorce when they never married is beyond me – poor Pam.

The party at Pam's. I was feeling a little better after being served tea by an Australian girl with an accent like fingernails on glass.

8 AUGUST

The sultry weather is driving people completely mad. I saw a crowd gathered round the spectacle of two drunken Scottish women, rolling on the ground, each attached to the other's hair. The one viciously bashing her red stiletto-heeled shoe to the other's face. The crowd tut-tutting.

10 AUGUST

[*In hospital.*]

Was given shots, several, five holes in my chest, they'd made me shave off the hair on my chest. I hated doing that. Sarah Cockrell is a surgical ward – it closes over the weekend. Last Monday, they got twelve patients in two hours.

I spent eleven days in August in room eleven on Mary Ward and they gave me eleven pints of blood intravenously. 'I tell you, you've got a few spelling mistakes there in that bit I just read, and I'm not British,' says a pretty young nurse whose accent I don't recognise. 'Oh really, not British, where are you from?' 'Dutch, I'm from Holland.' I shouldn't have had that glass of beer last night.'

11 AUGUST

Day to day, vomiting blood.

14 AUGUST

Flashback: I woke up at five o'clock parched, drank Perrier water and rushed into the bathroom and threw up in the toilet bowl. Horror – even worse it seemed in daylight – no it wasn't yet light, the great big orange moon filled the sky as I staggered into the kitchen to make camomile tea. I knew I had to ring for help but it took ½ an hour before I dialed 999 for an ambulance, which came in 15 minutes. The driver and his female assistant were very hostile because I walked down the stairs to the awaiting vehicle. She put herself physically between me and where I could have laid down – 'No, you can sit.' What's your name, how old are you . . . I answered clinging on, everything going round, thinking of Denton Welch and a voice through a cloud and Nil by Mouth.

When we arrived the driver said, 'That'll be £250.' I gave a feeble laugh, but he wasn't joking. 'That's what it costs, £250,' he shouted. They were both convinced that I was a charlatan and made their feelings clear. 'Here, he's been vomiting blood,' he said, handing over the hastily scribbled incorrect form to the night nurse. She took me into a little cubicle just off the Emergency Entrance with a high-cot – instructed me to undress and for a long time I thought I was in St Mary's Paddington because that's what it said on the gown she gave me to put on. I lay in the cold, unable to reach Beryl's last lovely sweater. I was questioned and prodded by a series of doctors while a glorious day dawned. I traced the sun as it shone across the wall of the little room, answered all the questions honestly. At 8 o'clock precisely I was wheeled in a chair to have three chest x-rays. Very cold and depressing was the x-ray department, as I waited I felt very old and decrepit.

The third doctor has lovely dark eyes. I connected with her on visuals. She is called Melanie Smith and again during all the tests I told her of champagne and good food in Paris and when I first threw up, the osteopath who made everything worse, the endless Anadin Extra, the endless pain throwing up, vomiting blood last night, the inhuman treatment of the ambulance crew. 'I'm not a charlatan,' I wailed.

Internal haemorrhage. Suddenly then all the stops were pulled out. Please lay back on the cot, Mr Clark, please, pulling me, but I know it comes up better standing, and I didn't want it get all the horrible, vile, multi-colour mucus and blood into my clean but dishevelled hair.

Finally, it was over and I sank down, panting, a named, numbered wrist tag attached.

Flinching in pain as the doctor jabbed an intravenous saline drip and Melanie almost screaming into me ear, 'Mr Clark, you must tell us honestly. We must know, are you in any danger from HIV contact?' – No.

No dates recorded, all in one narrative. Newton Ward was absolute bliss: cocooned in crisp cotton sheets, a great high ceiling, sunlight flooding in, drip-fed and monitored every half an hour, pulse rate and blood-pressure both, on my back and sitting upright. The first in a line of dedicated nurses, a cadaver in the next bed and later one opposite. A sleeping corpse.

I thought of Derek Jarman as I watched the saline fluid drip drip – felt very content except I longed for a major dump.

15 AUGUST

Bedlam in Mary Ward – I was transferred to Mary Ward because the other is short-term admissions. I felt as though I was being punished – in an open ward and into a bed someone had just died in, surrounded by old men suffering from Senile Dementia – the man in the next bed repeated everything anyone passing said – his name was Tom.

MONDAY, 24 AUGUST

Five to four in the afternoon, St Charles Hospital, W10, Mary Ward. Waiting for my blood analysis, if the hemoglobin is OK I can go home – can it really be all over? I've packed everything up, George has brought my flat keys, he arrived while I was bathing, after two. Oscar in the car.

13 SEPTEMBER

Anthony Perkins[35] died of AIDS last night in Los Angeles. I almost met him once – came face to face at a party at the top of the 6's in NY after a Rolling Stones concert at Madison Square Gardens – it was Mick[36]'s 30th birthday. 'Here's somebody I thought I'd never meet,' I said, very stoned and offering my hand – but Tony Perkins just took one look, turned and fled in the opposite direction. Bob Dylan treated me in a similar fashion but then somebody had given him a small bottle, ⅓ full of white powder labelled Pure Hydrochloric Merc, produce of Western Germany, and I got the mayor of New York City to autograph my back-stage pass.

22 SEPTEMBER

Dad, this is Albert. I'm terribly sorry to hear about Oscar. Hope you're taking it well. Phoned to say hi, see what you're doing. I'm at work, I was gonna pop around but can't now. See you later. Bye Bye.

17 OCTOBER

Ossie, hi, it's Bella. Very funny message, erm, I'm just ringing to say I'm going to Spain for 10 days today and I'm just ringing to see how you were, say goodbye and hope to see you when I come back. I just wanted to thank you for all your help. You've been absolutely incredible and it's been a real honour to have you helping, umm, anyway I would love to see you when I come back. I'll be back on the 27th and perhaps you could come and have tea or lunch or anything, anyway, lots of love. Clunk.

22 OCTOBER

Albert's 23rd birthday, and Oscar died 34 days ago. There, I've written it down.

29 DECEMBER

Not a day goes by without me thinking about Oscar. I miss him so very much and I'm reminded of him constantly.

Today Albert phoned me to see how I am. He had been in St Charles Hospital with a nasty burn and said he might come and see me. But he didn't, which is just as well because my flat is in a very untidy state and my morale very low. All I do is read and watch television in bed – no energy to do anything else. No enjoyment in food – everything I put in my stomach a gamble. Pains, vomiting and diarrhoea. I've given up chanting and feel very sorry for myself.

Albert too seemed a bit down. He had worked all over the Christmas holiday. Talked about going on holiday for a couple of weeks. I long to swim in the Caribbean but it just seems an impossible dream.

1 Sandra and Michael Kamen.
2 Carla Ames.
3 Henrietta Rous.
4 Hedley Marten.
5 Adie Hunter.
6 Richard O'Brien, British actor, famous for his role in *The Rocky Horror Picture Show*, which he also wrote.
7 The car Ossie crashed was on loan from Hedley Marten.
8 Billy Henry.
9 A lover of Ossie's.
10 Patrick Procktor.
11 Nick Balaban.
12 Henry Tennant.
13 Peter Lee's art dealer.
14 Notting Hill Gate.
15 Ulla Larson.
16 Marlene Dietrich.
17 Carol Hammond.
18 Kay Melia.
19 Gladys English.
20 Justine Silver, Buddhist friend.
21 Patrick Procktor's new boyfriend.
22 Morning gongyo.
23 Jose Fonseca. Ossie is designing her a yellow silk sari.
24 One of the organisers of the show.
25 John Hurt, British actor.
26 Lyle Lovett, American country and western singer/songwriter.
27 In the film *From Here to Eternity*.
28 Andre Agassi, American tennis star.
29 A Buddhist friend of Ossie.
30 Bianca Jagger.
31 Evening Gongyo.
32 Mrs Roberts was Henrietta Rous' cleaner. She and Ossie had a somewhat contentious relationship.
33 Mo McDermott.
34 A lover of Ossie's.
35 Anthony Perkins, American actor, the star of *Psycho*.
36 Mick Jagger.

1993

This year's diary is very thin. Ossie begins the year at an all-time low, having taken a break from his Buddhist practices at the end of 1992 and succumbed to his pain and sorrow at the loss of Oscar. Bill Weston, Ossie's Buddhist mentor, said that he felt that Ossie had real strength, but that the black dog, depression, would drag him right down; then he would realise that this was unsatisfactory and spring up again, reasserting himself. Ossie would argue with Bill about his failure to practise, saying that 'hitting the weed' was his alternative. Bill says, 'He could be very tough and selfish, but there would always be a candle burning in one little corner of himself, however dire circumstances were.'

The most important influence on Ossie this year was the acceleration of Nick's illness. His frailty and demoralisation had been charted in the previous year: 'Like a sledgehammer, the inescapable fact slams into my consciousness. Is he going to?' Ossie witnesses Nick's physical decline: in February he is in the Moorfield Eye Hospital with shingles in his right eye; by August he is back in hospital.

Despite numerous sexual encounters over the years since 1978, it has always been to Nick that Ossie has returned emotionally. Now he finds Nick's deterioration too painful to write about. Nick goes blind and wastes away in front of his friends and family in Chelsea and Westminster Hospital. Ossie is not in the regular group of school friends who visit him. He minds too much. He bursts into tears in the Orangery in Holland Park and confides to Guy Burch, Nick's closest friend, 'I can't bear it. I feel completely useless.' It will be Carla who comforts Ossie after the small, colourful funeral in January 1994; he will return with her and sob uncontrollably. Molly Balaban, Nick's mother, will remain very fond of Ossie; he had always treated her with respect and generosity.

Ossie seems calm and practical. He has to move his massive sewing machine out of Sutherland Place because the house has been sold. This is a blow; he had been a frequent and welcome guest and the house provided him with the space he needed to cut important commissions. Bella Freud helps him and he assists her with her pattern-cutting for the spring collection. 'I showed Bella how to cut the skirt and cut the collar on a jacket. Pattern-cutters are only taught to cut straight up and down.'

In February Ossie is acknowledged in an article by Liz Smith, a long-time admirer, in W Magazine. Liz traces the effect of 'Le Flou' in Karl Lagerfeld to Ossie's 'long fluid high-waisted seventies line'. 'Ossie' scrawled in a few notebooks at recent collections was the shorthand for this look. There is much nostalgic reference now in the fashion press to the seventies, and Thierry Mugler tells in Elle Magazine how his sculpted seaming was inspired by Ossie. Ossie accepts these compliments drily.

He is in touch with Michael Fish, Ulla, his sister Kay, and Pam Procter. He visits the sauna baths, but does not comment on his encounters. His flat is still a mess and he is dependent on sick notes from his psychiatrist, Michael a'Brook, from whom he has regular prescriptions for valium and amphetamines. In August some of his clothes are featured in a sixties night at the Kensington Hilton, but he makes no comment on this.

It is almost certainly the effect of Nick's death that prevents Ossie writing in his diary for almost a year – the last four months of 1993 and the first half of 1994. It seems that he is withdrawn and inwardly broken by this loss and cannot express his grief at the time.

20 JANUARY

Shit like lead.

2.35 'Why don't you go work in NY?' Albert here, on the telephone to George.

DH is keen to get Gregory[1] back who's keeping him at arm's length but busy spending on Hockney's credit card. David meanwhile is trying to tempt him with a groovy new chef.

Albert meanwhile told me all about his safari in Africa and showed me photographs with elephants and giraffes in the background.

3 FEBRUARY

There was a postcard from Nick[2] in Egypt when I got back from Devon on Monday. He rang at eleven. 'Did you have a good time?' I asked. 'Well, no. I had to come back early because I've got this infection in my left eye. I'm in the Moorfield eye hospital.' So I went to see him, taking the broken answerphone to Paddington on the way. I found him in a private room on the top corridor and lying on a bed with a drip to the vein in his neck. It's his right eye and he's got shingles in it.

10 FEBRUARY

11 stone in the sauna.

12 FEBRUARY
I woke after nine. It was quite pleasant to get up early for a change. The sick note from Michael a'Brook has been working. Done. So I've filled it in – it's dated 4/2/93 – and put it into an envelope addressed to Box 8, Glasgow. And I'm just about to put it into the post.

5 MARCH
Tanya[3]'s show at Café de Paris, Leicester Square.

9 MARCH
Streaming sunlight at 8 o'clock.
Percy Savage rang to tell me my picture's in the *Herald Tribune*.

9 AUGUST
Sick note to the DSS dated today.

13 AUGUST
Nick phoned from hospital. He is poorly again.

17 AUGUST
2.40 Kensington Hilton, Boardroom No. 1. BBC Sixties Night.

1 Gregory Evans.
2 Nick Balaban.
3 Tanya Sarne.

1994

There are three large diaries for 1994. One is written in the same type of day planner as 1993's diary and many of the September entries are written on the March and April pages; all three diaries are full of sketches, glued-in business cards and supermarket receipts, a reminder of Andy Warhol days. Ossie's handwriting is larger and more of a scrawl than previously. Some events are reported in all three diaries, and it is clear that Ossie returned to the diaries at a later date to revise or add information.

The year is dominated by the first diary entry; on 3 January Ossie wrote simply, 'Nick died.' The rest of the three journals is largely a record of Ossie's reaction to this. For the first seven months of the year Ossie was obviously in great pain and his entries are extremely sparse and concise. As at other times, after the deaths of friends or family, Ossie seems too upset to record his feelings in any depth or detail, unable to face the reality of his loss. In August he re-emerges, at first only to record his determination to 'restart the chemical way of life', a return to prescription drugs to get him through the physical and emotional pain.

Thereafter the diary is full of mood swings. Ossie had been in love with Nick since 1978 and had clung to the lingering hope that he would return to him, just as he had romantically and unrealistically pronounced in 1978, 'Celia and I were made for each other' years after she had declared that she could no longer bear the turmoil and cruelty. However, Nick's death also seems to have a liberating effect and in the last five months of the year he rediscovers himself and the determination to address his problems in a practical way. Then, he feels he is achieving a lot and charts his attempt to get back into business again. He becomes intensely social, often paying three or four calls a day. He sees a lot of his sons, but little of Celia; George is working in Celia's shop and Albert is head chef at 192, the chic restaurant in Kensington Park Road. Ossie does plenty of satisfactory gongyho with Justine Silver and his Gohonzon is re-enshrined by Bill Weston.

Again, Ossie transcribes answer-machine messages and he becomes obsessed by the precise timing of incidents and even the number of minutes between stations. He writes 700 words on Gerlinda Costiff's funeral.

Vanessa Denza, an old friend and international fashion consultant, believes in him and helps him set up his company with the help of Maggie Watson and solicitor Margaret Bennett. He hopes to raise £240,000 and attract investment from former friends in the music world including Mick Jagger and Dave Gilmour. The latter gives him £15,000 for 'business only', and Ossie is then busy throughout the year writing letters to other potential backers and viewing potential studios.

The recovery of his spirits and self-esteem are matched by renewed attention from the media. An article in the Evening Standard magazine, E.S., ends, 'Ossie, come back! Can anything coax this genius out of retirement?' Ossie is referred to as an icon in an industry where it is easy to become a 'has-been' if you skip a single season. In Bella Freud's opinion, there is a nostalgic move back to the romance of the seventies. Even Naomi Campbell and Susie Bick dress themselves in Ossie's romantic chiffons. He is encouraged by the numerous inclusions of his work in the *Vogue History of Twentieth-Century Fashion* and appears 'full of ideas'.

The highlight of the year is a trip to Dave Gilmour's house in Lindos. Ossie is in overdrive; he is a maestro in the kitchen, swims by starlight, draws and deliberately misses the plane home to see the new moon. He is definitely moving into a new phase of vigorous optimism and it seems for the first time in many years that he may be close to a comeback. There is still a very noticeable difference between him and his old friend Manolo Blahnik whom he declares has the look of a 'successful businessman'; Ossie can get good seats for the Vivienne Westwood show but not the best ones. Indeed, he does not seem to be as famous this year as Oz Clarke, the wine critic, for whom he is mistaken by the Daily Telegraph, something that causes him great indignation.

Ossie still has bad luck – another car crash and a fall from a donkey – and is frequently unwell. However, the last time we hear from him, he is feverishly working on a new design and full of enthusiasm. Instead of chanting for his emergence as a designer, he longs for love. Just as, in the past he was naive in his business dealings, soon he will prove himself to be unguarded in his final choice of a companion.

3 JANUARY

Nick[1] died.

7 JANUARY

Rugged is my favourite word.
If I had my way even workmen would wear velvet every day.

16 MARCH
Unprotected sex.

13 MAY
Oh, my God, another ulcer. This time at the top of my stomach. Hospital again.

27 JULY
Michael a'Brook at nine. I determined this time I'd ask for my old pills again.

1 AUGUST
I restart the chemical way of life. I heard the prescription (addressed in Michael a'Brook's shaky handwriting) as it fell through the letterbox. Gone his luxurious notepaper. Penned in biro from a state clinic in Southend-on-Sea. Something to get up for. First I thought I'd rush there unshaven. But once I got up I had second thoughts. On impulse I rang Patrick[2] and read the *Daily Mail* with extracts from Marianne's forthcoming book[3]. Deeply engrossed, I arrived outside the old chemist in Paddington Street, and it was gone. Bewildered, unbelieving, only glancing up the street trying to think of an alternative. I went on to Manchester Street. Patrick let me in, rubbing ointment into his jaws, had a long moan after he told me the chemist had moved over the road. 'Yes, but what am I going to do, Ossie? I'm drinking vodka. Already I drink bottles. I smoke and I'm not well. Will you have one, dear? It's frightfully early, but I've been having a hell of a time.'

Marianne Faithfull, still a loyal friend to Ossie.

I only took one pill to begin.

2 AUGUST
Dealing with a nasty letter from the Council.
I pick up my abandoned journal again.
Stopped taking Prozac.

4 AUGUST
Terrible pain. 2 hours of hell. Vomit. Shits.

8 AUGUST

I was very disappointed, still 11 stone 4lb in the sauna, but I met a very nice man called Tony. A drama teacher.

17 AUGUST

Wearing Nick's waistcoat. Chris Jagger rang again. 'It's all on with the *Saturday Express*, and guess what, they'll pay you five hundred[4].'

'Will they?' Flabbergasted.

18 AUGUST

Slept in the clean room. The bokara devoured by moths. Ugh. The dust of years swept and sucked into the vacuum cleaner.

20 AUGUST

Billy[5] very morbid and down, so I brought him breakfast. I dipped into my little stash of £50's I've saved since not spending in Tangiers last year.

23 AUGUST

'And do you empty your ashtrays? All I seem to do is go round emptying the ashtrays.' said Patrick Proctor on the telephone.

24 AUGUST

Woke before 8 in a sweat.

I've a desire to buy some fish from Shepherd's Bush Market. Seven little fishes with my dole money.

Daily Mail water test. Stupid cunt wanted Oz Clark the wine expert.

The day just fizzled away.

25 AUGUST

A nasty dream about rejection. Very horrid.

Walking through Holland Park, two policemen took my particulars because I stole a rosebud and a frond of yellow jasmine for my outgoing August posie.

Teatime. Henrietta[6] rushed in; her arms drop, releasing various bags, newspapers, *Hello* magazine with Richard Branson on the cover. They spilled on to the cushions and floor, not even noticing my great effort at the clean up – the space – 'Look, I've made a great effort at last.' She stopped in her tracks, mouth open. 'Look at the kitchen floor. I got on my hands and knees and scrubbed it. My back is killing me.'

I told Guy[7] of wearing Nick's boots and the good feelings I got. Since he died I've thought of him every morning when I woke up. 'Ugh, Nick's dead. I wish I could go back to sleep. And Oscar.' But the day after I wore his boots, and the waistcoat I'd already worn and fallen in love with – the wide safe pockets which hold the Gongyo book – something changed.

26 AUGUST

Walking around the Serpentine. All I wanted to do was to weigh myself in the sauna. I'm sure I've lost a couple of pounds.

News – Maggie Thatcher's got a drink problem.

28 AUGUST

Carnival Sunday at Carla[8]'s. Hard-core music and nine pretty policemen, I counted outside.

1 SEPTEMBER

Haywire day. Collected the miniature gold jacket I made for George from Nancy Howard. She gave me all the gossip about Polly Gilmour[9] and the Pink Floyd tour, which Tony[10] is on. (Ginger[11] wasn't the, how shall I put it . . .? But in comparison she was a pussycat.)

Say what you like about Steve O'Rourke; you must give him his due. They have got a number one album and the tour is sold out worldwide.

I spoke to Jose[12] who says I must make it up with Celia. Long chat. Cutting at Ghost.

I've told everyone the story of Nick's boots now – it's become a myth and a Buddhist legend already, and somewhat odd as I thought, even as I put them on, of Derek Jarman and his collection of dead men's shoes.

2 SEPTEMBER

Wonderful shits.

I've just spoken to Nancy Howard who had seen Ulla[13] in Fulham Road. So I went to collect her. She was so amazed by the transformation and admitted she'd thought I was never coming back.

3 SEPTEMBER

I went to collect Ulla at 1.30. It began to rain but we still walked down Portobello. The last crisp fifty pound note. A day with Ulla is exhausting.

4 SEPTEMBER

A swim in Highgate pond. Home at 5.30, bursting with ideas.

Started painting.

5 SEPTEMBER

A really fabulous shit. 12" at least. Fluffy cotton-wool floater. The diet really seems to be working – beanshoots, peppers, ginger, garlic, rice; orange juice freshly squeezed every day. Only one coffee to wake and I'm really off. I still haven't weighed myself but my belt two notches tighter.

Inadvertently I took the wrong pill before eating my dinner – I took 8 milligrams of Valium but ended up going to sleep.

Everything wonderful except for a mosquito bite.

7 SEPTEMBER

Five mins in Holland Park to steal a rose for Gladys[14] and hope to see the new moon and smoke a joint.

Beautiful evening, I changed into green.

During Gongyo I smashed the beautiful green vase I've been using for a gong. I've had a premonition it would happen. I took it lightly. Slept on the daybed with three cushions.

8 SEPTEMBER

A very sleepy morning Gongyo using the old gong. Desolate at the loss of my green vase which sounds so beautiful, and I just had to go back to bed.

I had the shits all day and – instead of facing Tanya at Ghost – I was staggering down Portobello and had to pay 20p.

And the new moon. Such a pale silver. Now everything will go right.

10 SEPTEMBER

Farting at Justine[15]'s. Eating delicious food. Came in a taxi from Bella Freud where I've been working all afternoon, chanting for Billy to appear. Where are you?

12 SEPTEMBER

Manolo Blahnik looks every inch the successful businessman.

Nobody knows how to cut anymore.

Was amazed by my red T-shirt I'd taken for the colour. Very good red.

Vivid as geraniums.

13 SEPTEMBER

Wonderful morning Gongyo at All Saints Road. But on the way I felt a bit queasy and realised I had forgotten to take my omeprozol. So now at Carla's where she is ironing the red, hoping it will fit Tanya.

'Make one that fits everybody.'

'Would you rather have the old me back?'

'You criticise everything I do.'

'No, I'm not greedy darling, I just like a lot.'

14 SEPTEMBER
Henrietta phoned, has to go somewhere ghastly called Brent's Cross.

15 SEPTEMBER
Long conversation with Britt[16]. I rang to thank her for the loan of the Rock Python coat[17]. She's going to be my first client.
I rang Bella, she thinks Chris Jagger's a bit of a joke and Tanya Sarne's clothes are passé.

16 SEPTEMBER
9.00 Cocaine. Naughty. The oh-so-familiar folded paper package. Still up at half five. Absolutely smashed out of our brains.
I cried at Ulla's reading about my hospital trip in this journal but it was actually the moment I realised both Oscar and Nick were going to die – that May Day in 1992 on Highgate ponds.

17 SEPTEMBER
Billy at the Venus and no more pills. The hashish doesn't seem to work without them and Gongyo more difficult. 'The paranoia is beginning to go.' Ian still here at 3.43. I'm just off to Bella Freud's studio to make Henri's dress and visit Carla.

18 SEPTEMBER
Woke with the shits and wondered what caused it. Carla's chicken cooked two ways and delicious or Justine's bread and butter pudding.

19 SEPTEMBER
10 stone 6 pounds in the sauna. Yippee. That means I've lost 12 pounds since 8th August.

20 SEPTEMBER
Bad news. The carpet has been stolen. I wish Michael a' Brook would phone.

24 SEPTEMBER
Today Billy came. Just as miserable.

25 SEPTEMBER
Vomiting. Diarrhoea.

26 SEPTEMBER
10st 5lb in the sauna.

Maggie Watson – long talk – she'll ring me on Thursday. Unlimited resources from a Greek accountant.

27 SEPTEMBER

[*Plans already seem up and running in relation to the creation of Ossie's new company. But there is little mention of them in the diaries.*]

Maggie Watson phoned. Her meeting went very well. Basically I can do what I want. But again the shits – just water pouring out of me. No pain, thank God, but up and down all night.

29 SEPTEMBER1

Early rise for the postman – a'Brook's handwriting. Gongyo with Justine then to Peter's Pharmacy in Paddington Street. 'You're looking better, Mr Clark.'

I listened to the new Pink Floyd album at Gillian Bobroff's, whose lyrics include, 'You can have everything you want.'

My God, I'm knackered. But so much achieved.

30 SEPTEMBER

With my weightlifter's belt on the tightest eyelet hole, I started to scrub the bedroom floor.

2 OCTOBER

[*Guy Buirch brings round some of Nick's belongings.*]

My place was a complete mess. I apologised. 'Oh, how unusual.' Sarcasm with an understanding smile – gentle. It was only when Nick was a real goner I can write it now, nine months later. When he was first in the Chelsea and Westminster in the end bed with the horrible view of a blank brick wall which, despite the modernity and vast atrium, I found it so deeply depressing.

4 OCTOBER

No money. No hashish, but feeling fine.

Tanya has lost a stone in weight.

5 OCTOBER

What a darling Tanya is. She gave me £50.

Found a Hockney drawing.

'I've got everything I've ever wanted, what have you got?' said Robert

Mapplethorpe to Derek Jarman when they met in Heaven. RM estate reputedly worth £250 million.

8 OCTOBER
Bella Freud's show.

14 OCTOBER
Chris Jagger rang up to tell me the *Express* article comes out in two weeks – and that he is a going away for 10 days and how can he get a stain out of his favourite green suede trousers.

18 OCTOBER
Mike the carpenter for help.
Michael a'Brook for a new sick note.
Tanya for whatever I can get.
It is the most beautiful day – the sky is so blue and cloudless. So tranquil. The leaves are turning gold. How to describe the blue? Organising a flight to Rhodes and talking to Kay[18] who doesn't want to go.

21 OCTOBER
Ghost to upgrade the safari jacket. Incredibly Henrietta was at the ground-floor door – so drove me to Ghost where everyone was smiling and I put my safari jacket pattern on to the computer and Tanya gave me 200 quid.

25 OCTOBER
Celia, Celia, when I am sad and weary,
When I think all hope has gone,
When I walk along High Holborn
I think of you with nothing on.

26 OCTOBER
[*Ossie, George, Roger Dixon and Henrietta Rous fly to Rhodes to spend a week in David Gilmour's house in Lindos*.]

Everyone relaxed and happy to have arrived safely. And the Lada – I can't wait to tell my friends that Dave Gilmour owns a Lada.

27 OCTOBER
Up at 8.20. Brilliant sunshine. Cloudless blue sky glittering on the sea. Butterflies all over the vine. Buzzing insects. I want to draw everything. But instead down to St Paul's Bay where I swam through and round the rocks.

I did morning Gongyo with Hen. A drawing lesson. 'My ego is going to wilt rather,' said Henrietta because I told her she can't read poetry.

30 OCTOBER

12.31 Tarot reading one hour. Actually took until 3.20 and it was a fabulous experience.

[*Here Ossie takes pages and pages of notes on his Tarot reading.*]

3.30 And I must go for a pee.

31 OCTOBER

Oddly enough, it was George who got it in the neck. Shouting at the top of my voice – in the kitchen for the others to overhear – I gave him a few home truths about DH and how he was very instrumental in breaking up my marriage to Celia.

3 NOVEMBER

Horrible day. I fell off a donkey, bruising my arm, hand and hip. In shock. We had to take a taxi to the airport, blew my last £40.

4 NOVEMBER

The phone pinged at 5 and I couldn't sleep, so I climbed the Acropolis where I saw the sun rise above the haze over the sea and did the first prayer of morning Gongyo. I made my way back, passing the skull and carcass of a goat. I sat in the amphitheatre and experienced a feeling of how it must have been in the past – the goat's farts echoing with perfect acoustics.

6 NOVEMBER

Athens international airport 9.15. Henrietta trying to get hold of her Greek millionaire friend Evangelos because we have got three hours until the 12.15 flight to London. My God, what a dramatic morning so far – unbelievable. Up at 5, we left Lindos in the white Lada before dawn. What could go wrong? Well, at 6.10 we ran out of petrol on an almost deserted road. For some unknown reason I remained completely calm while she went bananas, blaming everybody but herself, even though I'd said last night perhaps we should get more petrol because it would be dreadful if we ran out, knowing the garages don't open until 7. 'Bloody Dave Gilmour, fancy having a car with no petrol garage' etc. Bloody this, bloody that. We flagged down three cars before we got any sympathy from a huntsman with two dogs in the open back of his truck. No English. He was like Jack the Giant Killer, a true Greek from the interior, unbismirched by the greed of all the Greeks in the tourist villages. I insisted she go with him to the next village towards Rhodos and, chilly as it was, sat in the defunked car and recited first prayer of morning Gongyo, watching the precious minutes tick by on the turquoise blue Swatch. She came back at 6.30 with a smile on her face, but the plan to siphon some petrol from the tank didn't work – I tried, and even though I got a mouthful of vile gasoline and an inch of the precious fuel into the bottom of the plastic bucket, no more would come. I felt sick and longed to vomit. All seemed lost again. But miraculously two trucks stopped again, going towards Lindos – and two men very helpful indeed. One got on to the ground under the huntsman's vehicle and with a universal spanner drained off $^1/_2$ a bucketful of petrol and the other made a funnel out of a plastic washing-up bottle. And off we got, with Henrietta shivering in shock as we drove, complaining still about some wretched taxi man who was a complete cunt.

It was light now and imperative we find the short cut to the airport, marked only by a sign. A very suave, handsome young solider with perfect English directed us and promised to ring the airport. We arrived at 7.18 and the plane was held for us, unbelievable.

10 NOVEMBER

Kinky Gerlinka'[19]s funeral. I console Michael who pushes me away. 'Go take your seat.' Inside packed. An outrageous pink shocking dress. So many flowers everywhere. We are all given a candle as we enter. Incense. A beautiful church. A beautiful sea of colour against a medieval backdrop. 'If I could have my wishes, wishes, wishes, it would to be happy.' Gerlinka's favourite song. Tears and snuffling all around.

The organist arrives late. Caught up in traffic. The priest is telling us about her life. Born in Germany. 'Always give it a try, darling.' 'Darling, don't go into such a twitch about it. When you wake up with glitter in your house, you know you've had a good time.' Life is a song, game, challenge. A candle-lighting ceremony. 'Let's dance,' sings Donna Summer. A muscleman in a see-through T-shirt standing by the altar fights to hold back from crying. I say sansho as I light mine and write now, sitting at the back. Passing a bearded drag queen dressed in lime-green and pink. So I put my roses on the coffin. 'Let's dance' is played again, to cope with the crowd. There must be three of four hundred people here. Looking along my row, Chelita[20] looks directly into my eyes, but no more. I blank her. She looks ghastly, overpainted like a witch. Bright red lips, a checkered black and white hat, a tissue for her nose. The queue goes on from the outrageous to the very traditional. Oh! look at those three with black veils. Shaven heads. A lotta wigs. Black suits too tight around the hips. Of all the drag queens, Y was the most demure in a simple black cape and Manolo Blahnik suede slingbacks. Fabio, a South American boy who Gerlinde loved, is completely broken down in grief. The candles have set fire to a man. Outside a South American band of twenty, playing drums and maracas. Samba music. A fabulous finale. Then Carol[21] suddenly attacked me, I know you're on those pills again. Everybody knows. 'We're all worried about you.' Which completely brought me down. And I'm still down at twenty past four.

How Gerlinka died: she flew home from Miami four days early. She was alone when she got back from the airport. Opened the front door, put down her bags and boom, she dropped dead. Fabulous exit.

Chutzpah.

11 NOVEMBER

Woke at seven, hungover up to twenty to eight. Very good day. Altogether I organised and tidied my flat. More and more it's coming together. Did morning Gongyo while two handsome men began to install a fence.

Errol is so mean; he brought the smallest tube of KY. No comb. No poppers. 'Is it real?' he asked in total amazement when I pointed out the single lily from Gerlinde's funeral. He thought it was plastic, and I've got a bruised cock, I discover in the bath later.

Death slams like a sledgehammer. But so regularly since Nick, I'm desensitised.

12 NOVEMBER

The idiot children outside playing football. So I complain to the police rather than face the tall and gangling blonde 14-year-old. I hid the hashish but nothing happened. Just after one, a horrible scowling face confronted me through the glass of the front door. I had to force my way out, banging the door hard against his foot, ignoring him and using all my strength to bash my way. Barred by Ryan, an evil bully aged 13, already 6 foot tall.

Home at ten past four, having scored everything without money. Even the beige trousers from the cleaners without paying. To wear to the Vivienne Westwood show tomorrow at Liberty's.

13 NOVEMBER

[*Vivienne Westwood's show.*]

Twenty-five to four. We got the best seats in the house.

Rolling a joint in the basement toilet. Back upstairs we are still the only people in the front row. 'How can somebody of 5 foot 5 wear a hat like dat?' Tracy Ullman arrives. It's after 4. Nobody we know, says Ulla. Of course, the 6 o'clock show will be fabulous.

Well done, Vivienne. Fabulous girls. French milk maid, Venice masked balls, Punch and Judy, Spanish riding school. The show was just an exhibition of spending money.

16 NOVEMBER

Looking up the word 'ponce' in the dictionary.

17 NOVEMBER

Watching Dave Gilmour go through his once a week work-out. This isn't very vigorous.

21 NOVEMBER

Nadia[22] rang overjoyed, but Lorenzo[23] tells me she was sizzling like hot oil and she's had liposuction and she's still gross.

22 NOVEMBER

Gate-crashed Lord Snowdon's photographic exhibition.

23 NOVEMBER

[*Ossie has once again crashed Henrietta's car.*]

A message from Henrietta, fuming. 'Ossie, I'd like you to make a proper contribution for wrecking the car for the fourth time. You're unbelievable, absolutely irresponsible.' Oh, dear, I don't think I'll hear from Henri for a while. Not 'till after the weekend at least.

Michael a'Brook gave me three months prescription before he got up the stairs. We drank the last of the 12-year-old single malt whisky.

24 NOVEMBER

Brian Harris here crunching biscuits like a horse. Deaf as a post. 'He, who travels alone,' he tells me, 'travels farthest,' when I asked him if he had a lover yet.

Beautiful Nick Kamen[24] – you have got beautiful hands – while I tell him how much I adore Neil Young – 'The Needle and The Damage Done.'

25 NOVEMBER

Henrietta called, quite calm despite the £400 car bill.

26 NOVEMBER

Hate to admit it but I've got a pain in my chest.

The chrome yellow leaves cling on to the mild weather – it was 61 the other day, though now it's colder. The birds are behaving in a very peculiar way. I heard seagulls cry for the first time in ages. It's a bit Hitchcock, sparrows flocking or feeding in masses.

28 NOVEMBER

No money. I've still got a pain in my chest. Is it still getting worse? When I cough it feels like I've been punched in the chest. Ouch.

'Do you like Karate?' asked the shop girl, noticing my belt as I buy a bottle of Chardonnay. And I drink the whole bottle to myself.

29 NOVEMBER

Vanessa Denza. Basically I've got to raise 50 thousand pounds by the end of the year.

Lorenzo's going to take me to Jade[25]'s opening. Please be there, Mick[26]. Please, nam myoho rengi kyo.

[Later] At Jade's, 'How's your mother?'

'OK.'

'How's your father?'

'OK.'

Jade's pregnant and Lynn Franks so pleased I'm looking so good and keen to work.

30 NOVEMBER

Talk about mystic. I rushed out at three to go and see Sue at the Pink Floyd office. When Dave Gilmour drove by in his Merc.

Teddy Millington Drake dead. Death comes knocking every day.

1 DECEMBER

Oh, my bloody aching back. I must remake my belt.

At last I have pinned Dave Gilmour down for lunch next Weds at 192 – everything continues to go swimmingly. I just need £50,000 by the New Year and I'm in business again.

2 DECEMBER

I knew when I found the green perspex clothes-peg with little crabs and sea creatures trapped in it, that I would meet an interesting person born under the sign of Cancer. I knew he would be special, but I never dreamt it would be a 13-year-old boy with a thick American accent and perfect French.

I am a corrupter of youth; I am the tick in the sheep's flank. Corruption is the wrong word.

3 DECEMBER

Unprotected sex with a leatherman.

5 DECEMBER

People used to think of me as the frivolous young floozy. That's daft. Now I'm older and ugly, not so beautiful and successful, people are beginning to take me seriously.

7 DECEMBER

Lunch with Dave Gilmour at 192. Ask for the money and grab it.

Ulla's bash for Rosita but I didn't go. In the bath I decided evening Gongyo much more important. Whatever next?

Christopher Tennant talking about a Gala[27] in Mustique, telling me if I mention his father's name I can get a cheap ticket.

8 DECEMBER

3.30 Tea with Dave Gilmour.

9 DECEMBER

[*Ossie writes to Steve and Linda O'Rourke, looking for financial backing for his new company.*]

'Will you be an angel in the theatrical sense and match Dave Gilmour with a small sum to finance a new venture to set me up in a studio which I've already found in St George's Street so I can design and produce clothes again?'

Yippee, say all the girls. It was Dave's idea to go about it like the Groucho Club was launched and he has set the ball rolling with 15 thousand, because I'm an old friend and he likes me. I'm about to tax Jagger with this same proposal and I hear he wants some new frocks. I figure if I get the right three names first the rest will follow – Michael Caine, David Frost, Paul Getty, Eric Clapton, etc. Even Rick Wright maybe, with a pretty new wife.

'What do you think? Will you consider it? I'll cross my fingers and chant.

With love, Ossie.'

10 DECEMBER

Skip hunting.

'George Harrison, will you sign my book?' – I didn't dare ask him if he dyes his hair. He talked about some clinic in America, said, 'You find out when you reach the top you're at the bottom.'

'If you don't know where you're going, any road will take you there.'

11 DECEMBER

Writing on Ulla's balcony, looking down over a wonderfully green lawn that's rippling like water with wind on it. She farts leaving the room, saying Ooh! Like she stood on a squeaky floorboard.

[*Ossie goes to a party at The Chelsea Arts Club, where Jocelyn Steele is performing.*]

She's playing music that seems chosen because it is difficult to play. The chairs creak as she hits the wrong notes and her upper arms wobble violently when she hammers the bass vibrato. At first I don't even want to sit down. We stood at the bar until I spied this round table; it was the bowl of crisps that prompted me to move.

7.20 A snooty man looks down his nose at the remains of the crisps – I'm so hungry I've eaten half – and from the bar interjects, taking them away. 'Excuse me, can we just share these?'

'Was she very good?' asks the woman who lent me her programme, to no one in particular. She turns out to be Diane Hart, now my lord, 68 years old. I sued the Aga Khan about a building in Thurloe Square. I did very well out of that. Made a film in 1970 with 4 mins of games that lovers play. I ask you, my lord, why should I appear in a film with a penis erect or not? I used to buy clothes from a woman in Edgware Rd. I was voted best actress and all my clothes were second-hand.

12 DECEMBER

In the *Vogue History of 20th Century Fashion* by Jane Mulvagh I've got 13 entries in the index. Well, fantastic.

13 DECEMBER

A card from Johnnie Rozza in LA. He's coming in March but he's got that look which the glasses and big hat can't disguise.

14 DECEMBER

I woke at 5.30 full of ideas. It was still dark when I got up so I went for a walk in Holland Park and picked some pink camellias and was sick.

Guy came dressed in leather to go to the Coleherne. Trousers, jacket, chest harness and a waistcoat that belonged to Nick. 'Ah, green eyes,' he said when he saw my little painting of him. 'It's nice to see him looking like that. The rose madder and turquoise of the sunset are the colours of his complexion.'

Guy came to tea and said that he'd heard somewhere that Pink Floyd have given eight million to charity.

I rang Lorenzo – absolutely fabulous – he's had a mole removed from his chin by laser.

16 DECEMBER

[*Ossie receives a call from Steve O'Rourke's office telling him that Steve would like to know the exact proposed structure for Ossie's company. Steve has also remarked that 'Angels in the Theatre take all the first profit, then 50 or 60% of any subsequent profit.' Ossie writes back saying the company will be in the hands of two directors.*]

First – Vanessa Denza – perhaps one of the most powerful women in not just British fashion but on a global scale. Big in Hong Kong, helped Tanya Sarne set up Ghost, who will produce my first collection. 12 pieces to sell on merit, with no mention of OC. Second – Maggie Watson – nice Yorkshire lass, intimate knowledge of fabric supplies and a knack of knowing trends two years before they happen. For the last eight years she's been in men's boxer shorts making a killing. Margaret Bennett is my lawyer. Utterly divine. Two shareholders could be my sons, Albert and George. The discharge from bankruptcy is a chore, but will take time. Maybe three months.

So there's great excitement humming through the rag trade and press. The buyer from Liberty's actually ran after me when I went to the Vivienne Westwood show. Rent £12,000 a year, rates £3,400. Maggie Watson has ordered some delicious black fabrics through her company Playful Clothing.

Now the return on the investment – well, how does that work in the theatre? I'm looking for 16 people who can afford the gamble, exactly like a musical. I'm after £240,000. You would share in the profit after corporation tax, I think.

I'm also faxing a copy of this to Margaret Bennett so she can write a more businesslike structure of the company. But I want to send this while the moon is still ascending. It wanes from Monday.

So, waddaya think? With Love, Ossie.

17 DECEMBER

Henrietta crashed the Sierra last night.

The boy I bought home last night works in food. 26. Tattooed. Already his body is going to seed. I never got to draw him properly and he stole my stash. The benefit being I tidied up my flat completely looking for it.

18 DECEMBER

One message. 'Ossie, unless you produce the chits for the garage thing, I'll never speak to you again. I just can't afford £300 down the drain like that.'

19 DECEMBER

Vanessa Denza 4.30, and I haven't even got the tube fare. Kenny next door to the rescue. His nature is so sweet. I arrived on time but had to wait an hour. Poor Vanessa looked very harassed and even actually a little bit grubby – dirty hair, grey complexion, worn-out old suit in need of a good cleaning – but her Xmas cake delicious, and cut open especially for me. But not the champagne which the fridge is full of.

21 DECEMBER

Hungover. Soon cleared away with the blue of the sky as I rushed to get my dole. I even had time to go to the doctor for more omeprozol and collected a little December posie and much more freshly fallen leaves on Landsdowne Road for a dress idea.

Errol at 12.30, just what I need. He didn't arrive 'till after one-thirty, harassed with the traffic. I soon had him happy, moaning in pleasure with a big cock up his arse pinned down to my bed. He soon had an orgasm and I pretended I did just to please him.

22 DECEMBER

Things are never as good as they appear.

23 DECEMBER

I woke at ten past five after 6 mil Valium and began vomiting and vomiting. Couldn't sleep. Up and down for more than two hours. After seven up came vile bile – the acid of the wine. And diarrhoea to boot. It was truly horrible.

24 DECEMBER

Up at 8.30 after a very good sleep. Strange how I don't seem to dream anymore.

28 DECEMBER

Ulla hung up on me because I was shouting. However, she's a stupid cunt telling me to go to Art School.

29 DECEMBER

I rang Ulla and apologised.

30 DECEMBER

My belt is almost complete. I'm stoned on hash and I want to draw the blue fading light. The leaves of the camellia fall as I fiddle with the python skin. My belt, now almost finished, is truly worthy. I wore it under the newly pocketed leather coat to buy skins and then I switched to drawing.

1 Nick Balaban.
2 Patrick Procktor.
3 *Faithfull*, co-written with David Dalton. Ossie was not mentioned in the book, a fact which upset him considerably.
4 Chris Jagger was trying to arrange an interview for Ossie to gain publicity for his career relaunch.
5 Billy Henry.
6 Henrietta Rous.
7 Guy Burch.
8 Carla Ames.
9 Polly Gilmour, second wife of David Gilmour.
10 Tony Howard.
11 Ginger Gilmour.
12 Jose Fonseca.
13 Ulla Larson.
14 Gladys English.
15 Justine Silver.
16 Britt Ekland.
17 Ekland has lent Ossie a coat she purchased from him in the sixties so he can lend it to the Victoria and Albert museum.
18 Kay Melia.
19 Kinky Gerlinka, outrageous club promoter.
20 Chelita Secunda.
21 Carol Hammond.
22 Nadia La Vallée. She had undergone minor plastic surgery.
23 Lorenzo Poccianti, Italian art photographer with whom Ossie had a brief affair.
24 Nick Kamen, model and singer; he is also a Buddhist.
25 Jade Jagger. Ossie was going to the opening of an exhibition of her paintings.
26 Mick Jagger.
27 Gala Mitchell.

1995

Ossie's purposefulness and creative energy of late 1994 are eroded this year by an unpropitious meeting in Notting Hill. In January Ossie is in flamboyant form. Over a weekend in the west country he insists on decorating a friend's house with massive branches of greenery and, at a wedding, sits drawing like the Pied Piper with teenage youths thronging around him. He is happy in his little flat, sewing away with country and western music playing in the background. Buddhism is still important and he performs morning and evening Gongyho.

However, the regularity and discipline of his life is blown apart when, after an evening with the Australian Buddhist Justine Silver, he encounters Diego Cogolato, a twenty-seven-year-old Italian, in Holland Park Avenue. Diego is searching for the Youth Hostel in Holland Park; Ossie invites him home.

Diego was considered good-looking by some; to others he had the look of the devil. When I asked Ossie what he was doing with someone so primitive, he replied, 'I like the peasant quality - Caravaggio, Henri.' He was referring to the juxtaposition of softness and violence, of light and dark. Ulla, Ossie's mentor and close friend, was instinctively concerned, warning Ossie to 'remember Joe Orton'. As the relationship progressed, it was clear that Diego was Ossie's 'dark angel', again a comment from Ulla.

Ossie and Diego descend into a Genetesque world. Poverty stricken, they sometimes fish for money in Holland Park. Diego sits around glowering in Penzance Street and rather brutishly insists on listening to heavy metal music. When he eventually finds work, it doesn't last long. He has no inclination. 'I don't want to do shitty jobs that I only get two pounds an hour for.'

Diego's presence is disconcerting to Ossie's friends, because he has repulsive manners and can only think of consuming as much alcohol as possible. Eventually Diego is discouraged from coming to many homes. Sandra Kamen always felt he was 'casing the joint', and Marisa Masters remembers him pacing uneasily from room to room. When he and Ossie visited Yorkshire, my sister felt Diego must be from the Mafia and sensed a brutal strength - how prophetic. Nadia and Swami La VallÈe, great admirers of Ossie, were horrified when the pair arrived and glugged a whole bottle of vodka in front of them. But Ossie was proud and besotted by his new companion and identified with him. When they were together, Diego dragged Ossie further and further down, and Ossie had to descend to his level.

However, Ossie is still appreciated and is a stimulating, if sometimes perverse, guest. At the Pink Floyd wedding party he makes off with an elaborate display of lilies he plans to present to my mother at Clovelly. He runs off with Joss Ackland's grandchildren to chant in Devon with Pam Procter.

However, with Diego things get seriously worse. Diego drops in at Kevin Whitney's at the end of a dinner party and is antagonised by Clive Bendon, who corrects his English and pats him paternalistically on the shoulder. Diego's eyes go cold and he picks up a bottle threateningly. He and Clive dance round the table. 'It was like a scene from the O.K. Corral,' Clive says. Diego smashes his fist down on the twenty glasses remaining from the dinner party, breaking them and cutting himself in the process. Clive has to rugger tackle him to remove him from the flat. Ossie is very contrite about Diego's behaviour and rings Clive repeatedly to apologise. Clive Bendon feels that Ossie might still be alive if only he had alerted the police to the danger of Diego's psychotic behaviour following this debacle.

However, the incident which has the greatest impact on both Ossie and Diego is a hideous contretemps with the police. Ossie becomes high on champagne after a dress fitting at Peter Golding's in Chelsea. Driving home in the oppressive July heat, Ossie impatiently bumps another car, the driver of which turns out to be a plain clothes policewoman. She summons a van and a fracas takes place involving Ossie, Diego and the police.

On 14 August there is a preliminary hearing at Marylebone Magistrates Court where they are both charged with assault, and Ossie for failure to produce samples of blood and urine. In November there is a further hearing at Horseferry Road and on 18 December a magistrate gives Ossie and Diego a two-month prison sentence for assaulting police officers. Ossie's solicitors appeal against the sentence which they say shocks them: 'It was hardly likely that the diminutive Mr Clark would have much impact on a six-foot-three-inch policeman. From his injuries it would seem the reverse was the case. The whole scene was Pythonesque.'

Apart from these dire shenanigans, Ossie is invited backstage at the Rolling Stones concert on 16 July and is warmly welcomed by Mick

Jagger. Diego characteristically disgraces himself by getting uncontrollably drunk. Jane Rainey remembers Ossie being asked by security men to take him away.

Ossie is in touch with several friends, including Janet Street Porter, Johnny Rozza, Patrick Procktor, Ulla, Carla and Britt Ekland, and keeps up with gossip. Raynes and Patrick Minns in Primrose Hill are loving and hospitable, but the violent rows Ossie has with Diego - the one matching his intelligence against the other's brute strength - result in Diego being banned from yet another house. Despite Ossie receiving various commissions, the two are sometimes so poor that they are compelled to eat by courtesy of the Salvation Army.

Anna Chancellor's al fresco wedding in mid-August to Nigel Willoughby at Nettlecombe in Somerset, 'reminiscent of Italy', has Ossie in his element. But once again the drunken Diego disgraces himself and Ossie at a friend's house near Bristol by stealing a bottle of the best armagnac and being sick all over the curtains.

Later, Ossie is thrilled to design the dress for Linda Pugh's marriage to Andy McKay; cutting the toile he felt 'really happy for the first time in ages'. At the wedding lunch in October he is elated and capers around, happy to be with old friends like Richard O'Brien. The dusty pink bridal dress is a resounding success. However, later that day at the Groucho Club in Soho, there is a fracas where a drunken Diego threatens to throw Ossie out of a window.

Most of this year Ossie seems cheerful and the flat is kept pristine. Diego is at least physically fastidious. On the domestic front there is harmony; together they produce delicious, simple meals of pasta and fish. Ossie feels he is improving the life of this ex-heroin addict and in return has the physical companionship he has sought for so long, but at what personal expense?

Al Radley invites Ossie out to supper at La Famiglia. He admires his high spirits, self-sufficiency, fortitude and values, and attributes this to strength of character. He asks him to go back to work for him, but Ossie does not want to relinquish the relative security of the flat and the dole money, which he would lose if he had a full-time job. He has found a certain peace and pattern to his living. He told Gerogina Howell, who interviewed him that year, 'I am happy. I have my sons, my health and Diego.' Albert and George, however, express grave reservations about Diego and they are not alone. .

3 JANUARY

I walked to Holland Park at twilight, ice crunching under my feet. The new moon diamond right over Oakwood Court when suddenly a feeling of great sadness came over me and I realised it's a year today since Nick[1] died.

Found a fiver and the bankruptcy numbed.

9 JANUARY

[*Ossie attended the wedding of friends of Henrietta Rous in Bristol, then went to stay at Clovelly, North Devon, at Henrietta's mother's home.*]

I woke early in almost unbearable pain. Mary[2] called from the stairs, 'Ossie, I would like to be awff by 10 o'clock, 9.30 really, but you're OK.' So no time to bathe and I guess I looked pretty grim and grey-faced because everyone was extremely concerned. The local doctor was summoned and arrived while I was eating boiled eggs – a sweet and kind red-faced old man called Cook examined me with big gentle hands and decided I'd got a flailed rib – number 9 on my right side – I am so relieved that's it's not my internal organs.

11 JANUARY

Michael a'Brook rang – if it is a flailed rib then his son Jonathan can put it back in place. I rang Jose[3], begging for my phone bill: but this is the last time – I can't do it again. Thanks, Jose darling.

13 JANUARY

Oh dear. Tanya[4] shrieking at me. 'You've really upset her this time,' said Carol the machinist.

14 JANUARY

Worked, sewing all day. I performed a miracle in Indian red wild silk.

21 JANUARY

Woke at eight, up at nine. Gobbing phlegm every morning, how regular. MG[5] with Karen[6]. She really is so sweet, lent me a fiver, which I spent on cigs, candles and Aloe, getting soaked right down to my long johns in the process. Then big surprise: a wonderful evening with Henrietta and her sister Caroline. Pizza and stolen whisky, and Karen and Nick Kamen. FABULOUS DAY.

23 JANUARY

I rang Marie Helvin – she just turned in her second book, out in April.

24 JANUARY

A perfect day. I was late to Gongyo because I took time and care dressing. It was very good and after I phoned Lorenzo[7] and told his answerphone I've got the name of a tailor because actually I can't be bothered to alter his father's trousers. I've carefully prepared all the bias piping and cut the cherry-red corduroy – so I went on to Bella Freud's studio and made a cushion in an hour.

25 JANUARY

Three dead fish – who's next? It's scary.

30 JANUARY

I've spoken to Pattie Boyd and done my 20 mins EG.

9 FEBRUARY

Diego[8]. Went off to his meeting place. Well, first I had to mend the bed which walked off its supermarket wheels.

11 FEBRUARY

Tony Secunda dead. Red wine for breakfast. A walk in Holland Park.

14 FEBRUARY

Up at eight. Clear blue sky, mild, and one and a half hours' cleaning up after last night. Diego limps in the morning. 'You are not my father,' when I tried unsuccessfully to stop him snorting the amyl nitrate. We did the bed.

3–3.30 Pattie Boyd fitting. She came early. Her eyes like sapphires. Not as big as mine used to be. Mine used to be real zonkers.

17 FEBRUARY

I LOVE DIEGO.

[Diego's writing] 'We are going to a lake to steal Sony television and a video.'

21 FEBRUARY

11.40 Lorenzo – do I want to make a wedding dress for his friend Francesca? How much do I charge?

1 o'clock bath. Pouring rain and hail. Poor Diego out in it, on an errand for me while I did MG.

25 FEBRUARY

Awake before light, 6.30, up at 7. What shall we do today? We've got 82p; if we find another 53p we can buy 10 cigs. With cigarettes we can make a start.

27 FEBRUARY

Diego up at 9.45. 'Cigarette,' he wails and I provide from stubs collected on Holland Park Avenue. 'I want to find a job. Last night I dreamt my father had a pub in Venice and I got up in the night and drank all the alcohol.' I feel very let down.

2 MARCH

Diego let me fuck him and I gave him two pills. So nice to see Ben and Emily[9] so in love, so glowing after their hols in LA and Costa Rica.

5 MARCH

In the evening Henri took us to visit Raynesy[10], and Diego drank whisky and was very drunk. We rowed all night.

7 MARCH

Couldn't Diego get a job?

9 MARCH

Diego's dead drunk.

13 MARCH

Slept bad, worried about money. I phoned Pattie after determination to finish the dress today. She came at 6.45, still without the final payment. I was quite pissed off.

14 MARCH

Again I didn't sleep well – up before light and early to go fishing in Holland Park[11]. I got enough for 20 cigs and skins. We argued over the washing-up and he went out to walk (in Shepherd's Bush Library he found a book on Eric Clapton), but he was OK and smiling when he got back.

The dress goes well and is looking beautiful. Pattie came at seven with a bottle of Moët – she doesn't know about Eric's birthday. Is there going to be a party on the 30th? She spoke to him yesterday and right now he's more concerned with catching a flight to Antigua.

15 MARCH

'Not enough stoned,' said Diego. I planted nasturtiums and three kinds of pansy in pots to propagate on my windowsill.

16 MARCH

'6.30. Fleur de Fleur, Park Lane Hotel. Just say you're my guest.' But Margot,

Countess of Buckinghamshire, an ancient who must have been beautiful in her youth, who organised it (£85 a ticket to raise money for the Royal Marsden), came over and demanded rudely, 'What's your name?' We were enjoying the champagne, Diego especially. 'Ossie Clark,' I replied with a smile, looking down into her eyes – I could tell she was furious and agitated, but I wasn't about to be intimidated.

Then Patrick[12] came over and she set on him so we slipped away to refill our glasses at the bar and talk to Percy Savage and glug as much fizz as possible.

17 MARCH

10.25 Just had a wonderful conversation with Christopher Gibbs. I'd come across his number on a box of matches, and eight photos of Tahlita[13]. 'Do you think he might buy them?' I asked, meaning Paul Getty. 'No, I think that's a very bad idea – he's got hundreds of photos of her and a new wife – I think you should make some clothes for her when she comes back from her travels.'

Caught shoplifting.

17 MARCH

At 192, taking shelter. I'm not kidding now – hailstones lashing outside. Albert's on fine form downstairs – has shooed me away while he works. Frederic says Albert's the least nasty person here.

At Carla[14]'s, drinking. 'Are you feeling happy, darling?' 'Yeah.' 'Can I fuck you?' 'Maybe. Can I drink your wine?' 'No.' 'Then you can't fuck me.'

Don't like Miss Shere Hite[15]. She's a feminist mutton dressed as lamb without even eye-make-up.

24 MARCH

Ten to five. Tea at Marissa Masters'[16]. She's just spent £66 on dog food. Fake pearls set on a kitchen table. She says hello to Eric Clapton every Saturday in San Lorenzo when he dines with Terry O'Neill. The mad dog chewing a yellow ball makes him sound asthmatic. 'Only mad people put Hockney in the kitchen like me. I make all my own clothes but I'm so fat now. Oh, Ossie, I'm so sorry, I was going to make a proper tea party.' I'm sorry I was so flat.

25 MARCH

2.25 Glorious sunshine after a very successful shopping trip down Portobello, and maybe a job for Diego with Tom the florist. He gave me a fresia which smells so sweet.

25 MARCH

Up early. Fished with Diego in Holland Park for money and cigs. We walked through the market penniless. In the evening we got our spaghetti carbonara and a bottle of red wine, thanks to Ben who lent me a fiver willingly, plus the extra six pence from Laura. I was watching a very interesting programme about spiders when Hedley rang my door at 8.15. I was a bit concerned, leaving Diego without funds. 'Didn't he want to come?' asked Henrietta. 'He's frightened of you,' I replied. 'He thinks you don't like him.'

27 MARCH

[*Ossie has been to Wales with Henrietta.*]

HOSPITAL. Chelsea and Westminster – I had pain in my stomach when we left Wales last night. It got worse and worse and I started vomiting and vomiting ('Strange how it didn't smell,' said Henrietta later). The pain got worse and worse and I began to wish I would die to be free of it. They stuck me with drips, gave me the anti-nausea drugs and shot me with Panathol. I all the time squirming like a fish in agony while they asked me all the same stupid questions. 'Who is your next of kin? Have you had an HIV test? Have you got a partner? Is it male or female?' They put me on the fourth floor next to an ancient man who grumbled all night.

28 MARCH

[*Ossie returns home from hospital.*]

Diego was delighted to see me – the flat sparkling and clean. 'I'm so glad you are OK. When you was in hospital I was very nervous. I drank three bottles of red wine.'

30 MARCH

Prescription in the post but no money to get it. I rang PP[17]. Sally Fleetwood has been staying with him while Mike Upton had his leg amputated and she was a nightmare.

31 MARCH

Henrietta's not home – I promised to be here at 3 o'clock. She's in a panic because she's giving a dinner party tonight. I've come to help.

We had to walk home through the park, which I didn't mind at all because the weather is so mild with the promise of a really warm weekend. Diego, however, reading the *Evening Standard* opposite me, is surly, feeling sick. He's cross with me because I walked on and didn't wait for him.

1 APRIL

I spoke to Pattie Clapton about photographing her in the red dress. Smoking grass reluctantly paid for by Ulla[18].

3 APRIL

[*Ossie goes to Terrington in North Yorkshire with Henrietta to visit her sister. Unfortunately the trip is not a great success, as Ossie and Diego are thrown out of the house because of Diego's drunken behaviour and because he has stolen a bottle of rum.*]

Terrington is a very manicured village. Waiting for Henrietta, the plans have all changed. We are going back to London tonight – I'm really pissed off with Caroline[19]. I told Henrietta I was very hurt by Caroline's intolerance of Diego. Back in Dalby we packed up and I was very polite, but cold.

3 APRIL

So much has happened and I haven't been able to write it all down – since the hurried exit from Yorkshire with Henri screaming at me about her god-mother's broken plate. 'I'll put you out of the car,' she threatened at one point (I knew I was going to get it in the car). 'Just you try,' I growled. On the steps of York Minster at 7 o'clock exactly, I discovered Diego. He was hopelessly drunk on $^1/_2$ a bottle of rum stolen from Caroline's larder – maybe that's why she threw us out so unceremoniously. I was furious and blew my top, saying, 'That's it. It's all over,' which made him cry and I had to pretend to Henri that he was homesick and the Minster had reminded him of Milan cathedral, which she swallowed even though she was amazed at his tears.

4 APRIL

[*In light of Ossie's discharge from bankruptcy, he is hoping to re-negotiate the publication of his diaries which, while he was bankrupt, Bloomsbury was unable to agree to.*]

I spent the day in Bella Freud's studio making Ulla's long-promised top and sending faxes to David Reynolds at Bloomsbury suggesting lunch with Henrietta next week.

10 APRIL

I've got to get some money from somewhere. The Kamens[20] are away in America. Diego began work at Speck Deli. Kari Anne[21] on the phone – she is organising a fund-raising bash in Battersea Park for the Dalai Lama in July. Who should she approach?

15 APRIL

Nick Kamen's 33. We went shopping at Safeway's. Diego grumbled about spending £40 of his £120 wage packet. Diego home at 10.30. 'I got fired.'

A lovely day until the evening when Diego went too far – drinking two bottles of red wine, finishing off all the hash.

16 APRIL

Still angry.

20 APRIL

Spoke to Janet Street-Porter. She will pay my phone bill. 'One tries so desperately HARD.' 'What's happened to you? – I've heard you've fallen.' 'Yes, I fell long ago.'

At the Cobden Men's Working Club for Nick Kamen's birthday party. A crush to get in. It's beautiful like my blood inside.

24 APRIL

Walked to Ulla's and she gave me boiled eggs. We argued about how much Marianne got paid for her book, which doesn't mention me, and apparently Tony Secunda worked out the deal.

26 APRIL

Woken very early by thunder and lightning.

Went fishing in the Kyoto Garden.

Bought cigarettes and coffee. 'When you drink and smoke and I don't, we are not compatible.'

1 MAY

Sandra on the phone. I'd gone there with red satin and my scissors in the vague hope of cutting a dress for Janet Street-Porter, because this morning I received another threatening letter from the TV people which more or less said, 'Big Brother is watching you. We know you have a television, so if you don't buy a licence within the next 10 days we will fine you £1,000.'

2 MAY

Diego got himself a job washing up at Orsini and walked out after half an hour. In desperation we dined al fresco, courtesy of the Salvation Army.

4 MAY

With Margaret Bennet I ended up weeping as I read from my journals and told of Nick's death.

15 MAY

Diego telling me he enjoys reading English, and points out a Hockney book in the *Sunday Times Magazine*, knock-down from £14.95 to 3 quid.

16 MAY

It's a lovely new house, Raynesy's got. Backs on to Regents Park canal. Roses, masses in bud, tippling over the garden wall above the water where fish swim. Very disorganised and panic, so went to see Johnny Dewe Mathews.

17 MAY

Johnnie Rozza's coming from LA. He's looking good. I'm furious Emily's leather coat stinks of poppers since Diego wore it on the tube going to Camden Town.

19 MAY

Minah Bird Dead. Shocked.

20 MAY

Another DEATH – my beautiful mother-of-pearl goldfish. 'Stop sponging caffeine and get Diego a fucking job, Ossie.'

23 MAY

Up early in Holland Park to draw roses for the painting I'm working on for Johnnie Rozza, who was staying with Nick Kamen but now he's moved to Chelsea. He's coming at 5 to collect it and do EG.

26 MAY

Bathed early and dressed in my new sandals and Nick's blue and white striped shirt. Walked to Britt'[22]s house and plucked three roses for her from the cemetery, but she didn't buy my samples. So desperate we are for money – dirty sheets and no washing powder. We had a pathetic Sally Army dinner of tinned spag and cheese pasties with hidden fat.

31 MAY

We went to Sid[23]'s at 3 and smoked some very good hash.

1 JUNE

I put on my corset like an old warrior. Just one buckle holds my tender stomach. Tea with Bernard Neville 5 o'clock. He rang at seven minutes to five: 'I'm expecting you.' It was after 6 when we arrived. A proper tea all laid out and a lemon cake. Henrietta arrived five minutes later. He showed us all over his wonderful house and all his fabric designs on Japanese polyester. My head was reeling when we left. I found a 10 quid bottle of wine behind a lamp-post and we walked to Ulla's.

2 JUNE

I rang Johnnie Rozza at 9.20 to ask him if he wanted to come round. But he didn't, saying, 'You know, I don't think I will see you again. I'm away at the weekend and then on Monday I'm outta this place. See you in 10 years.' Which I thought very optimistic of him, since his eyes are so bad that he just points the camera and gets his assistant to focus everything for him. He says how good he looks, but I don't think so. He's definitely got that look.

I've been a whole week on the drawing of Diego, which is quite beautiful, and a third piece of paper added and many more roses. It is the most ambitious thing I've ever done. I've put myself in the corner and there's just enough space for the crescent moon – it is full of symbolism with the roses turning towards his face and paling at his beauty.

9 JUNE

My 53rd birthday. Nick Kamen came with a bouquet of blue corn flowers. The most wonderful birthday lunch provided by Ulla (but how much further I could have made 25 quid go). It was great fun – we went to meet them in the park. There was Philip Prowse[24] alone drinking a cappuccino. 'You're just a baby,' he said. Oh no, I'm much older than that.

12 JUNE

Stoned at twenty-five to ten. I start to write this as the smell of hash penetrates Diego's sleep. 'Sweetie pie, are you awake?'

PP was in bed when I rang – it was the wrong moment to ask for money.

16 JUNE

6.30 Gala Graduate Fashion Week. The guy who won dressed bald-headed and tattooed drag queens hideously – just disgusting.

9 p.m. Wedding, Walpole House, Strawberry Hill. A Venetian masked ball. Turned out to be Rick Wright's party. The first person I saw was Steve O'Rourke with a face painted white. He tweaked my arse. We drank champagne and didn't eat the food, it was so disgusting – apparently the whole bash cost £300,000. We drove through the night to Devon, arriving at 8 in the morning. I slept until 11.30 then bathed and dressed to go to a wedding in the local church.

The next morning I looked over the garden We went12 to Mouthmill to lots of nice people and red wine and an al fresco lunch which went on till after 6.

20 JUNE

Amanda Lear is going to some big gay shindig in Berlin to sing with Donna Summer and the Village People.

While I was in the bath Marisa phoned. Told me about Edith Foxwell – come down in the world and had to sell her house because she's been ripped off by a young black man – typical.

30 JUNE

Poor Diego, I drove him to shout and shout at me, and whispered don't shout at me and shouted back. Raynesy had mentioned his drinking too much. I tried to make conditions, offering the hash instead or only drinking to match me glass for glass, but in the end I had to leave without him.

13 JULY

10 o'clock with Cilla in the room where Jimi Hendrix wrote 'Purple Haze'. I got bit – the first mosquito of the year.

15 JULY

Dropped in to see PP – already drinking whisky and only midday. He's still besotted with Adam – he showed me a photo of him wearing an emerald he had bought for him.

16 JULY

[*Ossie and Diego go to a Rolling Stones concert courtesy of Mick Jagger.*]

FUMING WITH RAGE and Diego more stupid than ever at the Wembley Arena where the Stones are giving their final concert. It's 8.03. No later than 8.15 on stage.

8.19 Lulu[25] kisses me. Will she sign my book? [*Her handwriting*] I love you Ossie now, I loved you then. Love Lulu.

'We're gonna sing an old one, keep ya happy,' says Mick from the stage, 'because I used to love you but it's all over now.' A couple exit with a child and a yellow teddy bear. Mick wears blue and black stripes. Before the concert he gave me a big hug and I asked him for 15 grand. Diego begged. We smoke the joint.

On the huge screen, a computer graphics lips and tongue. SATISFACTION. Off come the stripes, revealing an electric blue T-shirt.

It's a roller coaster. 8.41. Mick's in the audience. The blue T-shirt seems to be getting shorter. He back on stage. Wooooooooling. Hey Hey Hey My My My Oh Oh Oh.

Ten to nine. What was that song called? 'I dunno,' says Lulu.

Keith in purple, a silver skull ring on his guitar-picking finger. Charlie wears Buddhist orange. Yellow crucifixes radiate outwards. Ronnie Woods' solo – he wears black and white to match his guitar and the screen goes black/white.

8.56 Diego has drunk ½ bottle of red wine. 'It's been a hard day.' Diego's gibbering.

He's actually asking, 'How long do you speak to Mick Jagger?' who is now dancing with a girl and wears another different coloured T-shirt. She's got a fabulous voice.

Worse than me and I'm 53. How old are you? Lulu is 46. Don't worry. I go WILD.

The roller coaster has gone purple, I mean peppermint green. I mean both. Mick wears a stripe down the side of his trousers. The black girl shakes her arse to the rhythm of the drums. 'Are you ready? OK.' The tongue gets spikier. 'Keith R is gonna sing for you – it's a good night for it, it's an old one, "I Need Your Love". I felt very well, and you brought me down . . . Babe, it's just another day . . .'

Slipping away. Like the light. 9.44. Soon it will be too dark to write. Just another song. Slippin' away.

Ten past ten. I know it's only rock and roll but I like it. I've LOST it.

[*Later*] I'm sorry Diego. Do forgive me. I do love you very much. Here, smoke this. Ossie. We'll have a better day tomorrow.

26 JULY

A man from the council came to replace the glass in my front door which Diego smashed with his fist the night of the Stones concert.

29 JULY

[*Stopping off at a garage in his car, Ossie had become impatient with a driver he believed was taking too long to fill up. He decided to give the car 'a little bump' to hurry along the owner. Unfortunately the owner was an off-duty policewoman. When Ossie began arguing with her she summoned police back-up and a van-load of policemen arrived, arrested Diego and Ossie and took them to Paddington Green Police station. They were charged with common assault but Ossie believed the officers themselves to have treated him and Diego with unnecessary brutality.*]

Police brutality.

1 AUGUST

Home to an attempted robbery and abuse from a gang of kids.

8 AUGUST
Al Radley phoned out of the blue. He has just lost his wife from skin cancer – sounds very distraught. He's taking us out to dinner at La Famiglia.

14 AUGUST
Marylebone Magistrates Court, 10 a.m. Diego wore his Free Tibet T-shirt and I wore a cross in my tie on a white shirt and the same linen pants that went through the ordeal with me. We walked there which took 45 mins, arriving at five to ten. I began to fret in case Dante didn't arrive. He did at ten past, cool and wearing a suit. We're in Court Two. He disappeared and came back with the police's photocopied report, 1/2 inch thick. I am now facing two more charges, of failing to provide blood, breath or urine, and of assaulting a police woman. Inside the walls are the colour of vomit or mucus. 'All rise for the judge.' Like *Alice in Wonderland* 3 trooped in – overweight, badly dressed woman – Plain Jane. The actual judge sat in the middle, and we both decided he was OK. Very thorough, almost a twinkle in his eye. The other man, a blob, was instantly forgettable. In front, sat sideways and lower down, a man easily flustered and an Asian woman who read out the charges in very bad English.

Ossie leaving court with Diego Cogolato, 1995.

16 AUGUST

Billy[26] here watching the news on TV. '*Star Trek* – this is not the news.' 'No, this is not child murder, water shortage, unemployment has gone up, Maggie Thatcher's got Alzheimer's disease and so has Thea Porter – poor bitch, no care for it – and old Tomb Stone Teeth is dead.' 'Who's that?' 'Jean Muir.'

I've really been neglecting writing since Diego entered my life. I've taken up bag-making and two frocks on the go.

22 AUGUST

DRAMA

23 AUGUST

[*On the night of 22 August Ossie and Diego had had a violent argument.*]

The sheets covered in blood, Diego's thumb a torn mess. The postman mentioned the scene of carnage downstairs. 'Er, what happened here last night?' Like a scene from *Psycho* – I cleaned it all up – smeared blood all over the intercom and glass from the front door, a trail up the stairs, floor, walls, banisters.

26 AUGUST

Andy McKay getting married on 26 October. I'm to make the wedding dress. Yippee!

30 AUGUST

[*Ulla Lawson has cast Ossie in a small part in Dennis Potter's* Cold Lazarus.]

Filming at Pinewood, 6 a.m. at Hammersmith. Vomiting on the way twice – made it on time but had to borrow 10p to crap. I sat with a very sweet mixed-race girl called Sonja – we laughed and got on very well through take after boring take – while Francis de la Tour acted and two amateurs fluffed it.

It was all very disorganised and boring. I'm afraid Dennis is not my favourite, and I don't share his gloomy vision of the future. The dialogue was crap. The clothes pathetic design and very badly made. The hairdos very *Babylon Five*. The crew got much better tea than we herded cattle.

5 SEPTEMBER

Michael Fish phoned to talk about the filming.

7 SEPTEMBER
Hospital. Oh my god, what is happening? Such incredible pain.

12 SEPTEMBER
The toile on my table already marked with Lucinda[27]'s bodice in three colours before the actual cut.

15 SEPTEMBER
I woke elated by my achievement – felt happy, really happy, for the first time in ages. Roxy Music on the radio had me dancing.

18 SEPTEMBER
Billy stayed the night. He went off at 8.30, really rather sad.
Lunch Chelsea Arts Club for Sylvia Polakov[28]. Ulla told me Sylvia had had plastic surgery on her eyes and, quite rightly, Sylvia was furious.

22 SEPTEMBER
In court.

2 OCTOBER
Lucinda rang at 9 a.m. 'Do you want my body today or don't you want my body today?'
I worked on the inner bodice and cut the outer shell.

19 OCTOBER
Diego says he is depressed.

26 OCTOBER
Wedding of Andy McKay and Lucinda Pugh. 10.30 a.m. 33 Astell Street.

27 OCTOBER
Ulla rang with dreadful news. Luciana Martinez[29] in a coma. Meningitis destroyed her liver, not expected to live. Diego in bed, feeling awful. I'd not done my Gongyo, so I did it as I walked to shop for oranges and paracetamol.

28 OCTOBER
Tea with Edward Bell[30].

8 NOVEMBER
Dinner with Wayne Sleep.

23 NOVEMBER

Horseferry Magistrates Court. Barrister Janet Weeks.

1 DECEMBER

A bloody parking ticket, the 1st, and due-for-removal sticker, yellow and black like a bee sting – a bugger to remove and given after 8.30. The bastard Gestapo parking warden must have watched me park it yesterday morning.

1 Nick Balaban.
2 Mary Rous.
3 Jose Fonseca.
4 Tanya Sarne.
5 Morning Gongyo.
6 Karen, Buddhist friend of Ossie.
7 Lorenzo Poccianti.
8 Diego Cogolato, Ossie's lover and eventual murderer. This is the first time Ossie mentions him in the diaries, though it is understood that they met in Holland Park Avenue one afternoon after Ossie had attended a Buddhist meeting at Justine Silver's – Diego had been trying to find the youth hostel in Holland Park.
9 Ben Brierly and his wife Emily. Ben by this time is running Benchmark, a shop selling 19th-century furniture, in Westbourne Grove.
10 Raynes Minns, writer and theatre designer; husband of architect Patrick Minns.
11 Ossie was occasionally reduced to 'fishing' money out of the wishing well in Holland Park.
12 Patrick Procktor.
13 Tahlita Getty.
14 Carla Ames.
15 Shere Hite, American feminist, author of *The Hite Report* and *Women as Agents Revolutionary Change*.
16 Marissa Masters, ex-wife of founder of Haymarket Press, Brian Masters.
17 Patrick Procktor.
18 Ulla Larson.
19 Lady Caroline Armstrong, Henrietta Rous' sister.
20 Sandra and Michael Kamen.
21 Kari-Anne Jagger.
22 Britt Ekland.
23 Sid Rotbart.
24 Philip Prowse, close friend of Celia.
25 Lulu, British singer/songwriter.
26 Billy Henry.
27 Lucinda Pugh was to marry Anthony McKay.
28 Sylvia Polakov, jewellery and artefacts designer.
29 Luciana Martinez, British portrait painter.
30 Edward Bell, painter who ran art classes which Ossie attended.

1996

The day-planner diary is sparse and has relatively few entries. Ossie feels undermined by his experiences in the courts and with the police the previous year. He and Diego are fighting an appeal against the two-month prison sentence given to them in December 1995. They have spent a frugal Christmas together, and the young Italian cannot bear the thought of New Year without wine or cigarettes. Gradually Ossie's disenchantment with Diego surfaces. Whereas the previous year Ossie proudly says he has spent a week on a drawing of his lover and comments on the beauty of his face, he now finds him volatile and writes, 'Scowling. Is he pretty?' and, later, 'second portrait is hardly a homage to him'.

Ossie's performance of morning gongyo is irregular and he seems to lack the motivation to write up his diary. He records his lecture at the Royal College in just two words. He sees Michael a'Brook regularly from February to April, and the diary is punctuated by accounts of the drink-driving course he has to attend.

Those who knew him well thought it would be wise for him to avoid a trial unless he was certain of winning it. However, Ossie is determined to go ahead and finds a good barrister, Oscar dell Fabbro. Ossie goes to court on 14 February and again on 6 March on legal aid. Despite the two young law students of 'shining integrity' who witnessed the incident at the Bayswater garage, the magistrates are not convinced that there is 'reasonable doubt'. Ossie's faith in justice is shattered and he records this in a letter to Vanessa Denza. His prison sentence is commuted and he is given twelve months' probation and Diego gets 120 hours community service. The reporters present seem dumbfounded at the verdict.

As the relationship cools, Ossie finds Diego's presence more and more obstructive to the progress he wants to make. Albert and George have long objected to Diego and give their father an ultimatum. Ossie is aware that he and Diego are becoming increasingly ostracised and a hostel is found in Bayswater for Diego to live in. Freed of his demanding presence, Ossie is able to work again and recreates a beautiful crimson outfit and undertakes other small commissions. Again, he wants to regain the respect of Celia and his sons, and wants to teach George how to tailor.

Susannah Handley from the Royal College of Art is thrilled to take up with her childhood hero and arranges for Ossie to give a lecture in February. She is deeply impressed by the intellect and civilised knowledge he displays in the lecture and in his conversations with her. Despite his predicament, close friends remain loyal. Ulla and Ossie are invited to Dave Gilmour's fiftieth birthday party at Fulham Town Hall, and Ossie is in good spirits at Nicolette Meere's exhibition in Carlton House Terrace at the beginning of June. He attends Christopher Tennant's wedding in the presence of Princess Margaret and is photographed alongside Jade Jagger in Hello. He goes to a cousin's fiftieth birthday in Yorkshire, but before he leaves seems apprehensive and preoccupied.

Certain incidents conspire to humiliate him. The ankle-length snakeskin coat that he designed in the sixties is shown at the Royal College of Art's Centenary Exhibition in February, along with an Ossie-designed leather jacket. However, the coat is later rejected by the Victoria and Albert Museum as a potential permanent exhibit and its owner, Britt Ekland, puts it up for sale at Christie's as part of a clear-out sale where it fetches a humiliatingly small sum of money. Bella Freud marvelled at its perfect elegance, and Ulla remembers that occurrences like this broke Ossie's spirit. Ulla, a major supporter of Ossie, was always with him at his most vulnerable moments and constantly entertains him at her Fulham Road flat. She followed the trajectories of his life with the consistent love and understanding he so desperately needed.

Ossie is preoccupied by Diego's depression and dependence on him. Diego considers returning to Italy but we are told his mother will not have him back unless he cleans up his drug-taking. He drops by to visit Ossie and lounges around often feeling very sorry for himself. They remain friends. Jenny Runacre, among others, is consulted about him at a party she gave, and Ossie announces that Prozac might help Diego with his depression.

The last time I saw Ossie was five days before his death. Although anxious about Diego, he seemed gentle, reflective and purposeful. He was about to design some skull caps for an Italian friend and took back a zany leopard-skin hat with ears and badges that he had lent me. He was full of amusing gossip about mutual friends.

The day before his death Ossie writes his last diary entry, a brief note to Diego saying that he has gone to the park. On the morning of 6

August Pam Procter goes to chant with him. Later in the morning he is seen by Chrissie Lewis, a neighbour and friend who lives in the flat opposite; he is on his way to buy cigarettes. Later in the day Chrissie Lewis sees him again, strolling through the courtyard, smartly dressed; when she asks where he is going, he smiles and shrugs his shoulders.

Chrissie Lewis sees Diego enter the small block of flats in Penzance Street at 8 pm with the mountain bike that he and Ossie shared. She hears nothing, but sees Diego leave an hour later.

The next morning, at 6 a.m., Chrissie hears Ossie's dog Pippin barking frenziedly and sees the dog at the window. At approximately the same time Diego rings the police from Richmond and confesses that he has killed Ossie. Soon afterwards an ambulance arrives, followed immediately by several police cars. The area is cordoned off. Four large white forensic vans arrive. The frightened dog is dragged across the courtyard. Several hours later a body is carried out in a black bag. Chrissie prays. 'Let it be anyone but Ossie.'

'He must have put up a fight,' said a distraught Albert. 'There was blood all over the bathroom wall.'

By the evening of 7 August family and close friends are informed of the ghastly truth. On 8 August newspapers around the world carry the news.

On 17 March 1997, Diego was sentenced to six years for manslaughter. Friends, family and members of the public were astounded by the leniency of the sentence.

Much later, certain of Ossie's friends visited Diego in prison. It seems that Ossie was resting in bed and not in the mood to see him when he arrived at 8 p.m. on 6 August. Diego lit a joss stick and Ossie said something. High and destabilised by a combination of Prozac and amphetamines, Diego reenacted a vision he had had the previous day, that he was the messiah and Ossie was the devil. Taking a long kitchen knife he stabbed Ossie thirty-seven times and then broke his skull with a terracotta pot. He left the flat and loped across the courtyard barefoot. He had killed his one and only friend.

31 DECEMBER

Poor Nero, the black fan-tailed carp, didn't make it to the end of the year. I couldn't see him as I did my evening Gongyo. Eventually I found him dead in the big white conch shell. He had been lethargic for weeks. I just flushed him down the toilet while Diego[1] lay in bed in a bad temper, out of sorts at the prospect of a miserable New Year without a drink or a smoke.

6 FEBRUARY

6.30 'Design of the Times.' 100 Years RCA opening.

22 FEBRUARY

[*Ossie spoke to students at the Royal College of Art at an event organised by Susanna Handley, about his aims as a designer and about his early career.*]

RCA lecture.

6 MARCH

In court again. Dave Gilmour's 50th birthday.

11 MARCH

The six a.m. alarm. I wake up simultaneously to pee and pat Pippin and pop my pills. Back to bed for another blissful 1½ hour's sleep. Diego already out with Pips to shop in Safeway with the £10 note Carla[2] tendered on Saturday night. I showed her the trousers off the machine, which I was sewing when she rang the door. 9.30. The plumbers came and while they mended the taps (no water pressure on the hot) I bashed the leather pants together. They fit pretty good. Diego came back – we all did morning Gongyo.

12 MARCH

Almost 9 a.m. Please let me write my diary every day. I'm in a mess. Bleak. Everything difficult – no money. Ulla has been a brick. I don't feel good inside. A pain when I kneel. The sewing machine breaking needle after needle. Pippin is a full time job – always hungry, barks at children, pulls at the lead, runs off in a flash. Later he chewed his leather lead in two. His white hairs an inch long, fall by the thousands. Diego complains I haven't been out for three days. He's grumpy. Volatile. 'Give me back the lighter!' he demands, pulling his face. Scowling. Is he pretty? Probation[3] at 12.30. Such a bore – until next Valentine's Day. Once a fortnight for four months – eight weekly drink-drive seminars – all such a drag. But it must be faced, unjust as it is. I told her about the second assault police charge and Buddhism and was out in ½ an hour.

20 MARCH

Probation 10.30. Vicky Brown.

22 MARCH

In court again.

28 MARCH

1.00 Python coat and gold leather jacket back from the RCA.

2.30 Carla came round.

Michael a' Brook 9.15. Dinner La Pomme d'Or with his two sons. Much younger than I expected.

31 MARCH

12 a.m.-ish. In Marissa[4]'s garden. Hideous Gigi attacked Pippin. Clamped his great big well-fed teeth on to my lovely one's pretty white face. In desperation I tried everything to get his jaw apart, to release poor Pippin's face. I kicked him, pulled him up by his tail. Finally I stuck my lighted cigarette into his nose and Pippin, whimpering and shaking, fell free. Marisa jabbering. No help and all her fault.

There was blood and my hands were bashed. Painful broken knuckles on both. She promised lunch out – pizza or fish and chips. So indoors, off red wine, sharp like vinegar, scrambled eggs, old cold turkey and ham. She answered the phone.

1 APRIL

2 p.m. Ralph Neville. Probation. He seemed quite nice. Why can't I have him to go and see? Such a nice day. I rang for permission to take Pippin who is becoming a monster. 4 p.m.

4 APRIL

I finished the leather trousers for Karen[5] to take on holiday to Morocco tomorrow. Or was that the week before? At 12.20 a.m. I saw the eclipse of the moon but I didn't see the comet.

6 APRIL

Ulla[6]'s gone to Sweden for at least a month.

10 APRIL

8.40 a.m. Diego to community service, but not till 10 a.m. Why don't you do the prayers with me, Diego? No! I wanna shave. 10.14. Bathed. I wish every day could be like this without Diego. Yet I still work on the 2nd portrait of him. This one unfinished is not a homage. Still the eucalyptus is very nice, and it's dole day.

23 APRIL

Diego to the DSS. Didn't get back till after one. Michael a'Brook rang. He's been laid low with a migraine. I carried on reading, wearing the blue towelling robe, till Pam[7] rang at 12.30. I did morning Gongyo with her after 2. Sid[8]'s gone to see his mother.

24 APRIL

Collected my dole at 9 a.m. Pippin tried to bite a child. Bought Marlboros for Diego. Community service. Went early. Johnnie Rozza phoned just as I'd finished morning Gongyo to thank me for dressing him last night – 'and you were so well behaved.' 11.30. Probation. 10 mins wait. 1.15. Reluctant to go shopping. Chicken for Pippin, oranges, pasta, eggs. Should buy black plastic bags, make the symbolic clear-out.

3 MAY

Pay my £15 fine fortnightly at Marylebone Magistrate's Court.

7 MAY

Derek Jarman in Retrospect, Barbican Court Gallery.

9 MAY

11 a.m. Probation officer home visit. She half an hour late.

28 MAY

An hour's daimoku. Then Diego came. He'd been earlier, and we had a wonderful day together. A bottle of Moroccan red wine. I cooked the sausages I'd bought on Saturday when I'd called him greedy and he'd stormed out, leaving Billy speechless. And he too went, sad that he wouldn't get fed. Me with a red face.

Anyway, today was the other side of the coin. Diego's mama phoned, just as we began to eat. 'She's got a psychic bond with you,' I said. It was he who instigated sex (even brought a condom). I was just getting into him when Billy's heavy hand hit the doorbell, sending Pippin into a frantic barking bout. I still can't come but I was glad I made him happy and went willingly to Safeway for another bottle of wine while he took a bath. Unfortunately it was corked. Then Billy came again and this time we let him in. He has had a hard day trying to sell a fax machine. I traipsed back to exchange the wine and cook dinner.

29 MAY

A plumber at 9 a.m. No apparent reason for the flooding. A joint at last. I made it too strong. It knocked me sideways. Of course, Diego smelt it immediately he walked in the door after community service.

30 MAY

Up before 7. Morning Gongyo and 40 mins chanting for Diego's money to arrive, which it did at 2.15. Still no word from my probation officer. Left a message for Julie – a' Brook's secretary – because I run out of pills tomorrow. A lovely warm, sunny day for a change.

7 JUNE

A bailiff at the door. Oh God, community charges. Still hasn't gone away. I kept the man outside and ranted at him. I've sorted it out with the Council.

9 JUNE

My 54th birthday. Not one card, 'even from Gladys,'[9] I thought as I sat on the toilet. But she rang later.

12 JUNE

Henrietta[10] came round with money. 'I love £50 notes,' she said, handing me one for the organza, having spent the day with darling Evan from Athens.

14 JUNE

Wedding – Christopher Tennant, Greek Orthodox Church, Moscow Road.

1 JULY

Mr Pip's castration. Oh dear. Read books.

2 JULY

Michael a'Brook rang at 10 to cancel tonight. Diego unhappy. Lent me 10 quid and the bicycle to shop. Poor Pippin in his lampshade. Horrible. Very, very hurt, pleading eyes. And why am I being punished, what have I done? Clinging to me.

3 JULY

5.15 First Drink-Drive Course.

17 JULY

A quandary. Britt Ekland phoned demanding, 'I want my coat back.' I've got it on the answerphone and pissed-off tone to her voice. And, darling,

Johnnie Rozza moved to New York. Left a message on the answerphone while I was walking Pippin in Holland Park. Written one week later, 24/7/96, breaking my rule never to use biro. Never again. But I'm desperately trying to catch up on my diary.

23 JULY

First Gongyo in 4 days, I think. A fabulous thunderstorm.

24 JULY

Morning Gongyo in Holland Park. Writing again with a biro.

31 JULY

£50 and 55p after the £7.50 rent and arrears. A new pension book till 11 December. Pippin's food, oranges, eggs, melons, cigarettes, soy sauce, coffee, apple juice.

5 AUGUST

[*A glued-in note.*]

Diego, gone to Holland Park. Come there if you like.

1 Diego Cogolato.
2 Carla Ames.
3 As part of Ossie's and Diego's conviction for common assault they were sentenced to two months in prison. However, on appeal Ossie was sentenced to 12 months' probation and Diego to 120 hours' community service.
4 Marissa Masters.
5 Karen, Buddhist friend of Ossie.
6 Ulla Larson.
7 Pam Procter.
8 Sid Rotbart.
9 Gladys English.
10 Henrietta Rous.

Index

Page numbers in *italic* refer to captions
Page numbers in **bold** indicate main footnotes

Pattie Boyd 1971.